BEER
LOVER'S
RATING GUIDE

BY BOB KLEIN

WORKMAN PUBLISHING
NEW YORK

Library of Congress Cataloging-in-Publication Data
Klein, Robert, 1941–
    The beer lover's rating guide / by Bob Klein—2nd ed.,
    rev. & updated
      p.   cm.
    ISBN 0-7611-1311-8
    1. Beer   I Title.

    TP577.K63   2000
    641.2'3—dc21   00-061453
                                                            CIP

Cover photograph by Michael Harris
Book illustrations by David Cain

Workman books are available at special discounts when
purchased in bulk for premiums and sales promotions as well
as for fund-raising or educational use. Special editions or book
excerpts can also be created to specification. For details,
contact the Special Sales Director at the address below.

Workman Publishing Company, Inc.
708 Broadway
New York, NY 10003-9555
www.workman.com

Manufactured in the United States of America

First printing October 2000
10 9 8 7 6 5 4 3 2 1

ACKNOWLEDGMENTS

This guide of (mostly) good cheer could not have happened, of course, without the glorious multitude of beer makers out there in breweryland, especially those who consciously strive to offer pleasure and quality in every barrel. I salute them all, with a beer in my hand and a glow of satisfaction on my face.

But there are others, too, who must be acknowledged for helping to make this book the catholic collection that I hope it is. Since I no longer can be certain of regularly finding new beers during my own travels or at home in Albuquerque, I must also rely on dedicated globe-trotting friends to selflessly schlep back the untried and unusual. Gayle Zieman, for example, returned from a South Pacific idyll with Western Samoan brews. On several other occasions, he heroically contended with customs officials, querulous shopkeepers, and airline weight restrictions in order to hand-deliver suitably packaged large bottles of beer from various spots in India, Hong Kong, Germany, and other countries.

My friends Scott and Toots Obenshain periodically bring me a bottle or two (occasionally a case) from their European and East Coast travels, and Spider Johnson, my connection from Mason, Texas, has sent in beer from the land of the Lone Star.

My appreciation as well to Anne Kass and Janeanne Snow (she with the exquisite taste buds) for scouring the local beer stores trying to find something I haven't had when they know I will be coming over for a visit. And thanks, too, for the cache of ten bottles from Brazil from someone I don't even know—a bank VP in New York who got my name from my sister. I thank them all.

In New York, I've always paid a visit to Alex Anastasiadis, the serious-minded proprietor of Alex's Deli in Manhattan's Greenwich Village. Alex is gone now, back to Greece. But the new owners carry on, and the extensive assortment in the large glass-door cooler still is one of the best in the city. I am particularly grateful to Brad Kraus, a certified Master Beer Judge (Brad would be in a higher category if there were one) and the extraordinarily knowledgeable and talented brewmaster at Wolf Canyon Brewing in Santa Fe, where, in my judgment, some of the country's finest stouts and ales are consistently made. Brad, and also Dan Baumann, former president of the Dukes of Ale and an experienced homebrewer in his own right, were kind enough to go through my original manuscript at various stages. Both were generous with their time—between the two of them, there wasn't a brewing question I couldn't get answered.

A very special thank you to John Zonski, owner of Jubilation Fine Wine and Spirits in Albuquerque (with his wife, Carol, whose next-door restaurant offers a wonderful green chile-chicken soup). Not only does John stock his shelves with care and consideration for his customers, but he also encouraged me to write my beer newsletter (and made available his photocopier). John was always patient and detailed with answers to my questions about the bottled beer he sold, and unfailingly went out of his way to obtain the sometimes esoteric information that I needed. Both his kindness and his inventory of quality beers were important to the completeness of this book.

To my agent, Jim Levine, and his stalwart crew: Thanks for your help, taste buds, and enthusiasm. My appreciation to Suzanne Rafer, my editor at Workman, who learned from me about beer while I learned from her about the sometimes subtle, sometimes arcane, but always helpful ways of a busy editor. And a special toast of thanks must be offered to Joni Miller, the Guide's intrepid and always ebullient copy editor, who brought erudition, tact, and a sense of humor to an occasionally tedious, if not frustrating, editing process. Alas, despite this solid lineup of aid and comfort, any errors, of omission or commission, are mine.

If gold medals were to be given out for personal attention and support, my wife, Norma, would have the world's largest collection, in all categories and every style (style, in fact, is her middle name). Endlessly supportive and resourceful, she provided me unsparingly and (usually) in good cheer all manner of assistance, from emergency scraps of paper on which to write my ratings to hour after (late) hour at the computer sorting out sometimes horrendous manuscript glitches and solving them with the aplomb and accuracy and mind-boggling tenacity of the talented professional that she is. She is also a most amiable and tolerant drinking companion (not to mention my wife and partner of 37 quite interesting years). Her help in putting this book together was enormous. It is safe as well as accurate to say, with no diminution of the generous input of those noted above, that Norma's contribution alone equals that of all the others combined. I trust that we all can drink to that.

—BOB KLEIN
Albuquerque, New Mexico

CONTENTS

APPENDIXES

INTRODUCTION
to the New Edition

A lot has happened in the world of beer since the first edition of *The Beer Lover's Rating Guide* was published in 1995. For one thing, I have more than doubled the number of beers I've tasted. My personal list now is past the 3,500 mark, and rapidly rising. Many of those beers are included in this new edition of the *Guide*. But, more important, the brewing industry in the United States, especially the micros and brewpubs, seems to be calming down after a whirlwind two decades or so. Although the market is far from settled—if, indeed, it ever will be—it's becoming clearer every day just who the survivors will be.

To begin with, several of the early successful brewers who helped spark the rejuvenation of the American beer market some twenty-plus years ago have merged with, been acquired by, or been invested in by larger, historically well-established operations. Seattle's Red Hook, one of the most successful of the upstarts, is also one of the first to become associated with a megabrewer, in this case Anheuser-Busch, brewers of Budweiser and owners of close to 50 percent of the domestic beer market. A-B has also invested in another of the Northwest's small brewery pioneers, Widmer Brothers. Miller Brewing, with a majority stake in formerly independent micros Leinenkugel and Celis, is a distant second, with approximately half of A-B's percentage of beer sales domestically. Next come Coors, Stroh's, and Pabst.

Other microbreweries that have proven their worth, and hence have achieved stability, are two California stalwarts, pioneering Anchor (San Francisco) and slow, steady, and superb Sierra Nevada (Chico), which continues to do well despite its refusal to advertise. Others include Full Sail and Rogue from Oregon (for across-the-board tasty, well-made beers, my personal favorite) and New Belgium in Colorado, one of the relatively newer breweries whose quality ales, and lately lagers, are appreciated by the drinking public. The Boston Beer Company, makers of Samuel Adams products, may be the biggest success story of them all. Established in 1985, the brewery was producing 1 million barrels annually by 1996. Today it is distributed nationally, even internationally, and by the end of the twentieth century it had become the fourteenth-largest brewer in the United States.

While these players have stayed the course, others have gone down the tubes—some for good reasons, others for various reasons. The initial excitement and curiosity created by anything new that claimed to be handcrafted and freshly brewed has worn off and no longer automatically brings 'em through the swinging doors. The American beer-buying public, at least that segment that continues to maintain an interest in buying and drinking the more flavorful and complex-tasting brews, no longer quite so uncritically ponies up three or four bucks a pint just because of the novelty. Quality and, equally important, predictable stability of flavor and character from glass to glass are now the determining hallmarks for choosing a beer. As a result, the poorly made beers, the unpredictable ones, the fad-of-the week beers (remember lemon beer? raspberry?), and the beers rushed onto the market by some who thought they could make some dough (many did) by calling it handbrewed and slapping a cutesy name on it—there are certainly fewer of those around today, thankfully.

Admittedly, part of the problem was that many customers who were curious enough to order a glass or two of the new stuff didn't know what the new stuff should taste like. When they got a bad one, which unfortunately occurred fairly often, they thought that's how it was supposed to taste (bad) and never returned. That, too, is happening less and less.

For this second edition of *The Beer Lover's Rating Guide,* I have set out to offer a wider range of examples from around the world. Instead of loading up on three, four, five, or more new brews from one brewer (as with the original listings), I have tried to list no more than three new beers from any one place, enough to give you an idea of what I think about a brewer's brews. This left me more room to rate single beers from areas as geographically or historically diverse as San Sebastian, Spain, Hurbanovo, Slovakia, and Mishawaka, Indiana.

As before, I have had the good fortune to know several beer devotees who unselfishly, and backbreakingly, carried back bottles from around the world so that I could present them to you in the *Guide.* In addition to those whose beer-toting efforts have continued over the years, I am particularly indebted to Danny Sutton, who knows a good beer when he drinks one, and who regularly returns with several examples from his worldwide travels, always carefully chilled for the intercontinental trip back to Albuquerque. Various retailers have made my searches a bit easier, too. Larry Robinson, who maintains the wide-ranging and eclectic beer inventory for Chevy Chase Wine and Spirits in Washington, D.C., was always there to help me ferret out a new beer or two, as was Doug Alberhasky of John's Grocery in Iowa City. In the end, of course, it's the brewers who define the industry, and the drinking pleasure. Once again, I thank them all.

A final word or two: Norma, among many other things my wonderful wife, durable traveling companion, and constant source of inspiration and delight, continues in her supportive ways. Her late-hour tenacity and expertise at the computer is nothing new of course, rescuing me time and again from computer-glitch and disordered-manuscript despair. But there's more. On the occasions when I go out drinking with a buddy or two—Richard Borthwick, Rick Reed, Phil Peterson—Norma cheerily sees me to the door, reminds me of the necessity of the task at hand, and pronounces the invariable admonition: "If you come back *before* eleven o'clock, I'm locking you out of the house." And she means it. All beer-drinking husbands should have a wife like that. I do, and I couldn't be happier.

WORDS FROM A BEER LOVER

I've been called a beer nut. And, despite the pun, I guess that's accurate.

I drink beer. Lots of it.

Not just any beer, mind you. Nor in copious, indiscriminate amounts. I don't chug barrels of Coors in front of the TV or cases of Bud at family picnics.

I'm more focused than that, and I have a goal: to judiciously locate, sip, and rate at least one beer from every nook and cranny of the globe. A gargantuan task, to be sure; may everyone have a job so stressful.

Amazingly, I have succeeded—to the point where I am now asked to judge sanctioned beer competitions. (Yes, there *are* such things—many of them.) I also have written and been a guest judge for the national publication *All About Beer*. And copies of *Jubilation News,* my monthly beer newsletter, which I published for a couple of years, are in the Anheuser-Busch library. That's what drinking and keeping a careful record of more than 3,500 beers can get you.

During the past two decades I have logged over 150,000 miles searching for the perfect—and, alas, also meeting up with the imperfect—beer, traveling to places like Prague, Vienna, Moscow, and Leningrad; Paris; Valdivia and Santiago, Chile; Quito, Ecuador; Shannon and Cahir, Ireland; and Helsinki, Finland. Nearer to home, I have sampled beer made in locations as far-flung as Pottsville, Pennsylvania, Olathe, Kansas, Hoboken, New Jersey, and Auburndale, Florida; Victoria and Toronto, Canada; and Mazatlán, Mexico. I have asked for seconds at brewpubs in Southern California, San Antonio, and central St. Louis (where I also had, not so incidentally, the best dessert in the world—but that's another story); Albuquerque, and New York City; and, of course, Oregon, Colorado, and Washington state, where brewpubs and microbreweries flourish like hops in the Yakima Valley region.

In order to keep track of my tastings, I have an assistant who logs each beer I drink into my computer. The electronic storage system allows me to sort, categorize, and rate the beers by state, city, and country; best and worst styles; lowest and highest rankings by different regions of the world and country; and a host of other breakdowns—all of which are yours for the page-turning in *The Beer Lover's Rating Guide.*

In 1987 my list showed a paltry 150 different beers rated;

by 1989 it had increased to 639. As the first edition of this book went to press in 1995, I had tasted and evaluated 1,298 brews from every part of the world—covering all five continents, several islands, and a jungle or two. Norma—who's found a new favorite in Negra Modelo—urged me ever onward to reach 2,000 brews by the year 2,000. I surpassed that marital mandate by a year and as of this writing (August 2000), I have tasted 3,591 brews. This second edition includes some 1,500 of them.

RATING GUIDELINES

Like many others, I drink beer socially, often requesting something different or unusual whenever I eat out or purchase a couple of bottles to take home. Over time I began to have difficulty recalling whether I had already tasted a particular beer, and if so, whether I cared to have it again. I also began to go to great lengths to locate unique beers or ones that were not readily available. I started to plan trips around the locations of breweries and brewpubs, sometimes extending or modifying vacations for the sole purpose of adding even one more new find to my list.

Finally, I decided to keep a record of what I drank. First I jotted down the pertinent information on a handy scrap of paper. Now, I carry my computerized alphabetical listing with me, adding new beers to it as I find them. I also note the city in which the beer is brewed (not always, as I soon learned, the same location as the company), my impression of what I'm paying for—taste, aroma, alcohol content, balance—and how it all goes with the food at hand. I always have food with beer.

As I drain the glass and make a judgment about its connection to the food, I rank the brew on a scale of 0 to 5. (In a few pages, I will show you how to do that.) Over time, I have come to learn which beers to avoid, which to try again, and which to order for my friends. After a while, I began to get requests for copies of my computer-generated, alphabetized list of ratings. I gave them out as birthday presents, holiday gifts, and just plain because I liked somebody and wanted him or her to have some guidance and pleasure when selecting a beer to drink.

IN THE FIELD WITH THE RATING GUIDE

Fifteen to twenty years ago, beer drinkers in the United States were limited in domestic choice to the half-dozen or so national megabreweries, a few regionals, a small handful of hard-to-locate microbreweries, and hardly any brewpubs. Even finding imports, particularly from lesser-producing countries, took some effort.

Today we can choose from over 1,300 brewed-in-the-U.S.A. local, regional, and national brands stretched across the landscape from Portland, Maine, and Utica, New York, to Boonville, California; from New Glarus, Wisconsin, and New Ulm, Minnesota, to Cave Creek and Tempe, Arizona—not to mention places like Fernandina Beach, Florida, Windsor, Vermont, or Strongsville and Willoughby, Ohio, and Kona, Hawaii (and an additional 100 to 200 in Canada). Mind you, each of these breweries—tiny, medium, large—typically has anywhere from three or four to a dozen or more styles available at any given time, plus a changing roster of seasonal and specialty offerings that pushes the total number of choices out of the barrel or the tap into the thousands. At the eighteenth annual Great American Beer Festival in 1999, 406 U.S. breweries poured a record 1,902 different beers. (For the first festival, in 1982, 20 breweries served up 35 brews.) And the numbers, varieties, and sources of beers coming into the country have increased markedly. For example, sales of imports jumped 14.1 percent from 1996 to 1997, bringing to 7.6 percent the import share of the total U.S. beer market. All in all, there are roughly 5,000 to 5,500 breweries throughout the world, give or take a merger or closure or two.

This burgeoning largesse has served to solidify at least one ranking that has remained constant: The U.S. is by volume the world's largest brewing nation. (Germany, Great Britain, Japan, and the former Soviet Union are two to five respectively, much of their production finding its way to our taverns, package stores, and restaurants.) Although, perhaps surprisingly, we now (since 1997) have more breweries than any other country in the world, and more beer styles and brands too, we don't drink all we produce: The United States is not even in the top ten in per capita consumption, hovering around twelfth in the world (the Czech Republic, Germany, Denmark, New Zealand, and Belgium are first to fifth).

Overall, close to 95 percent of American domestic producers are brewpubs (where draft beer is made in small batches and primarily sold and consumed on the premises) and/or microbreweries (small quantities of bottled beer distributed mostly to nearby retail outlets). Although the definition is still being debated, the latter are generally assumed to have a brewing capacity of no more than 15,000 barrels annually; by comparison, a commercial megabrewery like Anheuser-Busch, the largest in the world, regularly churns out 5 to 6 million barrels at one plant alone (in the U.S. 1 barrel equals

31 gallons). Still, the total output of brewpubs and micros combined adds up to perhaps 3 percent of U.S. beer production; this despite the fact that there are no more than approximately six national breweries, some 80–90 contract breweries and perhaps a dozen regional breweries remaining in the country. In addition, fast-paced changes in the industry have resulted in a new category: regional breweries. Mostly, these started as micros and grew. They are defined as having a brewing capacity of 15,000 to 2,000,000 barrels a year. Boston Brewing, Red Hook, Celis, Full Sail Brewing, and Boulevard Brewing are just a few that have expanded into this new category.

In general, brewpubs and micros are small craftsmanship-oriented outfits where quality often can vary as unpredictably as the weather outside. As a group, they are referred to as *craft breweries*. The mortality rate is high, and one year's favorite drinking spot may easily become next year's empty parking lot. Domestic industry failure rates through 1998 were 1-in-5 for brewpubs and 1-in-4 for micros, with a total of 123 closings (versus 183 openings) for the year. This guide is as up-to-date as it can be, but it's always best to check the status of the brewery—pub, micro, regional, or mega—that interests you prior to paying it a visit or searching out its product.

Riding this ever-cresting wave of malts, hops, yeast and water, *The Beer Lover's Rating Guide* will help you determine and select the very best beers of any type—lagers, ales, stouts, wheats, porters, fruit, specialty, whatever—from all over the United States and around the world.

By providing sections on style characteristics, serving temperatures, alcohol content, color variations, taste, aroma, ingredients, and foodworthiness—even a listing of the beers with the oddest names—this field guide to beer drinking pleasure will also identify those brews less deserving of your attention.

TAKING YOUR OWN FIELD TRIP

This is not a book portentously telling you what to drink or what to avoid; it is instead a guide meant to encourage you to select beers that *you* will enjoy, for your own personal pleasures and reasons. While the ratings and comments in *The Beer Lover's Rating Guide* reflect my standards and opinions, I have tried to present the information in a way that makes it easy for you to determine what you find tasty and satisfying and what not.

The guide is user-friendly, easy to read, and designed to be fun and informative. As my friends, and their friends, have come to rely on my list, I invite you to match your evaluations with those you find in this guide. Remember: one person's sip is another one's swallow.

What follows are the results of careful research. Hope you enjoy the tasting as much as I did. And, with the guidance of *The Beer Lover's Rating Guide,* may you Never Buy A Bad Beer Again—anywhere, anyplace, anytime.

—Bob Klein

BEER STYLES:
What's the Difference?

ALE

Ales tend to be sweet, fruity, and texturally smooth. Many ales are higher in alcohol content than lagers and may have a pronounced taste and flowery aroma. Ales are top-fermented, that is, the yeast rises to the top during the brewing process. Most are served at 50° to 55°F.

Types of Ale

BARLEY WINE: A strong, full-bodied dark ale with malt sweetness. Medium-to-strong hop bitterness with very high alcohol presence. Almost like wine.

BITTER: Highly hopped and quite bitter. Strength varies from Ordinary to Best to Extra Special Bitter (ESB). Usually served from the tap in England.

BLOND/GOLDEN ALE: A lighter version of pale ale, this offering is closer to a lager in flavor than most ales. It has a floral aroma with a light, dry taste.

BROWN ALE: A lightly hopped, sweet, full-bodied brew with low-to-medium alcohol content. Color ranges from reddish-brown to dark brown. Lower in alcohol than porter and not as dry.

INDIA PALE ALE (IPA): High in hops with a moderate amount of malt flavor. A dry, assertively bitter brew that ranges from pale (many IPAs fall into this category) to deep copper in color. It is fruity and flowery with evident alcohol.

PALE ALE: Pale ales combine distinct bitterness with some malt-based sweetness. Distinguishing characteristics are dryness and defined hop taste. So named to separate them from the darker porters, these ales range from amber to copper-brown and may be fairly mild to quite bitter.

PORTER: Black or chocolate malt contributes significantly to the dark-brown color. Well hopped and heavily malted. Hops help mitigate what might be a heavier drink. Porters can be malty sweet and range from bitter to mild and are drier than stouts—somewhere between stout and ale.

SCOTTISH ALE: Classically strong and amber to dark brown in color with a sweet, malty character. Rich and chewy. Low in hops; however, some variations brewed outside Scotland tend to be a bit bitter. Wide range of alcohol content. Also called "wee heavy."

STRONG ALE: Powerful flavor, highly alcoholic, but without clear-cut style characteristics. Usually dark in color with medium-to-low hops, producing a dry, bitter beverage.

ALCOHOL CONTENT

*T*he alcohol content of beer has traditionally been measured in the United States by percentage of alcohol by weight. Increasingly, American brewers, especially craft brewers, are switching to the general European standard: alcohol percentage by volume. You can easily convert one to the other by remembering that "by weight" is approximately 20 percent lower than "by volume." The chart below shows a general guideline for alcohol levels for major beer styles. Keep in mind that many beer styles—and therefore the defining amounts of alcohol—overlap.

BEER STYLE	% ALCOHOL BY VOLUME	BEER STYLE	% ALCOHOL BY VOLUME
U.S. Light	2.9–4.4	European Amber	4.9–5.9
Ale	3.2–7.5	Märzen/ Oktoberfest	5.5–6.3
Lager	3.9–5.4	Malt Liquor	5.5–7.5
Pilsener	4.0–5.5	Bock	5.9–8.8
Porter	4.3–6.3	Doppelbock	6.5–8.0
Stout	4.4–10.0	Barley Wine/ Abbey Ale	8.1–15.0
Wheat	4.5–5.6		

STOUT

NOTE: Stouts and porters are often visually mistaken for each other, as both are quite dark in color. Unlike porter, however, stout comes in a variety of types which are described below. Highly roasted barley is the keynote of this ale style.

GLOSSARY OF TERMS

Beer Language

BALANCE: The subjective impression of how well the various ingredients, especially malts and hops, go with one another. Ideal balance varies from style to style.

BODY: The thin-to-thick feel in the mouth. Beers can be full-bodied, medium-bodied, or light-bodied.

BOTTLE-CONDITIONED: Yeast continues fermentation process in the bottle, resulting in unpasteurized, naturally carbonated beer.

BOTTOM-FERMENTED: Lagers are made from a type of yeast that ferments at the bottom of the liquid; the brewing process involves longer brewing times and colder temperatures. During brewing, the beer is stored for periods ranging from weeks to months. Storing, or lagering, encourages a smoother, more settled taste in the beer.

BRUSSELS (or BELGIAN) LACE: Wisps of tightly packed small bubbles, or foam, that attach to the sides of the glass, often in intricate, spiderweb-like patterns or with a delicate curtain or sheeting effect. Usually a sign of a fresh, quality-made brew.

CLOYING: A sweet, sticky taste and feel on the tongue and sides of the mouth; often results in a thickish aftertaste.

Types of Stout

DRY STOUT: Plenty of hops, which produce a bitter taste; the addition of roasted unmalted barley or flaked barley result in a drink that is almost like a strong cup of coffee. Also called Irish Stout.

IMPERIAL STOUT: Created as an export to the frozen climate of Czarist Russia, this is very rich and malty with fruity overtones. Somewhat dry and strongly alcoholic.

MILK STOUT (also called English Stout or Sweet Stout): Malty sweet instead of dry, milk stout has a lower alcohol content than dry stout. The name reflects the addition of lactose (milk sugar) as a sweetener.

FERMENTATION: The process by which alcohol and carbon dioxide (carbonation) are produced as the yeast acts on sugars in the grain.

HOPS: Flowers that give beer its bitter and aromatic character. Specific hops are selected for their taste- or aroma-giving properties. They are also a natural preservative and enhance the alcohol effect. Hops slow the pulse rate and give a sense of euphoria.

MALT (MALTED BARLEY): The defining ingredient, malt gives the beer its distinctive roasted, grain, or sweet character by influencing color, flavor, aroma, and head retention.

MOUTHFEEL: Overall physical impression of the beer as it travels from the lips to the throat.

TOP-FERMENTED: Ales are made from a type of yeast that ferments at the top of the liquid; the process involves warmer brewing temperatures and a shorter brewing time, often only days. Prior to the advent of refrigeration and the introduction of hops as preservatives, ale was the only game in town.

YEAST: A single-celled organism that converts sugars to alcohol and carbon dioxide. Also contributes to the production of certain flavors (e.g., citrus) and aids in the expression of malt and hop flavors.

OATMEAL STOUT: Like milk stout, this is a sweeter product. The addition of oats is the sweetener in this case.

LAGER

Meant to be aged for 6 to 8 weeks or longer at cool temperatures, lagers should be clear, crisp, and distinctly carbonated. Most are maltier, less hoppy and aromatic, lighter colored, lighter in body, and often less alcoholic than other beers. Lagers are bottom-fermented; that is, the yeast settles at the bottom during the brewing process. *Lagern* means "to store" in German. Drink at 40° to 45°F.

Types of Lager

AMERICAN DRY LAGER: Despite the name, this product is a Japanese development. Pale to golden in color, it is distinguished by high carbonation but is low in bitterness, malt and hop flavors, and, often, taste. Dry (not sweet), low in alcohol, and scientifically balanced light body.

AMERICAN PILSENER: Crisp and more carbonated than European pilsener, but weaker and lighter in body and flavor. Prevalent style in the United States. Corn or rice adjuncts are often added during the brewing process, giving bulk and filler. Corn also imparts some flavor.

BOCK: Bock is traditionally full-bodied, strong, and high in alcohol content. It has an obvious malt and hop presence. Color is copper to dark brown. Bocks brewed in the United States often are brown or light brown, mild, and not complex. The more full-bodied doppelbock (double bock) is even higher in alcohol content. It is often identified by "ator" at the end of the name (for example, Celebrator). Helles Bock, a lighter version, in both color and taste, is somewhat sweeter and softer.

ENGLISH LAGER: Light variant of the American-brewed version, in both color and taste.

EUROPEAN DARK/MUNCHNER DUNKEL: Malt, as opposed to hop, taste predominates. Suggestion of caramel, although not as sweet as brown ales. Clean and crisp with nice carbonation. Roasted malts give this beer its dark amber-to-brown coloration.

EUROPEAN PILSENER: Light-bodied with high hop bitterness. Clean, dry, rich taste and restrained flowery finish. Pale color with medium alcohol content. Pilsener, the palest of all lagers, is the most widely brewed and copied beer style in the world.

EXPORT: Often, but not always, refers to Dortmund-style brew (named for that Rhineland city's classic style): smooth, pale, fuller-bodied, and higher alcoholic content. Also, as the name suggests, it may indicate beer sold only outside the country of origin, usually to meet specific, or assumed, foreign taste preferences. Sometimes it means nothing at all.

MALT LIQUOR: Generally pale in color with no particular flavor profile. Very high in alcohol (where allowed by law). Some may have a sweet finish. Essentially an American invention.

MARZEN/OKTOBERFEST: Amber to pale copper in color. Malty aroma and sweetness with lots of hops to balance the malt. Good carbonation with low-to-medium bitterness. Toasted malt flavor predominates. Originally brewed in March *(Märzen)* and stored until October.

VIENNA AMBER: Toasted malt flavor with some rich, malty sweetness. Low hop aroma. Similar in flavor to the American-made lagers but darker in color, which is amber to copper.

COMBINATION STYLES

Beers produced by a mix of ale and lager brewing techniques and/or ingredients.

ALTBIER: Well hopped and fairly malty, alt beers are quite aromatic and bitter. These beers are a well-defined amber color to a deep brown. *Alt* is the German word for "old" or "old style" and refers to the use of the old brewing method (warm ale-like fermentation) as opposed to the age of the beer. It basically the German equivalent of English ale, although alts are aged cold, like lagers, which puts them in the combination-style category. In southern Germany, ordering an alt will get you a dark lager.

BIERE DE PARIS/BIERE DE GARDE: Strongly hopped, high in alcohol, copper colored, vibrant palate, and bottle-conditioned, laid on its side to age. Some are top-fermented (ale), some are bottom-fermented (lager—Brasseurs, for example).

CREAM ALE: A mild, pale ale with hop aroma. Sometimes blended with a lager, or using both ale and lager yeasts. *Cream ale* is an American term. A close cousin to "steam beer." Also called American ale.

KOLSCH: A lighter-colored version of alt beer, Kölsch is pale gold. It is delicate, dry, and almost wine-like, with low hop flavor and less bitterness than the true alt beer.

STEAM: Brewed at warmer ale temperatures and made with lager yeast. Medium-bodied, amber, and tellingly hoppy, with a generous head. A beer style created in the U.S., it is generically known as California common. Anchor Brewing Company has copyrighted the "Steam Beer" name.

WHEAT/WEISSE/WEIZEN; WEISSBIER (White Beer): Offers wheat malt concentration, high carbonation, and lower alcohol content. Yeasty tartness is a distinctive characteristic with hints of fruity/spicy overtones, especially clove and apple or banana. Belgium's *witbier* has a honey-orange character. American wheat beers are not as well defined as European wheats. A good hot-weather thirst-quencher. Wheat beers that are conditioned in the bottle, with resulting cloudiness or sediment, carry the prefix *Hefe,* which means "yeast" in German.

SPECIALTY BEERS

These beers may be ales, lagers, or combination-style beers. What distinguishes them is the addition of flavorings, such as fruits (including chile peppers), herbs and spices, smoke, honey, or the use of uncommon brewing techniques. Specialty beers may fit into more than one category. Some of the most distinctive are listed here.

ABBEY or TRAPPIST: Dark, rich ales, these brews were traditionally produced at Trappist monasteries throughout Europe. Five Belgian Trappist monasteries still make the strong concoction using a centuries-old processes under the direction and supervision of monks. Only this quintet—Chimay, Orval, Rochefort, Westmalle, Westvleteren (St. Sixtus)—can use the appellation Trappist.

FARO: A kind of lambic enhanced in sweetness by candy sugar.

GUEUZE (pronounced *gerz*): A type of Lambic, blending aged and new lambics to produce a sweeter drink.

LAMBIC: Lambics are wheat beers, with fruit added. Essences or real cherries *(kriek),* raspberries *(framboise),* or peaches *(pêche)* are blended into the beer, giving it a distinct but not overpowering fruitiness. Often sour, with low carbonation. Brewers typically do not add yeast; fermentation is accomplished naturally and spontaneously by any one, or more, of hundreds of airborne wild yeast strains, resulting in an uncontrolled variation in flavor characteristics from one brewed batch to the next.

RAUCHBIER (Smoked Beer): The smoky flavor of these beers is produced by drying the malt with wood smoke. The flavor is quite intense, like some sausages and salamis.

SEASONAL/WINTER: Christmas beers are typical of this category. Cloves, coriander, ginger, cinnamon, spruce, licorice, nutmeg, and other herbs and spices are common additions. Often full-bodied ales and high in alcohol.

THE COLOR OF BEER
(Light to Dark)

Visual characteristics greatly enhance the enjoyment of a particular style of beer. The shading in the glass below will give you a general idea where within the range of beer coloring a beer style falls. Keep in mind that, contrary to popular belief, dark beers do not automatically mean higher alcohol content. They are generally stronger tasting, but the impact is often attributable to ingredients other than alcohol.

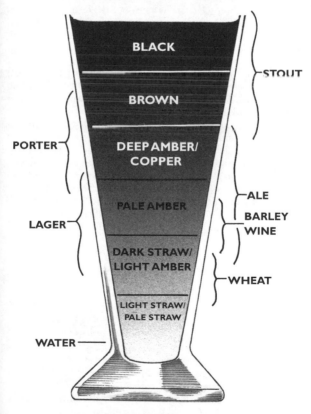

BREWERY TYPES

One hundred years ago, Americans had some 2,000 domestic breweries from which to select a favorite brew (down from 4,131 in 1873, the most ever). In the 1980s and into the 1990s, with six major brewers in the United States, the variety, if not the availability, became dramatically limited. But within the last two decades or so, a resurgence of interest in quality and in different styles of beer has moderated that trend. As a result, beer drinkers have become more familiar with—and appreciative of—both domestic and imported brands.

While domestic brews are still by far the cold one of choice, imported beers make up an increasingly large segment of the U.S. beer selection. Where once the focus was on readily available European brands, consumers in the United States now can find varieties from places like Russia, Nairobi, Ecuador, Belize, Korea, Togo, Western Samoa, and Hong Kong. Nonetheless, Europe remains the leading exporter. Number one is Holland, followed in descending order by Canada, Mexico, Germany, Great Britain, Ireland, and Japan. By brand, it's Corona, Heineken, Beck's, Molson Golden, and Labatt's Blue. Brands and styles of imported beer currently number in the thousands and comprise close to 8 percent of the total beer consumed in this country. In 1998 the nation's 480,000 licensed retailers sold over 196 million barrels of imported and domestic beer, amounting to $59.8 billion in sales. Twenty-five years ago, according to one report, no more than 100 different beers arrived at our shores from elsewhere.

This imported and domestic liquid cornucopia has altered our drinking habits in still another way: American beer drinkers now can get their brews from five distinct brewery sources.

CB COMMERCIAL BREWERY:

These are the megabreweries that market their bottled and canned beers for mass consumption. Annual production is in the 50 to 90 million barrel range for individual breweries such as Anheuser-Busch and Miller. While most foreign breweries do not approach the gargantuan output of the American giants—though some do, for example Ireland's Guinness and Brazil's Brahma—brewers with the capacity to export their products to the United

> NOTE: The abbreviations CB, MB, BP, CT, RB, and AB are used throughout the guide to identify brewery types.

States will also be identified in this category, except as specifically noted otherwise.

MB MICROBREWERY:
Producing 15,000 barrels or less each year (a changing benchmark often in dispute), these small operations offer an array of special handcrafted beers with the emphasis on quality ingredients and careful attention to brewing methods. There are now some 500 microbreweries in the United States and Canada, many of them also operating their own brewpubs. Distribution is usually limited and in bottles (cans are not used by these craft operations because they affect the taste). The success of some former micros (for example, Sierra Nevada in Chico, California, Red Hook in Seattle, Washington, Samuel Adams's Boston Beer Company, San Francisco's legendary Anchor Brewing) has allowed them to expand local operations to reach regional, national, and even international markets.

BP BREWPUB:
With far less brewing capacity than a microbrewery, the majority of brewpub beer is produced and consumed on the premises, as specified by local and state laws. No packaged sales are allowed, though some jurisdictions do permit customers to "take out" returnable half-gallon or gallon jugs. Further, brewpubs may sell small quantities to be tapped at nearby taverns. Capacity is usually measured in gallons, not barrels, and variety is often limited at any given time. Along with food, most brewpubs also offer several changing styles in honor of the season or a special occasion, or in response to customers' tastes. Approximately 1,000 brewpubs are in operation in the United States and Canada.

CT CONTRACT BREWERY:
Individual brewers that don't have their own production facilities contract with an idle brewery, or one functioning below capacity, to make a beer to the brewer's specification using the brewery's equipment. The brewer, not the brewery, is usually responsible for distribution and sales. Utica, New York; New Ulm, Minnesota; Monroe, Wisconsin; and Dubuque, Iowa, are sites of several contract breweries, the use of which has become quite popular in recent years. Check bottle labels to determine where the beer is made versus where the company is located. For example, many of the Boston Beer Company's popular Samuel Adams brands were originally brewed in Pittsburgh, Pennsylvania; more recently they've been coming out of Portland, Oregon, and Cincinnati, Ohio. Much smaller batches are also made at its Boston location. And Spanish-sounding Simpatico, found in the Mexican beer section of the cooler, is brewed in . . . Dubuque, Iowa, USA.

RB REGIONAL BREWERY

Too large to be considered a microbrewery but too small to be called a commercial brewery, regional breweries can now be found all over the American beermaking landscape (a total of about 60 in both the United States and Canada). Brewing capacity is within the 15,000 to 20,000 million barrel range. Many regional breweries were formally microbreweries; with increased production and distribution, they outgrew their micro status. Some are longtime operations that have successfully catered to loyal customers over the years and for one reason or another never were interested in significantly expanding their operations. Yuengling, Shiner, August Schell, and Rogue fall into this category.

AB ABBEY/TRAPPIST BREWERY:

Using centuries-old traditions, European monastery breweries turn out limited quantities of (usually) strong, stern stuff meant to warm the cockles of the medieval traveler's heart. Belgium is especially known for its monk-brewed ales. Today, not all abbey-style beer is made at a monastery.

BEER GLASSES ARE MORE THAN JUST CONTAINERS

ALE

Because ales often have a flowery, fruity aroma, the best glasses are tulip-shaped to capture the bouquet, or volatile odorants, thereby prolonging sensual enjoyment of the brew. Ales tend to be fruity-sweet with a smooth texture. In general, they also have more robust, complex flavors and deeper hues.

Ale Glass

STOUT

Large, hefty, thick-sided glasses or tumblers with lots of clear viewing space allow depth and shades of color to be enjoyed

in a variety of stouts and other heavy brews. Enough room is also needed for head foam to settle out at its own pace or rise to the occasion as it sees fit. A wide mouth permits access to the rich roasted aroma and taste as the liquid is drained to the bottom.

Stout Glasses

LAGER

Glasses with thick sides help keep cold beer cold—or at least chilled. Facets in the design help achieve that goal. Lagers in general are best served cold. Mugs with handles allow you to grasp the brew while keeping your hands off the glass, thereby minimizing the possibility of raising the beer's temperature by body warmth.

Lager Mug

**Faceted Lager Mug
(English Style)**

**Pint Lager or
Bitter Glass**

PILSENER

Pilseners, which feature an assertive carbonation, display their character best in a conical, distinctly tapered vessel. By forcing pressure upward within the liquid, the V shape helps to generate a constant stream of bubbles, adding to both the zestiness of the texture and the appealing foamy abundance of the head.

**Pilsener
Glass**

WHEAT

Because wheat beers combine the characteristics of different styles, the glass configuration should accommodate the variations. Serving multipurposes, the glass should restrict escaping aromas (in the upper bell-shaped portion), while also allowing for the relatively higher levels of carbonation (the lower straight portion forces the bubbles upward).

Wheat Glass

SNIFTERS, FLUTES, AND TULIPS

Because high-alcohol ales like barley wine and Christmas beers have especially concentrated aromas and tastes, a compact, rounded glass is best for forcing the senses to pay attention. To start, take several short, quick sniffs for aroma and enough of a brief sip to allow the liquid to touch all areas of the mouth—and then swallow. When sniffing, cup the hand around the rim of the glass to prevent the odors from escaping.

Brandy Snifter   **Flute Glass**   **Tulip**
(Barley Wine)   **(Lambic)**   **Champagne Glass**
(Abbey/Trappist Ale)

BEST STORAGE TEMPERATURES FOR BEER

REFRIGERATED TEMPERATURE	STYLES	
45°F	Light beer American lager	Australian lager Malt liquor
45°–50°F	Wheat beers	Bock beers
48°F	European lager Dark lager	Pilsener Kölsch
CELLAR TEMPERATURE	STYLES	
50°–55°F	Ale (Scottish, brown, pale, etc.) Stout Lambic	India pale ale Bitter Doppelbock
ROOM TEMPERATURE	STYLES	
55°–60°F	Barley wine Strong dark ale	Abbey/Trappist ale

PAIRING
BEER AND FOOD

While European beer drinkers have long known the pleasures of pairing beer and food, it is only recently that we in this country have come to appreciate the close connection between a good brew and a pleasurable meal. There are several reasons for this change, but two stand out. The increasing availability of tasty, quality beers has revolutionized our attitudes and taste buds about a drink that had come to be seen as uniformly bland and/or mainly for those desiring an alcoholic thirst-quencher at a ball game or picnic. Second, the new willingness to sample a broader spectrum of cuisines, both foreign and regional, coupled with their more universal accessibility, has encouraged a similar receptivity to different drink accompaniments, including beer. Also, beer is reasonably priced, is unlikely to spoil as easily as wine, and is there when you want it—at restaurants, pubs, grocery stores, and convenience stores—in quantities and serving sizes that minimize waste and are small enough to encourage sampling a wide enough variety to find favorites. In short, the renewed interest in beer (for that's what it is—the recalling of pleasures and quality hardly experienced since Prohibition) parallels our search for satisfying ways to enjoy what we eat and drink.

There are no hard-and-fast guidelines for choosing the "right" beer for particular foods. In truth, beer is so versatile it pretty much goes well with whatever food or meal your individual taste tells you is compatible. For some, and for some foods, that may mean, for example, a textural or flavor contrast between the beer and the food. At other times or locations, with other companionship, or following the mood of the moment, you may desire a beer that complements or integrates smoothly with the food. Whatever the situation, the choice is up to you. Unlike wine drinkers, we are not constrained by proscribed food/drink compatibility—allowing us a more varied, changing range of choices and pleasures.

The following chart lists traditional beer and food pairings. But remember, the final opinion is yours. Feel free to experiment and explore, with one goal in mind: to enjoy what you drink—and eat—regardless of what food may be on your plate or any preconceived notions you may have brought with you to the table.

Similarly, suggestions regarding the shape of the serving

glass are based on helping you get the most enjoyment from the characteristics of a particular brew. Don't worry if you can't locate just the right container; in the end, as long as it doesn't leak (and it's not made of plastic or metal), you've got the right one in your hand. Skoal! Prosit! Good cheer!

ALES

One of the four basic beer categories. Ale, top-fermented and the oldest of the brewing styles, takes only a few days to mature. Serve at cellar temperature (between 50° and 60°F).

STYLE	GLASS/ SERVING TEMP.	FOODS
BARLEY WINE	Snifter/60°F	Strong-flavored cheeses, nuts; as a complement to Cognac, sweet whiskeys, or as an *apéritif* or *digestif.*
BITTER	Straight-sided pint/55°F	Strong-flavored cheeses and good company.
BLOND/GOLDEN ALE	Straight-sided pint/55°F	Generally, fish or fowl.
BROWN ALE	Undulating (like old Coke glass)/55°F	Game, spicy foods, well-seasoned beef dishes.
DRY STOUT	Clear tumbler with wide mouth/60°F	Oysters, spiced shellfish dishes, hearty breads, game, chocolate.
IMPERIAL STOUT	Goblet or snifter/60°F	Best alone, or before a meal, with snack foods.
INDIA PALE ALE	V-shaped or pint glass/55°F	Smoked meats and cheeses; foods that need sharp, pointed contrast.
MILK/CREAM STOUT	Clear, gradually tapered tumbler with wide mouth/55°F	Lighter foods and sweeter desserts, or alone.

STYLE	GLASS/ SERVING TEMP.	FOODS
OATMEAL STOUT	Clear tumbler with wide mouth/55°F	Italian foods, beef dishes, stronger-flavored seafoods.
PALE ALE	Straight-sided pint glass/55°F	Fish, shellfish, sharp cheeses; also spicy foods, beef, and well-seasoned seafoods.
PORTER	Clear tumbler/ 55°F	Shellfish, veal, lighter flavored meats.
SCOTTISH ALE	Mug or thistle-shaped glass/ 55°F	Strong-flavored meats and cheeses; melons.
STRONG ALE	Goblet, tumbler, or snifter/50°F	Fruits, nuts, soft cheeses; rich foods in general.

LAGERS

These bottom-fermented brews require up to six weeks or more of storage at cool temperatures (*lagern* is German for "to store"). Serve them the way they came into this world—chilled (between 45° and 50°F).

STYLE	GLASS/ SERVING TEMP.	FOODS
AMERICAN DRY LAGER	Your choice/ 45°F	Your choice of bland foods.
AMERICAN PILSENER / EUROPEAN PILSENER	Tapering (V-shaped) glass from narrow bottom to wider top or elongated tulip-shaped glass/ 45°–48°F	Freshwater fish, salads, fresh tart fruits.

STYLE	GLASS/ SERVING TEMP.	FOODS
BOCK	Thick-sided stoneware mug or glass tumbler/50°–55°F	Smoked and unsmoked meats, garden salads.
DOPPELBOCK	Stemmed, rounded tumbler/50°F	Pastries, desserts, smoked meats, wild fowl.
ENGLISH LAGER	Faceted mug/ 45°–50°F	Light summer-type foods, or drink by itself.
EUROPEAN DARK/ MUNCHNER DUNKEL	Undulating (like old Coke glass)/ 48°–50°F	Well-seasoned pastas or chicken, but you decide for yourself.
EXPORT	Mug or thick-sided glass/ 45°F	Sliced cold meats, hearty meat dishes.
HELLES BOCK	Stemmed tumbler or straight-sided glass/45°F	Spicy foods, stronger-flavored meats with mustard and onions on the side.
MALT LIQUOR	Your choice/ 45°F	You name it.
MARZEN	Tall earthenware or glass mugs/ 48°–55°F	Sausages, German-style foods, heavier but simple foods.
OKTOBERFEST	Thick-sided glass or earthenware mug/ 48°–55°F	Sausages, sauerkraut, and lots of oompah music.
VIENNA AMBER	Straight glass or glass mug/ 48°–50°F	Mexican food, spicy pastas, sweet desserts.

SPECIALTY BEERS

Specialty beers usually contain some additive to give them a distinctive taste. Fruits, smoke, herbs, and spices are but some of the ingredients.

STYLE	GLASS/ SERVING TEMP.	FOODS
ABBEY/ TRAPPIST ALE	Snifter or goblet/60°F	Cheeses, breads, hard fruits, shellfish, freshwater fish, light seafoods.
FRUIT LAMBIC: CHERRY, RASPBERRY, PEACH	Champagne glass/45°–50°F	Foods that are flavored with or complement the particular lambic fruit flavor. Cherry goes well with other tart fruits, such as apricots, cranberries, and cherries. Raspberry is delicious with chocolate. Peach is nice with waffles covered with peach slices.
LAMBIC (NON-FRUIT)	Tumbler/55°F	Stronger cheeses, shellfish. Use lambic as you would a dry sherry *apéritif,* or *digestif.*
RED (OR GREEN) CHILE ALE	Tumbler or clear tankard/ 55°F	Mexican-style or other spicy foods. Pork-based meat dishes.
SEASONAL/WINTER ALE	Clear tumbler or goblet/ 55°–60°F	Smoked meats, game, hard fruits (pears and apples).

COMBINATION-STYLE BEERS

These beers blend the features of both lager- and ale-brewing processes.

STYLE	GLASS/ SERVING TEMP.	FOODS
ALT	Thin, straight glass/55°F	Tart fruits, breads, lighter meats, tomato-based dishes.
BIERE DE PARIS / BIERE DE GARDE	Snifter or champagne glass/50°–55°F	Gourmet foods—make believe this is wine.
CREAM ALE	Your choice	Anything.
KOLSCH	Thin, straight glass/48°F	Vegetables, less-than-tart fruit, white chicken meat, breads, appetizers.
STEAM	Sturdy mug/ 45°–50°F	Cheeses and moderately spicy foods.
WHEAT	Long vase-shaped glass or large tumbler with beveled top/48°–50°F	Smoked fish, meat; heavier but not highly-spiced foods; German-style dishes; alone as good summer thirst-quencher.

THE RATING GUIDE

HOW I JUDGE AND
RATE A BEER

Tasting and evaluating a beer is not a complicated or sophisticated process. Basically, all I need is a clean glass (very important), the beer, and, if I am planning to have more than one brand or style without a meal, some unsalted crackers (I prefer unsalted Nabisco Saltines) or French bread (or other bread made without sugar), and water to cleanse the palate between tastings.

I rank beers from 0 to 5. In official beer competitions, judges use a 50-point scale. That range can be useful in helping the commercial brewer or serious homebrewer to pinpoint trouble spots (for example, bacterial infection or too much bitterness for a particular style). Likewise, judges using this method can confirm for the brewer the attractive qualities of the product (for example, malt and hop balance, fruit subtlety, carbonation level).

However, I find the 50-point scale to be too cumbersome for the ordinary beer drinker, the interested consumer who wants to enjoy a freshly poured glass at home or at a restaurant, but who would also like to be able to sort out the various characteristics defining a good, bad, average, or exceptional beer. My 5-point scale takes the important elements from the 50-point scale and makes them manageable: It is meant to add to the enjoyment of the beer as well as serve as a guide, or aid, to the understanding of what makes a satisfying (or not-so-satisfying) brew.

The following section defines the overall qualities—separated by one-point intervals—I took for in assigning a rating: from *Bad* (0 to 1) to *Outstanding* (4 to 5). A separate chart outlines the five steps I use to arrive at a rating of the beers I sample. Each beer style and its defining characteristics can be found earlier in this book. On pages 17 to 19, I have included a chart that suggests the shape of glass to use with each style. Pictorial representations of the various shapes are shown as well.

BEFORE YOU TASTE

First, a few quick reminders:

• Pour the beer slowly and gently in a steady, thin cascade against the inside of the glass, gradually angling the liquid so that it becomes a vertical stream down the middle by the time the beginning of the head is about an inch from the rim of the glass. Careful pouring reduces the likelihood that you will wind up with a glass full of foam while simultaneously ensuring the presence of foam, in the form of a head, where it is desired—at the top of the glass.

• Beer should never be tasted straight from the container, whether bottle or can (cans in particular tend to impart a metallic or otherwise taste-distorting sensation). Pouring the beer into a glass or mug ensures that a beer's aromatic components, called "volatile odorants," will be slightly jostled in their journey through the air from container to glass. The relatively brief contact with the oxygen allows for a fuller release of the ingredients into your nose and mouth, where your senses—taste, aroma, tactile—await them.

• Remember: a clean glass is an absolute must. Dirty glasses destroy the head and cause the beer to go flat. Bubbles in the liquid that adhere to the side or bottom of your glass are a sign of a dirty glass—no bubbles sticking below the beer line is a wise formula to keep in mind.

• Also, stay away from those frosty, iced mugs. They may be appealing, especially on a hot day, but they cause thermal shock to the beer, essentially flattening and obscuring the beer's flavor.

Now, begin pouring and start enjoying. You're on your way to never having to tolerate a bad beer again.

JUDGING A BEER

1. LOOK

Hold the glass up to the light; note the head shape and uniformity of color.

CHARACTERISTICS

Color: according to style.
Clarity: according to style.
Head: according to style. Quality beers have tightly packed small bubbles. Large, quickly disappearing bubbles in the foam are a sign that artificial foaming agents have been added. *Note:* beers tend to have a bigger head at higher altitudes.

Points: 0–1 _____

2. SNIFF

• Leave 1 to 2 inches between the rim of the glass and the head to allow for the collection of volatile odorants (bouquet or aroma).
• Swirl the beer to release some carbonation.
• Place your nose inside the glass, cup your hands around the rim, and inhale deeply. (Some experts suggest taking three to four short, quick sniffs.)

CHARACTERISTICS

Malt: generally clean and fresh.
Hops: generally tonic and bracing, sharp.

Points: 0–1 _____

3. SIP

• A very personal process.
• Make sure the beer gets to all parts of the mouth.
• Swallow.
• Take another sip.

CHARACTERISTICS

Malt: generally sweet, clean-tasting.
Hops: generally bitter, perhaps flowery.
Balance: do the malts and hops balance or does one dominate?
Conditioning: e.g., carbonation, full- or light-bodied brewing flavors—does it adhere to beer style (flowery, fruity, for ale, for example)?
Aftertaste: is it pleasant, intrusive, nonexistent, long-lasting?

Points: 0–1 _____

4. ANOTHER LOOK

Beer can change while sitting in the glass waiting for you to take another sip.

CHARACTERISTICS

Bubbles: still rising (good) or nonexistent (bad).
Brussels lace: plentiful, ringing sides of glass in more or less parallel circles (good); erratic, thin and wispy (bad).
Clarity: according to style.
Color: according to style.
Head: according to style; should be at least one-half thickness of original after one minute.

Points: 0–1 _____

5. EVALUATE

This is an overall impression. Try to pay attention to the separate elements in steps 1 to 4. Better yet, pay heed to all of the senses, as suggested by Munich's Weihenstephen Brewing School: "To sight it must ring clear as a bell, it must snap in the ear, feel pleasantly sticky between the fingers, smell fresh and tempting and taste heavenly." In short, does this beer you have in your hand make you want to have more, or less, or none at all?

Points: 0–1 _____

TOTAL POINTS: 0–5 _____

RATING THE BEERS

Using the "Judging a Beer" information starting on page 29, rate each of the five components (look, sniff, sip, another look, evaluate) anywhere along the continuum from 0 to 1. Next, add the five scores to get your own total rating. For example, Brand X Lager receives the following: Look: 0.3; Sniff: 0.7; Sip: 0.2; Another look: 0.5; Evaluate: 0.5 (Total: 2.2). Or simply drink, enjoy, and come up with one overall rating anywhere from 0 to 5. Then, check the list on the following page to find out what your rating means. In this case, Brand X Lager is at the low end of the Average range.

One enjoyable approach is to gather several friends, give each a few ounces of the same beer, and rate it individually without any discussion. To add to the fun, you might also obscure the label, so no one knows what beer it is. When everyone is finished, compare the ratings, and go on to the next bottle.

RATING	DEFINITION
4 to 5	OUTSTANDING, with or without food. Makes you eager to share with friends and to keep stocked in your refrigerator.
3 to 4	ABOVE AVERAGE. Complements and adds to the enjoyment of food and is satisfying by itself. The choice when no 4 to 5 is available.
2 to 3	AVERAGE. Neither enhances nor detracts from the food and hardly satisfies by itself, but serviceable in a pinch. Okay for when your attention is directed elsewhere, for example at the TV.
1 to 2	BELOW AVERAGE, with few redeeming qualities except for being wet and/or cold and you are very thirsty. Ingredients may be apparent, but are weak and/or of poor quality.
0 to 1	BAD! Unfinishable under most circumstances.

AROMA AND TASTE

It always helps to know the right word to identify what your senses experience. Here are the basic terms to help convey your impressions as you sniff, taste, and swallow.

TERM/ DEFINITION	KEEP IT	SEND IT BACK	COMMENT
ASTRINGENT: dry, puckering mouthfeel, raw	✔		Too much is not a good sign.
BITTER: sharp taste • bitter hops taste • bitter non-hop taste	✔	✔	Particularly noticeable at the back of the tongue; intensity varies.
BUTTERY: • slickly smooth like butterscotch		✔	Bacteria in the processing; request another brand.
• slight suggestion of sweet butter	✔		Okay in some European beers and ales.

TERM/ DEFINITION	KEEP IT	SEND IT BACK	COMMENT
CABBAGEY: smells like cooked cabbage		✔	Improper boiling method, malting process, and in some cases, contamination.
CHEESY: smells like, well, like cheese		✔	Beer stored warm, or possibly old hops used in brewing.
FRUITY: the aroma and taste of banana, apple, raspberry, etc.	✔		Okay, especially in ale; generally not appropriate in lager.
GREEN APPLE: smells and tastes like unripened apples; raw tasting		✔	Brewing process is unfinished, or inappropriately high fermentation temperature.
MEDICINAL: smells like a hospital, iodine, or a chemical		✔	Due to unclean brewing container, wild yeast, sanitizing residues; get your money back.
METALLIC: may also taste tinny or blood-like		✔	Brewing error: exposed to metal.
MOLDY: smells like mold or damp earth		✔	Fungal contamination in the brewing process.
MUSKY: smells like a closed-up cellar		✔	Stale water or malt with fungal contamination.
NUTTY: similar to taste of fresh nuts	✔		Malt character; a pleasure if you can find it.
OXIDIZED/STALE: winey, or unpleasingly acidic and sour; cardboard, rotten vegetable-like odor		✔	Exposed to high temperatures in shipping/storage; old beer or air in bottle; demand another bottle.

TERM/DEFINITION	KEEP IT	SEND IT BACK	COMMENT
SALTY: tastes as if table salt has been added to the beer; generally noticed on the sides of tongue		✔	Too much sodium chloride or magnesium sulfate (both salts) used in the brewing process.
SKUNKY / LIGHT STRUCK: smells like a skunk		✔	Exposed to light; don't buy beer displayed in sunlight, under fluorescent bulbs, or bottled in green or clear glass.
SOUR/ACIDIC: tastes like very tart lemon or like vinegar; pungent aroma	✔ (sour)	✔ (acidic)	Good (e.g., Lambic, Berliner Weiss): citric/lactic acid. Bad: bacterial infection.
SPICY: odor should be present only if spice has been added to beer	✔		Common in Christmas beers and beers advertising the addition of spice. Should not overwhelm.
SULFUR-LIKE: taste/odor of rotten eggs/corn, burning matches		✔	Terrible yeast problem—demand a free bottle for you and your drinking partner.
TART: • fresh, full-bodied tartness	✔		Positive attribute in *weissbier* and some other beers. Tartness should not be present in a lager or overly present in an ale.
• dry and sour; no body		✔	Unacceptable in any beer.
TURPY: solvent or turpentine odor/taste		✔	Results from old hops or warm-temperature storage.

PUTTING IT ALL TOGETHER

Each of the beers in the Rating Guide is listed by its name as it appears on the label of the beer or as indicated in the brewery literature. (Similarly, brewery location is taken from the label, information which in some cases may change from time to time—make certain to check before-hand.) If the beer's style is capitalized, it is officially part of the beer's name. The lower-case boldface type indicates that I have added the beer's style for your information (for example, in the case of draft beer, when the beer tasted was, in fact, on tap, the word "draft" appears in parentheses). The boldface capital letters after the name indicate the type of brewery that produces the beer (for example, **CB** for commercial breweries), and the number at the far right indicates my overall rating of the beer.

It is my preference to drink beer with food, and to keep a record of beer-food compatibility. In order to organize my impressions so that I can accurately record them, I generally don't pour the beer until the meal has been served. (At restaurants, I make sure to ask the server not to bring my beer until the food has arrived.) Then I take a sniff and a sip or two before eating anything and record my perceptions. From that point on, I jot down my impressions—aroma, texture, color, mouthfeel, aftertaste—as they occur. As a result, some food/beer characteristics may be revealed by mid-bottle, and I make note of them in the middle of the entry; others do not clearly appear until the end, and accordingly, my comments about the relationship of the beer to the food appear later in the written observations. Still others may fluctuate from sip to sip, thereby sometimes making the comments appear to be contradictory. It's all part of the complete impression.

My tasting method is loose and flexible, although I admit that on occasion I do get carried away; but after all, this is meant to be fun, not preparation for a final exam in Advanced Malts and Hops. Indeed, I would encourage you to freely use the pages of the Rating Guide to record your own taste impressions and ratings.

In most entries, I offer a generalized food suggestion rather than a specific recommendation. Each is based on food I sampled with the beer and is meant to give you an idea of what type of dish to order or prepare. The suggestions are not meant to be limiting—"Klein says try this with chicken, but I'd rather have a burger." Instead, use them as a starting point. Then eat, drink, and enjoy.

AASS BOCK   **CB**   **3.2**
(Drammen, Norway)
Immediately pleasing fruity aroma followed by pleasant, round, natural-fruit taste; thin at the tip of the tongue, but more full-bodied going down; pleasant sweetness with smooth tang at the edge; basically warm, creamy, and comforting, though weak on flavor. Try it with hot dogs (and other spicier sausages) and beans.

B E E R   F A C T

*A*ass, the name of the country's oldest brewery, means "summit" in Norwegian.

AASS CLASSIC Lager   **CB**   **3.2**
(Drammen, Norway)
Oat-nut aroma; smooth and easily digestible; minimal head atop ruby-brown-peach color; malty nuttiness; moderated freshness; somewhat flat; suggestions of roasted smokiness—nice combination of style and cultural influences; well made, as is true of all Aass brews. Accompanies pasta dishes nicely.

AASS JULE ØL Lager   **CB**   **4.5**
(Drammen, Norway)
Very enticing initial aroma followed by burst of mild, mellow, dark nutty-caramel taste; water is clear and fresh; texture remains mellow and smooth; sweetness mists the palate nicely; calm, tasty, uncomplicated, and delicious. Accompanies deli-style foods.

AASS PILSNER   **CB**   **2.9**
(Drammen, Norway)
Smooth with an edge that fits comfortably into place; fresh and clean-tasting; moderate body somewhat manipulated by food reflects and mirrors the ingredients; semi-dry, thickish finish. Serve with barbecued ribs, coleslaw, and onion rings.

ABC EXTRA STOUT   **CB**   **3.7**
(Singapore)
Burnt taste becomes slowly integrated as it warms; musty and flat; food gets lost in its creamy maltiness and is ultimately enveloped by dominant richness; cherry-black color; very full-bodied, with a zest for life—watch that you don't get bowled over by this energetic brew. Goes well with Mexican food.

ABC VERY SUPERIOR STOUT   **CB**   **3.6**
(Singapore)
Moderated bitterness turns calm as it reaches the back of the mouth; combination of ambiguous wine/burnt taste; appropri-

ately thick and creamy without being obtrusive; onrushing bitterness significantly enhances the overall flavor, raising it above average. Fine with charbroiled steaks and salad.

T A P   T I P

Quenching the Fire on the Tongue

*N*o, it's not your imagination that beers high in alcohol seem to go well with hot, spicy foods. The scientific fact is, they actually do. Potent, highly alcoholic brews—typically malt liquors and strong lagers—are quicker to quiet the pain on your tongue. In spices such as chiles, certain compounds are specifically alcohol-soluble and as the concentration of alcohol increases, the fiery molecules are washed away. As a result, water is always less of a fire extinguisher than even the most minimally alcoholic beer.

ABITA AMBER Lager   **RB/BP**   2.6
(Abita Springs, Louisiana)
Thick on the tongue with a honeyed aroma; somewhat flat; maltiness predominates, as is appropriate for Vienna style lager; mild, toasted sweetness also adheres to style, though it gets washed out by spicy foods; satisfying but unexciting. Accompanies pasta carbonara and other non-tomato-sauced pasta dishes.

ABITA GOLDEN Lager   **RB/BP**   2.3
(Abita Springs, Louisiana)
Hardly any mouthfeel; flat with a hint of citrus taste; some slight mustiness; warming trend comes up at mid-bottle and beyond; good balance between hops and malt, though to be truthful, neither ingredient is really tangible or apparent; well made, but not overly exciting; pleasant, affecting sweetish finish. Try it with plain grain and vegetable dishes such as rice, green beans, and corn.

ABITA IRISH RED ALE   **RB/BP**   1.4
(Abita Springs, Louisiana)
Slightly skunky; meager carbonation and general flatness do not bode well; some back-of-the-throat fruitiness; not zesty or alcoholic; bland; some pleasant, mild, honey taste at the finish—too bad it wasn't present earlier.

ABITA TURBO DOG Dark Ale　　　**RB/BP**　　　**3.8**
(Abita Springs, Louisiana)
Mild, rough perfuminess both in the nose and on the tongue; glimmer of fruitiness, but not sweet or alcoholish; very malty with surrounding burnt-caramel ambiance; fresh water helps tie it all together; deep brown color with underlying auburn undertone is revealed in the light; softens and mellows food; smooth on the tongue, grizzled and rough on the throat; very textured and aromatic feast for all senses; substance and staying power. Complements all-American meals, such as roast turkey with stuffing or grilled cheese sandwiches.

BEER FACT

*T*he story goes that Brian Boru, the first king of Ireland, was out riding one day, when he was suddenly enveloped in a magic cloud. Therein he encountered a Celtic god, accompanied by a beautiful maiden. The young girl handed the king a glass of foaming red beer. Some say that was the beginning of Irish red ale.

ACADIAN VIENNA AMBER　　　**MB**　　　**3.2**
(New Orleans, Louisiana)
Malty, with a touch of fresh-out-of-the field hops; medium-bodied and quite tasty; sweetens at mid-glass; well-placed, balancing band of hops keeps the sweetness in check; a tint of caramel colors the pale gold body; finishes with a sweet swish of hops in tandem with a pleasant toasted-malt mouthfeel. Try this amber-style with spicy pasta dishes.

ACME PALE ALE　　　**MB/BP**　　　**1.4**
(Fort Bragg, California)
Bitter and sharp, with just the slightest hint of sweet honey; malt and hops are present, but just barely; vaguely fruity with no clearly defined taste features; a quick hit of flavor disappears and leaves a sour aftertaste; overall, too muddy to be ranked above average; cloudy pale apricot body and quarter-inch-thick head provide the visual focus. Best to avoid this one.

ADELSCOTT MALT LIQUOR　　　**CB**　　　**4.2**
(Schiltigheim, France)
Mellow, smoky aroma and taste set this off immediately as a beer to search for; fresh yeast taste and deep-seated earthy character with hints of spice (cloves?); peat-smoked malt contributes mightily to its smooth, whiskey-like presentation; finishes with all the ingredients respecting and complementing each other; delicious

alcoholic warmth emerges with sweet-sauced dishes; a delightful little beer full of zip and surprises.

ADLER-BRAU PILSNER   **BP**   **0.9**
(Appleton, Wisconsin)
Thick, bland, with no hint of complexity or ingredients; continues its crawl to nowhere although redeemed slightly when paired with food; take your business elsewhere.

ADMEERAL TYEYSKOYE Lager   **CB**   **0.4**
(Moscow, Russia)
Rough, raw graininess, with faint alcohol aroma; rough, raw graininess, with faint alcohol aroma; rough, raw graininess, with faint alcohol aroma—need anything further be said? Try at your own risk, one sip at a time.

ADNAMS SUFFOLK EXTRA ALE   **CB**   **3.1**
(Southwold, England)
Quick whiff of alcohol is followed by a mildly bitter taste that stays awhile in the throat; hops are more dry than bitter; faint pinpricks of spiciness come along at mid-bottle; hazy amber body contrasts nicely with the white frothy head; a good sessions beer—for drinking and talking with old friends.

BEER FACT

*H*orse-drawn drays, pulled by Percherons, the battle horses of medieval days, still make deliveries in Southwold and the surrounding region. Nearby locals insist that the Adnams brewery's location near the sea is the reason for the subtle taste of salt in its beers.

AEGEAN HELLAS Lager   **CB**   **4.2**
(Atalanti, Greece)
Nice, sweet barley taste lingers pleasantly on the tongue; subtly well-defined, soft and receptive; substantive and close to full-bodied, this is a quality brew. Goes well with fish and shellfish.

AFFLIGEM NOEL CHRISTMAS ALE   **CB**   **3.9**
(Opwijk, Belgium)
Sweetly and gently bitter; toying, playfully thick-sweet character, especially on the palate; as soft and buttery as the mouth of a champion bird dog; faintly chocolate; carefully calibrated alcohol infusion; becomes honey-sweet as you drink it; light richness entertains from start to finish. This is a wonderful sipping ale—gently warming and patient, and by the end of the bottle, you will be too.

AFFLIGEM TRIPEL ABBEY Ale   CB   3.6
(Opwijk, Belgium)

Distinct but passing burnt taste; very soft on the upper palate and sides of the mouth; head is creamy, soft, and delicately bubbled and remains on top of the cloudy, apple-cider body; enhanced by mild, fruity taste; consistent, predictable, and modest in its expectations; gets a little too winey as meal progresses; more appealing at the beginning than the end, though creamy fullness is especially tasty at the finish; rounded body and full in character. Accompanies meatballs and spaghetti.

AGUILA IMPERIAL ALE   CB   3.8
(Madrid, Spain)

Airy and light, with rice aftertaste; complex without making you pay too much attention; restrained hoppiness and maltiness make this a delightful, but not heavy-handed, beer for snacks and other light dishes. Try it with pistachio nuts, creamy dips, celery, carrots, and thinly sliced hard salami.

AKTIEN JUBILAUMS PILS   CB   2.8
(Kaufbeuren, Germany)

Slight clove mouthfeel with subdued, spritzy texture; dry and softly straightforward; soft, creamy head doesn't hang around too long, so enjoyment quickly fades; modulated crispness along with appropriate balance; faint hoppiness and enduring mild sharpness settle into a fuller workmanlike pilsener with food, including appropriate golden hue; no particular distinction or distraction; clove remains; texture could be thinner; not something you would seek out at the bar, home, or restaurant, yet there is no reason to refuse it if it's delivered to your table. Accompanies all types of poultry dishes.

AKTIEN ST. MARTIN
DUNKLER DOPPELBOCK   CB   2.8
(Kaufbeuren, Germany)

Soapy aroma and stuffy, roasted, almost burnt taste on first sip; too much syrupy sweetness; alcohol becomes more apparent as beer is imbibed—clearly needs help from food that is strong enough to absorb and neutralize its alcoholic excesses. Spicy dishes such as chili nicely absorb the cloying sweetness and sharpness of the alcohol, turning this doppelbock into a smoother, more drinkable brew.

AKTIEN WEIZEN   CB   2.6
(Kaufbeuren, Germany)

Definite spicy and yeast aroma, which becomes more defined as it picks up a complex fruity-clove character; tart and strong; straightforward—goes from mouth to throat without giving up any of its flavor; well made and sturdy; leaves a dry feeling on the roof of the mouth. Good with salty snacks, like popcorn and peanuts.

ALASKAN AMBER Alt   **RB**   **3.8**
(Juneau, Alaska)
Deep, attractive aroma greets your nose as full-bodied sharpness greets your mouth and upper palate; although smooth texture eventually weakens, it maintains its vitality and very pleasing balance; easy sipping and easy going down, but not particularly complex; maintains composure from start to finish; a frisky little brew. Try it with heavily sauced barbecued spareribs.

ALASKAN FRONTIER AMERICAN
AMBER ALE   **RB**   **0.7**
(Juneau, Alaska)
Malty sweetness is followed quickly by an unpleasant bitterness that lingers in the mouth; caramel-malt aroma lures you into expecting a similar taste—to your disappointment; fortunately, the bottom drops out and *all* the flavor seems to disappear about one-quarter through the bottle; aroma gallantly hangs on. Don't waste your money on this one. Bronze Medal winner at the 1996 Great American Beer Festival.

ALASKAN PALE ALE   **RB**   **1.0**
(Juneau, Alaska)
Fizzy but neutral-tasting with a faint hint of raw fruitiness; decidedly uncomplex; muddied copper color—not distinctive or defined; slight sneaker smell, as if it sat in the closet too long; no nuances. Remains neutral with food. Nonetheless, this beer clearly has its fans: It was a Bronze Medal winner at the 1993 Great American Beer Festival.

ALBA SCOTS PINE ALE   **CB**   **2.8**
(Alloa, Scotland)
As advertised, abundant liquid morsels of spruce and pine quickly identify this traditional Scottish ale; rich and complex; thick-smelling, as if it's still cooking; spruce character is enhanced by the lack of bitterness (there are no hops); reminiscent of sweet, freshly tapped pine sap; the texture is smooth as glass; ends with a woodsy taste and spicy aroma. Drink this alone and imagine you're quenching your thirst in the wilderness.

ALFA Pilsener   **CB**   **3.1**
(Schinnen, Holland)
Crisp with a comforting tastiness; mellow, unassuming; almost an afterthought to the food, but it's appealing enough, with sharp carbonation and light texture, to succeed on its own; finishes a touch dry. Accompanies barbecued pork dishes.

ALGONQUIN COUNTRY LAGER   **MB**   **0.5**
(Formosa, Ontario, Canada)
Old perfume aroma; slightly sour taste; flat texture; too bitter to even begin to be enjoyable, or palatable; flat and listless; even the

pale straw color seems washed out; turns musty on the upper palate; there may be some malt hidden in there somewhere; rough and unappetizing.

ALGONQUIN SPECIAL RESERVE ALE   CB   2.9
(Formosa, Ontario, Canada)
Immediate surge of barley malt followed by subdued tang and some fullness in the mouth; sort of lays back and lets the food do its thing; sharpness remains at the bottom of the throat while body fullness remains detached, to everyone's advantage; vague fruitiness confirms its ale character. Accompanies home-style meals.

ALIMONY ALE   CT   3.9
(Dubuque, Iowa)
Nicely integrated; balanced fruit and harsh hop aromas; neither too sweet nor too bitter; overall burnt taste is not demanding and carries along a trace of bitterness; full-bodied; loses some oomph at the end while its red-brown cola color turns muddy; mild fruity aroma persists; accommodates meat loaf and fried potatoes quite nicely; a surprisingly good beer. Label calls it "The Bitterest Brew in America."

ALLAGASH WHITE Wheat   MB   3.6
(Portland, Maine)
Nice, clean fruity/clove aroma is followed by a complementary spicy-clove mouthfeel; hazy, yellow body stays crisp and fresh-tasting; full-flavored without being pushy; hint of bitterness covers back of the tongue and stays in the aftertaste, along with minimal citrus presence; becomes sweeter along the way, but keeps its trademark clove-yeast complexity; pleasant, perfumey aroma at the very end; a top-notch wheat beer made with the knowledgeable beer drinker in mind. Drink alone or with fresh, crisp salads.

ALMAZA PILSENER   CB   3.9
(Beirut, Lebanon)
Sharp, crisp, and to the point, with a faint hint of mustiness; adds comfortable zestiness to food and gains sweetness and coherence as meal progresses; this surprisingly refreshing brew comes in a minuscule 9.5-ounce bottle—not enough to let you fully enjoy its tantalizing delights; delectable and light. I liked this a lot. Goes well with lightly flavored poultry dishes.

ALPINE VILLAGE HOFBRAU LAGER   MB   2.3
(Torrance, California)
Sour and vaguely oxidized on the first sip—almost like apples about to ferment; aroma and taste disappear and settle into somewhat flat and characterless interplay with food; malt is tasted as meal progresses, especially after a chew or two of bread; not much

head, but Brussels lace is present as glass tilts for a drink; ultimately falls somewhere between an American lager (relatively plain and featureless) and a European one (assertive, hoppier); less-than-solid presentation—lacks complexity, balance, and attraction. Accompanies Italian tomato-sauced dishes, such as veal Parmesan.

ALPINE VILLAGE HOFBRAU PILSENER   MB   2.3
(Torrance, California)
Slight hint of malt and skunkiness on the first sip; fast, up-rising bubbles are apparent in the glass, but less so on the palate; slight sourness and ambient sweetness; turns perfumey later on; a chameleon of a brew; too soft and sweet at the end—not brittle enough for a pilsener; finishes malty with a sweet honey trace. Deteriorates into thinnish ballpark beer.

ALTENMUNSTER EXPORT Lager   CB   2.0
(Marktoberdorf, Germany)
Full, creamy texture; bland, weak aroma; initial watery mouthfeel; mildly flavorful; hangs around, providing an unobtrusive, occasionally fruity, background setting for food; overall, undistinguished and lightweight—especially for a German brew; honey-colored; grainy taste fades rapidly; sort of the Schaefer of Germany—not filling or exciting. Accompanies barbecue flavors well.

ALTENMUNSTER MALT LIQUOR   CB   1.9
(Marktoberdorf, Germany)
Milky appearance; immediately distinctive flavor appears at first to be headed in flavorful direction but instead quickly fades into sour-stale taste; becomes appealingly neutralized with spicy food; can't stand alone; all in all, cheap-tasting and underpowered.

ALTES GOLDEN LAGER   MB   1.3
(Frankenmuth, Michigan)
Oxidation, greenness, and an obvious but unsuccessful attempt at draft freshness; no complexity or compelling interest, but that's okay with simple foods; easy-going, undemanding, just-drink-me-and-don't-pay-too-much-attention-to-my-taste beer; lightweight and hassle-free.

AMARIT LAGER   CB   2.2
(Bangkok, Thailand)
Smooth; slight rice presence comes through when the bottle is almost finished; additional overall flavor also appears as the end nears, especially without food; no aroma or taste markers to guide you through the bottle; some palates have detected an unlager-like fruitiness, but I couldn't find any; still, not bad-tasting, just not aggressive enough. Accompanies chicken breast covered with sharp cheddar cheese and green chile peppers.

AMBAR DOS ESPECIAL Lager   CB   3.3
(Zaragoza, Spain)
Mini-fizziness with sharp, honey taste on the tongue; tart hoppiness plays around with subdued serious malt presence; remains smart and tart with medium head (with, alas, big bubbles) on top of red-tinted, golden hue; hangs in there with strong qualities that are accommodating to food; dryness on the palate at the finish, as well as warmth in the throat; gentle sweetness gradually emerges with spicy chips and dips—beer matches dip in attraction on one-to-one basis; mellow, soft, and contented; finishes with just the perfect touch of hoppiness, letting you know that there is some bitterness hidden in there somewhere.

AMBER—VIENNA STYLE Lager   CT   3.1
(Monroe, Wisconsin)
Predictable and unprovocative; not unpleasant cheesy smell; almost crisp; small-bubbled; quickly fills the palate; deceptively bland and Americanized at first taste, quickly followed by creamy, mildly burnt undertone; soft and mellow, with follow-through of opposing bitterness; comforting, friendly beer; somewhat sweet in the end. Accompanies spaghetti and meat sauce.

ANCHOR LIBERTY ALE   CB   3.7
(San Francisco, California)
Sweet, mild taste with clear hop presence; not too sharp or sparkly; distinctively mellow and subtly dry; cloudy amber; natural carbonation; sips smoothly, quietly, and responsively; somewhat chewy, as if waiting for food to munch on; very pleasant, highly aromatic from mid-bottle to the bottom; nicely done; Silver Medal winner at the 1993 Great American Beer Festival. Makes for a fine combination with scallops or other mild seafood lightly sauced with butter and garlic.

BEER FACT

*A*nchor Brewing is an old San Francisco company that was resuscitated in 1965 by Fritz Maytag (of appliance fame) while he was a graduate student at Stanford University. One of the early microbreweries, Anchor's increased production, along with a full range of brews now distributed nationally, has moved it into the regional brewery category.

ANCHOR OLD FOGHORN ALE (draft)   CB   3.4
(San Francisco, California)
Immediately cheery, spicy-sweet, and fresh-tasting; sprucy-citrus, similar to Anchor's Our Special Ale; packs a punch that creeps

up on you; gets stickier and fruitier but maintains distinctive Anchor taste—all without food; subtle, continuing undertone of hops; surrounded by gummy spiciness; not a bashful brew; delicate, stenciled Brussels lace—cobwebby and long-lasting—adds to the party; well made. Good with desserts.

ANCHOR OUR SPECIAL ALE (annual)　CB　2.5–4.0
(San Francisco, California)

Anchor's annual Christmas beer since 1974, this is indeed something special—sort of like a liquid Christmas tree. I have had several bottles of this fruity, spicy confection every holiday season since 1988, and look forward to each year's incarnation (six-packs begin reaching retail outlets in early November; supplies are often gone by mid-December); a distinctive clove presence is a perennial feature, along with a fizzy, creamy texture and a full, restrained heartiness; unfortunately, a cloying, syrupy sweetness also shows up regularly as does (less regularly) some bitterness at the back of the throat; taste and aroma are richly complex, with modifications from year to year—spruce livened up the 1991 edition, while an orange pekoe tea aroma greeted 1992 consumers; celery and, more recently, an accommodating chocolate presence have also made appearances; articulately balanced, consistent, and predictably satisfying from bottle to bottle as well as from year to year. Goes well with pretty much any food, but I find it to be most enjoyable all by itself, slightly warmed. My average rating over the 12-year period is 3.7.

B E E R　F A C T

*C*arbonation "steam" released from warm-temperature brewing gives Anchor Steam its unusual name, although others say it was based on the original power source. Whatever the case, Anchor now owns the "Steam" trademark.

ANCHOR PILSENER　CB　2.5
(Singapore)

Slight, flowery taste, along with faint clove mouthfeel; quite pale; zesty and almost tart; smoother than many pilseners; tends to weaken and flatten as you drink it; well-meaning. Best imbibed alone or with chips and mildly spicy dip.

ANCHOR STEAM　CB　3.9
(San Francisco, California)

Full, rounded, and unpretentious with a ribbon of fruitiness along the edges; distinctive bite and attenuated bitterness don't chase you away; this unique cross of ale and lager massages the sides of the mouth with a subtle tang; integrated smoothness, responsive character, and overall quality presentation suggest this is a food-friendly beer you could drink in (moderate) quantities without tiring, getting bored, or feeling unduly filled; too much heartiness and zest are lost at the bottom of the glass; sample the draft version to fully enjoy its mellow grittiness and lasting charm. Try it with egg dishes or seafood pastas.

ANCHOR WHEAT   **CB**   **3.8**
(San Francisco, California)
Subdued and smooth; tamped-down fruitiness, with a slight lemon nuance; sheets of full Brussels lace enhance the ambiance; smooth and very swallowable; maintains mellowness and attraction with food; well hopped, but controlled and measured; citrus flavor emerges more pointedly at the end of the meal; color is weak for this style. Good with a turkey or tuna salad sandwich.

ANDERSON VALLEY BARNEY FLATS
OATMEAL STOUT   **MB/BP**   **4.0**
(Boonville, California)
Fresh and burnt-tasting malt; magnificent deep, deep-brown color; full and creamy with ongoing well-balanced mix of caramel and chocolate malts; smooth; expresses itself very well overall and does likewise with individual nuances in taste, color, and texture; well made; perhaps a little thin at the end; a bit chewy toward the bottom of the bottle. Blends almost seamlessly with plain foods.

B E E R   F A C T

*O*riginally called *entire,* porter was much preferred by eighteenth-century London porters (hence its name) who asked for a heady mixture of ale and several other beers at their local drinking spots. Only recently reclaiming interest among all types of beer drinkers, it is now a style of ale sometimes made with darker, roasted malt. Porterhouse steaks are so called after the popular cut of meat offered up at the early porter bars, or houses.

ANDERSON VALLEY DEEP ENDERS
DARK PORTER   **MB/BP**   **3.8**
(Boonville, California)
Soft and gently prickly; creamy with palpable backbone; a little too thin; gentle caramel/mild roasted flavor; rich, dark-brown opaque color with chocolate aroma, but not taste; needs a bit more integration and settling; creamy head, with a modicum of nicely patterned Brussels lace; watery richness; subdued, but ap-

propriate bitterness; sediment on bottom of glass; in the end a little too weak for porter. Retains even-handed bite with grilled chicken breast with Cajun-style sauce.

ANDERSON VALLEY HIGH
ROLLERS WHEAT   MB/BP   3.6
(Boonville, California)

Rounded, appealing, sweet-cider taste with just enough head to let you know it really is a beer; some freshness bordering on green; fruit remains in the nose, not on the palate; ripening floweriness as it warms; cloudy blond color as befits a wheat beer; fresh-tasting brew with hoppy strength and yeasty exuberance with a little tang. Good with dried fruit or whole-grain snack crackers.

ANDERSON VALLEY POLEEKO
GOLD LIGHT ALE   MB/BP   3.7
(Boonville, California)

Honey-gold, light-bodied ale; crisp, clear, and richly scented with hops; hint of English bitter gives it a zesty flavor and some bite; furry, citrus overtones; alcoholic with a foamy, long-lasting head; some bitterness and snap settle into a creamy fruitiness; perhaps a bit too fizzy; supportive and unobtrusive with food. A light accompaniment to linguine with clam sauce or sautéed chicken with fresh ginger.

ANDES Lager   CB   2.6
(Caracas, Venezuela)

Typical lager with more heartiness and grain flavor than most; flavor and texture even out and become more integrated with food; prickly sharpness also emerges; slight musty aftertaste detracts from graininess of this mid-range but not great South American beer.

ANDES PILSENER   CB   1.2
(Santiago, Chile)

Visually very bubbly, but alas, you can't taste the carbonation; rather tasteless overall with a hint of grain to catch your attention; exudes freshness due to what the label says is "pure Mountain water"—not to any other ingredients, certainly; no real substance; filled with adjuncts, it's sort of the Budweiser of Chile, but with better water; has a certain soft crispness; a touch skunky at the end.

ANKER PILSNER   CB   2.9
(Djakarta, Indonesia)

Mild, pleasant, grainy taste on first sips; sharp and spicy itself, it exacerbates and encourages hotness of Chinese food; smooth with a slight jolt of sharpness; nice, integrated balance of the texture and the water. Responsive to spicy or well-seasoned dishes.

ANTARCTICA Pilsener   CB   2.7
(Sao Paulo, Brazil)

Lightly perfumed, with sweet aftertaste; good carbonation; distant hint of cloves; thin, but nicely configured and visible Brussels lace; finishes with a coffee taste on the sides of the mouth. Compatible with Southwestern or Mexican food.

ARA BIER ALE   CB   3.8
(Essen, Belgium)

Fresh-tasting and yeasty-tart; banana and clove flavors touch the palate with pleasure; mouthfeel is rounded and complex; subtle, background honey taste is just the right complement to the soft, yeasty mouthfeel; mellow hop-malt-citrus interchange is very satisfying; pillowy, white head nicely caps the cloudy, light-blonde body; well-done blending of flavors at the end; this is a delicate, tasty morsel of an ale. Goes nicely with fruit pastry.

ARCTIC AMBER LAGER   CB   0.8
(Sault Ste. Marie, Ontario, Canada)

Flat, bland, and inflexible; no head; faded, weak-looking body; faint caramel taste is not entirely covered up by the more pronounced metallic taste; listless and unappetizing; harsh texture; also coarse and irritating.

ARCTIC BAY CLASSIC LAGER   MB   1.8
(Vancouver, British Columbia, Canada)

Hoppy ballpark beer, with just a hint of tang to keep you interested; somewhat thin and light with pallid golden color; sharpness diminishes and what little complexity it has disappears with food; okay if you want a pedestrian, low-denominator brew at the local tavern; otherwise, it's not worth the trouble—or the money.

ARIS GREEK LAGER   CB   2.5
(Thessaloniki, Greece)

Quite dry and amiably thirst-quenching, helped along by a tart bitterness that makes itself at home on the tongue; sharp and thoroughly carbonated; light, sweet grainy mouthfeel; flowery, textural sharpness lessens at mid-bottle and is replaced by flowing mild maltiness that stays until the end; faint hop presence at the finish makes for a balanced, gently bittersweet aftertaste. A delight with creamed pickled herring.

ARNOLD PILSNER   CB   1.3
(Bavaria, Germany)

Smooth and easy to swallow; slightly musty and somewhat bland, leaning toward mild; unobtrusive, tentatively sweet taste; light for a German beer; does nothing for food; slight, quickly dissipating aftertaste; definitely undistinguished.

ARROGANT BASTARD ALE MB 2.3
(San Marcos, California)
Sharply bitter with a fresh, fruity aroma and taste; thick, almost gummy mouthfeel; aggressively hoppy without any moderating maltiness (or anything else); heavily roasted malt taste only adds to the intensity, as does the alcohol potency (7.2%/vol.); aftertaste is bitter and unsatisfying; thankfully, it finishes fruitier and lighter than the beginning (or middle), but still is too unidimensional; flavorful, but a tough drink to handle, especially for the newcomer.

ARTEVELDE ALE CB 4.1
(Melle and Ghent, Belgium)
Fresh, breezy aroma reflects an equal balance of hops and malt; pours a heavy, large-bubbled head that literally hangs around when the bottle is finished; silky smooth with just a hint of grit to allow it to cling to your tongue and be savored a bit longer; nice and gentle, like a pat on the head; deep-rooted alcohol presence; remains refreshing without much fruitiness or yeastiness, but lacks a certain depth of character; full, creamy, off-white head and rich, deep-brown body make for a picture-perfect classic Belgian ale; improves with warmth; satisfying. Best with unadorned chicken or fish.

ASAHI DRAFT Pilsener CB 1.1
(Tokyo, Japan)
Nutty and relatively tasteless; more American than Japanese; smell and taste of adjuncts, particularly rice, are in the air (and in the glass); this is the least satisfying of Asahi's long line of beers.

ASAHI SUPER DRY DRAFT Pilsener
(bottle/can) CB 2.5
(Tokyo, Japan)
"Rigid" feel with unvarying taste; predictable; dull aftertaste is minimally apparent; unexciting, but of good quality; came in smallest commercial beer container I have ever seen: a 135-ml micro-mini can (about 4.5 ounces). Okay with plain food.

ASAHI Z DRAFT Pilsener (bottle/can) CB 3.7
(Tokyo, Japan)
Sharp, fresh, and refreshing with a quick thickness on the tongue; light, with a tasty complexity of hops, malts, yeast, and water; touch of sweetness comes and goes; no hint of impurities; good thirst-quenching summer beer. An almost perfect complement to just-caught rainbow trout.

ASMARA Lager CB 2.1
(Asmara, Ethiopia)
Sweet/sour, quickly resolving to light, fruity/syrupy ambiance; spritzy underlayer; evolving grain taste pushes aside initial fruitiness; holds creamy, quarter-inch-thick head throughout; in the

end there is too much of a weak, dusty off-taste with food; not complex or interesting.

ASSETS DUKE CITY AMBER LAGER   MB   1.9
(Albuquerque, New Mexico)

Slight, fruity aroma, but weak taste and minor toastedness; generic, nondescript; tastes more like ale than amber; color approaches appropriate (but so what?); pleasant hoppy aroma doesn't translate into zesty, integrated beer; sweetish finish is a bit cloying.

ASSETS HEFE WEIZEN   MB   2.2
(Albuquerque, New Mexico)

Creamy, smooth with a slight hint of clove, as advertised; perfumey aroma with thick, foamy Brussels lace that hangs like a curtain; not as pungent or sharply defined as it should be; needs to be drier and fruitier; remains smooth with a little snap only at the end; cloves fade rapidly—as does your interest.

ASSETS SANDIA STOUT   MB   2.5
(Albuquerque, New Mexico)

Light in body and soul; musty on the tongue with a flattened, roasted taste; thin; large, erratic bubbles form what passes for a head; gives evidence of proper ingredients and appropriate arrangement, but not enough of them, or not enough character to make them either distinctive or enjoyable; no aroma—a distinct loss for a stout; Brussels lace is okay, while it lasts; if this could be pumped up, it could be a decent beer.

ASTICA PREMIUM LAGER   CB   3.6
(Haskowo, Bulgaria)

Flavorful; steadfast head greets you with a continuing hoppy taste; lots of grain present; rounded sharpness mellows and becomes even more agreeable with spicy dishes; stable, firm, full-bodied, with character and aplomb. A beer to enjoy with a variety of foods.

ATHENIAN—THE GREEK BEER Lager   CB   0.8
(Athens, Greece)

Vaguely sour; very thin and textureless; no head and no body to speak of; minor fizziness provides the only continuous suggestion that this might be beer; light and undistinguished with a bitter off-taste; finishes flatter than it begins; those may be hops lamely bringing up the rear, but they're too late—and too faint— to help.

AUGSBURGER BOCK   CB   2.5
(St. Paul, Minnesota)

Lightweight, dark beer with mild, fruity fizziness; smooth, watery consistency with hollow innards; warm, cozy, and somewhat insipid with food; a pleasant, easy-to-get-along-with beer of no real consequence; lazy and unassertive; a surprising freshness at the end.

AUGSBURGER DARK Lager CB 1.8
(St. Paul, Minnesota)
Smooth, gentle, and basically tasteless; easy-going background beer; acceptable alone, with an appetizer, or with a main dish; taste of both malt and hops is suppressed; thin reddish-brown color detracts from overall ambiance; in the end, uncaring and neutral; friendlier companions are easy to find.

AUGSBURGER GOLDEN Pilsener CB 1.1
(St. Paul, Minnesota)
Gritty taste with an expectation of similar texture that never occurs, so you wait for a balance or at least a presence of an important ingredient and are left hanging; remains flat and straight-line in taste with no variation; thin-to-nonexistent head; light honey-golden color; actually seems to lose taste when accompanied by food; surprisingly bland.

AUGSBURGER PILSENER CB 3.5
(Monroe, Wisconsin)
Smooth taste and flavor, with an almost-crispness from start to finish; detectable hoppiness; end is sharp and engagingly sweet, with gentle, muted alcohol presence; agreeable, no-effort refreshment, which, after all, is what enjoyment should be all about. Enjoy with raw bar shellfish.

AUGSBURGER ROT LAGER CB 2.3
(St. Paul, Minnesota)
Basically aromaless with a non-distinctive taste and a head not even worth discussing, somewhat spritzy, with thin texture; washed-out amber color (*rot* means "red" in German) is the only sign of roasted caramel malt; neutral taste and semi-solid backbone of tangible hops; mellow, malty sweetness finally emerges (how come it took so long to find its way out?); oddly for a lager, this appears to improve as it warms; no bad aftertaste, just no taste at all. Try it with broiled or grilled beef dishes.

AUGSBURGER WINTER FESTBIER CB 2.6
(St. Paul, Minnesota)
The gentle aroma of nutmeg and cinnamon is accompanied by hints of honey and perhaps molasses; full-bodied and mouth-filling; orange pekoe flavor emerges after a while; spices swirl around the auburn-colored liquid; at the finish, the spicy energy settles down and warms the cockles of your heart, throat, and palate. A festive Festbier that goes with cookies and fruitcake.

AUGUST SCHELL BOCK CB 2.2
(New Ulm, Minnesota)
Fizzy, medium-light body and spritzy, highly caramelized taste; dissolves into smoothness with heavyish sweetness at the back of the tongue; too sweet and goes off in the wrong direction with

spicy foods; mellows out in the end, with no pizzazz to speak of; low alcohol presence; not very bock-like.

B E E R   F A C T

*T*he August Schell brewery's public gardens and lovely park grounds, listed on the National Register of Historic Sites, compete for attention with the company's lineup of beers. Contract brews from the across the country are a major part of the business at this family-run regional brewery.

AUGUST SCHELL ORIGINAL
DEER BRAND Lager   CB   3.8
(New Ulm, Minnesota)

Mild, light, and fizzy—this immediately strikes you as a good common beer; not complicated; tasty and flavorful; easy to drink several bottles; appears to contain adjuncts, but never mind; a bit of a thick aftertaste on the tongue. Perfect accompaniment to kosher hot dogs with ballpark mustard or baked beans.

AUGUST SCHELL PILS   CB   2.8
(New Ulm, Minnesota)

Nice light-caramel sheen; golden amber color is romantic and appealing; variable sweetness winds its way through each sip; tends toward sourness in contact with spicy foods. Best with plain chicken.

AUSTRAL POLAR PILSENER   CB   2.8
(Punta Arenas, Chile)

Sharp, modulated hoppiness; soft on the tongue; astringent; fading tang makes taste linger too long on the roof of the mouth; initial aroma is strong, somewhat acrid, and uninviting; pale-yellow, airy, fluffy head remains thick and clingy; pleasant and unassuming with a tinge of fizziness to remind you that it's a pilsener; smooth; a little too weak for ballpark beer, but the overall taste and texture are there—where's the hot dog?; nicely decorated with intricate and tenacious Brussels lace; warmth in finish that is missing earlier; heavy German style with a hoppy touch at the end; well made, but not outstanding. Try with beef or chicken fajitas.

AUSTRALIAN PREMIUM LAGER   CB   1.4
(Brisbane, Australia)

Blunted crispness with rounded, hoppy, winey mouthfeel on first sip; wineyness lingers on the tongue; taste in general is distracting even with simple foods; dwindles to bland at the bottom of the glass; yellow-brown color doesn't add to the attraction; medium-dry finish; a beer of less-than-average rating.

AVENTINUS WHEAT—DOPPELBOCK   CB   3.3
(Munich, Germany)

Intense clove taste makes you think of apple pie spiciness, especially when a helping of fruitiness kicks in after the third or fourth sip; clove character integrates well with the unfiltered wheat and high concentration of alcohol; there is a hint of smoked flavor in there somewhere as well; full, ivory-colored head lends a graceful note to the overall ambiance; this beer can be overwhelming if you drink it too fast; take your time and don't fret if you don't finish it all. Quite good with provolone cheese and basil.

AYINGER BAVARIAN WHEAT   CB   2.9
(Aying, Germany)

Nice light flavor with fine, solid wheat undertow; sharp and bubbly; milky color; maintains its grainy taste throughout; not enough individuality—could be any one of a number of similar Bavarian wheats. Okay with unspicy foods.

AYINGER CELEBRATOR DOPPELBOCK   CB   3.7
(Aying, Germany)

Sweet, toasted, and smooth on first contact; deep, dark, nutty flavor, almost fruity; full-bodied, robust, rich and flavorful; hearty caramel taste wells up after several sips; just a touch too sweet on the tongue, burnt at the back of the mouth; remains chewy, while richness begins to mellow into a dry

> *NOTE:* In Germany, Celebrator is known as *Fortunator.*

finish; hearty, deeply powerful. Try it with German sausage, onion rings, and mounds of creamy coleslaw.

AYINGER DUNKLES UR-WEISSE   CB   4.0
(Aying, Germany)

Fresh-baked-bread aroma, with accompanying sweet wheat flavor; chewy, textural, malty head remains thick throughout; tasty and remarkably smooth; other than a relative coolness that lightens the burden, it doesn't react to spicy foods; nice complexity of fruitiness and maltiness; color of apple cider; a bit too thin for my taste, but very satisfying, especially in hot weather; 40% wheat. Good at brunch with egg dishes and fresh fruit.

B E E R   F A C T

*U*r means "source of" or "origin" in German; in this case it is just a way of emphasizing the style of beer.

AYINGER JAHRHUNDERT BIER
Pale Lager   CB   2.9
(Aying, Germany)
Appealing, rounded fruitiness à la fresh Concord grapes welcomes
you on the first sip; gets a little tough around the edges with
food, essentially reflecting the ambiance of the food rather than
complementing or supplementing it; tastes okay by itself, but
doesn't enhance the enjoyment of most meals; no head or Brussels lace to speak of; a better beer with snacks, such as nuts or
pretzels.

AYINGER MAIBOCK   CB   2.0
(Aying, Germany)
Medium-soft with a mildly fruity, metallic flavor reflecting the
bock-increased alcohol—or possibly a brewing defect; slight
caramel taste flattens and mellows with food; sweetness surrounds
the alcohol at the end, but this still is an attractive beer.

AYINGER OKFOBERFEST-MARZEN
Lager   CB   3.9
(Aying, Germany)
Dusty-honey mouthfeel at the back of the throat along with honey
color and no head; remains fresh and substantive in taste; loses
some vitality and self-confidence if strong food flavors take hold;
character is probably best expressed with unassertive food or alone.

T A P   T I P

Ensuring Palate Pleasure

When sampling different beers, a bite of French
or Italian bread and a few sips of water
between tastings help rinse the palate. So does
a piece or two of a plain, bland cracker (many beer
judges use unsalted soda crackers) washed down with
clean fresh water.

AZTECA Pilsener   CB   0.3
(Tecate, Mexico)
Light and sweetish, but barely palatable; mildly skunky mouthfeel; watery and slightly sour; weak in flavor; slight hint of malt
in the taste and aroma; dominating sour bitterness is unpleasant;
a rather unappetizing beer.

BAD FROG ORIGINAL LAGER CT 1.4
(Evansville, Indiana)

Bad Frog was originally less known for its beer than its contro-
versial, whimsical label, which got it banned in a number of states;
the brewer's motto, "Give 'em the bird," is exactly what the grin-
ning frog is doing; the beer itself is not nearly as emphatic; fizzily
bitter and soft on the tongue; fleeting suggestion of richness,
which may be a mirage in any event; bubbly, foamy head stays
forever; this drink is mainly for the collectors of amusing brew-
eriana, not the brew itself.

BAILEY'S ALE MB 3.1
(Nantucket, Massachusetts)

Sharply hoppy, tart, and fruity; near-lemon aroma; gentle, spicy
flavors stay throughout; snappy effervescence delivers a grape-
fruit-like character; bitterness lingers and stays prominently in
the aftertaste; airy, pure-white head leaves picturesque clumps of
Brussels lace on inside of glass; citrus-hop bite and malt presence
team up at the end. Try with fruit-impregnated pastry, especially
the cherry or apple variety.

BAJAN BEER Lager CB 2.7
(Bridgetown, Barbados)

Aggressive maltiness wrapped in a swirl of softly fizzing bubbles,
with just a hint of fruity, honey sweetness—a nice, if light, beginning; fluffy, big-bodied head sits quietly on straw-colored body;
malts and hops pleasantly interwoven with each other; musty, but
not unattractive, aroma; Brussels lace is sketchily patterned and
follows the liquid down to the bottom of the glass; finishes mildly
bitter; overall, a gentle, rather unusual-tasting beer. Try it with
lightly sautéed mild-tasting fish or with scrambled eggs for brunch.

BALLANTINE PALE ALE CB 2.0
(San Antonio, Texas)

Sweet and bitter in quick succession; stays malty rather than
hoppy; medium amount of fizz; weakens somewhat, but hop
presence remains tangible; needs to be pumped up, tastewise; finishes watery and malty sweet; grows weaker and weaker until it
finishes a poor shadow of its former self. For old times' sake, at
least, sit with this beer in front of the TV, watch some baseball,
and munch on a hot dog or some peanuts.

LABEL LORE

*B*ottles and cans of Ballantine still display the
beer's famous three-ring logo—Purity, Body,
Flavor.

BALLYARD BROWN ALE (draft)   BP   2.5
(Phoenix, Arizona—by Leinenkugel, at Bank One Ballpark)
Quite fizzy; light caramel taste; alcohol cuts through the caramel;
overroasted malt edge, as if the balance is out of kilter; a bit
harsh and stiff in the mouth; sweetness turns into a sugary
mouthfeel; definite strawberry notes at the end of the swallow
briefly linger in the aftertaste; finishes somewhat more integrated, but still rather sweet, with sweetness clinging to the surface of the tongue; needs refining; freshly brewed; sold, along
with several other choices, right next to the main gate to the
Arizona Diamondbacks' creatively designed baseball stadium.
Since you're at the ballpark, have Ballyard Brown with—what
else?—pizza.

BANDERSNATCH BIG HORN
PREMIUM ALE (draft)   BP   3.4
(Tempe, Arizona)
Sweet and a bit heavy, with a thickish hop taste pretty much hidden from view; flowery aroma and yeast presence make for an
attractive combination; continued hoppiness; a bit thin, with a
finish that is too sweet. Try it with summery seafood salads.

BANDERSNATCH MILK STOUT (draft)   BP   4.0
(Tempe, Arizona)
Burnt, subdued taste is an immediate hit; smoothly creamy and
mellow; less thick than traditional stouts; moderate alcohol presence creeps up quickly and pleasantly, leaving you with a final,
mellowing buzz; perfect deep-brown color; a virtual meal in a
glass; a different process now makes it even creamier than before;
I always look forward to sampling this delightful concoction. Accompanies cooked fish and shellfish.

BANDERSNATCH PALE ALE (draft)   BP   1.8
(Tempe, Arizona)
Citrusy and light with a mild, sour aftertaste; relatively flat and
not very balanced or integrated, with or without food.

BANGKOK BEER Pilsener   CB   1.6
(Bangkok, Thailand)
Highly carbonated; a thick, knotty taste at the back of the throat;
somewhat cold and aloof with no ingratiating components; keeps
you at arm's length; cloudy paleness adds to the depressed, un-
warm feeling; hint of rawness also comes through; for export
only—which perhaps tells us something.

BANKS BEER Lager   CB   2.1
(Cincinnati, Ohio)
Light, a bit yeasty, and soft; pleasant, mild, and unassuming; re-
mains weak with food; very pale color with robust, nicely shaped
Brussels lace; low-grade in taste, temperament, and overall satis-

faction; more fulfilling with salted peanuts; alone, its tenacious blandness becomes too boring to finish; touted as a Guyana Caribbean product on the label.

BANKS LAGER   CB   2.3
(Wildey, Barbados)
A bit of honey-sweetness strikes the back of the tongue and stays as an aftertaste that is rather pleasant; visually, there appears to be more carbonation that you actually experience; thin and essentially bodyless; some malt overtones break through two-thirds through the bottle; one-dimensional, but interesting.

BARBAR BELGIAN HONEY ALE   CB   3.7
(Quenast, Belgium)
Complex taste and aroma give off sensations of yeast, coriander, and a tart orange mouthfeel, all mixed together; soft, creamy, stark-white head feels like your first kiss; gentle honey taste cushions the more intense flavors at mid-bottle and beyond; impact of the yeast eventually softens and spreads out; texturally fragile; finishes with a sugary warmth tinged with the essence of mandarin orange—a delectable ending, indeed. I don't recommend this often, but try Barbär in the morning, with your toast and scrambled eggs.

BARLEY BOYS ED'S RED PALE ALE   CT   2.4
(St. Paul, Minnesota)
Very malty, unlike typical pale ale; hoppiness and bitterness do increase after several sips; improved balance is apparent at mid-bottle, but caramel malt taste remains clear and present throughout; nicely configured Brussels lace; finishes quite malty and sweet; definitely not in the pale ale style, but passingly enjoyable nonetheless. Try with salty snacks—peanuts, chips, pretzels.

BARLEY BOYS JACK'S BLACK PORTER   CT   3.7
(St. Paul, Minnesota)
Plummy-winey aroma is immediately apparent as soon as you open the bottle; hint of chocolate and coffee is also present; smooth, blended malt-chocolate flavor; minimal bitterness seamlessly melds into the folds of the coffee-chocolate taste; balanced and integrated; sweetens and mellows further at the end; finishes with a plum-wine taste; definitely a finely crafted beer. Goes great with a variety of shellfish dishes.

BARLEY BOYS PHIL'S PILS   CT   2.8
(St. Paul, Minnesota)
Immediately fills (pardon the pun) the mouth with flavor—hops, malt, and what tastes like a hint of coconut; much fuller body than other pilseners; hoppiness shades into a honeyed sourness toward the end; pretty sheets of Brussels lace fill the sides of the glass; thin, creamy head stays in position from start to finish; fla-

vors finish smooth and well integrated. A good partner with fresh-water fish or Caesar salad with lots of anchovies.

BARON'S STRONG BREW Lager   CB   2.9
(Singapore)

Simultaneously honey-sweet and puckeringly bitter; obvious alcohol presence becomes even more evident at each sip; hops, too, increase their intensity; body is golden, clear and sparkling; rough edges get tamped down as the mouthfeel smooths out toward the end; finishes with a nice balancing hop aroma. Drink this properly named brew with hot and spicy Chinese or Indian dishes.

BARRE BRAU Pilsener   CB   3.8
(Lubbecke, Germany)

A well-tempered gathering of sensations reaches your taste buds at the same time—hoppy, grainy, sweet, bitter; fresh, clean, and crisp; light-bodied, thirst-quenching, and most assuredly palate-pleasing; airy, foamy white head leaves a twisting trail of irregular patterns of Brussels lace; finishes integrated, balanced, and yummy. Try this fine pilsener with white-meat dishes.

BARRIL CLARA Pilsener (draft)   CB   3.8
(Mexico City, Mexico)

Light blond; maltier and a touch more carbonated than the Barril Oscura; slight musty aroma; thin head and reasonable Brussels lace; refreshing and thirst-quenching even without the requisite lime; acceptable and appropriate with any kind of meal. Knows how to please the food before it.

BARRIL OSCURA Pilsener (draft)   CB   4.0
(Mexico City, Mexico)

Soft, creamy, smooth, and delicious, even (especially?) when served on the warm side; somewhat light mouthfeel which, with minimum carbonation, makes for good sipping; fluctuating balance of malts and hops; gains appealing thickness with spicy, garlicky foods; subdued, but clearly present, ingredients; eventually weakens, not surprisingly, from the onslaught of spiciness, but that in no way diminishes the overall enjoyment; an unassuming, quite entertaining red-copper beer. Also excellent with shellfish.

BASS PALE ALE   CB   3.8
(Burton-on-Trent, England)

Calm, quick, sweet initial taste; malt-sweet, unobtrusive, zesty aroma has a hint of caramel; while it has difficulty holding its own with spicy dishes, it is subtle and understated with plainer foods; not flashy, but very predictable in a comforting way.

BEER FACT

*T*he red triangle on the Bass label is England's first registered trademark (1876). Bass is the largest brewery in England.

BATEMAN'S DARK VICTORY ALE   CB   3.8
(Wainfleet, England)

Nice, erect copper head sits atop sparkling, roasted maltiness with just the right touch of burnt flavor; certainly stands up to food; mild fruitiness leads to a stately finish and caps a winsomeness that encourages you to ask for more; cool, appealing fullness adds to the spiciness and texture of food. Accompanies meatballs and spaghetti, and other pastas with tomato-based sauce.

BATEMAN'S XXXB ALE   CB   3.7
(Wainfleet, England)

Bitter flavor with abundant hops from start to last sip, with clearly defined maltiness to complete the balance; dizziness drops away as air comes in contact with beer; fine nutty warmth eventually takes over; maintains soft, foamy head throughout; high alcohol content is obvious; typical English bitter, with abundant hop strength; substance and character add to the pleasure of the meal. Goes well with Chinese food. (The B after the XXX indicates "bitter.")

BEER FACT

*O*n a label, "X" traditionally denotes the relative amount of alcohol: "XXX" means there is more alcohol in this bottle than in an "X" or "XX" bottle.

BAVARIA LAGER   CB   3.0
(Lieshout, Holland)

Nice initial balance between hops and malt with moderated sharpness; slight, but pleasant, hint of yeast-hoppiness emerges and blends effortlessly with spicy foods, as a weaker partner; tasty and flavorful by itself at the end, with a warmth that is beguiling; a beer with substance, it takes its time announcing itself; more or less worth the wait. Goes well with Mexican favorites.

BEAMISH IRISH CREAM STOUT   CB   3.7
(Cork, Ireland)

A crisp stout with some underlying softness; complex coffee mouthfeel; satisfying fizzy head; a bit thinner and sharper than other stouts; classically put together with its own special twist. Perhaps better alone than with food, but compatible with pastas and salads.

BEAR REPUBLIC HEFEWEIZEN (draft)   MB/BP   3.3
(Healdsburg, California)

This up-and-coming brewery makes good beer; its hefeweizen is smooth and the lemony aspect adds appropriate tartness; lovely, soft-pedaled clove character is present throughout; underlying cocoa taste adds a pleasant surprise to the sweet aftertaste; texture flattens a bit toward the end; finishes mildly effervescent and well-balanced, with clove in ascendance. A versatile beer that is a good partner to meat dishes as well as lighter fare, like steamed mussels.

BECKETT'S ALE (draft)   CB   3.3
(Dublin, Ireland)

Fruity, with just the right amount of mild bitterness; dry; medium-bodied with a warming mouthfeel that tastes yummy; sweet, but constrained; well balanced and well delivered; sheets of lasting Brussels lace form random patterns that nicely shade the golden-straw-colored body; bitterness weakens a bit at the end but retains its tasty, if reduced, essence; a very satisfying mild ale. Have this with the usual sitting-at-the-bar snack fare.

BECK'S Pilsener   CB   3.1
(Bremen, Germany)

Sharp, light, and likeable; predictable and unchanging from start to finish, with dominating hop presence that makes you take notice; good, but not distinguished or unique; certainly an amiable companion, though not one to create excitement or produce new thoughts; nice with a tuna salad sandwich.

BECK'S DARK Pilsener CB 2.6
(Bremen, Germany)
Mildly roasted, familiarly carbonated, and filled with reassuring hints of standard hops and malts, especially malts; straightforward sharp sweetness that is not cute or cloying; too demanding for spicy foods; though the beer itself is well made, it is clearly a commercial product; essentially no head, no Brussels lace, and a somewhat muddied, deep-auburn color; finish is sweet and malty; good choice for someone who wants a different beer, but without an abrupt taste departure from the usual fare.

BECK'S OKTOBERFEST Lager
(seasonal) CB 3.7
(Bremen, Germany)
Nice effervescence with apple taste, all preceded by a hint of caramel; well-balanced malt and hops; charming ruby-red amber sets off accelerating sharpness of hops; very grainy, with matching alcohol content; maintains robust composure throughout; strong and wholesome, with staying power; finishes with soothing caramel aroma; similar to typical European amber; far better warm than cold; worth looking for as the leaves start turning gold.

BEER Lager CB 0.7
(Calgary, Alberta, Canada)
Harsh, crisp, neighborhood-bar beer; a hint of greenness is present; not meant for fancy meals or fancy restaurants—or even other locations where you are looking for a decent beer accompaniment.

BEER SWISS MOUNTAIN Lager CB 3.1
(Appenzell, Switzerland)
Quite bitter-sour taste and honey-malt aroma create a clash of sensations that makes you sit up and take notice; warming malty sweetness emerges after several sips; hops, malt, and texture interact at mid-bottle, creating a tasty complexity only hinted at earlier; finishes with a charming malty sweetness in the nose and on the tongue; this beer evolves as you drink it. Sample it with sharp Swiss or sharp cheddar cheese.

BEL PILS CB 3.8
(Puurs, Belgium)
Hint of citrus aroma as soon as you open the bottle; sharp grainy taste rushes down the throat and stays sharp in the aftertaste; suggestion of hops; dainty Brussels lace clings to the sides of the glass, adding to the overall fragile impression of this blond, bubbly pilsener; light-bodied, but eminently mouth-filling; finishes fresh and clean-smelling. Goes great with salads loaded with lettuce and other greens.

BELGRADE GOLD Pilsener   CB   2.9
(Belgrade, Serbia; former Yugoslavia)
Sweet, honeyed thickness with visual, but not tangible, effervescence; turns sour and citrusy with sauces and dressings; bitter hoppiness emerges and remains to the end of the bottle, along with honey taste; cloudy pale-golden color with no head; variable, but not unappealing; sweet finish. Goes best with Middle Eastern dishes such as falafel, couscous, and tabouleh.

BELHAVEN SCOTTISH ALE   CB   4.0
(Dunbar, Scotland)
Tiny bubbles, tingly carbonation; constrained high-quality alcohol and gentle, sweetish hops; creamy, gentle fruitiness; effervescence doesn't push itself on you—mellow, thick, light-tan, foamy head encourages enjoyment; I can't say enough about the marvelous support and delectability this ale adds to food; light and easy to handle, it keeps its composure through thick (a favorite barbecue sauce) and thin (corn on the cob); mild, playful presence of caramel aroma and taste at the end, with a hint of what seems to be licorice flavor; stylish and composed. An excellent match for chicken main dishes.

BEER FACT

*D*unbar, the birthplace of the famed conservationist John Muir, is also the site of a Benedictine monastery brewery that dates to the Middle Ages.

BELL'S AMBER ALE   RB   0.0
(Kalamazoo, Michigan)
A faint odor of bile affronts your nose; turns fruity, sour, and bitter in the mouth; harsh and aggressively hoppy; no complexity, just straightforward unpleasantness; raw and unripe; I will spare you the rest.

BELMONT LONG BEACH CRUDE Porter MB/BP   2.1
(Long Beach, California)
Immediately weak, though smooth and mildly chocolatey; roastiness is well hidden, but mild toasty bitterness becomes apparent at mid-glass, providing motivation for finishing the drink; the promise is more satisfying than the reality; in the end, too weak, thin, and one-dimensional to rave about. Try it with a hamburger and a tossed salad.

BELMONT MARATHON WHEAT ALE   MB/BP   1.8
(Long Beach, California)
Clear, textureless, and essentially aromaless, with a hint of soap
mixed in; no guts and no body; dull and placid; too fluffy for its
own good; definitely a beer made for American taste and consumption.

BELMONT STRAWBERRY BLONDE Ale   MB/BP   2.2
(Long Beach, California)
Smells like Barbie doll perfume—very soda pop–like, but thankfully not overwhelmingly so; flat texture makes for a watery,
lighthearted concoction; more plain than bitter; a strawberry
summertime drink that is easy to handle, if you like a beer that
is really not a beer.

BELMONT TOP SAIL ALE   MB/BP   2.8
(Long Beach, California)
Sweet maltiness presents something tangible with which to deal;
reasonably balanced between hops and malt; mild bitterness creates interest if not idolatry; light-amber color. Try it with salty
chips, nuts, or pretzels.

BERGHOFF FAMOUS BOCK   RB   2.4
(Monroe, Wisconsin)
Variable honey-sweet initial aroma collides head-on with a tangy
dollop of taste that ends flat and unexciting; texture remains surprisingly bland; expected alcohol zestiness never materializes;
muddy brown, with little redeeming red to it; mild maltiness remains and becomes essentially the sole distinguishing feature in
its uphill battle with food; heartiness and fullness finally become
evident, but remain far removed from the malty alcohol features
expected from a good bock; slightly acidic at the finish; this
isn't a bad beer, just not a good beer. Okay with Italian food.

BERGHOFF GENUINE DARK Lager   RB   3.3
(Monroe, Wisconsin)
Vague but persistent caramel flavor is complemented by relative
thickness that is charming and encouraging; a little watery with
food; deep red-amber color matches "feel" of the beer perfectly;
head hardly exists; good American dark beer; Silver Medal winner at the 1993 Great American Beer Festival. Accompanies steak
and salad.

BERGHOFF OKTOBER FEST BEER
(annual)   RB   2.3
(Monroe, Wisconsin)
Fizzy and slightly fruity with a malt flavor that passes through
very quickly; sharpness appears, either from the hops (good) or
brewing/distribution defect (bad); sugary sweetness kicks in midway through the bottle; moderated hop bitterness emerges as the

beer loses some of its coldness; rather harsh and unforgiving—
you constantly have to do battle with it. Try it with a knish
slathered with ballpark mustard.

BERGHOFF ORIGINAL LAGER—
DORTMUNDER Lager   **RB**   **2.6**
(Monroe, Wisconsin)
Fresh, slightly yeasty aroma, but stale, uninvigorating first taste;
cranky sharpness accompanies this full-bodied representative of
the style; remains malty sharp and texturally kind with food; Brussels lace is nicely wispy and has staying power; finishes warm and
almost sweet. Good with standard American fare such meat loaf.

B E E R   F A C T

*D*ortmund was one of the four dominant lager
styles in 19th-century Europe. Each was named
after the city in which it was first brewed; the
other three are Munich, Vienna, and Pilsen. The city of
Dortmund, in western Germany, brews more beer than
any other city in a country that boasts well over one-
third of the world's breweries.

BERKSHIRE TRADITIONAL PALE ALE   MB   3.4
(South Deerfield, Massachusetts)
Assertive hop character is laced with a milk-chocolate mouthfeel
that permeates all areas of the palate; full-flavored and hearty; intense, concentrated flavor evolves into caramel sweetness; strong,
dried fruit aroma has sweet chocolate high notes; finishes with a
full malty character decorated with caramel and fruit overtones;
this is a beer's beer. Drink with a double-decker sandwich filled
with meat and cheeses.

BERLINER PILS   **CB**   **2.5**
(Berlin, Germany)
Dry, crisp, and light—fits right in at the ballpark—but has a bit
more character; depressed texture and flavor don't integrate well
with food; mild honey taste rises to the top, along with a wispy
warmth and decreased sharpness; okay for a quick thirst-quencher
on the run.

BERLINER RATSKELLER LAGER   **CB**   **2.2**
(Berlin, Germany)
Typical crisp lager with hoppy undertone; sudsy Brussels lace on
sides of the glass and thin, sudsy head on top of the beer; individual ingredients suggest that the totality should be more inviting than the overall taste, but that is not to be; in the end it is

boring and uneventful, though balanced; a run-of-the-mill brew. Probably best with salted nuts or pretzels.

BERT GRANT'S IMPERIAL STOUT   BP/RB   4.2
(Yakima, Washington)

Incredibly dark, rich, and full of body; sweetness surrounds a burnt taste, resulting in an essence of chocolate syrup dipped in espresso; made with locally gathered honey, it gets sweeter, mellower, and more incredibly integrated with grilled New York strip steak and green chiles; chocolate dessert would be fine, too; character strengthens until the bottom of the glass; a classy, sturdy offering.

B E E R   F A C T

*I*mperial stout was the winter warmer of choice of Czar Alexander's troops, on the battlefield and in peacetime. Its significantly higher alcohol content helped preserve its freshness as it traveled from England to Moscow, St. Petersburg, and beyond. Several breweries carry on the potent part of the tradition, though far less of it finds its way to the former Soviet Union nowadays.

BERT GRANT'S INDIA PALE ALE   BP/RB   3.6
(Yakima, Washington)

Crisp and bitter-sharp with an ebb and flow of mildly fruity wine taste; sweetness with a hint of sourness emerges, then mellows into an obviously well-made brew, retaining sharpness and pungency at the edges; there is an anticipated, but not quite obtained, warmth on the tongue; you certainly can taste the hops; cloudy appearance; neck label pronounces this a "faithful reproduction of the 19th century ale." Delicious with smoked or grilled fresh fish and crusty bread.

BERT GRANT'S SCOTTISH ALE   BP/RB   2.0
(Yakima, Washington)

Sour fruitiness pervades, coats the mouth and stays there; remains too winey to be satisfying or greatly appreciated; a letdown compared to other Grant's styles, although a sturdy cheese sandwich improves the taste.

BGI Pilsener   CB   1.7
(Ho Chi Minh City, Vietnam)

Hint of sweetness on first sip disappears and never returns; sharp-tasting, but not very carbonated; watery and not complex; no ongoing flavor or textural interest; hint of sweetness at the end; overall, plain and ultimately bland.

BIECKERT ESPECIAL Pilsener   **CB**   **4.2**
(Antartida, Argentina)
Strikingly fresh, crisp, attentive, and immediately very satisfying; malt and hops are in pleasant, interactive balance, depending on the food requirements of the moment; just the right amount of fizz, but a flat-to-nonexistent head; maintains its own delectable dignity with food; excellent. Goes well with Mexican fare.

BIERE DU DESERT   **CB**   **3.7**
(Douai Cedex, France)
Mellow, malty aroma and tart, very dry taste make a very appealing opening combination; rather intense, focused hop bitterness carries it all along; sourness and alcoholic strength enhance the firm, unyielding mouthfeel; light-bodied; bitterness increases markedly by the end of the bottle; though the alcohol content is relatively high, its impact far exceeds its measure; finishes surprisingly sweet and under control; a well-done, quality beer. Good with pork tenderloin.

BIG APPLE PREMIUM Pilsener   **CT**   **2.4**
(brewed in Milwaukee, Wisconsin, by Pabst)
Sour-sweet with restrained cloying sensation; soft sweetness trails off to a mild backdrop to food; residual fruitiness lingers on the tongue—essentially flat with no complexity; according to the label, brewed for that "exquisite New York taste," whatever that might be.

BIG BARREL Lager   **CB**   **3.0**
(Leabrook, South Australia, Australia)
Smooth and easy going down; vague corn flavor subtly hidden behind first swallow, awaiting contact with deeper taste buds at the back of the mouth, where slight bitterness emerges; calm, tepid brew; taste is maintained throughout a meal, not necessarily a favor to the beer. Accompanies barbecued burgers served with plenty of condiments.

BIG HOUSE MA BARKER Ale   **BP**   **0.2**
(Albany, New York)
Grainy, grassy mouthfeel; sour and unpleasant; nasty aftertaste; poorly put together; not worth your attention.

BIG PIG ALE (draft)   **MB**   **2.5**
(Seattle, Washington)
Malty aroma and malty taste with a hop edge to it; hops and malt continuously compete for your attention, though malt finally gets the upper hand; flavor sensations flatten a bit and your mind begins to wander; unpredictable and confusing, it finishes with a splash of caramel only hinted at earlier; in the end, too much effort is needed to get a grip on where this beer is headed; too many ups and downs.

BIG ROCK COCK O' THE ROCK
PORTER   RB   2.4
(Calgary, Alberta, Canada)
Too sweet on first sip; a bit too thin; uncomplex and rather uninspiring; hint of roastedness tentatively appears, then fades away, leaving no taste trace in the mouth. Becomes more integrated and flavorful with broiled meat dishes.

BIG ROCK COLD COCK WINTER
PORTER   RB   3.1
(Calgary, Alberta, Canada)
Mellow, subdued, appealing burnt taste, with passing whiff of same as this relatively high-alcohol concoction settles into the glass; medium-bodied; remains constant and consistent with spicy Cajun dishes, but turns a bit sharp with milder fare—sautéed Dover sole or linguine with clam sauce, for example—which is okay, given that the food is soft and relatively bland; cooling sweetness at the end reveals molasses provenance; a little too watery, but still has substance.

BIG ROCK GRASSHOPPER WHEAT ALE RB   2.5
(Calgary, Alberta, Canada)
Faintly sweet, faintly honey, and definitely smooth and silky; becomes tart and fizzy, with a downplaying of the major ingredients; tantalizing malt flavor is coaxed out by seafood accompaniment; a calm, gentle yeastiness settles on the tongue alongside the food; malt and hops become more noticeable at the end of the bottle, with a malt imbalance; amiable, though unexciting. Nicely suited to shrimp salad and other seafood salad sandwiches.

BIG ROCK MAGPIE RYE BREW Lager   RB   0.4
(Calgary, Alberta, Canada)
Weak, flat, and not very tasty; there's an off-taste in there somewhere; and where's the rye? Somewhat hoppy and harsh, even with pretzels; ingredients finally integrate at the end, finishes tasteless and uninteresting.

BIG ROCK McNALLYS EXTRA ALE   RB   1.3
(Calgary, Alberta, Canada)
No head; full apple-juice flavor with no fizz or pizzazz—almost as if it came right out of the cider press; aromatic flavor; not a good match with food; more filling at the end, but not enough to change my opinion.

BIG ROCK SPRINGBOK ALE   RB   2.1
(Calgary, Alberta, Canada)
Plain, unassuming, but not unpleasant; hard to sort out any definite qualities; does leave slight whisper of aftertaste at the back of the tongue; fizzy apple fruitiness with a dry finish and an increased physical presence. Accompanies pork dishes.

BIG ROCK WARTHOG ALE   **RB**   **2.5**
(Calgary, Alberta, Canada)
Misleading fruit presence on first sip; distinctive plum-apple taste
fades as beer is consumed; thin head presages and reflects thin
mouthfeel, but flavor nonetheless is teased out by food; hops and
malts and yeast all remain unintegrated; yeast aroma and slight
fruity zippiness finish the bottle; not a beer to drink without
food; a step or two short of being memorable, but I would drink
it again. Good with egg dishes—plain or spicy.

BIG TIME BHAGWANS BEST INDIA
PALE ALE   **MB/BP**   **2.0**
(Seattle, Washington)
Insufficiently hoppy; too obviously citrusy (grapefruit) without
enough zest, though some oomph is present; too little carbonation; won't hold up over the long haul (say, a second bottle); too
much red in the color spoils overall effect; too many departures
from style to even begin to make this attractive—not to mention that, regardless of style, it doesn't have a good flavor.

BIG TIME OLD WOOLY BARLEY WINE   **MB/BP**   **2.8**
(Seattle, Washington)
Moderated alcohol presence; typical bittersweet barley wine taste;
thick and full but, pleasantly, not too potent; light, somewhat
murky copper color; grainy undertone; too weak, it needs more
work to define itself as a clear example of the style; Bronze Medal
winner at the 1993 Great American Beer Festival. Fine with a
fresh fruit salad served early in the meal.

BINTANG PILSENER   **CB**   **3.9**
(Surabaya, Indonesia)
Appealing creaminess, overlaid with smartly crackling carbonation; zesty freshness; light-golden color; subdued, flavorful, restrained hoppy bitterness; grains move to the foreground with
red meats; stays sharp and clear throughout; fine Brussels lace remaining at the end; typical dry finish with a light, feathery touch.
Match with steak and potatoes.

BIOS COPPER ALE   **CB**   **1.4**
(Ertvelde, Belgium)
Weak, but distinct, lemon-tart taste; layered, rather than full,
mouthfeel evolves into cherry and/or pear taste which diminishes
when accompanying food; thick, bubbly head tops off the strange-
ness of the body; very fruity; yeast residue at the bottom. Better
as an after-dinner drink.

BISON CHOCOLATE STOUT   **MB/BP**   **2.1**
(Berkeley, California)
Rich and chocolatey, with a complementing bite at back of the
throat; the calibrated balance between bitter and chocolate be-

comes more accommodating as the dark, coffee-colored liquid warms to room temperature; a distinct sweet, charcoal mouth-feel appears at mid-bottle; finishes increasingly bitter, but over-all, it doesn't reach its potential.

BITBURGER PILSENER CB 3.3
(Bitburg, Germany)
Quickly sparkly and quite hoppy with an ingratiating ambiance; mellow and cooling with spicy food; lends a tempered balance to hot foods; not bitter but quite dry; relatively low alcohol content; almost delicate in taste and quite pale in color; a very light, able-bodied pilsener to while away the day, rather than concentrate on the drinking experience; a nice little beer. Try it with Indian food, especially curries.

BITTER END MODULATOR
DOPPELBOCK BP 3.4
(Austin, Texas)
Spicy, complex, and quite charming; becomes bitter with a hint of apple after several sips; ingredients get along very well with each other and pop up individually here and there; dry; thick, foamy, long-lasting old-lace-colored head; full of malt flavor and full of well-placed alcohol; filled with tasty surprises, all of which come together at the end. Pick out a pastry and order up another Modulator.

BLACK LABEL Lager CB 2.1
(Seattle, Washington; La Crosse, Wisconsin, et al.)
Although clear and crisp, this beer is also watery and weak with more mini-fizz than taste; it does remain evenhanded and pre-dictable, however, a testament to this big commercial brewery's quality control; mixed with tomato juice, it attains a body and palate that are more satisfying and appropriately layered; this combination of juice and beer is particularly satisfying with pepper steak, rice, and tomatoes.

BLACK LION PREMIUM DARK Lager CB 3.1
(Hradecky, Czech Republic)
Pervasive chocolate-malt flavor is full and rounded; the multi-layered taste evolves from malty-sweet to chocolate-bitter as it fills the mouth; clean and crisp on the palate; finishes with a lusty vanilla-malt flourish that stays around awhile on the tongue; shiny amber body. Spicy food, like Indian dishes, helps to draw out the malt and adds body to the beer.

BLACK TOAD DARK ALE CT 1.8
(St. Paul, Minnesota)
Quite bitter and not as dark as advertised; hint of whiskey-like alcohol arises at mid-bottle; stays bitter, but there are suggestions, never realized, that this is a decent beer; eventually weakens, leav-

ing nothing noteworthy; remains a one-note brew, even when accompanied by pizza.

BLACKSTONE NUT BROWN ALE   BP   3.4
(Nashville, Tennessee)

Smells nutty and malty; well-timed zestiness keeps things moving along in good order; judicious infusion of hops is balanced and bountiful; sweetens perceptibly at mid-glass; faint, bitter hazelnut aroma is welcome and very yummy; nutty bitterness continues into the aftertaste; not demanding, but smooth and accommodating; an evolving, tasty brew with well-calibrated flavor mixes. Pick a spicy dish of your choice and order up some of this brown ale.

BLANCHE DE BRUGES Wheat   CB   3.9
(Bruges, Belgium)

Very yeasty, pale, and delicate, like champagne; taste and effect are enhanced in bowl-shaped wine or snifter glass; blond in color; bottle-conditioned, it makes good use of the grain; almost wine-like in character and in relation to food; wispy Brussels lace stays under the liquid. Gentleness and citrus ambiance are comforting alongside meat and potatoes.

BLANCHE DE CHAMBLY WHITE BEER
ON LEES   CB   3.1
(Chambly, Quebec, Canada)

Immediately quite yeasty and immediately quite thirst-quenching; soft feel on the palate; spry and invigorating; gentle, fruity mouthfeel is the primary taste sensation; stays refreshing throughout; nuance of honey presence appears toward the end; bottle-conditioned; light-bodied; diminished yeast character at the finish. Try this with a lemon or other tart-fruit pastry.

B E E R   F A C T

*L*ees refers to the yeast sediment at the bottom of the bottle, a sign that fermentation, or conditioning, is continuing. The process is called bottle-conditioning.

BLANCHE DES NEIGES ALE   CB   2.3
(Melle and Ghent, Belgium)

Smells lemony and oily, like Pledge, rather than fresh-squeezed; tastes light and airy like a lemon-flavored Life Saver; surprisingly refreshing quality on each swallow; perfumed yeastiness becomes the predominant taste; hint of cloves; texture flattens considerably at the end; this is a mixed bag, not consistent enough to be rated highly, though it does have some worthwhile characteristics. Accompanies salty crackers and salty hors d'oeuvres.

BLUE CORN PLAZA PORTER BP 2.3
(Santa Fe, New Mexico)
Tasty, creamy, and sweet; minimal sharpness; hard to tease out the chocolate and smokiness; instead, you get chocolate aroma and weak coffee taste; not complex; doesn't pack the punch of the style, or enough pushiness simply to be satisfying; a decent facsimile, but other than its deep-brown color, not the real thing; sort of like much of contemporary Santa Fe. Order this with chips and salsa, what else?

BLUE HEN TRADITIONAL Lager MB 2.9
(Philadelphia, Pennsylvania)
Flowery, sharp, very slight citrus-honey taste; relatively complex with favorable hop presence; slight upper-palate aftertaste; an all-malt beer (no adjuncts), it serves up a reasonable balance with malty sweetness; balance and sweetness diminish, but don't disappear, with food; carefully made. Try it with cold cuts and other deli favorites.

BLUE MOON HARVEST PUMPKIN Ale CB 2.5
(Cincinnati, Ohio)
Rose-petal aroma is quickly followed by a chocolate-flowery taste that sits comfortably on the tongue; a bit of spiciness is also present, but somewhat muddied in presentation; suggestion of pie crust is in there as well; malty aroma at the end, along with a shy malty sweetness; loses a fair amount of texture on final swallows. Keeps its integrity with roast turkey and the usual trimmings.

BLUE RIDGE HOPFEST BROWN ALE RB 3.9
(Frederick, Maryland)
Fizzy and fruity bitterness is accompanied by subtle carmel sweetness; peppery background character supports the bitter mouthfeel; pungent hop aroma; remains tangy in the mouth even after swallowing; passing flowery taste is nicely integrated into the tangy, fruity-flowery, hoppy melange; finishes with a generous hoppy mouthfeel that settles happily into the taste buds. Try this well-done Oktoberfest beer with something spicy.

BLUE RIDGE SNOWBALL'S CHANCE Ale RB 2.4
(Frederick, Maryland)
Coffee and chocolate flavors stay neck-and-neck in the aroma and taste, reflecting the five different malts used in this brew; at first the taste seems heavy-handed, but after a few sips, the flavors stretch out to become uniform and medium-bodied; smooth and dry; finishes with more hop mouthfeel than when it started. Goes with hot dogs and baked beans.

BLUE RIDGE SUNRAGE SOUR MASH   RB   2.0
(Frederick, Maryland)
Light-honey, sour-citrus smell accompanies a similar flavor; too
acidic; grapefruit taste; appropriately light for summertime drinking; close-to-perfumey aftertaste dissipates quickly and is not
pleasant; uncomplex. It's helped along somewhat by tunafish sandwich sprinkled with lemon.

BLUE STAR PALE ALE   BP   2.8
(San Antonio, Texas)
Fruity-sweet at the outset, with a pervasive thread of moderated
hoppiness; newly arrived fruit-nuanced bitterness does not cling
to the tongue as long as a pale ale lover might wish; taste sensations stay too muddied and not delineated enough; hop presence
fades in the stretch, though it does linger awhile in the aftertaste;
good, but not great. Make this more drinker-friendly with a crisp,
fresh salad filled with lots of crunchy lettuce.

BLUE STAR STOUT   BP   3.5
(San Antonio, Texas)
Mild, chocolate-malt taste offers up a gentle tickle of hop-spiciness; robust and fresh; consistent, characterful underpinning of
a roasty, toasty presence; this voluptuous stout just bursts with
flavor; gets creamier as the evening wears on; the touch of spice
is an unexpected, generous extra; carefully brewed quality is apparent here. Goes exceptionally well with any hardshell seafood.

BLUEGRASS HELL FOR CERTAIN
BELGIAN SPICED ALE   BP   0.4
(Louisville, Kentucky)
Filled with alcohol and not much else; a bit of turpentine in the
mouth; raw; hard-to-discern flavors are at odds with each other;
seems unfinished; leave it that way in your glass.

BOAGS PREMIUM LAGER   CB   2.2
(Hobart, Tasmania, Australia)
Skunky aroma and fizzily sharp; remains thick and unappetizing
with food; prickliness remains in mouth for a while after the beer
is gone; lasting impression, both literally and figuratively, is not
a good one.

BEER FACT

*B*oags, named for one of its founders, is the longest
continuously operating manufacturing company
in Australia.

BODDINGTON'S GOLD Ale   **CB**   **2.3**
(Manchester, England)
Slightly hoppy and very smooth; lovely blending of malt and
hops; sweet caramel aroma is almost buttery in presentation; well-
rounded and soft on the palate; more noticeable veneer of hops
is apparent after awhile; thinner bitterness and thinner caramel
mouthfeel ultimately make up the defining quality; fizzy sweetness marks the last sip; in the end, a so-so brew.

BOHANNON MARKET STREET
GOLDEN ALE   **MB/BP**   **2.1**
(Nashville, Tennessee)
Chemical sweetness fades quickly; Brussels lace is also chemically
induced, with random, rather than even, pattern; slight warm
citrus/fruity mouthfeel; clearly weak, but a bit more palatable at
the finish, with a touch of hops that was missing earlier.

BOHANNON MARKET STREET
OKTOBERFEST Lager   **MB/BP**   **0.3**
(Nashville, Tennessee)
Too sweet, no strength, no body, no carbonation, and sticks too
much to the roof of the mouth; big bubbles suggest artificial car-
bonation; not in the Oktoberfest style.

BEER FACT

*T*he mid-South's first microbrewery, Bohannon is
located on the river overlook site of Nashville's
now defunct pioneer commercial brewery, Cross-
man & Drucker, which started pouring beer before the
Civil War, in 1859.

BOHEMIA PILSENER   **CB**   **1.7**
(Monterrey, Mexico)
Slight, bitter hoppiness, with smooth, fizzy accompaniment;
warmth, unexpectedly, brings out the sweetish, bitter, malty complexity of flavors; hint of perfume comes and goes; settles into
slightly sour, flattish, far less complex offering with salty foods;
finishes more integrated than the beginning, but still several
notches below average.

BOILER ROOM RED Bock   **BP**   **3.0**
(Laughlin, Nevada)
Cool, calm, and collected; thin layer of maltiness coats the roof
of the mouth; mildly hopped, providing a slick underpinning to
the sweet malt mouthfeel; well balanced; medium-bodied, bronzey-
red body; small dose of alcohol at the back of the mouth punc-

tuates the last few sips; smooth and patient. Try this with a garden salad.

B E E R   F A C T

*T*he Boiler Room Brew Pub is a fully operational brewery located on the casino level of the Colorado Belle Hotel, a full-scale (docked) riverboat catering to tourists, gamblers, and beer lovers.

BOLTON ALT   CB   4.0
(Korschenbroich, Germany)
Smell and enjoy that grainy aroma, filled with malt, pleasure, and even a little bit of fruity essence; berry-like taste has nutty and woody notes; no harsh mouthfeel; easy going down; aromatic and bitter; although rich and full-bodied, no food is needed to temper it; drink this by itself, and take your time doing so; a joy to savor.

BOON GUEUZE Lambic   CB   2.2
(Lembeek, Belgium)
Very yeasty and acidic; skunky (an intentional flavor element); very light, dainty head stays at about a quarter-inch thick throughout—a very good sign (generally, heads should be half the thickness of the original after one minute); soft mouthfeel encourages liquid to go down gently; settles into an even keel with alcohol finally offering up its warmth; finish remains very yeasty, almost to the exclusion of all else; Brussels lace stays in sheets on sides of glass; tartly sweet, like a just-ripening grape; bottle-conditioned, and it shows. Best savored as an *apéritif* or with dessert.

BORSOD PREMIUM Pilsener   CB   2.5
(Bocsarlapujto, Hungary)
Hint of pleasant bitterness greets the tongue, followed by a whisper of maltiness at the back of the mouth; light, airy, and dry; crisp and relatively sharp—far more texture than taste, though taste itself is at best benign, at worst nonexistent; irregular, thick Brussels lace suggests more substance than is actually present in the pale-golden body; an inoffensive summer drink that doesn't interfere with food; unexpected fullness at the end, along with a mild sweetness and mild bitterness, as if all the substance of this beer sank to the bottom of the bottle. Serve with bagels, cream cheese, and a generous helping of smoked salmon.

BOS KEUN SPECIAL PAASBIER Ale   CB   2.7
(Essen, Belgium)
Very sugary-sweet yeasty taste is light on the tongue and undercuts the expected sourness; smooth, essentially textureless liquid; ingredients mingle more noticeably as the beer warms; sugges-

tions of fruity/cidery aspects at the end; rocky head overshadows the clouded pale-straw body; an unusual, odd beer that is strangely appealing, though not for everyone. Try with cold, crisp salads covered with croutons.

BOULDER PALE ALE   RB   3.6
(Boulder, Colorado)
Pleasantly light, smoothly refreshing; muted amber color is eye-catching, and crisp hop aroma is nose-catching—both are a beer lover's joy; remains unencumbering; a bit of an off-taste rapidly disappears; solid-tasting and sweet; don't gulp this one down. Stands up to spicy finger foods, such as barbecued chicken wings.

B E E R   F A C T

*B*oulder Brewing, started in 1979 and now called Rockies Brewing, is the oldest operating micro-brewery in the United States.

BOULDER PORTER   RB   2.7
(Boulder, Colorado)
Bitter hops and bland texture—not a good combination; burnt taste is acceptable, but not intense enough; more effective chilled than warm; lacks alcoholic strength and depth, but is mildly interesting and satisfying enough to want more. Serve with munchies such as potato chips, nuts, and crackers.

BOULDER STOUT   RB   2.2
(Boulder, Colorado)
Very smooth and creamy; initially sweet, then mixed sweet-sour taste that eventually turns stale in the mouth; essentially more texture than taste; chocolatey burnt feel at the end of the bottle with no food accompaniment; hairy mouthfeel also at the finish; aftertaste reduces the rating precipitously. Silver Medal winner at the 1994 Great American Beer Festival.

BOULEVARD "BULLY" PORTER   RB   3.8
(Kansas City, Missouri)
Tasty, with a sizzle of zest embedded in the balance of sweet and tart; deep red-brown stops short of deeper black associated with most porters; entertaining, but doesn't fully live up to its promise; foamy and relatively long-lasting head, leaving an even, substantial ring of Brussels lace; predictable. Quite appealing with a rich bread pudding or similar dessert; beer and food leave a comfortable, nostalgic taste in the mouth.

BOULEVARD NUTCRACKER ALE   RB   2.8
(Kansas City, Missouri)
Crackling fruity taste fills the mouth and slides pleasantly down
the throat; great sweet/grapefruit flavors balance each other nicely;
sweet nutty character creeps up at mid-bottle, adding some depth
to the ongoing maltiness and coaxing out even more of the grape-
fruitiness; accommodating bitterness in the aftertaste; leaves patterns of thick, cobwebby Brussels lace long after you've enjoyed
the last sip. Try this with chips and dip.

BOULEVARD WHEAT BEER   RB   2.3
(Kansas City, Missouri)
Clear Bartlett pear color with a swirl of bubbles is reminiscent
of those children's snow globes; light; slightly yeasty and barely
sweet; earthy, grassy aroma appears at mid-bottle as does a mildly
bitter-mild sweet balance; finishes light and fluffy; weak for a
wheat beer.

BRAHMA Pilsener   CB   3.8
(Rio de Janeiro, Brazil)
Very nice malty sweetness reminiscent of better Mexican beers;
fresh in bouquet and palate; although light, it does retain a stable heartiness without food; tends to weaken against only mildly
hot guacamole and chips; pleasant and attractive; crisp throughout; the label calls it "the best selling beer in all Latin America."

BRAHMA CHOPP Pilsener   CB   3.7
(Rio de Janeiro, Brazil)
Light, fluffy, and slightly carbonated; mild graininess; very feathery on the tongue and palate; nicely integrated with a sweet blend
of malt and hops that stays politely in the background; pretty
wisps of Brussels lace dance on top of straw-colored body, all in
perfect symmetry and balance; finish is weak with a hint of earlier strength that includes a thickish sweetness that is not true of
the rest of the can; appropriate for a beginner interested in building a foreign beer portfolio. Try it with your next Mexican meal.

B E E R   F A C T

*B*razil, the largest country in South America, is
the sixth-ranked brewing nation in the world,
just ahead of China and a step behind Japan. Rio
de Janeiro–based Brahma is the world's tenth-largest
brewer. Oddly, Brazil doesn't even show up on the top-
twenty list of beer-consuming countries.

TAP TIP

Air and Space

*T*he air space between bottle cap and liquid, called
ullage, should not be more than 1 to 1½ inches.
Extra air causes oxidation, which spoils the taste
and aroma of the beer in rather short order. Too much
space also means you're paying more per ounce of liquid in the bottle and getting less. While you're at it,
check the inside of the bottle neck; grit is highly suggestive of bacterial contamination. In this case, you're
paying for more than you want; you don't want that,
either.

BRAINS TRADITIONAL WELSH ALE   CB   3.9
(Cardiff, Wales)
Despite the name, a pretty picture is presented here: a settled,
pencil-thin head sits neatly atop the ripe-peach-colored body with
blond overtones; the Brussels lace looks like freshly laundered
Irish linen; tastewise, the well-defined bitterness releases its pleasures in measured steps like a flavor-filled time-release capsule;
delicate and airy, though there is a rough-suede feel on the tongue;
finishes mildly bitter and quite smooth. Enjoy this with lightly
seasoned fowl.

BRAND Pilsener   CB   2.5
(Limburg, Holland)
Acidic with light undertaste; very hoppy and some skunkiness;
all taste differential—good, bad, indifferent—is flattened out and
rendered irrelevant with food; keeps minimal but recognizable
head; flavors and aroma are not that attractive; dry from start to
finish. Should accompany bland dishes such as spaghetti with
unspicy meat sauce.

BRASSEURS BIERE DE PARIS Lager   CB   1.3
(Bonneuil, France)
Wimpy, unpleasant aroma and palate; cloudy reddish color, just
short of caramel; smooth, bland, and very unassuming; ingredients aside (please), it tastes more like good, fresh spring water
than anything else; pleasant head, but appearance doesn't make
up for lack of substance.

BRASSEURS GRAND CRU Lager   CB   3.5
(Bounneuil, France)
Sweet honey taste with moderate body; mild caramel flavor takes
over from honey as the beer warms; cloudy amber color suggests
a softness versus flattened sparkle of carbonation on the tongue;
a bit too sweet for, say, a spicy meal, but evolves into a gentle
pastime by itself or with pre-meal snack food.

BRAUMEISTER PILSENER   CT   2.5
(Monroe, Wisconsin)
Brittle top layer with softer fullness underneath; not particularly
fizzy; filmy aftertaste lingers at the top and sides of the mouth;
quick initial freshness fades into the throat, leaving behind moderate thirst-quenching qualities; typical, predictable pilsener—
friendly but not overly solicitous; good for a couple of quick ones
while waiting for the game to start.

BRECKENRIDGE AVALANCHE
AMBER Ale   MB/BP   0.4
(Breckenridge, Colorado)
Too smooth and too much off-taste; no real roasted flavor; sticks
to the roof of the mouth; feels somewhat raw and stomach-
turning; stay away from this one.

BRECKENRIDGE CHRISTMAS ALE   MB/BP   4.0
(annual)
(Denver, Colorado)
This annual ale teems with seasonal treats, ranging from a well-
delineated fruity nutmeg aroma and taste to a warming, spicy
bitterness that gently eases its way into your taste buds; and
don't forget (actually, you can't) the whiskey-like taste at the
back of the throat; chocolate is also present; rich, oak-leaf-brown
color; finishes smooth, with an invigorating edge; full-bodied
and very tasty. Drink this when you have a long, free evening
in front of you.

BRECKENRIDGE INDIA PALE ALE   MB/BP   2.4
(Denver, Colorado)
Cardboardy, papery taste, mildly bitter, and relatively uncarbonated; yeasty; moderately sour; soft, smooth texture—not bold as
the label proclaims; decent, circumscribed Brussels lace stays layered in thin sheets; hint of sweetness; essentially, quality ingredients make their presence known, but still not bitter, full, or
bold enough to be a fullblown IPA; hoppy finish; has the mak-
ings to become a decent beer.

BREUG LAGER   CB   2.7
(Roubaix, France)
Hoppy and a bit skunky; tart and sharp; strong maltiness quickly
comes up; achieves good balance with sandwiches, hors d'oeu-

vres, dip, and marinated olives; also integrates aroma, taste, and visual appeal, light golden color; tangy and lighter than most lagers, but surprisingly tasty for a French beer; it helps that it's from Flanders.

BREWER'S ALLEY MAIBOCK BP 2.7
(Frederick, Maryland)

Smooth and tea-sweet; rich malty character fills the mouth and coats the tongue; caramel sweetness goes and returns and goes again; moderately bitter; finishes with a charming grassy maltiness; good-tasting and easy to drink, but not especially memorable. Salty peanuts would be a good accompaniment.

BREWMASTER'S BREWER'S PRIDE
PORTER BP 1.6
(Cincinnati, Ohio)

Light; quickly receding roastedness; sugar-sweet and watery; coffee-chocolate flavor kicks in after three or four sips, but too late and not enough; much too weak for a porter, or anything else in the beer category; not worth the trip up to the bar.

BRICK LAGER CB 3.1
(Waterloo, Ontario, Canada)

Quick rush of flavor along with sharp bubbles that dissipate at the back of the mouth; texture is flat but taste is flavorful and apparent; not filled with adjuncts typically found in American lagers; somewhat smooth and silky. Accompanies oversized sandwiches on crusty bread.

BRIDGEPORT BLUE HERON PALE ALE MB/BP 2.4
(Portland, Oregon)

Fruity, viscous; leaves thin layer of aftertaste on the roof of the mouth; remains staunchly fruity and warm with an herbal tang alongside Southwestern and Mexican foods; flattens at the end, losing much of its effervescence; finishes slightly heavy and gamey. Try with green chile stew, grilled seafood, and vegetables.

BRIDGEPORT OLD KNUCKLEHEAD
BARLEY WINE STYLE ALE MB/BP 4.0
(Portland, Oregon)

Rounded, honey taste with barley sharpness; lastingly sweet, but fades and turns mildly cloying on the tongue; firmly entrenched grain taste; very high in alcohol; rich and strong; label identifies it as a sipping ale—it would be hard to down it any quicker; recommended for those wishing a powerful, tasty, well-made mouthful. A delightful *digestif* to sip slowly after a hearty meal.

BRIGAND BELGIAN ALE   **CB**   **3.8**
(Ingelmunster, Belgium)
Old-straw aroma and pungent sweetness greet first sip; soft, spongy
mouthfeel; highly yeasty and hoppy; cloudy, pale, creamy orange
bordering on peach-blush color; almost opaque; tingly robustness forthrightly integrates and balances the various ingredients
into a coherent alcoholic whole; well made, but doesn't appeal
to me personally; finishes smooth and sharply sweet, with some
roughness at the edges. Serve with smoked salmon, soft cheeses,
or fresh fruit.

BRIMSTONE HONEY RED ALE   **MB**   **2.6**
(Baltimore, Maryland)
Balanced in taste, aroma, and texture—part sweet, part bitter,
part rough at the edges; predictable and evenhanded—no highs,
lows, or anything unexpected; thick, foamy head stays around
awhile; fermented with pure honey; this is a friendly beer with
no ax to grind. Pairs well with slices of glazed ham.

BRIMSTONE RASPBERRY PORTER   **MB**   **1.9**
(Baltimore, Maryland)
Like a chocolate cake with fruit on top; light, somewhat fluffy,
and definitely sugary; fizzier than the usual porters; rather light
in texture; finishes more raspberry than anything else, although
there is a glancing chocolate aftertaste; makes for an interesting
dessert by itself; redeems itself slightly as a sipping beer after a
savory holiday meal.

BRISA Lager   **CB**   **2.8**
(Guadalajara, Mexico)
Light, sharp, good-tasting; simultaneously malty and sparkly;
good brew to sip during a ball game. Fine with hot dogs.

BROAD RIPPLE EXTRA
SPECIAL BITTER Ale   **BP**   **2.6**
(Indianapolis, Indiana)
Harsh, aromatic, and refreshing with bright deep-golden color;
keeps foamy head (with large bubbles); citrus/hoppiness helps retain freshness throughout; despite nonassertiveness, it is good-
tasting, but weak for a bitter—extra special or otherwise.

BROKEN HILL LAGER   **CB**   **2.0**
(Thebarton and Adelaide, South Australia, Australia)
Too bitter for a lager; sharp and hoppy; stays crisp with golden,
slight honey impression underneath; smooth and full, Broken
Hill is just one step up from bland; even when food is not particularly spicy, it overshadows this beer that goes nowhere; finishes watery with hint of hop graininess.

TAP TIP

Measuring Alcohol Strength

*T*he amount of alcohol in a beer is measured in two ways: by weight (percentage of weight of alcohol compared to weight of total amount of beer in the container) and by volume (percentage of alcohol in a given volume of liquid, e.g., pint, quart, liter). Brewers in the United States typically have used the alcohol/weight standard; elsewhere (and in the U.S. wine industry), the rule is alcohol/volume, although in recent years domestic brewers have increasingly switched to the volume criterion. A rough rule of thumb: alcohol/weight is approximately 20% less than alcohol/volume; for example, 4% alcohol/weight (fairly standard for an American lager) = approximately 5% alcohol/volume (fairly standard for a British lager).

BROKEN HILL OLD STOUT CB 1.2
(Adelaide, South Australia, Australia)
Pungent alcohol taste and bitter flavor make you sit up and take notice on first sip; bitter, dark chocolate mouthfeel; remains tart and astringent; sweet, syrupy aftertaste; head collapses into a small pond of brown flecks; finishes with a bitter chocolate taste, strong alcohol presence, and an overall rather unpleasant mouthfeel; the Aussies may like this, but I don't.

BROKEN HILL REAL ALE CB 2.9
(Adelaide, South Australia, Australia)
Fruity-sour aroma turns sweet, then fruity-sour in the mouth; texturally keeps your attention, offering a roughness reflective of the mythical Australian character; much maltier and smoother when warm, though less thirst-quenching; sourness eventually is surrounded by ragged sweetness—a nice combo; settles into a soothing, if not entirely smooth, drink; certainly keeps your interest from first to last. Drink with something hot off the grill—beef and chicken come to mind.

BROOKLYN BLACK CHOCOLATE STOUT MB 4.1
(Brooklyn, New York)
Go out right now and buy a six-pack of this stout; full roasted-malt-chocolate taste with a chewy, transitional aftertaste; muscular and strong; rich and robust; sweetens considerably, but still maintains the balance among a complexity of malts—sweet, burnt, and chocolate; pours smooth and golden-black; finishes with a

gentle alcohol-malt flourish; this is a top-notch beer that has quickly gained a large and devoted following. Particularly yummy with moist chocolate cake.

BROOKLYN BROWN DARK ALE   MB   3.1
(Brooklyn, New York)

Fresh flowery aroma; dainty on the back of the tongue; reddish-caramel color is not overly pleasing to the eye; a complement and adjunct to food; possesses warmth with cool alcoholic core, especially as the beer itself warms up; not complex or particularly integrated. Serve alongside steak and other grilled beef dishes.

BROOKLYN EAST INDIA PALE ALE   MB   4.1
(Brooklyn, New York)

This stylish and engaging IPA is mesmerizingly hoppy-sharp and taste-bud-popping juicy; delightful fruity aroma with a delicate, flowery thread underpins the taste trip from sip to swallow; quite refreshing and downright satisfying; appropriate hazy-golden color; a worthy successor to the much-missed Ballantine IPA of yore. Enjoy it with fish and chips, or your local equivalent.

BROYHAN PREMIUM Lager   CB   1.8
(Hannover, Germany)

Tartly hoppy with a mushy mouthfeel; texture flattens rather rapidly, becoming mild and reserved; food may coax a bit of hoppiness back out—this beer obviously needs to be urged to give up anything positive; light-bodied and light-colored, with thin, faint Brussels lace; musty, mild malty finish; an uninteresting brew.

BRUIN PALE ALE   CB   1.0
(Cincinnati, Ohio)

Slight light-struck mouthfeel, followed by a flat aftertaste after an initial sip or two; mildly perfumey; mild hoppy taste with a chemical underflow; not bitter, sharp, or particularly alcoholic as this ale should be, rather like a watered-down pilsener without the carbonated punch; tepid alone or with food; weak-tea color with no visual texture; minor softness and sweetness surfaces at end of bottle (but at this point, so what?); lowest-common-denominator beer.

B E E R   F A C T

"Pale ale" is the term often used to indicate a brewery's premium bitter. Traditionally offered in a bottle, it is increasingly served from the tap.

**BUCKERFIELD'S APPLETON
BROWN ALE** BP 3.3
(Victoria, British Columbia, Canada)
Nice, tender, smooth flow from the tip of the tongue to the back of the throat; remains friendly throughout; good and quasi-creamy. Goes nicely with fried finger foods, such as chicken wings and mushrooms.

BUCKERFIELD'S ARCTIC ALE BP 2.0
(Victoria, British Columbia, Canada)
A little watery; retains very mild, fruity taste; becomes more palpable with bland cooked foods but fades into mild sourness; not really worth the effort.

BUCKERFELD'S PANDORA PALE ALE BP 2.9
(Victoria, British Columbia, Canada)
Immediate citrus (orange-grapefruit) taste; fresh, buttery ambiance; soft, rounded fragrance; ends up being something of a lightweight, but creates some fun getting there. Goes well with shellfish.

**BUCKERFIELD'S SWANS
OATMEAL STOUT** BP 3.8
(Victoria, British Columbia, Canada)
Subdued, rounded, burnt taste; much less threatening than the deep-brown color would suggest; retains nicely moderated richness; roasted malts stay unobtrusive; very well balanced; surprisingly refreshing and not filling; well deserving of several pints and a return engagement. Serve with pork.

BUCKHORN Pilsener CB 0.1
(Milwaukee, Wisconsin)
Light, uncarbonated, toxic-tasting, and downright repellent; several sips are all you need, and several sips was all I needed; one of the worst American beers I have ever tasted.

BUCKHORN BOCK CT 1.6
(Torrance, California)
Malty, with a bit of unwanted sourness; what should be richly malty comes across as spoiled grain; strong and unpleasantly overpowering; hard to tell it's a bock, other than the hint of malt; touch of coffee at the end; this is the kind of beer that gives cute labels a bad name.

BUDWEISER Pilsener CB 1.1
(St. Louis, Missouri)
Crackly, thin, and watery; sweetish rice flavor floats up immediately; visually bland, thin, and faded; head disappears quickly; no aroma or even a suggestion that hops are present; some bitterness is coaxed out by food; absolutely no nuance or subtlety, or for that matter, taste; thickens a bit at the finish; very pre-

dictable at a low, superficial (or is it artificial?) level; blandness is so predominant that a negative taste or aroma sensation would raise the rating. It has to be the savvy advertising campaigns and not the beer that makes Budweiser so popular. Gold Medal winner at the 1996 Great American Beer Festival.

BUDWEISER BUDVAR Pilsener   CB   3.5
(Budejovice, Czech Republic)

Clover-sweet aroma and taste greet the palate on first sip; despite its delicate and relatively uncarbonated texture, there is a rich, round flavor that increases in strength and complexity; smooth, full-bodied mouthfeel; light golden body sparkles in the sunlight; pleasant hop-malt aftertaste; deliciously thirst-quenching; one of Europe's classic premier beers. Best to enjoy this alone, unspoiled by food.

BUFFALO BILL'S PUMPKIN ALE   CT   2.4
(Dubuque, Iowa)

Nutmeg-spicy; baked pumpkin pie mouthfeel overall, almost to the exclusion of the beeriness of the liquid; all that's missing is the crust; some hop bitterness relieves the monotony; light amber color is sort of autumnal, with hints of orange pumpkin hue; not so much overspiced as it is underbeered; this ale is fermented with real pumpkin. Try it alone or with the appropriate holiday meal.

BUFFALO BLIZZARD BOCK (draft)   MB   0.9
(Buffalo, New York)

Rather shallow and uncomplicated, hardly resembling bock; not very alcoholic or substantive; very fuzzy gray-brown color is too light for an American bock, which is usually dark or deep brown; lightly malted; more carbonation than beer taste, as if to hide its overall lackluster presentation; finishes with characterless warmth.

BUFFALO GOLD PREMIUM ALE   RB   2.9
(Boulder, Colorado)

Sharp and crisp, unlike the typical ale style; tasty and slightly alcoholic with understated sweetness; mild texture, but rough enough to raise your interest; gentle, integrated blend; flavor is too flat and tends to fade; slight cloudiness dilutes the pale gold color; finishes with a welcoming moderate bitterness. Accompanies pasta salads and traditional Italian favorites.

BULL ICE MALT LIQUOR   CB   1.0
(Detroit, Michigan)

Peach perfume in a malt liquor!—not the best beginning; chemical taste at the top of the palate, followed by unpleasant exhalation; quickly fading crispness and rapidly diminishing head don't distract you enough from slight sour alcohol taste; full-bodied with a sneaky, perfumey sweetness; settles into a no-frills, bulldozing attempt to get you polluted (6.13% alcohol/weight), even with a texture that is squishy-soft.

BULLDOG Pale Ale   CB   3.3
(Reading, England)

Pointed, sharp yeastiness with a clean-tasting fruitiness; body is light to medium; finishes nicely complex, hoppy and dry, but leaves a slight bitter aftertaste. Fine with roast beef and a baked potato.

BUNKER HILL LAGER   RB   1.8
(Wilkes-Barre, Pennsylvania)

Quite hoppy and sharp; more effervescent than flavorful, with dullish aftertaste on the roof of the mouth; no complexity, thin head; adds nothing in taste or as a general accompaniment to food; lackluster in color and mouthfeel; somewhat malty finish with a touch of sweetness doesn't fully redeem this beer by any means.

BUSCH Lager   CB   1.0
(St. Louis, Missouri)

Lightweight with a lot of fizz; adjuncts predominate, making flavor bland, light, but acceptable to many; in the end, uneventful and tasteless.

BUUR BEER DELUXE Lager   CB   3.4
(Randers, Denmark)

Rounded and sugary, with no head to speak of; sharply alcoholic, but not otherwise texturally complex; evenhanded malt-hop balance; a bit winey at the top of the mouth; gets warmer as the bottle bottoms out; clearly a well-made beer, crafted attentively and with quality in mind. Good with a barbecued burger.

BUZZARD BREATH ALE   RB   1.7
(Calgary, Alberta, Canada)

Smells of overripe apples on the ground in an orchard; flavor itself is flat and uninspiring; no head; amber color is too faded to be appealing; some emerging fruitiness and depth as it warms, but not enough to change the thumbs-down on this bland, uncomplex, and unmotivated beer.

CABRO EXTRA Pilsener   CB   1.7
(Guatemala City, Guatemala)

Flat, unrevealing taste—you wait for something to happen and it doesn't; slight, quickly fading fizziness; weak undercurrent of sweetness is evident midway, along with some graininess, with hops predominating; in the end, a low-end, palatable beer with minimal interest; doesn't come close to meeting expectations; flat, semi-bland, and steady-as-it-goes—which isn't very far.

CAESARUS IMPERATOR
HELLER BOCK   CB   0.0
(Zurich, Switzerland)
Extremely honey-sweet—so sweet it makes you thirsty; smooth in texture; cloying and syrupy; apple-juice color has no complexity; flat and almost medicinal in taste, suggesting you should drink this only if you're sick.

CAFRI PREMIUM BEER Pilsener   CB   3.4
(Seoul, South Korea)
Malt-grain mouthfeel is reminiscent of cereal; smooth and light-bodied; quick, knife-like sharpness; clear pale-wheat body; sweetens at mid-bottle; rounded rice flavor (jasmine rice?) goes well with sweet peach aroma, all very constrained; delicately presented; finishes with a full, sweet rice mouthfeel that is almost chewy; a dainty, complex beer. Goes best with cooked vegetable dishes.

CALGARY AMBER LAGER   CB   2.4
(Toronto, Ontario, Canada)
Sharp at the front of the tongue and mellower than usual Canadian beer; not complex; almost woody taste, good draft-style bar beer; no head to speak of; obviously not interested in going beyond the beginnings of a run-of-the-mill brew. Okay with tortilla chips and dip.

CALIFORNIA LIGHT BLONDE ALE   MB   0.0
(Torrance, California)
One sniff and sip, and you're out—phew! Sour, raw, green, uncarbonated; slight medicinal taste; unfinishable; brush your teeth after this one.

CALLAO PILSEN   CB   2.3
(Callao, Peru)
Acidic; some yeasty bitterness; very mild aroma; not bland, but undistinguished; like ginger ale in texture; smooth and unobtrusive; unexciting and rather routine. Compatible with deli-style foods.

CANADA COUNTRY LAGER   CB   3.0
(Vancouver, British Columbia, Canada)
Sharp and lusty mouthful; surprising but pleasant sweetness as it is swallowed; retains crispness and freshness even as frosted mug loses its iciness; decent, but not noteworthy. Try it with bland pastas.

CANADIAN LAGER   CB   2.0
(Vancouver, British Columbia, Canada)
Smooth, light, and easy to drink with light food, musty and day-old-tasting without; somewhat thin and watery. Label proclaims "An honest brew makes its own friends"; a good brew, of course, makes even more friends.

CAPITAL DARK Lager   **MB**   **3.2**
(Middleton, Wisconsin)

Mellow, slightly coffee-sweet, and full in the mouth; rounded with sharpness at the edges; piles on tingliness on the tongue; deep, ruby-red body makes the long-lasting, quarter-inch-thick head seem to float gently on the liquid; makes for soft and gentle sipping throughout a warm spring afternoon; unsophisticated taste—just aims to please. Nice accompaniment to chips and dips.

CAPITAL BAVARIAN LAGER   **MB**   **3.3**
(Middleton, Wisconsin)

Deep golden hue accompanied by average texture; nice rounded, malty fullness not generally found in American beers; stern with abundant touches of grain taste; as meal progresses, it becomes an integrated and pleasantly unobtrusive part of the meal; lingering unpleasant aftertaste mars overall effect, however. Try it with cold soups such as gazpacho or vichyssoise.

CAPITAL OKTOBERFEST Lager   **MB**   **2.5**
(Middleton, Wisconsin)

Mild, burnt maltiness and soft palate give immediate attractive impression; its hallmarks are warmth and softness; remains a one-note beer, with some slight but noticeable increase in sweetness as bottle empties; cloying at the roof of the mouth with thickish honey-like feel—not a good impression to leave. Accompanies green olives, pickled tomatoes, garlic-cheese bread, and other cocktail hour nibbles.

CAPITAL WILD RICE Lager   **MB**   **2.4**
(Middleton, Wisconsin)

Underpinning of honey; somewhat flat with no head; eventually displays warmth that envelops tongue and insulates entire mouth from the flavor of accompanying food; disappointing in its simplicity; more honey aroma at finish, with associated sweetness.

CARDINAL LAGER   **CB**   **4.0**
(Fribourg, Switzerland)

Very light and fluffy, with a mild, quite attractive astringency; wonderful use of hops which appear to be timid at first, but blossom into a complex, moderated fullness as you swallow; head is thick and captivating, leaving substantial, well-configured Brussels lace to linger on the sides of the frosty mug; aromaless, but more than made up for in taste and texture; very similar to a wheat beer, including its thirst-quenching abilities; easy to drink, it finishes smooth and satisfying. Light enough for tuna salad and interesting enough to be enjoyed alone.

CARIBE Lager CB 3.3
(Champs Fleurs, Trinidad)
Mild but insinuating in a pleasant way; light-honey taste emerges; maintains its identity even with a variety of food flavors contending for attention; distinctive and noticeable; ranges from fruity balance to mild spiciness; minimal sour aftertaste smoothly attenuates the honey taste; pale-yellow color inadvertently signifies more lightness than actually is present. Accompanies thick deli sandwiches.

CARLSBERG Lager CB 3.3
(Copenhagen, Denmark)
Pilsener-like, typical pale lager; thick sweetness deteriorates in the mouth; continuing interplay of barley and hops maintains interest and pleasant unpredictability, settles down into a slightly rough but stylish rhythm; attractive, thickly bubbled head is a soft preface to the sharpness of the body and its mild maltiness. Goes well with the usual pilsener-appropriate foods, from fresh pineapple to freshwater fish.

B E E R   F A C T

*T*he Carlsberg headquarters in Copenhagen boasts what many call the prettiest brewhouse in the world. While the company still is brewing beer (lots of it), it has also set itself up as a foundation in support of the sciences and arts.

CARLSBERG ELEPHANT MALT LIQUOR CB 3.1
(Copenhagen, Denmark)
Crisp, relatively full taste with muted floweriness; nice malt/yeast aroma is a good counterpoint to the sharpness of the texture. Pick your food carefully with this beer: it is enhanced by New York strip steak, at odds with shellfish.

CARNEGIE HILL GOLDEN ALE BP 2.3
(New York, New York)
Strong malty aroma; light, not unattractive perfumey taste; semicrisp, with circumscribed bitterness; fresh bitter aftertaste; too smooth and watery; obviously uses quality ingredients and is made with forethought, but fails to engage anywhere along the way. Accompanies light snacks.

CARNEGIE HILL HEFE-WEIZEN BP 2.1
(New York, New York)
Smooth clove taste and pleasant citrus-musty flavor; hard to find the yeast; Brussels lace is erratic and much too sparse; too sweet, like weak sun-brewed tea; not thirst-quenching; too faded and

unfocused for the style; almost like lemon juice. Like its cousin Golden Ale, hefe-weizen does okay with light snacks.

CARNEGIE STARK-PORTER CB 2.7
(Sundsvall, Sweden)

Smooth and silky, with a deep, full-of-flavor roastedness that's thick and full-bodied; very noticeable chocolate presence pleases the throat; abrupt gain in bitterness near the end adds to its generally strong character; finishes with a pungent, malty aroma and coffee taste; dark-brown body is attractively shaded with yellow-red. Companionable with well-prepared pork roast.

CARTA BLANCA Lager CB 3.6
(Monterrey, Mexico)

Light but with significant body; flavorful without being obtrusive; good workman-like beer that still has style and creativity; can be sipped alone without embarrassment or loss of enjoyment; I get teased a lot about this, but Carta Blanca is one of my favorite everyday, drink-with-anything-or-nothing-at-all brews; taste for yourself.

CARVER IRON HORSE STOUT BP 2.6
(Durango, Colorado)

Appealing light-chocolate aroma; soft milk stout with quick flash of malty roastiness; thick Brussels lace; opaque deep-brown color; medium-bodied; close to coffee-tasting with lingering dryness on the roof of the mouth; not zesty or pungent enough; improves with each additional sip; overall, too fragile—needs more hop backbone. Good with this brewpub's pastry desserts.

CARVER OLD OAK AMBER ALE BP 2.5
(Durango, Colorado)

Soft and weak; hops in evidence, but passive and subservient; doesn't go anywhere after first swallow or two; Brussels lace is spotty and head is less than minimal; no alcohol presence to speak of, but stays within style; dry, with less malt than advertised.

CARVER RASPBERRY WHEAT BP 0.5
(Durango, Colorado)

Wispy raspberry aroma and taste, but not sweet; essentially raspberry juice—watery, flat, with no characteristics of wheat beer; orange-copper color; no head to speak of.

CASS FRESH Ale CB 3.4
(Seoul, South Korea)

Mildly and daintily hopped; minimal fizziness feels good going down; sharp and fresh-tasting; thirst-quenching; medium-bodied; light, perfumey note is noticeable at the end; sweetens, and stays very tasty; finishes smooth and satisfying; a very well balanced beer that keeps your interest. Try with light sandwich fare, like tunafish on rye toast.

CASSEL SCHLOSS Amber Lager   **CB**   1.7
(Noerten-Hardenberg, Germany)
Sweet and yeasty; slightly spicy odor is more attractive than the
taste, which is like modeling clay; pale champagne color; zero head;
flat-looking texture; taste sharpness dulls halfway through; turns a
bit sour; remains absolutely listless from start to finish in the company of food; malt-hop balance seems to fluctuate from sip to sip.

CASTELLO Pilsener   **CB**   2.2
(San Giorgio di Nogaro, Italy)
Sweet, dry taste typical of pilsener; fresh with a subdued, musty
crispness; in the end weak and somewhat watery. Not bad with
Mexican food.

CASTLEMAINE XXXX LAGER   **CB**   3.3
(Brisbane, Queensland, Australia)
Crisp and a bit flowery with a swift thirst-quenching rush when
well chilled; some hoppiness becomes apparent with grilled red
meats; cloudiness, atypical of lager, misleads you into expecting
some yeastiness and grain taste; interest fades as meal progresses;
more entertaining at the beginning than the end.

CATAMOUNT AMBER ALE   **MB**   0.2
(Windsor, Vermont)
Flat, watery, and some skunkiness; faint, wispy, fruity aroma that
clears out quickly; deep-down sulfur taste sticks like a lump in
the throat and is reminiscent of a polluted river; turns into simple blandness as it warms; this beer is obviously weak and poorly
thought out.

CATAMOUNT PALE ALE   **MB**   2.7
(Windsor, Vermont)
Take a sip and immediately enjoy the pleasant, mild, somewhat
fruity aroma wafting gently to your nose; comprehensive doses
of malt and hops add substance to this full-bodied brew; feisty
and increasingly bitter; wisps of Brussels lace patiently follow the
cloudy orange-blond body down the sides of the glass; a fresh hit
of malt aroma decorates the finish. Pairs well with freshwater fish.

CATAMOUNT PORTER   **MB**   3.8
(Windsor, Vermont)
Sharper than expected, with attenuated bitterness that is slightly
off-flavor; head is immediately thin but it doesn't matter, given
the luscious deep purple-brown color throughout; warms into
mellower, more exactingly balanced brew as it embraces mild
foods; reaches nice bittersweet, hop-malt balanced stride at the
bottom of the bottle, but also gets a bit watery; mildly bitter aftertaste; sharp, clean finish—a handsome brew. Try it with roast
chicken or turkey.

CELIS DUBBLE ALE RB 3.7
(Austin, Texas)

Fresh, tangy aroma meets fresh, alcohol-laced taste; deep-seated maltiness; long-lasting sweetness is almost cloying; underlying thin texture is a satisfying surprise that adds balance to the strong, forward-marching flavor; tamped-down bitterness at mid-bottle further adds to the complexity; pungent alcohol mouthfeel remains predominant; well made and distinctive. A good companion with cheese and hard fruit.

CELIS GRAND CRU Ale RB 2.4
(Austin, Texas)

Vague fruity aroma followed by somewhat spoiled-fruit taste, coming close, but not quite to, rotten-egg taste; highly yeasty with very little carbonation; tart sweetness, along with off-flavored fruitiness, is reined in by curries and other traditional Indian dishes; engaging crispness emerges; tightly packed Brussels lace adheres to the sides of the glass; finishes with a sharp hoppiness that redeems (somewhat) the earlier spoiled presentation; yeast aroma, however, remains throughout; clearly quality ingredients, but only a knowledgeable palate can begin to appreciate the totality of their taste, if even that is possible.

CELIS PALE BOCK RB 3.4
(Austin, Texas)

Pleasant warming rush on first sip, with dry aftertaste at the roof of the mouth; accommodatingly bristly with an alcoholic undercurrent; light and tingly; alcohol presence less than it should be; reasonable balance between sweet maltiness and moderately bitter hops; well made, but essentially a weakened American bock; sweet, dainty finish. Accompanies broiled meats.

CELIS WHITE Hefe-Weizen RB 4.0
(Austin, Texas)

Sharp and highly yeasty; quick lemon aftertaste matches cloudy weak-lemonade color; wispy Brussels lace slides gracefully down sides of mug; remains steady and forthcoming, maintaining its integrity and predictability despite the potential roadblocks and derailing possibilities of spicy food; throws off the spiciness and cuts forward with pronounced dryness; steady threat of cloves and pungent yeastiness make the brew exciting; clearly brewed by someone who knows what to do; a good representative of this style—and made in the U.S., no less. Silver Medal winner at the 1994 Great American Beer Festival.

CERES ROYAL EXPORT Lager CB 3.3
(Arthus, Denmark)

Full and hoppy; quickly sweetens and warms up with food; yeast and grains emerge at mid-bottle, lending a nice balance to the sharp hoppiness and adding a mellow, understated mouthfeel;

faint bitterness/sourness clings to the roof of the mouth, even after swallowing; needs to be highly chilled for full enjoyment—an iced mug would be appropriate; flavor continues throughout; neatly patterned Brussels lace remains until the last drop is gone—a sign of brewing quality; finishes warm, with a hint of hop bitterness. Goes well with fish dishes of all kinds—try it with a fresh tuna salad niçoise or poached salmon with dill sauce. A fried flounder sandwich on a toasted roll partners nicely, as well.

B E E R   F A C T

*C*eres is the Roman goddess of agriculture, a telling reference to the beer's earthy hop character. Interestingly, *cerveza*, the Spanish word for "beer," comes from the name Ceres.

CERVEZA AGUILA Pilsener   CB   2.3
(Barranquilla, Colombia)

Malty effervescence and lighthearted ambiance; light straw color with some integrity; remains quite grainy; minimal solidity fades in the stretch while at the same time it turns somewhat bland texturally; light, weak, but tasty; finishes gently sweet and freshly grainy, but remains so-so overall. Accompanies vegetable salads composed of a mix of any of the following: steamed and coarsely chopped carrots, broccoli, cauliflower, zucchini, and yellow squash; uncooked tomatoes, avocado, and sweet onion.

CHANGLEE LAGER   CB   2.6
(Sanshui, China)

Zesty and ricey with clean, fresh water taste (brewed with mineral water—you can tell); barest hint of honey on the throat arrives slowly and leaves quickly when food is introduced; somewhat wimpy overall, including faded honey color; entertaining without food, it slides down without any complexity; but it is certainly not unpalatable.

B E E R   F A C T

*D*espite comparatively low per-capita consumption, China is the third-largest beer market in the world. Consumer spending on beer there has increased around 14% in each of the past several years.

CHAPEAU FARO LAMBIC CB 2.6
(Wambeek, Belgium)
Sweet and sour simultaneously; smooth and textureless on the
roof of the mouth; tastes slightly rubbery, as if you had just applied the brakes; subtly complex, with a variety of yeasty sensations; sugary sweetness has a tart, yeasty bite; cloudy brown-yellow
body; finishes sugary-sweet, with a slightly woody character. Drink
this without food.

CHAPEAU GUEUZE LAMBIC CB 1.1
(Wambeek, Belgium)
Flat, and minimally satisfying; sour; a bit moldy and appley;
placid, limpid taste mirrors the light-straw flat-looking body; becomes fruitier, as if apples were sliced open to allow more taste
and aroma; uninvigorating and disappointing, unusual for a Belgian beer.

CHECKER CAB BLONDE ALE MB 1.3
(New York, New York)
Somewhat skunky, too bitter and rather flat texturally; second
sniff reveals a malt sweetness and faint lemony aroma; acidity
gives it some interest; cloudy light-blond body, with no head;
lifeless; drink this with something sweet to counteract the sour-
tart mouthfeel.

CHERRYLAND CHERRY RAIL LAGER CT 2.9
(located in Sturgeon Bay, Wisconsin;
brewed in Dubuque, Iowa)
A shot of cherries is quickly and forcefully present, and stays
around; never gets nasty or presumptuously sweet or tacky, though
it has the ingredients to head off in that direction; with light
coming through the glass, golden ruby-brown color echoes a
thick, newly ripe Bing cherry; acceptable fruit beer with little attention to malt, even though it is all-malt. Looking for something slightly different? You could do worse. Best imbibed without
food.

CHERRYLAND GOLDEN RAIL LAGER CT 2.8
(located in Sturgeon Bay, Wisconsin;
brewed in Dubuque, Iowa)
Sour and thin, with only a hint of texture; settles down and the
balance becomes apparent; mid-bottle warmth comes through as
sharpness remains at the edges; gets sweeter with malty features;
finishes more palatable than it began; worth trying.

CHERRYLAND SILVER RAIL LAGER CT 2.2
(located in Sturgeon Bay, Wisconsin;
brewed in Dubuque, Iowa)
Sweet and sour, leaning toward the former; light and fluffy, with
little complexity; warm with a bit of snap, but mushy and mild

with food; no head; generally flat texture; decent starter beer for those worried about sharpness and surprises—neither of which is present here.

CHESTER GOLDEN ALE   CB   2.9
(Cheshire, England)

Very appropriate hint of bitters with fresh, almost sweet wheat/grain ambiance; modulated crispness that flatters the palate unaccompanied by food; not as creamy as other similarly styled English ales; honest aroma; leaves you somewhat thirsty after the last sip (too much sugar?); good and sweet, but flags at the end.

CHIHUAHUA Lager   CB   2.7
(Monterrey, Mexico)

Middle-of-the-road taste; good for homey foods; familiar, everyday beer; light, mildly hopped, sharp, and fresh-tasting; the choice at the neighborhood bar. Goes well with salsa and chips.

CHIMAY PERES TRAPPISTES ALE—
GRANDE RESERVE (gold label)   AB   2.5
(Chimay Abbey, Belgium)

Fizzier and more wine-like than its red-labeled Premiere cousin; alcohol predominates from tip of the tongue to back of the throat, tending to overwhelm the anticipated fruitiness; amber cloudiness from fresh yeast added just prior to bottling; in the end, too sharp and harsh, with an unfortunate hint of greenness. Try with red meats.

BEER FACT

*T*he Trappist fathers of Chimay produce a trio of very strong ales (of which I've tasted and rated two), each identified by a different-colored cork; gold-corked Grande Réserve is the highest in alcohol content of the three (8.9%/volume). Each of these ales is vintage-dated. While true of all sedimented ales, it is especially important that Chimay be poured slowly, to make certain that sediment stays at the bottom of the bottle.

CHIMAY PERES TRAPPISTES ALE—
PREMIERE (red label)   AB   4.7
(Chimay Abbey, Belgium)

Soft, sweet taste is mellow going in, integrated going down; lots and lots of yeast—in the nose, on the palate, at the bottom of the glass, in the color, which is milky brown; sly fruitiness edges around the tongue while you're dealing with the yeast; soft with gentle but pervasive alcohol presence; apple-juice appearance and implication; delicious, like a good sipping port; best alone, as a gentle and appealing *digestif* without culinary distraction; one of the best I've tasted.

BEER FACT

*B*rewed by French-speaking monks in a Belgian monastery, the Chimay ales have been called the "burgundies of Belgium." Chimay Abbey was the first monastery in Belgium to brew beer commercially.

CHINA CLIPPER Lager   CB   2.5
(Guangzhou, China)

Fresh, with vague medicinal undercurrent; strikingly unnuanced, with malts and hops clearly defined and unintegrated; light, unobtrusive texture; dry finish and humdrum memory; best to sample this without food.

CHINA GOLD Pilsener   CB   1.8
(Guangzhou, China)

No effervescence and slightly watery; strong physical mouthfeel; essentially bland with a slight ping; not a memorable brew. Okay with a hamburger.

CHINA LUXURY LAGER   CB   2.9
(Taipei, Taiwan)

Immediate rice-wine taste with soft crispness; clean, fresh, faintly vanilla mouthfeel; smooth and easy going down; not very complex, suggesting that boredom would set in after several bottles; trace of burnt molasses serves as a good finish, with sharpness and sourness not noticed before. Subdued companion to linguine with clam sauce and other Italian food.

CHRISTIAN MOERLEIN BOCK   CB   2.6
(Cincinnati, Ohio)

Watery on first sip, but a jolt of textural graininess catches you at the back of the throat; almost satisfying in its attempt at bock richness; less creamy and rich than advertised; clearly better without spicy or sharp food; tantalizes with the promise, but not the fulfillment, of satisfaction.

**CHRISTIAN MOERLEIN-CINCINNATI
SELECT BEER Pilsener**   CB   2.5
(Cincinnati, Ohio)

Relatively full and undistinguished on first sip; smartly rising bubbles end in a big-bubbled, rather airy head; exhibits reasonable balance of malt and hops; neither-here-nor-there textural ambiance lightens up a bit and serves as calming, settling balance/counterpoint to food; not particularly exciting without a meal. Try it with a burger or grilled chicken breast sandwich piled high with green chiles.

BEER FACT

*C*ontrary to a seemingly indestructible myth, bock beer, such as the Christian Moerlein Bock, is not the residue scrubbed out of the kettles during a brewery's annual spring cleaning. It is a distinct style, a strong warming lager meant to be consumed when cool weather is changing. Perhaps the myth stems from confusion about the brewing of Marzenbier (Oktoberfest), which was traditionally brewed in March, placed in cool caves, and consumed each fall in celebratory fashion. The kegs were then ceremonially drained of their fully fermented and enjoyable contents.

CHRISTOFFEL BIER LAGER   CB   2.5
(Roermond, Holland)
Fresh, doughy taste with bitterness at the back of the throat; fruitier than the usual lager; prolonged sharpness matches pinprick-by-pinprick sharpness of spicy foods; somewhat moderating after food is gone, with potential warmth that never really arrives; noticeable graininess, but too hoppy in the end. Goes well with Southwestern dishes.

CHRISTOFFEL ROBERTUS Ale   CB   2.6
(Roermond, Holland)
Caramel aroma and flavor are obvious and insistent; accompanying yeast taste is also somewhat demanding; vague lemon taste stays underneath the caramel; kind of sticky on the lips; loses some substance and zip halfway through, as the caramel malt is absorbed into the cloudy apple-cider-colored liquid; uncomplex and essentially a one-note brew; good, but not particularly interesting. Drink with melon or other cold fresh fruit.

CH'TI BLOND BIERE DE GARDE   CB   3.3
(Benifontaine, France)
Smooth and not very hoppy; mild, subdued yeasty aroma and taste stay throughout; sweet citrus presence at back of the throat; sweetly champagne-like, but without the bubbles; taste recalls *les pommes* when they are slightly bruised and fermenting in the field;

soft and silky, like cognac; a gentle, lulling drink that cautiously sneaks up on you. It makes for a good pre-bedtime *digestif.*

LABEL LORE

*T*he shadowy image of a coal miner on the Ch'ti label is a tribute to the once vigorous mining industry in northern France. *Ch'ti* is Picardy dialect for *c'est toi,* meaning "it suits you."

CHUNG HUA Pilsener CB 3.4
(Guangzhou, China)
Fresh, crisp taste with sweet undertone; pleasant, with an easy-going rhythm; a bit on the dry side, it remains appealing and enjoyable from start to finish. A good match with Asian food.

CHURCHILL AMBER Lager CB 3.3
(Redruth, England)
Slight molasses-malty taste disappears after passing over the tongue; this is not a bowl-you-over beer, but instead a gentle sipping brew to enjoy at the neighborhood pub; smooth, fading in-and-out maltiness stays throughout, alternatingly enticing and neutral (or is it a mild caramel taste that comes and goes?); come-hither attraction leaves you with a desire for more. Try this with bagels and lox—a surprise delight.

CHURCHILL LAGER CB 3.6
(Redruth, England)
Full, hoppy taste quickly followed by pinpricks of subdued fruity bitterness; hearty and somewhat assertive; very pale color; spring water plays leading role in the taste; full, balanced, and maturely integrated at the end with a sweet, lingering taste on the tongue; smooth and medium-dry; appropriate for the novice interested in something different. Try with broiled or roasted pork.

CLARA ESTRELLA DORADA Lager CB 0.6
(Guadalajara, Mexico)
Rather musty and a bit raw; hard to discern any particular ingredients; sly sweetness creeps out when a slice of citrus fruit is squeezed into the glass; essentially no distinctive character—texture, taste, or otherwise; light and thin; pass on this one.

CLARK'S GREAT CANADIAN Lager CB 1.0
(Vancouver, British Columbia, Canada)
Bold and rugged, just as the label proclaims, but without much flavor or aroma to go with those northern Canadian virtues; the goal here is to muscle its way onto your taste buds, minus much

evident concern for the niceties of, say, balance, nuance, and/or consistency; label also boasts, in italics, about its "genuine rugged Canadian bottles"; when the packaging is of more interest than the ingredients, watch out.

TAP TIP

What Time of Day Is It Best to Drink?

While it is not recommended that you make a habit of drinking beer shortly after getting out of bed, that time of the day, especially mid-morning to lunchtime, is in fact the period when your senses are at their most acute. Taste and smell are just getting revved up and are receptive to sensory input, making the two- to three-hour window of opportunity ideal for pure judging and taste-comparison purposes. More appropriate for the ordinary social pleasures of tasting and drinking beer, however, are the several hours prior to suppertime, which, as fortune should have it, is the period generally considered the next-best sense-sensitivity time frame. Alas, fortune is not always precisely prescient: The senses lose some of their sharpness during and immediately after a meal, and flavor, olfactory, and other characteristics become less readily identifiable.

CLAUSEN EXPORT Pilsener   CB   2.8
(Bogota, Colombia)
Faded off-taste, but crisp and tangible; rice presence is covered by freshness of the water and sweet tang of malt; ingredients become more integrated toward end of can; serviceable and thirst-quenching; tasty by itself. Good with chowder or gumbo.

CLIPPER CITY INDIA PALE ALE   MB   0.7
(Baltimore, Maryland)
Very malty and caramely; attenuated hop taste flattens on roof of mouth; sour and bitter; more physical sensation than flavor; not hoppy, not fruity, not tasty; mild unpleasant aftertaste; gave me heartburn.

CLUB Lager CB 2.7
(brewed by Labatt in Toronto, Ontario,
 and elsewhere in Canada)
Straightforward classic lager with fading taste as it is swallowed; bland toward the bottom; in the end, too weak for highly flavored food; evolves into moderately sweet, rounded finish. Try it with relatively bland pasta or vegetable dishes.

CLUB PREMIUM Lager CB 2.1
(Quito, Ecuador)
Weak and not charming; minimal fizz; builds airy head quickly; very foamy and full of air; average but apparent grain/malt ambiance; glimmer of interest at end of bottle with a hint of character via a malty finish; pedestrian and run-of-the-mill. Serviceable with pureed soups such as tomato, pea, or potato.

COAST RANGE MERRY MAKER ALE
(draft) MB 1.5
(Gilroy, California)
Actually, this draft version is not very merry; it has a weak, lemony taste and vinegary aroma; light, textureless, and much too airy; a partially redeeming doughy aroma is apparent after several sips; far too soft on the palate; not complex and rather uninteresting.

COCHONNETTE PETITE VAPEUR
COCHONNE ALE CB 3.1
(Pipaix, Belgium)
Coppery glow to the body sets it off visually right away; applebrandy flavor is tart and yeasty; smooth, gently increasing alcohol taste makes your cheeks light up; good blending of orange peel and coriander flavors is bolstered by roasted chicory; sweetens into a delicious, full-bodied fruitiness at the end. Made for after-dinner or pre-bedtime sipping, accompanied by a rich dessert, like chocolate pudding or toffee.

COLT 45 MALT LIQUOR CB 0.3
(Detroit, Michigan)
Thin, perfumey, and otherwise tasteless; a slight bitter sensation makes an appearance, but that may just be my imagination; watery, too; what less would you want in a beer?

COLTS BERG Pilsener CB 2.1
(Bangalore, India)
Hint of clove, with some sourness; thinnish, light-yellow concoction; vague sharpness; some malty warmth surfaces occasionally; prickly on the tongue; in the end, more benign than unappealing; weak and undemanding.

COMMONWEALTH HEFE-WEIZEN BP 2.4
(New York, New York)
Clove and banana-cherry tastes intermingle on first sips; textu-

rally too smooth for wheat beer; a bit buttery; neither the wheat, barley malt, nor yeast is clearly distinguishable, though the body is wheat-colored; could be more thirst-quenching, tastier, crisper, and thinner; flavor shifts from clove to banana and back too often to be predictable or enjoyable. Snack foods only with this beer.

COMMONWEALTH HUDSON RIVER PORTER   BP   2.5
(New York, New York)

Silky smooth; tasty, mild roastedness; hops and malts are nicely integrated, though neither is assertive nor aggressive; a decent bitterness is present, as is accommodating nuttiness; deep-brown body flashes orange-red hues; finishes with a gentle sweetness that contains a hint of sourness in the aftertaste; perhaps the best of the Commonwealth brews. Goes reasonably well with heavier pub fare.

COMMONWEALTH OCTOBERFEST   BP   2.4
(New York, New York)

Bold and fruity; lightly bitter; clean on the palate; vinegary aroma is a significant distraction; slight mustiness at back of mouth eventually subsides; continuing sweet malt taste contains just the slightest hint of hops; weakens at the finish; okay, but not great. A beer made for pretzels or other light pub fare.

COOK'S GOLDBLUME Lager   CB   0.5
(Evansville, Indiana)

Sharply carbonated; slight sour odor; apparently loaded with adjuncts, giving it taste uniformity, not to mention taste boredom; light, weak, and inattentive with food; carbonation disappears at the end; leaves a slight musty aftertaste; standard, low-priced, barroom can of beer with nothing really to recommend it.

COOPERS BEST EXTRA STOUT   CB   3.4
(Leabrook, South Australia, Australia)

Smartly and strongly roasted with a touch of sugary maltiness; roastedness has a smoky character reminiscent of Rausch beer; not for the faint of heart, or palate; coffee taste is refined and laid-back; black, syrupy body glides smoothly out of the glass and onto your tongue; sturdy and robust; generous coffee-colored head. Goes with raw oysters or other shellfish.

COOPERS SPARKLING ALE   CB   2.5
(Leabrook, South Australia, Australia)

Lightly hopped with a tea-like essence in the aroma; yeasty sweet, close to puckering; light mouthfeel; faint clove spiciness; slight perfumey taste; alcohol presence is noticeable about two-thirds down the glass; raggedy head stays from start to finish; yeast sediment is plentiful at bottom of bottle; finishes with a decidedly apple cider mouthfeel. Stick to light fare here, like sandwiches and cold soup.

COOPERSMITH'S ALBERT
DAMM BITTER Ale   BP   3.0
(Fort Collins, Colorado)
High hoppiness is brought down to acceptable size with yeasty maltiness that is encouraging and beguiling; not very bitter; the predominant texture is smooth and tending to flatness; attractive yeast aroma counterbalances the appropriate diminishing fruitiness as ale warms; while alcohol content makes up for some of the lack of carbonation texture, this bitter ale could still use more working-class grittiness; deep hoppiness is missing. Nice with a variety of cheeses and tart fresh fruit.

COOPERSMITH'S CHRISTMAS ALE
(annual)   BP   3.2
(Fort Collins, Colorado)
Though ingredients and nuances are modified from year to year, you can generally expect to find a holiday treat that is gently and subtly spiced; mellow cider feel on first sip; thin, but bulked up with many tasty Christmas ingredients, including cloves, ginger, nutmeg, cinnamon; maintains integrity and balance with food; though too thin and texturally weak, remains smooth; allows spices a nice showcase. Try it with a bowl of chili or hearty winter soup.

COOPERSMITH'S HORSETOOTH
STOUT   BP   4.0
(Fort Collins, Colorado)
Luscious, rich, burnt, roasted-malt flavor; relatively flat and texturally smooth and silky; deep, deep brown, almost-black color mirrors the rich flavor—classic example of a milk stout; a second gallon was too alcoholic. (At this brewpub, as at many others, you can get a returnable gallon jug to go.) Overall, the richness of the ingredients and diminished alcohol are just right with oysters and other shellfish.

COOPERSMITH'S IMPERIAL STOUT   BP   3.0
(Fort Collins, Colorado)
Rich, smooth, and thinly creamy with no sparkly zest at all; deeply luminescent dark, dark brown sets off nicely in conjunction with tongue-tantalizing light burnt-molasses taste that almost in passing becomes the core of this stout; milky and silky, but where's the alcohol?; some spicy tones are almost indistinguishable from one another. Best with chowders and deli foods; meatballs and linguine also do well.

COOPERSMITH'S MOUNTAIN
AVENUE WHEAT   BP   1.8
(Fort Collins, Colorado)
Yeasty aroma; burst of flavor in the mouth with clear citrus feel; yeast sediment on bottom clouds this thin pale ale; no clove taste

at all; quite hoppy and somewhat rough; far too yeasty for its own good; tastes unfinished.

COOPERSMITH'S NOT BROWN ALE   BP   2.7
(Fort Collins, Colorado)

Touch of sweet maltiness; smooth, with no ripples; slightly toasted; deep, rich color; nice interacting Brussels lace; sweetish aroma; hint of annoying cloying aftertaste. Okay with Asian food.

COOPERSMITH'S POUDRE ALE   BP   2.4
(Fort Collins, Colorado)

Flowery, almost perfumey, with continuing aftertaste; smooth with wine-like feel, but alcohol is not noticeable until the end; stays stable and uninteresting with very little carbonation; finishes with some mild sharpness; disappointing in the weakness of its ingredients.

COOPERSMITH'S PUNJABI
INDIA PALE ALE   BP   3.8
(Fort Collins, Colorado)

Yeasty and fruity (especially grapefruity); light mouthful settles fully and more thickly on the tongue; hops are unassuming, but present in the form of tangy, moderated bitterness; substance rises to the occasion, but falls a hair short with food; smooth but not gritty; the genteel alcohol accumulates subtly and engagingly, but quality fades rapidly. Bronze Medal winner at the 1993 Great American Beer Festival. Fine with pasta.

COOPERSMITH'S SIGDA'S
GREEN CHILE Ale   BP   2.2
(Fort Collins, Colorado)

Sharply pungent chile taste comes and lingers; overwhelms bland foods; nice in balance with spicy dishes; chile taste has depth and subtlety with spirited spike of texture; strong, powerful, almost overwhelming.

COORS Pilsener   CB   1.4
(Golden, Colorado)

I agree with the ads: It's the water. Take away that crisp, clean, fresh liquid, and it's hard to tell what you have left; the malt, hops, and adjuncts, such as they are, are very difficult to discern, although a thin, faint maltiness does make its presence known, if you pay close enough attention; very light, almost prim texture. Featureless with food, it doesn't get much tastier alone.

COORS EXTRA GOLD Pilsener   CB   1.8
(Golden, Colorado)

Sharp, light, and tasteless; at first it seems to be a quality beer, but it quickly subsides into a typical pedestrian brew, even on a summer picnic with cold cuts and salads. Touted as "a full-bodied beer"—yes, in comparison to Coors' regular pilsener.

COORS WINTERFEST Lager (annual)　CB　　　3.1
(Golden, Colorado)
I have found a fair amount of variability from year to year with this annual offering; more recent editions have been weaker in alcohol content than other Christmas beers and moderate-bodied rather than full-bodied; at least one earlier version was quite smooth and palpably sweet-tasting (it had a pleasant glow of color and a friendly aroma; more beer-like than the close-to-water stuff of regular Coors); with the unevenness of past experience, there's probably a 50-50 chance that you will wind up with something at least nearly worthy of the holiday season; try to cajole a sample sip beforehand.

CORDOBA-DORADA Pilsener　　　CB　　　3.7
(Cordoba, Argentina)
Simultaneously dull and sharp texture, especially when cold; hint of rice with good everyday journeyman's taste; soothing undertone with spicy foods; essentially a good, tasty, middle-of-the-road brew that accommodates itself to the food at hand; recommended. Good with broiled or roasted chicken, steaks, and most spicy foods.

CORONA EXTRA Pilsener　　　CB　　　0.8
(Mexico City, Mexico)
Slight fizzy acidity; very light, airy, and essentially tasteless, unless lemon slice is added; hard put to keep up with even mildly salty snacks; hint of skunkiness—not surprising from this clear glass bottle; weak and mass-produced; cold, it is refreshing, but then so is plain water; we need a little more textural and taste heft in Corona.

CORSENDONK MONK'S BROWN ALE　　AB　　3.9
(Sigillum Monastery, Ertevelde, Belgium)
Silky smooth and clean-smelling, with color of luscious dark chocolate and commensurate appeal; not complicated at all; nice, unobtrusive fruity undertone; bottled with its natural yeast, the yeastiness emerges calmly and accommodatingly as beer warms at the end of the bottle; gentle and slightly aromatic, with qualities for the novice as well as the more experienced drinker; a visual delight. Perfect for relatively bland food.

CORSENDONK MONK'S PALE ALE　　AB　　4.0
(Sigillum Monastery, Ertevelde, Belgium)
Highly yeasty, but moderated and calm; creamy finger-thick head tops off warm golden body with a touch of red; plenty of fast-rising bubbles; a bit murky, as expected; mildly bitter sweetness; tart citrus taste emerges out of nowhere in mid-bottle; Brussels lace hangs in sheets like finely webbed curtain on sides of glass; hearty and to the point; strikingly smooth and warm; well put together. Good with spicy shrimp cocktail.

BEER FACT

*T*he Corsendonk monks started their brewery in 1400 and closed it in 1784, when the entire abbey was shuttered by Austria's Jozef II. The religious order's brewing tradition was revived in 1906 with the founding of a secular brewery by Antonius Keersmaekers. Responding to consumers' presumed sensibilities, what is known as Monk's Brown Ale in the United States is called Pater Noster (Our Father) in Europe. Sic transit marketing.

COTTONWOOD LIFT YOUR KILT
SCOTTISH ALE   BP   3.5
(Boone, North Carolina)
Nice full flavor; slightly smoky from the peated malt; rounded, filling mouthfeel; sweet and chewy; light and flavorful; a bit perfumey in the mouth; aftertaste is somewhat woody; becomes more intense as you drink it—and do drink it; understated tart finish punctuates the subtlety of the previous flavors; a well-done, craftsmanlike beer. Try with fresh trout or other light fish.

COUGAN'S MARZEN (seasonal)   BP   2.2
(Glendale, Arizona)
Fresh, fruity, and vigorous in presentation; quite bitter; lingering grapefruit taste; diminishing sparkle in the light-amber body; becomes fizzy and soda-like toward the end and seems to lose its flavor grip; thins out too much, though the hops remain viable; starts well, ends poorly.

COUGAN'S PORTER   BP   2.6
(Glendale, Arizona)
Unfortunate hint of metal right at the start; quickly rebounds with a mildly bitter mouthfeel that includes a touch of coffee in the taste; doesn't have the depth or complexity of a top-notch porter; cobwebs of Brussels lace on sides of glass enhance the experience; for any chance at enjoyment, make certain this is served at room temperature.

CRAZY ED'S BLACK MOUNTAIN GOLD
Lager   MB/BP   2.5
(Cave Creek, Arizona)
Surprisingly soft in texture but harsh, with a touch of greenness, in taste; meshes wonderfully with marinated green olives—in fact, the two go together divinely; cloudy-pale; good barroom drink; fullness and controlled sweetness at the end; has character for a

rather commonplace beer. Companionable with appetizers like stuffed mushrooms.

CRAZY ED'S ORIGINAL CHILI BEER
Lager   MB/BP   0.6
(Cave Creek, Arizona)

Rapidly rising, very sharp jalapeño taste and texture immediately lodge in the throat—sort of like inhaling a mouthful of crushed red peppers; set in light pale liquid with no mouthfeel of its own, the beer just says hot-hot-hot; harsh and much too distracting for plain foods; slim, small jalapeño pepper in bottle is difficult to remove, unfortunately; defiantly a one-note (very sharp) beer with no accompanying melody or rhythm; gimmicky with few redeeming qualities.

CRAZY HORSE MALT LIQUOR   CB   1.9
(La Crosse, Wisconsin)

Hint of skunkiness; taste varies, bordering on a honey-sweetness sometimes, other times on a sour acidity; head is full and foamy but, alas, artificially induced; fast-rising bubbles provide good visual carbonation effect in the glass; soft mouthfeel, with no real oomph; lacking the punch associated with malt liquor; sweet finish with, finally, a dollop of alcohol; generally unappealing.

B E E R   F A C T

A Minnesota law, effective August 1, 1994, prohibited the use of the Crazy Horse name on malt liquor or any similar product that suggests "a connection with an actual living or dead American Indian leader." The brewers of Crazy Horse claimed the ban violated its free speech rights. As a result, Crazy Horse Malt Liquor is still being sold. Minnesota and Washington were the only two states where agencies banned the sale of Crazy Horse.

CRESTED BUTTE RED LADY ALE   BP   2.3
(Crested Butte, Colorado)

Sour citrus taste emphasizes the alcohol; hint of hoppiness helps to propel this ale forward; bland and yeasty; thin head; reasonably filigreed Brussels lace; yeasty finish; not flavorful enough; malt is too subdued.

CRISTAL Pilsener CB 2.2
(Leca Do Balio, Portugal)
Tastily grainy with a honey background that makes this pilsener very easy to drink; light on the palate; gently and lightly hopped; minimal bitterness; rather weak-flavored, though the underlying grain character does its best to keep your interest; finishes a bit snappier than it started, but by then it's too late; a borderline beer.

CRISTAL PILSENER CB 1.3
(Limache, Chile)
Very flat with quickly passing thick taste at the back of tongue; benzene taste starts at mid-bottle and lingers; a no-frills beer; sole interest is a minimal sharpness; no character. Matches the mildness of cheese empanadas.

CRISTAL PREMIUM Lager CB 2.4
(Chiclayo and Lima, Peru)
Quickly and convincingly refreshing with initial brief touch of alcohol; bubbly and even-tempered, but not particularly flavorful or nuanced; not pushy or intrusive with food; has the same thirst-satisfying qualities of water with added quality of being beer; slightly soapy aftertaste. Enhances Southwestern foods.

CROOKED RIVER BLACK FOREST
LAGER MB/BP 3.2
(Cleveland, Ohio)
Full-bodied, with a texturally assertive presence; spice, perhaps clove, is noticeable throughout; plenty of malt-hop flavor is filling and fulfilling; less carbonated than expected for lager; dry; some honey taste is coaxed out by plain grilled seafood. This is a beer with style and distinction.

CROOKED RIVER SETTLERS ALE MB 2.4
(Cleveland, Ohio)
Mildly fruity, mildly hoppy; flattish texture offers a slight buzz on the tongue; creeping bitterness after a few sips; interesting base of malt holds up and carries the hop bitterness along; remains calm and predictable, neither offending nor pleasing; has hints of promise, but in general doesn't deliver. Try with Polish sausage and kraut.

CROWN Lager CB 2.2
(Seoul, South Korea)
Weak Asian beer without much zest—typical of the area; lacks distinction; watery and lifeless; essentially unassertive; ingredients are hard to discern; okay in a pinch. Picks up somewhat with plain pork chops and baked potato.

CROWN LAGER CB 2.3
(Belize City, Belize)
Very soft; mild fizziness; distinctive grain taste; musty, almost dusty aroma goes up nose with a little irritation; nice complexity; some wine-like flavor; foam clings to sides of glass but otherwise does not do justice to the beer; head also stays intact with bubbly, lighthearted airiness. Some fruitiness emerges with beef stew; remains uncomplicated and relatively lifeless with food.

CRUZCAMPO LAGER CB 2.7
(Campo, Spain)
An underlying stream of bitterness accompanies a crisp, grainy mouthfeel; slight sweet honey taste; bitter character stays throughout, but settles into a composed, restrained presence; clear, crystalline pale-straw body; finishes crisp and dry. Goes nicely with shrimp and rice dishes.

CRYSTAL DIPLOMAT DARK BEER CB 3.8
(Wurtenberg, Czech Republic)
Full-bodied; rich chocolate taste and aroma; lush and luscious tan-white head; faint bitterness suggests faint coffee overtones; chocolate forms the core of the taste; some roughness in the texture adds to the winning ambiance; rich without being filling; maltiness sidles up toward the end to create a one-two chocolate-malt finish; loses some complexity at the end, but you hardly care. Try this with strong-tasting fish from the sea.

CUSQUENA PREMIUM PERUVIAN
BEER Lager CB 2.4
(Cuzco, Peru)
Consistent background bitterness carries along a gentle hint of graininess; sweetens perceptibly after several sips; soft touch on the palate; light-bodied; though it weakens texturally, it finishes with a noticeable hop mouthfeel. This is a light summertime drink, and nothing more.

CUZCO Pilsener CB 3.2
(Cuzco, Peru)
Mixture of tastes and textures: fizzy, fruity, and malty, sharp and smooth; pale gold with intense coppery core; moderate carbonation; user-friendly and mellow-minded—it's there to please, not to dominate or intrude; some citrus aftertaste spoils the finish; good beer for the novice drinker. Retains delightful filigree of malt grains even up against spicy foods.

DAB TRADITIONAL GERMAN
DARK BEER Lager CB 1.7
(Dortmund, Germany)
Malty and hoppy, but mildly so; you need to concentrate to experience any of the flavor; mellow, it goes with the flow; rather

weak and uncomplicated; even the ruby-amber color is undistinguished; malty aroma emerges, but doesn't add much; in general, not as tasty as it would like to be; snack foods seem to give it some much-needed muscle.

DALLAS GOLD Pilsener   MB   1.0
(Dallas, Texas)

Malty, far too watery and textureless, with no head; hint of toastedness, in Vienna amber style, but even then falls short; some acidity spoils overall effect; tastes too much like a home brew —unfinished, unintegrated, unbalanced; deep malty aroma accompanies definite chocolate taste at the finish, but there is no texture or nuance to mitigate the strong sensations; some orange fruity aroma at last sniff; definitely not in the pilsener style at all; soothes the stomach at the end; lifeless; unappealing with food.

DAMM Pilsener   CB   3.8
(Barcelona and Valencia, Spain)

Nice grainy, zesty flavor fills the mouth; similar aroma fills the nose; smooth with a bit of an off-taste, but gets back on track; neither heavy nor light, it appears to be just right for the food at hand, as well as later on, when a meal is finished; thirst-quenching and satisfying. Good with a thick cheddar cheese sandwich.

D'AQUINO ITALIAN BEER Pilsener   CB   2.3
(Induno, Italy)

Malty, fruity, and quite zesty with light pale color; becomes somewhat Spartan, letting texture overwhelm taste; workmanlike, soccer-stadium beer that would go well with pasta and other everyday food; unprepossessing when all is said and done; finish is malty and without much flash.

DARK MOUNTAIN PORTER   MB   1.4
(Vail, Arizona)

Plummy-winey sharpness dispenses a nice, full sweetness; thins quickly into a dried fruit taste, losing its richness while gaining roughness on the palate; well-defined sour character is similar to weak plum wine; lackluster in taste and aroma; no depth, just a lot of screeching high notes; lots of promise, not much delivery.

DARRYL'S PREMIUM LAGER   CT   2.6
(Dubuque, Iowa)

Surprisingly soft and agreeable on first sip; subdued sharpness turns flat at sides of the tongue; creamy, relatively lasting head tastes a little soapy; not particularly complex; pedestrian, with hints of impending surprise and potential interest—all undelivered; unexciting accompaniment to food; good try for a contracted beer.

DB DRAUGHT Lager   **CB**   **2.3**
(Auckland, New Zealand)
DB presents a faint bitterness that is dry and thirst-quenching; the slight flavor and light body add minimal support to the otherwise refreshing summer-sensitive character; sweet unlit-tobacco aroma offers some much-needed substance; reddish-gold body is not filling; a semi-pleasant afternoon diversion for those interested in a cooling, nonassertive drink. Chips and dips should be paired with this one.

DE KONINCK ALE   **CB**   **3.9**
(Antwerp, Belgium)
Exquisite grassy mouthfeel is coupled with a balancing, toned-down maltiness; spicy, close to peppery aroma; sweet and warm all over the palate; lush, coffee-cream colored head; hint of clove presence is refreshing and energizing; sweet and juicy toward the end, which makes you want to roll it in your mouth just to prolong the savory satisfaction. Fruits, nuts, and soft cheeses will enhance the enjoyment of this ale.

DEAD ARMADILLO ROASTED RED
Lager   **CT**   **2.5**
(Lake Oswego, Oregon)
Vague roastedness, with hint of dark chocolate; medium-bodied and rich-tasting; roasted malt aroma; loses some textural punch at mid-bottle; burnt caramel color with red hue; eventually attains a degree of complexity and bitterness, though overall it weakens too much at the end. I like this with cream filled cookies.

DEEP CREEK GOLDEN ALE   **CT**   **0.2**
(Frederick, Maryland)
Rough-edged and harsh; vaguely fruity, but essentially the experience is flat-to-stale and ultimately beside the point; a poor example of this or any other style; diluted hop aroma surfaces at mid-bottle; hard to find anything good about this beer.

DEEP CREEK YOUGHIOGHENY RED
AMBER ALE   **CT**   **1.1**
(Frederick, Maryland)
Noticeable nutty malt aroma along with a light maple syrup taste that turns maltier as you drink it; flavors gain in stature and complexity as it warms; turns grumpy early on—thickens, loses flavor, flattens, and sticks to roof of mouth; winds up uninteresting, except for some hints of malt hanging on for dear life; finishes relatively tasteless.

DEGROEN'S PILS   **MB/BP**   **1.1**
(Baltimore, Maryland)
Fruity, with emphatic bitterness; far too uncarbonated for a pilsener; where's the balancing malt? Too cloudy; wisps of Brussels

lace fade slowly; hops fade quickly; weak and uninteresting. Gold Medal winner at the 1996 Great American Beer Festival.

DEGROEN'S WEIZEN   MB/BP   2.4
(Baltimore, Maryland)
Sharply bitter with a healthy dose of clove; soft texture; faint sulfur smell evolves into a flowery-fruity aroma; mildly yeasty; nicely designed Brussels lace stays attached to the glass; approaches the wheat style, but doesn't quite pull it off.

DEININGER KRISTALL WEIZEN   CB   2.2
(Hof, Germany)
Yeasty, with rounded crispness and fullness on first sip; lighter than usual sweetness, but overall not above average; maintains mild tartness; a bit less bitter and more palatable when warmed. Nice counterpoint to spicy, big-flavored foods.

DELIRIUM NOCTURNUM   CB   3.5
(Melle and Ghent, Belgium)
Plummy, raisiny, fruity aroma; similar, but fuller taste also has a gentle yeasty-fruitiness; lessened carbonation level lets you enjoy the yummy flavors without undue interference; background character suggests a nice blending of coffee and chocolate; warming sugary sweetness complements the slightly sharp alcohol taste; long finish is smooth and full of plum and raisin notes. Goes great with light cheeses and fresh fruit.

DELIRIUM TREMENS BELGIAN ALE   CB   1.7
(Melle and Ghent, Belgium)
Nothing but thick creamy foam fills three-quarters of the glass; in a moment or two, the light golden hue peers from beneath the cloud cover and glacially supplants some of the huge head; sour and sharp; light and fizzy; highly yeasty, with a stringy dollop of honey maltiness; yeast aroma crawls upward into the nostrils; too strong for my palate. Hard to match with any food, but try hard cheese for starters.

DEMPSEYS ALE   CB   2.4
(Monroe, Wisconsin)
Flat aroma and somewhat salty, acrid taste on first sip; rather musty and old-tasting; basically bland and ticklish on the roof of the mouth; neatly, but uninterestingly, goes hand-in-hand with food; undistinguished by itself, even as it warms; tastes more like Scotch than ale. Accompanies roasted pork dishes.

DENTERGEMS WHITE ALE   CB   0.6
(Dentergem, Belgium)
Rose-petal perfumey taste and aroma; blond and bland with essentially very little texture; a disappointing boudoir beer—pale, light, and very frivolous, like chamomile tea; conditioned in the bottle, which is painted white to give it a ceramic look; feh!

DESCHUTES BACHELOR BITTER   MB/BP   3.1
(Bend, Oregon)

Mildly malty and less than mildly bitter, but decently flavored; increases in circumscribed bitterness with food, becoming mellower and creamier; red coppery color; increasing complexity makes it pleasing and easy to drink; keeps its strength at the finish, and retains its quality character. Upgraded a year or so ago—more hops, malt, and alcohol—Bachelor Bitter is better than ever.

DESCHUTES BLACK BUTTE PORTER
(draft)   MB/BP   3.7
(Bend, Oregon)

Relatively light for porter, with forthright alcohol presence (appropriate for porter); deep velvety-brown-nearly-black color is a real attraction; emerging fruitiness and toastiness are refreshing, though texture remains flat; almost food-like in its ability to be filling; calming, satisfying, with even-tempered complexity; fuller-bodied and mellower at the end of the glass. Goes well with shellfish—oysters, clams, and shrimp, for example.

DESCHUTES MIRROR POND
PALE ALE (draft)   MB/BP   1.2
(Bend, Oregon)

Wispy and fruity with similar aftertaste; I find it to be not much of a drink with or without food, but over the years it has improved. Try it for yourself and decide; Gold Medal winner at the 1994 Great American Beer Festival.

DESCHUTES OBSIDIAN STOUT   MB/BP   2.5
(Bend, Oregon)

Roasted, then bitter, then sweet—all in quick succession; malty sweetness stays for a while, accompanied by a vaguely plummy, wine-like taste; a nugget of malt flavor forms on back of tongue; gets a bit watery, but the flavor is persistent; pleasant mild roasted aroma pops up at the end; a subdued but accurate rendition of the style. Goes nicely with chocolate dessert.

DESPERADOS Pilsener   CB   0.1
(Schiltigheim, France)
This beer is what Dr. Dementia is to radio—a novelty in poor taste, a little off-kilter, silly, and wacky; with its citrus and spices and essential oils (!), it tastes and smells like aftershave; splash it on, don't drink it; it also contains tequila, but you'd never know it; flat and cloying, too; to make matters worse (if that's possible), it comes in a clear, sunray-penetrating bottle; keep Desperados at arm's length.

DIEKIRCH Pilsener   CB   2.9
(Diekirch, Luxembourg)
Nice sweet grain aroma with muddied yellow appearance; sharp, with quickly rounded end note; crisp and clean from head to toe with fulfilling mid-range body, does yeoman service against hot, spicy dishes; still, it is more appropriate with blander food.

DINKELACKER Pilsener   CB   2.9
(Stuttgart, Germany)
Cloudy, milky, unobtrusive; good complementary background taste; dry, minimally fruity, and light-bodied; hop taste is soft, but present; a good, sturdy beer that is not particularly complex. Serve it with fresh salmon or other favorite fish.

DINKELACKER DARK Lager   CB   3.4
(Stuttgart, Germany)
Moderate, chewy sweetness that almost immediately turns a bit sharp and yummy; slight burnt-caramel taste lingers and remains tantalizingly around the roof of the mouth; maltier, rather than hoppier, with attendant, almost bland smoothness; not really dark in color, but medium-brown with orange-red overtones and some murkiness; weakens at bottom of the bottle. With this malt liquor, try a barbecued chicken sandwich.

B E E R   F A C T

*W*ood barrels made of Louisiana cypress are used to age Dixie lager. Once in the bottle, however, Dixie, like most beers, does not improve with age. A good rule: drink your beer within one week of purchase.

DIXIE Lager   CB   3.5
(New Orleans, Louisiana)
Great uplifting spirit entering and leaving the palate; crisp and refreshing; brewed for an appreciative popular taste; texture outplays flavor, but end result is a comprehensive beer worthy of

repeat performances. Accompanies (what else?) oysters on the half-shell, crawfish, and spicy shrimp.

DIXIE BLACKENED VOODOO LAGER   CB   2.4
(New Orleans, Louisiana)

Teasing sweetness with pungency in background, punctuated by snappy pinpricks of fizz; texture is tamped down and smoothed out in mid-bottle; flatness rapidly settles in, underscoring lack of complexity and integration of ingredients; fades toward water; rich reddish-brown with hint of purple when held up to the light; faint fruity, molasses feel at finish, along with the return of a malty aroma; in the end, disappointing. Full and almost fruity with linguine with clam sauce.

BEER FACT

*D*ixie Blackened Voodoo Lager gained a measure of notoriety when it was introduced to the public in 1992. A number of localities tried to ban the brew because, it was alleged, images on the label were too suggestive of sorcery, charms, and other voodoo practices. The company, of course, couldn't have bought better publicity, and the fledgling boycotts quickly disappeared into the swamps.

DIXIE CRIMSON VOODOO RED ALE   CB   2.3
(New Orleans, Louisiana)

Quick honey aroma and taste, both of which edge toward sourness; light-bodied and hardly carbonated; flavor lessens after three or four sips, but still remains distinctive; malt gradually rises up at mid-bottle; no subtlety or complexity, just a straight-on honey mouthfeel. Okay with American cheese sandwich.

DOCK STREET AMBER Ale   MB/BP   3.1
(Philadelphia, Pennsylvania)

Front-of-mouth fruitiness, followed by fizziness at the back of the throat; thick and robust with grilled London broil—noticeable sweetness mellows out and integrates, nicely enhancing the red meat; body gets fuller, too; warmth and fruitiness are finishing trademarks.

DOCK STREET BOHEMIAN PILSNER   MB/BP   3.5
(Philadelphia, Pennsylvania)

Spritzily hoppy with a fine tingle of texture that gently tickles your throat; good, persistent hop mouthfeel; pale straw color supports a reasonably thick head; aromatic and tasty; pleasurably long-lasting hints of flavor remain long after the last sip; this is a well-crafted pilsener that enhances a variety of uncomplicated dishes, including seafood salad and pasta.

DOCK STREET ILLUMINATOR Lager   **MB/BP**   **3.1**
(Philadelphia, Pennsylvania)
Lots of alcohol here, along with a strong surge of hops that covers the tongue; plenty of ongoing malty sweetness helps to round things out; rich brown color is typical of the double bock style; finishes with a big, all-encompassing malt aroma; bold, balanced, and bountiful. With a meal, try smoked meats, like ham or pork; after a meal, fruit-filled pastries.

DOGFISH HEAD CHICORY STOUT   **MB/BP**   **3.2**
(Rehoboth Beach, Delaware)
Milk-chocolate flavor provides a gentle balance to a subdued roasted bitterness; smooth, mouth-filling coffee taste glides down the throat effortlessly; relatively light-bodied for a stout, almost airy; coffee flavor blossoms as the liquid reaches room temperature; deep rich black body shows off a purple cast; finishes as smooth as it starts; a good-natured, easy-drinking beer. As you might with a fresh cup of coffee, savor this with a flaky pastry filled with cream or fruit.

DOGFISH HEAD SHELTER PALE ALE   **MB/BP**   **1.4**
(Rehoboth Beach, Delaware)
Bittersweet and full in the mouth; hoppiness gradually emerges, though it never gets really bitter or sharp; suddenly, a sweet-tea flavor intrudes—a nice taste, but not one normally associated with this style; remains flat, as if all the flavor was sucked out of it; weak and uninspiring.

DOGWOOD WHEAT   **MB**   **3.0**
(Atlanta, Georgia)
Spice-clove taste is immediate and quite pleasant; fresh and sharp; clove presence increases and teams up with a distinctive banana aroma; there's a bit of citrus in there as well; this German-style wheat beer is made up of a progression of appropriate flavor changes, much like a tasty chain reaction; turns a bit bitter toward the end; nice cobwebs of Brussels lace decorate the glass; finishes with—what else?—a good dose of cloves. Quench your thirst with this before settling in for lunch; then have another with your tunafish sandwich or tossed salad.

DOJLIDY PORTER   **CB**   **3.2**
(Bialystok, Poland)
Constrained roastedness accompanies a mild bitter presence; creamy smooth on the palate; intense roasted aroma is molasses-like in character; sweet, heavy, and laden with subtle flavors, this porter is on the verge of becoming a barleywine; rich, raisiny taste

has a decided alcohol kick; finishes with a fruity/plummy character and lush, dense mouthfeel. While it goes well with red meat, I suggest you take advantage of its characterful presentation and drink it without food.

DOMINION LAGER   RB   1.0
(Ashburn, Virginia)
Smells soapy but inexplicably tastes like a mixture of spice and clove; flat and unfizzy; citrusy and bitter; dry and almost puckering; did they put the wrong label on this beer?—it's certainly not lager; hard to fathom and equally hard to digest.

DORADA PILSENER   CB   3.3
(Talca, Chile)
Starts off with fresh on-rushing hops taste that calms down to an integrated, more balanced drink with some mellowness; hoppiness remains ascendant and agreeable; a heavy pilsener that continues to weigh heavily. Serve with solid, meat-and-potatoes-style meals.

DORTMUNDER AKTIEN ALT   CB   1.2
(Dortmund, Germany)
Complex and balanced aromatic interaction between malts and hops is featured at the outset; sweet, fresh wood taste quickly disappears, to be replaced by a rather bland, unentertaining, and cloying mouthfeel that stays for the duration; a curious beer that holds promise, but ultimately doesn't deliver.

DORTMUNDER UNION DARK Lager   CB   0.1
(Dortmund, Germany)
Creamy head; hint of bitterness at the back of the throat; has a funny fish-like taste with some foods; mild and smooth with a medium body; exudes an almost rancid chocolate taste; remains creamy and slightly chewy throughout.

DORTMUNDER UNION ORIGINAL
Pilsener   CB   3.6
(Dortmund, Germany)
Cold, this mildly bitter creation squarely hits the spot after an hour or so of lazing in the sun; aftertaste is dry and hoppy; head is thinnish but smooth and very much a part of the full body; achieves faint sweetness with kalamata olives, as the salt of the olives appears to draw out the flavor of the hops; nicely put together; low carbonation level, with resultant smooth texture.

DOS EQUIS CLARA—LAGER ESPECIAL   CB   3.2
(Guadalajara, Mexico)
Mild, pleasant, and responsive; light rice taste appears to come from brewing ingredients rather than addition of adjuncts; flattened sharpness is well balanced; weakens after a bottle or two. Appropriate with pasta in a garlicky seafood sauce.

DOUBLE DIAMOND ALE CB 2.5
(Burton-on-Trent, England)
Starts with a honeyed, fruity palate; cold on the sides of the tongue; wraparound taste quickly dissipates with food; sharp finish with unexpected savory sourness to match; overall, more texture than taste, but that's not necessarily a drawback; malty warmth along with roughened smoothness finally emerge at the end. Accompanies roast chicken with plain vegetables.

B E E R   F A C T

*D*ouble Diamond gets its name from the twin diamonds chalked a century ago on the brewery's wooden casks to mark the best of the brew. Today the bottle label shows an updated version of the original geometric design.

DOUBLE HAPPINESS Lager CB 2.3
(Guangzhou, China)
Pedestrian Asian beer with faint rice taste that is plain rather than enhancing; thin and somewhat pallid; completely overwhelmed by spicy or highly flavorful foods; clearly tries to be a good companion to food, but ingredients are not integrated enough to allow it to perform the task; I would come back to this in a year or two, to see if any changes have been made. (I did, and there haven't.)

DOUGLAS SCOTCH BRAND ALE CB 3.9
(Antwerp, Belgium)
Creamy, alcoholic fruitiness greets the nose and mouth with just a hint of underlying cloyingness; constant burnt-caramel taste, particularly on the tongue; alcohol emerges with great depth and insistence with food; tightly bubbled Brussels lace surrounds the beer, adding to the creamy, smooth context; cream-white head sits like a crown on deep-red body; malt accent; drink this nifty concoction in a brandy snifter for best results, or try it with pasta dishes and lightly seasoned pork chops.

DOWN UNDER Lager CB 2.6
(Perth, Western Australia, Australia)
Creamier than other Australian beers, with a smoky aftertaste; smooth, mellow, and easy going down; in the end, turns thin and a bit sour; ultimately less robust than at first sip. Pleasant with pan-fried fish.

TAP TIP

Empty Glasses

*B*eer brewing is often a fleeting enterprise. Brews and breweries come and go, and it is not unusual to unexpectedly discover that a familiar companion—or just-acquired friend—is no longer available. Sometimes they reappear in a different guise (different company, different label, hoppier, smoother). Over the years, several good beers, as well as some that perhaps should never have been made in the first place, have disappeared. Here are a few remembered favorites, offered to you fondly and with the hope that someday they may return—for my renewed, and your newfound, enjoyment.

An ale and two lagers stand out: Marthasville Sweet Georgia Brown Ale (Atlanta, Georgia), Trapper (Red Deer, Ontario, Canada), and Dark Horse Amber (Virginia Beach, Virginia). Dark Horse, which I rated 4.0, was one of the best American beers I've ever had—fresh-tasting, fruity, and well balanced. Marthasville, which I savored at the popular ambience-loaded Manvel's Tavern in Atlanta, had a refreshing fruitiness and a dry, constrained, hoppy mouthfeel which still makes me weep at the thought of its demise. Trapper (3.7) was crisp and effervescent, with a mild, sweetish tartness. You still can buy a product called Trapper, but although it's made in Canada, it's not the same beer, company, or brewery location.

The moral? Enjoy your beer, but don't get too attached to it. Although smaller breweries have a higher overall success rate than, say, restaurants, the mortality level still warrants caution. A conservative figure suggests that 1 in every 5 brewpubs goes belly-up shortly after opening, and 1 of every 4 microbreweries. The death rate for Canadian counterparts is roughly twice the American ratio. On the other hand, more than three breweries a week opened somewhere in the country at the end of the century. A second moral (*caveat emptor* division): The success of a beer is not necessarily related to its taste—as if most of us didn't already know that.

DRAGON STOUT   CB   3.3
(Kingston, Jamaica)
Creamy and very sweet, with mild burnt follow-through; warmth, comfort, and emerging alcohol strength make your heart (and cheeks) glow; deep-brown color is classic in its luminescence; strong high-alcohol aroma; finishes pleasingly bitter and smooth, smooth, smooth; typical milk stout, but perhaps too sweet. A nice *digestif;* try this with chocolate cake or chocolate pudding after a meal.

DRAKE'S ALE (draft)   MB   2.1
(San Leandro, California)
Smooth and malty with faint fizz; good when warm; hint of apple comes and goes; relatively uncomplex, with no predictable distinctive taste; too weak for a true ale.

DREHER PILSENER   CB   2.1
(Milan, Italy)
Creamy, smooth head tops off mild, laid-back hoppiness; soft, gentle fizziness, but virtually tasteless; parallel, uniform Brussels lace circumnavigates the glass; beer plays second fiddle to heavy food; more balanced visually than texturally; pale golden color; some integration in the palpably dry finish; subdued—not exciting, but neither is it a turnoff. Try it with pasta, fish, or chicken.

DRESSLER Pilsener   CB   2.0
(Bremen, Germany)
Honey taste and aroma as if from bees using very strong malt flavor source; almost like a mild Scotch whiskey; no effervescence; flat, sparkleless texture; alcohol seems to be more spread out, not concentrated; not unlike water, but with some backbone; ends with continuing honey taste, but overall rather lifeless and dull.

DRUMMOND DRAFT LAGER   CB   2.4
(Calgary, Alberta, Canada)
Light and citrusy; pale color underneath airy, rapidly diminishing head; very plain with no pretensions; not filling or obtrusive.

DRUMMOND DRY Lager   CB   0.8
(Red Deer, Alberta, Canada)
Light and faint-tasting, reminiscent of other Canadian beers; sharp at the top of the mouth, but that's about all it has to offer in the way of impact; some greenness; continuing less-than-bland taste/texture is completely irrelevant to and submerged by even the plainest food; cheap-tasting, almost perfumey.

DUESSELDORFER PALE ALE   MB   2.9
(Indianapolis, Indiana)
Pleasant and mild; complex with a well-done circumscribed hoppiness; overall grainy taste and aroma; nice malt-hop balance

makes you look forward to the next sip; faint hint of honey emerges when accompanied by roasted chicken breast.

DURANGO Pilsener   CB   0.8
(Del Sur, Guatemala)

Tastes as pale as its color, which is very pale—virtually colorless through green glass of the bottle; sort of like flavored water, it's the Guatemalan answer to Coors; old, musty taste with faintly sweet undertone doesn't deviate with food; the colder it is, the more it tastes like water; an obviously mass-produced beer with little to recommend it.

DURANGO DARK Lager   MB   2.7
(Durango, Colorado)

Immediate light-chocolate aroma and taste are essentially its most telling features; gentle roastedness obscures both malt and hops, though malt is a bit more apparent; medium-bodied; connects to antipasto-type hors d'oeuvres; no head to speak of; middle-of-the-road—a beer for all foods and all seasons.

DUTCH GOLD LAGER   CB   2.7
(Breda, Holland)

Light-tasting and lightly hopped; slight cornmeal presence emerges, adding a rounded, dainty balance to the hops; hop aftertaste on roof of mouth; fuller and more complex flavor as you drink it; fluffy, rocky, stark-white head; grainy aroma percolates up toward the end; finishes light-hearted and mellow. Serve with crisp warm bread and pats of creamy butter.

DUVEL Ale   CB   2.9
(Breendonk, Belgium)

Big head with flat, musty taste does not make for a good introduction; fruity wine flavor; soft, thin, and obviously highly alcoholic by both weight and volume; gains in warmth and mellowness; rather light body; all-malt; smells like raw yeast, but that's the trade-off for its distinctive fruitiness; for those of you who ask a little more from your beer. Perfect with poultry.

B E E R   F A C T

*D*uvel means "devil" in the Flemish language, making this ale from Belgium one helluva beer.

EDDIE McSTIFF'S CANYON
CREAM ALE   MB/BP   0.0
(Moab, Utah)

Flat and cloying; remains drab and odd-tasting, even with spaghetti

and tomato sauce; listless medium-yellow body has a vague hint
of bitterness which may or may not be due to the hops; a bread-
like yeastiness creeps in at the end; raw and almost gasoline-
tasting; I couldn't finish it.

EDELWEISS DUNKEL DARK Wheat   CB   3.0
(Salzburg, Austria)

Apparent but more subdued clove taste than its cousin Hefetrub;
with clove diminished, the taste is more enchanting; retains freshness without cloyingness, somewhat unexpected for a dark beer;
unassuming and clear-tasting; circumscribed warmth. A good
companion with baked or roasted chicken.

EDELWEISS HEFETRUB Wheat   CB   2.4
(Salzburg, Austria)

Very light and fizzy, with distinct hint of clove; becomes rather
airy, almost nondescript; golden, translucent cloudiness gives the
iced glass a frosty appearance; delicate flavor is a bit too cute, not
to say disconcerting, in an Austrian/German brew; lightly hopped;
drink with lemon slice, as recommended on the label. Food is
unnecessary with this beer.

B E E R   F A C T

*N*ow privately owned, the Edelweiss brewery was
founded in 1475 and remained under the control of a succession of archbishops for three centuries. Edelweiss products are Austria's best-selling
weizenbiers.

EDELWEISS KRISTALLKLAR
WEIZENBIER   CB   4.0
(Salzburg, Austria)

Immediate clove palate and softened sharpness; dry; golden, pale
color with long-lasting creamy-puffy head; soothing in the stomach while nourishing in the mouth; fresh and hardy for wheat
beer; textural sweetness, clove-like in substance, finishes the bottle; like a well-tempered symphony with engaging opening, sublime middle, and smooth finish; strong, thirst-quenching example
of this style. (Labeled malt liquor for U.S. consumption.) Serve
with spicy food or fish.

EDELWEISS LUXURY GRADE
MALT LIQUOR   CB   1.4
(Dresden, Germany)

Flat and stolid in texture with faint, hard taste of honey; no complexity; hops are evident with accompanying dryness; malt is

downplayed; mild cloudiness subverts light amber color; even the alcohol in this malt liquor is not apparent; an unattractive, much-too-predictable brew.

EFES Pilsener   CB   0.9
(Izmir, Turkey)

Fresh and restrained on the first sip; sweet and sour at the same time; mixed aftertaste is more unpleasant than pleasant; reminiscent of cheap perfume or old turpentine; an aroma better suited to cleaning fluid than to beer.

EFES PILSENER PREMIUM BEER   CB   3.3
(Istanbul, Turkey)

Quick to satisfy, with its delectable fizzy, sharp, grainy combination; malty grain aroma complements the honey-toned sweetness; controlled, patient bitterness; compact flavor offers a concentrated, focused mouthfeel; truly refreshing and thirst-quenching. A good companion to thin slices of freshly cooked rare roast beef.

EGGENBERG URBOCK   CB   2.0
(Salzburg and Linz, Austria)

Sweet at the tip of the tongue, bitter at the back of the tongue, smooth aft over the tongue; golden color draws attention away from the taste; sort of parallels food rather than complementing it; some fruity taste; a bit sour and cloying; round alcoholic taste; far from memorable.

EINBECKER UR BOCK   CB   2.7
(Einbeck, Germany)

Smooth; pleasantly integrated with unexpected lightness; weakly alcoholic, mellow, and somewhat undistinguished, but not without distinctiveness; tastes far better without food, which obscures its gentle nature.

EISBOCK ICE BEER   MB   2.9
(Niagara Falls, Ontario, Canada)

Very malty; sweet, vinegary aroma; vivacious and sparkly; taste is fruity-sweet, but not cloying; maltiness increases and gets more assertive after several swallows; malty alcohol character fills the mouth; full-bodied; rings of Brussels lace encircle the inside of the glass in parallel patterns; mellow, smooth alcohol presence is noticeable at the end; self-proclaimed "North America's First Ice Beer;" this is a straightforward, forthright brew from the North Country.

B E E R   F A C T

*I*ce beer is made by lowering the temperature to the freezing point of water during the brewing process. The resultant iced water is then removed, thereby increasing the alcohol strength. Eisbock is the strongest type of bock beer, sometimes reaching more than 14%/volume. *Eis* is *ice* in German.

EKU DARK HEFE WEISBIER   **CB**   **3.8**
(Kulmbach, Germany)
Pinprick sharpness with underlying smoothness, accompanied by lemon-clove taste; mild and gentle on the palate; creamy tan head remains thick and comforting with tiny well-shaped bubbles; tart, tangy, and richly yeasty; dry bite; no aftertaste; contrast between head and copper-brown body is aesthetically pleasing and emotionally calming; well made; nice stately brew you can serve proudly to guests. A pleasant companion to pasta dishes.

EKU EDELBOCK   **CB**   **3.7**
(Kulmbach, Germany)
Sweetly and sharply hopped with restrained alcoholic upflow on just the first sip, sturdy and assertive thereafter; aroma and taste match each other perfectly, while texture remains supple and smooth; malt can be ascertained in the aroma; relatively higher alcohol content remains under control and presents itself gradually rather than being overwhelming; a step above the usual brews of this style; nice warm maltiness finishes the bottle. Accompanies various types of deli meats and cheeses.

EKU KULMBACHER PILS   **CB**   **3.9**
(Kulmbach, Germany)
Fresh taste; appropriately sweet graininess; smooth, yet agreeably textured; sparkly and well proportioned; finish is mildly dry. Serve with clams or oysters on the half-shell; taste circulates and seems to improve after every bite of food, not to mention every swallow of beer.

EKU KULMBACHER RUBIN Lager   **CB**   **1.9**
(Kulmbach, Germany)
Rather mild and run-of-the-mill with tantalizing hint of slight fruity sweetness; flat texture; imbalanced in the direction of maltiness; attractive ruby-red amber leads you to believe it's a better brew than performance suggests; uninteresting and fades further in the stretch.

EKU KULMINATOR URTYP HELL
MALT LIQUOR CB 0.2
(Kulmbach, Germany)

Overwhelmingly sweet and syrupy, with lasting coating all over the mouth; remains strongly unpalatable, with increased alcohol content adding to the unpleasantness; food is ruined by the taste of the beer; even deep-red color doesn't take attention away from its sticky cloyingness; far too strong, potent, and aggressive for food, and by itself, it is unfinishable.

BEER FACT

*M*alt liquors come in the same range as do other beers: dark, pale, hoppy, sweet, dry, and so forth. However, malt liquors, while malty (though not strongly so), are not true liquors; that is, they are not distilled, as is vodka or gin.

ELEPHANT RED LAGER CB 2.2
(London, Ontario, Canada)

Smells like lettuce and has about the same nutritional value; relatively tasteless except for a nasty sourness after the swallow; hint of malt emerges when accompanied by pizza with black olives; mellows out a bit after drinking most of the bottle; tastes better than it smells; has pretensions, but doesn't quite make it; nothing to rave about.

EMPERORS GOLD Pilsener CB 3.5
(Guangzhou, China)

Somewhat vivacious, with a touch of hoppy aroma at first sip; pale golden color and minimal head suggest lighter feel than is actually the case; almost perfect balance between malt and hops; loses some fizziness as bottle is drained; good and serviceable—unusual from this country; finish is warm, attractive, and satisfying. Serve with broiled meat.

ENAME DUBBEL ABBEY ALE CB 4.0
(Oudenaarde, Belgium)

Alcohol is clearly present, so be prepared for quite a ride; heavy yeastiness is also a major factor; alcohol makes its most potent statement at about mid-bottle, blending well with the ever-present light fruitiness of the yeast; head is composed of a thick, compact pile of little beads that turn into perfectly rounded bubbles —a very impressive sight; very well made and very well received. Lovely with tomato-based chowders.

ERBACHER GERMAN LAGER   CB   2.4
(Erbach, Germany)

Pungently hoppy, with a pleasant malty background; initial zestiness flattens fairly quickly; a sturdy, straightforward lager with a hint of lemon flavor and a malty aroma at the finish; though the pale-golden color is rather lifeless, the mouthfeel is strong and able to deal with spicy ketchup on roasted potatoes; workmanlike, but not outstanding.

ERDINGER WEISSBIER—DUNKEL   CB   4.0
(Erding, Germany)

Tawny-tan, thick, creamy head sits atop a root-beer-brown body, a great visual beginning; controlled mild yeastiness is chewy and very attractive, with just the right hint of lemon-clove taste; about midway through the bottle, a charming vanilla flavor emerges as a delightful accompaniment; fresh, with a constrained tartness and appealing rich maltiness—marks of a good *dunkel weissbier;* quite spritzy and invigorating; slight roasted taste keeps things interesting; remains tart throughout; yeast sediment collected at the bottom of the bottle turns the color apple-cider hazy; quality product from this reliable Bavarian brewery. Goes well with veal scallopini and fresh vegetables.

ERDINGER WEISSBIER HEFETRUB   CB   4.4
(Erding, Germany)

Fluffy, with a wonderful clove-lemon balance and blend; crisp and nicely carbonated, making it delightful to drink and savor; smells like fresh air off a mountain lake—so much so, you might want to keep your nose in the glass all evening; head stays thick and creamy; tastes every bit as fresh as the aroma; slightly opaque, though relatively clear, despite presence of yeast in the bottle; small, moderately fast-rising bubbles continue until the last sip; quality ingredients and quality-brewed; finish is mildly pungent and sweetly tangy—a joy to behold and to drink. Goes perfectly with shrimp and other seafood salads.

ERDINGER WEIZENBOCK   CB   3.8
(Erding, Germany)

Spicy and flowery, with a moderated pungency; finely tuned caramel taste and accompanying smooth mouthfeel; creamy at the front of the mouth and bitter at the back, adding just the right touch of character; muddy nut-brown color is the result of sediment in the bottle; aroma is reminiscent of macaroni and cheese; cloyingness on the tongue at mid-bottle wears off and the beer remains quite dependable from there forward; thick maltiness intrudes toward the end, detracting from the previous good cheer; surging alcoholic finish caps this dark, flavorful beer. Try it with fried fresh fish.

ERIN'S ROCK STOUT & AMBER LAGER CT   2.4
(Wilkes-Barre, Pennsylvania)
Strong-tasting, with a slightly malty aroma; a touch of malt contributes to the smooth, rich mouthfeel; overall, the flavors meld into one another, lessening the impact of each individual ingredient; settles into a run-of-the-mill beer; color looks like flat cola; finishes with a weak-coffee presence. Strictly a pretzels and peanuts brew.

B E E R   F A C T

*I*n Chile, *pilsener* signifies more hops; *cerveza* ("beer" in Spanish) means less.

ESCUDO PILSENER   **CB**   2.9
(Osorno, Chile)
Very hoppy; bubbly head; not subtle—direct and to the point; strong graininess; for those who want their beer cold, but with some taste so as to know they're not drinking water. Assertive with pickled cold meats and cheese, and with spicy empanadas.

ESCUDO SCHOP (draft) Pilsener   **CB**   2.4
(Santiago, Chile)
Somewhat thick-tasting with a hint of sourness; provokes some interest, which is passive rather than active; thickness at back of tongue doesn't linger; flat and unmotivating at the end.

B E E R   F A C T

*I*n South America, where many countries have a large German population, *schop(p)* means "draft." It is based on *Schoppen,* which in German means a "glass of beer."

ESKE'S ALT BIER   **BP**   1.4
(Taos, New Mexico)
Somewhat fruity and acidic; weak, without staying power; flat; tends to lose its taste; in the end, undistinguished and not worth the effort.

ESKE'S BOCK   **BP**   3.8
(Taos, New Mexico)
Creamy, smooth, and roasted; fine, strong example of this higher-alcohol style; slips down the throat without a hitch, while rela-

tively unassertive flavor clings to the roof of the mouth; a little too supple, with no backbone to speak of; light-headed concoction of charm and piquancy; a bit cloying in the end, but why quibble? Appropriately assertive with strongly flavored meats such as mutton, lamb, and game.

ESKE'S EL JEFE WEIZEN   **BP**   **3.0**
(Taos, New Mexico)
Clearly filled with wheat malt; diminished hoppiness; thickish aftertaste on the back of the tongue turns somewhat acidic as it remains there; dry, with rounded sharpness; full, with light underpinning of citrus presence. Try it with a tuna salad or American cheese sandwich.

ESKE'S SPECIAL BITTER Ale   **BP**   **3.5**
(Taos, New Mexico)
Fresh and fruity, but not sweet or sappy; nice restrained taste with some flat, fizzy aftertaste at mid-glass; flavor and texture fade with some foods; drink first half of glass quickly to get the best out of it; finishes warm and comforting. Match with a hamburger and French fries.

ESKE'S TAOS GREEN CHILI Lager   **BP**   **2.7**
(Taos, New Mexico)
Fresh green-chile aroma and taste with lingering, roasted mouthfeel; texture is flat and liquid without much pizzazz; gentle roll on the tongue accompanies nice mild chile aftertaste; chile presence is handled well—subdued, but clearly a player; agreeable change of pace. Try it with a grilled cheese sandwich.

ESQUIRE EXTRA DRY Lager   **MB**   **0.9**
(Smithton, Pennsylvania)
Dry, light, and tasteless; very pale faded color; uninspiring, uninteresting, unintegrated; possesses a certain fruitiness that saves it from complete condemnation; someone must have liked it: Silver Medal winner at the 1993 Great American Beer Festival.

ESTRELLA GALICIA ESPECIAL Pilsener CB   **2.5**
(La Coruña, Spain)
Plenty of carbonation here, as demonstrated by the rapidly rising bubbles; grainy sharpness at back of the throat; somewhat dry and lightly bitter—a workable, if not outstanding combination; white foamy head forms a rocky cover to the clean golden liquid; dry bitterness lingers in the aftertaste; finishes warm and relatively sweet. Pair this with a meat-and-cheese-stuffed hero sandwich.

ETTALER KLOSTER DUNKEL Lager   **AB**   **4.5**
(Ettal, Germany)
Rich, flavorful, and immediately—and immensely—satisfying; flat hoppy taste is tantalizingly bitter and quite fresh, even after

its journey across the ocean; golden red-brown color suggests it is lighter than it actually is, but who's complaining? A lovely gentle blend of aroma, taste, and texture with an integrated, layered complexity; out of the tap, this beer must be a knockout; finishes with a hint of caramel and sturdy malt sweetness; an exciting import. Sweetens gently, while malt mellows into a feathery texture with couscous and chicken breast with honey-mustard sauce.

EUROPA Lager   CB   3.1
(Lisbon, Portugal)
Mild hoppiness; easy on the nose, palate, and tongue; slightly perfumey; light, somewhat airy taste and pale-blond color; uncomplicated; calm honey-sweetness emerges with determination, pleasantly balancing and complementing saltiness of some foods; malts take over gently and gradually, turning this brew into a more interesting and desirable drink, finishes smooth and mellow; good to have with food or without. Try it with an Italian hero sandwich.

TAP TIP

Changing Temperatures

Bitter flavors are intensified by colder temperatures, which also lessen malt sweetness and body fullness. Beers meant to be served at warmer temperatures, like many ales, are generally less bitter, more full-bodied, and less dry (sweeter).

EUROPEAN EXPORT LAGER   CB   3.0
(Assen, Holland)
Complex honey-malt taste has a faint hint of caramel; quite dry; increasingly malty, in both flavor and aroma; this is one of the maltiest lagers I have ever tasted; far less crisp at the end, but the trademark sweet maltiness stays until the finish; a one-note taste sensation that makes for the beginning of a good tune; needs more complexity to raise it to the level of greatness. Goes with thick pork chops.

F AND A Lager   CB   3.1
(Toronto, Ontario, Canada)
Subdued freshness fills the palate; more texture than taste; sweet, soft, and variably mellow; unintrusive malt-hop mix stays in the background; worth trying. Serve with warm bread and soft cheeses.

FALSTAFF Lager   **CB**   **2.3**
(San Antonio, Texas)
Quickly refreshing and crisp, but just as quickly develops a thickness on the tongue and palate; freshness and some zip; taste is rather attenuated and bland, but like a cold glass of water, it does offer thirst-quenching qualities; too many adjuncts to be anywhere near distinctive; decent lightweight brew. Try it with Indian food.

FAMOSA 1896 LAGER   **CB**   **2.7**
(Guatemala City, Guatemala)
Slight fruity aroma; many bubbles; light and crackling, with a gradually growing hoppiness; minimally fluffy; carbonation diminishes along the way; less integrated and tasty at the end, as if competing with itself to see if the beer in the bottle or all the flavor fades first; still, there is character and substance at the end; not a bad medium-ranked beer. Accommodates stuffed shrimp and couscous quite well.

FAXE PREMIUM Lager   **CB**   **2.7**
(Faxe, Denmark)
Starts with a pleasurable grain-malt flavor and a charming grain aroma; before things get out of hand, malt sweetness reins in some of the graininess about midway; good bitter-sweet balance, with emphasis on the bitter; big full head is soft and easy on the tongue; the light-golden body could use more texture and oomph. An equal partner to thick cheese pizza topped with anchovies.

FEST BIER Malt Liquor   **CB**   **2.4**
(Bayreuth, Germany)
Soft taste at the top of the glass, with sharp underlay on first sip; rather neutral with food; unassuming and uneventful except for quantity (comes in 16.9-ounce bottle); ordinary.

FIEDLERS BOCK IM STEIN   **CB**   **2.5**
(Koblenz, Germany)
Sweet and somewhat cloying; smooth and easy going down; remains constant and predictable; almost plain, with diminished sweetness when imbibed with food; alcohol gets warm and comforting about halfway through the crock; in the end it has an up-and-down attraction, quite different from the beginning sips; doesn't reflect a typical bock in ingredients or quality; bottled in a stoneware crock, traditionally used to "shield its contents from harmful light and heat for thousands of years," according to the label. Accompanies grilled poultry dishes.

FIEDLERS PILS IM STEIN   **CB**   **2.3**
(Koblenz, Germany)
Mild freshness immediately followed by a dullness that lasts as slight tannic aftertaste; changes and becomes unpleasantly filling,

eventually subsiding—all this without food; filmy aftertaste remains on the roof of the mouth; mellows and sweetens considerably with food; better at the beginning, but still a little too flat and thick-tasting for a pilsener. Try it with broiled meat dishes.

FIRE FOX BELGIAN ALE CB 4.2
(Melle and Ghent, Belgium)
Starts with a gentle yeasty aroma and taste, followed by a cornucopia of fruit flavors—peaches, apricots, a bit of apple; malt sweetness tempers the restrained bitterness; alcohol is clearly present, but is an equal and participating partner to the other main players; hazy caramel-tinged body is topped by an airy but full old-lace head; this is a tasty morsel of a beer. Try it with a hearty roast cooked to medium-well.

FIREHOUSE KEY LIME WHEAT MB 2.8
(Miami, Florida)
Smells like lime aftershave and tastes like key lime pie—an interesting effect; tart; suggestion of musty-grainy aftertaste; light-bodied; not complex; very pale light-straw body; key lime character becomes more apparent after several sips, though overall it remains a one-note brew; nonetheless, it deserves your attention, especially on a warm, muggy afternoon (or night). No need to accompany this with food.

FIREHOUSE PILSENER MB 0.2
(Miami, Florida)
Subdued, calm mix of hops and malt includes a flash of medicinal taste—not a good sign; increasing bitterness covers up the iodine-like character a bit, which then takes on the aspects of motor oil; sweetens a little, but remains poor-tasting; all the off-tastes stay in the mouth, even after a rinse with water; obviously, stay away from this one.

FIRESTONE DOUBLE BARREL ALE
(draft) MB 2.6
(Los Olivos, California)
Fresh yeasty aroma, with fresh fruity taste; a dash of hops adds a bitterness that is welcome and appreciated; by midpoint, fruitiness and hops come into good balance; has a harshness that takes some getting used to; some maltiness can be discerned underneath the other ingredients; leaves a layer of roughness that detracts from paying attention to the next sip. A good outdoor patio beer with grilled shrimp.

FISCHER D'ALSACE AMBER
Malt Liquor CB 3.2
(Schiltigheim, France)
Hearty, thick, and creamy; full-bodied with hint of sharpness; not much alcohol presence; soothing, smooth; some dryness

and flatness at the end. Appropriate accompaniment to pork dishes.

FISH EYE IPA (draft)   MB/BP   0.5
(Olympia, Washington)

Fruity aroma; mellow and faintly sweet with a hint of acrid lemon flavor; peach/almond marzipan taste adds to the impression that the brewing process was incomplete—more reminiscent of a homebrew; yeast is sour and off-tasting; weak and hard to finish; skip this one until further notice.

FISH TALE MUDSHARK PORTER   MB/BP   2.7
(Olympia, Washington)

Mild burnt/roasted aroma is accompanied by mild drinker-friendly bitterness; full creamy smoothness becomes the dominant feature; hoped-for flavor intensity never materializes; vague hint of chocolate—or is it only wishful thinking? Sticks a bit to the roof of the mouth; remains mild, which makes it a good introduction to porter for novices; weakens far too much at the end. Try Mudshark with shellfish.

FISH TALE WILD SALMON PALE ALE   MB/BP   1.2
(Olympia, Washington)

Weakly fruity flavored; somewhat bitter and hoppy; all the appropriate ingredients are present, but the taste is too staid and not as fresh as it should be; traditional hop bitterness suddenly increases, bringing some redemption; finishes sweeter, but never really makes the grade.

FITSPATRICK STOUT   BP   3.1
(Seattle, Washington)

Creamy-smooth and soft; roasted-barley taste is obvious, even with food; clearly quality-made; integrated and complex throughout; gives feeling of lightness and airiness, although its substance is tangibly present. Try it with seafood dishes.

FLENS Lager   CB   2.6
(Flensburg, Germany)

Light-bodied and grainy; smooth at each swallow; aroma is reminiscent of imported hard candy, with an herbal taste of horehound; hints of bitterness and grassiness are apparent toward the end of the bottle; finishes with a sharp grainy aroma and smoothed-out earthy character; unusual mix of flavor characteristics not often found in the United States. Cleanse the palate after each sip with unsalted crackers or pieces of French bread in order to gain a full appreciation of the taste complexities.

FLOSSMOOR STATION IMPERIAL
ECLIPSE STOUT   BP   3.4
(Flossmoor, Illinois)

Sweetly alcoholic at first; soft touch of roastedness on the palate;

gentle roasted mouthfeel becomes slightly chocolatey, like a fruit-filled dark chocolate candy; complex malt character from a near-record sixteen different malts; opaque black body; strong alcohol presence doesn't let up and powers this stout until the last swallow; finishes fruity and full of alcohol; a very good representation of the style. A slice, or two, of chocolate cake adds to the enjoyment.

FLYING DOG DOGGIE STYLE ALE   MB   1.9
(Denver, Colorado)
Begins with slight apple perfume and a brief hit of bitterness; stale taste follows immediately and dies quickly; settles into a sharply bitter, watery drink with a faint musty-hop aftertaste; slight hint of chocolate comes and goes; finishes harsh and green.

FLYING HORSE ROYAL LAGER CB 2.7
(Bangalore, India)
Sour citrusy taste and a bit gauzy; turns pleasantly bitter early on; dainty sheets of Brussels lace enhance the ambiance, while a touch of medicinal taste at the back of the throat inhibits it; hoppy rather than malty, but overall rather evenhanded and middle-of-the-road; aromatic hops are pleasant if not exciting; medium-bodied; in the end, the whole turns out to be more interesting than the individual parts. Goes well with seafood salads.

FLYING MONKEY AMBER ALE   MB   2.0
(Merriam, Kansas)
Combination of caramel and nut flavors seeks and finds every taste bud in your mouth; mild hoppiness follows close on its heels; soft mouthfeel; caramel presence lessens, eventually veering off into sourness; complexity is also lost toward the end; too acrid for my taste. A creamy dip of some sort siphons some of the bite away, but not enough.

FLYING MONKEY PALE ALE   MB   2.1
(Merriam, Kansas)
Mildly hoppy; flavors are not well integrated; sweetens and gets flowery, but not intensely so; hints of spiciness in the aroma; more like pilsener than pale ale; hops are evident, but not over-powering; not terribly distinguished; flowery-talcum aftertaste; a little soapy at the end.

FLYING MONKEY WHEAT BEER
(seasonal)   MB   1.3
(Merriam, Kansas)
Sprightly, doughy aroma; accompanying orange-citrus character incorporates a complementary bitterness; leaves a little acidic presence in the aftertaste; flattens and loses more of the already minimal complexity; watery and underpowered; gets unpleasantly perfumey toward the end.

FOECKING PREMIUM Lager   CT   0.3
(Monroe, Wisconsin)
Sour winey taste accompanies hint of honey sweetness—the latter planned, the former not; thick, brutish texture as well; flat
and watery with no carbonation; muddy-gold color; insults the
taste of food; blotches of stuff (yeast?) float around the glass; its
only redeeming feature is the honey aroma and flavor, even at
the end.

FOSTER'S LAGER   CB   3.4
(Melbourne, Victoria, Australia; Toronto, Ontario, Canada)
Expectedly fresh and crisp on contact; full palate and smoothness around the sides of the mouth; generally even-tempered and
predictable throughout; head is very white with clearly distinguishable bubbles; nicely patterned Brussels lace adds to the soft
feel; a quite pleasing, flavorful lager with backbone; Australian
version is essentially identical, except for definitely lighter carbonation. Try it with spicy Mexican fare.

FOSTER'S LIGHT LAGER   CB   3.2
(Melbourne, Victoria, Australia)
Light, citrusy flavor; typical lager texture and body; mild hoppiness fades into background after several sips; as beer warms, ingredients seem to flow and blend; head is creamy-looking, but
appears to be pumped up by additives, not naturally. Accompanies Chinese food nicely.

FOUR PEAKS SCOTTISH AMBER ALE   MB/BP   1.1
(Tempe, Arizona)
Sugar-sweet taste is restrained, but overall this is a relatively complex ale with a moderated, understated bitterness; malty aroma;
medicinal presence becomes overwhelming; underneath the unpleasantness there appears to be a decent-tasting beer, but it's not
enough to redeem the negatives.

FRANKENMUTH DARK Lager   MB   3.1
(Frankenmuth, Michigan)
Very pleasant honey-fruit aroma with underlying tartness; consistent flavor that doesn't attack your taste buds; not as texturally firm or full-bodied as it should be; warmth is relatively characterless—minimal integration of ingredients; hint of clove spiciness at the bottom of the bottle; creamy head quickly thins out;
good but not great. Drink alongside broiled pork chops and other
broiled meat dishes.

FRANKENMUTH GERMAN-STYLE
BOCK   MB   2.4
(Frankenmuth, Michigan)
Full and darkly hearty; mushy taste with a cloying mouthfeel;
heavy maltiness disrupts enjoyment of a variety of ordinary foods—

this is not a food-friendly beer; slight bitterness disappears very quickly; deep brown matches color of the bottle; malty sweetness turns a bit bitter at the end, and is not pleasant; malt aroma, however, redeems the overall impression somewhat.

FRANKENMUTH PILSENER   MB   1.2
(Frankenmuth, Michigan)

Immediate juicy flavor, followed by sharp, tangy citrus taste; full and satisfying; many bubbles suggest high carbonation, but texture is flat, flat, flat; provides very little energy for food; weakens further as bottle is drained; intricate, thin, relatively short-lived Brussels lace; weak, cloudy pale-yellow color adds to the overall poor presentation; gets downright blah and watery at the end, with low-level sourness.

B E E R   F A C T

*T*he Picts, a group of fierce warriors storied for their brewing and war-making skills, made the first heather ale around 325 B.C. Some historians maintain that the leprechaun myths originated with the Picts. *Fraoch* is Gaelic for "heather."

FRAOCH HEATHER ALE   CB   2.9
(Alloa, Scotland)

Smells like scented wood in a field of . . . well, heather; filled with the essence of lively Scottish malt and wild heather tips, but it is not flowery; mild whiskey pungency offers the right balance to the herbal-spice mouthfeel; hints of licorice fill out the aroma; dry, doughy malt aftertaste; there are no hops in this rare, old, apple-cider-colored brew immortalized by the poet Robert Louis Stevenson.

FREE STATE OATMEAL STOUT   BP   1.2
(Lawrence, Kansas)

Rather bland; medium-light; no burnt-roasted flavor; tame, with faint underlying complexity, too weak and uninteresting.

B E E R   F A C T

*F*ree State Brewing Company was founded in 1989—the first (legal) brewery to be established in Kansas since state prohibition, begun in 1880, was repealed. It occupies a renovated interurban trolley station in downtown Lawrence. "Free State" refers to Kansas' role in the Civil War.

FRYDENLUND Pilsener   CB   2.5
(Oslo, Norway)
Sharp with rounded, restrained edge; remains crisp and concise throughout; taste stays consistently attenuated; texture is far more exciting; aroma is essentially nonexistent. Okay alongside smoked fish and the like.

FULL SAIL BROWN ALE (draft)   RB   2.8
(Hood River, Oregon)
Immediate malt hit on the tongue and palate; deep, roasted mouthfeel, with lovely sidebar of hops; no aftertaste; full-bodied and almost succulent in its richness; not as complex as it should be; needs more alcoholic pizzazz to lift it above average; increased hop presence finally enters the picture at the end. Good with pub fare.

FULL SAIL GOLDEN ALE   RB   2.3
(Hood River, Oregon)
Mild, quickly dissipating fruitiness; melts into background and lets the flavor of the food have its way; gentle and unassuming, with moderate fullness and dryness at the roof of the mouth; fruitiness increases again at the end of a meal; finish is weak-kneed. Okay with grilled steak and a tossed salad.

FULL SAIL WASSAIL WINTER ALE
(annual)   RB   2.9
(Hood River, Oregon)
Strong, almost perfumey, chocolatey burnt-caramel taste and aroma, with prominent lacing of bitterness; full-bodied and smooth, with a core of softness; becomes more pungent and citrus-flowery with hot foods; emerging spiciness at the bottom of the bottle proves this is a seasoned beer; very hoppy beginning, middle, finish, and aroma—wow!—strong stuff; more than two are likely to produce some discomfort. Very good match with Southwestern/Mexican food.

FULLER'S E.S.B. EXPORT ALE   CB   2.5
(London, England)
Full, mushy (slightly gooey) mouthful with sweet taste of mustiness; similar to London Pride but with more bite; maintains a consistent, forward-thrusting, unfading presence from the tip of the tongue to the back of the throat; its advertised bitterness can be clearly dominant (and off-putting); a good beer to share with a friend; voted "Britain's Best" at the Great British Beer Festival in 1985. Nicely complements lightly barbecued pork chops.

FULLER'S LONDON PRIDE Ale   CB   3.8
(London, England)
Tastes like Sugar Daddy lollipops with nuttiness thrown in; reasonably full-bodied; caramel flavor; overall, a delicious, soft, slosh-

around-the-mouth taste/texture; sip this gently, take your time, and swallow slowly. Delicious with maple syrup–enhanced baked beans.

FURSTENBERG Pilsener   CB   3.3
(Donaueschingen, Germany)

Fresh and hoppy but without sparkle, despite the many quickly rising bubbles; smooth, almost to the point of becoming bland; conservative and constrained; keeps its distance, but its gentle presence has subtle strength and backbone. Try it with pastas, salads, and fruit (it turns a bit sour, but remains a worthwhile food companion nonetheless).

GALA DE LUXE EXPORT BEER Lager   CB   1.5
(Logone, Chad)

Weak grain taste; faint aroma of aftershave lotion quickly fades; somewhat harsh texturally; not particularly fresh tasting; thin-bodied; has a touch of honey in it; hops are not evident; some hard to identify flotsam floats around at the bottom of the glass; moderate malt-honey sweetness emerges with spicy dishes, though the beer stays aloof from the food.

GAMBRINUS LAGER   CB   2.9
(Pilsen, Czechoslovakia)

Crisp and edgy with underlying composed flatness; emerging sweetness counterbalances the earlier sharpness; not fizzy; no head to speak of; malt takes precedence over hops toward the end, then reverts to a hoppy, dry finish. Remains sharp enough to slice right to the core of an open-face deli sandwich.

GATOR LAGER   CT   2.3
(New Ulm, Minnesota)

Very neutral in taste, aroma, and ambiance; no bite, though it does have a comforting nothingness that has a nice calming or settling effect on hot foods, almost like a friendly analgesic; relative robustness not found in similar, locally brewed American lagers; only the texture has any lasting impact, and that's relative;

the label proclaims "The beer with a bite"—toothless, at best. Try it with hot dogs topped with everything.

GEARY'S LONDON STYLE PORTER   RB   3.0
(Portland, Maine)
Nicely roasted; rich Baker's chocolate character has a balancing acidic-bitter mouthfeel; surprising amount of fizz; well timed and attractively arranged blending of malts, hops, chocolate, and roast-edness makes for a pleasant if not outstanding porter; deep-brown body with burnt-orange overtones at the edges; finishes with some malty sweetness. Try it with lighter-flavored meats like veal or chicken.

GEARY'S PALE ALE   RB   2.4
(Portland, Maine)
Crisp caramel ale taste with core of sweetness and body; holds its own with food, but syrupy sweetness detracts from any kind of well-rounded flavor; devoid of hop presence for about two-thirds of the bottle; not unfriendly, just standoffish.

GENESEE 12 HORSE ALE   CB   3.4
(Rochester, New York)
Fittingly light-tasting; full-bodied core makes the first sips very pleasant and fulfilling; evolves into smooth, relatively soft drink; a beer to sit back with on the front porch while shooting the breeze; creamy with a quick-to-detect underlying fruitiness; not difficult to enjoy. Try it with pizza.

GENGHIS KHAN Lager   CB   1.1
(Guangzhou, China)
Muddled sharpness, with no particular evidence of taste; remains unflavorful although somewhat thirst-quenching; not obnoxious, but essentially not worth the effort.

GENNY BEER Lager   CB   2.5
(Rochester, New York)
Opens crisp and to the point with the quick disappearance of both characteristics as it is swallowed; light-bodied with some complexity of hops and barley—a taste that can easily become tiring; forget food with this brew, but feel free to call it up in a local bar with friends; nice Brussels lace evolves from head on sides of glass; highly carbonated; gains in fullness and satisfaction as evening progresses; slight touch of sourness in the finish.

GENNY CREAM ALE   CB   2.7
(Rochester, New York)
Creamy, smooth, and mellow; maintains this pattern evenly and consistently with food, for which it provides good working background; modulated thickness occasionally intrudes; texture more noteworthy than taste; Silver Medal winner at the 1993 and 1994 Great American Beer Festivals. Goes well with grilled shrimp.

GENTLE BEN'S COPPERHEAD ALE   BP   0.6
(Tucson, Arizona)
Musty, soapy smell; nondescript, washed-out taste; not exactly unpalatable, but gets close.

**GENTLE BEN'S MACBLANE'S
OATMEAL STOUT**   BP   2.2
(Tucson, Arizona)
Burnt-malt taste with a bitter finish that stays on the sides of the mouth and interferes with food; not thick or creamy enough; as it warms, it balances well with red meats but loses flavor with other foods; too constrained without the complexity necessary for a top stout; aroma is more attractive (and appropriate to style) than taste.

GENTLE BEN'S RED CAT AMBER Ale   BP   2.3
(Tucson, Arizona)
Lightly malted with a faint warmth and a gentle dollop of alcohol; color is appropriate, with good balance and integration of ingredients; approximates traditional amber but is not hefty or malted enough.

GENTLE BEN'S T.J.'S RASPBERRY Ale   BP   2.4
(Tucson, Arizona)
Gently fruited, with a lot of fizz making it more like raspberry soda; light and gentle with good Brussels lace; too weak but not too sweet, it teeters between beer and a frilly summertime drink; malt and hoppiness are subdued, so any balance is hard to detect; sip this without food to whet your appetite, then order a real lager—without fruit in it.

GEORGE GALE PRIZE OLD ALE   CB   3.9
(Horndean, Hampshire, England)
Plummy taste is paired with high alcohol content; thick-bodied and strong tasting; from a distance, the aroma suggests scotch or bourbon, not beer; complex and subtle; rich, smooth, and fruity, like an expensive, fine brandy; more like food than drink; robust Prize Old Ale will knock you on your rear if you're not careful, so sit down and enjoy this with some soft cheese, crackers, and a good book.

GERST AMBER Ale   CB   3.2
(Evansville, Indiana)
Beautiful newly polished ruby-copper color prefaces a very fizzy, smooth mouthfeel; light and watery with sweet malt taste; nice Midwestern beer—rather direct and accommodating; got universal rave reviews from a mixture of indifferent and experienced beer drinkers during a recent holiday season. Great for mild premeal snacks.

GIRAF MALT LIQUOR   CB   2.3
(Odense, Denmark)
Slight, quick, initial bitter taste, then crisp and undistinguished; never seems to get started and recedes as full impact of food is felt; well-meaning, but not assertive enough.

GLACIER BAY LAGER   CB   1.1
(Toronto, Ontario, Canada)
Crisp and oozing adjuncts; a notch or two above ballpark beer, especially with hot dogs on a bun smeared with yellow mustard; flat-tasting and off-tasting as meal progresses; a bit more filling than most lagers, but repellent by the time you get to the bottom of the bottle; much too variable to risk buying again.

GLARNER LAGER   CB   3.1
(Zurich, Switzerland)
Hoppy fullness with strength at the back (bitter) and sides (sour) of the tongue; depth and charm remain circumscribed and "top out" just when you expect the beer to continue its interest and your enjoyment; while the texture is flat, the taste with food is appealingly sharp and almost palpable; a food's beer—well made but not particularly distinctive. Try it with caviar or other salty hors d'oeuvres.

GLOSSNER HOPFENGARTEN PILS   CB   3.6
(Neumarkt, Germany)
Lovely, fragile grainy aroma is followed by a sharply bitter hop-grainy mouthfeel that fills the mouth; delightfully crisp; pleasant sour aftertaste; there's a little bit of lemon character nestled in the clear, golden body; sharp carbonation spikes the tongue with pin-pricks of tiny bubbles; good blending of hops and malts; a vigorous, active pilsener. Particularly appetizing with broiled freshwater fish.

GLOSSNER TORSCHMIED'S DUNKEL   CB   3.2
(Neumarkt, Germany)
Immediate malt taste gives way to a gentle, spicy-hop character; settles down into a steady, middle-of-the-road dunkel, but with significant malt presence; sweet, caramel aroma parallels the flavor, which expands to fill the mouth; deep-amber body has pretty purple tones; the final sips are very smooth and marked by a circumscribed but full maltiness. Goes with seasoned pastas or chicken. Glossner is hard to find in the U.S., but it's worth searching for in Germany.

GLUEK DARK BEER Pilsener   RB   2.7
(Cold Spring, Minnesota)
Complex nutty aroma is followed by a sweet-nutty malty taste that lingers in the crevices of the mouth; deep-seated, flavorful

sweetness acquires an easy-going grassy character; alcohol-infused bitterness increases sip after sip; cola body shines with a red glow; finishes with a hint of fresh grassiness and a fullness not present earlier; good, but not great. Strictly a hearty meat-and-potatoes brew.

GLUEK PILSNER RB 0.5
(Cold Spring, Minnesota)
Blessedly ephemeral; lightly metallic taste, which disappears quickly; no fizz; quickly becomes tasteless and textureless; light, watery and without interest; starts off pretty bad and dribbles away to nothing.

GOA PILSNER DRY CB 2.9
(Goa, India)
Full and immediately satisfying; hint of rich maltiness; texturally too smooth for this style; sharply sweet, with improving flavor as you drink it; cloudy, pale yellow with barest suggestion of golden color; no head; wispy Brussels lace; in general, not compatible with food; too filling; finishes with an autumnal smell.

GOEBEL GOLDEN LAGER CB 2.1
(Detroit, Michigan)
Filled with taste-flattening adjuncts; starts off bland and watery, although there is some amount of fizzy sharpness; not awful, but remains rather tasteless, uninspired, and completely inattentive to food; hint of warmth/sweetness hardly makes its presence felt; light and thin.

GOLDEN CITY CENTURION
BARLEYWINE ALE MB 0.2
(Golden, Colorado)
Smells alcoholic and malty, and tastes the same; silky-smooth texture is essentially flat; flavors stay separate, never integrating or creating any kind of complexity; dense malty taste becomes quite salty; flat cola color; sour and off-tasting; like mouthwash without the refreshing qualities; unpalatable.

GOLDEN DRAGON Pilsener CB 3.1
(Guangzhou, China)
Flattish liquid with bubbly effervescence on the surface; immediately undistinguished; however, it gets more interestingly complex and attractive—developing a honeyish, almost fruity, overtone—as food interacts with the brew; if you don't believe a beer can grow and improve before your very eyes, or on your own lips, try this one, but with mild-mannered food.

GOLDEN EAGLE LAGER   CB   3.5
(Madras, India)
Strong, sweet wine bouquet; smooth, full-bodied texture; blond color; a bit watery with food, but comfortable and palatable; a touch lightweight in the end. Goes well with flavorful hors d'oeurves, such as sweet-and-sour meatballs and chicken wings.

GOLDEN PHEASANT Lager   CB   3.9
(Hurbanovo, Slovakia)
The smooth, sweet maltiness here is mild but engaging, like expensive hard candy; delicate, nuanced flavors, tastefully reminiscent of distilled bruised peaches; texturally unruffled on the tongue; complexity increases as you drink, adding even more depth and character; thinnish, rich head adds to the overall pleasure. An engaging beer that goes well with fowl—seasoned duck or chicken, in particular.

GOLDEN PROMISE ALE   CB   2.8
(Edinburgh, Scotland)
Subdued, integrated fruitiness and yeastiness; thin texture; weak but balanced; splash of alcohol occurs on second or third sip; generally attends to the differing demands and flavors of food; reddish-copper color (not golden) with thin head; a little too rough around the edges.

GOLDEN VALLEY RED THISTLE ALE
(draft)   BP   1.0
(McMinnville, Oregon)
Burnt aroma, perfumey taste, and black-coffee color greet the senses; less-than-mild bitterness parallels an emerging grassy aroma, which ultimately predominates; caramel maltiness offers some hope (false, it turns out) that things will get better; taste comes and goes quickly, which in this case is a blessing; too weak and watery for the style; where are the alcohol and hops?

GOLDHORN CLUB Pilsener   CB   3.4
(Lasko, Slovenia; former Yugoslavia)
Fresh, fruity aroma and sharp clove taste greet first sips; soft, quickly diminishing head; honey-like sweetness plays second fiddle as bottle is emptied; I like the way this beer and food interact—grainy ingredients are well matched; cloudy yeast haze creates translucent blond color; slightly sour dry/sweet finish, suggesting a cross between wheat and pilsener styles.

GOLFER'S CHOICE GERMAN ALE   CB   2.6
(Schwäbisch Gmünd, Germany)
Constrained sweetness is accompanied by a mild, but tasty grassiness that transforms into a malty honeyed mouthfeel; soft texture; malt-hop aroma; slight increase in bitterness at mid-bottle;

loses some solidity and oomph at the end; finishes sweet and mild, balanced and calm on the palate; not outstanding, but certainly drinkable, particularly with freshwater fish.

GOOSE ISLAND DUNKEL WEIZEN
BOCK   **BP**   **2.2**
(Chicago, Illinois)
Light and a bit perfumey; slight roof-of-the-mouth cloyingness; deep malty sweetness is distinctive and creates a furry aftertaste; minimal hint of alcohol; strength weakens further with even plain-cooked foods; apparently a bock that prefers no competition—especially from food.

GOOSE ISLAND HONKERS ALE   **RB**   **2.7**
(Chicago, Illinois)
Fresh-smelling with a nutty-hop mouthfeel that's dry and long-lasting; bitter-fruity taste arrives in short order and becomes the main flavor presence; integrates comfortably with chicken wings and rice; light caramel body and thin ivory head; not a very taxing beer, but has enough flavor to keep you interested; finishes gently bitter with a touch of malty sweetness; respectable, but not exciting.

GOOSE ISLAND MILD ALE   **MB**   **2.9**
(Chicago, Illinois)
Firm, sturdy mouthfeel; balanced, smoky character; mild, malty aroma; tends toward sweet-tasting, with emphasis on the malts; in fact, the sweet, roasted malt aspect remains the dominant feature; as a result, it is rather uni dimensional both in flavor and aroma; maltier and more integrated at the end. Try with sliced cold meats, like turkey.

GOSSER PALE Lager   **CB**   **2.6**
(Leaben Goss, Austria)
Creamy, smooth, fluffy, and lots of air; dark taste belies its mildly cloudy pale color; restrained flavor ends at the back of the tongue; overall, more American in its blandness, although it does have a fuller body generally absent in U.S. brews; foam bunches up thickly as a head, even when most of the beer in the glass is gone; the steel (not aluminum) can says, "Especially brewed for export, ships and aircraft." Appropriate with sandwiches.

GOSSER STIFTSBRAU Lager   **CB**   **3.5**
(Graz, Austria)
Mild-mellow burnt taste with very little carbonation; relative thinness; remains consistent and evenhanded by itself and with salty snacks; modest depth and hearty, well-defined, sweet, malty taste; clearly defined textural boundaries—you easily can tell when

strength gives way to smoothness, for example; gets stronger at the end of the bottle. Serve with barbecue- or mesquite-flavored potato chips.

GOUDEN CAROLUS ALE   CB   3.9
(Mechelen, Belgium)
Sweet, almost cherry, aroma turns into mild, tentative clove aroma; well made; deep golden-amber color with a dollop of red; rich, tan, long-lasting head and haphazard Brussels lace; strong, warming alcoholic presence that tenderly envelops food; yeast at bottom clouds the end of the drink; sweet, very malty finish. Nicely accompanies Italian food.

> ### B E E R   F A C T
>
> *G*ouden Carolus, Latin for "Golden Charles," is named for the bright metal coinage of the Holy Roman Emperors Charlemagne and at least one Charles V. Brewed since the middle of the 14th century, this brown ale is reported in historical documents to have been popular at royal fox hunts because "it fired both rider and steed with such enthusiasm for galloping that the hunt took place in the best possible atmosphere." Later, when he was no longer monarch, Charles V declared "this daughter of the grain [to be] superior to the blood of the grape."

GRAIN BELT Lager   CB   2.8
(St. Paul, Minnesota)
Lightly hopped; fresh, Concord-grape taste; reminds you of the way beer used to taste—light on the palate, with a mellow grain-hop character; hop mouthfeel diminishes at the end, making for a sweeter, more flavorful beer; texturally sharp and thirst-quenching; thick, foamy head leaves delicate traces of Brussels lace in its wake; very companionable. Grain Belt has been a regional favorite since 1891, and it's easy to see why. Goes with informal social and conversational food—pretzels, hot dogs, sandwiches, hamburgers.

GRAIN D'ORGE BIERE DE GARDE   CB   2.6
(Ronchin, France)
Quite yeasty and quite tasty; prickly bitterness tastes a bit soapy and lasts a while on the tongue; an underlying orange flavor is present; malt sweetness increases perceptibly at the end, as does the alcohol; yeast stays strong throughout; okay, but not out-

standing; needs more complexity and textural oomph. Its wine-like character suggests a choice of wine-friendly foods.

GRANVILLE ISLAND ENGLISH BAY
PALE ALE Lager   RB   2.6
(Vancouver, British Columbia, Canada)

Very effervescent; light and airy with ginger-ale ambiance; settles into calming, no-waves beer; mild, honey-like taste remains as an undercurrent throughout; basically falls in the range of average Canadian lagers, with perhaps a bit more complexity. Accompanies Asian food.

GRANVILLE ISLAND LAGER   RB   2.9
(Vancouver, British Columbia, Canada)

Mild fruity-caramel taste with little carbonation, but sustaining interest; taste is silky and pleasantly grainy; professionally done brew. Nice with main-course pork dishes, baked beans, or winter vegetables.

GRAY'S HONEY ALE   MB   2.5
(Janesville, Wisconsin)

Light honey taste; seems to get lighter still as you drink it; hard to discern anything of substance other than rapidly diminishing honey presence; promisingly sweet, but no follow-through; smooth; teeters between gentle honey taste and fresh water; could be a good beer if there simply was more taste to it. Drink this alone so nothing else interferes with the hard-to-coax-out flavor.

GREAT BASIN RYE PATCH ALE   RP   3.3
(Sparks, Nevada)

Rye-fruity and smooth, with a hint of perfume in the mouth; sweetens surprisingly, but appropriately, then returns to the rye-fruitiness that initially got your attention; nice controlled rye taste makes this a lovely beer; as smooth as a well-developed liqueur and just as appealing. Try this with strong cheeses for a challenging and unforgettable change of pace.

GREAT DIVIDE SAINT BRIGID'S
PORTER   MB   2.9
(Denver, Colorado)

Mild burnt aroma and a more intense but similar taste accompany a soft, gentle mouthfeel; complexity is present, though it is diminished and vague; medium-bodied; some chocolate is present and lingers on the roof of the mouth; flattens too much at the end; a good choice for those who enjoy dark beers but not the flavor intensity that comes with many of them. Have this porter with spicy chicken wings and dip.

GREAT LAKES CONWAY'S IRISH ALE
(draft)   **MB**   **2.9**
(Cleveland, Ohio)

Takes two or three sips for the sweet maltiness to emerge, but it's worth the wait; reserved in its heartiness; decently flavorful, but not intensely so; complexity of malt and hops make it intriguing, if not outstanding.

GREAT WALL Lager   **CB**   **2.9**
(Hebei, China)

Immediate, sweet, honey-like taste; sharp with rounded edges; faint back-of-the-mouth rice presence; needs bland food, like rice or egg noodles, to show off the complexity and malt character that is only hinted at; the first super-premium Chinese beer.

GREEN ROOSTER Lager   **CB**   **0.0**
(Copenhagen, Denmark)

Soapy, sticky, unpleasant, green (I'm not making that up); reminiscent of dishwashing liquid, only not as tasty; color was chosen as an alcoholic bow to spring; perhaps the worst beer I ever have encountered; I couldn't finish it.

GREENALL'S BITTER Ale   **CB**   **2.4**
(Warrington, England)

Deft, creamy smoothness and attractive softness circulate around the mouth and then gently slide down the throat; turns acidic, then ultimately fades in the presence of the food; thin, with a bubbly head; expected bitterness is surprisingly low-key; clearly not a connoisseur's beer, but a pleasant pub diversion with a few chips rather than hot/spicy food; complexity diminishes at the middle and almost disappears at the end.

GREENALL'S CHESHIRE ENGLISH
PUB BEER Ale   **CB**   **3.1**
(Warrington, England)

Thin, fruity, winey foretaste with nicely layered maltiness primarily at the back of the tongue; warm honeyness evolves underneath a fizziness that is a little too sharply intrusive; settles into a droll companion with hints of excitement and unpredictability; too much imbalance between taste (fruity warmth) and texture (sharp, cold, and prickly). Try it with pork or lamb dishes.

GRENZQUELL GERMAN PILSNER   **CB**   **3.1**
(Hamburg, Germany)

Smooth hops feel, enticing Old-World aroma (complex and dainty); sharp bitterness turns into a film all over the mouth; 100% barley malt. Best with food, such as veal or white meat of turkey.

GRIMBERGEN DOUBLE ALE   **MY**   **4.0**
(Waterloo, Belgium)
Soft, creamy, and richly medium-bodied with a weighty lightness; emerging fruity sweetness with an unwanted hint of cloying mouthfeel; thick, creamy foam lasts down to the bottom of the bottle—sits like meringue atop the beer; durable softness and changing flavor with food (from minimal sweetness to appropriately mild bitterness); a laid-back, mellow delight that sort of surrounds and gently absorbs the food in a cushion of deep amber; texture is especially attractive; the alcohol tastes like the alcohol in a delicious fruitcake—very easy to get along with. Good company with London broil and green chile stew.

B E E R   F A C T

*G*rimbergen Abbey, constructed in 1128 by St. Norbert, is typical of the monastery brewing tradition; abbeys doubled as inns for pilgrims, providing room, board, and good drink. Many centuries-old brewing recipes remain appealing today. The monks recommend serving their ale in a chalice glass at 53°F.

GRIMBERGEN TRIPLE AMBER
ABBEY ALE   **CB**   **4.0**
(Waterloo, Belgium)
A heavy storm-at-sea-type head—rocky, foamy, and white—is a great visual welcome; light, yeasty champagne-like mouthfeel is a great gustatory welcome; honey-tempered sweetness is airy and long-lasting; gentle effervescence effortlessly lifts the integrated sweet yeast flavor to your lips; finishes strong and compelling; wonderfully made, but for selected tastes. Sit back and relax with this abbey ale after a filling dinner.

GRINGO EXTRA LAGER   **CT**   **0.8**
(Evansville, Indiana)
Light, fluffy, airy, with a faint, seemingly pleasant whiff of fruitiness; very, very faint hop taste, as if it were put in just to prove this is actually beer—not unpleasant, but ultimately rather pointless; Brussels lace sticks to the sides of an iced mug in clumps, suggesting poor carbonation and/or too many artificial ingredients; finish is a little sweet and a bit chewy, but also somewhat metallic; contains cereal grains as adjuncts (unspecified—undoubtedly corn, perhaps rice). From "original 1877 recipe, Santa Fe, New Mexico Territory"; obviously bad beers were made back then too, but why advertise the fact?

GRITTY McDUFF'S BEST BITTER Ale   MB   2.3
(Portland, Maine)

Sharp bitter-to-sour taste; somewhat soft texture; remains quite bitter and the sensation is not offset by any hint of malt; not balanced enough, even considering this is made in the bitter style; aroma matches the taste; finishes on a down, one-dimensional note. Taste improves when accompanied by honey-saturated tortilla.

GRIZZLY Lager   CB   0.4
(Hamilton, Ontario, Canada)

Heavy, obtrusive odor; off-taste; green-tasting—all of which strongly suggested I forego the possibility of having my meal spoiled by this beer; so, no food with this one, and no expectation of trying another bottle, either.

GROLSCH Pilsener   CB   3.1
(Groenlo, Holland)

Fresh, crisp, and sharp with a quick, dulling aftertaste; mildly distinctive almost-malt taste; relatively full-bodied; dry; unpasteurized (pasteurization tends to dull the flavors and subtleties of a beer); levered stopper in the bottle. Works well with Caesar salad with lots of anchovies and crunchy croutons.

GROLSCH AUTUMN AMBER ALE   CB   3.6
(Groenlo, Holland)

Mellow and pleasant with immediately apparent fresh mouthfeel; slight hint of caramel malt adds to the increasing enjoyment; tasty and mild—makes you want more of whatever they put in this; rich amber-brown color with creamy tan head is ad-copy perfect and quite inviting; rising hoppiness; unpasteurized, it holds its flavor; despite being a beer without an intense taste, it nonetheless has lasting flavor; finishes malty, carbonated, and alcoholic—all to its credit. Good with shellfish.

GROLSCH DARK LAGER   CB   3.2
(Groenlo, Holland)

Mild aroma and taste greet the first sip; balanced sharpness and creaminess make this beer pleasantly unpredictable, though its relative lightness (for a dark beer) remains constant; laid-back dark malt/slightly burnt taste emerges and increases in mellowness and flavor when interacting with food—a good sign; not the best-quality ingredients, however; a decent mass-market beer; Brussels lace forms at the bottom of the glass. Try it with broiled or roasted meats, especially pork or ham.

GROLSCH DRY DRAFT Pilsener   CB   3.0
(Groenlo, Holland)

Crisp, fresh, substantive texture—a good thirst-quencher on a hot day; a bit of staleness in mid-taste; with food, the beer becomes more mellow and seamless; nicely calibrated; strong, holds its own nicely. Accompanies guacamole, salsa, other favorite dips with chips.

GROZET GOOSEBERRY & WHEAT ALE   CB   3.1
(Glasgow, Scotland)

This peach-colored ale is served up with a potent mixture of malts, wild spices, and gooseberries; sweet and perfumey, rather than fruity; wheat blends comfortably with the spice-berry character; complex and stays that way; the berry flavor is kind of like that found in import-quality candy; has a nice touch of sophistication. Drink this for dessert.

LABEL LORE

*T*he somewhat unusual brown and green Grozet bottle label, based on a 1st-millennium Celtic rendering of a maze, was designed by third-year students at the Glasgow School of Art. *Grozet,* from the Gaelic *groseid,* is auld Scots for "gooseberry."

GUINNESS EXTRA STOUT   CB   3.8
(Dublin, Ireland)

Rich, brown, toasted bouquet and palate; exudes a warmth both charming and insulating against the tasty hot breath of a hamburger with green chiles; interestingly, the burnt-toasted taste fades rather quickly and emerges as a firm underpinning to the food; soft, creamy, calming, and smooth at the end; a sturdy, yeasty presence brings this classic brew to a pleasant close. Guinness Extra Stout is traditionally used to create a Black and Tan (see page 148).

GUINNESS PUB DRAUGHT Stout   CB   3.9
(Dublin, Ireland)

Mushy, mellow, soft, mildly bitter with an almost roasted-chocolatey elegance; stays smoothly balanced in texture and taste with food; constrained, expertly calibrated maltiness; classy and very satisfying; they've come winningly close to having this packaged beer taste as if it just came out of the tap; it is now my canned beer of choice, although a bit too foamy and airy—a mechanical problem with the clever nitrogen gas capsule in the specially designed can, which needs re-engineering; nonetheless, a clear winner. Especially good with baked fish or roasted chicken.

B E E R   F A C T

*B*lack and Tan is a popular mixture of draft lager or ale and stout (usually Harp or Bass and Guinness), and apparently is a political reference to the color of the uniforms of the English military busy in certain parts of Ireland in the 1920s. The practiced barkeep first pours a half-pint of the golden lager. Then, placing a spoon under the tap containing the stout, the bartender carefully rolls the darker liquid from the spigot onto the spoon and onto the top of the lager. When done properly, the two styles don't mix in the glass—brown-black on top, pristine gold on the bottom—producing perhaps the most esthetically appealing glass of beer in all the world. In response to its popularity among the current generation of drinkers, several companies now bottle a blend of the two styles; alas, so far they haven't figured out how to keep the black and the tan separate. The precursor to Black and Tan was a mixture of bitter ale and stout called "Arf 'n' Arf."

GULDEN DRAAK Ale	CB	3.8

(Ertvelde, Belgium)

Alcohol presence is noticed immediately; full, malty-sweet flavor with an underlying touch of spiciness; smooth, with prickly edges; flavor complexity and strength increase as you drink; glowing amber body is topped by a thin strip of off-white head; finishes strong and sprinkled with yeasty-appley overtones; a tasty and flavorful ale. Drink with strong hard cheeses.

GULDER LAGER	CB	2.5

(Lagos, Nigeria)

Mild, sugary mouthfeel gently complements a smooth, compellingly sweet malt presence; medium-bodied; soft on the mouth and tongue; grainy background character is present from start to finish; mild hoppiness appears about midway through and stays until the last swallow; ends with a surge of bitterness that stays awhile on the roof of the mouth; this is an unassuming, easy-going beer. Drink Gulder with light summer fare, salads in particular.

GULF BEER Lager	CB	1.4

(Indooroopilly, Queensland, Australia)

Crisp and carbonated; strong hop presence, without the attendant bitterness; gentle, sweet maltiness appears after two or three sips; full mouthfeel; suddenly and unexpectedly loses fizziness; taste dulls as well—where did it all go? Flavors get muddied and give up their individuality and taste clarity—not a good way to end a beer.

GULL Pilsener   CB   2.5
(Reykjavík, Iceland)

Quite grainy, with an undertone of mild bitterness; touch of mild sweetness appears after several sips; soft mouthfeel; rather subdued, but complex character overall; clear golden body supports a fluffy white head; nice, unaggressive grainy finish; non-threatening and easy to drink; one of just two domestic breweries in Iceland, Gull (*gold* or *golden* in Icelandic) is not available in this country; if you don't mind paying $5.71 for a glass, order one next time you're in Reykjavík.

GURU LAGER   CT   2.2
(London, England)

Tangy, citrusy, and sharp; settles down after a few sips into a malt-oriented lager that is a bit too soft and uncertain about where it's going; citrus theme and mini-fizziness continue throughout; no head or other distractions to speak of, a bit watery under the quickly disappearing fizz; in the end, uninspired. Okay with roasted meats.

HACKER-PSCHORR WEISSE BOCK   CB   3.3
(Munich, Germany)

Immediate taste of alcohol, with bittersweet overtones, mostly bitter; evolves into a soft caramel malty flavor that is smooth on the palate; caramelized malt sweetness lingers well into the aftertaste; some coming together of malt and alcohol gives it an upbeat, pushy finish; nice malty flourish is the last thing you taste from this constrained, rather unassuming beer. Goes with heavier foods, like German sausage.

HACKER-PSCHORR WEISSE DARK   CB   2.5
(Munich, Germany)

Reasonable dark taste, but too watery for any depth to take hold; initial sweetness dissipates and appropriately disappears into food; somewhat dry; decent, middling beer. Weakly soothing with hot/spicy foods.

HACKERBRAU EDELHELL MUNICH
LAGER MALT LIQUOR   CB   3.3
(Munich, Germany)

Obviously a lager with too much alcohol for the U.S. authorities (hence the malt liquor appellation) and typically high enough for German consumption (hence the Munich-style prefix); starts off very grainy, slightly fizzy, and mildly bitter; rich pale-golden color with a touch of red; bitterness sweetens and increases with food; emerging strong alcohol presence; ongoing, clean aroma; medium-bodied; consistent texture and mouthfeel; tasty and attractive, though not my cup of tea; malty, mellow finish; well made, it progresses and changes, all in a positive direction; a strong lager, regardless of what it's called in this country. Try it with Mexican as well as German dishes.

**HAIR OF THE DOG ADAMBIER Ale   MB/BP   3.8
(Portland, Oregon)**
You want rich flavor in your beer? Here it is, beginning with a generous dose of tart sweet-sour fruit aroma with an aromatic roasted nimbus wrapped around it; burnt chocolate taste rolls around your mouth and fills every groove in your tongue; intense and complex, this is definitely not a beginner's beer; smooth, velvet mouthfeel graciously balances the pervasive maltiness; thick and almost syrupy in texture; strong whiff of yeast throughout accompanies a mouthful of sweet, chewy alcohol; strong and hearty. Drink this with something that battles back, like highly flavored fish such as salmon.

**HAIR OF THE DOG GOLDEN ROSE
BELGIAN TRIPEL STYLE ALE   MB   4.0
(Portland, Oregon)**
Prepare yourself for something different and something delicious, especially you yeast fanatics out there; this knockout of a beer has a slight honey sweetness that is gently tempered, and appropriately absorbed, by starchy foods; there is a full fruity hoppiness and enough alcohol (7.5%/volume) to keep you glowing for a week; you can definitely taste the rock sugar candy at the end; this is a tricky beer to brew, and it has been done very well. Serve it alongside a baked potato and thick slabs of crusty bread.

**HALE'S AMBER ALE (draft)   MB/BP   1.0
(Seattle, Washington)**
Fruity at the beginning; full-bodied character and complexity disappear almost completely after the beer sits for five minutes or so—and I got this fresh out of the tap; retains a slight floral taste, but everything else dramatically flattens out; some roasted aroma pops up momentarily but is really of no consequence; starts out with promise, but ends up as forgettable.

**HALE'S IPA (draft)   MB/BP   4.4
(Seattle, Washington)**
Hoppy, hoppy, hoppy—but well controlled and smoothed over by healthy dollops of malt; fruity fermented initial aroma; bitterness takes over your entire mouth, but it is so well done, you can't complain; lovely patterned curtains of Brussels lace stick around in wide parallel configurations; retains perfect balance, with all ingredients in convivial harmony; lusty, musty grain scent finishes the glass along with a full-bodied fruitiness; slight hop

weakness at the end, but so what—getting there was fun; a well-crafted, tasty beer; I couldn't stop drinking this, with food or without, although I enjoyed it more with seared chicken breast topped with almonds.

HALE'S PALE ALE   MB/BP   2.2
(Seattle, Washington)

Deep fruitiness with subdued bitterness; soft throughout the mouth; flowery aura is evident; a little too precious and thin to make this worthwhile, even with food.

HAMMER & NAIL AMERICAN ALE   MB   3.4
(Watertown, Connecticut)

Nice fruitiness contains a balancing and complementary light caramel presence; feisty, well-built hoppiness is apparent after several sips; slightly spicy aroma; fruity character gains a citrus component as you drink; smooth, evolving caramel-fruit combo is easy on the throat; some aromatic nut character appears at the end; an interesting gathering of flavors and sensations. Try this ale with fish from the sea.

HAMMER & NAIL EXTRA SPECIAL
BITTER ALE   MB   3.7
(Watertown, Connecticut)

Caramel, vanilla-like aroma and fruity-malty taste are slick, well-presented, and very satisfying; bitterness increases subtly and gradually, eventually reaching all areas of the palate; flavor is evenly distributed; slight caramel character appears at the start of each swallow and disappears at the end; generous, ivory-colored head sits patiently atop the orange-yellow body that nicely catches the light; fine, fruity-caramel aroma and trademark, caramel-tinged hoppy mouthfeel offer a final, pleasurable salute. A good drinking partner with sliced ham and sweet potatoes.

HAMM'S Pilsener   CB   2.5
(brewed by Pabst in Milwaukee, Wisconsin)

Fruity aroma that turns musty; sharp swallow at the back of the throat; offers some warmth and some substance and complexity, though not enough; fuller than other megabrews, with longer-lasting flavor; hops and malt are virtually impossible to discern; carries a certain grittiness, providing texture to let you know it went through a brewing, rather than a blanching, process; if you need a six-pack of mass-produced beer, this is it.

HAMPSHIRE SPECIAL ALE (annual)   MB   2.4
(Portland, Maine)

An annual event, this Christmas beer has proven to be alcoholic, spicy, and clove-like with a smooth small-bubble mouthfeel; echoes of strength and quality with depth; mellows, but remains distinctly alcoholic with food; tamps down into calm, organized, somewhat complicated brew; still, compared with other Christmas beers, it leaves much to be desired, though as a seasonal offering, changes do occur yearly; among other things, it's not spicy enough; higher alcohol content is not integrated with the other ingredients and complexity fluctuates; musty reddish color with tannish foamy head; finishes with a fresh yeasty aroma—but pay attention from year to year.

HANSA DARK Pilsener	**CB**	**4.1**

(Bergen, Norway)
Hint of burnt caramel doesn't alienate; constrained sweetness; distinctive; mellow yet sharp and crackling at the back of the tongue; defined, subtle roasted taste combines with an undertone of malt, resulting in a pleasant, pungent package; taste comes around subtly, smoothly, and uniformly. Complements oysters or boiled shrimp with sharp horseradish or cocktail sauce.

HANSA LIGHT Pilsener	**CB**	**2.6**

(Bergen, Norway)
Significantly thinner, paler texture than the dark, but same overall taste and aroma. Too tame for oysters, shrimp, and similar seafoods; much better alone.

HARD GAUGE BEER Lager	**CT**	**0.8**

(Detroit, Michigan)
Hard Gauge is one of the new generation of private-label beers brewed for specific mass-market tastes for what are essentially PR purposes. In this instance, the national Hard Rock restaurant chain has packaged a light and flimsy pilsener in what looks like a happening soda can. Completing the pop image is an uncomplex, very pale gold body that is sweet from an overdose of corn adjuncts. If your tastes run to, say, beer, then this imitation is not for you.

HARDY COUNTRY BITTER	**CB**	**2.3**

(Dorchester, Dorset, England)
Thick white luscious head tops off the cloudy medium-amber body; hardly any aroma at all; taste has depth, but the ingredients, especially the hops, are ill-defined; lightly carbonated; slightly sour yeast character at the back of the throat; mellow and simple in presentation; this is a laid-back, awfully gentle, unassertive bottle-conditioned bitter—almost a contradiction in terms. A beer for fish and chips.

HARLEY-DAVIDSON HEAVY BEER

Pilsener (annual)	**CT**	**2.4**

(brewed by Joseph Huber Brewing in Monroe, Wisconsin, for the Harley-Davidson Co.)
Surprising softness and engaging thinness given the name, which immediately raises expectations; however, finish is bland and a

bit flat; slight greenness; even with its gimmicky packaging (the 1989 edition was designed to look like an oil can), it is more appealing than anticipated; two to three at a time would probably help improve its taste; sweetness surfaces throughout; about average for an American beer; brewed annually for motorcycle events in Daytona, Florida, and Sturges, South Dakota, so check the date on this. Try it with a turkey sausage sandwich.

HARP Lager	**CB**	**3.5**

(Dublin, Ireland)

Immediate rich taste without being overwhelming; balanced blend of flavors lingers on the tongue; sharp and very pleasantly fizzy; for people who have not fully developed their beer taste buds, this may come close to top-of-the-line; nice and solid, with integrity; a good food beer. It stands up to pizza with lots of cheese and has the guts to stand up to stronger dishes. Harp is also my lager of choice in a Black and Tan (see page 148).

HARPOON ALE	**RB**	**2.7**

(Boston, Massachusetts)

Vaguely sour, almost bitter, with a citrus fruitiness; thin body; gentle fuzziness with flowery dryness at the back of the throat; soothing; engages several senses at once; classy presentation, but still not up to the great ones; dry and austere; meant for the connoisseur rather than the casual beer lover, but misses the mark with both. It doesn't miss the mark, however, with mildly spicy Thai food.

HARPOON OCTOBERFEST (seasonal)	**RB**	**4.0**

(Boston, Massachusetts)

Malty and spicy for you and your holiday guests; presents the rich flavor of a stout, but without the heavy mouthfeel; aroma is reminiscent of scented soap, but eminently drinkable; appealing give-and-take of full-bodied sweetness and pinpricks of citrus-rind spiciness; malty aroma remains throughout as a happy reminder of the taste that inevitably follows; finishes with a seasonal snap of malt-encased bitterness; a premier Oktoberfest. Do try it with sauerkraut and sizzling sausage on a crusty bun.

HARPOON PILSNER	**RB**	**2.2**

(Boston, Massachusetts)

Tea-like flavor and richly malty in aroma; thin-bodied; clean-tasting with suggestions of grain throughout; could be crisper and more textural; visually, the quarter-inch head and golden-blond body present a classic pilsener picture; malty sweetness, almost honey in character, emerges at the end; though the tastes ultimately meld into an integrated whole, the effect is not satisfying. Fresh vegetable salad helps boost it up a notch or two.

TAP TIP

Listen When Your Beer Speaks

*A*s with our other senses, hearing plays a role in the appreciation of drinking beer, though we aren't always aware of it. Listen to the "psssst" of the air escaping as you open the can or bottle. Is it strong and steady, or weak and very brief? The more noticeable the hiss, the more certain it is that the liquid has been packaged correctly and is ready to drink. Return the bottle or can if no sound is heard as you pop the top. Similarly, once beer has been poured, cock your ear to the top of the glass. Are the bubbles crackling and sharp-sounding, especially in a lager or pilsener? If so, carbonation levels are probably okay, and that pleasing, appropriate sound is likely to translate to a pleasing, enjoyable taste on the palate. As they say at Munich's Weihenstephan School of Brewing, a good beer "must snap in the ear." So listen up.

HATUEY Lager   **CB**   **2.3**
(Baltimore, Maryland)

There's more "feel" to this beer than taste; concentrate, and you might experience a constrained sweetness; minimal hoppiness comes and goes after several sips; improves as you drink, gaining in body and strength; there's nothing to dislike here, nor is there anything exciting; fuller and tastier at the end, with even a glimmer of alcohol, but that's not enough. A true peanuts and popcorn brew.

BEER FACT

*H*atuey is named after a legendary Cuban Indian chief. Originally brewed in Cuba by the Bacardi family, of rum renown, today it is made by Bacardi in this country, using the original Caribbean island formula.

HAZEL DELL RED ZONE PALE ALE
(draft) BP 0.2
(Vancouver, Washington)
Sharply fruity taste and aroma; somewhat hoppy with a tart aftertaste on the roof of the mouth; apple-cider color; begins to
taste like burnt rubber and coats the mouth; unpleasant ensuing
citrus taste curls in on itself; simply not well made.

H.C. BERGER RED RASPBERRY
WHEAT ALE MB 2.6
(Fort Collins, Colorado)
Crackly sharp all over the mouth; sweet, restrained raspberry taste;
hints of yeasty sourness integrate companionably with the tart
berry character; fruit flavor gets further absorbed into the mainstream and propels the taste forward, though the carefully laid-
down yeast presence cannot be ignored; refreshing and flavorful;
nothing complicated or fancy here, just plain, straightforward,
thirst-quenching satisfaction.

H.C. BERGER WHISTLEPIN
WHEAT ALE MB 2.7
(Fort Collins, Colorado)
Light on the tongue and sharp at back of throat; bright, vivacious fizziness; malty sweetness mingles nicely with the hop and
sharp wheat-yeast flavors; gains balance as it warms to room temperature, with the mouthfeel becoming more complex in the
process; finishes with a slight hint of citrus tartness; let this sit
out of the fridge for a half-hour or so before drinking. A nice
summertime refresher.

HE'BREW GENESIS ALE CT 0.8
(Boonville, California)
Sugary-sweet; cotton-candy aroma; tart, sharp, and hard to digest; continuing bitterness stays after you swallow; only hint of
relief is a telltale smidgen of malt and a hint of honey hidden in
the bitterness; there's no getting away from its sour-bitter taste,
unless you stop drinking it; harsh and unfinished.

HEINEKEN LAGER CB 3.4
(Amsterdam, Holland)
An old, familiar standby with crunchy sharpness in both taste
and texture; substantive quality and predictable rhythm; consistent palate; although its taste is not the most inspiring, it is a
solid all-around beer. As good with a burger as it is with shrimp
and other seafood.

B E E R   F A C T

*H*eineken Lager is the number-two imported beer in the United States, overtaken by Corona in 1997 after decades as number one. It is reputed to be the first beer legally brought into the United States after Prohibition. Its presence and initial popularity in this country are attributed to Leo van Munching, a baggage manager with a transatlantic shipping line who carted a few cases westward on the S.S. *Statendam* at the behest of a friend of his who was well placed with Heineken. The New York response to the beer was so positive that sales quickly zoomed, and in short order van Munching was made Heineken's distributor in the U.S. With the change in management several years ago, his name no longer appears on all cans and bottles of the brand sold here.

HEINEKEN SPECIAL DARK Lager   CB   2.4
(Amsterdam, Holland)
Light, sharp, and fizzy, unlike the usual middle-European darks; taste is mild, clammy, and accompanies an uninteresting seltzer-like texture; best alone rather than with food; not worth the hype and label.

HENNINGER DARK Lager   CB   2.5
(Frankfurt, Germany)
Mild, slightly burnt taste; pretty much zestless and punchless; the taste at the back of the throat turns a bit acrid as it settles in; hint of caramel; stays unperturbed, neither bolstering nor subtracting from a variety of foods; some musty mouthfeel at the end, along with sweetish accompaniment; neither exciting nor unexciting.

HENNINGER KAISER PILSNER   CB   3.0
(Frankfurt, Germany)
Sharp, crisp, and "guzzleable" on first sips; smooth and prickly in moderation, with a hint of non-fruity sweetness; modest and unobtrusive, with a vague hint of hoppy floweriness in the finish; moderately dry; malty flourish at the bottom of the bottle. Needs food to add interest, so serve with a deli sandwich and fries.

HENNINGER LIGHT Pilsener   CB   1.9
(Frankfurt, Germany)
Quick mustiness develops rapidly into flat, superficial taste; ef-

fervescence and staying power save this from being labeled nondescript; somewhat wispy and light, with similar color; for a weak-appearing beer it remains determined to help out in whatever way it can. Try it with lamb, or at brunch with spicy scrambled eggs.

HENNINGER MEISTER PILS   CB   3.2
(Hamilton, Ontario, Canada)
Simultaneously lightly crinkly and smooth; taste and freshness remain constant with food; quality ingredients enhance the enjoyment; overall, keeps your interest, though not exciting. Goes well with a crab salad.

HENRY WEINHARD'S DARK Lager   CB   2.3
(Portland, Oregon)
Sharp to bland, with no head to speak of; thin, with a slight malty, roasted flavor that just manages to differentiate it from the usual American beer; no depth or character; an attempt at giving the impression of a quality brew, but in the end rather ordinary; slight warmth comes through at the bottom of the glass; Bronze Medal winner at the 1993 Great American Beer Festival. Try it with salami on rye.

HERRENBRAU PILSNER MALT LIQUOR   CB   2.4
(Bayreuth, Germany)
Strong, very appetizing, honey/grainy taste and aroma; slides a little roughly down the gullet; maintains honey flavor with blander dishes although the texture is too watery to fully complement most foods; fades in interest as meal continues; encroaching sourness further pushes it downhill.

HERRENHAUSER PILSENER
MALT LIQUOR   CB   1.2
(Hannover, Germany)
Odorless, tasteless, and textureless; hints of clove and honey appear midway with food; smooth and dry, but so what? More complexity at the end of bottle—slight acidity and thickness on the tongue.

HEXEN BRAU SWISS DUNKEL
MALT LIQUOR   CB   3.9
(Zurich, Switzerland)
Full of malt and caramel; texturally a bit sharp; rich, with a restraining tartness that is not filling; caramel malt has a crystal sugar character that is pleasant and not overly sweet; lingers sweetly and gently on the lips, like a first kiss; settles into a smooth, almost watery liquid; a tasteful beer that is "traditionally brewed only when the moon is full." Have this with bread and hard fruit, such as apples.

HIGHFALLS INDIA PALE ALE   **CB**   **2.9**
(Rochester, New York)
Nothing on the first sip, but the second swallow is filled with a surge of spice that floats to the roof of the mouth; underlying layer of malt supports the sweet, flowery taste; aroma is slightly sweet and slightly fruity; sweetness seems to lift off the tongue and slowly change to bitter; finishes with a fine peppery character that stays in the aftertaste. Nice with cold salmon or tuna.

HIMALAYAN BLUE PREMIUM LAGER   **CB**   **2.5**
(Malli, Sikkum, India)
Sweet and malty; pinpricks of bitterness remain on roof of mouth; quite smooth overall; hints of graininess in the aroma and flavor stay throughout; sparkling clear gold body; uncomplex; weakens with snack foods like olives and peppers; there is an upsurge of grain and hops at the last few sips.

HINANO Lager   **CB**   **2.1**
(Papeete, Tahiti)
Slightly sour and flat-tasting on the tongue; mild fizziness quickly dissipates; French brewing influence is evident in the cutting texture and winey sharpness; has a fullness not always found in better-tasting beers; better with food than by itself. Try it with seafood.

HOBGOBLIN TRADITIONAL
ENGLISH ALE   **CB**   **3.8**
(Witney, England)
Mellow; interactive hop and chocolate tastes fill the mouth and stay after you swallow; malt then catches up with the hop-chocolate character and all intermingle in joyous taste harmony; pale cola color with yellow and brown highlights; sweetens slightly at the end; full-bodied mouthful of rich hops, complex malts, and traditional chocolate make this ale well worth having. Try with spicy foods, like peppered beef.

HOEGAARDEN GRAND CRU ALE   **CB**   **0.9**
(Hoegaarden, Belgium)
Perfumey aroma and taste discourage finishing this ale; made exclusively with barley malt; fruity, almost rancid, sourness and pale-golden haze leave a great deal to be desired; unpasteurized and bottle-conditioned; according to the label, Grand Cru was the secret of medieval noblemen, but the reputed allure of its flavor still remains a secret.

HOEGAARDEN WHITE Wheat   **CB**   **2.6**
(Hoegaarden Belgium)
Immediate winey, almost vinegary, aroma; fruity, perfumey sour taste at the sides of the tongue; quickly dissipating fresh, flat texture; sweetens to a honey mouthfeel with food; much more palat-

able at the end than at the beginning, shimmering cloudiness; hints of coriander and curaçao, both common flavoring ingredients used before hops. Good with Italian food as well as brunch dishes.

HOFBRAU BAVARIA DARK RESERVE
Lager   **CB**   **2.5**
(Kulmbach, Germany)
No aroma; ripe-apple flavor; texture wavers between thin and thicker; remains balanced (sweet/bland) with foods; a friendly, unassuming beer for the novice who wants to start trying dark beers; decent drink for any food regardless of spiciness; eventually fades into the woodwork.

HOFBRAU BAVARIA LIGHT RESERVE
Lager   **CB**   **2.7**
(Kulmbach, Germany)
Light, flavorful, and crisp with a smooth blend of hops and malt; flat aftertaste leaves slight burnt feel, even several minutes after last sip; sturdy and predictable. Fine with deli sandwiches.

HOFBRAU MUNCHENER OKTOBERFEST
Lager (annual)   **CB**   **3.3**
(Munich, Germany)
Full in the mouth and slightly bitter, with a minimum of fizziness; nice balance between taste and texture; mild burnt-caramel taste appears throughout; this beer doesn't overwhelm you—it remains steady from start to finish with manageable complexity, balance, and overall flavor; good choice for those wanting an introduction to Marzenbier. Accompanies lemon chicken and rice nicely.

BEER FACT

*H*ofbrau, "court brew" in German, is made by Hofbrauhaus, the famous beer garden in Munich that was originally the Bavarian Royal Court Brewery, founded in 1589.

HOFBRAU ROYAL BAVARIAN LAGER **CB**   **3.1**
(Munich, Germany)
Zippy, hoppy, crisp, and grainy; classic lager mouthfeel, but with more fullness and complexity; aroma and taste match perfectly; a good beer for those wanting something basic, yet somewhat challenging; well made, but not overly exciting. Goes well with thick meat loaf or meatball sandwiches.

HOLSTEN Pilsener   CB   3.0
(Hamburg, Germany)
Neutral taste and texture, leaning toward soft; hop aroma increases as food is consumed; still, you have to pay close attention to appreciate this beer; tapers off to a more pronounced dryness at the end. Enhances sushi and gazpacho.

HOLSTEN DRY Pilsener   CB   2.9
(Hamburg, Germany)
Sharp graininess at outset; sourness and sharpness increase with spicy foods; medium body with mellow golden hue; well-presented balance of sweetness and dryness, essentially substituting taste for texture; good example of a dry beer. Try it with bagels, lox, and cream cheese.

HOMBRE Lager   CB   2.9
(Ciudad Juarez, Mexico)
Sweet-tasting; very smooth and easy going down; gritty character is more malt- than hop-based; a little watery, but I would drink it again. Enjoy with corn on the cob.

HOOD CANAL AGATE PASS AMBER
Lager (draft)   MB   1.9
(Poulsbo, Washington)
Intense sweet-fruity taste has just the barest suggestion of chocolate; turns a bit hoppy after several sips, but is spoiled by the soapy finish; eventually pretty uninteresting; ends with a maltiness that unfortunately is not really evident earlier; has too many missing ingredients to be recommended.

HOPFENPERLE Pilsener   CB   2.6
(Rheinfelden, Switzerland)
Affecting fruit aroma on first sniff, followed by pleasantly flat maltiness that lingers on the tongue; surprisingly mild for a Swiss beer; no acidity or alcohol bitterness; good basis for a malt beverage, but taste, texture, color, and body all need to be built up. Goes well with Sloppy Joes and the like.

HOPFENPERLE SPECIAL Lager   CB   2.9
(Rheinfelden, Switzerland)
Dry, light, and flat on the tongue with an accompanying thickness; turns warming and honeyed with the right food—nicely mellows out the fire of grilled chicken with green chiles; kinder at the end than the beginning.

HOPPY HOLIDAZE FLAVORED ALE   MB/BP   2.8
(annual)
(Larkspur, California)
Gently and comprehensively spiced; although the label says cinnamon, nutmeg, mace, and pure vanilla extract, there is a clove character mixed in with everything else; nutmeg, however, even-

tually becomes the dominant flavor, balancing nicely with the four varieties of sweetly exuberant malts; vanilla mellows out some of the more insistent spice flavors; definite nutmeg-cinnamon aroma at the end. Drink this traditional Christmas ale with traditional holiday foods.

HOPS AMBER ALE   BP   2.4
(Scottsdale, Arizona)

Long-lasting head; perfumey, light, and dainty; minimally cloying, but enough to negatively affect pairing it with food; an unpredictable ebb and flow of sweetness, which is submerged by the end of the bottle, may surface without warning.

HOPS BOCK   BP   3.1
(Scottsdale, Arizona)

Sheets of Brussels lace set off the deep brown of this seasonal beer, making for a charming visual context; gently alcoholic and somewhat sticky; appropriately hopped; remains weak to mild for a bock, which in this case makes for an acceptable mellowness; I enjoyed this, but would not return for another.

HOPS PILSENER   BP   3.2
(Scottsdale, Arizona)

I first sampled this at the 1991 Great American Beer Festival in Denver. Served in tiny plastic glasses, it was not fizzy, too sweet, and too malty; the color was too yellow. I didn't consider it a true pilsener, and rated it close to 0. A year or so later, I tried it again, fresh from the tap at the brewery in Scottsdale, and *voilà!* Without the knocking around, it tasted sweet, sharp, and crisp, with more appropriate carbonation; though still a bit flat on the tongue, it was an attractive malty brew; firm and fulfilling; pale color was still too faded; and now, with a well-filled glass, Brussels lace tantalizingly coated the sides. Try it with a toasted bagel and smoked trout—a delightful combination.

HOPS WHEAT   BP   2.3
(Scottsdale, Arizona)

Restrained citrus taste; fresh and alluring; sweetness is weak but lasting; not as thirst-quenching as a wheat should be; an ordinary beer; dryish finish.

HOSTER HEFE WEIZEN (seasonal)   MB/BP   2.5
(Columbus, Ohio)

Much too faint clove aroma; not sharp or thirst-quenching enough for a wheat beer; much more like a plain, run-of-the-mill lager; flat but not unattractive; undistinguished; a beer without a style. Improves with plain foods such as liverwurst or ham sandwiches.

HUA NAN Lager   CB   3.8
(Guangzhou, China)

Very sweet, light, and delicately refreshing; easy on the hops, it is a little too weak for spicy or barbecued food; enjoyable alone or with plain beans and rice or steamed vegetables.

HUBCAP RAZZLE DAZZLE BERRY
Wheat Ale (seasonal)   BP   1.0
(Vail, Colorado)

Weak, watery cranberry juice; consistency of cheap wine; weak red-brown color doesn't help; not unpleasantly sweet with hint of counterbalancing bitterness; more gimmick than beer.

HUBSCH LAGER   MB/BP   1.4
(Davis, California)

The first thing you notice is the clear orange-hued color, which certainly does not scream "beer"; the next thing you notice is how flat and uncarbonated it is, with no head; looks like a bald guy with the beginnings of a bad sunburn; uncomplex and rather tasteless; malt is the only hint of an ingredient, and even that is vague; slight sweetness detracts from spicy food. Hubsch is a well-regarded brewery, but this example doesn't do it justice.

HUBSCH MARZEN   MB/BP   2.4
(Davis, California)

Sweet chewing-gum flavor and, less so, aroma; vague but acceptable sweetness continues, with just a hint of hoppy bitterness; keeps a mild floral aroma; some flavor harshness appears at the back of the throat; carbonation diminishes significantly at the end; not bad, not great. Choose something spicy or tart to eat with this beer, like spiced beef or Mexican food.

HUE BEER Lager   CB   0.6
(Hue, Vietnam)

Salty, sour, and bitter with sharp carbonation—all obscuring any real taste sensations; sweet, perfumey presence is felt at the back of the throat as the fizziness subsides; dry, flat aftertaste lingers on the roof of the mouth; no head, no lace, and no complexity; cloudy, faded yellow-golden color; while some malt appears at the end, this concoction is oddly un-beer-like; finishes cold and unforgiving.

HUMBOLDT PALE ALE   RB/BP   2.1
(Arcata, California)

Bitter and medium-bodied, with a tingle of fruity bitterness; begins to weaken and stays weak; light amber body; bitterness softens and gains an off-taste; texturally too smooth; hint of clove at the end doesn't quite redeem things; flat and not complex enough.

HUMBOLDT RED NECTAR ALE   RB/BP   2.8
(Arcata, California)

Fresh-baked aroma with emerging citrus taste, particularly at the back of the throat; maintains its keen bite; gets into the crevices of the mouth with a comforting watery feel; each pour creates a new, somewhat fluffy/spongy head that lasts until the next pour; raw at the end; this is a serviceable beer, rather than an outstanding one.

HURLIMANN SWISS DARK LAGER CB 2.4
(Zurich, Switzerland)

Malty and pinprick-sharp at the beginning of the bottle, followed by a light backbone with concentrated yet short-lived boldness; unenticing dryness flattens on the tongue and, thankfully, goes away; sharpness fades into fizziness; overall integration of ingredients as beer warms—surprising for a lager, which usually does its best when chilled. Fine with bread and a hard cheese, such as an aged gouda.

HUSKE HARDWARE HOUSE ROUGH
HOUSE INDIA PALE ALE BP 3.3
(Fayetteville, North Carolina)

Fruity and hoppy, with an apple note or two—all in good balance; the fresh, crisp character softens as you drink; dry and satisfying; gradually increasing subtle hop taste becomes more noticeable as the bitterness accumulates; finishes with a delicately hopped mouthfeel. A good beer for shellfish salads or a fried fish sandwich.

ICEHOUSE ICE BEER MALT LIQUOR CB 3.3
(Milwaukee, Wisconsin)

Stiff-backed and bold; surprising hop bitterness that slowly erodes; harsh, full sweetness follows first swallow with food; remains fresh and invigorating, very dry; plain and clean-tasting; not bothered by complexity or nuances in texture or flavor; malts and hops are carefully calibrated; a tangible physical "feel" distinguishes this beer; the taste is almost an afterthought, but there is a purity that is central to its appeal, not to mention the 5.5% alcohol/volume; Bronze Medal winner at the 1994 Great American Beer Festival. An uncomplicated companion for hearty corned beef sandwiches and snacks.

ICHTEGEM'S OLD BROWN ALE CB 3.9
(Ichtegem, Belgium)

Very sweet, almost syrupy, but don't let that stop you from drinking more; as it warms, a fruitiness reminiscent of fresh peach or apricot appears; slightly sour, in keeping with the traditional old brown ales of Flanders; foamy, moderately bubbled head rests comfortably on top of the deep nutty-brown body; this is an intriguing beer; well made, but not for everyone's taste. Try with red meat that is not heavily spiced.

IL VICINO WET MOUNTAIN INDIA
PALE ALE   **MB/BP**   **3.3**
(Albuquerque, New Mexico; Salida, Colorado)
Fresh and sharp-smelling, with a touch of sweet-spicy fruitiness, followed by a compact bitter taste—all in all quite inviting; settles into a gentle, satisfying hop-malt balance, with both ingredients patiently playing off against one another; texture flattens too soon, but the sweet-hop flavor just rolls along; finishes with a hint of orange pekoe taste; the complexity of the three types of hops keeps this appealing IPA moving along. Goes very well with any fresh-made pizzas.

IMPERIAL Lager   **CB**   **1.3**
(San José, Costa Rica)
Brief front-end flavor that quickly goes flat and bland; mild hops and almost nonexistent malt make this beer weak at the end.

IMPERIAL PILSENER   **CB**   **2.7**
(Punta Arenas, Chile)
Crisp, with warmth and minimal sweetness alongside food; malt and hops play off each other with finesse; thick high head with flat, uncomplex taste and a faraway sharpness that forces you to rely on the food at hand for flavor; some thick, bitter aftertaste around the tongue and sides of the mouth doesn't make you look forward to drinking this alone; color is impure, off-yellow. A thirst-quenching companion to salty salamis and pickled condiments.

INDEPENDENCE FRANKLINFEST Lager MB   **2.3**
(Philadelphia, Pennsylvania)
Thin maltiness exposes twinkles of bitterness; somewhat fizzy; minimal hop aroma; medium-bodied; thin head; sharper and more bitter than other Oktoberfests; sweet, toasted malt character; slightly malty-fruity aftertaste; light but flavorful. Okay in a pinch.

INDIA Lager   **CB**   **1.1**
(Mayaguez, Puerto Rico)
Thick, essentially indiscernible taste and texture; ginger-ale color; barely satisfying; remains stale-tasting with food; "La Cerveza de Puerto Rico" is rather harsh and discordant; fortunately, it comes in a nonstandard 10-ounce can.

INDIAN RIVER AMBERJACK Alt   **MB**   **2.2**
(Melbourne, Florida)
Malty; texturally too heavy on the tongue; sweet and calming; not complex and too weak in taste; whatever flavor is present is pleasant enough, but there's simply not enough of it; finishes sweet and hoppy, but so what?

INDIO OSCURA Lager   **CB**   **1.6**
(Monterrey, Mexico)
Minimally thick, sweet, and somewhat bland; no zest or carbon-

ation; almost smoky, musty aftertaste toward the end, at which point it begins to lose its flavor and rapidly goes downhill; rich amber color rescues it from visual obscurity.

IRISH BRIGADE Ale   CB   3.0
(Warrington, England)

Toasty; slightly winey taste; mellow; dark red; smooth; soothingly works its way around the mouth and tongue, encouraging food to display its full flavor and texture; finishes warm and mature, like a good friend. Just right with hearty meat dishes such as stews, barbecue, grilled steaks with onion rings.

IRONWORKS CONDOR LAGER   BP   2.0
(Lakewood, Colorado)

Far too foamy, with large bubbles in a thick head that sops up too much of the flavor; a bit of bitterness remains a tease throughout; hazy and cloudy, as if yeast is swirling around, which it shouldn't be in a lager. Improves with chicken potpie and onion bread.

ISENBECK Lager   CB   3.4
(Hamm, Germany)

Smooth, pleasant, fruity taste; lacks zest; hoppiness at the end helps; goes down easily, with grainy finish that is not harsh or bothersome. A good match for sharp cheeses and mustards, specialty meats such as smoked ham, spicy salamis, and German wursts.

J W DUNDEE'S HONEY BROWN LAGER CB   2.4
(Rochester, New York)

Aggressively effervescent and definitely bitter, this lustrous copper-amber lager gives your mouth a good workout; some help comes along in the form of a mild honey flavor that seeps into the strong texture after four or five sips; as it warms it settles down further and achieves a balance and smoothness missing earlier; second half of the bottle is more integrated and flavorful, so ignore the first half. Munch on roasted peanuts with this one.

JAMAICA BRAND RED ALE   MB   3.3
(Blue Lake, California)

Rich-looking and rich-tasting, with a quickly disappearing bitterness; turns thin as you swallow; gentle, light fruitiness has a suggestion of nutty undertones; flowery hop taste becomes quite powerful after several sips, presaging a big flavor that emerges with food; yeasty apple-cider aroma provides an invigorating uplift halfway through the bottle at the same time the beer regains its full-bodied stature; not as crisp as label suggests, but still well done; milk-chocolate color and yeast cloudiness and sediment at the bottom of the glass; considering the complexity and balance requirements of this style, the brewer is to be commended for displaying a certain degree of daring to produce this commercially and with panache. Goes well with grain dishes.

JAMAICA BRAND SUNSET
INDIA PALE ALE   MB   1.1
(Blue Lake, California)

Sharply bitter, hoppy and fruity; fruit aroma is noticeable at arm's length; citrus-fruity character turns sugary-sweet, but bitterness stays in the aftertaste; rubber-plastic taste is strong and persistent; rough and raw on the tongue; very relentless and insistent, which would be okay if there were something to be pushy about; not a good beer.

JAMES BOWIE KENTUCKY HILLS LTD.
PILSNER   CB   2.0
(La Crosse, Wisconsin)

Raw, tart, and flat, with a sharpness at the back of the mouth that keeps your attention; tea color is beguiling and un-pilsener-like; plain and less invigorating than most American pilseners, but with slightly more taste; aftertaste lacks complexity or strength; gets blander as the bottle drains; boredom is a distinct possibility, but patience reveals that stage to be a precursor: the 40-ounce container, packaged to resemble a large whiskey bottle, offers a (very) slow mellowing out, giving you the chance to decide whether the wait is worth it. Best suited to light luncheon fare and plain sandwiches.

JAMES PAGE IRON RANGE AMBER
Lager   MB   3.4
(Minneapolis, Minnesota)

Pleasant uncomplex flavor features a gentle whisper of mild, sweet maltiness that lingers on the tongue; a kiss of hops wanders forward and nicely balances the malt; thick head is long-lasting, but Brussels lace fades too rapidly; finishes with a vague but charming fruitiness; this is a quality beer that needs a little fine-tuning to make it thoroughly enjoyable; serve it cool, neither warm nor cold. Makes for an interesting partner with slices of barbecued beef or pork on a roll.

JAMES PAGE BOUNDARY WATERS
WILD RICE BEER Lager   MB   4.1
(Minneapolis, Minnesota)

The combination of a faint rice-alcohol taste coupled with the fresh graininess almost takes your breath away; medium- to full-bodied; crisp and very tasty; slight bitter hop flavor is evident at mid-bottle and stays judiciously in the background; mild and dainty; foamy, full, long-lasting head leaves promiscuous sheets of Brussels lace; inscrutably delicious, it grows on you; this is one of my favorite beers. Goes very well with chicken and rice dishes.

JAX Pilsener   **CB**   **3.0**
(San Antonio, Texas)
Light, but with enough grit to go along with hot or spicy foods; visually and nosewise similar to its even lighter cousin, Pearl; sweet malt presence and carbonated vivacity distinguish it from other summertime throwaways; unpretentious; a tried-and-true thirst-quencher. I had my first one in Gulfport, Mississippi, back when the county was legally dry. A bottle went for 25¢, and you and your friends could have five longnecks brought to the table for a grand total of $1. It helped pass the dog days of August, and will likely do the same for you. Well suited to spicy Cajun and hot Southwestern dishes; also fried fish.

JENLAIN FRENCH COUNTRY ALE   **CB**   **2.3**
Jenlain, France)
Sweet plum-like taste with silky wine smoothness; similar to a pale rosé wine; remains warm and somewhat removed from itself. Best after a meal, as a mellow *digestif.*

BEER FACT

*T*echnically, Jenlain is in the specialty French *bière de garde* style—traditionally strong, full-flavored, fruity, cask-aged or bottle-conditioned, and all malt. The style, often produced by family brewers, originated in northern France near the Belgian border. Up until the early 1900s, more than 2,000 farmhouse breweries operated in France; Jenlain is one of about 30 that remain active today.

JET CITY ALE   **CT**   **2.4**
(Seattle, Washington)
Aroma is slightly oxidized, but taste is smooth and creamy with apple-cider tang; medium-bodied and not complex at all—indeed, hops and malt and yeast kind of just sit there, neither asserting themselves nor interacting with each other; malt finally takes over as the ale warms; eventually turns watery and uninteresting; starts much better than it finishes. (Although a major brewery actually produces this beer, Jet City owner-brewer Jeff Leggett uses his own recipe and ingredients and oversees the brewing process.)

JEVER PILSENER   **CB**   **3.0**
(Jever, Germany)
Crispy, tangy, and sharp with a wonderful zing of hops that stays put on your tongue for a while; subtle spiciness and aroma along with a bit of bitterness; clean taste is accompanied by a slight

grainy presence; bitterness increases and livens things up even further; finishes with a moderated bitterness and good-tasting graininess; a nice everyman's (and -woman's) beer. Goes well with light fish from a mountain lake or stream.

JINDAO Lager   **CB**   **4.0**
(Qingdao, China)

Fresh, creamy, and refreshing—something of a surprise given its cloudy paleness; lends a not-overwhelming sweetness to a meal; could be a bit heavier texturally; holds its own overall; a very drinkable beer. Excellent accompaniment to Chinese food, especially seafood-based dishes with shrimp or lobster.

**JOHN BARLEYCORN BARLEYWINE
STYLE ALE**   **CB**   **3.0**
(Blue Lake, California)

Complexly spicy and soft on the palate; quite sweet, too; easygoing alcohol character belies its strength (8%/volume) and creeps up on you unnoticed; continuing sweetness provides a good balance to the underlying alcohol sharpness; aroma and taste match on a one-to-one basis; it finishes fruity, spicy, and sharp. Best before or after dinner.

JOHN BULL Ale   **CB**   **2.4**
(Burton-on-Trent, England)

Rather flat and tasteless with a cold crispness that makes for the only excitement; decent, but essentially uninteresting; there is substance to the texture, but that's not enough to put it over the top. Good with heroes and other overstuffed sandwiches.

B E E R   F A C T

*B*urton-on-Trent, known especially for its ales, is probably the most famous brewing center in Britain. It originally gained renown because of the quality of its drinking water, which may be the hardest in the world used in commercial brewing.

**JOHN COURAGE AMBER BEER
Lager**   **CB**   **3.5**
(Staines, England)

Creamy, malty, and caramely, with a sharp slice of alcohol running through it all; soft-tasting and moderately flavorful; accommodating and pleasant in a run-of-the-mill way; remains tame and sensible from start to finish; mellow and medium-bodied; though it's deceptively high in alcohol, you could probably keep on drinking this forever without much effect one way or the other (but don't). Try with something prickly or abrasive, like sharp cheddar or spiced crackers.

JOHN COURAGE EXPORT Lager   CB   2.8
(Bristol, England)
Cross between pale and dark beer, leaning toward dark; so-so in the bottle, without the positive attributes of either pale (prominent bitterness) or dark (crisp and clean); the draft version is much more mellow, smooth, and satisfying. An all-purpose accompaniment to most cuisines.

JOHN LABATT CLASSIC Lager   CB   3.8
(Toronto, Ontario, Canada)
Smooth and mellow, with some fizziness at the back of the throat; subtle complexity; smooth maltiness is the centerpiece of this calming, unaffected quality brew; conservative, but with presence; gets a little too flat and a touch thick at the bottom of the glass; companionable and easy—very easy—going down. Try it with grilled salmon steaks.

JOHN PEEL Ale   CB   2.8
(Blackburn, England)
Sweet caramel taste, soft and smooth; rising pleasant, modulated sharpness as beer integrates with food; subtle fruit flavor, almost cider-like in its wateriness; in the end, however, flatness pervades and comes to be what is remembered. Try it with raw vegetables and dips.

JOHN'S GENERATIONS WHITE ALE   CT   2.9
(Solon, Iowa)
Dainty balance of cloves and spices makes for a welcome opener; aggressively fresh and lively; keeps its characteristic zip even with strong-tasting foods; mouthfeel becomes more tea-like, leaving a tart-fruity-yeast presence in the aftertaste; cloudy, pearlescent body and small-bubbled, clean white head are visually attractive. Appropriate with smoked fish or alone as a summer thirst-quencher.

JOSEPH MEENS' HOLLAND PREMIUM
Lager   CB   1.0
(Schinnen, Holland)
Nondescript sweetness rises to flatness on the roof of the mouth; remains unchallenging and rather devoid of balance and tangible ingredients; pale-golden color and very white head are the only things that attract your attention; slight off-tasting maltiness is the last memory—not a good beer.

JULIUS ECHTER HEFE-WEISSBIER   CB   3.0
(Wurzburg, Germany)
Combination buttered popcorn and distinct clove taste, with tart citrus accompaniment; passing sweetness; becomes a warmer, gentler blend as ingredients settle down; ultimately dry, with no after-

taste; somewhat watery; cloudy faded-blond color, as expected from bottle-conditioning; drink when warm. Best with moderately seasoned pastas, turkey or chicken potpies, and other dishes with crusts to absorb and mellow the harshness of the yeast and alcohol.

JUMPING COW AMBER ALE   MB   2.3
(Paso Robles, California, and New Ulm, Minnesota)
Fruity aroma, malty taste, smooth texture; goes from sweet to bitter to sour in one mouthful; fruitiness disappears and is replaced by sweet maltiness; sour finish; mildly filling; slight chocolate taste creates some excitement, but in the end this is a run-of-the-mill brew; doesn't grow on you, though it does tell you what it is right up front and goes downhill from there; it is finishable, however.

KB AUSTRALIAN LAGER   CB   2.9
(Mendocino, California)
Tasty and full of verve and gumption; leaves a somewhat dry mouthfeel at the back of the throat; sharp, grainy presence comes and goes, eventually staying until the end; crispy on the tongue; medium- to full-bodied; forthright, workman-like character readily becomes comfortable and familiar; though no longer brewed Down Under, it still is better than many Australian brews. Goes very well with grilled meats.

KAISER Pilsener   CB   0.8
(Queimados, Brazil)
Light, light, light; faint hint of old-fashioned ballpark beer, which really is nothing more (quite literally) than a canful of adjuncts— or cereals, as the label points out in Portuguese; something of a head, perhaps due more to the travails of travel and the wonders of brewing chemistry than to anything intrinsic to the beer; slightly sour at the back of the tongue; wispy mustiness lazily reaches the nose; quite weak texturally; cheaply made and cheap-tasting.

KAISER PILSENER   CB   0.5
(Frankfurt, Germany)
Very malty and flat; quite un-pilsener-like; more reminiscent of a chocolate malted; mild burnt flavor; no pizzazz at all; watery, flat, and entirely uninspiring; no hops of any consequence.

KAISERDOM EXTRA DRY Lager   CB   3.9
(Bamberg, Germany)
Very nicely balanced between malt and hops; homey, attractive malt aroma; remains crisp and evenly balanced with knife-like dryness and keen texture; durable yet fancy at the same time; mild enhancing honey taste and aroma add to the strong finish; comes in a tasteful all-black bottle with prominent gold lettering on the label; a nice package, inside and out. Try it with baked ham, pork chops, or a bacon, lettuce, and tomato sandwich.

KAISERDOM RAUCHBIER—SMOKED
BAVARIAN DARK Lager   CB   3.9
(Bamberg, Germany)

Immediately smoky-tasting, but subordinated to a clear coldness on the palate; distinctive, restrained, and not overwhelming; a truly interesting and enlightening brew; reportedly the first smoked beer imported into the U.S. Goes with smoked trout, smoked oysters, or lox and cream cheese on a bagel.

BEER FACT

*R*auch is the German word for "smoke." The area around Bamberg is famous for the smoked malts that characterize this unusual specialty beer.

KALAMAZOO TWO HEARTED ALE   RB   3.2
(Kalamazoo, Michigan)

Quite hoppy, leaving a nice bitter tingle on the tongue; perfumey taste; pleasant floral scent; flavor blossoms in the mouth, filling it with hoppy delights; peach taste eventually floats up from the bottom of the glass and blends well with the hops and floral character; this is a beer that is constantly striving to reach your taste buds. A good match with tuna salad.

KALIK–BEER OF THE BAHAMAS   CB   2.9
(Nassau, Bahamas)

Quite hoppy and prickly for a Caribbean beer; hold a sip in your mouth before swallowing in order to experience the exquisite sharpness all over the mouth; full and filling; sweet bitterness appears at mid-bottle and stays until the end; clean, refreshing mouthfeel; malt becomes more noticeable, balancing the hops at the finish; a cold bottle of this lager takes the edge off a humid, hot day at the beach; add some potato chips, and its thirst-quenching nature really becomes apparent.

KALYANI BLACK LABEL
PREMIUM LAGER   CB   3.5
(Bangalore, India)

Tart, sharp, and hoppy with dry, satisfying swallow; balanced and complex, with strong backbone; surprisingly smooth; tasty and serviceable for beginners and experienced drinkers alike; finish is full and fresh. Works well with Mexican fare.

KAPUZINER WEIZEN KRISTALLKLAR   CB   3.1
(Kulmbach, Germany)

Subdued smooth clove taste and creamy texture; full white head nicely tops red-golden body; clear and filtered, rather than the more typical *weizen* cloudiness from the bottle-conditioned yeast;

emerging yeast taste at the finish; remains settled and creamy to the end; could be a bit spritzier; lasting quality. Remains evenly balanced and tempered with Chinese food.

KAREL IV LAGER   CB   3.6
(Karlovy Vary, Czech Republic)

Lots of fresh graininess on first sip; mild hoppiness is appropriately gritty at the back of the throat; dry and a bit musty on the roof of the mouth; damp soil/wet straw aroma attests to its earthy origins, with a similar, but less enchanting, aftertaste; typical pale-golden color with small-bubbled head presents a classic lager picture; substantial sheets of Brussels lace add to the enjoyment; firm, forthright body from beginning to end; malty aromatic finish tops off a solid representation of the style. Fine with rice dishes such as risotto and pilaf, and with veal.

KARL STRAUSS AMBER LAGER   MB/BP   2.9
(San Diego, California)

Smooth texture and hop spiciness sit together nicely on first sip; sweetness slips through almost unnoticed, providing soothing, cooling backdrop to spicy food; increasing complexity stops short of full-blown integrated charm; has more presence with milder-flavored foods; its ready responsiveness to food makes it hard to evaluate—not necessarily a bad sign, just a gentle warning. Karl Strauss considers this its signature beer; only problem is, it's a little too hard to read.

KARL STRAUSS BLACK'S BEACH
EXTRA DARK PORTER (draft)   MB/BP   4.0
(San Diego, California)

Nutty, toasty, and surprisingly easy to drink, this distinctive porter has an unusually light body, nicely calibrated, not overwhelming or intrusive; respects food while retaining its own dignity; very satisfying and smooth. Fine with charbroiled burgers.

KARL STRAUSS DOWNTOWN AFTER
DARK BROWN ALE (draft)   MB/BP   3.3
(San Diego, California)

Firm, very malty, and toasty; more complex than its namesake cousins; appropriate sweetness is modulated and does not linger; fresh, rich, and not cloying. Try it with minestrone or tomato soup and a grilled cheese sandwich.

KARL STRAUSS GAS LAMP
GOLD ALE (draft)   MB/BP   2.7
(San Diego, California)

Nicely moderated sweetness, thin creaminess, and pale-amber color with a sweet lingering aftertaste; not as bold or creamy as advertised. Goes with light pasta main courses.

KARL STRAUSS PORT LOMA
LIGHTHOUSE LIGHT LAGER (draft)   MB/BP   1.1
(San Diego, California)

Tasty for a light beer, but too musty and, ultimately, uninspiring; leaves thick aftertaste on the roof of the mouth, which is as thick—or substantial—as this lager gets.

KARL STRAUSS RED TROLLEY ALE
(draft)   MB/BP   3.1
(San Diego, California)

Super fruitiness wells up as you're drinking; aftertaste is less compelling and dissipates relatively quickly; without food, it's too fruity; bright-red color; well made, but not a favorite of mine. Good with salty snacks such as nuts or potato chips; believe it or not, an interesting match with apple pie à la mode.

KARLOVACKO lager   CB   2.9
(Karlovac, Croatia; former Yugoslavia)

Mild and flavorful; balancing sweet, malty presence; increased bitterness is savory and well-targeted; grainy hoppiness lingers in the aftertaste; creamy, densely-packed head keeps its shape atop the effervescent, clear, gold body; pleasant earthy-grassy aroma and taste make the finish especially satisfying. A good, refreshing beer that goes well with light fare.

KARLSBEER Pilsener   CB   3.2
(Karlovac, Croatia; former Yugoslavia)

Rounded honeyed taste that quickly flattens and becomes a bit musty; somewhat thick on the tongue, but with a hoppy sharpness; malty aroma emerges as does an attenuated hop bitterness that is contained, not widespread, over the palate; may lose some of its complexity in its travels from the brewery; settles into a predictable, smooth companion. Try with vegetarian Japanese dishes such as vegetable teriyaki or tempura.

KARMI OKOCIM LOW ALCOHOL
CONTENT BEER   CB   3.8
(Brzesko, Poland)

Sweet, toasted, tobacco-like aroma is immediately followed by a surprisingly strong, and unexpected, malt-molasses-corn sugar flavor; fortunately, there are just enough compatible hops to cut the sweetness down to manageable—in fact, satisfying—size; malt-molasses character remains primary, however; suggestion of fresh-cut grass stays in the background; medium-bodied; zippy mouthfeel; with an alcohol content of 1.2%/volume, this is not legally a non-alcoholic brew (which can't have more than 0.5%). Good accompaniment to crisp, tart apples or pears.

KELER LAGER   **CB**   **3.4**
(San Sebastian, Spain)
Lightly carbonated, lightly colored, lightly hopped, and lightly
malty, all capped with a heavy-looking inch-thick head—a very
pleasurable mouthful, indeed; hoppiness shortly emerges from
the pack, providing a welcoming bite to a well-designed beer;
what's more, the accompanying grain taste aids and abets the
hops; head remains creamy and full; finishes balanced and easy-
going. A yummy brew with medium-rare slices of roast beef and
new potatoes.

KELLY'S HAVANA RED ALE   **BP**   **2.4**
(Key West, Florida)
Sugar-sweet, fruity, and smooth, with just a touch of what appears to be West Indian spice; quite malty; slightly nutty; texture
is too flat; low in alcohol, giving the impression that you can
drink this indefinitely, though I don't suggest you try; flavor, complexity, and texture weaken precipitously at the end, which pushes
this ale right out of the average or above-average range. Partially
redeemed when imbibed with shellfish.

KELLY'S SOUTHERN CLIPPER WHEAT   **BP**   **0.7**
(Key West, Florida)
Weak, with no clove taste; not lightbodied and not particularly
thirst-quenching; slice of lemon overwhelms rather than complements the flavor; slightly bitter, but so what? Seems to be devoid
of alcohol, or anything else with even minimal vivacity, liveliness,
or zest.

KEO Lager   **CB**   **3.1**
(Limassol, Cyprus)
Malty aroma, hoppy taste, with a dash of fishiness just to make
things interesting; grainy presence comes forward, especially with
spicy or salty foods; improves—tastier, more complex, better
balanced—the more you drink it; reasonably steady Brussels lace
diverts the eye from washed-out yellow color; finishes pleasantly
grainy, but with little to no carbonation and definitely no head;
generally friendly beer. Try with cheese/jalapeño nachos, kalamata olives, and salty snack foods.

KESSLER ALE   **MB**   **2.3**
(Helena, Montana)
Fruity and slightly bitter and spicy; otherwise a rather run-of-
the-mill beer taste, though there is a following hint of malt flavor and aroma; never really defines itself; finishes like tea with
lemon. Try it with lightly salted snack foods.

**KESSLER LORELEI EXTRA PALE
LAGER**   **MB**   **3.2**
(Helena, Montana)

Soft crispness and mild, placid flavor make it easy to handle; fruitiness emerges at mid-bottle; appropriate balance and complexity finish this surprisingly approachable beer. Try it with meat or chicken potpies, rice and beans, or sourdough bread with cheese.

QUAFF QUOTE

" **W** hat a beautiful world it was once. . . . You could leave beer to cool in the river, and it would be so cold when you got back it wouldn't foam much. It would be a beer made in the next town if the town were ten thousand or over. So it was either Kessler Beer made in Helena or Highlander Beer made in Missoula . . . . What a wonderful world it was once when all the beer was not made in Milwaukee, Minneapolis, or Saint Louis."

—**Norman Maclean,** *A River Runs Through It*

KEY DARK Lager   **CB**   **1.2**
(Victoria, British Columbia, Canada)

Too smooth and watery, no immediate—or eventual—discernible taste; mildly bitter, but that's about it; slight alcoholic warmth eventually pushes its way through, but not enough to really notice; try something else.

KEYSTONE Pilsener   **CB**   **0.9**
(Golden, Colorado)

Mildly acrid citrus flavor, with paper-thin body and somewhat old mouthfeel; chemically induced head stays throughout; remains green-tasting and unfulfilling despite can's special inner lining designed to reduce metallic taste; what we have here is not the "Quality bottled beer taste" it bills itself as providing.

KEY WEST LAGER   **MB**   **0.4**
(Key West, Florida)

Sweet and sour rather than bitter; somewhat medicinal mouthfeel; off-putting in its off-taste; looks like sauterne wine; aroma is old in presentation and unpleasant; close to unpalatable, even with a faint increase in maltiness toward the end.

KEY WEST SUNSET ALE   MB   2.2
(Key West, Florida)

Fresh, fruity aroma; caramel-malt taste is seamlessly followed by a citrus-fruit mouthfeel; malty, but doesn't taste like top-of-the-line malt—weak and not particularly flavorful; faint metallic aspect masquerades as bitter; a decent effort at the beginning, but then too many negatives take over; redeemed somewhat at the end as malt resurfaces and brings back some of the flavor; a rather iffy beer.

KILKENNY IRISH BEER—EXPORT
Lager   CB   3.0
(St. Francis Abbey in Kilkenny, Ireland)

Persistently hoppy mouthfeel defines this beer; rapidly disappearing bitterness; soft mouthfeel, especially from the pillowy head; concentrated malt aroma; not particularly complex; chestnut-red body; finishes with a creamy malt taste that stays on the tongue until the last swallow; a pleasant enough brew, with no outstanding features. Sitting at the bar, order up some peanuts for substance.

KILLIAN'S RED ALE   CB   2.0
(brewed by Coors in Golden, Colorado)

Vague cherry lollipop taste with sharp pinprick texture; cloying sweetness at the back of the tongue needs starchy, absorbent food to temper it; distinctive non-American taste; thin in texture; bad tendency for the round, sweet caramel-like taste to rapidly give way to modulated sharpness.

KING & BARNES IPA   CB   2.7
(Horsham, England)

Floral aroma; hop taste tinged with caramel; prickly, then smooth on the roof of the mouth; vanilla overtones help make this sweet and rich for an IPA; chocolate undertone in the aftertaste; finishes with a coffee-grind aroma and slightly bitter and buttery mouthfeel. Well made, but too many interfering blemishes. Try with raw vegetables, like carrot sticks and celery stalks.

KING COBRA MALT LIQUOR   CB   2.2
(St. Louis, Missouri)

Rounded mild flavor with raw green overlay; remains even-tasting throughout a meal; some fizziness, though it is essentially flat-tasting; not much body; Bronze Medal winner at the 1993 Great American Beer Festival.

KINGFISHER LAGER   CT   2.8
(brewed and bottled in England for United Breweries, Bangalore, India)

Robust and tasty grain presence; integrated flavor is underpinned by cold-water blandness; early on, the taste unpredictably peaks and flattens out from sip to sip; persistent tangy sweetness offers a cooling balance to spicy foods; oddly enough, with food the up-and-down vagaries of the beer settle into an interesting routine. A calming complement to curried rice, tandoori chicken, and other Indian dishes.

KINGPIN Lager CB 1.0
(Mansfield, England)
Pallid, flat, thin, and essentially unexpressive; slight body appears tentatively and fleetingly; label advises "Best consumed within 3 days of opening"—that's being presumptuous, and optimistic; a "college" beer meant for large-scale consumption, without much attention to quality. Drink with dorm or pub food.

KIRIN DRAFT Lager CB 2.0
(Tokyo, Japan; brewed for the Japanese market, not for export)
Brewed for the Japanese market, not exported; sharp and attention-getting, with brief flowery follow-through; close to full-bodied; flavor comes and quickly goes, replaced by flat, almost metallic taste; doesn't integrate well with food; leaves a thickish aftertaste on the tongue; hard to discern the ingredients in this beer; too sharp and unforgiving.

KIRIN DRAFT Pilsener CB 3.9
(Vancouver, British Columbia, Canada)
Sharp, straightforward taste and texture; mellow crispness accompanies an airy top with a heavy underpinning; emotionally and spiritually satisfying, but not physically filling, making it easy to enjoy more than one; retains aesthetic vigor to the last drop; smooth and charming throughout. Nice with crisp raw vegetables, salads with sprouts, or mild soft cheeses with unsalted crackers.

KIRIN ICHIBAN MALT LIQUOR CB 4.0
(Tokyo, Japan)
Hoppy, sweet tang greets nose immediately, with follow-up cold, rounded sharp taste that prepares the tongue for more; grain presence is full and complex; dry; tends to cling to the roof of the mouth; strength and character mesh well with food; higher alcohol content is well hidden within the nuances of malt and hops; strong and full of character; clearly a quality, well-thought-out product. Goes well with barbecued and grilled foods.

KIRIN LAGER CB 3.9
(Tokyo, Japan)
Crisp, but not sharp on the first and subsequent sips; malt is tangible and accommodating to food; clearly high quality, and clearly made for mass consumption, with none of the nuances or little touches that often personalize a beer as well put together as this one. Excellent with fruited meat dishes and Japanese cuisine.

KIWI LAGER CB 4.0
(Timaru, New Zealand)
Nicely crisp and fresh throughout; satisfyingly fills the mouth with tantalizing faint hop/barley taste that perfectly fits ongoing crackliness of texture; grain taste is even more deliciously apparent; fresh and invigorating—have more than one to gain full pleasure. A good complement to all but hot/spicy foods.

KLOSTER SCHWARZBIER—MONKSHOF
Lager CB 2.9
(Kulmbach, Germany)
Texturally complex, with a thread of sweetness from start to finish; pleasant lingering taste; dark and brooding; too syrupy to be rated higher, but a good complement to a barbecued chicken sandwich.

KLOSTERBOCK MONKSHOF
Malt Liquor CB 2.3
(Kulmbach, Germany)
Faint, quickly disappearing burnt taste that is more acute at the back of the mouth; sweet but not cloying; transient, somewhat watery flavor; drink this without food.

KOBANYAI VILAGOS SOR pilsener CB 2.3
(Budapest, Hungary)
Sweet at the outset; sheet of sharpness melts into a faintly grainy taste with hints of sourness; flavors come together at mid-bottle, offering some previously missing complexity; malty aroma emerges as beer reaches room temperature; texture becomes smooth and lifeless; loses its fizz too soon; an up-and-down beer with, alas, more downs than ups. Redeemed somewhat with vegetable stew.

LABEL LORE

*I*n Hungarian, *világos* means "pilsener" and *sör* translates to "beer."

KODIAK PREMIUM LAGER CT 2.5
(Saskatoon, Saskatchewan, Canada)
Mild; a bit sour, but pleasantly hoppy; well balanced, crisp, and roughly smooth; becomes more subdued with food; sweetness stretches toward the end; mild and somewhat matter-of-fact; recommended for those just beginning to sample the wonderful world of beer and others who just want a nonthreatening, easy sipping drink; finishes with a hint of yeasty aroma; disappoints in the end—clearly its potential has not been approached.

KOFF Lager   **CB**   **3.6**
(Helsinki, Finland)

Flat on first sip; restrained aftertaste with small bubbles provides a nice fizziness at the back of the throat; in general, invigorating, playing very well to taste expectations; soft, modulated finish is somewhat surprising, but certainly acceptable. Quite compatible with chicken and pasta.

KOKANEE GLACIER PILSENER (draft) CB   **3.4**
(Creston, British Columbia, Canada)

Creamy, soft, and chewy; calm and laid-back; flavorful and substantive, with integrated graininess that remains intact and consistent with food; crisp, with staying power; appropriate for a warm, not hot, day, with time to idle away. Try it with summer seafood dishes.

KONA PACIFIC GOLDEN ALE   **MB**   **2.6**
(Kailua-Kona, Hawaii)

Fruity sweetness has some appropriate grit on the roof of the mouth; gradual increase in bitterness slices through the sweetness, nicely balancing the mouthfeel; perfumey, flowery character steps up at mid-bottle; smooth, insidious bitterness wells up and vies for your attention; nice, light-honey presence is evident in the last few sips. Drink this with light, warm-weather fare or a refreshing fruit salad for dessert.

KOSMOS RESERVE LAGER (draft)   **CB**   **3.0**
(Shiner, Texas)

Full-bodied and quite chewy, with distinct hop bitterness that follows a rounded bittersweet presence on the roof of the mouth; gentle, lasting, figurative Brussels lace—its presence enhances your enjoyment of the undulating, alive taste and texture; vague citrus feel lurks in background; enjoyable fullness three-quarters of the way through. Good—but be careful of the follow-through: it may pucker the sides of your mouth without warning. Pair with a good old mustard-slathered American hot dog.

B E E R   F A C T

*K*osmos, brewed by the Spoetzl Brewery, makers of Shiner beer, was named in honor of the company's original brewmaster, Kosmos Spoetzl.

KOZEL PREMIUM CZECH
MALT LIQUOR   **CB**   **4.0**
(Velké Popovice, Czech Republic)

Strong and assertive; refreshing bitterness carries everything else along; texturally sharp; hearty and to the point, with hops galore; bright white foamy head unfortunately quickly disappears; softens at the end; otherwise a tough, tasty, and tenacious beer that has a life of its own, like mustard spicing up a tasty morsel. An appropriate partner with simple sandwiches of sliced meat.

QUAFF QUOTE

"Malt liquors undoubtedly assist in the support of the body, and are in practical effect equivalent to so much easily digested food."
—John Bickerdyke,
The Curiosities of Ale & Beer (ca. 1890)

KRAKUS LIGHT Pilsener　　　　CB　　　　2.1
(Zywiec, Poland)
Very pleasant wheat aroma that quickly falters; thin and watery, with virtually no zest or fizz; no head or smoothness; sweet and pleasant, though clearly not fully developed; charming, but unable to offer a whole lot with food.

KRONEN CLASSIC ALL DARK Lager　　CB　　2.1
(Dortmund, Germany)
Rather undistinguished—you wait for an increase in appeal and nothing happens; flat to no head with faded deep-red body; hint of warmth and caramel sweetness toward the end; flat, bland, and, unfortunately, very predictable.

KRONENBOURG BIERE DE NOEL
Lager　　　　　　　　　　　CB　　　　2.8
(annual)
(Strasbourg, France)
Very, very mild taste; mainly sweetness at the front edges of the tongue and bitterness at the back of the mouth; vaguely cloying; quite malty, like drinking caramel, but not overwhelmingly so; full-bodied; good soft, foamy head stays and nicely tops off the light-amber body; caramel malt wafts up gently at the finish; this beer engages a lot of senses but unfortunately not all at the same time or in equivalent measure. Appropriate with hearty Christmas dinner of sliced ham and sweet potatoes.

KRONENBOURG PALE Lager　　　CB　　　3.1
(Strasbourg, France)
Rich golden color; sparkling, malty, and strong; combined wine/ beer taste, as befits its geographic location; medium-bodied and nicely balanced; some sharpness; has potential to wear thin too soon. Goes very well with duck and chicken.

KROPF DARK DRAFT Lager CB 2.6
(Kassel, Germany)

Molasses aroma precedes light, but sharp, fizziness with a rounded appealing swallow; satisfying without being challenging or pushy; finishes with a hint of sweetness and subtle malt; pleasant but not exciting. A friendly backdrop to casual lunch foods such as a grilled cheese sandwich.

KROPF DRAFT Lager CB 2.3
(Kassel, Germany)

Fruity, musty taste with sharp texture on first sip; fullness grows but fades into the background; some solidity and mild warmth are maintained; complexity tentatively emerges along with an appealing roundedness at the end of the bottle. Good with steaks and hamburgers.

TAP TIP

Your Nose, Your Glass, and You

Proper attention to glasses can make a great difference when tasting beers. Lack of a good head of foam might indicate the presence of grease or detergent film on the glass. Next time you're at a bar, smell an empty glass. A musty odor indicates the probable presence of dishwashing detergent. At home, rinse the glass with hot water—and nonperfumed detergent—and let it stand to dry.

Also, the thinner the sides of the glass, the quicker your beer will warm up, particularly if you wrap your hand around the glass. That's one reason beers meant to be consumed warm—most ales, for example—are generally served in goblets or tumblers that can be held by wrapping your hand around the glass; on the other hand, cold beers, like lagers, are often offered in mugs with handles to keep body warmth away from the thick glass surrounding the liquid.

KROPF EDEL PILS CB 2.5
(Kassel, Germany)

Kind of hoppy at the outset; bland foretaste succeeded by subtle, complex ongoing taste involving the malts and yeast and hops; after the first bottle, the beer becomes lifeless and loses distinction; lack of depth hinders its staying power. Good with hot dogs with sauerkraut or grilled sausage sandwiches.

KUNSTMANN LAGER   MB   2.7
(Valdivia, Chile)
Uplifting effervescence brings along a sweetish clove taste that is
a little flat on the tongue; sharp; slowly evolving licorice taste;
texture tends toward flatness; pleasurable malt-hop balance.

KWAK Ale   CB   2.1
(Buggenhout, Belgium)
Wine aroma with dull, sweet, fruity wine taste that settles generously on the tongue; sweet acidity lingers on the palate, detracting from the taste of food; deep-amber color misleads you
into expecting a more full-bodied, caramel taste, though there is
some of that; sweetness increases as the glass is emptied, turning
it into a rather unwanted experience; you do need a particular
interest in this assertively tart, dry style (known as *zuur* in Flanders) to enjoy it; food is important to help absorb some of the
alcohol and acidity. Try with strong cheese before a meal.

LA BELLE STRASBOURGEOISE Lager   CB   2.9
(Schiltigheim, France)
Heartier and sharper than some German and/or Austrian beers,
but not as heavy or hoppy; pleasing sharpness distracts you, but
not enough to keep you from wondering why you didn't order
a stronger beer. Overwhelmed by full-flavored foods.

LA FIN DU MONDE Ale   CB   3.3
(Chambly, Quebec, Canada)
Increasing clove taste integrates smoothly with fruity yeast aroma
and flavor; assertive and strong, in various combinations; thick
airy head on top of blond body gives off a light, evanescent feel;
malt-yeast interaction takes center stage, though yeast keeps the
upper hand; sweetens perceptibly at the end; this is for experienced beer drinkers only, not for the faint of heart. Sip it after
the meal, when everyone else has gone home.

LA GAILLARDE ALE ON LEES   RB   2.4
(Chambly, Quebec, Canada)
Fresh, full yeast aroma; yeast tartness provides a good counterpoint to the sweet and deliciously fruity mouthfeel; a redeeming
sharpness cuts across all the ingredients and then goes away;
wheat-colored body has a charming peach blush; flat matte-like
character eases the yeast and cereal grains into a generous, full-
bodied aftertaste; starts to weaken just as you're settling back to
enjoy it; could be heartier and zestier; runs out of gas at the end.

LA GUILLOTINE BELGIAN ALE   CB   3.2
(Melle and Ghent, Belgium)
Yeasty and tart, with a very spicy nutmeg aroma; eye-catching,
strikingly white rocky head of foam leaves scattered irregular patterns of Brussels lace at different spots on the inside of the glass;

yeast becomes a more integrated part of the beer, imparting a mild fruitiness that balances the continuing tartness; finishes smooth with a definite clove sweetness, which in turn softens all the sharpness that came before; nicely done. Pair with freshwater fish or light seafood.

LA TRAPPE ALE   AB   3.9
(Tilburg, Holland)

Not overwhelmingly fruity; mildly acidic; moderated sweetness with sharp after-bite; hazy reddish-brown color adds to the European ambiance; remains crisp and fresh with cidery overtones; fizzy, loosely bubbled head diminishes quickly, but adds to the sharpness while it lasts; holds character and balance from start to finish; predominance of tangy hops makes itself apparent; good example of style; nicely settled sediment on the bottom; definitely well made but not to my taste; ends on a sweet note. Works well with sweetened pork dishes.

LA TRAPPE TRAPPIST ALE—
QUADRUPEL   CB   3.9
(Tilburg, Holland)

A strong core of alcohol anchors a finely calibrated apple cider taste; the high alcohol content makes you sit up and take notice, but it fits in just right, never overwhelming or intrusive; crystalline sheets of Brussels lace nicely complement the cratered off-white head; understated interplay of malt, hops, yeast, and alcohol is in just the right balance. A delightful after-dinner drink, especially with spiced pie or cake.

LABATT'S Pilsener   CB   3.1
(Vancouver, British Columbia, Canada)

Uncomplicated but good taste in the back of the mouth; some crispness offset by rounded, sweetish malt body; flavor tends to flatten relatively quickly; label proudly announces "Union Made." Okay with hamburgers and other sandwiches.

LABATT'S BLUE PILSENER   CB   3.1
(Vancouver, British Columbia, Canada)

Flavorful and fresh; consistent taste and texture, though lacking in subtlety; crispness increases with food, but ingredients remain relatively subdued; falls short of its promise. Compatible with fresh seafood.

LABATT'S 50 Ale   CB   3.7
(Vancouver, British Columbia, Canada)

Understatedly crisp and fresh, with not-quite-fruity aroma; taste grows on you, steadily and consistently; finishes with a hint of sourness that may or may not be attributable to food; warm and friendly enough to request another bottle. Subtly compatible with Italian foods.

LABATT CLASSIC LAGER (see John Labatt Classic, page 169)

**LABATT'S VELVET CREAM STOUT   CB   3.1
(Edmonton, Alberta, Canada)**
Full at the back of the throat, thin at the sides of the tongue; sweet fullness with a rim of bitterness at the back of the tongue; deep brown-black color is a bit muddy with a hint of red; no head to speak of; mushy at the end. Good with mildly flavored chicken dishes and relatively bland grain and rice dishes.

**LAGUNA BAY AUSTRALIAN PALE ALE   MB   2.8
(Indooroopilly, Queensland, Australia)**
Light caramel malt taste is accompanied by a hint of bitterness, but nothing serious; moderately prickly on the tongue; flavor could be richer, but that's not the Australian way; nothing subtle here, everything is direct and pointed; gains flavor and appropriate sourness as it warms; smooth, almost flat at the end—it doesn't insist that you enjoy what it has to offer; a refreshing summertime drink.

**LAGUNITAS DOG TOWN PALE ALE   MB   3.4
(Petaluma, California)**
Tastes fresh-brewed out of the bottle, with a medium hoppiness that's just right; the hint of fruitiness is snapped off at the swallow by a bitter bite; aroma is fresh and bready, accompanied by a sharp, hoppy aromatic character underneath; suggestions of nuttiness arise from the careful blending of sweet and bitter; dry; finishes with a nicely calibrated hop-spiciness; very satisfying. Try with light sandwich fare.

**LAKEFRONT CHERRY LAGER   MB   2.7
(Milwaukee, Wisconsin)**
Slightly bitter and slightly cherry; mini-fizziness on the tongue; sweetens a bit; calm and smooth; light and easy to swallow; grows on you sip after sip; tasty and charming, but not balanced enough to send it above average; label calls it "a hand-crafted seasonal delight." Goes surprisingly well with cheese pizza.

**LAKEFRONT CREAM CITY PALE ALE   MB   2.3
(Milwaukee, Wisconsin)**
Tart, with a hop punch that is felt from the front of the mouth to the back of the throat; taste fades at mid-bottle, settling into a milder, more equitably balanced brew; malt becomes more of a partner to the hops, rather than being dominant and subservient; almost full-bodied; finishes a bit malty; sudsy ivory-colored head stays thick and foamy. Good with sharp cheeses or seafood.

**LAKEFRONT PUMPKIN LAGER   MB   3.8
(Milwaukee, Wisconsin)**
Immediate spice and pumpkin aroma and taste make you want more, more, more; sharply smooth and entirely beguiling; pump-

kin is brewed right into the beer, along with well-integrated cinnamon and nutmeg; the only thing missing is the pie crust; this
is not a gimmick beer, it is definitely the real thing; try it year-
round, if you can get it. Perfect with turkey dinner. Surprised?

LAL TOOFAN INDIAN PILSENER   CB   2.1
(Trowbridge, England)

Mild carbonated texture is soft and fizzy, almost soda-like; mildly
bitter; uncomplicated, dry, and almost mouth-puckering; thickish mouthfeel, due to the rice, offers a fullness in the mouth; balance of ingredients at the end is too little and too late; not a
pilsener with punch or verve, but rather sedate and uninvigorating. Try with not-too-spicy Indian food.

L A B E L   L O R E

*L*al Toofan means "Red Storm" in Hindi, which
seems an odd name for a pretty sleepy pilsener.

LANCASTER MILK STOUT   MB   2.3
(Lancaster, Pennsylvania)

Soft and smooth, with a milky-sweet flavor and faint burnt taste
reminiscent of roasted chestnuts; there is, as well, a definite roasted-
coffee character; tarry, sticky mouthfeel kind of gums things up
a bit; coffee presence increases, but overall remains relatively passive and uncomplex; burnt-brown body. Goes with bonbons or
other chocolate candy.

LANDLORD STRONG PALE ALE   CB   2.9
(Keighley, England)

Clover-honey sweetness goes directly to the upper palate; restrained hoppiness settles into the main flow of the liquid; emerging bitterness is acceptable after sweetness passes; definitely mellows
as it warms; ends dry with subtle character; a beer that definitely
improves during the course of a meal; the rating is primarily based
on its finish. Up-and-coming graininess matches nicely with well-
spiced dishes like beef fajitas.

LANDSKRON PILS   CB   3.8
(Radeberg, Germany)

Immediate yeast/grain aroma and taste; texture is duller than expected; appealing honey sweetness remains central; color is light
and golden; less carbonation and not as zippy and zesty as many
other pilseners, but pleasing and almost sensuous. A good match
with barbecue, spicy sausages, or choucroute garni.

LAPIN KULTA Lager   **CB**   **2.2**
(Helsinki, Finland)

Fresh, clean, and semi-sharp; relatively tasteless and short on nuance; remains low-key and unassertive, but not unpleasant; hard to detect alcohol content, though it is supposedly present; ditto for hops and malt; texture is more attractive than taste, leaving you less than half satisfied, which is not enough to try this again.

B E E R   F A C T

*F*inland, like its neighboring countries, restricts beer advertising, usually allowing it only for the lowest-alcohol-content brews. Unadvertised Lapin Kulta is in Class IVA, giving it an alcohol strength a little above the typical American pilsener (3.6% to 4.9%/volume) and about the same as an American premium pilsener (4.5% to 5.5%/volume).

LCL PILS   **CB**   **2.4**
(Newcastle-upon-Tyne, England)

Lightly spiced aroma, with a touch of easy-going hoppiness; not very fizzy or complex; pale-straw body is overshadowed by the thick, slowly diminishing head; picturesque cobwebby strands of Brussels lace adhere tenaciously to the sides of the glass; overall, too weak and unexciting; ingredients are too well hidden, if they are there at all.

B E E R   F A C T

*L*CL Pils is made by the Federation Brewery, a northern England brewery owned by a group of workingman's clubs from the area. Its beer is served in the House of Commons.

L'EAU BENITE TRIPLE Ale   **CB**   **2.4**
(Chambly, Quebec, Canada)

Somewhat doughy, with a very noticeable yeasty taste; honey flavor expands to take in a tingle of spice; increasingly complex as it warms; yeast aroma becomes sharper and more apparent; overall, more sweet than bitter; late-arriving fruit-juice mouthfeel joins up with the residual honey, resulting in a mildly bitter finish. Try with soft cheese and crackers.

LEAVENWORTH BLIND PIG
DUNKEL WEIZEN (draft)   BP   3.0
(Leavenworth, Washington)

A flavorful and understated beer that makes you sit up and take immediate notice; yeasty citrus presence is precise and fulfilling; tantalizingly dry; muted malty taste exudes chocolate overtones; muddy brown body suggests it's heavier than it actually is; finishes a bit watery; with just a little work, this brew can go far. Try it with smoked cheeses.

LEAVENWORTH HODGSON'S IPA
(draft)   MB   2.5
(Leavenworth, Washington)

Filling and fruity, but lacking in strength; zesty and fresh-tasting, though not particularly complex; malty fruitiness makes for a nice balance with the less-than-full hops flavor; light-amber color; minimal carbonation; keeps your interest; on the way to being a good IPA, but not yet there. Try it with pizza.

LECH PILS
                                           CB   0.2
(Lech, Poland)

Tasteless, unless you call "sour" and "metallic" tastes to be reckoned with; perhaps spoiled; no head; smells like gunpowder; thin and watery; no redeeming qualities are apparent except for a hint of malt aroma halfway through; label reads "Official Sponsor of the Polish Olympic Team in the USA '96."

LEEUW PILSENER
                                           CB   3.2
(Limburg, Holland)

Clean and flavorful overall; moderate effervescence; soft, inviting taste; invigorating, distinctive mouthfeel slides into mildly sour aftertaste; well made; good example of a Dutch pilsener without any pretensions. Goes with cheese or ham sandwiches.

LEFFE BLOND ALE
                                           CB   3.1
(Leffe, Belgium)

Tart and sharp with slight mustiness; full yeast taste increases as beer warms; nice balance between hops and malt, with gentle bitterness predominating; slight haze fuzzes up pale-blond color; minimal winey aroma; sweet alcohol finish; in general, a good representative of the style. A nice match for Southern-style foods, such as fried chicken and honey-glazed baked ham.

LEINENKUGEL'S BERRY WEISS
                                           CB   2.1
(Chippewa Falls, Wisconsin)

Rather intense, concentrated raspberry/blueberry-cross taste is enveloped in fizzy soda-like texture; might be a slight touch of hops in there somewhere, absorbing, thankfully, some of the fruity sweetness; foamy, creamy Brussels lace adheres to sides of glass as liquid goes down; when poured, the stream of liquid is a translucent light purple-violet; more like soda than beer, thereby making it appropriate with potato chips or other junk food.

LEINENKUGEL'S BIG BUTT
DOPPELBOCK   CB   2.2
(Chippewa Falls, Wisconsin)
Smooth; hint of spices and fresh vegetables; faint fresh doughy aroma; rather creamy in texture; rich, thick mouthfeel; more subtle than your usual bock; malty sweetness becomes too annoying; needs more alcohol balance; a bit sour at the end; finishes too weak and uninteresting for a bock, much less a doppelbock, which should be stronger still. Try with lightly smoked beef.

LEINENKUGEL'S ORIGINAL PREMIUM
Lager   CB   3.1
(Chippewa Falls, Wisconsin)
Thin, light, and sweet; thick, airy head remains for at least half of the bottle; even-tasting; almost flat, but not distracting; distinctive in its mildly sweet blandness; may just grow on you after two to three bottles; typically Midwestern: mild, beguiling, and undemanding; Gold Medal winner at the 1993 Great American Beer Festival. Try it with grilled or barbecued red meats, baked beans, or a hearty black bean soup.

LEINENKUGEL'S RED LAGER   CB   2.1
(Chippewa Falls, Wisconsin)
Brutish and fizzy, with no complexity; a nasty undertone; unstylish and straightforward; hint of sweetness; fast-disappearing Brussels lace and dirty amber-chocolate color reflect neither a good lager nor a good example of the namesake color; some substance struggles through at the end, but essentially a disappointment; flat and uninvigorating.

LENINGRAD COWBOY LAGER   CT   2.3
(Helsinki, Finland)
Somewhat rough and raw; underlying pleasant malty sweetness; focus is on the sweetness; uncomplex; mid-bottle brings a slight malty aroma; hop-malt balance improves at the end; pale-gold body; taste fluctuates too much to be predictable and therefore it's not entirely satisfying. It's a hamburger and French fries beer.

LEON DE ORO CERVEZA ESPECIAL
Lager   CB   3.8
(Antartida, Argentina)
Warm, enveloping honey aroma accompanies warm, filling honey taste underpinned by lightning strike of carbonation/fizziness and hint of lemon; flattens and weakens but hangs on to its core flavor by the end of the bottle; essentially tasty and attractive; based on one note, it still holds promise. Satisfying with burritos, empanadas, and other South-of-the-border foods.

LEONA CERVEZA Pilsener   CB   2.2
(Bogota, Colombia)
Fresh honey-like aroma; sharp, thin mouthfeel reminiscent of
ginger ale, including the light-straw color; texture has liveliness;
overall flavor sensation is rather lifeless and bland, with vague
hints of flavor to come (which never does); no head or Brussels
lace; no suggestion of malt or hops, though some perfumey sweetness is present at the end; not bad, just not there when you want
it. Goes with hot dogs and hamburgers.

LEOPARD DELUXE Pilsener   CB   3.0
(Hastings, New Zealand)
Bland but tasty; bitter initial mouthfeel; smooth and unobtrusive; appealing mild hop presence and faint fruitiness enhance
this light-to-medium-bodied brew; increasing strength halfway
through the bottle. A reliable seafood companion.

LIEFMANS KRIEKBIER Ale   CB   3.9
(seasonal)
(Oudenaarde, Belgium)
Queen Anne cherry-red color; mild and smooth with a sweet and
sour balance; cross between beer and wine; minor sparkle on the
tongue; if this were a delicate wine, it would be overwhelmed by
any food; subdued cherry flavor nicely balanced by fermentation
and the yeastiness itself, charming and delightful; some stick-to-
your-tongue texture; full and musty at the end. Perfect for sipping after dinner with a chocolate dessert.

B E E R   F A C T

*B*rewed once a year at the time of the July harvest of Schaerbeeck cherries, Liefmans Kriekbier is made with the addition of 1 pound of this
relatively scarce shiny red fruit to each gallon of
6-months-aged Goudenband Brown Ale. The resulting
product is then matured for 8 months, after which it
is filtered and bottled in champagne-like bottles and
stored in the brewery's caves. It is at least 2 years old
by the time it reaches the retailer's shelves.

LIMACHE CERVEZA TIPO CRUDA
Lager   CB   3.2
(Limache, Chile)
Fills the mouth on the first sip; fresh and peppy in the throat,
with a hint of acidity that is acceptable and refreshing; flavors
are uninhibited, allowed to circulate and percolate though the

texture is a bit flat; it maintains its integrity and character nonetheless; a little thin and almost salty at the end; when this beer is drunk fresh, it is integrated and has interest. Try with a *completo* (Chilean sausage with garnishes).

LIND RASPBERRY WHEAT   MB   0.9
(San Leandro, California)

Raspberry flavor is full and genuine, but tastes and smells like soda pop, without the fizz; overall, flat and boring; uncomplicated, with no interesting features.

LINDEMANS KRIEK-LAMBIC   CB   2.0
(Vlezenbeek, Belgium)

This red Belgian cherry-flavored brew tastes and smells like the cherry sodas I knew as a kid—with more bite, of course, but the same amount of sparkle; resembles a spritzy wine cooler; indeed, more of a wine than a beer; label touts it as one of the five best beers in the world, but it's too thin, light, and sweetly fruity to be on my best beer list; comes in a thick green corked bottle; drink in a champagne glass. Clearly a pre-dinner drink or an after-meal companion with a fresh fruit dessert and cheese.

LINDEMANS PECHE LAMBIC   CB   1.3
(Vlezenbeek, Belgium)

Immediate peach aroma—like a peach liqueur mixed with Sprite: sweet and overachieving; similar to peach-flavored champagne—hard to know it's a beer; ingredients from different worlds are brought together in a cheap wine-cooler taste; too fruity to go with food; finish is like old canned juice or semi-alcoholic cider; sticks to the roof of the mouth. An after-dinner drink.

LION RED lager   CB   2.5
(Auckland, New Zealand)

Hoppily bitter and tart with a sharp balancing texture; malty mouthfeel crawls forward at mid-bottle; underlying malty mellowness is the main positive feature of this firm, stalwart beer; rather charming sweet aroma is also a plus; sits a little too heavily on the stomach; hint of alcohol becomes more of a presence toward the end. Pub food supports the already noticeable hop-malt balance.

LITTLE KING'S CREAM ALE   CB   2.0
(Cincinnati, Ohio)

Soft and creamy; hint of bitterness; mellow quick refreshment with little substance or flavor profile; basically it does its appointed job, which is to cool you down, quench your thirst, and encourage enjoyment of the food—so why complain? Good with grilled meat or poultry.

LOBKO BOHEMIAN LAGER VYSOKY   CB   4.1
(Chlumec, Czech Republic)
Highly grainy, with a continuing and balancing touch of hops;
a dash of malt sweetness enhances the very pleasant mouthfeel;
shiny clear gold body showcases the tiny, rapidly rising bubbles
as they bump against the bottom of the airy, tightly woven, white
creamy head; subtly increasing bitterness adds a flavorful punch
that stays until the end, where it meets up with a reinvigorated
hoppy-sweet character; complex and finely tuned, this is a damn
fine beer. Goes well with a variety of traditional middle-
European dishes.

LONDON LIGHT Pilsener   CB   2.2
(London, England)
Watery and very lightly carbonated; empty-tasting, as if there are
no innards; not unpleasant going down; a bit sour at the end—
but at least that suggests it's alive. Nice with tomato soup and a
ham sandwich.

LONE STAR Lager   CB   3.1
(San Antonio, Texas)
Traditional crisp, common-beer mouthfeel; a workingman's brew
with minimal body; fresh-tasting and to the point; a beer you
could drink a lot of, but wouldn't necessarily write home about;
"The National Beer of Texas"; Silver Medal winner at the 1993
Great American Beer Festival and Bronze Medal winner in 1994.
Pour with down-home dishes such as chicken-fried steak with
mashed potatoes and black-eyed peas.

LONG TRAIL ALE   MB   3.3
(Bridgewater Corners, Vermont)
Fine-tuned bitterness; fluffy, soft head serves as a filter for the
smooth, integrated clove taste that greets the first sips; clove presence then gives way to the gently dispensed hop flavor which
lingers in the aftertaste; clean-tasting and fullbodied; fresh, malty
aroma arises toward the end; flavorful hop bite completes this
well-done ale. Drink with a comforting dessert, like apple pie or
applesauce.

LONGXIANG Pilsner   CB   2.1
(Beijing, China)
Mildly fruity with thickness on the tongue; lightly carbonated;
remains flat, but with promise that unfortunately goes nowhere;
sweet, benign malt taste; not quite bland but certainly not full of
flavor; actually more watery taste as bottle is emptied; needs good,
zesty fistful of roasted nuts to pep it up. Match with Szechuan
and Hunan food.

LORD CHESTERFIELD ALE   CB   2.5
(Pottsville, Pennsylvania)
Light and fizzy with ongoing aftertaste; ordinary golden color; moderate hop aroma; rather unassuming, without hint of briskness; sweetness emerges after a while, so it is more flavorful at mid-bottle than at outset; quietly competent and unexceptional. Serve with pork chops or simple chicken entrees.

LORIMER'S SCOTTISH BEER Ale   CB   2.6
(Edinburgh, Scotland)
Sharp honey aroma and taste; expected jolt from fizz doesn't materialize; burnt, smoky paper taste comes on quickly and dominates; dark apple-cider color with gilt-brown undertones, shades, and shadows; malty and mildly pungent at the finish, with a thinnish texture as if running out of oomph; almost, but not quite, an ale. Doesn't keep up with accompanying foods.

LOS GATOS OKTOBERFEST Ale (draft) BP   0.1
(seasonal)
(Los Gatos, California)
A little bit of citrus with a taste of sulfur that even the hops can't hide; remains uninviting, with an unpleasantly sour emphasis; green and raw; hard to finish (starting wasn't easy, either). FYI: This is a seasonal beer brewed in October.

LOST COAST DOWNTOWN
BROWN ALE   MB   3.2
(Eureka, California)
Full, tasty, and entertainingly balanced; smooth, with pleasant yeast aroma; nice creamy smoothness, with thin but consistent head; lends mildly fruity, faint, and tart counterbalance to roasted main dishes; well made; taste and texture flatten at the end; Bronze Medal winner at the 1993 Great American Beer Festival. Fine with roasted poultry and meats or a green salad.

LOST COAST STOUT   MB   3.3
(Eureka, California)
Appropriately bitter burnt-malt taste; smooth with rough edges; coppery, somewhat thin head; quickly becomes flat, especially up against spicy dishes; not as mouth-filling as a stout should be, but otherwise has most style characteristics; a step or two away from being a top-quality confection; sweet, gentle finish; very good beginning, but brewer must learn to master the ending as well. Serve with game meats with grilled mushrooms.

LOWENBRAU PREMIUM DARK   CB   2.8
(Toronto, Canada)
Immediately exudes a sweet, rich maltiness that unashamedly shows off its depth and character; subtly complex; pleasant, lightly roasted malty aroma delicately balances the restrained hop taste;

sweet maltiness lingers comfortably on the palate; dark amber liquid has clear, red highlights; easy-going and medium-bodied from stem to stern; not challenging, but pleasant and well-made. Try with mildly-flavored meats.

L A B E L   L O R E

*L*öwenbräu, one of German brewing's Big Six, is produced and distributed in North America by Labatt's under the slogan "Original Munich Formula." It has been Canadian brewed since October 1999, in accordance with the centuries-old German Purity Law. The yeast strain is the same one used continuously at Löwenbräu's Munich brewery since 1890.

LOWENBRAU PREMIUM LAGER   **CB**   **2.7**
(Toronto, Canada)
Brewed with attention to its German heritage, this lager has regained its sparkly mouthfeel and full grainy flavor and aroma; lightly malted and nicely balanced; slight bitterness spreads evenly on the tongue; holds its flavor and lets you savor it over time; finishes slightly bitter, with a grapefruity sweetness at the final swallow. Good with a meat sandwich, but the bread should be flavorful like rye or pumpernickel.

LUCIFER Ale/Lager   **CB**   **1.1**
(Dentergem, Belgium)
Sour bitterness with thin texture; faint odor of fresh varnish (turpey); needs to be forced down to finish it; unlike its stronger, more assertive cousin, Duvel, this beer is less sharp and lacking in character; not the best example of the usually well-regarded Belgian beers.

LUCKY LAGER   **CT**   **0.8**
(Tumwater, Washington)
Tasteless, light, watery, and bland, with almost undetectable harshness that thankfully breaks up the monotony; despite relatively average alcohol content (5%/volume), this is a weak beer.

LYNX PILSNER   **CT**   **2.1**
(brewed/canned for Malt House Vintners in London, England)
Sweet, dusty aroma; taste is neither soft nor flexible; suggestion of bitterness, but no direct evidence; has a refreshing nip, but not assertively so; very low in alcohol content (2.38%/weight); the lack of zest is reminiscent of nonalcoholic beers; finish is flat and even less complex than before; water is the dominant ingredient at the end. An appropriate beer for saltless snacks.

MacANDREW'S SCOTCH ALE   CB   3.2
(Edinburgh, Scotland)

Amazingly creamy, with a satisfying mix of bitter and sweet, the emphasis on the former; lovely clouded-amber color, topped nicely with a waxy, milky foam; distinct wine taste emerges as the food settles; appears to be more sour with food, sweeter and more mellow alone; contains some surprises, not all of them pleasant. Goes with sausages, sharp cheeses.

MACARDLES TRADITIONAL ALE   CB   2.4
(Dublin, Ireland)

A little bit of doughy aroma is followed by a whiff of malt, followed by a thin-bodied taste of bitterness; somewhat astringent with a wee bit of caramel malt underneath; achieves an interesting malt-hop balance that emphasizes both ingredients; pale-amber body with orange-ish glow supports the thin constant head; touch of whiskey aroma at the end; finishes light and slightly bitter. Pair with bland fish.

MACCABEE Lager   CB   1.8
(Netanya, Israel)

Sharp and bitter with flat aftertaste; evolves into sourness with some rounding off at the edges; bile-like at the back of the throat; hint of grain; end is clearly better than the beginning; establishes some warmth and calmness, but still no complexity.

MACKESON TRIPLE XXX STOUT   CB   4.1
(London, England)

Good dark, sweet, burnt taste; silky and enjoyable; tasty with a wide range of dishes as its subdued zest quickly integrates with the food; remarkably balanced, with taste and texture very close to perfectly complementing each other; a good example of a traditional milk stout. I've never had a better match of food and beer. Fantastic with any highly spiced or barbecued foods; equally good with rich stews, duck, and game.

MACK-ØL ARCTIC BEER PILSNER   CB   2.9
(Tromsø, Norway)

Wheat taste at the back of the mouth on first sip, but fades quickly; even-tempered and sharp; nicely subtle texture and taste go well with sweet grain mouthfeel with a bit of edge on it. Accompanies a broad range of foods.

B E E R   F A C T

*S*ituated north of the Arctic Circle, Mack claims to be the most northerly brewery in the world. *Øl* means "beer" in Norwegian.

MACLAY WALLACE PALE ALE   **CB**   **3.8**
(Alloa, Scotland)

Quite bitter on first sip, this coppery pale ale evolves into a creamier milk chocolate mouthfeel that sits happily at the back of the tongue; milk chocolate/cocoa aroma respectfully coexists with an equally satisfying malty-sweet aroma; a certain spiciness showcases the malts and hops; finishes with malt in the nose, and hops and spice on the tongue. Makes for easy drinking with well-prepared shellfish—lobster, for example.

MacQUEEN'S NESSIE ORIGINAL
RED ALE   **CB**   **4.0**
(Vorchdorf, Austria)

Complex and tasty; bitter, sweet, and lightly fruity—a yummy combo; tastes succulent, like a ripe peach; extraordinarily satisfying and quenching; slight bitterness in the aftertaste urges you to take another sip; retains its sharpness throughout; a triumphant malty flourish punctuates the finish; a great beer. You might want to try Nessie with after-dinner bonbons or pastries.

MacTARNAHAN'S SCOTTISH STYLE
AMBER ALE   **MB**   **3.8**
(Portland, Oregon)

Nice malty, food-like aroma with a hint of floweriness; almost like drinking bread; rich, creamy mouthfeel with light-caramel color and taste; finishes with a pleasant caramel aroma, taste, warmth, and color; well made and professionally balanced; perfect with roast chicken.

MADCAP ZEBRA EUROPEAN PEACH
Lager   **CT**   **2.7**
(Longview, Texas)

Very peachy, indeed; underlying mild bitter fizziness; well balanced and surprisingly crisp; hops play a more distinct role later on, but maintain their appropriate role in the hop-peach balancing act; no cloying sweetness here, just a straightforward fruity presence. Drink when the weather is hot, accompanied by light summer fare, or no fare at all.

MAES PILS   **CB**   **3.0**
(Waarloos, Belgium)

Sharp and mildly sour with a cleansing palate; no head and very light color make it look puny; mellows into tart sweetness at the end of a meal; prickly edge, not unappetizing, remains—attributable to the hops; delicate aroma is reflected in the light texture of the beer; passively dry; tantalizing, but not entirely satisfying. Bland thickness holds steady alongside grilled meats and mild cheeses.

MAGIC HAT NOT QUITE PALE ALE   MB   2.4
(Portland, Maine)

Brisk and feisty on the palate; hop bitterness reaches to the back of the throat and stops, as if running into a taste-bud barrier; very little balance to redeem the unrelenting, almost runaway bitterness; calms down somewhat at the end; blond body and pencil-thin white head are by default more appealing than the taste; this is certainly drinkable, but be prepared to hang in there.

MAGIC HAT RED ALE   MB   2.4
(Portland, Maine)

Light grainy aroma, with a slightly floral character; malty-caramel taste floats from tongue to throat; subtle underlying bitterness threads its way from start to finish; ingredients mix and ultimately lose their individual identity; finishes smooth and diminished in character. Accompanies the white meat of chicken or an unadorned slice of ham.

MAGNOLIA SPUD BOY IPA   BP   3.5
(San Francisco, California)

Silky and smooth, with lovely apple-fruity bitterness; well-rounded, fruity aroma; nicely packaged hop bitterness becomes more noticeable; consistently and evenly distributed alcohol is a cheerful, constant presence throughout; firm textural backbone; finishes strong, but not pushy, with a great alcohol-bitter combination. Goes very well with standard bar food, like that found at Magnolia, the only brewpub in San Francisco's Haight-Ashbury section.

MAGNOLIA THUNDERPUSSY
BARLEYWINE   BP   3.9
(San Francisco, California)

Chocolatey aroma precedes a characterful soft and nutty mouthfeel; a streak of alcohol bolsters the well-placed, faint cocoa flavor at mid-glass; alcohol is definitely present (10.2%/volume), but nicely integrated and not aggressive; malty sweet and wonderfully mouth-filling; sweetens considerably as you sip; delicious and highly satisfying. No need to spoil the ambiance of this strong and complex barleywine with food. The name is a tribute to the late Magnolia Thunderpussy, once the most famous tenant of the brewpub's historic building in the Haight-Ashbury section of San Francisco.

MAGNUM MALT LIQUOR   CB   0.7
(brewed by Miller in Milwaukee, Wisconsin; Fort Wayne, Indiana; et al.)

Silky smooth to the point of being wishy-washy; tasteless; no texture or complexity—indeed, no hint of any ingredients; no gustatory intrusions, except for a bit of perfume; a beer no one can complain about since it doesn't engage you when you drink it; the makers of this beer clearly had the goal of not scaring off any potential American drinkers—except, of course, those who enjoy beer; Silver Medal winner at the 1993 Great American Beer Festival.

MAIN STREET ABIGAIL'S AMBER Ale
(draft)   MB/BP   2.8
(Cincinnati, Ohio)

Attenuated fruity aroma and taste; quick splash of hop bitterness; not malty sweet, as advertised; retains its moderated bitterness; is this really an amber? Good picturesque sheets of Brussels lace; appropriate alcohol content is unobtrusive but present; flavor flattens toward the end, though its memory does linger. Try it with moderately seasoned seafood.

MAIN STREET STEAMBOAT STOUT
(draft)   MB/BP   3.5
(Cincinnati, Ohio)

Immediate chocolate-malt aroma and taste; subdued and smooth; chocolate toys with coffee in a gentle, motivating interplay—mmmmm; silky and satisfying; well balanced and appropriately restrained; roasted taste lingers tantalizingly on the tongue; an accommodating beer. Drink alone to fully savor the flavor, or with a sweet dessert, a chocolate bar perhaps.

MAIN STREET WOODY'S
AMERICAN WHEAT (draft)   MB/BP   2.3
(Cincinnati, Ohio)

Flavorful but not zesty—in line with American wheat beers; dry enough, but where's the tang? Some appropriate cloudiness; honey mouthfeel appears at mid-glass, faint but appreciated; neither sharp nor crisp enough to take it over the average mark. Drink this alone as a thirst-quencher.

MAISEL'S HEFE WEISSE   CB   4.0
(Bayreuth, Germany)

Pinch of clove kicks in on the second sip and lingers long after you get your mouth out of the creamy foam that tops off the hazy amber color pockmarked with gently rising golden bubbles; cloves remain dominant, gently turning sweet; a touch of astringency trickles down the throat; texture, taste, and aroma balance and integrate about halfway through the bottle, resulting in a pleasant, good example of what *weissbier* is supposed to be; matches the nuances of food very well; tinge of sharpness permeates the inner recesses of the mouth; quite yeasty and rather softly full-bodied; finishes with a clove/yeast flourish. A good pairing with barbecued baby spareribs.

MAISEL'S WEIZEN   CB   2.0
(Bayreuth, Germany)

Light for a *weizen;* almost tasteless with well-seasoned or spicy foods; very foamy; unimpressive and without redeeming characteristics; no real negative qualities, just no positive ones.

MAISEL'S WEIZEN KRISTALL-KLAR   CB   2.5
(Bayreuth, Germany)
Very fine bubbles and a direct hit of cloves as the first swallow finds the back of the mouth; finely tuned with a soft, lacy backbone; remains soft and pliable with soft-textured foods; head stays creamy and smooth throughout; hint of rising bitterness toward the bottom of the bottle; warming and sweetish at the end. Enveloping pungent sweetness develops with barbecued foods.

MAMBA Malt Liquor   CB   3.1
(Abidjan, Ivory Coast)
Surprising chewiness along with a prickly sharpness that evolve into a flatness on the sides of the tongue; this is a golden beer with a substantial but rapidly disappearing head; creamy texture in the entire mouth, along with fruity wine notes; becomes more mellow and even-tempered well into a meal; almost syrupy in its wine-like mouthfeel; not complex; silky; tending toward bland; aftertaste is too sweet. Good with duck, steaks, and cold cuts.

MANHATTAN BEACH BOHEMIAN
PILSNER   BP   2.5
(Manhattan Beach, California)
Light graininess accompanies a bit of spice at every sip; faint bitter character lingers on the tongue after each swallow; hint of vanilla blends in well, adding flavor and dimension to the mouthfeel; thirst-quenching in a gentle, unassuming way; pleasant, slightly grainy aroma; not complex; ideal for summer drinking. Enjoyable with pub fare.

MANHATTAN BEACH HOPHEAD I.P.A.   BP   2.6
(Manhattan Beach, California)
Full-tasting, with a gentle but definite presence of hops; bitterness contains hints of spice in the aftertaste; fruity aroma; a bit too watery; sweetness at mid-glass engages the malt and hops, increasing the complexity in each; soft on the palate; patina of hoppiness appears on the tongue at the finish. Like its pilsner partner, this too goes well with pub fare—fortunately so, since you can only get it at the namesake pub.

MANILA GOLD PALE PILSEN   CB   3.1
(Cabuyao, Philippines)
Moderated freshness, quickly flattening into prolonged dryness; remains appropriately malty and thick on the roof of the mouth with food; a little heavier than a standard pilsener; generally flat and not complex; sharpness on the edges of the tongue; unassuming dry finish with a tantalizing hint of rice; tasty and flavorful, as is true of Filipino beers in general. Good with deli food.

MARATHON—THE GREEK BEER
Lager   **CB**   **3.8**
(Athens, Greece)

Earthy, fresh, and grainy; hearty, crisp, and refreshing; dainty well-placed maltiness stays throughout; hop presence is minimal; filling and satisfying, but leaves a little bit of thickness/furriness on the roof of the mouth. Goes very nicely with Greek lemon soup.

MAREDSOUS ABBEY ALE   **AB**   **4.1**
(Denee, Belgium)

Fresh, clean aroma greets first sip, with a nice fruity backdrop; cloudy, yeasty look gives off a glowing frosty appearance topped by a thin layer of long-lasting head; sharp, readily apparent alcohol mouthfeel; full-bodied, very obvious yeast presence; appropriately balanced fruitiness has banana overtones; heavy on the hops and malt, with reduced fruitiness and increased alcohol as the bottle is finished; good example of solid, traditional abbey ale with backbone and palpable presence; not for the fainthearted; finish is warm and satisfying. Sip this slowly, like a brandy, after a hearty meal.

MARIN OLD DIPSEA BARLEYWINE
STYLE ALE   **MB/BP**   **3.0**
(Larkspur, California)

Strong; rich fruity taste fills the mouth nicely; quite hoppy, with subtle maltiness; almost whiskey-like; a bit thin texturally; has staying power; be careful not to drink too much—its potency is potentially overwhelming. Sip and savor after dinner, accompanied by chocolates.

MARITIME FLAGSHIP RED ALE (draft) **MB**   **3.0**
(Seattle, Washington)

Flowery and bitter caramel tastes balance each other on initial sip, while a toasted aroma wafts pleasantly in the background; malty smoothness with a touch of coffee taste; copper-brown color; a bit cloying, but not enough to be troublesome. A friendly accompaniment to a bagel with cream cheese.

MARITIME ISLANDER PALE ALE
(draft)   **MB**   **2.8**
(Seattle, Washington)

Fresh, clean aroma with the pleasant bitterness of a pale ale plus a sharp fruitiness; color is classically pale-gold; highly hopped and a little chewy; stimulates the appetite, thereby increasing the enjoyment of food; one-dimensional, uncomplex hop character; sheets of Brussels lace testify to its freshness; finishes as it started: clean and bitter/dry; unfortunately, it leaves you thirstier than when you started. Goes with a tomato-and-cheese sandwich.

MARITIME NIGHTWATCH ALE (draft)   MB   3.0
(Seattle, Washington)
Warm and smooth, with tantalizing pinch of hops at the back
of the mouth; auburn-brown color and curtains of Brussels lace
make for an attractive visual package; fresh-bread aroma stays
throughout; calm maltiness; no apparent fruitiness or yeast presence; tepid but flavorful—a beer to calm your stomach and mas-
sage your senses. Complements bean and grain dishes, especially
black bean soup.

TAP TIP

Flat, Fizzy Fixes

*I*s your draft beer flat? A leak in the keg or lines
or improper keg pressure can cause a freshly
tapped brew to lose its zest. Bottom-of-the-barrel
remnants could also be the culprit.

Is your beer too fizzy? Partially clogged or dented
lines, or lines not kept sufficiently cold, may result in
too much carbonation.

Ask the bartender or server for bottled beer if you
are served a draft with either of these defects.

MARKSMAN LAGER   CB   3.3
(Mansfield, England)
Sharply crisp with mild mustiness; light-hearted and direct, with
restrained sweetness that underpins a sparkling vigor; maintains
a certain fruitiness that is not interfering; pleasant and entertaining; smooth and robust in the English manner. A subtle complement to seafood pasta dishes.

MARSTON'S ALBION PORTER   CB   2.8
(Burton-on-Trent, England)
Roasty maltiness goes down easy; smooth and not biting or astringent; light-bodied; dry and hoppy; sweet caramel aroma has
high notes which suggest a bit of coffee-like acidity; deep-brown
body glows red when held to the light; touch of nuttiness caps
the last sips. A good accompaniment to pork roast.

MARTIN'S PALE ALE   CB   3.5
(Antwerp, Belgium)
Honeyed smoothness and soft backbone greet the palate; steady
retained head tops off the slight acidity underlying the rest of the
body; subtle balance with a warmth and mild maltiness; fluffy
pieces of foam cling to the sides of the glass; some complexity

and strength are lost at the end—a shame. Delicious with broiled steak or a snack of aged cheddar cheese with crunchy apple wedges.

MASTER BREW PREMIUM ALE CB 2.1
(Faversham, England)
Faint sour-perfumey aroma contrasts with a fizzy, fruity, caramel taste; gentle malty caramel presence increases as the ale warms; flavors are unintegrated and distant and fade with food; big, broad-shouldered bottle is reminiscent of a whiskey bottle and suggests the liquid inside should be stronger than the actual low (2.5%/volume) reading; in this case, the packaging is more attractive than the contents.

MATEEN TRIPLE ALE AB 3.4
(Melle and Ghent, Belgium)
Light and dainty, with a beguiling combination of alcohol and mild hops; brewed in the abbey style, its soft, foamy head remains thick and bubbly; soothing, accommodating, unobtrusive light color is a bit (appropriately) cloudy; finish is a touch fruity; yeasty in taste and visually quite pleasant but stumbles briefly at the end of the bottle, then recovers nicely, thanks to the presence of yeast. A tasty companion for a bagel with smoked salmon and cream cheese.

MAXIMATOR DARK DOPPELBOCK CB 3.5
(Munich, Germany)
Cola-colored; smoky-tasting with very little carbonation; very flavorful, with body and character; malt dominates; increasing complexity, strength, and backbone with food; smooths out at the end of the bottle with a touch of fruity aroma; strong and chewy; gives you a run for your money. Try it with Danish pastry or similar desserts.

McEWAN'S EXPORT INDIA PALE ALE CB 4.0
(Edinburgh, Scotland)
Attractive hoppy fruitiness and sharp fizziness greet you; full in flavor and satisfying; remains fresh and zesty throughout; dainty Brussels lace in layered patterns lasts until the glass is empty, and beyond; thick head; overall, flavor stays strong, constant, and predictable; clearly a quality, well-thought-out product. Accompanies rare roast beef, baked ham, beef Wellington.

McEWAN'S SCOTCH ALE CB 3.8
(Edinburgh, Scotland)
Full, thick, and perhaps too sweet; virtually chewable; deep-bodied; flavorful burnt-caramel taste; food should be chosen carefully for this handsome silky, molasses-like brew. Best as an after-dinner drink, but pleasant with Virginia ham or smoked turkey.

McFARLAND GOLDEN FIRE Ale CB 3.9
(Milan, Italy)

Restrained crispness with perimeter of sharp hoppiness that sticks to the roof of the mouth; malt kicks in after two to three sips; remains fresh and motivates you to drink more, even though balance is sequential rather than simultaneous; passive golden color; mere hint of head appropriately tops off this understated and not entirely satisfying brew; full of taste, but quietly so; grain and malt aroma emerges in the finish; malt flavor is nicely hidden, though it clearly contributes. I drank this in a tulip-shaped wine glass, quite suitable to the gentleness of the ingredients. Good with cheese and fresh fruit.

McMENAMINS BLACK RABBIT
PORTER BP 2.7
(Portland, Oregon)

Gentle roasted malts and smooth mouthfeel make this a well-calibrated beer with pleasant taste and textural balance; unfortunately, the texture part of the equation is relatively thin, ultimately resulting in the mellow roastedness becoming the main player; rich amber-brown color; some spiciness pops up at the end—a nice touch; an attractive, though not outstanding, porter. Good with shellfish.

McMENAMINS HAMMERHEAD
AMBER ALE BP 2.0
(Portland, Oregon)

Somewhat flat and deficient in hops; vague fruity aroma kind of drifts around; medium-bodied; spotty, unpatterned Brussels lace; exudes some warmth with food, but stops short of any real interest; intimations of being good, but doesn't deliver; finishes with a surprisingly gentle hoppiness.

McMENAMINS NEBRASKA
BITTER Ale BP 2.9
(Portland, Oregon)

Light, fruity, and gently bitter; fantastic patterns of Brussels lace decorate the circumference of the glass; rich yellow color adds to the visuals (and orals); fizzy hoppiness increases alongside food; citrus aroma emerges and becomes full-blown at the end; unfortunately, the flavor flattens at the same time—too bad: This beer is definitely headed in the right direction. Try it with chicken dishes.

McMENAMINS RUBY RASPBERRY
ALE BP 3.0
(Portland, Oregon)

Looks like pink grapefruit juice, tastes mildly of raspberries; sipping sweet, not cloying or overwhelming like many other fruit beers; light and texturally unobtrusive; quite appealing as a novelty drink, and a good match with a pastry dessert, especially a chocolate one.

McMENAMINS TERMINATOR STOUT   BP   2.1
(Portland, Oregon)

More bitter than roasted; remains too flat and simplistic, lacking nuance and alcohol; bitterness increases further, along with an insignificant sweet taste; mild roasted aroma; the brewer has calibrated it to be an obvious stout that is also palatable to the general public; good commercial instincts, but shy of the real thing. Ask for oysters with this, and hope for the best.

McMULLEN'S AK ORIGINAL BITTER   CB   2.8
(Hertford, England)

Starts very bitter, with faint hint of underlying malt sweetness; maltiness overtakes the bitterness and eventually the two achieve a workable balance, though hops continue to predominate; complexity also increases; finishes lightly bitter, with a smooth, cooling sweetness. Goes surprisingly well with lamb garnished with mint.

McSORLEYS ALE   CT   2.0
(Detroit, Michigan)

Pungent citrus-honey aroma mellows after two or three sniffs; warm, gentle taste with faint hops and quality water; rather simple and uncomplicated; light-bodied and unfruity; some yeasty fruitiness begins to emerge as it warms, but remains faint; pleasant and undemanding; overall, weak and lacking character; go to McSorleys for the ambiance, not for this ale.

MEDALLA DE ORO LAGER   CB   2.3
(Guatemala City, Guatemala)

Dull and fruity on first sip; relatively rapid flatness occurs on surface of the tongue; some flavor and relative warmth oozes up at the end of the bottle; fruity aroma, but stale smelliness remains throughout; cereal/grain taste is also evident from start to finish.

MEDALLA LIGHT Pilsener   CB   0.8
(San Juan, Puerto Rico)

Very fizzy; mildly light, with a back-of-the-tongue aftertaste; doesn't contribute to or detract from food; clearly is attempting to appeal to the lowest common denominator; hint of warmth is its only redeeming feature; thickness occurs at the end; it's not bad-tasting, just no-tasting.

MELBOURN BROS. APRICOT BEER
Lager   **MB**   **3.8**
(Stamford, England)

Fruity apricot aroma precedes a startlingly sour taste; more complex than American fruit-flavored wheat beers; more like apricot cider than beer, or champagne without the frivolity; light and lightly effervescent; aroma remains distinctly fruity; hops make an appearance at mid-bottle; a good choice for fruit beer fans. Have this with, or for, dessert.

MELO ABREU ESPECIAL   **CB**   **3.0**
(Ponta Delgada, Azores)

Light, frothy head gently filters the soft, light malty-grainy taste; subtle hop aroma arises after several sips; maltiness increases and becomes the dominant character, giving off tantalizing hints of vanilla and grassiness; tasty and light on the palate; characterful hop interaction becomes more nuanced and balanced, though malt remains primary throughout; well-done and quite satisfying. Good with mountain trout or similar mildly-flavored fish.

MENDOCINO BLACK HAWK STOUT   **MB/BP**   **3.4**
(Hopland, California)

Somewhat flat, with no head and a fizzy bitter undertone; burnt flavor dissipates quickly; deep-brown color and malty nose underscore the stout definition; a good sweet balance with smoked fish—the food enhances and sets off the stout and vice versa, a sweet combination; settles into a predictable languid flow with smoother texture, peak-performing hops, and modulated sweetness; appears to have enviable ability to reflect the best in the food though it retains some immaturity throughout. Delicious with smoked salmon; an equally interesting match with barbecued ribs.

MENDOCINO RED TAIL ALE   **MB/BP**   **2.3**
(Hopland, California)

Sharply fruity with fast-disappearing fizziness; too much tang at the outset; with warmth, the unwanted zip diminishes; better without food; some energizing fruitiness, but not outstanding.

MENDOCINO YULETIDE PORTER   **MB**   **2.5**
(seasonal)
(Hopland, California)

Rather sharp texturally; coffee-mocha character insinuates itself into your taste buds; flavor is applied with a fairly light hand; pleasant, somewhat bitter aftertaste; lighter mouthfeel than the cola-brown color would suggest; goes down very easily, leaving no lasting impression in its wake; could be more complex with greater taste definition; as it is, this is a glib little beer. Trying Yuletide Porter with the fruit and rum in seasonal fruitcake significantly enhances its attraction.

MERLIN'S ALE   CB   3.7
(Broughton, Peebleshire, Scotland)

The very essence of Scotland wells up as you take the first sips and savor the scruffy earthy/grassy aroma; a cooked maltiness and sweetly aromatic hoppiness simultaneously soothe and enchant; heather-honey flavor settles in at mid-bottle and stays in the aftertaste; creamy half-inch head leaves a crazy-quilt of thick, tenacious Brussels lace that adheres to the inside of the glass; finishes balanced and very tasty. Merlin's goes magically well with any style of egg, either on a sandwich or on a plate.

MERRIMAN'S OLD FART Ale   CB   2.5
(Leeds, England)

Malty-sweet caramel taste; mild bitterness comes and goes; malt presence increases after each swallow; tellingly carbonated; big-tasting and full-bodied; not complex; sweetness is the featured player in the bitter-sweet interaction; finishes with a more sugary-caramel combination; drink cold in order to minimize the sweet mouthfeel. Try this with hot pretzels and hot mustard.

MESSINA PILSENER   CB   4.1
(Milan, Italy)

Typical pilsener, reminiscent of Rheingold and Schaefer at the ballpark; hoppy and purely satisfying in a direct, uninhibited way; nicely balanced, with constantly refreshing palate; light and uplifting, with substance and piquancy; fun to drink. Tasty accompaniment to antipasto, pastas, and Italian specialty meats.

MEXICALI BEER Pilsener   CT   2.5
(San Antonio, Texas)

Yeasty-doughy aroma and complementary malt flavor all rise up with a fair degree of bubbly carbonation; wispy taste of malt comes and goes quickly; more full-bodied and more complex than other brewed-in-the-USA pilseners; finishes with a light but pleasant grainy aroma; made with style and gusto. Clearly a chips and tacos beer.

MICHAEL SHEA'S IRISH AMBER
Lager (draft)   CB   3.0
(Utica, New York)

Light and fluffy, with sedate hoppiness that fades into a soda-like texture; similar to flavored water, but in a positive, tasty sense; foggy deep-amber color is reminiscent of Irish bogs; remains clean and unfilling, yet satisfying; you could probably drink gallons of this stuff without feeling it too much; pleasant, even without food. Try it with salty snacks such as nuts and pretzels.

MICHELOB CLASSIC DARK Lager   CB   1.8
(brewed by Anheuser-Busch in St. Louis, Missouri)
Tastier and maltier than its dry cousin, but still weak and relatively boring; toasted flavor redeems it somewhat; diminishing hop presence makes it seem sweeter than it actually is; a minimally serviceable brew.

MICHELOB DRY Lager   CB   2.1
(brewed by Anheuser-Busch in St. Louis, Missouri)
Softly pallid, clean, and bold, but with flavor that doesn't match the promise; relies on texture rather than aroma, taste, or complexity; distinctive but not significantly so; not a good complement to food.

BEER FACT

*T*he Michelob name was adapted from Michalovce, a town in the Czech Republic. It's not the first time Anheuser-Busch found inspiration in European geography to name a beer, however. In 1876, Adolphus Busch wished to invest his newly created brew with Old World character, so he named it Budweiser, after the royal Bohemian town of Budweis (formerly Ceské Budjovice). The local brew in Budweis, known as the "beer of kings," also inspired Busch to call his the "king of beers."

MICHELOB PALE ALE   CB   1.9
(brewed by Anheuser-Busch in St. Louis, Missouri)
Mild hoppy aroma with grain-honey taste; smooth texture; washed-out amber color; malt and hops are not complex or particularly well balanced; malt presence is hardly there at all; ends even flatter than it started; bland; needs to be punched up a notch or two. Drink this with light fare, like an egg salad sandwich on white toast.

MICKEY'S MALT LIQUOR   CB   3.1
(La Crosse, Wisconsin)
Smooth, light, and easy-flowing; even-tempered and predictable throughout; surprisingly pleasant. Gold Medal winner at the 1993 Great American Beer Festival. Accompanies virtually anything.

MIDNIGHT DRAGON GOLD
RESERVE ALE   CT   1.5
(Winston-Salem, North Carolina)
Malty, hoppy, sweet-and-sour on first sips; ingredients quickly settle down into uniform, slightly sweetish, thickish mixture; not

enough bulk and backbone; eventually becomes mildly interesting; gives too little, too late; no fruitiness, no alcohol presence, and hardly any yeast—not exactly the signs of a good ale.

MIDNIGHT DRAGON MALT LIQUOR   CT   1.1
(Winston-Salem, North Carolina)
Alternatingly strong and weak, and very soft on the palate—hard to tell it's malt liquor; slight chunky sweetness emerges; essentially benign and sympathetic with plain foods; pale, almost pallid color, with thin "look" overall; bland and tasteless—close to tea, except tea usually has more pizzazz; finishes weaker than it began.

MIDNIGHT DRAGON ROYAL
RESERVE LAGER   CT   0.5
(Winston-Salem, North Carolina)
High prickly carbonation with orange-juice-concentrate aroma that rapidly rises through the nostrils; not especially disgusting, but certainly not wonderful; rounded sourness; carbonation almost completely disappears; very tea-like; begins to turn skunky; this is a sequential beer—it goes from bad to worse; rough texture at the end; hard to finish.

MIDNIGHT SUN FIREWEED HONEY
WHEAT BEER (seasonal)   MB   1.9
(Anchorage, Alaska)
Slight sourness is wrapped inside a soft cushion of honey sweetness; regains a focused sharpness after several sips; texture and flavor weaken and flatten at about the same time; definitely loses much of its vim and vigor at about mid-bottle; faint hint of malt offers some solace toward the end, but certainly not enough to even begin to redeem this brew.

MILLER HIGH LIFE Pilsener   CB   2.4
(Milwaukee, Wisconsin)
Attractive clean smell, with no grit that might make it interesting; on the other hand, it's clear, inoffensive, and devoid of chemical taste; no intimations of adventure, but no signs of danger, either; compared to other mass-produced beers, this at least has the beginnings of complexity; stays restrainedly refreshing and mildly interesting with food; tissue-thin dusting of foam stays on top of the liquid, while some adheres tentatively to the sides of the glass; very faint grainy odor at the end; one of the better of the mega-brewed products. Try with a bacon-wrapped filet mignon and a tossed green salad.

MILLER HIGHLIFE Pilsener   CB   2.2
(Toronto, Ontario, Canada)
Smoother and softer than the American version, with a flavor built from quality adjuncts and the usual malt and barley; cool-

ing and refreshing at first; in the end, watery and washed out as far as taste, texture, and visual "feel" are concerned; no aroma or complexity—just your basic okay bland beer with some hint of interest.

MILLSTREAM LAGER   MB   3.8
(Amana, Iowa)

Fresh and malty at the beginning, which leads you to expect a fuller, mellower taste; sharp and effervescent; good malt-hop balance; straightforward; zestier than other Midwestern beers; finish is medium-dry with a flavor that makes you want to try another; crosscurrents of texture make it interesting with or without food; a touch flat and metallic, leaving you disappointed and perplexed on final sip. Sweetness comes through with dishes such as chicken with Cajun spices or gumbo.

MILLSTREAM SCHILD BRAU
AMBER Lager   MB   2.7
(Amana, Iowa)

Nice rounded maltiness with complementary minimal carbonation; faint lasting sweetness adds upbeat note; remains relatively consistent throughout; appropriate sourness emerges with food; bland, yet a bit interesting, with subtle, tangible complexity; food is necessary to add substance to this beer—not a brew that creates excitement by itself. Good with mustard-slathered hot dogs or wurst.

MILLSTREAM WHEAT   MB   0.3
(Amana, Iowa)

Not in wheat style at all—no cloves, no fruitiness, no zip, not even refreshing; hard to tell this is even beer; rather staid and unassertive, especially with spicy foods; dry and characterless.

MILWAUKEE 1851 Pilsener   CB   0.4
(La Crosse, Wisconsin)

Chemical-tasting and somewhat sharp; water is the predominant feature, though some hop suggestion is also present in the far background; light- to medium-bodied; starts going flat one-quarter of the way through the can; taste turns unpleasantly bitter, metallic, coarse, intrusive; gives a new meaning to the cliché "It leaves a bad taste in your mouth"; forget about this one.

MINOTT'S BLACK STAR
AMBER EXPORT   MB   1.9
(Whitefish, Montana)

Brief pleasant whiff of aromatic hops accompanies a hint of hop bitterness in the mouth; no real bitterness at the core of the hop character, however, and what is there fades rapidly; lightly perfumed aroma; and, by the way, where's the malt in this so-called amber ale? Taste eventually disintegrates into a hodge-podge of sour-bitter flavors; thins and becomes watery, too; the label is interesting, though.

MINOTT'S BLACK STAR
GOLDEN LAGER   MB   2.4
(Whitefish, Montana)
Sharp, hoppy-acidic mouthfeel stimulates the taste buds; mellows and sweetens, turning into an easy-going balance of hops and malts; soft-pedaled hops eventually achieve a more noticeable bitterness; hop graininess also emerges and enlivens things a bit; lightly-flavored and not intrusive; a general drinking beer with no outstanding qualities, but okay when just sitting around and schmoozing.

MISHAWAKA HOP HEAD ALE IV   BP   3.3
(Mishawaka, Indiana)
Prickly hop aroma on first sniff; flowery hop taste with perfumey aftertaste; tastefully complex; a bit of a citrus-sugary character comes along and helps balance the aggressive hop presence; light and quite dry; this beer has a carefully programmed progression of flavors that moves things along at a comfortable pace; a well-done, delicately hopped ale that's not ashamed of its hop lineage. Grilled sausage makes for a sure-fire partner.

MODELO ESPECIAL Vienna Lager   CB   2.9
(Mexico City, Mexico)
Sharp, with a tantalizing sweetness that comes to the upper palate and then diffuses; slight after-bite; golden hue suggests it's more lightweight than it is; there's chocolate in there somewhere; flavorful and motivating. Maintains malty sweetness and character with Mexican food and pasta.

MOERLEIN'S CINCINNATI BOCK BEER   CB   2.9
(Cincinnati, Ohio)
Sweet, bitter, burnt flavor all rolled into one accommodating mouthful; robustness is not overpowering; malt character drops back after a while, increasing the beer's sharp, bitter taste; malt aroma remains, however; finishes full and complex; a changeable beer that makes the experience interesting, if not overwhelmingly so. Goes with smoked ham or smoked turkey.

MOGOLLON SUPERSTITION PALE ALE   MB   2.0
(Flagstaff, Arizona)
A mild, flowery aroma is followed by a mild, well-balanced malt-hop taste; smooth, flowing mouthfeel; vague buttery character; at mid-bottle attains apple cider flavor that is too sweet and too cloying; texture and moderate effervescence diminish to zero at the end; this pale ale fades too much to be ranked average. See how this goes with sharp cheese on crackers.

MOGOLLON WAPITI AMBER ALE   **MB**   **2.9**
(Flagstaff, Arizona)

Very fruity and juicy, with a sweet orange kick that is filling, complex, and very tasty; subtle maltiness provides a soothing sweet backdrop; bitterness is pleasant and short-lived; finishes with a beguiling, restrained spicy-malty sweetness and a curl of hops that lingers on your taste buds; perhaps a bit too sweet in the end. Goes with chicken and rice dishes.

MOJO HIGHWAY GOLDEN ALE   **CT**   **3.3**
(Frederick, Maryland)

Sprightly, light, and very tasty, Mojo Highway quickly draws your interest; delicate, nicely alternating hop-malt balance—hop on the tongue, malt toward the back of mouth; some gentle bitterness in the aftertaste; placid, pillowy white head leaves puffs of Brussels lace clinging to the sides of the glass; gains a smoothness and fullness missing earlier; some banana notes in the finish. Try this well-built golden ale with fish and chips.

MOLSON BRADOR MALT LIQUOR   **CB**   **2.7**
**(Montreal, Quebec; Toronto, Ontario; Vancouver,
British Columbia, Canada)**

Fading crispness on first sip; predictable, somewhat malty, without much kick from the supposedly higher alcohol content; a lager-like beer; neither offensive nor attractive. A fitting partner for a burger topped with green chiles.

MOLSON EXPORT ALE   **CB**   **3.2**
**(Montreal, Quebec; Toronto, Ontario; Vancouver,
British Columbia, Canada)**

A little stronger and fuller than the lager, with a hoppier taste; crispness is a bit rounded at the edges; remains satisfying, filling, and fresh; straightforward; satisfies different tastes; thirst-quenching when very cold; not much complexity. Good with grilled chicken or fish.

MOLSON GOLDEN Ale   **CB**   **2.4**
**(Montreal, Quebec; Toronto, Ontario; Vancouver,
British Columbia, Canada)**

Immediate first impression of substance begins to fade into relatively bland taste and nonexistent aroma after a swallow or two; a certain crispness remains as long as the beer stays cold; light, thin hoppiness; creamy head and unpredictable, intricate Brussels lace last until final drop; attractive mild bitterness finishes the bottle, with accompanying hop aroma; a one-sip, one-whiff beer—beyond that, not much to experience. "An Honest Beer," claims the label, "Makes Its Own Friends"—true enough. Fine with a ham and cheese or salami sandwich.

MOLSON ICE Lager CB 3.5
(Vancouver, British Columbia, Canada)
Fresh, crisp, and cold (it's from Canada, after all), with a predominance of hops; medium-bodied; uncomplicated; remains firm; strong brew for hot-weather thirst (5.6% alcohol by volume—higher than most American lagers). Serve with hearty beef stew, well-seasoned meat loaf, or braised oxtail.

MOLSON SPECIAL DRY Lager CB 2.5
(Toronto, Ontario, Canada)
Smooth and soothing; a seriously dry beer, with no hint of sweetness or cloyingness; remains cool, calm, and collected; hangs together tenuously, as if the wrong food would destroy its attractiveness; not flavorful or complex enough to be ranked very high. Compatible with relatively bland foods such as a turkey burger or a club sandwich.

MONKEY WRENCH ALE CB 4.2
(Harrogate, England)
Sit back and enjoy the rich, plummy raisin-malt taste and aroma; then look at the picturesque small golden-white bubbles making up the creamy quarter-inch head that glows in the sunlight; smooth and silky all over the mouth; finishes with a nicely calibrated touch of alcohol that turns the satisfaction up another notch; "freakin' delicious," according to one of my more reliable drinking buddies; I agree. Just sit around and savor a Monkey Wrench or two with some friends. No food necessary.

MON-LEI Lager CB 2.6
(Beijing, China)
Immediate wheat/wine taste, fading into some sourness; settles into a balance between grain and acidity; sharpness at the back of the throat remains even several minutes after swallowing; alcoholic presence throughout; some spritziness; thin and watery; complexity increases from start to finish. Try it with pasta dishes.

MONROVIA CLUB BEER Lager CB 3.0
(Monrovia, Liberia)
European-style lager; dry without much carbonation; settles into tasty, nicely balanced beer that sets off food well; dry, flattish finish lingers. Companionable accompaniment to Caesar salad with grilled chicken breast or a chef salad.

MONTE CARLO LAGER CB 2.8
(Guatemala City, Guatemala)
Crisp, sharp, and neutral-tasting on first sip; medium body with nice spritziness; flavor develops when matched with food, but texture flattens out—greenness toward the end; slight attractive fruitiness. Goes with spicy Mexican foods.

MONTEJO Pilsener   CB   2.5
(Merida, Yucatán, Mexico)
An underlying grain taste moves this middle-of-the-road drinking beer along; there is a touch of honey at the swallow, along with a pleasant smoothness that accommodates the malty-grain mouthfeel; a little raw and unfinished; light and not filling; finishes with a semi-satisfying earthy ambiance. I had this in my favorite Mexican city, Oaxaca, with *crepas de elote*. I hope that you are able to do likewise.

MONTEZUMA DE BARRIL Lager (draft) CB   3.3
(Mexico City, Mexico)
Dark and tasty; I sampled it with street food in Mexico City's Zona Rosa, where the beer is served mainly as a grease-cutter, but its deep maltiness and faintly sharp hops hinted that it could be enjoyed without food. It is a delectable choice on its own or as a perfect foil for snacks such as Buffalo-style chicken wings and jalapeño-topped nachos.

MOONLIGHT TWIST OF FATE
BITTER ALE   MB   3.3
(Windsor, California)
Harsh with citrus overtones, but appealing—a true bitter, with hop aroma to match; delicate Brussels lace belies the strength of the contents; musty aftertaste at the roof of the mouth; dry finish, sturdy and forthright. Serve as an intriguing *apéritif* accompanied by unsalted walnuts, cashews, and smoked almonds.

MOONRAKER OLD ALE   CB   3.3
(Middleton and Manchester, England)
Highly alcoholic (7.5%/volume); plummy and caramel flavors wind around each other as you sip, taste, and swallow; strong, firm body; alcohol presence increases and remains strong and compelling; slight presence of malt in the aroma and on the tongue begins to moderate the alcohol strength at mid-bottle; coffee-plum aroma arises as the russet-brown body warms; finishes sweeter as the alcohol is absorbed into the mainstream of the taste. Goes with nuts and cheeses.

MOOSEHEAD CANADIAN LAGER   CB   1.1
(St. John, New Brunswick, Canada)
Foamy, creamy head covers a very pale, less-than-carbonated, weak body; dainty light-lemon mouthfeel suggests a barely flavored bottled spring water; faint beery aroma fades rapidly, as does the transient bitterness; a hardly-there beer; the best word for this brew is flimsy—no taste buds need apply.

MORDUE WORKIE TICKET Ale   CT   3.4
(Newcastle-upon-Tyne, England)
Pungent caramel sweetness is smooth at the front of the mouth,

but stern at the back of the throat; full-bodied and quite filling; malt flavor spreads all over the mouth, accompanied by a touch of bitterness; caramel aroma and caramel-sugary taste increase along the way; distinctive burnt character is noted in the swallow; ingredients are tightly bonded to each other, making for a predictable, balanced, full-flavored ale. Goes well with red meat.

L A B E L   L O R E

"Workie Ticket," a geordie term for mischief-maker, was named Supreme Champion Beer of Britain in 1997. The original 19th-century brewery was located on the town green in Wallsend, a small city alongside the Tyne river in northern England, not far from where the beer is now contract-brewed.

MORETTI BIRRA FRIULANA Pilsener   CB   1.3
(Udine, Italy)
Immediate cardboard/paper aroma, the dreaded hallmark of oxidation; very perfumey; mild, light-bodied, flat, uncomplex, airy, sweet, corn-like taste; finish is soda-like, with fizz and raspberry flavor; a second bottle doesn't contain the oxidized off-flavor; drinkable, but not enough stamina to stand up to bland foods; too variable to recommend.

MORETTI LA ROSSA ALL MALT Lager   CB   3.1
(Udine, Italy)
Caramel flavor, thick foam, and full body—all unexpected from an Italian beer; very much like an ale, except for the alcohol—there doesn't seem to be any; silky and smooth throughout; malty with a hint of acidity and sweetness; malt-rich aroma and taste from start to finish; deep-red color. Try with Cornish hens or veal chops.

MORETTI LA ROSSA DOPPIOMALTO
Amber Lager   CB   2.7
(Udine, Italy)
Malty and mildly roasted, as expected; smooth; light- to medium-bodied; increasingly cloying; happiness arises at mid-bottle, nicely counterbalancing the slight fruity sweetness; rather unobtrusive; unappetizing without food. Good with chicken and seafood pasta dishes.

*T*he familiar captivating image of the intent, preoccupied man with the moustache on the Moretti label (see page 213) is based on a real-life beer lover. Brewer Menazzi Moretti was so taken by the scene of the patron enjoying his favorite brew in a Udine trattoria in 1942 that he took his photograph. That photo is the basis for the painting on the label that now identifies Moretti's beers worldwide. Moretti is Italy's third-largest brewer.

MORGAN STREET DOPPELBOCK   BP   1.9
(St. Louis, Missouri)

First a fragile sugary sweetness, then a blast of in-depth layered chocolate offers lip-smacking goodness; malt sweetens perceptibly as it warms, evolving into a cola syrup-wine taste; a gummy sensation on the tongue is present in the aftertaste; finishes with some bitterness and lots of caramel malt; an uncertain beer still searching for its own identity.

MORLAND "OLD SPECKLED HEN"
ENGLISH FINE ALE   CB   4.1
(Abingdon, England)

Subtle apple pie–spice aroma combines exquisitely with a very light caramelized flavor to offer oodles of pleasure—and this is just the beginning; then there is the bready mouthfeel, adding fullness to the overall pleasure; dry and sweetly yeasty, reminiscent of a fine blended bourbon; thick, creamy full-bodied head; carefully prepared and nicely balanced, this hen is tuned to perfection. Enjoy before a meal or sip slowly while dining on veal or pork.

MORT SUBITE PECHE LAMBIC   CB   3.4
(Kobbegem, Belgium)

Peachy keen, indeed, with a snap of yeastiness that immediately activates the saliva juices; slight peach aroma is not intrusive; nuanced sour yeast mouthfeel changes at every swallow, as if the molecules are dancing to their own engaging tune; light and dainty; noisy carbonation adds vitality and interest; simultaneously sweet and dry; aged in oak casks and flavored with peach juice, this well-made lambic is a pleasant way to finish just about any meal.

MOSCOVA Lager CB 1.3
(Moscow, Russia)
Malty and hoppy at the same time, with a hint of spoilage; flat and relatively textureless; rather indifferent, both by itself and with food; slight honey aroma and taste appear at the end of the bottle; medium-dry; flat viscosity; typical of Russian beer; uninteresting and unpleasant mouthfeel.

MOUNTAIN CREST Pilsener CB 0.9
(Toronto, Ontario, Canada)
Tries to imitate American beers and unfortunately has succeeded; undistinguished; drink water instead.

MOYLAN'S INDIA PALE ALE MB/BP 2.9
(Novato, California)
Complex mix of spice, grapefruit, and floral-hop aromas start this IPA off with an aromatic bang; some grapefruit tartness clings to the back of the tongue; bold and crisp; the continuing strong hoppy-citrus mouthfeel invigorates; also present is a tantalizing hint of chocolate; finishes less sharp, but the interweaving of flavors and textures remains; a frisky little beer. Try with smoked clams or smoked cheese.

LABEL LORE

*I*n 1927 the MG car factory in Abingdon built a one-of-a-kind model covered in canvas that had been painted gold and flecked with black. Local residents affectionately dubbed it the "Old Speckled Hen." On the 50th anniversary of the factory in 1977, MG asked the Morland brewery to produce a special ale to honor the event. The result is Old Speckled Hen (see facing page), a delicious ale, which you are hereby advised to go out and buy. The beer company's founder, George Morland, was a celebrated 18th-century painter of scenes of the rustic English countryside.

MOZA BOCK CB 2.9
(Guatemala City, Guatemala)
Spritzy and flavorful; texture a bit watery; maintains appealing slightly sour mustiness; flattens out to a pleasant blandness; mildly agreeable burnt taste at the back of the throat; not complex; weakens at the end of the bottle. Good with rice or grain dishes.

MURPHY'S IRISH STOUT   CB   2.5
(Cork, Ireland)

Surprisingly flat and tasteless, though soft and creamy, almost velvety; hint of wine meanders in and out; predictable creamy smoothness gently, seamlessly insinuates itself into food, mainly because it has no real core of its own; deep, dark brown; thick tan head; virtually nonexistent aroma; neither complex nor balanced; more integrated, textured presence at finish, with some emerging warmth; a disappointment despite its new pressurized-can packaging, especially compared to the real draft version. Okay with a grilled chicken or sharp cheddar cheese sandwich.

MURPHY'S STOUT (draft)   CB   3.5
(Cork, Ireland)

Soft on the mouth, lips, and palate; sharp hoppiness evolves into mellow, smooth, burnt flavor; brown-black body and milky-brown level head create perfect visual balance for this spicy-tart stout; stays smooth throughout, with evergreen spiciness; classic clinging Brussels lace; solid and above average. Good with raw oysters, chips and salsa, or potato chips with clam dip.

MYTHOS HELLENIC LAGER BEER   CB   3.0
(Sindos, Greece)

Nice hop-malt arrangement; fulfilling, grainy-hop emphasis goes down the throat smoothly and comfortably; clean, effervescent mouthfeel; bitterness becomes dominant at mid-bottle, but definitely not overwhelmingly so; medium, pale gold body has backbone and substance; this is a predictable, thirst-quenching lager. Appropriate with Greek olives and similar condiments.

NAKED ASPEN BROWN ALE   CT   3.3
(Cold Spring, Minnesota)

Warm, nutty flavor is set in a rich, medium-bitter hoppiness; gentle and soothing on the palate; subtle, nuanced spiciness is hidden within all the mellowness; while the head doesn't last too long, it is creamy; chocolate taste comes on gently toward the end; this is a pleasant enough beer that finishes with a mini-bite of bitterness. Try with well-seasoned beef dishes.

NAKED ASPEN HONEY WHEAT   CT   2.2
(Cold Spring, Minnesota)

Harsh, rough, and semi-honeyish, as if the beer didn't quite finish its pollination, or fermentation; rough mouthfeel lightens up a bit as more honey gets pressed into service; begins to taste like plastic; pale-straw color reflects the thinness of the flavor; weak and watery at the end.

TAP TIP

Where's the Brewery?

Not all beers are brewed where the company is located. Now an established phenomenon, contract brewing allows individuals and, increasingly, companies with a beer recipe to contract with a functioning brewery to produce and package the beer. Often the contract brewery is located many miles from the home company—even out of state. Thus you get such anomalies as the Naked Aspen beers brewed in Cold Spring, Minnesota, not Aspen, Colorado. Some major contract brewing locations are Utica, New York (Portland Lager, Michael Shea's Irish Amber), Pittsburgh (many Samuel Adams styles—it has also contracted with a brewery in Cincinnati), and Wilkes-Barre, Pennsylvania (Erin's Rock Stout & Amber Lager, Neuweiler Black and Tan). Pete's Wicked Ale and other Pete's brews are made in Seattle and Winston-Salem, while Pete's Brewing Company itself is based in Palo Alto, California.

Caveat emptor: Check the label to make certain the handsomely packaged beer you think is made from the delicious local spring water is not in reality bottled across the country in some time-worn urban zone. The beer may be just as good, but it's always wise to know what you're getting.

NAPA VALLEY RED ALE   **MB**   **3.5**
(Napa, California)

Malty, warm, and smooth; trailing sourness provides a tasty exclamation point after 2 or 3 sips; very malty aroma, with the barest touch of accompanying fruitiness; full of flavor; bubbly texture; ivory-colored head leaves thick clumps of foam on the sides of the glass; hops, fruit, and malt merge seamlessly at the finish, providing a tasty ending to an already pleasant beer. Try with shellfish or lighter-flavored meat.

NAVIDAD CERVEZA
COMMEMORATIVA Lager (annual)   **CB**   **0.1–3.4**
(Monterrey, Mexico)

A popular Christmas beer that has, in my experience, varied wildly in acceptability; my first bottle in 1986 was flat and lifeless—no zip, no zest; some fruitiness was present, but it was pallid, thin, and weak. More recently I have found the body to be pleasing—not too heavy, with a flavorful, unobtrusive toasty taste; sharpness on the front of the tongue turns sweet with spicy foods; not fully thirst-quenching, but worth searching for during the year-end holiday season.

NEUWEILER BLACK AND TAN
Porter/Lager   **CT**   **2.5**
(Allentown, Pennsylvania)

No aroma; bland-tasting; deep copper-red color; a hint of malty sweetness pops up now and then; remains frustratingly predictable, given its quality ingredients and thoughtful brewing; this beer, unfortunately, goes nowhere. (For more on Black and Tan, see page 148.)

NEW AMSTERDAM AMBER Lager   **CT**   **3.6**
(Utica, New York)

Watery apple flavor with sharpness early and flatness later; smooth, malty mouthfeel; enhances the sharpness of very spicy foods; roasted freshness throughout; amber color is too light, but gustatory sensations more than make up for the visual deficit. A nice match with Thai food.

NEW AMSTERDAM INDIA PALE ALE   **CT**   **2.4**
(Utica, New York)

Tamped-down bitterness and tamped-down fruitiness indicate at the outset that this is a tamped-down IPA; hops become sharper and more appropriately bitter as the bottle progresses; fluffy, uneven head is full, well bubbled, and lasting; finishes with too many mixed flavors and mixed messages. Try it with a bacon, lettuce, and tomato sandwich on rye.

NEW AMSTERDAM NEW YORK ALE   **CT**   **3.3**
(Utica, New York)

Fruity aroma and strong citrus taste on first sip; appropriately thin and texturally evenhanded; some complexity and balance emerge as it warms; bitter aftertaste and spiciness trail the main part of the drink; zesty; all ingredients come together pleasantly at the end, making for a good adolescent beer that would gain from maturity. Try it with Mexican food.

NEW BELGIUM ABBEY BELGIAN
STYLE ALE   **MB**   **4.1**
(Fort Collins, Colorado)

This strong, well-made ale opens with a full, rich aroma and taste that never quit; hints of fruit and spice tantalize and tickle the nose; alcohol presence increases subtly and jauntily; yeast is present but judiciously placed, ultimately adding a low-key citrus-apple fruitiness; handsome rich-toned body shines with an ebullient deep-brown color and a red glow of enchantment; New Belgium continuously releases a panoply of pleasure. Particularly good with crusty, doughy peasant bread; dip a piece in the liquid and enjoy.

NEW BELGIUM BLUE PADDLE
PILSENER   MB   3.8
(Fort Collins, Colorado)
Sparkly, lively array of hops coats the tongue with a very tasty and invigorating bitterness; flowery aroma is a good counterbalance to the sharp mouthfeel; refreshingly and engagingly bitter; finishes with a malt-hop balance marked by a nuanced interplay of flavors; cobwebby sheets of Brussels lace hang tenaciously to the insides of the glass; nice, complex hoppy aroma caps things off at the end. Blue Paddle makes a fine partner with cold chicken and potato salad.

NEW BELGIUM FAT TIRE AMBER ALE   MB   3.9
(Fort Collins, Colorado)
Tightly compacted, fizzily foaming bubbles in head; attenuated fruitiness is immediately and appropriately cut down to manageable size with the first bite of food; bounces back with a modulated sweetness that plays off a hoppy aroma and slightly nutty malt flavor; some yeast in the bottle helps to give it body and a cloudy amber color; an even-tempered, respectful ale, though lacking complexity; too sweet without food. Accommodating with foods such as lamb chops with mint sauce.

NEW ENGLAND ATLANTIC AMBER Alt   MB   3.1
(Norwalk, Connecticut)
Far too fruity and alcoholic for this style, but inviting and satisfying nonetheless; a nice foamy head; soft and mellow; hint of tangy sourness passes quickly; carbonation is quickly minimized; lively fruitiness combines with rich, hoppy bitterness; finishes with an attractive mustiness and warmth, although too thin; Gold Medal winner at the 1993 Great American Beer Festival. Try this with spicy boiled jumbo shrimp.

NEW ENGLAND HOLIDAY ALE
(annual)   MB   4.0
(Norwalk, Connecticut)
A little sweet, even a little gummy; a mini-concoction of delectable scents and spices, mainly evergreen and cloves, in varying intensities; full and tasty, with a rich velvety red-brown color giving it an enticing glow; an undertone of chocolate unites all of the diverse but complementary ingredients; the ale's spiciness heats up the tongue and ultimately takes over most foods; perfect, discernible alliance of aroma and flavor—you get what you smell; remains consistent from beginning to end; an enchanting holiday drink; highly recommended. A festive match for a traditional roast turkey dinner with all the trimmings.

NEW ZEALAND LAGER   **CB**   **2.4**
(Auckland, New Zealand)
Thin and grainy, with minimal spritziness; takes on an attractive
molasses-like sweetness when served with pork; pale-golden color
with a ruby undertone; head thins down very quickly; hint of
hoppiness and dryness finishes off this good-hearted but uninteresting beer.

T A P   T I P

What About the Bubbles?

*C*arbonation offers a clue to the quality of the
beer you drink—or don't drink. Small bubbles
are found in a naturally carbonated product, generally resulting in a smoother, creamier brew. Larger,
fast-rising bubbles are usually an indication that carbonation has been artificially introduced. This commercial carbonic injection process results in shorter
brewing and aging periods and generally less care than
is required for naturally carbonated beverages, potentially rushing the beer to market before its time.
It also allows for fewer carbonation-related serving
problems at the tap, and hence the potential for fewer
irritated customers. Large bubbles and a rapidly collapsing head may also be the result of insufficient malt.

NEWCASTLE BROWN ALE (draft)   **CB**   **3.3**
(Newcastle-upon-Tyne, England)
Full-bodied and very satisfying—gets to the core of your taste
buds on the first sip; fresh malty aroma; hearty and stalwart, with
minimal carbonation; quality medium-brown color and sweet
chewy maltiness create a smooth, soft mellowness; hops slowly
creep up onto the roof of the mouth about halfway through the
glass; bit of thickish aftertaste lowers the rating; finishes smooth,
smooth, smooth. I had this with chewy strips of licorice candy—
an unusual combination I recommend highly—but it would also
be good with a tuna salad sandwich.

NGOK' MALT LIQUOR   **CB**   **1.8**
(Pointe Noire, Congo)
Skunky and strong-tasting—a surprise, given its light-golden
color; turns tasteless and lifeless; hoppy presence and relatively
dry finish; disappointing; lacks interest, even with the hoppy
punch.

NGOMA MALT LIQUOR   CB   2.1
(Lome, Togo)
Musty aroma with a mild caramel flavor; increasing taste of old alcohol; sharply hoppy with a cloying hint of malt sweetness; alcohol predominates and detracts from the texture and flavor of most foods; finish is milder, sweeter, and less alcoholic, but still somewhat raw.

NGOMA TOGO PILS   CB   2.7
(Lome, Togo)
Immediate grain taste with subdued but evenhanded texture; no head or Brussels lace to speak of; goes flat halfway through the bottle; a rather bland drink for foods; flavor is better than texture; mildly warming; rating is based primarily on strength of its taste.

NICOLAS DARK ALE (seasonal)   CT   3.1
(Helena, Montana)
Creamy, moist, and sweet, unlike many other Christmas brews; typical burnt-malt taste nicely tempered by smooth texture and restrained sweetness; enchanting specialty beer whose attitude appears to make it welcome with any food—spicy, plain, or in-between; some fading of already weak strength at the end; uncomplicated and straightforward; above average.

NIKSICKO PIVO Pilsener   CB   3.1
(Niksic, Montenegro; former Yugoslavia)
Slight musky odor followed by mellow warm taste with little pizzazz; rather flat texture; much more flavorful alone than with food; gentle sweetness, almost juiciness, remains throughout; won awards in (among other places) London, 1976; Paris, 1932, 1973, 1979; Brussels, 1971, 1974, 1987; Lisbon, 1985; Plovidiv, 1985; Luxembourg, 1977—decide for yourself.

NINE STAR Lager   CB   2.9
(Beijing, China)
Sharp and rice-tasting, but overwhelmed by spicy or highly seasoned foods; comes out refreshed and balanced, and not as weak as at the outset; a grain-hoppiness begins to take over at the finish; label calls this the "Beer For State Banquets." Try it with rice and beans.

NITTANY ALE   CT   3.0
(Philadelphia, Pennsylvania)
Honey-sweet, with the faintest hint of smooth graininess; bitterness is mild and soft-pedaled; smells like fresh-made toast and presents a warm, toasty feel, as if you can go to a wintry football game and wrap your hands around the bottle for warmth and comfort; clear brass color; gains in complexity as it warms; distinctive softness to the mouthfeel; malt character stretches out toward the end. Try this with sweet sausages on a roll.

NOCHE BUENA Lager (annual)   CB   2.4–3.3
(brewed by Moctezuma in Orizaba, Mexico)
A much-sought-after Christmas beer that, in my experience, is above average, though it has been known to fail to reach that level occasionally; negative qualities include a mild, cloying sweetness with bland texture; can switch gears quickly and without warning; sometimes too watery; however, at its best it is strong, full, and flavorful with a richness that complements salty foods; its sweetness and sharpness make a nicely balanced beer; a taste of clove; thick, rich, and bountiful; start looking for this annual release in late October, as it is often difficult to find in the U.S.

NORTH COAST BLUE STAR
GREAT AMERICAN WHEAT BEER   MB/BP   2.3
(Fort Bragg, California)
Too sweet and malty for a wheat beer, though a certain bitterness is present; full; not very fizzy; bitterness becomes increasingly apparent as bottle is emptied; thickish taste continues to stick to roof of mouth; not especially thirst-quenching; uninspired. Pretzels help here.

NORTH COAST OKTOBERFEST ALE
(annual)   MB/BP   0.8
(Fort Bragg, California)
Sweet-sour accent with mild aroma and taste; fruitiness has been sapped out of this ale, leaving it wimpy and without substance; even alcohol content is diminished; clouded brown color with purple overtones; these folks need to scrap everything and start this one all over again.

NORTH COAST OLD NO. 38 STOUT   MB/BP   3.1
(Fort Bragg, California)
Malty aroma; astringent, with flat taste on first sip; crusty, chocolatey underlying flavor moves into caramel; on second pouring, it displays a thick tan head; smooth; vanilla hidden in the deep brown-red body; sweet milkiness emerges when served with poultry, remains "green"-tasting; overall, integrates nicely as the bottle empties; representative of the style; Silver Medal winner at the 1993 Great American Beer Festival. A very good match with duck.

NORTH COAST RED SEAL ALE   MB/BP   2.4
(Fort Bragg, California)
Fruity and flat, but encourages you to have more; nice reddish-amber color complements flavor; remains watery and textureless—you can tell this is made by unskilled, but presumably well-intentioned, hands; premise is promising but not fulfilled; a mild, essentially textureless ale that is subtle enough to interact with food flavors; mild, in the English tradition; alas, the label is more enchanting than the beer. Try it with barley or cream of mushroom soup served with rustic whole-grain bread.

**NORTHAMPTON OLD BROWN
DOG ALE (draft)** BP 3.3
(Northampton, Massachusetts)
Strongly alcoholic and malty in taste and aroma; this is clearly a
strong beer, even after having traveled cross-country; fresh and
sharp, with staying power; good flavorful mixture of malt, hops,
and yeast; some chewiness adds to the enjoyment; well-coordinated
and pleasantly balanced; a calm, attractive brew that finishes with
a mild caramel taste. Goes well with mild cheeses and flavorful
crackers.

NORVIG ALE CB 2.4
(Wisbech, England)
A definite yeasty fruitiness and fresh flowery aroma in the beginning are followed by a hop bite at the back of the throat at
first swallow; thin-bodied; smooth texture; malt sweetness becomes predominant, otherwise there is almost a primitive mouthfeel: basic, uncomplex, eventually almost no hoppiness anywhere;
washed-out red-blond body; finishes weak. Hard cheeses seem to
pep this up a bit. (Not currently available in the U.S.)

NORWEGIAN ICE Pilsener CT 1.6
(Trondheim, Norway)
Not as crisp or sharp as expected; watery and weak—where's the
alcohol? Where's the taste? Slight malty flavor seeps out at mid-
bottle, but that's it; pale, very transparent straw color lets you see
all the bubbles rising and settling; head is gone in a New York
minute, leaving an overall ginger-ale visual effect; this is obviously a product for export to the U.S.

NUTFIELD NOR'EASTER ALE MB 3.5
(Derry, New Hampshire)
Charming malt-hop blend and delightful hit of nutty spiciness
make your mouth water; slight caramel-malt taste and hazelnut
aroma add to the pleasure; wonderfully complex and satisfying;
clear ruby body; finishes with a sharper, more compelling spicy
character; a very tasty beer. Drink with sharp cheese and crackers.

NUTFIELD OLD MAN ALE MB 2.9
(Derry, New Hampshire)
Here's a pretty picture: creamy, rocky, old-lace-colored head atop
a muddy orange-hued caramel body; aroma and taste are light
and substantive, consisting mainly of sweet-caramel; loses some
zip and zest as the glass empties, but the memory of the caramel
alone is worth the effort; a flash of alcohol comes bopping along
at the end, finishing the bottle on an upbeat, but constrained,
note. Interesting accompaniment to beef barley soup.

OASIS CAPSTONE ESB   MB   3.3
(Boulder, Colorado)
Smooth; not as bitter as it should be, but it tastes quite good; prevailing sweetness nicely supports the mildly bitter hoppiness; alcohol is insidious and creeps up on you, prompting a mellow, comforting glow; vague hint of fruit at the end of the bottle; nice and easygoing; remains soft and surprisingly underpowered with barbecued chicken breast and onion rings.

OASIS PALE ALE   MB   2.5
(Boulder, Colorado)
Fresh, tangy hit of orangey-citrus taste on first sip; some fishy mouthfeel, as well, particularly on exhalation; not complex; light-bodied but invigorating; hoppy aroma lingers longer than the hop taste, which begins to fade quickly toward the end. Chinese food helps it to retain its freshness and flavor.

OB LAGER   CB   2.5
(Seoul, Korea)
Light, not very tasty; some wine overtones; neither complicated nor simple; nonassertive and predictable, it follows the lead of food. Good with mild-flavored pasta and noodle dishes.

OBERDORFER DARK HEFEWEIZEN   CB   3.1
(Marktoberdorf, Germany)
Apple aroma; slightly musty; maintains soft fizziness throughout, adding tang to its already smooth character; head stays foamy but thin; nice interplay of taste, texture, and aroma; interesting by itself, but not outstanding, even with a twist of lemon. A thirst-quencher to drink with salty snacks such as potato chips and olives.

ODELL CURMUDGEON'S NIP
BARLEY WINE   RB   2.2
(Fort Collins, Colorado)
Obviously high in alcohol, with a thin stream of malt on the tongue; nice malty sweetness on second sip; alcohol has a sharpness to it; malty flavor and aroma increase as the beer warms; light amber body should have fuller mouthfeel; a malt-alcohol feast, but nothing much else; has all the right ingredients, but they're not put together properly. Best to sip this alone, without food accompaniment.

ODELL EASY STREET WHEAT   MB   3.7
(Fort Collins, Colorado)
Like grapefruit juice with malt and alcohol; citrus fruitiness settles into predictable, smooth palate; nicely integrated; light, and not too fluffy; consistent foam from start to finish.

ODELL 90 SHILLING ALE   MB   3.7
(Fort Collins, Colorado)
Sweet, syrupy-malty aroma is quite attractive; fresh, mildly hoppy mouthfeel gently coats the palate; hints of smoke in the aftertaste intermingle nicely with a touch of nuttiness; a tasty morsel of an ale.

OERBIER ALE   CB   3.2
(Essen, Belgium)
Lots of yeast, lots of alcohol, all accompanied by a surprising amount of fizziness; rich malty aroma has a spicy undertone; like a lollipop with alcohol; thick creamy head helps to deflect some of the stronger taste sensations; some malt-hop complexity is noticed underneath; not for everyone, this is a beer for experienced tastes or for the more adventurous. Best before or after dinner.

**OKANAGAN SPRING PREMIUM
LAGER**   MB   1.1
(Vernon, British Columbia, Canada)
Flat texture, woody taste, some water; poor integration of ingredients; but it does leave a nice layer of Brussels lace.

**OKANAGAN SPRING ST. PATRICK
STOUT**   MB   1.3
(Vernon, British Columbia, Canada)
Shallow caramel flavor is too flat for maximum savoring; thin, with nice tartness and a fruity tang; watery and lacks punch with food; no flavor develops as this stout warms up, dashing initial expectations; no maltiness or any real feel for this brew's ingredients, other than water; at bottom of glass, a burnt flavor emerges as it should have earlier; not full-bodied; so smooth it puts you to sleep—but not soon enough.

O'KEEFE ALE   CB   3.1
(Toronto, Ontario, Canada)
Soft head contrasts with the sharpness of the hazy pale-golden color of the body; moderate complexity in the rounded, almost fruity taste; a hint of alcohol; unassuming, nonintrusive Canadian overtones; grows warm and comforting; pleasant, but not scintillating company. A good match with Chinese or Japanese noodle dishes.

**O'KEEFE'S EXTRA OLD STOCK
MALT LIQUOR**   CB   2.9
(Vancouver, British Columbia, Canada)
Stark, crisp, and light, with unexpected substance; reasonable head; relatively high alcohol content (5.65%/volume); nice balance of taste and texture—at least by itself, without food; not exceptional, but a decent everyday companion; proudly proclaims "Union Made" on the can. A good partner with virtually any food.

OKOCIM O.K. FULL LIGHT Pilsener   CB   2.2
(Warsaw, Poland)

Sweet and airy; flattened texture; smooth mouthfeel; back-of-the-throat sourness comes through with food; mild fruitiness ebbs and flows; pleasantly bland; neither surprising nor memorable.

OKOCIM O.K. PILS   CB   0.3
(Warsaw, Poland)

Lacks flavor and has minimal zest; odd lamb chop taste; pallid honey-yellow color with no head; does not resemble a pilsener; Brussels lace is spotty and ragged—dribbles sit on top of the liquid in the glass; spoiled-fruit aroma with vague malt; far from delightful.

OKOCIM PORTER   CB   3.1
(Okocim, Poland)

Fermented raisiny-fruity aroma wafts up as soon as the beer is poured; the rich, full, hefty taste is similar, but with a bite; strong and demanding all over the mouth; thick with alcohol (8.1%/volume), it sweetens a bit and stays fruity; powerful and stubborn, it keeps its taste presence regardless of what food you have with it.

OKOCIM PREMIUM BEER Pilsener   CB   3.1
(Okocim, Poland)

Hops rapidly become dominant and remain steady and predictable; rounded maltiness is earthy and filling; pinch of bitterness is apparent after most swallows; more balanced and nuanced malt-hop interaction around mid-bottle; unexpectedly soft on the palate; restrained carbonation allows for a fuller appreciation of the distinct flavors; a friendly beer; finishes with grainy sweetness. Enjoy this with red meat cooked medium-well.

OLD AUSTRALIA STOUT   CB   3.8
(Thebarton, South Australia, Australia)

Inviting head, substantive body, almost black color, and pleasant caramel taste on first sip; a hint of sweetness/syrupyness; tangy and sharp; with a bit more body, this would be a very good example of traditional stout; winey aftertaste turns sour in the throat; still, worth asking for. Enjoy with shepherd's pie and other pub grub.

OLD CHICAGO LAGER   CB   1.2
(Chicago, Illinois)

Somewhat stale and quite hoppy; pale straw color; poorly integrated ingredients; slightly sour, with citrus overtones; for the fainthearted.

OLD DETROIT AMBER ALE   CT   3.8
(Frankenmuth, Michigan)

Fruitiness stays in the background while a sweet nuttiness takes over; nicely restrained overall ambiance, as if waiting for food;

full and sharp; not as rich as it should or could be; distinct fruitiness emerges as it warms, as does a touch of caramel flavor; a surprise find. Good with a steak and baked potato dinner.

OLD MILWAUKEE Lager   **CB**   **0.8**
(Detroit, Michigan)
Sour mustiness greets you and stays throughout; no complexity to speak of; hint of greenness; loaded with adjuncts (corn, for example), which make for a weak overall impression.

OLD PECULIER ALE   **CB**   **3.8**
(Masham, England)
Rounded burnt-caramel flavor thickens into fuzzy aftertaste; rich and creamy without food; mildly sticky aftertaste adheres to the roof of the mouth; faint nut aroma; lightly carbonated; increasing sweetness suggests this would not go well with food, though this turns out not to be the case; immediately frothy and creamy; smooth and texturally appealing; flavorful, well balanced; complements the taste of red meats; whiff of alcohol lingers; warm finish and caramel aroma; the label calls this "traditionally brewed Yorkshire Ale"; an excellent choice for the newcomer who wishes to try a moderately dark, moderately alcoholic, distinctive style of ale. Good with prime beef dishes.

OLD RASPUTIN RUSSIAN
IMPERIAL STOUT   **MB**   **3.1**
(Fort Bragg, California)
This beer is filled with alcohol (Imperial stouts usually are) and chocolate; short-lived bite of hoppiness gets renewed with every sip; very smooth, but a bit on the thin side; sits quietly in the glass, with no bubbles to speak of; muddy-brown body glows ruby-red in the right light; comes close to overwhelming the malts and hops at the end; a stout with presence. Add to the delight and have this with rich chocolate cake.

OLD STYLE PILSNER   **CB**   **2.4**
(Vancouver, British Columbia, Canada)
Both light and thick; fuzzy aftertaste; bubbly head thins down and stays down; hops are evident; a rather ordinary beer with some character and strength. Fine with plain everyday fare.

OLD THUMPER EXTRA SPECIAL ALE   **RB**   **2.5**
(Kennebunk, Maine)
Fruity-caramel taste on first sip, along with bruised fruit/appley aroma; sugar-malt flavor is not intrusive; cloudy caramel color supports the thinnest of heads; a tick of alcohol comes along at mid-bottle; tangible caramel-alcohol interaction livens up the proceedings somewhat; finishes malty and caramely. Goes with a sticky-sweet dessert.

OLD VIENNA Lager   **CB**   **3.0**
(Toronto, Ontario, Canada)
Fresh, with a beguiling hint of mustiness; has more complexity than American lagers; fullness and sweetness emerge with sweet-and-sour foods; typically crisp, though lighter than most Canadian beers; retains its freshness; better than average. A good choice with barbecued spare ribs.

OLDE ENGLISH 800 Malt Liquor   **CB**   **2.9**
(brewed by Heileman in La Crosse, Wisconsin)
Very smooth; appropriately sweet; flavorful but unobtrusive with food; adequately balanced between hops and malts; surprisingly pleasant warming finish; Gold Medal winner at the 1994 Great American Beer Festival. Good with roast beef or ham.

OLDE HEURICH MAERZEN   **CT**   **2.6**
(Pittsburgh, Pennsylvania)
Mildly fruity and pleasantly sweet; relatively flat in texture; somewhat watery as the bottle progresses; tea-like color and taste; on the mild side; similar in caramel maltiness to Vienna amber, with little intrusion by the hops; not as smooth as advertised on the label; sweet malt finish and aroma. Good with pizza.

OLDE RED EYE RED ALE   **MB**   **0.4**
(brewed by Southern California Brewing Co.
in Torrance, California)
Sludge-brown color; intense sour-grapefruit taste is noticeable just by inhaling; sharply fizzy; green-tasting; fruity, with a nasty bite that scratches the throat; too rough and raw even to tolerate; obviously a brew designed to capitalize on the current interest in microbrews, without regard for flavor or interest.

OLDE WYNDHAM FROG 'N HOUND
CREAM ALE   **MB**   **2.3**
(Willimantic, Connecticut)
Lightly hopped and mildly grassy, with a winsome hoppiness that emerges dominant; mild and unobtrusive, but surprisingly appealing, at least for a while; suggestions of vanilla come and go; smooth; in the end it's the bitterness that comes through, fleshing out the otherwise relatively bland taste; finishes with a last gasp of grassiness. Drink this with something that has zest—pretzels, chips, etc.

OLDENBERG PIOUS PALE ALE   **MB**   **2.5**
(Fort Mitchell, Kentucky)
Moderated hoppiness from tip of the tongue to back of the throat; steady, predictable hop drumbeat, just what a good pale ale should have; unruffled, almost smooth texture; with your nose over the pale amber liquid, take a deep breath about mid-bottle and smell the hint of caramel-malt; finishes too flat; three-quarters of a

good bottle of beer; the remainder is disappointing. Pretty good with bacon-lettuce-tomato sandwich and lots of potato chips.

OLDENBERG PREMIUM VERUM Lager   MB   2.6
(Fort Mitchell, Kentucky)

Malty Vienna amber sweetness is struck immediately in the middle of the tongue by a (purposefully) sour jolt; full-bodied, with no head to speak of; strong and uncompromising with too little complexity to make it genuinely interesting; deep burnt-caramel aroma and hazy yellow-amber color; a mixed bag. Fine with most pasta or rice dishes.

OLIVER'S SCOTTISH ALE   BP   2.2
(Baltimore, Maryland)

Tawny, smooth, and unbalanced; mildly fruity; not much zestiness or texture; quite weak in alcohol and overall mouthfeel; somewhat watery; neither strong nor full-bodied; other than the color, I'm not sure why they call this a Scottish ale.

OLYMPIA Pilsener   CB   2.1
(San Antonio, Texas)

Clean and light in taste, texture, and appearance; mild malt aroma tantalizes your interest, but never really satisfies—you keep waiting for the taste to kick in or hint that this beer is alive and breathing; perhaps it's the advertising exerting its influence, but the water is ultimately what moves this pale, limp brew along; drink alone or with cheese and crackers; it's not bad—there's just not much to it

OMMEGANG BELGIAN-STYLE
ABBEY ALE   MB   4.0
(Cooperstown, New York)

Rich, fruity, and yeasty; pungent mouthfeel is rounded and reserved; light dusting of spice, including licorice; restrained sugary sweetness; alcohol aroma is full and everywhere, suggesting a full-flavored burgundy with chutzpah; concentrate and you'll pick up berry notes in the aroma; deep-garnet body holds aloft a wavy old-ivory long-lasting head; this is a wonderful American-made abbey-style ale that you'd swear was brewed in Belgium; go out right now and get a bottle. Goes great with sliced pork and mashed potatoes.

OMMEGANG HENNEPIN
BELGIAN-STYLE ALE   MB   4.2
(Cooperstown, New York)

Tart and clovey, with an excellent balancing yeast-hoppy character; crisp and invigorating; hints of banana add to the charm; soft on the palate; time-released sugary sweetness threads its way through the deftly calibrated bitterness; beautiful contoured head stays throughout and tastes like the beer itself—a noteworthy accomplishment in itself; plenty of alcohol to tie it all together; gains in yeasty tartness a day after the bottle is opened; this is an excellent beer, no question. Versatile enough to be imbibed without food or with, such as medium-well roast beef.

LABEL LORE

*T*hough relatively new on the brewing scene (it started operations in 1997), Ommegang has made a quick and lasting impression on beer lovers from coast to coast. The Belgian-style brewery, located on a 136-acre former hops farm in upstate New York, makes beers in the tradition of the European artisanal breweries, known for their complex bottle-conditioned ales. It is the only brewery of its kind in the United States and is a joint venture with the Belgian breweries Affligem, Dubuisson, and Moortgat.

ORANJEBOOM PREMIUM LAGER   **CB**   **3.4**
(Breda and Rotterdam, Holland)
Strong hops; sharp texture; reasonable head; reddish-golden color; blunt yet restrained; fuller flavor, including rice graininess, as texture diminishes; becomes full-bodied and bold; increasing smooth maltiness; virtues are magnified when imbibed by itself; well made, firm, and moderately lively; label boasts "Crown Prince of Lagers." Goes well alongside a hamburger with green chiles.

ORCHARD STREET GOLDEN ALE   **MB**   **2.4**
(Bellingham, Washington)
Sour-bitter first sip changes to a more definite, and acceptable, hop-bitter taste, which stays on the roof of the mouth; light-bodied and quite dry; minimal hit of spiciness is noted at mid-bottle; finishes with some sugary sweetness and a following dash of tartness; flavor kind of pushes itself on you, so drink in small doses.

OREGON ORIGINAL HONEY Ale   **MB/BP**   **1.5**
(Portland, Oregon)
Obviously honey-based at first, then sweetness fades; flat and zipless; soda-like fizziness toward the bottom of the glass doesn't help nor does weak off-blond color; in the end, quite forgettable.

ORKNEY DARK ISLAND BEER Ale   **CB**   **2.9**
(Quoyloo, Scotland)
Slightly smoky in the nose and mouth; maltiness becomes full-flavored as it trickles down the throat; soft, foamy head sticks to your moustache (or upper lip); vague roasted character and light

chocolate mouthfeel are inevitably followed by the ever-present complex maltiness; quite smooth; fresh flash of grassiness makes a delightful surprise near the end of the bottle; a blend of chocolate, earthy, and smoky flavors finishes this off in style. Try it with strong-flavored fish and chips.

ORKNEY SKULLSPLITTER ALE   CB   3.8
(Quoyloo, Scotland)
Full, sweet caramely mouthfeel goes hand-in-hand with a mildly nutty flavor that expands at the back of the mouth; pleasantly accommodating bitterness offers just the right balance; vague but definitely present nutty aroma grows in character as the beer warms; alcohol slowly but surely has an effect; nicely layered and subtly complex; very easy to drink. Treat yourself to a snifter or two after a hearty meal, while sitting in front of a gently burning peat fire.

ORVAL TRAPPIST ALE   AB   2.1
(Florenville, Belgium)
Expensive, distinctive wine/musty/perfume taste; high alcohol content contributes to the bitter mouthfeel; cloudy color; many knowledgeable beer drinkers claim this is one of the best made; complex and rich, it can be stored for several years; but sample first before deciding if it's worth the shelf space. Best as an *apéritif* or *digestif*.

OSB STOCK ALE   MB   3.0
(Bellingham, Washington)
Soft and fruity; mildly sweet; tamped-down hop character; gradual, hardly noticeable emergence of malt eventually matches the impact of the hops, placing both ingredients in an even, equitable balance; finishes quickly, with a fleeting hint of sugar; a mild, accommodating beer that offers enjoyment at it own pace. Drink this with light fish dishes.

OSTANKINSKOYE BEER Pilsener   CB   0.7
(Moscow, Russia)
Tart, sharp, and tasting of alcohol; gains in malt sweetness after three or four sips; tastes cabbagey; remains harsh and astringent, with a hard-edged mouthfeel; stiff and not complex; weakens at the end, so the earlier unpleasant tastes seem even more intense in retrospect. Pour yourself some vodka instead.

OTTAKRINGER GOLD FASSL PILS   CB   2.9
(Vienna, Austria)
Nice rice taste, but also wine sourness; light, even for a pilsener; underlying tastiness isn't readily detected, especially a shame since the pleasant malt sweetness is too deeply hidden to be easily savored. Try it with a cheese pizza.

OTTAKRINGER GOLD FASSL VIENNA
Lager   CB   2.5
(Vienna, Austria)
Full, with an edge; undercurrent of honey; bit of flat aftertaste; not bad, but not memorable, either; a run-of-the-mill beer for run-of-the-mill food.

OTTER CREEK HICKORY SWITCH
SMOKED AMBER ALE   RB   2.9
(Middlebury, Vermont)
Roasted and woody flavors settle pleasantly on the back of the throat; toasted nutty character stays in the aftertaste; smoky character becomes noticeable as the shiny amber body warms, and is reminiscent of tasty bacon bits; smoked mouthfeel remains dominant, but not dominating; texturally soft, almost creamy; finishes with a stretched-out smokiness and a suggestion of chocolate, of all things. A good beer to have with chestnuts warming on an open fire.

OTTER CREEK OKTOBERFEST
AUTUMN ALE (seasonal)   MB   2.5
(Middlebury, Vermont)
Grassy, with a nice sprinkling of hops that neatly balances an even-tempered malty sweetness; hop character changes into a number of different taste sensations, not all of them wonderful; makes fizzy sounds in the mouth just before you swallow; evolves into a maltier rather than hoppier brew, but the last hurrah is a mild hop mouthfeel; take it or leave it.

OTTO BROTHERS MOOSE JUICE
STOUT   MB/BP   3.0
(Wilson, Wyoming)
Reserved, as if the malt and roasted sensations are being experienced from afar; mildly and nicely unassertive; fresh just-brewed aroma; very appealing latte-colored body, touched off by a faint red glow; hints of chocolate malt toward the end; a very attractive stout that needs to be wound up a notch or two. A good beer to have with oysters and hot sauce.

OTTO BROTHERS TETON ALE   MB/BP   3.4
(Wilson, Wyoming)
Soft and mellow; continuing tangy fruitiness along with citrus-spice mouthfeel; acquires more grapefruit presence while it warms; substantial, long-lasting sheets of Brussels lace; loses some texture as it goes along; maintains its composure and finishes in mouth-watering style. Try this with fresh mountain trout.

OXFORD WHITE OX WHEAT ALE   MB   3.2
(Baltimore, Maryland)
Dry, with a vague citrus–orange peel aroma and flavor; slight

spiciness lingers on the tongue but comes and goes elsewhere in the mouth; flavor becomes fuller after several swallows, evolving into a well-balanced bitter-orange taste; far hoppier and more palatable after warming to room temperature; light-bodied. The choice of accompanying food is tuna fish on toasted rye bread.

PABST BLUE RIBBON DRAFT Lager   CB   2.1
(San Antonio, Texas)

Tastes a little like draft, if you concentrate hard and there aren't too many distractions; too many filling adjuncts; relatively soft and creamy for an American beer. Good with salted chips and a creamy dip.

PACENA CENTENARIO Pilsener   CB   2.6
(La Paz, Bolivia)

Light, sweet, and smooth; some emerging citrus with counterpoint of gentleness; head is medium-to-wispy; modulated grain character lowers assertiveness of the 5% alcohol content; easygoing; fizzy; bland except for a pungent yeastiness; thin and sharp; very pale. Primarily a thirst-quencher, but could be matched with mildly seasoned pork dishes.

PACIFIC DRAFT Pilsener   CT   1.7
(Vancouver, British Columbia, Canada)

Genuine draft taste (this came in a can); slightly sour; rough texture without food; not high-quality or high-interest; pedestrian at best—why walk with this when you can run with something better? Passable with hot dogs or hamburgers.

PACIFICO CLARA Pilsener   CB   3.1
(Mazatlán, Mexico)

Sharp, clean mouthfeel that veers toward an off-taste as it is swallowed; remains smooth and easy; not fancy or complex; spicy food easily blunts and dulls its effects; workmanlike, with no pretensions. Fine for non-spicy Mexican seafood dishes served with rice and beans.

PADERBORNER PILSENER   CB   0.2
(Paderborn, Germany)

Cheesy aroma; rough and raw-tasting; what discernible taste there is is sour, odd, and unpleasant; this is unfinishable—ugh; has the lightest beer color I've ever seen; malty aroma peeks out briefly, thereby keeping it from getting a 0.0 rating. Can announces "More than a Pounder." It also says, "Mit Einem Paderborner Haaben Sie Mehr." Whatever . . .

PALERMO ESTRASBURGO Lager   CB   2.2
(Quilmes, Argentina)

Slight skunky odor; flat taste and a touch of grain on first sip; faded flavor may be the result of long travels and time in the bottle; too bland for a serious beer, especially when the flavor withers next to an egg burrito; tastes like zesty water; moderate body suggests somebody gave some thought to quality, but was apparently overruled in other areas.

PALM ALE   CB   3.2
(Brussels, Belgium)

Thickish, with a nice balance of fruitiness and modulated strength; cloudy red-golden color adds to the enjoyment; maintains a richness, though there's a hint of interfering sweetness; smoky and toasted malt aroma; taste reminiscent of apples and oranges; easygoing character is not up to hot or spicy food; quickly dissolving head makes you long for more body; retains its interest and appeal throughout, like a longtime friend. Overall, a substantial beer that goes with food you can sink your teeth into.

PANAMA CERVEZA ALLEMANA STYLE
Lager   CB   3.6
(Panama City, Panama)

More texture than taste; evenhanded, compact malt/hop balance stays throughout; sparkly to start; becomes more integrated as meal progresses; grows on you. Good with shrimp jambalaya or shrimp with hot sauce.

PANDA Pilsener   CB   3.5
(Shanghai, China)

Nice immediate rice taste; light, but holds its ground with food; even-tempered and predictable; pleasing aftertaste; a good friendly beer. A thirst-quenching choice with barbecued spare ribs; good light match for meat-and-potatoes suppers.

PAPER CITY CAPTAIN ELIZUR'S
HERITAGE RED ALE   MB   3.2
(Holyoke, Massachusetts)

Slight, toasted-malt taste; minimal bitterness at each swallow; sweet, mildly spicy aroma; slight bitterness sits on the center of the tongue and spreads slowly as you drink it; intimations of chocolate come and go; well-balanced between hop-bitterness and malt-sweetness; hazy, reddish-brown body; fruity-malty aroma and mild malty taste at the end. Interesting confrontation with chocolate chip cookies.

PASADENA LAGER NATURAL DRAFT   CT   1.0
(Vancouver, British Columbia, Canada)

Sharp, with quickly diminishing textural breadth and depth; faded background taste with a hint of rancidity; bad aftertaste.

PASQUINI'S RED ALE   CT   3.8
(brewed in Denver, Colorado)

Smart and tart, with just the right amount of fruitiness; crisply bitter; somewhat perfumey; increasing bitterness adds to the lively finish; just this side of hearty; picturesque configuration of cobwebby Brussels lace; a parting swoosh of tasty maltiness ends things on the right flavor note. If you're in Denver make sure you have this house brew at Pasquini's Pizzeria, with the Pizzetta Margherita. Everyone else does.

PAULANER ALT MUNCHER DUNKEL   CB   3.9
(Munich, Germany)

Sharp and sparkly; dark; lightly burnt taste, making for an interesting balance and combination; almost a layered taste effect; dry and quite malty at the end; think of this mellow brew as a deeply satisfying, good example of the German style. Just right with hamburgers or shish kabob.

B E E R   F A C T

*D*unkel means "dark" in German and identifies the classic Munich (Munchner) dark-brown malty style.

PAULANER BAVARIAN ALPINE
EXTREME ALE   CB   2.6
(Munich, Germany)

Sour and skunky; pale-straw, almost ginger-ale color; sharp, cutting alcohol taste; on second day (after bottle is recapped and placed in fridge), malts, hops, and texture were more integrated and balanced; a certain warmth is also present; finishes with a powerful but manageable grain aroma. Goes well with fruits and nuts.

PAULANER HEFE-WEIZEN   CB   2.9
(Munich, Germany)

As expected, very yeasty and spritzy; head remains foamy and cohesive atop cloudy opaqueness; too yeasty and rancid-fruit-tasting to be acceptable overall (rancid=oxidized=rotten, harsh, sour); mellows and warms as meal progresses; dry, firm finish grudgingly comes and quickly goes; not an all-star, but a beer for individual tastes. Compatible with most red meats.

PAULANER MUNCHEN NR. 1 LAGER
(seasonal)   CB   2.2
(Munich, Germany)

Slightly sour; attractive maltiness greets you and remains; well integrated and balanced with food, but dull and plodding by itself. Good matched with grilled red meats, green salads with creamy or blue cheese dressing, baked potatoes with sour cream.

PAULANER OKTOBERFEST Lager   CB   3.8
(Munich, Germany)

As close to dark beer as you can get without actually being dark-colored, though, fortunately, many dark-beer attributes are present; full-bodied; some effervescence, but not obtrusive. Good with simple broiled or grilled chicken dishes.

PAULANER PREMIUM LAGER   CB   3.0
(Santiago, Chile)

Malty and clove-like with fluffy but decreasing head; grains emerge and provide roughness against the smoothness of the texture; gentle fizz ends the bottle, and the evening. Nice with lemon-baked chicken.

B E E R   F A C T

*M*unich's largest brewery, Paulaner, is close to 400 years old. It was one of the first in Germany to use electrified cooling units.

PAULANER SALVATOR DOPPELBOCK   CB   4.0
(Munich, Germany)

Molasses flavor and apple fruitiness with bite and backbone make you take notice immediately; obvious alcohol content is nicely wrapped in a creamy, mellow texture with, surprisingly, no head to speak of; rich, roasted, and filling; drier at the end; roasted malt mouthfeel remains throughout; strong, resilient, and memorable; a top-notch doppelbock with complexity and balance. An excellent choice with spaghetti and meatballs or other red-sauced pastas.

B E E R   F A C T

*D*oppel means "double" in German; *bock* means "strong, malty, and highly alcoholic" (literally, it means "goat"). Not surprisingly, then, doppelbocks, with their particularly potent warmth, are available, and popular, in late winter and early spring. Of course, if you can find them, you are allowed to drink them at other times of the year.

PEARL LAGER   CB   2.3
(San Antonio, Texas)

Solid down the middle, but raggedy at the far reaches of the mouth and throat; the water is fresh and sharp, overshadowing weakish hops and washed-out malt; minimal grain taste appears at the bottom of the can; a reasonable choice if you need a quick, straightforward thirst-quencher, but not worth going out of your way to find. Try it with all-American classics such as hot dogs, meat loaf, or fried chicken.

PECAN STREET Lager   CT   2.5
(Shiner, Texas)
Immediate perfumey taste; heavier than the usual lager; soft texture with virtually no head; perfume taste fades and becomes more interesting, more acceptable, and sharper with grilled meats; respectable, but far from exciting.

PEDAVENA PILS CLASSICA   CB   2.1
(Italy)
Soft; faintly hoppy; hint of perfume in the taste; playful mustiness is a nice balance to the sharp hoppiness; firm, ungiving mouthfeel; not texturally assertive enough; flavor and pizzazz weaken at mid-bottle and stay that way; head is thick at first, then rapidly disappears; ultimately flat and unfulfilling.

PELICAN DORYMAN'S DARK ALE   BP   1.3
(Pacific City, Oregon)
Raisin flavor and aroma—you can almost taste the iron content; definitely a metallic aftertaste; fruitiness increases, but stays flat and uninvigorating; leaves a musty feel all over the mouth; stronger raisin presence at the bottom of the glass; not complex; overriding flavor is reminiscent of iron filings.

PENNSYLVANIA PENN PILSNER   RB   3.7
(Pittsburgh, Pennsylvania)
Tingly with warm, comforting undercurrent; nicely balanced between barley malt and hops; refined textural quality usually found in more expensive beers; rounded body provides rolling satisfaction along the tongue; heftier than the usual pilsener; good for two to three bottles at a time with or without food—won't give you any unexpected taste jolts; a very satisfying beer. Best with chiliburgers, roast beef sandwiches, or a pot of baked beans.

PERONI Lager   CB   3.1
(Rome, Italy)
Fresh up front and full at the throat; creamy head; steady flavor remains with food; sharpness on the upper palate persists; retains its fizz throughout; gentle malt taste, reminiscent of bread; mild but ever-present thickness detracts somewhat; some muddiness at the end; quality with mass appeal. Serve with shrimp and a piquant cocktail sauce or herb-broiled chicken.

PERRY'S MAJESTIC LAGER   CT   2.6
(Frankenmuth, Michigan)
Light and fluffy with a hint of varnish; maltiness evolves into

hoppiness, but overall is too weak for strongly flavored foods; light and hardly carbonated; retains a freshness; a thirst-quenching, pleasant, friendly beer that doesn't tax you or your taste buds; nicely integrated at the end; made from organically grown barley and hops. Pair with bland foods such as turkey burgers or plain grilled fish.

PERTOTALE FARO LAMBIC   **CB**   **2.9**
(Lembeek, Belgium)
Strong yeast aroma, thick head, slightly sour fruity taste, and a rush of warmth all greet the senses as soon as you pop the cork from this elongated green bottle; classic off-white head sits atop the medium-amber liquid; surprising hints of orange pekoe and a heavy dose of cloves appear in the alcohol; yeast taste remains subdued, allowing for mellow orange taste; a sweetened, less assertive version of the lambic style (faro is a type of lambic, with additional sugar or caramel); finish is warm, spicy, and hoppy; orange taste becomes more sweetly pungent as beer warms; dry, lightly fruity finish; toasty and satisfying. Customarily poured with dessert or as an after-dinner drink.

PETE'S GOLD COAST LAGER   **CT**   **3.2**
(Seattle, Washington; Winston-Salem, North Carolina)
Golden (as advertised) quintessential lager (as advertised); hops practically bounce around in your mouth; dry, creamy aftertaste coats the palate; distinctive mellow taste; flowery aroma appears as long-neck bottle is finished; heady balance of taste, texture, and aroma; hops have the last word; not top-of-the-line, but a better American lager than most. A mellow match for a hot pastrami on rye or an olive-topped pizza.

BEER FACT

*P*ete's Brewing Company, one of the most successful of the first wave of U.S. microbreweries, was bought by Gambrinus Importers in 1998 for $68 million. Gambrinus is an importer of Corona, Modelo, and Moosehead. It also owns the pioneering BridgePort Brewing Company in Portland, Oregon.

PETE'S SUMMER BREW PALE ALE   **CT**   **2.7**
(Seattle, Washington; Winston-Salem, North Carolina)
Thickish, with a balanced malt-hop feel throughout the mouth; highly carbonated, as it should be; lemon taste is present, but not readily apparent; gains a moderated sharpness that complements crisp-crust pizza; flavorful, without revealing individual ingredients; a bit too cumbersome to be a truly refreshing light

summer brew. Makes a decent partner with an egg salad sand-wich on toast.

PETE'S WICKED ALE   **CT**   **3.8**
(Seattle, Washington; Winston-Salem, North Carolina)
Lovely burnt-caramel taste with fizziness; emerging sweetness as ale warms; silky texture on the tongue fades to dull undertaste at the back of the throat when drunk with smoked foods; grows sweeter with bread and rolls; not as thick and full-bodied as it could be, but still welcoming with its blend of warmth, fruiti-ness, and smoothness; texture weakens, however; this may be best one bottle at a time rather than multiple bottles at one sitting—too many sips would quickly diminish its attractive textural and taste qualities, which are not insubstantial. Compatible with Chi-nese noodle dishes, pasta primavera, or pasta with pesto sauce.

BEER FACT

*P*ete's beers no longer sport the distinctive and attractive picture of Millie, the brewery co-founder's English bull terrier, on their labels. The original packaging was changed because the desired image was getting uncomfortably muddied by the logo's resemblance to another canine, the once-ubiquitous Budweiser dog. Millie has been replaced by a photo of Pete's grandfather.

PETE'S WINTER BREW—
AMBER ALE (annual)   **CT**   **3.1**
(Seattle, Washington; Winston-Salem, North Carolina)
Mellow spiciness; deep root-beer color; fresh-tasting; subdued fla-vor; tasty; light, dainty, yet substantive; more complexity and ap-peal than many other winter brews; oddly, the half-inch tan-white head foams and stays after most of the bottle has been poured; hint of nutmeg fittingly supports the raspberry taste; despite the fruity sweetness, this is an unusually adaptable drink; finish is thin and creamy smooth, almost textureless; my local supplier ran out of this quickly once the locals discovered it. Tasty ac-companiment to spicy Chinese food or peppery-hot main dishes.

PETER'S BRAND PILSENER   **CB**   **2.3**
(Amersfoort, Holland)
Rounded sharpness; large bubbles in head suggest artificial car-bonation; flattens as bottle empties; consistency of flavor doesn't remain in place from start to finish; ends with dull mild citrus taste, which lessens its attraction. Good with sweet barbecue sauces, herbed pasta salads, and dishes with a lot of cilantro.

PETRUS OAK AGED DARK BEER   CB   2.8
(Bavikhore, Belgium)

Gentle cherry and wood taste follows a soft cherry-wine aroma that is mild and easygoing; thick tan head emits a continuous noisy fizz; malt and hops are kept well hidden; smooth and easy going down the throat; some sourness toward the end of the bottle; sugary sweetness saves the day at the last sip; this is not a beer to analyze, just to enjoy. Garlicky green olives and pickled vegetables add to the enjoyment.

PHILADELPHIA'S IPA   BP   2.9
(Portland, Oregon)

Dry and to the point, with a slightly bitter fruitiness that lasts into the aftertaste; bitterness puckers the mouth, letting you know this is a well-made IPA; significantly carbonated; finely configured Brussels lace disappears too quickly; weakens too much at the end. Makes for a brisk accompaniment to this small brewpub's tasty meatball sandwich.

PHILADELPHIA'S TUGBOAT STOUT   BP   1.0
(Portland, Oregon)

Smooth, somewhat watery and lackluster; too smooth for its own good; very vague chocolate taste; hint of roastedness, but not enough for the style, or for taste excitement; musty aftertaste on the tongue—not a good sign; cask-conditioned, meaning flavor should be even more intense; needs work overall.

PICKWICK ALE   MB   2.5
(Boston, Massachusetts)

Sharp on the throat, complete with a husky fruitiness that emits a growing, but controlled, hoppy mouthfeel; nice, sweet patch of malt pops up after several sips; mix of hops and malt is like a veneer, rather than a display of depth and character; lingering toffee-sweet mouthfeel after each swallow; burnt-match aroma intrudes unexpectedly; no taste is overwhelming, which may be a good thing.

LABEL LORE

*O*riginally brewed in the mid-'teens by the Harvard Brewery, Pickwick was Boston's best-selling beer brand in the 1950s and 1960s. Reintroduced by Harpoon Brewery, it bears the name of Charles Dickens' popular character in *The Pickwick Papers*.

PIELS DRAFT Pilsener   **CB**   **1.0**
(Detroit, Michigan)

Thin and mildly crisp; flat, no complexity; very pale, almost lemon in color, which reflects the lack of real substance in the taste; passing hint of skunkiness; no distinctiveness or even a glimmer of identifiable ingredients, other than corn as a filler and lightener; food makes the beer taste better than it really is; a nonbeer.

PIG'S EYE PILSNER   **MB**   **2.5**
(St. Paul, Minnesota)

Undistinguished; not as carbonated as it should be; nice Brussels lace, which fades too quickly to really enjoy; some malt presence at mid-bottle; too sharp and too hard to serve with a meal; remains fresh but uninteresting; oddly, for a pilsener, it improves as it warms—more flavor and complexity emerge; malty aroma also makes a (tentative) appearance. Serve with salted nuts or potato chips.

B E E R   F A C T

According to legend, Pig's Eye was the original name and site of what is today St. Paul, Minnesota. The town allegedly was named after a famous one-eyed local bootlegger whose snouty features and tiny eyes were reminiscent of a certain portly animal.

PIKE INDIA PALE ALE   **MB**   **3.8**
(Seattle, Washington)

Juicy Fruit gum aroma, alongside a balanced thickish bitterness; well-crafted balance between malt and bitter flavor sensations; pungent and strong, it keeps your attention; placid, shapely head; a pale ale with backbone that finishes with just the right combination of smooth and bitter. Pair this with a fresh catch from the sea.

PIKE PALE ALE   **MB**   **3.6**
(Seattle, Washington)

Perfumey grapefruit taste and aroma with emerging clove background; ingredients become well balanced, but weaken with food; interesting and different; thinner than I'd like, but lovely copper-brown color compensates; mellows, with grapefruit flavor tantalizingly at the forefront, even at the last sip; Bronze Medal winner at the 1993 Great American Beer Festival. Very tasty with lamb.

PILSENER   CB   4.0
(Quito, Ecuador)
Soft and velvety; smooth going down; wispy Belgian lace lasts
the length of the drink; subdued grain; fresh and enlivening—a
very good pilsener. An assertive partner for a hero (submarine)
sandwich.

PILSENER CLUB PREMIUM   CB   1.0
(San Antonio and Galveston, Texas)
Green unfinished taste; cheap perfumey flavor and aroma; chemical mouthfeel; some yeast makes a fleeting appearance, but overall a narrow band of taste prevails; no aftertaste; it has some
thirst-quenching qualities; good in comparison to Old Milwaukee and Schaefer.

PILSENER OF EL SALVADOR   CB   2.5
(San Salvador, El Salvador)
Immediately sweet and appealing, but changes quickly to sharp
bitterness; fades into a run-of-the-mill beer with food; alone, it
has more body and a modicum of taste integrity; light and dry,
with corn adjunct—a workingman's beer; the clerk at the store
referred to it not by its proper name, but as *Corazon de Rojo* (Red
Heart)—exactly what is found on the stark white-and-red label.
A versatile companion for a wide range of foods.

PILSNER URQUELL   CB   3.5
(Pilsen, Czechoslovakia)
Crisp, fresh, and mustily hoppy pleasant, understated aroma; intensely carbonated; floral mouthfeel contains some bitterness, but
it is subtle and well calibrated; admirable textural strength; slides
into tempered sweetness with spicy foods; a first-class beer to be
enjoyed in multiples; considered noteworthy from an historical
point of view.

B E E R   F A C T

*P*ilsner Urquell is the original pilsener, introduced
in 1842. It still sets the standard for pilseners.

**PINEHURST VILLAGE DOUBLE
EAGLE SCOTCH ALE**   MB   3.3
(Aberdeen, North Carolina)
Wonderful nutty taste and aroma evolve into a faint nutmeg character in the aftertaste; lasting, lingering hoppiness is a little bit
bitter, with a compact, snappish bite; a scrim of tiny bubbles
coats the sides of the glass; medium-bodied; rich with flavor and
brewing integrity; to take full advantage of the brewer's obvious

ability, the overall character should be fleshed out just a bit more; finishing creamy and smooth, it leaves malt and the signature nuttiness in its wake. A great match with strong-flavored cheeses.

PINKUS ORGANIC MUNSTER ALT   CB   1.5
(Munster, Germany)

Sour and tangy; astringent, which fades after a swallow or two; texture is smooth and punchless; maintains a "hard" taste; flat and uninspiring; malt aroma helps mellow overall harshness; aroma is the only element of interest; some honeyed sweetness appears at the end of the bottle.

PINKUS ORGANIC UR PILS   CB   1.9
(Munster, Germany)

Sour, flattening off-taste that evolves into overly hoppy floweriness; light, firm, and typically dry; a bit too astringent; retains rich, creamy head—a nice contrast to the body's pungency; improves and becomes more pilsener-like with food, but never reaches a truly acceptable level; unexpectedly weak; leaves a trellis of Brussels lace the length of the tall pilsener glass. Okay with tuna or salmon steaks.

PINKUS HOME BREW WEIZEN   CB   1.3
(Munster, Germany)

Sparkly, sharp, and somewhat sour; thin and unassuming; no hint texturally or flavorwise of wheat, clove, or tartness; disappointing with food; smells like the beer left in a glass after a party.

PIRAAT ALE   CB   4.0
(Ertvelde, Belgium)

This strong, yeast-laden Belgian ale is high in alcohol content (10.5%/volume); it is also tart, sharp, and full-bodied; the intricately constructed spicy-honey flavor fills the crevices of the mouth; sweet and bitter at the same time; pieces of Brussels lace rain down onto the 24-carat-gold-colored body, creating visual pleasure as well; aged and fermented in the keg, it finishes yeasty and deliciously satisfying. Best to sip this slowly in a place with no distractions so you can fully concentrate on its many nuances.

POINT MAPLE WHEAT (seasonal)   MB   2.2
(Stevens Point, Wisconsin)

Nicely done maple syrup mouthfeel parallels a mildly sharp wheat character; maple, however, remains the dominating presence; placing a wedge of lemon into the pale-amber body brings the syrup into just the right balance; despite this first aid, it eventually settles into being a one-note beer—maple syrup; begins to taste a lot like cough syrup; interesting, but not really a beer worth having.

POINT SPECIAL PREMIUM LAGER   CB   2.9
(Stevens Point, Wisconsin)

Smooth; "cool" in texture; laid-back; somewhat dry; interesting not-quite-spicy taste; pretensions of being full-bodied (contains corn grits); smooths out toward the end; an unexciting but well-made beer; Bronze Medal winner at the 1993 Great American Beer Festival. Serve with snack foods such as nachos, olives, and flavored crackers.

T A P   T I P

Nice Legs

"*L*egs" refers to the mini-streams of liquid that drip down the inside of the glass. They are usually found in higher-alcohol brews and denote strength and quality.

POLANDER BEER Lager   **CB**   **3.1**
(Koszalin, Poland)
Grainy, tea-like flavor is quickly followed by a sharp, compelling, malty mouthfeel; crisp and fresh-tasting; grainy taste stays consistent and strong; faint perfumey presence in the aftertaste; gains bitterness as you drink; grainy-hop character at back of tongue; sturdy and straightforward in presentation; tasty and well-balanced; tough and self-confident enough to go well with just about all kinds of foods, from red meat to light fish to fresh salads.

POLAR Lager   **CB**   **1.0**
(Caracas, Venezuela)
Weak nose (no aroma) and bad legs (low alcohol presence); not complex; raw and harsh; like a homebrew; doesn't aspire to greatness; take it for what it is.

PONY EXPRESS HONEY BLONDE ALE   **MB**   **0.7**
(Olathe, Kansas)
Rather sour, harsh, and spoiled-tasting; flat texture; slight malt aroma, but nothing to write home about; musty feel on the tongue; not complex; uninteresting.

PONY EXPRESS NUT BROWN ALE   **MB**   **2.6**
(Olathe, Kansas)
Nutty-coffee taste and plummy aroma present a pleasing introduction; quite malty; faint acidity and faint spicy mouthfeel; flavors seem to meld together, producing a rich, soft, tasty complexity; body shines with a brown-amber glow; takes on a calming roastedness toward the end; finishes with a pleasant nutty-spicy aftertaste. Try this nut brown ale with a dessert pastry.

PONY EXPRESS RATTLESNAKE
PALE ALE   MB   1.6
(Olathe, Kansas)
Background hoppiness is clean and crisp and non-assertive; some
increase in hop character, but not enough; lacks depth; quick
touch of bitterness disappears just as quickly; harsh on the palate;
sours at the end; not worth the effort.

POPE'S "1880" Ale   MB/BP   3.6
(Dorchester, England)
Wine-like fire-brewed taste; very close to a light-style dark beer;
similar to Watney's but a bit more bitter; evident freshness; heightened aroma—due to the type of hops as well as special process-
ing methods—makes this strong ale an aromatic delight and
enjoyable experience. Good with mild cheeses or shellfish.

PORT ROYAL EXPORT Pilsener CB   1.3
(San Pedro Sula, Honduras)
Off-tasting, crisp mouthfeel in the body, accompanied by softness attributable to immediately foaming head; deeper taste at
the back of the tongue does little for food; uninteresting, inconsistent, and uncertain (can you enjoy it or not? the next sip may
change your mind); continuing fullness is a positive that keeps
it from being a complete dud.

B E E R   F A C T

*P*ort Royal, made by a transplanted Bavarian brewmaster, boasts that its beer is imported in
refrigerated ships. "We certify: The draft pilsener
character of this beer has been safeguarded during
ocean shipment by refrigeration at a constant temperature." A good thing, too, since heat and fluctuating temperatures speed spoilage.

PORTERHOUSE RED ALE (draft) BP   3.0
(Dublin, Ireland)
Smooth; bitterness is tamped down at first but measurably increases
after a few sips; pale ale-like fruitiness with emphasis on the lighter
top notes; bitterness continues to increase, though it never gets out
of hand; touch of malt is apparent at mid-bottle, but the hops remain paramount; although it is cask-conditioned, it is not intensely
flavored; Porterhouse is Ireland's first modern brewpub.

PORTLAND BAVARIAN STYLE WEIZEN MB/BP   1.8
(Portland, Oregon)
Spicy and crisp; requisite touch of clove flavor makes this wheat

beer immediately refreshing; loses some of its pizzazz fairly quickly, though effervescence and pieces of clove sweetness remain; finishes maltier and far less complex than at the beginning—too bad; it could have been a winner.

PORTLAND SUMMER PALE ALE   MB/BP   1.4
(Portland, Oregon)
Fruity and malty with minimum hoppiness; light- to medium-bodied; not much zip or pizzazz; flavors, such as they are, turn muddy; texture flattens; weak and unfulfilling; not a good rendition of the style.

PORTSMOUTH BLACK CAT STOUT   MB/BP   2.4
(Portsmouth, New Hampshire)
Dainty fruity aroma with fanciful lightly roasted flavor; smooth, with weak but appealing finish; too light and watery for a stout; very little complexity.

POST ROAD PALE ALE   CT   3.6
(Utica, New York)
Circumscribed bitterness and somewhat fruity-flowery mouthfeel; sharp taste brings along occasional rough edges, adding scintillation; hops are nicely controlled and apportioned throughout the hazy golden-brown body and remain a consistent, reliable taste pleasure; very well done; this is a charmer of a pale ale. Goes well with fresh fruits, which flesh out the tantalizing fruity overtones in the aroma.

POST ROAD REAL ALE   CT   3.6
(Utica, New York)
Nicely balanced, with mild fruitiness; settles into a subtle consistency; some greenness; slight flavor loss as you drink it; nicely nuanced; not pretentious or overly strong; a good introduction to ale. Complements lamb and pork.

POST ROAD SNOWSHOE ALE   MB   1.5
(Utica, NY)
Chocolate and banana notes; some bitterness; medium-bodied; early metallic taste finally disappears; increasing sharpness crosses the tongue toward the end and becomes too acrid and sour; this beer does not encourage you to drink it—so don't.

PRESIDENTE PILSENER   CB   3.5
(Santo Domingo, Dominican Republic)
Foamy first sip with hoppy taste and fine texture; huskiness is appealing, particularly on the sides of the mouth; solid, with tangible body; pleasant sharp hoppiness; leaves some nicely patterned Brussels lace; there is German influence here. A good choice with spicy Thai food.

PRESTIGE STOUT   CB   4.0
(Port-au-Prince, Haiti)

Fresh sweet start subsides quickly and abruptly, but your interest is recaptivated by the hearty texture; musty controlled sweetness emerges; dark robust color; sudden wine taste quickly, and thankfully, dissipates; turns silky, smooth, and mellow; provides sweet/bitter balance with poultry; heavily malted, with sediment that looks like tea leaves; reaches fullness of character at last sip; chocolatey, caramely, and rich-bodied. A good match with duck or chicken.

PRIMO Lager   CB   2.2
(Van Nuys, California)

Sharp and watery with an appealing hoppy undertone; some body with food; turns even more watery by itself without food; just a notch above run-of-the-mill; stale and thin at the end; everyman's beer.

PRIOR DOUBLE DARK Bock   CT   3.7
(Norristown, Pennsylvania)

Not as strong-tasting as expected; good burnt taste; could be creamier; rather unobtrusive, but complements hearty food—in short, a meat-and-potatoes kind of beer; finishes full and smooth, but leaves room for more; worth a second bottle. Pair with pot roast or braised veal shanks.

PRIPPS LAGER   CB   2.9
(Gothenburg, Sweden)

Rounded bitter taste with strong hoppy bouquet; creamy, smooth, thick, long-lasting artificial-looking head on top of a pale-gold body; crisp and straightforward hops; a typical lager; subdued freshness; dry finish; nearly better than average. Good with simply prepared fish such as cod, snapper, sole, or flounder.

PRIVATE STOCK MALT LIQUOR   CB   1.1
(Cranston, Rhode Island)

Very watery, somewhat fruity, and generally textureless; slight sourness underpins the fruitiness; tongue-coating aftertaste remains tangible throughout; virtually no redeeming flavor; vinegary taste tracks throughout and increases—or seems to—toward the end of a meal (and bottle). Label suggests serving it on the rocks—a sure sign this beer is headed for oblivion, and deservedly so.

PSCHORR-BRAU WEISSE   CB   3.5
(Munich, Germany)

Tangy apple-citrus taste; yeasty, with soft, gentle mouthfeel; fat bubbles support half-inch-thick head; carbonation holds up, as does dusty-yellow color; taste, aroma, texture, color, are all nicely arranged and balanced, but tame for this particular style; flavor ful chewiness ends this dry beer on an attractive note. Try it with Indian curries or Middle Eastern rice and grain dishes.

PUNTIGAMER DARK MALT DRAFT
Lager   **CB**   **2.5**
(Graz, Austria)
It does have, as advertised, a draft beer "feel"; bland in a pleasant way, with no carbonation to speak of; some faint burnt taste, a result of dark malt; warming and fuller at the bottom of the bottle; best drunk by itself.

PUNTIGAMER PANTHER DRAFT
Lager   **CB**   **3.1**
(Graz, Austria)
Mixture of citrus and honey with a creamy head and solid, hearty body; forthright hops and malt presence keep this beer moving along; fruit taste lessens somewhat at mid-bottle, but not to its overall detriment; finishes with character and balance. Good with shrimp, chicken, or pasta salads.

PURGATORY PORTER   **MB**   **2.4**
(Wichita, Kansas)
Purple-black body, like a moonless, starless night; mild coffee bitterness; very smooth, almost no texture at all; slight roastedness comes along but leaves too quickly; could be more flavorful and less watery; finishes lifeless, leaving bottle-conditioned residue at the bottom of the bottle; all in all, a disappointment. Try it with cheese and crackers.

PYRAMID BEST BROWN ALE   **RB/BP**   **2.9**
(Seattle, Washington)
Mildly malty; sweet with a frisson of hoppiness; smooth, reassuring, and unprovocative; sort of like a thin layer of brown sugar on a piece of cinnamon toast; tantalizingly gains in hop-malt balance, but never reaches satisfaction. Clams or oysters are okay with Best Brown.

L A B E L   L O R E

*T*he bottle label reads: "A pint of your Best, landlord." Commonly overheard in local pubs, the request is for the brewery's premier draft, simply referred to as "Best."

PYRAMID PALE ALE   **RB/BP**   **2.5**
(Seattle, Washington)
Perfumey and flat with a thin layer of warmth; an even thinner layer of complexity while it warms; fullness emerges, along with

a touch of acidity, when drunk with a combination of spicy and sweet foods; not complex; fruity finish. Fine with barbecued beef and a slice of cornbread.

PYRAMID SNOW CAP ALE (seasonal)   RB/BP   2.5
(Seattle, Washington)
Red-black color; roasted bitterness on the sides of the tongue; watery; flowery hoppiness in an otherwise textureless liquid; slightly cloying as the glass is finished; taste is more appropriate to style than are texture and complexity; some balance creeps in at the end; this is an annual winter offering, so expect some variability. Perfect for traditional holiday meats such as roast turkey and baked ham.

PYRAMID WHEATEN ALE (draft)   RB/BP   3.3
(Seattle, Washington)
Chewy with a bit of wateriness; light, smooth, and sweet; nice citrus bitterness is boosted with a slice of lemon; fresh and light; recommended as a summer beer. No food was eaten with this, but it would probably go well with salad of mixed summer greens.

QUELQUE CHOSE SOMETHING Ale   RB   3.9
(Chambly, Quebec, Canada)
The label instructs you to warm this cherry-infused beer to 160°F before drinking; the resulting mellow tartness and prune-raisin-cherry mouthfeel is delicious; cloves and ginger are also present; a herb/yeast underflavor props things up along the way; opaque brown body with purple cast; alcohol (8%/volume) is smooth and unintimidating; ginger aroma is especially pronounced at the bottom of the glass; a very good alternative to mulled wine. A great match with light meat like turkey or pork, or just to sip after dinner.

QUILMES CRISTAL Pilsener   CB   1.6
(Buenos Aires, Argentina)
Too light and dainty for its own good; low-key and thin, but not too watery; loses tartness as it goes from the front of the mouth to the back; uninteresting and dull; pale ginger-ale color matches washed-out taste.

RADEGAST ORIGINAL LAGER   CB   3.1
(Nosovice, Czechoslovakia)
Texturally pallid; quite hoppy, with minimum fizz; consistent, though relatively bland, taste; typical of a Czech pilsener, with its requisite hint of bitterness and hop backbone; soft, long-lasting, spongy head; in the end, the weak core undermines the strength of the hops; still too hoppy for my taste, but a solid beer that will make an adventurous beer connoisseur happy. Accompanies pretzels.

RAFFO Pilsener   CB   3.9
(Rome, Italy)
Light, somewhat fizzy; pleasant balanced taste; mellow, "warm" texture; not as full as I generally like, but certainly a good "local" beer; lacks the typical flowery pilsener aroma, which in this case would enhance its attractiveness. Try it with knockwurst or Italian sausages.

RAFTMAN Ale   RB   2.9
(Chambly, Quebec, Canada)
Extraordinarily fizzy—listen to it as you pour; very yeasty, almost overpowering on first sip; hard at first to discern anything but yeast, except perhaps the very unpleasant smell; malt rises up at mid-bottle, adding a sweet close-to-apple fruitiness that is unexpectedly charming; made with whiskey malt, there is a faint hint of smokiness; finishes yeasty-malty-fruity, almost tea-like; a veritable swirl of unusual taste sensations. See how you like this alone, then choose a food accompaniment.

RAINIER ALE   CB   3.6
(Seattle, Washington)
Mellow, sweet, creamy, and just fruity enough to titillate the salivary glands; pale red-amber color adds to the enjoyment; maintains warmth and some complexity—certainly more so than most other mass-produced U.S. ales; thinner than comparable European brews—a good American beer. Try it with a cheese or chicken salad sandwich.

RAINIER BEER Pilsener   CB   2.7
(Seattle, Washington)
Rounded hop presence recalls the bleacher seats at your favorite ballpark with a cup of suds in your hand; light, refreshing, and quite drinkable; unfortunately, the hop taste decreases along the way, making this a more ordinary brew; a satisfying no-frills accompaniment to the usual summer stadium fare.

RAJ INDIAN BEER Lager   CB   2.4
(Bangalore, India)
Lots of bubbles in the head create a softness on the palate that accommodates a beguiling bittersweet taste; however, there is a rapid transition to sweet, as the bitter presence quickly fades; this beer doesn't have much staying power and you get bored fairly soon; some metallic taste on the sides of the mouth. Improves significantly with pecans.

RATTLESNAKE PREMIUM Lager   CT   2.4
(Shiner, Texas)
Light; flavorful, with unexpected fullness at the back of the throat; tantalizing warmth doesn't come close to fruition; serviceable in a pinch.

RAZOR EDGE LAGER   CB   2.5
(Ukiah, California)

Sharp; mild citrus flavor; freshness increases with food; two levels of taste: one relatively bland, the other with more pizzazz and complexity; ingredients are less than top-quality, with some roughness and rawness; too thin and not crisp enough; on the verge of becoming a good beer.

RECCOW T'MAVE   BP   2.5
(San Francisco, California)

This dark Czech-style lager is semi-crisp and full of chocolate-malt taste that leads to a toasty-tasty climax at the end of each sip; unfortunately, the flavors get increasingly muddled along the way, as does the cloudy caramel-brown body; leaves a film of indiscernible taste characteristics on the tongue; decent-tasting, but somehow not satisfying. Hamburger helps to pull Reccow T'Mave out of its doldrums, but not by much.

RED BACK MALTED WHEAT BEER   CB   2.2
(Fremantle, Western Australia, Australia)

Baked-bread aroma on first sniff—enough yeast to make it almost taste warm and just out of the oven—but the enjoyment stops there; tangy citrus accent; highly malty, so there's little hop bitterness to deal with the yeast; flavor and ambiance are too unfocused; soft texture, almost mushy.

RED BARON Lager   MB   1.9
(Waterloo, Ontario, Canada)

Fresh and purposely sour; quickly fading presence; even-tempered; a bit bland; flat, with a somewhat pasty taste, in the Canadian tradition; warms to turpentine essence at the end; light and very easy going down.

RED BONE RED LAGER   ?CT   1.9
(San Antonio, Texas)

Nice flattened fruitiness, which disappears too quickly; caramel-sugary taste is full and wholesome; could be more complex; rather textureless; taste turns harsh and hard, obscuring some of the more attractive qualities, which are not many to begin with; ultimately, not enjoyable. Strictly a peanuts and chips beer.

RED BREW-STER Pilsener   CB   2.2
(Ljubljana, Slovenia; former Yugoslavia)

Skunky smell yields to fresh malt taste, all packaged in pale, faded liquid with rapidly rising bubbles, which don't quite impact on the palate—or anywhere else; slightly honeyed, creating a warming balance to spicy foods; remains unfizzy and uncomplicated as honey sweetness increases; light, yet with a dollop of body for the European customer; pleasant and entertaining, but not top-notch; in the end, too thin and lackluster.

RED BRICK ALE   MB   2.4
(Atlanta, Georgia)
Semidark and brooding; inflexible taste contains some hint of roasted malt, but the ingredients never really become integrated; unsubtle and texturally a bit harsh; finishes with a hard-to-discern maltiness; obviously a well-made beer, but too rigid and devoid of nuance; sweetness sneaks through with meat loaf and mashed potatoes.

RED BULL MALT LIQUOR   CB   1.4
(Detroit, Michigan)
Pretty much what you'd expect from a mass-market, higher-alcohol product—drinkable but lacking distinction; a beer to swill; untamed and mildly raw; weak with food.

RED DOG Lager   CB   1.1
(Milwaukee, Wisconsin)
Somewhat harsh; slight hint of turpentine; visually flaccid, with no head; becomes mildly sweet with no offsetting bitterness; stale-tasting; smoother and more pleasant at the finish than at the beginning; faded light-straw color doesn't help; watery and unassertive; essentially run-of-the-mill.

RED HOOK BALLARD BITTER
INDIA PALE ALE   CB   3.0
(Seattle, Washington)
Caramel-sweet, watery, and beguiling at first taste; musty after-taste wends its way down the tongue as you swallow; the taste is okay, but the texture is too light; hop tang is present, carbonation is not; label cheerfully proclaims "Ya sure, Ya betcha," a local high school sports cheer. Pleasant with Chinese hot-and-sour soup, and Asian pork and shrimp dishes.

RED HOOK BLACKHOOK PORTER   CB   4.0
(Seattle, Washington)
Nice prickly smoothness with very appealing black barley taste; mildly rich; well-balanced fullness; achieves well-earned, attractive grittiness at the end as it warms; satisfying with or without food; clearly well made and very carefully prepared; an American-made porter on a par with English versions. A smooth match for barbecued foods.

RED HOOK BLONDE ALE   CB   2.0
(Seattle, Washington)
Nice sweet smell and corresponding taste; very smooth; tangy mouthfeel comes from the presence of wheat; sweet aftertaste; not complex, and not very interesting; unidimensional in its presentation; ingredients noted on label are not discernible in the bottle. Drink this with something distracting, like a thick hero sandwich with lots of mustard.

RED HOOK ESB ALE　　　　　　**CB**　　　　　　3.1
(Seattle, Washington)
Watery bittersweetness coats the tongue and sides of the mouth on first sip; becomes more integrated and smoother with food; increasingly satisfying as it warms; smoother, rounded, and more body with emerging citrus sweetness; ends as a very nicely balanced beer; probably not more than a two-bottle brew because it's prone to over-sweetness; check the label for detailed information on how to drink this representation of the classic style. Good with hearty pub food.

RED HOOK WHEAT HOOK ALE　　　　**CB**　　　　　　2.9
(Seattle, Washington)
Thirst-quenching subdued freshness; clear, crisp, and sparkling in taste and feel; simpatico with spicy, salty foods; briny, sharp, and musky; well made, but it gets less than rave reviews due to its weak fruitiness. Match with strongly flavored foods served with hot sauce.

RED HOOK WINTERHOOK
CHRISTMAS ALE (annual)　　　　**CB**　　　　　　3.6
(Seattle, Washington)
Apple aroma with moderated back-of-the-mouth spritzy sharpness on first sip; nicely balanced between smoothness and some prickliness; unobtrusive, but maintains its identity with food; perhaps a little too watery and thin; segues into bland at the end; may vary from year to year. Just right with holiday cookies and cakes.

B E E R　　F A C T

"*M*alt liquor" is a misnomer. Often an American brewery's strongest non-ale offering, malt liquors are in fact lagers that are too high in alcohol to be labeled beer—usually 4% to 4.5% and up. That limit is reached in Texas at 4% by weight, at 7% by weight in Montana, and at 3.2% by weight in Missouri, where an exception at 5% is made specifically for malt liquor. Several states—including New Mexico, Connecticut, and Nevada—have no legal limits. But because of national distribution constraints, the lowest limit becomes the common denominator.

RED HORSE MALT LIQUOR　　　　**CB**　　　　　　3.2
(Manila, Philippines)
Neutral to pleasantly sweet, with soft, lightweight taste and color; evolves into a mild, calm drink; unobtrusive and not particularly

engaging on its own; best with bland foods; a good choice for those who prefer a nonassertive brew. Try it with chicken noodle soup or fried rice.

RED STAR SELECT Lager   CB   2.2
(Berlin, Germany)

Flat, with minimal fizzy citrus bubbles; grainy hoppiness ranges from subtle to hard, depending on the food it accompanies; clear golden color suggests it will taste cleaner and fresher than it does; dull, workmanlike ambiance; relatively light body; a thick slice of lemon enhances the beer tremendously, adding zest and encouraging the hops to do their thing. Okay with a pastrami-on-rye sandwich.

RED STRIPE LAGER   CB   2.2
(Kingston, Jamaica)

Weak hops, malt, and color, with immediate overall ballpark-beer ambiance; weakens still further after a sip or two; some lively flavor holds your interest, but not for long; soft fizziness saves it from blandness; faintly stale odor; plain and not especially memorable; appropriate for novices building their imported-beer library; still, remains in the low-average range. Serve with a salami and cheese sandwich or sourdough pretzels.

B E E R   F A C T

Jamaica is one of at least ten islands in the Caribbean that have one or more breweries—a legacy from the early European colonists. Some others include Barbados, Cuba, the Dominican Republic, Haiti, Puerto Rico, Trinidad, and the British Virgin Islands.

RED, WHITE AND BLUE
SPECIAL LAGER   CB   3.2
(La Crosse, Wisconsin)

Inexpensive, good baseball beer; tastes like Pabst; I'd probably tire of it quickly; light and thin, typical for an American beer, but still maintains a slightly effervescent feel and some distinction in taste with spicy foods; for a mass-produced brew, this is a surprisingly enjoyable find. Good with a mustard-slathered hot dog.

REDDING PREMIUM GOLDEN ALE   CT   1.1
(New Ulm, Minnesota)

Malty-sweet caramel-honey taste with not much hop balance to reduce the sweetness; weakens and loses its complexity fairly quickly; flattens out to bland; weak tea color doesn't add to its overall character; fruity aroma is weak and uninspiring; finishes sweet and sappy.

REGIA EXTRA Lager — CB — 2.4
(San Salvador, El Salvador)

Mild, sugary sweetness parallels the quick, sharp hop taste; light-bodied, with a surprisingly smooth texture; subtly sweet, spicy aroma makes a quiet impact; corn sweetness is fuller at mid-bottle; low alcohol content encourages drinking more than one bottle at a sitting, though the overall character doesn't; more punch at the end than at the beginning. A so-so everyday beer for everyday, home-cooked meals

REICHELBRAU BAVARIAN DARK Lager — CB — 3.1
(Kulmbach, Germany)

Soft honey aroma is not reflected in the taste, which is, initially at least, sharp and cold; mild burnt mouthfeel emerges around the edges and increases in vigor as the bottle empties; a bit too sweet in the end; reasonable balance and complement to sweetish meat that by itself would be bland or neutral. Try it with braised pork chops, stir-fried pork with vegetables, or roast turkey.

REMBRANDT MASTERPIECE
LAGER BEER — CB — 2.3
(Nijkerk, Holland)

Bitter; surprisingly flat despite the obvious bubbles; not noticeably balanced; texturally weak, but aggressive and assertive in taste and presentation; hops deal directly and strongly with the anchovies in a hero sandwich; overall, this is a tough beer to contend with; finishes with a smoothness not present earlier.

RESCHS PILSNER — CB — 2.9
(Sydney, New South Wales, Australia)

Full-bodied for a non-dark beer; background taste is so subtle that too often it appears as if there is no substantive flavor; drink alone or with pizza.

RHEINGOLD PREMIUM Pilsener — CB — 1.1
(Philadelphia, Pennsylvania)

Some body along with immediate taste of adjuncts (corn, definitely; rice, perhaps); sharpness quickly fades to blandness; a hint of rawness; some complexity saves it from complete failure; still, it's generally unappealing.

RHINELANDER Lager — CB — 2.4
(Monroe, Wisconsin)

Light, with a thick backbone and weak citrus fruitiness at the back of the mouth; maintains slight sour taste throughout; far more complex and nuanced than most American lagers; smoother, sweeter, and less flavorful at the end. Try it with black beans and rice or other Central American dishes.

RHINO CHASERS AMBER ALE   CT   **3.7**
(Chatsworth, California)
Well balanced; delicate intertwining of sweet and dry makes for interest and mature taste; citrus fruitiness accompanies all sips; somewhat mushy texture, but unobtrusive; milky/hazy amber color doesn't match the interest and appeal of the flavor; soft; more of a beer than an ale; tepid but competent. Good with sturdy, uncomplicated dishes such as meat loaf, roast beef, or chicken.

B E E R   F A C T

*P*roceeds from Rhino Chasers products are shared with the African Wildlife Foundation for the protection of the rhinoceros and other endangered species.

RHINO CHASERS AMERICAN ALE   CT   **2.2**
(Chatsworth, California)
Soft on the tongue and palate; hint of acridness in the nose and at the back of the throat; a little too bland; settles down into a mildly sweet ale with no real distinguishing characteristics; hops presence asserts itself midway through; weak tea color echoes the pallid texture and taste; malt touches the tongue at the end; drink this ale shortly after purchase, as it tends to quickly lose its freshness.

RHINO CHASERS LAGER   CT   **3.7**
(Chatsworth, California)
Highly grainy and sharp, with an earthy country aroma that reminds you of health and goodness; crisp and pointed; texture continues to outweigh flavor; hops are evident; gritty sweetness emerges toward the bottom of the bottle; pale-yellow color belies the strength of the drink; smooths out, but maintains an attractive boozy interplay. Good with grilled salmon, spicy boiled crawfish, or Chinese seafood combinations.

RHINO CHASERS WINTERFUL Ale
(annual)   CT   **2.5**
(St. Paul, Minnesota)
Brewed during the winter holiday season; light touch of orange mixed with soft spiciness; pale amber-copper color; cloves rise up as it warms; too sweet and timidly spicy; suggests alcohol strength heartier than is actually present; fruity aroma toward the end; thickish sweetish finish is not counterbalanced enough with alcohol—a disappointment when all is said and done; comes in a bottle with what appears to be a cloudy, milky film coating the glass, obscuring the contents; a holiday ale that, ironically, does

not go well with holiday foods; warm the glass in your hand and sip it without food.

RICKARD'S RED DRAUGHT ALE CB 2.5
(Calgary, Alberta; Vancouver, British Columbia, Canada)
Malty-sweet beginning becomes aftertaste at the back of the mouth; mildly sharp, but mainly smooth, almost milky texture; generally a middle-of-the-road brew; hard to define one way or the other. Best alone or with simple pasta dishes.

RIEGELER SPEZIAL EXPORT Lager CB 2.9
(Kaiserstuhl, Germany)
Strong musky, malty aroma with nearly equivalent initial taste; distinct alcohol presence remains throughout; grainy undertone significantly enhances enjoyment; surprising molasses taste at mid-glass gives the beer a lift; fuller and more complex at the end than at the beginning—warming seems to help; light golden color contrasts with the full-bodied taste and texture; somewhat hoppy finish. Good with broiled or grilled steaks.

RINGNES EXPORT PALE Pilsener CB 4.0
(Oslo, Norway)
Very warm, mellow wheat-rice flavor lasts with food; taste is consistent, not too sharp, and pleasingly integrated; a touch of sweetness gives this light brew a certain roundness; crisp and clean overall, it has more taste than texture; a beer made with the enjoyment of food in mind. Very good with Buffalo-style chicken wings or chicken nuggets with dipping sauce.

RINGNES SPECIAL JUBILEE ALE CB 2.7
(Oslo, Norway)
Malty roastiness disappears and goes flat almost immediately; slowly rising integrated warmth with food; mellow moderate sweetness also emerges; lovely maltiness appears further on; ultimately lacks the silky firmness and pungency of a first-class ale; basically no head; in the end, a restrained but changeable drink. Serve with grilled chicken.

RIO GRANDE OUTLAW LAGER MB 2.8
(Albuquerque, New Mexico)
Thickly fruity, with a hefty hop sharpness; malt sweetness creeps in on second sip, lending beguiling balance to the flavorful bitterness; rather flat and too smooth texturally; ingredients, especially the water, come together in a neat package; yeasty sourness floats forward as the fruity taste diminishes; weakens considerably at the finish. For an interesting taste sensation, try with chocolate cookies or a piece of rich, chocolatey devil's food cake.

RITTERBRAU PALE Lager CB 4.0
(Dortmund, Germany)
Dark and attractive on first sip—and last; malt and hops appear

to be of high quality and professionally brewed, making for delectable spritzy mouthfeel; worth savoring alone, as well as with food—remains fresh and inviting, with slight mustiness as the bottle empties; finely tuned and unresponsive. A good choice with snapper, mahi mahi, or pompano.

T A P   T I P

Clouds, Agitation, and Beer Storage

More and more breweries are marking their bottles with dates to indicate optimal shelf life. While some clearly identify the pull dates on the label, usually with delineated punch marks, others place essentially indecipherable codes, generally meant for the retailer, on the bottle, can bottom, or neck. One quick and easy way to make some determination about the age of the bottle you have in your hand is to gently turn it upside down. Hold it up to the light; you can be fairly certain it is past its prime if you observe any cloudiness or sediment (this, of course, doesn't work for a wheat or bottle-conditioned product, since its defining characteristics are, in fact, cloudiness and/or sediment). Checking dates is not a futile exercise. I once purchased an expensive French bitter, only to discover that, according to the date markings on the label, it was almost three years old. I returned it to the retailer, who not only gave me credit for future purchases, but immediately had one of his clerks call up the wholesaler and tell him to come by and pick up the whole rotting batch.

Beer should be stored standing up, in order to minimize oxidation and to reduce the possibility of contact between beer and metal (in the cap). Further, don't agitate the liquid, which means keep your bottles and cans in the back of the fridge, not on the door shelf.

RIVA BLANCHE ALE   **CB**   **2.2**
(Dentergem, Belgium)
Perfumey, yeasty aroma; mini-fizziness; yeast continues to dominate; pale-straw color, with no head; sour and moderately bitter;

very cloudy; uninspired vision; meets the style of white ale—a bit orangey (citrus increases) at the end; yeast sediment on the bottom of the glass; you really need to like this style to finish this bottle-conditioned brew.

RIVER HORSE CREAM ALE   MB   3.2
(Lambertville, New Jersey)

Mildly bitter, bordering on tart; quickly changes to mellow and gentle on the palate; following malty taste is mouthfilling and soothing; frothy white head enhances the rich body's golden color; hint of cherry flavor spreads over the tongue; ongoing, placid graininess accompanies the increasingly malty character; creamy aspect is also evident; this is an interesting and evolving beer. Try with sweet, fruity desserts.

RIVER HORSE HOP HAZARD
PALE ALE   MB   3.2
(Lambertville, New Jersey)

Opens with a very nice grapefruit aroma and similar tart taste, which lasts well after each swallow; smooth, underlying maltiness comfortably absorbs and cushions the hop bitterness without diminishing its appealingly complex character; faint caramel aroma appears toward the end; mild cider and malt tastes wrap things up in fine style; a well put-together pale ale. Complements and compliments well-seasoned pasta salads.

RIVERSIDE GOLDEN SPIKE PILSNER   MB/BP   0.9
(Riverside, California)

Muddy in taste and color; rapidly fading off-taste; almost flavorless, except for a sour bitterness that clings to the palate; no texture to speak of; harsh and astringent; some maltiness emerges, if you pay close attention; gains some flavor and accountability with burritos; finishes with a faint rancid-fruit aroma.

RIVERSIDE PULLMAN PALE ALE   MB/BP   2.4
(Riverside, California)

Straightforward, but not particularly complex; circumscribed fruitiness comes and goes quickly with each sip; bitterness is present, but not for long; weakens at the core; fades into pedestrian, though baked salmon succeeds in adding flavor; slight soapy taste at finish; fresh out of the tap, this would be quite good; in the bottle, it's routine and run-down.

RIVERSIDE RAINCROSS CREAM ALE   MB/BP   0.5
(Riverside, California)

Harsh, rough, and tasteless; leaves a sour and bitter taste at back of the mouth; vague hint of fruity hoppiness is hidden underneath an unyielding coldness; no nuances or integration; some malt sweetness tries to surface at the end, but fails; pass this one up.

RIVERSIDE 7TH STREET STOUT   MB/BP   3.1
(Riverside, California)

Slight, well-controlled hop-roasted bite; smooth all over the mouth; some of the toastedness becomes burnt-bitter, almost pungent; sweetness emerges around mid-bottle to take the edge off things; a solid, well-meaning stout that needs a little fine-tuning; I look forward to future incarnations. Try it with spicy pasta dishes.

ROCK CREEK WINTER PASSION
SPICED ALE (seasonal)   MB   3.7
(Richmond, Virginia)

Warm, rising cocoa aroma precedes a more intense, similar-tasting mouthfeel; full, nutty character joins up with the chocolate after several sips—a sophisticated, well-calibrated combo; the slightest suggestion of spices offers a counterbalancing grittiness to this smooth, malt-based juggernaut; a jolt of alcohol (5.9%/volume) helps, too; aroma and taste remain strong and vigorous from start to finish, caressed by a trace of pure malt at the last swallow; match with a box of high-quality chocolates.

ROCKIES BUFFALO GOLD
PREMIUM ALE   MB   3.7
(Boulder, Colorado)

Sharp and crisp, unlike ale style; tasty and lightly alcoholic with understated sweetness; mild texture, but rough enough to raise your interest; gentle, integrated blend; flavor is too flat and tends to fade; slight cloudiness detracts from pale-gold color; finishes with a welcoming slight bitterness. Accompanies pasta salads and traditional Italian favorites.

RODENBACH ALEXANDER
BELGIAN RED ALE   CB   4.3
(Roeselare, Belgium)

Aroma and taste are filled with cherry flavor and tantalizing touches of yeast—boy, what a mouthful; initial wine-cork aroma is wonderful and too short-lived; perfectly sweet and bitter; tangy and zesty at the same time; delicate and dainty; contains a flavor punch that makes you want more, much more; brandy color enhances its use as a dessert ale; buy one for yourself and one for a favorite friend, and then keep both.

RODENBACH BELGIAN RED ALE   CB   2.7
(Roeselare, Belgium)

Immediate light-struck (skunky) odor along with highly tart but normal sourness and orange spiciness; chocolate taste comes up with shellfish; rich deep-copper color leads you to expect more fullness; spice and yeastiness don't really sort themselves out; individual flavors are somewhat muddied; at the end, spicy hot sauces pleasantly cut through the yeast's tartness; finishes harsh, dry, and fruity; naturally aged for 2 years in oak casks, it lays

claim to being the "most refreshing beer in the world." Try it
with hard cheese and sliced cold meats.

ROGUE GOLDEN ALE   MB/BP   2.4
(Newport, Oregon)

Fruitiness with an edge of sharpness in the throat; airy, as befits
a golden ale; thin layer of aftertaste; murky, faded golden color
suggests that further maturing is needed; tastes like an unfinished
(green) product; everything softens as it warms, but premature
bottling remains evident; to best enjoy this ale, drink a bit and
let the remainder stay capped in the cooler for a day or two. A
match for pasta with Italian sausages.

ROGUE MAIERBOCK ALE   MB/BP   3.9
(Newport, Oregon)

Delightfully malty aroma offers not-so-sneak preview of pleasure
and enjoyment; light, syrupy berry taste lingers, but doesn't spoil
the aftertaste; light-golden color daintily supports fuzzy, mossy
head which pours to a delicious thickness; quick, sharp taste gets
nicely lost in sweet smoothness; random sheets of Brussels lace
enhance the ambiance; rich and moderately hearty; well balanced
in taste, aroma, and color; finishes a touch weak, but with a full,
grainy candied-malt aroma. A good choice with pizza or calzones.

ROGUE MEXICALI ALE   MB/BP   2.5
(Newport, Oregon)

Very pleasant aroma of restrained citrus and spice on first sip,
along with cloudy (yeast-laden) light-amber color; almost rea-
like in texture, taste, and coloring; weak but satisfying with fizzy
carbonation and faint hop taste; lingering tartness perks up the
end of the bottle; too watery—not the best representative of this
gem of a microbrewery. Nice with roast chicken and a garden
salad.

ROGUE MOGUL ALE   MB/BP   3.6
(Newport, Oregon)

Immediate honey-pine aroma that makes you go "Yummm. . ."
and eagerly look forward to tasting it; soft around the edges, with
a bite of hops underneath and throughout; good, lasting Brussels lace is nice counterpoint to the medium-deep red-brown
body; clear and balanced; light orange fruitiness becomes more
evident with barbecued foods; appears to be less alcoholic than
other Rogue ales; smooth, hoppy finish, preceded by subdued
liveliness. Pairs well with barbecued or smoked meats.

ROGUE NEW PORTER   MB/BP   3.7
(Newport, Oregon)

Even with the hyperbolic advertising, this label doesn't mislead:
"a bittersweet balance of malt and hops yet a surprisingly light
and refreshing finish." Thickish head and hearty Brussels lace; in

general, too texturally weak; substantial, fulfilling mouthfeel; finishes mellow, gentle, and soft. Wonderful with medium-rare roast beef and a baked potato, or with venison.

ROGUE OLD CRUSTACEAN
BARLEY WINE   **MB/BP**   **3.6**
(Newport, Oregon)

Tentative apple-cider aroma gently wafts up as soon as the cap comes off the tiny (6.4-ounce) bottle; full mouthfeel as alcohol revs up and takes over, though fruitiness lingers; quite bitter and texturally weak; hazy brandy color is the result of yeast in the bottle; slight mustiness comes along toward the end; a warming, compassionate brew; a bit too thin and unassertive; aroma is simply wonderful and stays steady and available throughout; smooth, not biting; well made and carefully crafted—a Rogue trademark. A companionable *digestif.*

B E E R   F A C T

*H*op content is measured in a brewer's convention called International Bitterness Units (IBUs). For most drinkers, hop bitterness first becomes noticeable at around 10 IBUs (Budweiser, Miller). A hearty stout like Guinness checks in at about 50 IBUs. Rogue's Old Crustacean, by strong contrast, is rated at 80 IBUs. Caveat emptor.

ROGUE SHAKESPEARE STOUT   **MB/BP**   **4.8**
(Newport, Oregon)

This may well be my favorite bottled beer of all time; deeply roasted and creamy, with tantalizing bitterness; thick, smooth, and attractive; deeply satisfying; I have sampled this many times with a variety of foods—red meat, pasta, vegetables, and sweet desserts—and my enthusiasm remains at every sip and swallow; a conversation stopper; do try it.

ROGUE SMOKE ALE   **MB/BP**   **2.0**
(Newport, Oregon)

Smells and tastes like smoked salami but without the spicy edge; hint of garlic; velvety smooth; mild, smoky ambiance; deep-amber color; nicely configured Brussels lace quickly slides down the sides of the glass and disappears; too thin and watery; weakens at the end; mild, lesser version of German *Rauchbier;* a rare below-average offering from this otherwise fine microbrewery. Drink with beer nuts.

ROGUE ST. ROGUE RED ALE   MB/BP   4.4
(Newport, Oregon)

Fresh yeasty aroma immediately creates interest; smooth, foamy texture perfectly balances the hoppy fizziness; just the right kick of alcohol; remains fresh, if just a bit raw, throughout the bottle; mellow, foamy head sits jauntily atop deep copper-red body; frothy, fresh, and appropriately complex; toastiness everywhere; stunning achievement; belongs in anyone's book of the best beers; cheers for this American brewery; may be the freshest-tasting bottled beer I've ever had. Savor this with thick Bavarian-style pretzels and honey mustard.

ROLLING ROCK EXTRA PALE Lager   CB   3.6
(Latrobe, Pennsylvania)

Very American, but with more flavor than the average domestic beer; taste is evenly distributed on the tongue, palate, and throat; blunted crispness sits well at the back of the tongue; paints its own texture and color; tasty, but not complex or dynamic; one of the better mass-market American beers. Goes with virtually any food.

B E E R   F A C T

Nobody knows for sure, not even the folks at Rolling Rock, why the number "33" is featured prominently on the brewery's green bottles. The three most popular possibilities refer to the 33 letters in the ingredients listed on the bottle (water, malt, rice, corn, hops, brewer's yeast), the 33 words on the back of the bottle, and the fact that Prohibition ended in 1933. Take your pick. By the way, the beer was introduced in 1939.

ROYAL BRAND Pilsener   CB   3.4
(Wijlre, Holland)

Sharp texture entering the mouth, dull at the back of the tongue; slight off-taste, but in general not much flavor at all: initial distinctive taste becomes integrated at the back of the tongue; retains an interesting and invigorating complexity with food; a second bottle would not be unwarranted. Serve along with olives, morsels of cheese, crackers, and other savory pre-dinner nibbles.

ROYAL DUTCH POST HORN Lager   CB   3.9
(Breda, Holland)

Sharp, grainy, and mouth-filling; mild, complex hoppiness changes to dominating bitterness at mid-bottle; charmingly full-bodied; dry and vivacious; alcohol insinuates itself toward the end, bolstering the firm, bold mouthfeel of this hearty lager; finishes with a strong, lasting hop aftertaste and a warming undertone of sweetness; this is one fine brew. Pork and chicken dishes go well here.

ROYAL EXTRA STOUT   CB   3.4
(Champs Fleurs, Trinidad)

Sweet, chocolatey, and full; doesn't present an immediately attractive ambiance; sweetness calms down and becomes relatively complementary; deep dark-brown color with thin reddish-tan head; still, this is a good example of a mild stout; delectable toasted malt aroma at the end; hint of alcohol also helps dampen the sweetness. Compatible with Caribbean cuisines.

ROYAL GUARD CERVEZA—TIPO
DORTMUND Lager   CB   2.5
(Santiago, Chile)

Thickish on the tongue; clearly less hoppy and bitter than its pilsener cousin (see below); also more run-of-the-mill; medium body; rather uninteresting without food, but still a cut above most other Chilean beers; malty sweetness eventually appears; in the end, too thick, too much aftertaste, which is moderated somewhat by food. Goes with savory tidbits such as nachos, Spanish *tapas,* or Greek *meze.*

ROYAL GUARD PILSENER   CB   3.8
(Santiago, Chile)

Some fizziness; attractive complexity with emphasis on hops; maintains character throughout; golden wheat color; almost winelike in character (body, balance, and integration); rich and satisfying with or without food. Good with a wide range of foods from mild cheese with crackers to steaks and chicken.

ROYAL OAK PALE ALE   CB   4.4
(Dorchester, England)

Appealingly soft and fruity, complemented by subtle bitterness; like a soothing smooth brandy but fuller, with more body; copper color at outset, which diminishes but remains at the edges; creamy head; finishes with a moderated sweet fruitiness that makes you ask for more; round and mobile at the back of the tongue— a classy act; mouth-filling flavor increases with warmth, though a bit watery. Very good alone; delicious with pork.

RUBENS GOLD Ale   CT   3.0
(Kontich, Belgium)

Crisp and slightly metallic with a bitter, hoppy presence on the tongue; thick, harsh-tasting head; exquisitely patterned small bubbles mutate into irregular big ones toward the top of the foam; grating, rough texture grabs your attention while the taste remains secondary; head stays foamy, if somewhat light and airy; finish is mild and unassuming; best without food. Style is indeterminate; label says top-fermenting, serve chilled, the importer says it has the character of a pilsener; sort of a eunuch beer, but I'd try it again.

B E E R   F A C T

*R*ubens Gold is named for the 17th-century Flemish painter, Peter Paul Rubens, whose vibrant, exuberant, animated style is claimed by the importer to be represented in this lively ale.

RUDDLES BITTER Ale   CB   1.4
(Rutland, England)
Sweet to tasteless with hint of cloyingness; possesses a lightness that is not expected due to its (thin) amber color; certainly not bitter, in fact weak; taste of hops is feeble; an undistinguished beer.

RUDDLES COUNTRY ALE   CB   2.3
(Rutland, England)
Golden-amber color complements thickish, burnt quality of the initial taste; constant flat-tasting overtone; slightly unpleasant aftertaste; with food, taste begins to wither in strength and palatability; sweet and robust; best alone, but can be paired with seafood pilaf or chicken with yellow rice.

RUSKI Lager   CB   3.3
(Kiev, Ukraine)
Immediate sourdough-rye bread aroma with a similar follow-up taste; solid body; dry and thirst-quenching; reduces to cold-water mouthfeel, albeit from a relatively fresh spring; decent head appears to be artificially carbonated; very wispy Brussels lace; effortless to swallow, easy to take—a good beginner's beer; finishes with a hint of clove; refreshing. (Note that there is sometimes a residue in the rubber liner of the bottle cap—mold?) Serve with cold meats or fish.

RUSSKOYE LAGER   CB   0.2
(Kiev, Ukraine)
Full grain aroma followed by cold, sharp mouthfeel; relatively flavorless and almost green-tasting; chemical ambiance (to stabilize it) doesn't help; really has no quality features—no complexity, no enduring taste, no aroma, no lasting head; faded translucent yellow-orange color; basically unappetizing.

SACRAMENTO RED HORSE ALE   BP   3.3
(Sacramento and Citrus Heights, California)
Aggressively hopped and full of flavor; hints of fruit and hop-spiciness; alcohol content is getting up there (6.2%/volume), but

patiently remains in the background; deep amber body throws off a rich, ruby glow; pure, fresh-smelling, appley aroma; balanced, nicely defined bitterness lingers on the palate; finishes as fresh-tasting as it began. Goes well with a bagel and cream cheese.

SAGRES PREMIUM Lager   CB   2.1
(Lisbon, Portugal)
Gentle and flat, with faded texture as it hits the sides of the tongue; negligible head with nondescript yellow color; some acidity creeps in with food, paradoxically adding character otherwise missing; hop imbalance; overall, rather unimpressive.

SAIGON LAGER BEER   CB   0.0
(Ho Chi Minh City, Vietnam)
Hoppy, fuel oil/kerosene combo does not make for a good start, or anything else; thin and textureless; smells positively unnatural, reminiscent of cleaning fluid; toss this away or see if it will power your lawnmower.

SAILER PILS   CB   2.8
(Marktoberdorf, Germany)
Not-unpleasant sour taste on first sip; wine-like aftertaste; reminiscent of heavier beer; highly flavored and fills the mouth with bland but determined hoppiness; faint metallic presence makes your appreciation more cautious and tentative, but it disappears quickly and the beer regains its earlier attraction; clearly makes an effort to please, and except for a momentary lapse, it does. It is often not available in the U.S., so try tracking down a bottle on your next jaunt to Europe. Compatible with Asian cuisines.

SAINT ARNOLD CHRISTMAS ALE   MB   3.1
(seasonal)
(Houston, Texas)
Hoppy and malty-sweet at the same time, with a sweet, malty aftertaste; vague but clearly present mix of spices and fruitiness; rich and hearty; definite presence of alcohol, which is spread out and well integrated; leaves a certain roughness on the tongue, but overall it is relatively smooth in texture; ends up hoppy and spicy; nicely done. Goes well with seasonal fruitcake.

SAINT ARNOLD KRISTALL WEIZEN   MB   3.2
(Houston, Texas)
Hoppy rather than wheaty, but no complaints here—that doesn't at all diminish the taste pleasure; it's fresh, flavorful and smooth going down; sharp and clean-tasting, too; attractive, even-tempered bitterness keeps its character throughout; flowery taste in the swallow; a sturdy, appealing beer. Try it with light, lunchtime fare.

SAKU ESTONIAN PILSENER   CB   3.0
(Eesti, Estonia)
Immediately noticeable high level of effervescence is neatly ab-

sorbed by the very soft, thick, foamy head; well hopped and quite grainy; mild bitterness provides a balancing, complementary mouthfeel; heavier-bodied and more textural substance than the typical domestic pilsener; finishes in malt-hop harmony. Good with a hearty meal, like beef stew.

SAKU ESTONIAN PORTER   CB   2.7
(Eesti, Estonia)
Potent but subdued wine aroma in first whiff; slightly bitter and fleeting roasted taste; full-bodied maltiness suddenly emerges after several sips; thickish caramel character is also present; very soft mouthfeel; far too fruity for a porter; flavor kind of rolls around in the mouth, shifting nuances before it goes down the gullet; hit of alcohol is a nice send-off at the end. Try this with fresh fruit.

SALMON CREEK SWEET STOUT (draft) BP   3.8
(Vancouver, Washington)
Heavy mouthfeel, with intense bittersweet chocolate flavor; deep, dark, and roasted; in spite of the intense character, it doesn't take over your mouth, instead melting slowly and patiently into the taste buds; filling and full-bodied; a well-crafted stout; goes fabulously with a piece, or two, of rich chocolatey chocolate cake.

SALVA VIDA Lager   CB   2.6
(San Pedro Sula, Honduras)
Harsh but compelling malt graininess; high-powered carbonation; incisively sharp; creeping subtle bitterness; medium-bodied; almost as light in color as Coors; substantial, well-developed Brussels lace; some sourness comes and goes; hint of malt at the end; straightforward and unpretentious. Surprisingly assertive with spaghetti with sausages and tomato sauce.

SAMUEL ADAMS CREAM STOUT   CB   2.3
(Utica, New York; Pittsburgh, Pennsylvania)
Burnt, bitter, and roasted—the way a stout should be—although not hearty or integrated enough to be up there with the best stouts, nor is it as rich or smooth; malt needs to be more fully roasted and perhaps also increased in quality, or at least the ratio altered; weak alcohol presence; maybe brewing this at the company's Boston site rather than contracting it out would improve the mix and match.

SAMUEL ADAMS DARK WHEAT   CB   2.7
(Pittsburgh, Pennsylvania)
Subdued wheat taste with musty-dusty aroma; evenhanded and predictable, with fine sheets of Brussels lace; integrated balance of hops and malt fits nicely and comfortably with relatively bland foods; emerging hop bitterness with slight carbonation toward the end of the bottle—not very complex or intimidating; good starter for the wheat-drinking newcomer. Accompanies chicken dishes.

SAMUEL ADAMS DOUBLE BOCK
DARK LAGER   CB   3.7
(Pittsburgh, Pennsylvania)
Creamy, tangy, and full; highly malted; deep red-amber color is
clear and makes for a nice initial impression; sweet alcohol presence emerges at mid-stride, quickly subsiding before it gets too
cloying or too sweet; thick on the tongue; more than one glass
or bottle at a time might prove to be too rich and full-bodied
for the average drinker; starchy foods help temper the richness;
smooth and entertaining, with a high percentage of malt; Bronze
Medal winner at the 1993 Great American Beer Festival. Try it
with a broiled steak and a baked potato.

SAMUEL ADAMS HONEY PORTER   CB   3.3
(Lehigh Valley, Pennsylvania)
Tangy coffee taste follows a pour of deep ruby-red color; medium-
bodied with, as the label rightly proclaims, a full, round flavor;
honey tones emerge one by one: a very charming balance between constrained sweetness and bitter roastedness—makes you
pay attention to what you are drinking; mild malty aroma caps
things off as the glass is finished; effortlessly done and well worth
looking for; delicious by itself or with nuts and dried fruit.

SAMUEL ADAMS OCTOBERFEST
Lager (seasonal)   CB   3.7
(Boston, Massachusetts; Pittsburgh, Pennsylvania)
Immediate tangy hops, sparkling but subdued carbonation, and
fruity/hoppy nose; malts taste roasted; overall, a strong, deeply
textured brew; sprightly, rounded, balanced character, but doesn't
integrate well with food; alcohol is felt by the time the bottle is
finished; good American version of a traditional German beer.

SAMUEL ADAMS TRIPLE BOCK   CB   4.7
**(brewed at Bronco Winery in Ceres, California,
for the Boston Brewing Co.)**
First whiff (even at a distance) is alcohol, second is maple syrup;
deep tawny color is reminiscent of a beautiful port; wonderfully
fruity and woody, filling the mouth with delectable subtleties and
nuances; a sweet, ripe, prune-like taste emerges—all delicate and
exquisitely balanced; silky smooth and gentle, with none of the
burning roughness of a cognac or whiskey; remains layered, rich,
and absolutely compelling—the subtle delicacy is memorable;
warm maple-syrup aroma with hints of sweet vanilla lasts throughout; mellow, with a coaxing, tantalizing buzz; one negative: a
fuzzy, distinct aftertaste stays on the roof of the mouth for several hours after the last sip, but the good news is that it continues to evoke the sultry bock's maple and fruit essence; savor slowly
at room temperature in a brandy snifter after dinner. On the
other hand, one of my sources tells me it goes great with elk.

BEER FACT

*I*ntroduced to the public in 1994 in a sleek "designer" 8.45-ounce cobalt-blue bottle with gilt lettering, Samuel Adams Triple Bock claims a record-breaking alcohol content of 17%/volume. Commercially brewed for Samuel Adams at the Bronco Winery in Ceres, California, it is aged for 45 to 60 days in oak barrels that once contained Jack Daniel's whiskey. The company anticipates that the triple bock will improve with age and invites interested parties to contact it for periodic updates. I have five bottles resting comfortably in the back of my refrigerator, alongside 14 bottles of Thomas Hardy's Ale and four Rogue Old Crustacean Barley Wine.

SAMUEL ADAMS WINTER LAGER
(annual)   CB   2.2–3.9
(Portland, Oregon)

A seasonal beer with a warm, spicy caramel aroma and similar taste; a bit too thickishly sweet; strong hoppiness; not particularly complex though clearly well made; rich red amber color; generally unexciting; mellows out toward the end, but still remains essentially bland and unobtrusive; indistinct and lumbering. As an annual brew, the quality and enjoyment are necessarily variable; as a general rule, one way to maximize the likelihood of getting a fresh quality product is to buy a bottle produced at the brewery site closest to where you live (read the label carefully).

SAMUEL SMITH OATMEAL STOUT   CB   4.0
(Tadcaster, England)

Full-bodied without being filling; good burnt taste; strong, smooth—almost silky; generously sweet, but not to the point of interfering with food; well made and well worth the expense. Delicious with roast beef, steaks, and game.

SAMUEL SMITH TADCASTER
TADDY PORTER   CB   3.7
(Tadcaster, England)

Subdued wine aroma on first sniff resolves into mini-sharpness, with mild caramel on the palate; deep-brown color looks like a full-throated burgundy wine in a tulip-shaped glass; settles down into a rounded, full-bodied drink with slight sourness; interesting juice taste/texture (sugary, thin, just-off-the-vine) is present at the end of the bottle; quality wine-like finish; sequential rather than integrated taste; since I don't like wine, my ranking is probably less than a wine devotee might give it. Try with breaded pork chops or veal cutlets.

SAMUEL SMITH'S IMPERIAL STOUT   CB   4.0
(Tadcaster, England)

Wine/berry aroma; dark, roasted, creamy taste with a dollop of appropriate sourness; incredibly full-bodied, integrated, and robust, particularly at the end; extraordinarily rich throughout; cheery and refreshing, with more than a hint of alcohol; caramel color and burnt-currant taste fill the entire mouth, with the taste memory lasting long afterward; one of my favorite high-alcohol brews. Stay away from food with this distinctive beer; savor as either an *apéritif* or *digestif.*

SAMUEL SMITH'S LAGER   CB   4.0
(Tadcaster, England)

Full-bodied, appealingly hoppy, and clean-tasting, with pale-golden, healthy-looking hue; a professionally done beer with undiminished backbone; maintains its zest and balance of hops and malt from fresh start to exuberant finish; rounded and made to fit comfortably in the mouth. A versatile, quality lager that can be enjoyed with nearly any food.

SAMUEL SMITH'S NUT BROWN ALE   CB   3.4
(Tadcaster, England)

Mild and pleasantly sweet; slight winey taste; palate-pleasing and smooth; very similar to Fuller's London Pride; a more full-bodied taste at the back of the tongue; very complementary to plain foods.

B E E R   F A C T

*T*adcaster, home of the Samuel Smith brewery, was originally a Roman encampment. Its lake water lies atop a bed of limestone and is ideal for producing pale ale—the predominant style of beer in Great Britain.

SAMUEL SMITH'S OLD BREWERY
PALE ALE   CB   3.0
(Tadcaster, England)

Sharpness obscures slight caramel-burnt taste; copper-tan color; minimal sourness; not as satisfying as the heavier, darker, richer Smith's beers. Good with a chicken salad sandwich on toasted rye bread.

SAMUEL SMITH'S WINTER
WELCOME ALE (annual)   CB   2.3–3.8
(Tadcaster, England)
As an annual offering, there is variability from year to year; over-all, I find this to indeed be a warm winter welcome: opening aroma can be musty and dry, with a hint of perfume in the air; first sip is fizzy and crisp, smooth and elegant; straightforward, strong, and hearty, with high alcohol content adding to the sea-sonal cheer; refreshing and almost perfectly balanced, though it can be too textureless for the punch of the taste and aroma; im-parts a warm, friendly glow, but in the end is sometimes not as flavorful as it could be. Check out the label: it's a joyous multi-colored testament to attractive packaging, offering a visual sug-gestion as to what you may find inside. Alcoholic strength seems to have increased over the years; sip as a *digestif,* or serve with rice and other grain dishes.

SAN ANDREAS EARTHQUAKE
PALE ALE   MB/BP   3.0
(Hollister, California)
Very fruity aroma and mouthfeel with flowery smoothness; tastes like its color: cloudy pale amber; aftertaste bite is pleasantly fleet-ing, ends with integrated but conflicting appeal of flavor, smell, and texture; remains fresh throughout; invites you back again, although its name might suggest otherwise. Try it with crispy chips and dip.

SAN ANDREAS KIT FOX AMBER Ale   MB/BP   1.1
(Hollister, California)
Flat, flat, flat; tasteless, too, as if the flavor has been drained from it; only taste characteristic is hint of fruity sourness that is coaxed out by food; seems to have the promise of a balanced, flavorful brew, but never quite makes it; perhaps it's not fresh enough; caveat emptor.

SAN ANDREAS SEISMIC ALE   MB/BP   1.8
(Hollister, California)
Sour, with barely perceptible fizziness; settles into bland taste and texture; very slight hint of fruity aroma; improves 24 hours after bottle is opened; better without food.

SAN CARLOS ESPECIAL Pilsener   CB   2.3
(San Carlos, Argentina)
Very pale light-bodied pilsener with a sharp but very restrained opening tang; fluffy, moderately disappearing head is a good coun-terpoint to slight acridness of the body; relatively satisfying with-out food (the operative word here is "relatively"); some complexity raises it a notch or so above other ordinary brews.

SAN MIGUEL DARK Pilsener   **CB**   **4.4**
(Manila, Philippines)
Buoyant and uplifting, fulfilling both its promise and your expectations; creamy richness with very mild burnt maltiness that's integrated into the fullness and warmth of the texture; finishes a little too watery for my taste, thereby lessening its overall effect; this is a very good beer, one of the best imported beers of those most readily available at local retailers. One of the things I like is its compatibility with both plain and fancy dishes—from a salami sandwich to a butterflied leg of lamb.

SAN MIGUEL PALE PILSEN   **CB**   **2.9**
(Manila, Philippines)
Light and fizzy with no stimulating aroma; hint of wheat/grain flavor gently enlivens a mouthfeel that initially fails to gain your attention; sweetens and becomes pleasantly even-tempered with food; moves along; a far cry from San Miguel Dark. Fine with a hamburger or linguine with clam sauce.

B E E R   F A C T

Although San Miguel is often associated with the Philippines, it is actually a Spanish company, with headquarters in Manila.

SAND PIPER EXTRA GOLD LAGER   **CB**   **2.5**
(Dharuhera, Harvana, India)
Flowery, attractive bitterness; not as effervescent as other lagers; sweet, clover-honey taste; grainy-grassy aroma; interweaving of mild hoppiness and mild honey-sweetness gives this pale-gold beer a pleasurable but not outstanding presence; thin, clean white head; placid in taste and delivery; maintains its flavor characteristics, but just barely; brewed by Inertia Industries Limited, which may or may not explain its rather passive approach to flavor conveyance.

SANTA BARBARA PACIFIC PALE ALE
(draft)   **BP**   **2.9**
(Santa Barbara, California)
Starts with the vaguest perfumey aroma, but quickly gains a stronger perfumey/fruity taste and texture that lets you know you have just swallowed an IPA; fruity rather than hoppy, though bitterness is present throughout; a bit too thin; textural pizzazz is lost late in the glass; variable but satisfying, especially with chips and dip.

SANTA BARBARA RINCON RED ALE
(draft)   BP   2.6
(Santa Barbara, California)

Fruity, with a fringe of hop bitterness; very faint malty aroma is so brief you're not sure it's there; medium-bodied; fruity-maltiness stays throughout with Caesar salad; loses some vivacity toward the bottom of the glass; flavorful but unchallenging; finishes bitter, not sweet, though too weak on both counts.

SANTA CRUZ LIGHTHOUSE
AMBER Lager   BP   1.1
(Santa Cruz, California)

While the aroma is rose-sweet on first contact, it is too sour on the throat; oxidized, which in this case may not be the brewer's fault—but the taste effect is the same, regardless of the culprit.

SANTA CRUZ LIGHTHOUSE LAGER   BP   0.3
(Santa Cruz, California)

Sour and tart, almost like spoiled wheat beer; essentially textureless; fruity and acrid—clearly not a lager—this beer is either spoiled or mislabeled; no head, no fizz, no nothing.

SANTA FE CHICKEN KILLER
BARLEY WINE   MB   1.3
(Santa Fe, New Mexico)

Light, soft, and balanced; alcohol is gentle rather than harsh; medium amber color; yeasty and young—not fully developed; with short-term storage in the bottle, hops and sweetness diminish and balance changes: bitterness increases while hop flavors stay put; clingy coating on the tongue; chalky; should age longer—a beer that's not done yet.

SANTA FE FIESTA ALE   MB   1.9
(Santa Fe, New Mexico)

Very fruity nose with accompanying flowery taste; not yet ready for drinking; weak with foods; flat texture and noncommanding taste; sweet curlicue at the end doesn't really improve taste sufficiently.

SANTA FE OLD POJOAQUE PORTER   MB   3.5
(Santa Fe, New Mexico)

Creamy, moderated, and full; subtle roasted taste and aroma; perhaps a bit too smooth and watery in the end; slightly, but not unpleasantly, bitter; understated and satisfying even with a hint of premature bottling; nice creamy head. Accompanies chips and spicy dips as well as smoked meats and poultry.

SANTA FE PALE ALE   MB   2.3
(Santa Fe, New Mexico)

Variety of flavors: mild, sweet palate followed by slightly sour taste that dead ends back to mild and sweet; fresh, piquant, and fruity, but somewhat watery; settles into an average, evenhanded beer with a thick, foamy head; an acrid taste emerges with bland foods, interfering with their enjoyment; faint, flatly sour aftertaste; lingering hint of mustiness clouds the freshness; could use more depth and character.

SANTA FE RUBIA ESPECIAL Lager   CB   3.9
(Santa Fe, Argentina)
Very apparent, appealing graininess; conveys a fleeting impression of freshness that probably isn't really there; remains steady; evenly distributed head stays around; good body and mouthfeel; creamy smoothness emerges with continuing attractive malt and grain taste; unusually flavorful; hint of auburn in the color. Accompanies Chinese food.

SAPPORO BLACK MALT LIQUOR   CB   4.0
(Tokyo, Japan)
Lovely modulated caramel-roasted flavor with a touch of wine taste reflective of its higher alcohol content; as the liquid warms, balanced complexity and integrity meander pleasantly from the tip of the tongue to the back of the mouth—all this without food accompaniment; with food, it remains calm, cushioning spiciness nicely and unobtrusively; sweetness lingers at the end; not as chewy as it should be. A good choice with sturdy main courses such as spaghetti and meatballs.

SAPPORO BLACK MALT LIQUOR   CB   4.1
(Tokyo, Japan; brewed for the Japanese market, not for export)
Smooth, malty, and mildly pungent; muddy brown color with short-lived head; relatively sharp backdrop to food; leaves musty afterglow on the roof of the mouth; strikingly similar to Sapporo Black Malt Liquor (above), purchased in the U.S. Try it with spaghetti and meatballs or pork dishes.

BEER FACT

*S*apporo, brewing since 1876, is Japan's oldest brand of beer. Named after its city of origin, the brewery was founded by the Japanese government. Now privately owned, the firm has breweries in Tokyo as well as Sapporo.

SAPPORO DRAFT Pilsener   CB   2.4
(Tokyo, Japan)
Slightly sour and acidic with thick texture on the tongue; very little carbonation or balance; unsweet and grainy, especially for a Japanese beer; thin pale-gold color with absolutely no head; needs a redesign of taste, texture, and visual appeal.

SARAH HUGHES DARK RUBY ALE   CB   2.2
(Sedgeley, England)
Highly touted, bottle-conditioned Sarah Hughes disappoints; not particularly complex or nuanced; the tiny core of fruity and toasty flavors doesn't spread out, leaving instead an empty, hollowed-out mouthfeel; well-hidden wine-like presence suggests a bit more character after awhile, but it comes across stilted and rigid; deep, ruby-red body is much too thin on the palate; faint oaky aroma; finishes with a bleak, tea-like taste.

SARANAC ADIRONDACK SEASON'S
BEST ALE (annual)   CT   3.4
(Utica, New York)
Piney aroma and sharp, crisp taste with lots of malt overtones are the hallmarks of this holiday brew; quite alcoholic; not complex, too much of a one-note taste; smooths out its rough edges when paired with food; stays a bit bitter while showcasing its alcohol; could have more body; finish is nice and relaxed for a beer meant to offer good cheer. A festive accompaniment to baked chicken or roast turkey served with wild rice.

B E E R   F A C T

Saranac Black and Tan is a blend of Irish stout and all-malt German-style lager, a bottled version of the draft of the same name. The visuals in the bottle are quite different from those observed out of the tap. (See page 148.)

SARANAC BLACK AND TAN
Stout/Lager   CT   3.8
(Utica, New York)
Immediate freshness, depth, and balanced malt-hops; merely a whiff of sweet malty aroma at the start; hearty and flavorful; minimal but tangible fizziness nicely counters the beer's smoothness and mellow strength; loses strength and flavors turn a mite thin at the end of the bottle; dark-amber color adds to the enjoyment; late in the bottle, a pine-spice aroma whispers in the nose, which adds to an underlying subtle bitterness. Tasty with typical pub fare.

SARANAC ADIRONDACK AMBER Lager   CT   2.2
(Utica, New York)
Simultaneously acrid and fruity, with a hard edge; both qualities remain with food but display a much lower profile; taste flattens out; in the end, any pizzazz and spiffiness are leached out, leaving a chalky aftertaste.

SARASOTA IPA   BP   2.5
(Sarasota, Florida)

Fruity, musty aroma; sharp fruity taste; gently and happily hoppy; hop aftertaste fades a bit but keeps its character long enough for minimal enjoyment; dry and a bit sour; this is a delicately hopped IPA—not powerful, not memorable, but reasonably satisfying for the moment; more muscle than form; flavor needs to be increased to really make it worth your while.

SATZENBRAU PREMIUM PILS   CB   3.0
(Dublin, Ireland)

Virtually odorless, with medium-strength hop bite; rather sweet, with a hint of perfumey tastiness; hop bitterness is nicely contained by the sweetish malt, making for a tamped-down but tasty pilsener; large-bubbled head sits atop the golden-blond body; dry and smooth; finishes hoppier than it started. Fish and chips, for sure, with this one.

SAXER THREE FINGER JACK
HEFEDUNKEL   MB/RB   2.3
(Lake Oswego, Oregon)

Sweet close-to-cherry taste is quickly overtaken by a sharp-sour mouthfeel; lightly hopped; fizzy, with the barest hints of chocolate; as the beer settles down, some flavors are lost, particularly at the back of the throat; gains in sweetness but loses character; makes a comeback at the end, with a mild but definite malt aroma; too uneven to be highly recommended. A beer for snacks.

SCALDIS BELGIAN SPECIAL ALE   CB   3.7
(Pipaix, Belgium)

Fruity and sharply yeasty—enough to make your mouth water just smelling it right out of the bottle; mouthfeel is very strong-tasting and quite sour, almost grapefruity; bitterness and sourness increase, but that's the name of the game with this powerful yeast-laden ale; full-tasting and dry, but not as smooth as advertised; finishes with a malty sweetness that wasn't present earlier; thick, lumpy head makes you want to drink more—and you should; a professional, well-done brew that takes a special palate to enjoy. Fruits, nuts, and strong cheeses make good partners for Scaldis.

SCALDIS NOEL ALE (annual)   CB   2.1
(Pipaix, Belgium)

Caramel taste with thickish, not-quite-cloying mouthfeel; smooth and strong-bodied; thick, big-bubbled light-tan head stays a while and complements light-copper color of the body; slight bitterness tends to hide any fruitiness; triple-hopped, it is more of a routine high-alcohol brown ale than a special seasonal drink; harsh and biting; far too strong and thick for most foods. Goes with crackers and slightly sweet creamy spreads or dips.

SCHAEFER Pilsener   **CB**   **2.3**
(Detroit, Michigan)
Sour bouquet, with similar but quickly fading taste; overall, taste-less and unmotivating, even with aggressively flavored foods; strangely, it gets mellower and sweeter at the bottom of the glass; good for the ballpark. (It tasted better when I was younger, watching the Brooklyn Dodgers at Ebbets Field on TV.)

SCHINCARIOL PILSEN   **CB**   **0.2**
(Schincariol, Brazil)
Increasing cabbage odor that almost reaches full flower toward the end of the glass; bland texture; spoiled-food ambiance con-tinues, along with unexciting, not-going-anywhere mouthfeel; dull, heavy, and generally unpleasant; raw—forget it.

SCHLAFLY BARLEYWINE (draft)   **BP**   **3.0**
(St. Louis, Missouri)
Fine fruity apple aroma; smooth, fresh-made caramel-chocolate flavor sits pleasantly on the tongue; plenty of alcohol to go around (9.5%/weight; 11.88%/volume); sweet and full-bodied; deep, rich orange-amber body enhances the depth-in-character feel; finishes with an integrated flourish of apple flavor and alcohol; this is one strong barley wine. Savor this before or after a hearty meal.

SCHLAFLY HEFEWEIZEN (draft)   **BP**   **1.1**
(St. Louis, Missouri)
Citrusy, weak, and much too flat; sourness at the end of a swal-low; too light, too sweet, and not complex enough; too much yeast without proper malt balance; thin and shallow; Busch, an-other local product, is more satisfying.

SCHLAFLY OATMEAL STOUT (draft)   **BP**   **4.0**
(St. Louis, Missouri)
Mellow and soft; nice laid-back burnt taste with a hint of tang that's virtually perfect; a great example of the style—and tastes great, too; finishes with complexity balanced with a surge of thick-ness; suave and malty with charbroiled chicken; try one, and ask for another . . . and another. Good with game and rich stews.

SCHLAFLY PALE ALE (draft)   **BP**   **2.5**
(St. Louis, Missouri)
Fruity aroma and taste, but neither is overwhelming; light touch and feel; tempered sweetness with a circumference of citrus that is mellow and appropriately close to, but not quite making, the bitterness that helps define this style of ale; too weak to entice a second helping—or to fully enjoy the first one.

SCHLAFLY ROBERT BURNS
SCOTCH ALE (draft)   **BP**   **3.5**
(St. Louis, Missouri)
Fresh malty aroma, followed by an intense, quickly spreading

strawberry taste; nice fizziness quickly dissolves into the warm strawberry-like flavor; creamy and smooth; sweet aftertaste is properly restrained by the alcohol; deep ruby-garnet body is pleasant to the eye, with a sheen through the glass; clean sugar-water mouthfeel; finishes with an increasing alcohol presence that leaves you with a mellow, happy feeling; very well done. Goes great with the toffee pudding dessert.

SCHLENKERLA SMOKED BEER— MARZEN   CB   3.7
(Bamberg, Germany)

Just like a bacon slab sliced to perfection, Schlenkerla is sweetly smoky, with the emphasis on smoky; smooth and almost textureless; concentrate and you can experience the malt underneath all that smoke; the lingering taste makes you thirsty, as you might expect; cumulatively overwhelming; a well-made *Rauchbier,* but only for those who appreciate a strong brew. It's a good breakfast drink, since it goes well with scrambled eggs (and bacon).

SCHLITZ Lager   CB   1.8
(Detroit, Michigan)

Quite thin, with a feeble attempt at crispness; surprisingly unfizzy; musty "old" aroma; no complexity or intricacy; adjuncts safely hidden from view and taste, except for a slight, weak corn/graininess in the background; somewhat turpey (turpentine-like) at the finish, but sweetly so, not acrid or sour; more body at the end, as if everything sank to the bottom in order to prove this really is a beer. It is, but just barely.

SCHLITZ MALT LIQUOR   CB   1.3
(Milwaukee, Wisconsin)

More suggestive of high alcohol content than is actually the case; harshly grainy, with no discernible flavor nuances; ingredients become relatively more integrated toward the end, raising this mass-produced beer to the mediocre level.

B E E R   F A C T

*S*chmaltz came on the market in 1993 and was named after a founder of the August Schell brewery.

SCHMALTZ'S ALT ALE   CB   3.3
(New Ulm, Minnesota)

Sweet chocolate, burnt-malt taste, with smooth texture and a hit of alcohol; rich and full-bodied, with heft and hoppy character; deep dark-copper, almost-black color is appropriate match for taste and overall ambiance; warming sweetness of the alcohol is too overpowering for most foods; more like a porter than an ale, but tasty nonetheless; intimations of nuttiness float forward at the finish—a charming surprise. Fine with hero sandwiches.

SCHMIDT Lager   CB   1.8
(La Crosse, Wisconsin)
Sour, carbonated, and somewhat green mouthfeel; cheap taste; softer, warmer, and more flavorful at the end of the bottle. Better with pasta and grain dishes.

TAP TIP

Pass the Woodruff, Please

*M*ost beers suffer if you add anything to them once the beer is poured and waiting to be savored. After all, the brewer has done his or her job, and now you are expected to do yours: Drink it. True, you can add tomato juice. And in the case of some beers served in the traditional manner in a warm clime like Mexico, a slice of lime in a cold glass aids the battle against the tropical heat. However, there are beer styles that are peculiarly accommodating to an intrusion on the finished product. The southern German *weizenbier* is made more refreshing with a lemon slice added or with fresh lemon juice squirted directly into the full-flavored liquid. Some examples are August Schell Weizen, Witkap-Pater Singel Abbey Ale, Edelweiss Kristallklar Weizenbier, and Paulaner Hefe-Weizen.

An even more tantalizing tradition is the addition of a dollop of raspberry or cherry syrup, or a pinch of essence of woodruff, to help take the wheat-generated astringent edge off a cold *Berliner Weisse*. If neither of those sweeteners is available, a splash of fruit-flavored liqueur can be a more-than-adequate substitute. It is also not unheard of to use mashed fresh raspberries in place of the syrup. Good candidates are Pschorr-Brau Weisse, Schultheiss Berliner Weisse, Celis White, and Erdinger Weissbier Hefetrub.

SCHMIDT'S Lager   CB   2.4
(Baltimore, Maryland)
Smooth neighborhood-bar beer; slight tingle in tandem with smooth wave-like texture; mellowness swerves off to a bit of sour-

ness with food; in the end, cereal grains predominate and enhance the off-taste sourness that becomes increasingly apparent; starts good, but doesn't end well. Okay with a hamburger.

SCHNEIDER CERVEZA RUBIA
ESPECIAL Lager   CB   2.2
(Santa Fe, Argentina)
Tamped-down texture and taste; prickly and fizzy on the palate; some fruitiness continues throughout; hazy reddish color with little head; nice ring of Brussels lace; uninspired, almost wispy; leaves a fermented presence on the roof of the mouth, which is not unpleasant; sharp hoppiness. Nice accompaniment to barbecued pork dishes.

SCHOONER LAGER   CB   1.8
(Montreal, Quebec, Canada)
Very fizzy; nice bite initially, but fades and gets thin and watery; doesn't develop on the palate, or anywhere else; in the end, weak and uninteresting drunk by itself. Accompany it with a slice of pizza.

SCHOP OSCURO Pilsener   CB   3.4
(Osorno, Chile)
Mildly roasted, mildly sweet, and generously appealing; light on the outside, fuller in the middle; almost soda-like in texture, but with minimal fizz; smooth going down; nicely malted; a bit thin and almost watery; easy to enjoy. (Made by Compania Cervecerias Unidas, S.A., a monopoly that makes all of the beers in southern Chile and most of them elsewhere in the country.) Compatible with mild cheeses, olives, or a sliced tomato and avocado salad.

SCHULTHEISS BERLINER WEISSE   CB   3.0
(Berlin, Germany)
Astringent and highly citrusy; adding a dollop of raspberry syrup (a common practice with this beer style) quickly moderates any sourness or astringency, though it remains palatable without it; typical of the style; sharp, highly carbonated, and acidic; satisfying thirst-quencher; pale opaque color; almost like drinking grapefruit juice with alcohol; for highly individualized tastes—you may like it, but watch out for its tart bite.

SCHULTHEISS GERMAN PILSENER   CB   0.3
(Berlin, Germany)
Slightly light-struck; pale-golden color is clear and bright; tangy, with tangible carbonation; retains semi-fresh yeasty taste, yet becomes increasingly sour and spoiled-tasting; in the end harsh, green, and unsatisfying; too many off-tastes for its own good.

SCHUTZ BIERE D'ALSACE PILS   CB   2.4
(Schiltigheim, France)

Yeasty and quite malty, soft and gentle on the tongue; hop presence increasingly makes itself felt; airy, empty head lingers, but adds nothing of substance except some interest in comparison to the light, faded, pale body; very filling—don't drink too many of these; a slackness at the finish adds to the unappealing, but typically Alsatian, character; a curl of honey offers a semi-fond farewell. Try it with spicy pasta dishes.

SCHUTZENBERGER JUBILATOR Bock   CB   3.8
(Schiltigheim, France)

Fruity sweetness with a thickness that settles at the back of the tongue; delicately balanced, though a bit biased toward the hops; slightly golden cloudiness; nicely formed Brussels lace, indicating quality ingredients and manufacture; pleasant thread of alcohol remains present throughout; a good French beer, but thins out at the end. Try it with baked Virginia ham accompanied by sweet potatoes.

B E E R   F A C T

*B*ock beer names with the ending "-ator" (for example, Celebrator, Maximator) have a relatively high alcohol content. Doppelbocks, required in Germany to be brewed at 7.5%/volume or stronger, fall into this category. A good source of nutrition, bocks were originally created by monks to drink when they were fasting.

SCHWEIZERHOF-BRAU LAGER   CB   2.9
(Marktoberdorf, Germany)

Soft and gently carbonated; hop bitterness at the back of the throat; low-level flavor is rather flat and certainly not complex; amazingly untasty for a German beer—light, a bit fluffy, and airy; mild hoppiness finally emerges at the end of the bottle; also becomes more full-bodied, tastier, and maltier; gives the impression that it needs time to gather its strength in order to perform at an acceptable level—which it eventually does. Try it with pasta salads.

SCORPION MALT LIQUOR   CB   2.4
(Evansville, Indiana)

Hint of skunkiness, but sweet and sharply smooth, remains mild and somewhat malty; balanced overall, though there's really not much malt or hops to balance; stays prickly in the mouth without interfering with food; aroma remains lightly skunky (due, no doubt, to its clear-glass bottle); weak for a malt liquor, though reasonably flavorful—not a bad trade-off. Try it with ham and Swiss cheese on rye.

SEA DOG BROWN ALE   MB/BP   2.5
(Bangor, Maine)

Light caramel and fruity aroma dances into your nose; quite hoppy, even a bit astringent; thin, creamy, ivory-colored head; sweetens perceptibly, arriving at a good malt-hop balance; sheets of Brussels lace are topped off by a thin but well-configured ivory-colored head, making this ale visually interesting; smooths and mellows as it finishes, though it weakens somewhat at the end; more promise than delivery. An appropriate partner with light meat dishes, like thin slices of pork.

SEA DOG WINDJAMMER BLONDE ALE   MB/BP   3.8
(Bangor, Maine)

Sharp fruity aroma and similar taste, with an added bite in the mouth that keeps you alert; continues on with a subtle interacting balance of bitter and malty-sweet; light, but filled with flavor; rocky head stays a mesmerizing half-inch thick and moves around like an ice floe in a sea of gold; taste gets a little muddied at the end; finishes fuller and more bitter than at the start; fruity aroma is there to say goodbye at the last sip; nicely done. A good partner with chicken breasts or turkey legs.

SEABRIGHT BANTY ROOSTER IPA   BP   2.4
(Santa Cruz, California)

Fruity, sharp, and within the IPA style, but needs more bitterness; dry and appealing; hoppiness fades a bit at end, though in general holds its own; could be even sharper and zestier.

SECOND STREET INDIA PALE ALE   BP   1.4
(Santa Fe, New Mexico)

Quite hoppy, with an attendant spicy-floral aroma; dry and a bit salty-tasting; salty character eventually obscures the hops, malt and pretty much all else, even the alcohol (6.0%/volume); faint hint of malt and hops appears at mid-glass; hop presence fights its way through at the end, but it's not enough; flattens texturally, too, at the same time; leaves you thirstier than when you started.

SEPTANTE 5 MALT LIQUOR   CB   3.7
(Roubaix, France)

You know this is not a routine malt liquor on the first sip—it's highly malted, with a bitter alcoholic taste; a hint of caramel tames the malt and alcohol, making the beer vertically rather than horizontally balanced; surprisingly unobtrusive with food; softens as it warms; segues into a touch of cloyingness; sweetness increases at the finish; ends better than it starts; I don't particularly care for the *bière de garde* style, as it has a more distinctive flavor profile than most imported so-called malt liquors, but I think this is a good example of it. Try it with a spicy pizza or a garden salad with creamy dressing.

SEPTANTE ROUGE Ale   CB   2.2
(Roubaix, France)
Smoky taste reminiscent of smoked fish; silky texture; muddy color; distinctive but not distinguished, with a wine-like finish.

75th STREET BROWN ALE   MB   2.5
(Kansas City, Missouri)
A vague spicy presence is immediately followed by a smooth, gliding chocolate taste; nutty aroma and eventual nutty taste, similar to hazelnut; nutty character predominates well into the aftertaste; not aggressive; medium-bodied and uncomplex; dark cola color has an orangey-red glow; palatable.

75th STREET ROYAL RASPBERRY
WHEAT   MB   3.3
(Olathe, Kansas)
Lightly fizzy and lightly raspberry, with a wheat-hoppiness that quickly subdues any extraneous sweetness; fresh and lively strawberry aroma; surprisingly robust and full-flavored; keeps its appealing wheat-berry balance throughout; hazy blond body; a remarkably satisfying summer refresher; finishes with just the right amount of sweet and bitter mouthfeel. If you're thirsty, drink this.

SEZOENS ALE   CB   3.0
(Bocholt, Belgium)
Rather fresh-smelling, with promise of pleasantness; crispness turns sweet with red meat; gives an impression of thinness but is filling; daintiness remains on the tongue; a finishing warmth at the back of the mouth; a summertime ale from Flanders with a fresh hoppy aroma; hearty dryness. A pleasant companion with light picnic fare, such as cold chicken or turkey sandwiches.

SHAN SUI YEN SUM Pilsener   CT   2.5
(Utica, New York)
Definite aroma and taste of ginseng; bittersweet balance obscures the individuality of the hops and malt; needs non-spicy snack food; artificial-tasting fullness—the result, no doubt, of rice and/or corn adjuncts—makes this beer more American than Asian; indeed, it was brewed in the U.S. for a Hong Kong company; in the end, an average commercial American brew; finishes a bit sweet. Compatible with crackers and mild cheese.

SHANDY CARIB Lager   CB   0.2
(Port of Spain, Trinidad)
Overpowering ginger smell, albeit fresh and invigorating; taste packs a ginger wallop also; full and softly sweet; too strong in

the mouth; tastes more like ginger ale than beer, but without the carbonation; this might go over better with non-beer drinkers; I had trouble finishing it, and it's not even a 12-ounce bottle; too syrupy; light-caramel color adds to the soda-pop feel; ugh.

SHEAF STOUT   CB   2.5
(Sydney, New South Wales, Australia)
Yeasty, immediately attractive aroma; looks like a good cup of coffee—strong, deep black, and silky smooth; burnt taste does not turn overly bitter; almost overpowering, it needs to be cut with another, lighter beer; tough stuff—too much for one sitting; interestingly, it calms down with sweet foods; obviously a well-brewed product that will be satisfying to those who like heavy, bitter beer; I personally don't care for it. Compatible with sweet desserts, Danish pastries, cinnamon buns.

SHEPHERD NEAME INDIA PALE ALE   CB   3.2
(Faversham, England)
Full malt mouthfeel and smooth, accommodating texture are the first impressions; hops creep up and finally become the dominating factor; citrus-tang aroma; malts and hops balance well and produce a fine, delicate nutty taste sensation; orange pekoe color; an easy-to-drink, and easy-to-like, IPA. Goes well with smoked pork and smoked cheese.

SHINER BOCK   CB   2.4
(Shiner, Texas)
Indistinct aroma; brownish-red color; hardly any head; not unpleasant mustiness at the back of the throat; somewhat flabby; satisfying warmth redeems it partially; seems to be on the verge of tasting good, but in the end disappoints; pedestrian with food.

SHINER PREMIUM Pilsener   CB   2.5
(Shiner, Texas)
Light, quickly fading taste; some passing hops and rice mouthfeel; sweet and mellow; thin but serviceable; taste and energy appear capable of holding up through several cans; give it time, and it will grow on you. An interesting companion to veal dishes and white bean salads.

SHIPYARD BROWN ALE   MB   2.5
(Kennebunk and Portland, Maine)
Cocoa-chocolate aroma and taste; foamy, formidable, thick, heavily bubbled head sits elegantly atop the peach-amber body; mildly bitter; not very complex; chocolate flavor keeps coming through; designer lumps of aged-ivory Brussels lace on sides of glass; mild hoppy character is suggested toward the end; pleasant but not outstanding. Try with spicy red meat.

SIAM ALE CB 3.8
(Bangkok, Thailand)

Sweet, excellent mouthfeel; honey taste with mellow accompaniment; unfortunately, honey presence fades fast and is not replaced; a pleasant emerging charcoal undertone; better at the beginning than at the end; a lovely, finely tuned special brew; finishes spicy and with conviction; a beer this good should have an affinity for food, but alas, it does not.

SIERRA BLANCA PILSNER MB 2.4
(Carrizozo, New Mexico)

The fresh-fruit aroma and complementary taste get this pilsener off to a promising start; compact iced-tea sweetness borders on caramel; thick mouthfeel and lack of carbonation are unusual for a pilsener; solid sheets of Brussels lace line the sides of the glass; runs down at the end, finishing sadly; needs more work; order a glass, not a pint.

SIERRA NEVADA BIGFOOT
BARLEYWINE STYLE ALE (annual) RB 0.2–1.3
(Chico, California)

Fruity in taste and aroma, but also creamy and smooth; distinct wineyness; highly hopped and alcoholic, producing a strong, hearty flavor; rich deep-red amber color and lush aroma reminiscent of apple cider, but tending toward perfumey; lacks balance; some cloyingness on the tongue; thick, creamy foam helps moderate the strident bitterness—a good thing, too; fits the style and, apparently, the taste of judges at the Great American Beer Festival (it's a multiple award-winner), but I couldn't finish it; after five years in cold storage or under refrigeration, the cloyingness should lessen and the ingredients should blend (this style of ale is *intended* to improve with age).

SIERRA NEVADA CELEBRATION ALE
(annual) RB 2.3–3.9
(Chico, California)

Vibrantly fresh fruity aroma; flat, less aromatic taste brings a citrus tang to the roof of the mouth and is sidetracked by an astringent alcohol rawness; hops impart a pleasant bitterness; comforting warmth and alcohol sharpness remain throughout; finishes with a yeasty freshness and a touch of fruity alcoholic sweetness; in short, a true red ale, and a very decent one at that; Silver Medal winner at the 1994 Great American Beer Festival. Good with simply prepared red meats, beef potpie, and meat loaf.

SIERRA NEVADA PALE ALE RB 3.2
(Chico, California)

Musty, smoky; some bitter back-of-the-mouth taste and aftertaste; barley malt aroma is present, but not overwhelming; subdued fruitiness authenticates its ale lineage; hops are prominent, which also confirms the style; lacks punch with strongly fla-vored foods, though the oomph has definitely increased over the years; Gold Medal winner at the 1993 Great American Beer Festival. Best with lean fish, such as red snapper, flounder, and halibut.

SIERRA NEVADA PALE BOCK (draft)   RB   2.5
(Chico, California)

Attenuated freshness; dull richness and body; clean; hint of flow-eriness keeps food in place; sharpness turns a bit edgy and fresh-ness deflates; decent beginning, lackluster ending. Good with unspicy Chinese dishes such as pork chow mein, vegetable fried rice, and noodle soups.

SIERRA NEVADA PORTER   RB   2.6
(Chico, California)

Molasses aroma; very smooth; easy to swallow; has an enigmatic quality; bitter first, sweeter afterward. Not a particularly food-friendly beer.

SIERRA NEVADA STOUT   RB   2.5
(Chico, California)

Restrained in taste, texture, and overall impression; dark burnt-caramel taste eventually comes to the fore; soft and palatable in the mouth with food, but once food is swallowed, beer turns acrid and hard to savor; entirely handmade in the "old-world tra-dition," according to the label.

SIERRA NEVADA SUMMERFEST
(annual)   RB   3.5–3.8
(Chico, California)

Fresh, fruity, and zesty, with palate-cleansing initial taste and tex-ture; simultaneously sweet and bitter; mustiness is also present; heavy yeastiness turns comfortingly sweet; heavy quality head clings to the sides of the mug, putting a lid on the washed-out golden body; nicely pungent hoppiness takes over from the cit-rus fruitiness; mellows into a balanced, integrated brew; finishes with an ale thrust—warmish and slightly alcoholic; a quality prod-uct. Tasty with light summer fare such as cold pasta salads or tossed green salads.

SILETZ NUT BROWN ALE   BP   3.7
(Siletz, Oregon)

Creamy-smooth and very mouth-friendly; initially quite malty, then a deep chocolate taste comes along with a substantial hit of alcohol, or so it seems; appears to be an essence of berry (raspberry?) sweet-tartness underneath it all; carefully balanced and well prepared; civilized and reassuring; weakens a bit at the end. A beer made to coax out the delicacies of a bowl of seafood stew.

SIMPATICO AMBER Lager   CB   2.4
(Dubuque, Iowa)
Deep fruity essence; crisp and sharp with some thick cloyingness
at the back of the tongue; rather bland texture with an underlay
of malty warmth; in the end, spicy food overtakes any nuances
that this beer may have; closes with a faux-caramel taste that is
cool rather than warm; a run-of-the-mill amber. A beer nuts and
pretzels companion.

SIMPATICO GOLDEN LAGER   CB   1.2
(Dubuque, Iowa)
Light and artificial-tasting, apparently from a clear abundance of
chemicals and adjuncts; flat; watery, and goes nowhere; cloudy, almost muddy, especially for a lager; sharp without redeeming flavor; finishes with a tart honey flavor that belatedly raises its status.

SINGHA Lager   CB   2.5
(Bangkok, Thailand)
Smooth at first, followed by a sour citrus taste that overwhelms
anything other than bland food; gentle and mildly tingly on the
tongue; okay in a pinch. A match for pasta with a simple fresh
tomato sauce.

SINGHA GOLD Pilsener   CB   0.9
(Bangkok, Thailand)
Light and bitter; watery; tastes too much like a weak American-
brewed commercial product; harsh graininess becomes apparent
and then quickly dissipates; clear light-golden color holds no fizziness; kind of the Coors Light of Asia.

SKOL CERVEJA PILSEN   CB   1.0
(Rio Claro, Brazil)
Fruity, a touch spunky, and almost fizzless; nicely configured
Brussels lace remains throughout; milky haze obscures pale-blond
body; obviously old and punchless, but some malt flavor remains;
textureless and unaromatic.

SKOL HOLLAND PILSENER   CB   2.2
(Rotterdam, Holland)
Faint smokiness; no texture/fizziness; quite unpilsener-like;
unassertive; bland, but pleasantly so; hint of honeyed fruitiness
emerges at the finish; tea leaf–like sediment collects at the bottom; bland, bland, boring, blah.

SKOL INTERNATIONAL Pilsener   CB   1.2
(Linz, Austria)
Weakly sweet, with only the barest hint of hops (or is even that
a result of my hopeful imagination?); slight bitterness fades rapidly
after each sip; coats the mouth with a mildly unsatisfactory flavor; pale straw-colored body looks flat and undistinguished; distinctly mediocre; finishes lifeless.

SLAVAYANSKY Lager   CB   0.3
(Moscow, Russia)

This beer is so bad that the Russian waiter at first said I shouldn't have it, then claimed he didn't have any on hand; foolishly, I prevailed. Lacking effervescence, as if it had come straight from a water tap; fortunately, it was served warmish, so that the only identifiable characteristic—an almost palatable potato-like aroma—made itself known; I can only presume the vodka was of a higher quality.

SLEEMAN CREAM ALE   MB   3.0
(Guelph, Ontario, Canada)

Tastes like a soft lager; refreshing and mellow; exhibits no extremes in texture, aroma, or taste; a good brew by itself, or try it with a T-bone steak and baked potato.

SLEEMAN LAGER   MB   2.7
(Guelph, Ontario, Canada)

Hoppy, with surprisingly invigorating adjuncts—a beer for the ballpark if there ever was one; spritzy, with some body—designed to satisfy all comers; overall an easygoing brew for those who like it cold and with some pizzazz; refreshing and predictable at the same time; a convivial beer to share with friends; hint of greenness mars some of the good feelings; I liked it, though it is definitely not high-quality, just one with which to while away the time. Best with hot dogs and other ballpark foods.

SLEEMAN ORIGINAL DARK ALE   MB   2.3
(Guelph, Ontario, Canada)

A bit oxidized; mellow, mild toastedness becomes almost honeylike; weak, watery maltiness fades quickly, leaving a core of obvious quality in its wake; just as quickly, it becomes flat and uninteresting; mild malty aroma; very accommodating sweetness evolves with foods; in the end, there is more promise than delivery; faintly bitter finish within a too watery context; try drinking this closer to the source. Okay with a tuna salad sandwich.

SLO GARDEN ALLEY AMBER ALE   MB/BP   2.4
(Paso Robles and San Luis Obispo, California)

Rush of malty-honey aroma accompanies bittersweet taste; fruity and astringent; makes its presence known on the upper palate; minimally cloying; texture is smooth and lifeless; starts vigorous but ends aversive, though the pleasant malty aroma remains; let this beer warm in order to coax out whatever flavor it has. Try it with a well-seasoned meat dish.

SMITH AND REILLY HONEST BEER
Pilsener   CT   2.7
(Tumwater, Washington)

Variable initial tastes and texture, with an eventual strengthening of body and overall mouthfeel; hops reminiscent of a mildly bitter grassiness; the malt is plain and remains in the background; not quite bland, but not a challenge to your taste buds, either; a beer out to offend no one while giving the impression there's something of substance in the bottle. Fine with raw vegetable snacks, chips and dip.

SMUTTYNOSE OLD BROWN DOG ALE   MB   2.5
(Portsmouth, New Hampshire)
Harsh chocolate-malt taste; diminishing carbonation; a certain maltiness creeps up, reminiscent of a Vienna amber; there's some roasted flavor in there, too; appears to have some tangible alcohol presence as well as a hint of aromatic fruitiness, but it may be imaginary; finishes full-bodied and texturally flat. Best with fried fish dishes.

SNAKE RIVER ZONKER STOUT   MB/BP   2.2
(Jackson Hole, Wyoming)
Mellow, tangy roastedness sits on the back of the tongue after first swallow; increasingly apparent burnt, rather than roasted, taste; slightly bitter wine-like aspect; suddenly turns sharp and sour with no redeeming balancing character; warms and sweetens somewhat at the end, but it's too late; doesn't seem to be calibrated just right.

SNOWFLAKE Pilsener   CB   2.3
(Shenyang, China)
Mellow and mild, with a hint of carbonation; suggestion of sweetness at the beginning; smells like it's been sitting a little too long; while texture remains watery, mild hop sharpness is present; too light and gentle for spicy foods; rice flavor ultimately floats to the top as the beer warms; pale-golden color adds to light ambiance of this pilsener; best enjoyed on its own or with a bowl of nuts.

SOL Pilsener   CB   2.5
(Guadalajara, Mexico)
Light, some tang; first bottle or two creates excitement; a simplistic presentation of malt, hops, and yeast; a good common beer you can sip, and enjoy, for hours. Savor with spicy snacks such as Buffalo-style chicken wings, chili dogs, and nachos.

SOLANA BEACH PIZZA PORTS PORTER BP   2.8
(Solana Beach, California)
Smooth and laid-back; understated roasted-malt taste; almost melts in your mouth; thick, foamy Brussels lace covers sides of the glass in sheets like a frosty curtain; nice balance; chewy and accommodating; roasted flavor fades much too quickly; color not quite dark enough for the style. Try it with California-style pizzas or focaccia bread.

SOULARD OUR SPECIAL LAGER   **MB**   **2.5**
(Cold Spring, Minnesota)
Soft on the palate without expected zest; not unsatisfying; unique root beer–like taste; flat texture; soft, gentle maltiness with a vague hint of mildly roasted caramel; rather trite and plain, fading further in the stretch; best alone, but would also go with a garden salad.

SOUTH PACIFIC SPECIAL EXPORT
LAGER   **CB**   **2.0**
(Papua, New Guinea)
Off-taste odor is off-putting; undistinguished and somewhat watery sparkling crispness; texture gets more attention than the flat, somewhat bland taste; a hint of warmth and sweetness; predictable rather than changeable or complex; thickness lingers in the mouth; despite its pretty label, it remains a below-par beer.

SOUTHAMPTON SAISON Ale   **BP**   **2.5**
(Southampton, New York)
Immediate liqueur mouthfeel is attention-getting and quite tasty; tight bonding of malts and hops produces a well-defined tartness that characterizes this seasonal beer from start to end; some appropriate sourness appears at mid-glass and pushes the beer forward; finishes bitter-sour and puckering. Good by itself, or with fish from the sea.

SOUTHWARK GOLD LAGER   **CB**   **2.1**
(Thebarton, South Australia, Australia)
Faintly sour, acrid flavor with intimations of citrus; aroma reminiscent of butter; goes poorly with light summer fare, revealing an essentially undemanding character; respectable head; gains bitterness toward the end, but not enough to make a difference; a middling beer with lots of burps in the bottle; best without food.

SOUTHWARK PREMIUM Pilsener   **CB**   **4.1**
(Adelaide, South Australia, Australia)
Nice and hoppy, almost fruity, smooth; sweet, then gently tart at the back of the tongue; some dull aftertaste, which subsides with food; more flavor and continuity than other Australian beers; invigorating sharpness is predictable and continuous. Try with chicken teriyaki or mesquite-grilled meat and poultry.

SPANISH PEAKS BLACK DOG ALE   **MB**   **2.5**
(Bozeman, Montana)
Fresh-tasting, but somewhat amateurish in execution; not fully developed, though initial aroma and first sip or two do suggest potential; hops eventually dominate; only a hint of fruitiness or yeastiness (more of latter than former) suggests this is ale; malt presence pops up as it warms; with work, it might become a tasty

brew—but how long before we find out? Good with chicken fajitas, nachos, or guacamole and tortilla chips.

SPARTAN LAGER CB 4.0
(Atlanti, Greece)

Fine-tasting light, medium-bodied beer with even crispness; fresh-smelling, holding its aroma from start to finish; nice blend of flavor and sharpness; hops and malts relate well to each other, providing an easygoing, well-tuned interaction; rich and complex, Spartan is anything but. Try it with stuffed grape leaves, olives, figs, or hearty American soup classics like beef-barley.

SPATEN FRANZISKANER
HEFE-WEISSBIER CB 2.6
(Munich, Germany)

Yeast bite on first sip; full-bodied but light, lively, and fluffy, with pervasive fizziness; very noisy (put your ear to the top of a pilsener glass and listen); spicy (clove) and dry; bottle-sedimented; clean and fresh-tasting; more like wake-up juice for breakfast than a partner for dinner; cloudy pale color is typical of this beer style; too sweet; add a slice of lemon to the glass and enjoy on its own without food.

B E E R   F A C T

*S*paten, like all other Bavarian beers, adheres to the *Reinheitsgebot*, or German Pure Beer Law, of 1516, which mandates that all beer be made only from barley malts, hops, and water. Yeast, now required, was not included in the original list, as the function of this important ingredient was not yet identified or understood. Today many breweries, including an increasing number in the United States, voluntarily adhere to the 479-year-old guideline. To underscore the quality of their products, they often advertise this fact on the label.

SPATEN FRANZISKUS HELLER BOCK CB 3.1
(Munich, Germany)

Prickly and sharp; sweet, with an edge; clean and fresh-tasting; malty and a tad sour; wine-like alcohol is increasingly apparent at the end; very serviceable, but not award-winning; malty finish. A good choice with a burger or cold cuts.

SPATEN MUNCHEN CLUB—WEISSE CB 3.5
(Munich, Germany)

Attractive sweet aroma with pleasant fruitiness that, unfortunately, turns sour at the base of the throat; spritzy overlay tops off mellow smoothness underneath; moves around a great deal on the palate, providing interest at each sip; warm and comfortable, with a slight tang at the end. Try this at brunch with waffles or pancakes.

B E E R   F A C T

*S*paten, which means "spade" in German, was one of the first companies to apply scientific methods to brewing. The brewery still delivers some of its product in Munich by horse and wagon.

SPATEN MUNICH OPTIMATOR
DOPPELSPATEN BOCK   CB   3.4
(Munich, Germany)

Sharp and pleasantly caramelized with full burnt taste; soft and subtle; warm sweetness settles on the back of the tongue, while mild hoppiness attaches itself at the front of the tongue; smoothly malted, creamy, and consistently pleasant going down, though too much too soon produces a syrupy accumulation in the mouth and stomach; good, slightly chewy example of strong German bock; too sweet to be rated higher. Compatible with veal and lamb dishes.

SPATEN OKTOBERFEST UR-MARZEN   CB   2.8
(Munich, Germany)

Zestiness appears on first sip, along with a mild rounded texture that fades away down the throat; pleasurable balance of hops, malt, and sweetness; flat texture; slight caramel flavor emerges with spicy Italian foods; head disappears quickly; sweet taste, but no texture in this beer. Scrumptious with salty snacks such as barbecue potato chips; also good with an Italian salami sandwich.

SPATEN PILS   CB   2.5
(Munich, Germany)

Spritzy; distinct hoppiness floats to the back of the throat; puffy, airy head steps aside as the body of this pale brew slides past; tightly controlled balance and complexity; makes a partially successful effort at Brussels lace; in the end, rather undistinguished. Compatible with grain dishes such as risotto, polenta, and couscous.

SPATEN PREMIUM Lager   CB   3.3
(Munich, Germany)

Well hopped; pervasive light grain taste; less sharp, more rounded than other pilseners; earthy, pungent flavor; maintains a steady textural presence throughout; stays moderately bitter; spring-fresh water is pervasive; ingredients clearly make their individual presence known, generously helped along with barbecued breast of chicken.

SPECIAL EXPORT Lager   **CB**   **3.4**
(brewed by Stroh in La Crosse, Wisconsin)
This above-average Midwestern brew has a beguiling complex flavor; characteristic fizziness provides textural balance, making it especially agreeable when blended with tomato juice (mixed half-and-half, or to taste); smoothly layered ingredients and some depth make for a good American beer. Compatible with most foods, though it tends toward sourness with highly spiced dishes.

B E E R   F A C T

*S*pecial Export, like many other beers, is krausened —a double fermentation process that naturally results in more carbonation, additional smoothness, and a richer, foamier head.

SPENCER'S MCKENZIE PALE ALE   **MB**   **3.7**
(Springfield, Oregon)
Opening taste is variously sweet, then bitter, then sweet, all containing a sweet-grapefruit character that puckers the mouth; flavors are distinct on the palate, not muddy or blended; thick, creamy head looks like a fluffy upside-down Jell-O mold, quite dry and quite tasty; a woody presence can be discerned about halfway through; banana character, too, as it warms; finishes soft on the palate, with a bitter patina of hops; this is a fine pale ale. Goes nicely with cold cuts on sandwich bread.

SPENCES PALE ALE   **CT**   **2.2**
(Chatsworth, California)
Bitter fruitiness; watery; hardly aromatic except for the initial whiff; settles into minimal fruitiness with a touch of hops at the back of the mouth; maintains a sour citrus taste that seems to blot out other taste qualities; flat texture; wispy head quickly settles into thin gray line; yeast cloudiness muddies up color. Match with starchy foods to help absorb some of the sourness.

SPRECHER AMBER Lager   **MB**   **3.5**
(Milwaukee, Wisconsin)
Smooth and malty; big fruity aroma, which blossoms as it goes; constrained hop presence; a quality, nicely calibrated bitterness lasts and lasts; well balanced and very accommodating; attractive medium-amber color contains just a hint of red; a tasty drink that's filling and fulfilling. Pairs quite nicely with sautéed shellfish.

SPRECHER PUB BROWN ALE   MB   2.9
(Milwaukee, Wisconsin)
Slightly malty with a balancing hint of fruit in the aroma and
taste; smooth and quite quaffable; rounded, in-depth caramel
sweetness; soft and buttery on the palate; bitter quality is present, but barely noticeable; laidback and unassertive; at the end,
it becomes moderately sweet, smooth and very drinker-friendly;
take home a bottle or two for dinner, regardless of what you're
having.

ST. ANDREW'S ALE   CB   3.9
(Dunbar, Scotland)
In-depth fruitiness and fresh aroma; slight earthy burnt taste; watery caramel flavor is pleasant and persistent; smooth and medium-
bodied; well-tended malt sweetness and constrained hoppiness
are in good balance; crystal-clear medium-ruby body and patient
head form a pretty picture; this is a quality product. Goes very
nicely with roast chicken.

ST. BERNARD GERMAN LAGER
PILSNER   CT   3.2
(Dublin, Ireland; London, England)
Malty aroma and taste are immediately evident, accompanied by
just the slightest bite from hops; deep-roasted and strong-tasting; refreshing malty presence is full and mouth-filling; maintains its strong flavor throughout; more noticeable hop-malt
balance toward the end; standard amber-colored body supports
a less-standard frothy, big-bubbled head. Goes well with cold
cooked shrimp and hot sauce.

ST. CROIX MAPLE ALE   CT   2.8
(New Ulm, Minnesota)
Nice foamy, thick head stands upright on the light amber body;
taste gives off mixed signals—a calming sweetness mixed in with
pinpricks of sourness; a more defined mouthfeel finally emerges
in the form of a harsh, but not unpleasant, hoppiness; the fermented maple flavor is not directly apparent, but it seems to
moderate the fickle hop bitterness; faint maple aroma at the end,
if you take a deep whiff. A molasses cookie does bring up a more
substantial sweet maple character.

ST. GEORGEN KELLER BIER—
ungespundet-hefetrub Lager   CB   2.3
(Buttengheim, Germany)
Mildly but obviously bitter; nice gentle fruit-juice aroma and flavor; bitter honey-sweet fruitiness comes into balance, with the
bitterness lasting into the aftertaste; texture weakens along the
way and *really* weakens at the end; watery, no flavor, no texture—
what a shame. Drink the first two-thirds of this with lightly
breaded freshwater fish.

ST. IDES MALT LIQUOR   CT   1.1
(brewed by Heileman in San Antonio, Texas)
Syrupy ginger-ale taste, but flatter in texture than a pancake; almost candy-like all over the mouth; continuous mild after-dinner-liqueur mouthfeel. Serve as an *apéritif* or *digestif,* if at all.

ST. PAULI GIRL Pilsener   CB   3.4
(Bremen, Germany)
Fresh, tart, and sharp, with a hint of wateriness; very clear light-blond color; tender mouthfeel; nicely contained hops mix well with rice and grain dishes; an unintrusive player with food; traditional and predictable, with a dry finish. Try it with salty tortilla chips and spicy black bean dip.

ST. PAULI GIRL DARK Pilsener   CB   3.5
(Bremen, Germany)
Lightly toasted and lightly fizzy, with no apparent complexity; given on the color—thin yet rich brown, like Coca-Cola—you expect a more intense aroma and stronger taste; smoked meats sweeten the liquid and bring out the hoppiness; much fuller and sweeter at the end; more than one bottle is needed to fully appreciate what this popular pilsener has to offer; clearly well made. A good match with smoked meats and salty snack foods.

ST. SEBASTIAN CROCK ALE   CB   2.6
(Meer, Belgium)
Sharp, with a surprising mellow undercurrent of warmth at the front of the mouth, but lacks depth at the back of the tongue; effervescence pricks the roof of the mouth and the throat; a magnificent intact head on top of the light-amber body enhances the overall effect; color holds unfulfilled promise—without seeing the label, it would be hard to know it's a Belgian brown ale; without food, it warms up a bit; lots of Brussels lace—it's from Belgium, after all; in the end, lacks the usual distinctiveness of an abbey-style brew. Match with fresh and/or dried fruit, or brunch dishes such as waffles or French toast with syrup.

ST. SIXTUS ABBEY ALE   AB   3.1
(Watou, Belgium)
No question this contains alcohol; starts with a creamy, soft palate; pleasant fruitiness; some vinegary odor; alcohol and hoppiness mellow toward the end; subdued tartness remains; a sheath of tiny bubbles coats the sides of the glass; some yeastiness emerges at the very bottom of the bottle, as does an acidic component; dry finish; best alone, without food.

ST. STAN'S AMBER ALT   MB/BP   3.8
(Modesto, California)

Cidery aroma, taste, and color; soft and smooth on the palate; citrus fruitiness gently turns into an appealing sweetness and draws out the flavor and nuances of food; remains soft and creamy throughout; somehow plain and tasty at the same time; very pleasant simple, warm brew with staying power; no highs or lows; brewed with dark malts, adding to flavor intensity; "creamy head evokes its natural ingredients," according to the neck label, which also has other bits of interesting information; strongly recommended. Good with nearly any pork or lamb dish.

B E E R   F A C T

*O*riginated in Dusseldorf, *alt* (or *altbier*) refers to old-style methods and ingredients and designates a light- or copper-colored beer. St. Stan's version was the first produced in the United States after the end of Prohibition.

ST. STAN'S DARK ALT   MB/BP   3.9
(Modesto, California)

Mild burnt taste on first sip; fresh-tasting; dark rich chocolate color; thick body texture; very pleasant and rewarding; distinctively mellow and full-bodied. Quite nice with barbecued chicken or pork with a fruit sauce.

ST. STAN'S FEST BIER Alt   MB/BP   3.5
(Modesto, California)

Pungent citrus fruitiness makes its mark on the roof of the mouth; less robust and less sweet than the other St. Stan's I've had, but simultaneously possesses a nice bite with mellowness; subdued alcohol presence; some muddiness and aftertaste, however, spoil the show at the end; final sips are cool and fruity. Try it with a bacon-wrapped filet mignon.

ST. STAN'S GRAFFITI WHEAT
(annual)   MB/BP   1.9
(Modesto, California)

Brewed each summer to celebrate the Modesto Graffiti Festival; yeast all over the place: overwhelms the aroma, dulls the golden-yellow color, ruins the taste, making it rough and raw; no head; no zip; gradual mild citrus aroma pushes its way through; increasing lemon taste with or without food; too fruity, too thick, and not thirst-quenching enough for this style; needs work.

STAG Lager   CB   2.1
(La Crosse, Wisconsin)
Typical light American lager, with a calm, unprovocative approach; transient tart sharpness distinguishes it a bit from the rest; overall the hops, malt, and yeast are played down and successfully hidden; a certain textural crudeness is part of its beer-to-be-swilled charm; no surprises, nuances, or pretension, this is definitely a no-frills approach to brewing. Fine with a hot dog.

STAR LAGER   CB   1.0
(Lagos, Nigeria)
Sharp and pointed; underlying sweetness anchors the hop bitterness; taste turns sour and skunky; no texture and less and less taste; light blond body; stale and winey; deteriorates too rapidly for any real enjoyment.

STAROPRAMEN Pilsener   CB   3.9
(Prague, Czech Republic)
Full-bodied, crisp, clean, and flavorful; immediate playful interaction of hops and malt; pervasive smooth, grainy mouthfeel; clean aroma; delicate bitterness with no offensive aftertaste; direct, with few nuances; substantial irregular Brussels lace; well made and invigorating; finish is refreshingly hoppy, a credit to the style. Goes nicely with green vegetables or salads.

STEEL RESERVE 211 HIGH GRAVITY
LAGER   CT   2.5
(La Crosse, Wisconsin; Longview, Texas; Tampa, Florida)
Juicy Fruit gum (or ripe peach) aroma and taste on first and succeeding sips; sweet ripeness rises to the back of the mouth; high alcohol content (8.1%/volume), yet it doesn't taste particularly alcoholic; grainy malted barley taste is intense; sturdy body; has many ale qualities, like flavor intensity and sweeter/fruitier character; this is a maverick beer that may take some time getting used to. First try this alone, then choose food that seems suitable.

STEELER LAGER   CB   0.5
(Hamilton, Ontario, Canada)
Bleached, weak, prosaic; slight banana taste, suggesting too-high fermentation temperatures or an inappropriate type of yeast strain.

STEELHEAD BOMBAY BOMBER IPA
(draft)   MB/BP   2.2
(Eugene, Oregon)
Clean-cut citrus/grapefruit aroma suggests long-lasting taste; becomes tiresome and boring much too quickly; bitter toward the back of the mouth and soapy at the end of the glass; pale apple-cider color continues the outdoorsy fruit character, but with no real gain in overall enjoyment; needs a lot more pizzazz and snap before I'd try it again.

STEELHEAD EXTRA PALE ALE MB/BP 3.3
(Eugene, Oregon)
Strongly hopped on first sip, with a lingering citrus punch as the liquid goes down; fruity and smooth; predictably even-tempered from start to finish; possesses a sharply defined but restrained cutting edge that bites nicely into red meat; not particularly complex, with each ingredient well defined and offering its own separate note and balance; not as crisp as it should be for the style; leaves a slightly yeasty aftertaste and a somewhat uneventful finish. Good with steak or roast beef and a baked potato.

STEENDONK WHITE ALE CB 3.9
(Breendonk, Belgium)
Yeasty, flavorful, and fruity (kiwi?) with a clove theme; moderated sharpness keeps it from being too acidic; phosphorescent white paleness; sustains a high level of interest; assertive and charmingly wine-like with food; bottle-conditioned, there is sediment at the bottom of the bottle; exhibits a rare quality—it maintains its high overall standards in taste, texture, and aroma from start to finish; a gift from the hands of careful craftspeople. Try it with pasta or seafood.

STEFFL VIENNA LAGER CB 2.1
(Linz, Austria)
Fruity hops taste from start to finish, though diminishes over time; odd, unexpected whitefish taste at the back of the mouth; thin; quite weak with food; not assertive at all.

STEGMAIER 1857 PREMIUM LAGER CB 3.2
(Wilkes-Barre, Pennsylvania)
Fresh, with a hint of fruitiness; dry and approachable, with some aftertaste; clear and golden; aromatic hoppiness; comes close to typical lager style; good everyday beer with or without food; Gold Medal winner at the 1994 Great American Beer Festival. Appropriate with brunch.

B E E R   F A C T

Stegmaier is produced by Lion, Inc., one of only a handful of independent regional brewers that remain in the U.S. Along with its own brands, it also does a lot of contract brewing for other companies.

STEGMAIER PORTER CB 2.4
(Wilkes-Barre, Pennsylvania)
Roasted and mildly malty with matching aroma; bitterness creeps in—an acceptable nuance; smooth and perhaps too silky;

appropriately dark; taste fades much too quickly, almost abruptly; too weak at the finish.

STEINGADENER WEISSE DUNKEL   **CB**   **2.9**
(Kaufbeuren, Germany)
Musty fruit aroma is quickly overtaken by a hit of clove taste that becomes smooth, sweet, and mildly fruity itself; hop bitterness catches up to the clove flavor, creating a well-balanced, almost tender character; very thick head softens the mouthfeel further; settles down into a nicely integrated, satisfying dark wheat beer. Perhaps surprisingly, this is a good match for pretzels and mustard.

STEINHAUSER BIER Pilsener   **CB**   **3.5**
(Frankfurt, Germany)
Mild but attractive ginger aroma—almost nutty; smooth with soft surrounding prickliness nicely balancing the warmth and maltiness of the beer; slightly thick, with a continuing nutty/honey taste; sturdy and consistent; cloudiness detracts from overall ambiance; thin to nonexistent head and thin Brussels lace; finishes gluey, thick, and honey-sweet. Good with broiled fish.

STEINLAGER Pilsener   **CB**   **3.8**
(Auckland, New Zealand)
Appealing and light with initial flatness; mild and dry; quickly mellows into balanced smooth-sharpness, especially when matched with a robust meal; since it comes in a large (25.4-ounce) green bottle, there is more than enough to unhurriedly savor its limited but well-defined nuances; some aftertaste. Just right with roast beef and mashed potatoes.

B E E R   F A C T

*G*reen bottles do not screen out fluorescent lighting or sunlight as well as brown bottles. Clear glass is worst of all. Even small amounts of exposure to light can damage the flavor and aroma of the beer. Remember: Always choose your bottle or six-pack from the darker areas of the cooler.

STELLA ARTOIS Pilsener   **CB**   **2.5**
(Leuven, Belgium)
Watery at first taste, but carbonation fills out the body after two or three sips; flavor remains a little flat; virtually no aroma; label proclaims "Belgium's premium Beer." Versatile enough to go with a range of foods, from poached eggs at brunch to seafood or steak.

STER ALE   **CB**   **3.1**
(Meer, Belgium)
Charming quick hint of malt aroma followed by flat, bland taste; unlike many Belgian ales, this one is not overtly alcoholic; unfruity, unsweet, and unwine-like, thereby making it, in my opinion, an attractive companion with food; malt and yeast combine for solid grain texture with slightly warming sweetness; hazy reddish-brown color; gets a little stiffer toward the bottom of the bottle; never reveals much complexity or changing nuances; aroma continues to dominate flavor. A good match with meat loaf.

STERLING Pilsener   **CT**   **1.5**
(Evansville, Indiana)
Rounded mouthfeel; bitter hop taste quickly disappears; light and wispy; bitterness evolves into an uncomplicated sweetness; bland below-average beer. One redemption: water is fresh and invigorating; find the water source and forget the added brewing ingredients.

STIEGL COLUMBUS PILS   **CB**   **3.1**
(Salzburg, Austria)
Thick head atop a thin golden body with a hint of red; no effervescence to speak of—indeed, a rather mild texture; fresh and dainty; turns smooth and comforting and gains a slight acidic taste with smoked fish; even-tempered and quite appealing; some thickish aftertaste; weak with spicy foods and beef; not zippy; predictable; balanced equitably between malt and hops. Good with plainly prepared fish.

STONE CITY MANSION STOUT   **MB**   **2.9**
(Solon, Iowa)
Sweetly roasted mouthfeel is gentle on the tongue; malty-nutty aroma is compelling; increasingly intense deep-roasted taste is rife with nutty overtones; pleasantly effervescent; attractive frisson of bitterness on the tongue adds needed zestiness; midnight-brown body finishes smooth, composed, and slightly bitter. Pair this with a half-dozen fresh oysters.

STONE CITY STONE BLUFF PILS   **MB**   **0.9**
(Solon, Iowa)
Sour, and much too flat for a pilsener; bottle-conditioned, which is also highly suspect for a pilsener; slight, doughy aroma; unsettling sulfury-plastic character certainly doesn't help; unpleasant, sour presence pervades the mouth; poorly done.

STONE PALE ALE   **MB**   **2.6**
(San Marcos, California)
Full, rounded malt taste is tempered by a delicate subdued hoppiness; flowery character reaches a hearty fullness at mid-bottle and stays that way; fresh-tasting malt mingles haphazardly among

the other ingredients; slight hint of caramel creeps up late in the bottle and enlivens things; in the end, ingredients are not tied together uniformly enough, creating too much imbalance overall; finishes with a bitterness that needs taming. Complements salami and cheese on a Kaiser roll.

STONEY CREEK LAGER   **CT**   **0.7**
(St. Paul, Minnesota)
More soft than crisp on the palate; slightly fruity; superficially smooth honey sweetness; uncomplex; touch of bitter and spice crops up at mid-bottle; tastes like honey-infused plastic; after a brief sip or two, the ingredients seem to go off on their own—fortunately; watery and unsatisfying.

STOUDT'S ABBEY TRIPLE   **MB**   **3.8**
(Adamstown, Pennsylvania)
Lovely intermingling of yeast and light spiciness greets the first sips; sharp character of the yeast remains in the aftertaste; gains in complexity after each swallow; fresh fruity aroma; full and mouth-filling; the gradual cumulative effect of the alcohol stimulates the appetite; continues to sweeten as it warms; body looks like a peach in full blush; leaves a glow on the cheeks and a pleasure in the mouth; very nicely done. Best to drink alone—that is, with companions but no food.

STOUDT'S HOLIDAY RESERVE BEER—
SMOKED PORTER   **MB**   **3.4**
(Adamstown, Pennsylvania)
Smoky and roasted-coffee taste, all in one flavorful, filling mouthful; well balanced and relatively soft on the tongue; smokiness is more noticeable at mid-bottle; so is the smoky aroma; eventually the intensity of the smokiness decreases as it gets absorbed by the body, which is an opaque deep brown that evidences a ruby glow when held to the sunlight; a pleasant and pleasing porter. Try it with smoked fish.

B E E R   F A C T

*S*toudt Brewing Company was established in 1987 by Carol Stoudt, the first woman brewmaster in the United States since Prohibition. Her beers have won more than twenty medals at the Great American Beer Festival since that time.

STOUDT'S HONEY DOUBLE BOCK   **MB**   **4.0**
(Adamstown, Pennsylvania)
The first sip says it all: there is alcohol and malt in this beer, both

in the aroma and in the taste; full-bodied and mouth-filling; dense and yummy, like a chunk of dark chocolate; bitterness gently teases the back of the tongue; deep, luscious reddish-brown body and ivory head are the picture of brewing perfection; finishes upbeat, strong and compelling. Suitable for poultry, like turkey or Cornish game hen.

STROH'S Lager   CB   2.4
(Detroit, Michigan)

Stark and mildly malty; more substantive and flavorful than some American brews; brings a solid bite to spicy foods; noticeable textural punch—zingy and crisp; ruddy brown color is perfect, reminiscent of porter hue; good choice when more exotic beers are not available.

STUDLEY ALE   CT   0.0
(Fernandina Beach, Florida)

Old, spoiled, sour, and skunky; malt aroma has tired, poorly treated character; don't even think of buying this one.

SUMMIT GREAT NORTHERN PORTER   MB   2.8
(St. Paul, Minnesota)

Mild roasted taste floats along on a cushiony current of malt sweetness that lingers in the mouth; robust and filling; thin thread of bitterness arises at mid-glass and nicely counterbalances the ongoing bitter-chocolate sweetness; finishes smooth and mildly roasty; unaggressive and easy-drinking, this is a good introduction to the style. Try with standard porter fare, like lighter-flavored meats such as veal or pork.

SUMMIT INDIA PALE ALE   MB   2.7
(St. Paul, Minnesota)

Tangy and bitter; bitterness lasts into the aftertaste; there's a snappy bite to the mouthfeel; the quiet presence of malt is soft on the palate and offers a counterpoint to the tenacious, well-placed hop character; the tap version of this pale ale is somewhat less insistent in its hop presentation. Smoked cheeses are good accompaniments here.

SUN LIK Pilsener   CB   3.5
(Hong Kong, China)

Attenuated sourness; surprisingly smooth, with practically no fizziness or sharpness; diminishes with spicy foods; minimal balance of malt and hops, but essentially weak-kneed; some warmth pops out on occasion; smooth grainy sweetness; immediate sweet/pungent aroma and crisp rice flavor emerge with pork and pasta dishes; taste fades quickly on the palate; feels dry on the roof of the mouth; worth having again.

SUN VALLEY GOLD LAGER   **MB/BP**   **0.5**
(Hailey, Idaho)
Sour taste followed by flatness; the most striking thing about this beer is its creamy, very thick, long-lasting head; gains some complexity; thickness around the mouth and the tongue; they need to start over with this one.

SUN VALLEY HOLIDAY ALE (annual)   **MB/BP**   **3.9**
(Hailey, Idaho)
Lovely, undulating, malted-barley aroma wafts upward, and flavor lazily coats the tongue; sweetness veers toward cloying but backs off into balanced fullness without much zest or tang; soothing, not texturally complex, but remains evenhanded and predictable; leaves thin lacework on the sides of the glass; appealing sipping beer with relatively high alcoholic content; also fits well with a grilled cheese sandwich, which actually enhances the beer's substance and taste complexity; as with any annual like this Christmas brew, character and quality may vary from year to year. I tasted the last version that was brewed in Montana; the brewery is now located in Idaho.

SUN VALLEY WHITE CLOUD ALE   **MB/BP**   **3.8**
(Hailey, Idaho)
Mildly creamy with moderated fruity taste; cloudy amber color leans toward blond; hint of sharpness surrounds the liquid and permeates the mouth; tart fruitiness is relatively subdued without food; as the beer sits in the glass, the texture and taste spread out, becoming even more integrated, smooth, and seamless; a good ale for those who understand ale; nice malty finish. Goes nicely with flavorful snacks such as barbecue potato chips or cold shrimp with zippy cocktail sauce.

SUNTORY DRAFT Pilsener   **CB**   **2.2**
(Osaka, Japan)
Pale yellow-gold color with fizzy texture preceding a rather mellow, unassuming character; nearly tasteless undercurrent interrupted by some peripheral graininess; large quantities can be imbibed practically without realizing it; made with corn filler; expensive, and not worth it.

SUNTORY GINJO DRAFT Pilsener   **CB**   **2.6**
(Osaka, Japan)
Very pale; rapidly rising bubbles clearly evident; modulated hoppiness with rice adjunct reminiscent of ballpark beer, but of significantly better quality; clean, fresh taste; remains pleasant with food; gets a bit flat and fuzzy on the tongue toward the end; not complex, and that fact makes it too predictable; still, it's drinkable with simple foods such as hamburgers and Sloppy Joes.

SUNTORY GOLD DRAFT—
100% MALT BEER Pilsener   CB   3.3
(Osaka, Japan)
Thick and creamy with some sharpness at the back of the throat; warm and rounded and mild; pleasant, easy to drink; gets finished without your realizing it's gone. Try it with steak and a baked potato.

SUPER 49 MALT LIQUOR   CB   2.8
(Roubaix, France)
Muddy, undefined flavor on first sip, with an alcohol presence; honey-like mouthfeel; mellows out with peripheral fizziness with hot foods; resonating yeastiness continues to play on the tongue and sides of the mouth after food is finished; easily drinkable. Serve with caviar, thick slices of glazed ham, or fruit tarts.

SUPERIOR Pilsener   CB   3.1
(Guadalajara, Mexico)
Good smooth taste; circumscribed hoppiness, with a vague hint of citrus; very satisfying; I generally drink this without food—it's light, not filling, doesn't get you tipsy easily, and is reminiscent of old Mexico; toss in a slice of lime, and you'll swear you're there.

SWALE INDIAN SUMMER PALE ALE   CB   2.6
(Sittingbourne, England)
Highly and intensely hopped, leaving little room for other taste sensations; some fruity sweetness rides along the sides of the mouth as bitterness makes its imprint in the center; caramel-sugary aroma has an undertone of fruitiness, including a tease of citrus; deep-gold body shows peach-blush shades; aftertaste seems sweet rather than bitter, unlike most pale ales. A very good drink with light summer fare—for example, mild cheese sandwiches.

SWAN LAGER   CB   3.3
(Perth, Western Australia, Australia)
Nicely smooth and immediately satisfying; light-bodied, with an easy-to-drink manner; the flavor is present but not intrusive; a bit of sourness as meal progresses, along with mild bitterness; finishes relatively dry—a good thirst-quencher. Tasty with a seafood salad, oysters, or clams.

SWEET CHINA Lager   CB   0.2
(Guangzhou, China)
Immediate pineapple/hard candy aroma, followed by the same thing in the mouth; sweeter pineapple taste than fizzy-hoppy beer taste; far too frothy and sweet for most foods; more like soda pop than beer; label proclaims "beer with natural pineapple juice"—true enough; but why draw attention to the fact? I didn't finish it.

SWEETHEART STOUT CB 3.5
(Glasgow, Scotland)
Prominent and appealing taste of Concord grapes; rather flat, but smooth texture; clearly a "sweetheart" of a milk stout with very attractive, full, sugary sweetness and a distinguishing milky flavor; nice deep-red to dark-brown color in the stout tradition; grapey finish with fermented aroma; very low alcohol content; all in all, this is one of the most unique beers I have ever had; classic milk stouts like this one have long been considered restoratives. Serve as a *digestif.*

SWEETWATER EXODUS PORTER MB 0.4
(Atlanta, Georgia)
Watery; overly smooth; not complex, though there is some spice buried deep in there somewhere; weak and uninteresting; hint of sweetness, but not much else; needs work—lots of it.

SWEETWATER KOKOPELLI IPA BP 2.7
(Centreville, Virginia)
Fresh, fruity, mouth-puckering hoppiness makes you sit up and take notice; complex hop character spreads uniformly throughout the mouth; turns a bit sour along the way, then regains its composure; leaves a transparent film of Brussels lace; strictly a hop lover's IPA, focused and mouthwatering; could be more complex and balanced, but still worth visiting the brewpub for a pint or two. A nice beer to have with a chicken breast sandwich.

SWINKELS Pilsener CB 2.4
(Lieshout, Holland)
Calm, mild-tasting—actually, hard to detect a taste, though there is a slight pleasant grainy flavor with salty snacks; interesting aroma; in short, a mixed bag. Fine with salted crackers, pretzels, black olives, and pistachios.

**TABERNASH AMBER COLORADO
LAGER** MB 2.5
(Longmont, Colorado)
Faint fruity aroma; warm, complex malt-hop combo; delicate floral aftertaste is placid and filling; nice one-two punch of malt and hops characterizes the last half of the bottle; slightly more bitter and crisp at the end, but not by much; flavor weakens at the end. Goes well with fresh-caught mountain trout.

TABERNASH WEISS (draft) MB 3.0
(Longmont, Colorado)
Lemon and ginger—interesting, but is it beer? The answer is yes, with its floating yeast and circumscribed, but clearly evident, clove presence, giving it a ginger-ale-like zip; not as sharp as it should be, but thirst-quenching nevertheless; cloudy and straw-colored; needs more body, but worth a try. A good match with marinated bean dishes.

TAIWAN BEER Lager CB 1.8
(Taipei, Taiwan)
Immediate aroma is stale; minimal bubbly, crackly essence; quiet dullness at the back of the tongue; overall rounded taste with a hint of body; unassuming, rather run-of-the-mill; uneventful with food; presumably there are both malt and hops hidden somewhere amidst the slight fizziness; among the few English words on the label, other than the beer's name, are "Taiwan Tobacco and Wine Monopoly Bureau."

TAJ MAHAL LAGER CB 3.1
(Calcutta, India)
Smooth and mini-bubbled with vague clove presence; intermittent hoppiness varies from sip to sip; the level of hoppiness stays true, steady, and predictable throughout—a good sign; flattened bitterness balances nicely with a late-blooming maltiness; thick, rocky head and thick chunks of Brussels lace stay from start to finish; slight alcohol presence; a moderate, serviceable beer with substance and style. A good match with Indian food or fish and chips.

TAMPA BAY OATMEAL STOUT BP 0.8
(Tampa, Florida)
Bland; tasteless, despite 10% oatmeal content; nothing there except the pretty deep-brown-black body—nothing.

TANNEN BOMB Ale (annual) MB/BP 3.8
(McMinnville, Oregon)
Deliciously malty, full, complex, and bold; strong caramel aroma is sweet and easy in the nose; minimal caramel character mixes well with the mild bitterness; thick, full mouthfeel; though high in alcohol (8%/volume), it is restrained and essentially plays a background role of moving things forward; the alcohol and the fresh malty yumminess come together at the end; a nicely configured package of taste. Lift a glass and toast the Christmas season with Tannen Bomb.

TAQUINA EXPORT BEER CB 2.5
(Cochabamba, Bolivia)
Crackling mouthfeel is full and sharp on the tongue; full-bodied malt aroma and thin taste include hints of corn; stays crisp and tasty; continuing underlying mellowness balances the lightly-hopped character; uncomplicated and not very inspiring; smooth, subdued malt-hop presence defines the last few sips; check this out in Bolivia, but in the U.S. first see what else is available.

TECATE Pilsener CB 3.0
(Monterrey, Mexico)
Popular south of the border, this strong-bodied brew is both gentle and rough on the palate; unvarying in its narrow-range malt-

hop balance, it goes well with a variety of foods; each meal component responds differently to the unyielding taste and texture of the beer, while the beer itself stays composed and predictable; there are no extremes here, just a familiar strength that increases with time. Drink it alone or with Mexican dishes, especially ones topped with plenty of salsa.

TENNENT'S LAGER　　　　　**CB**　　　**1.8**
(Glasgow, Scotland)
Flat, bitter, and uninteresting; maltiness lurks in the background; patterns of white Brussels lace help the ambiance; a bland, dulled, slightly malted brew; sweetish molasses finish—too little, late. Match with hearty winter soups such as beef-barley.

TERKEN BIERE DE LUXE
MALT LIQUOR　　　　　　**CB**　　　**2.9**
(Roubaix, France)
Immediate pleasant perfume odor quickly degenerates to sour; muddy fizziness with big head remains; warming softness; more complex taste—grainy and fruity—emerges with plain foods; alcohol is quite apparent with a meal, perhaps not surprising for a fermented French beverage; possesses ale characteristics but basically is a mixed style. Okay with a simple supper of meat loaf, mashed potatoes, and a green vegetable.

TERKEN BRUNE MALT LIQUOR　　**CB**　　　**2.5**
(Roubaix, France)
Brewed in the brown ale style—sweet, malty, and caramely with a mild texture; highly alcoholic and on the cloying side; much too sweet with food; minimal head; too much maltiness, not enough balancing hoppiness spoil the fun; they've probably been brewing this for centuries, or decades at least, but I find it to be unfinished and uncertain, with no bond holding it together.

TEXAS COWBOY VIENNA LAGER
(draft)　　　　　　　　　**BP**　　　**0.5**
(Dallas, Texas)
Cold and tasteless; when the wind is right, you get a faint odor of beer; vague hint of bitterness is a plus in this case, since its presence lets you know you're drinking something; some citrus taste creeps forward, but doesn't last long; this beer wasn't lagered (stored) long enough.

TEXAS CRUDE BOCK　　　　　**CT**　　　**2.1**
(Longview, Texas)
Smooth in texture, soft in the mouth, and a hint of honey at the outset; initial sweetness turns bitter, almost sour; medium-bodied; whiskey-colored, with big-bubbled head that stays thick throughout; texture winds up being too flat; finishes with a roasted aroma

and flavor that weaken and fade in the stretch. Drink this without food, or not at all.

TEXAS PRIDE Pilsener   CB   0.1
(San Antonio, Texas)

Green-tasting and sweet; raw and unintegrated; faint varnish taste; rather unappealing; unaccompanied by any food, it has no qualities, redeeming or otherwise; gave me a stomachache.

THAMES FESTIVE ALE   CB   2.5
(Llanelli, Wales)

Soft caramel mouthfeel, with a deep malt-sugar sweetness; slight brandy overtones; relatively weak for a holiday ale, allowing you to concentrate more on the flavor than on the alcohol; no Brussels lace; minimum but patient head. Drink this with nothing more challenging than Christmas cookies.

THE SPIRIT OF ST. LOUIS ALE   CT   1.6
(Fort Mitchell, Kentucky)

Stream of sour bitterness parallels a caramel-malt mouthfeel; just the gentlest hint of citrus fruitiness; plastic taste clings to the roof of the mouth; thin; turns watery and flat and weakens perceptibly; a disappointment.

36.15 PECHEUR Lager   CB   0.3
(Schiltigheim, France)

Mild skunkiness that dissipates rather quickly; fine spritziness can't detract from the perfumey clash of not very complementary fruit and spice flavors and aromas (including cardamom, cinnamon, ginger, gin-seng, kola, licorice, mango, myrrh, myrtle); aroma of myrrh is discernible, while no one flavor predominates; almost literally a boutique beer—really too cute for words (or for drinking); motto on label: *La Bière Amoureuse* ("the beer for intimate occasions"). Interestingly, this concoction goes with toasted almonds.

33 EXPORT Pilsener   CB   2.0
(Ho Chi Minh City, Vietnam)

Light, with a pleasant mild bitterness; uncomplex; has barely distinguishable grains in it; bitter aftertaste; pale wheat color adds to the impression of weakness; finishes quite dry; a light summer drink for hot, humid weather. Try it with lake trout or other mild fish dishes.

33 EXPORT Lager   CB   3.1
(Paris, France)

Mildly sour-sharp on the back of the mouth; integrates well with Indian dishes; allows spiciness to take over, but not overwhelmingly; understated, quickly disappearing taste; slightly cloying and watery; finish is warm, sweet, and quite comforting. Good with curries and spicy Indian dishes.

THOMAS COOPER ADELAIDE LAGER   CB   2.4
(Leabrook, South Australia, Australia)
Crisp and musty on first sip, with hints of sourness and acidity;
ebbs and flows as you drink it—changes from bittersweet to sharp
and musty and back again; turns acridly sweet with food, playing second fiddle to it; a fair-to-middling beer.

THOMAS HARDY'S ALE-1989 (annual) CB   0.4
(Dorchester, England)
Aroma of old yeast; fruity, with alcoholic backdrop; sweetness
turns to a dryness reminiscent of oak-aged sherry; unattractive
overripe quality has a hint of mustiness; some caramel remains
when drunk alone after a hearty meal; its wine-like rosy-amber
color and lack of head or lace suggest that this is a *digestif* rather
than a more versatile beer; still, obviously has quality ingredients
and substance; hint of redeeming warmth during the last few
sips—indeed, it can be imbibed only in small doses. Though
many people like this beer, I had trouble finishing it; high alcohol content makes it inappropriate with most foods, if you insist on trying this strong drink, do so before or after a meal; for
highly individualized tastes only; I hope it's better after 25 years
(see below).

BEER FACT

*B*ecause of the continuing bottle fermentation
(look for yeast sediment on the bottom), Thomas
Hardy's Ale, named for the British poet and novelist, is one of the few beers that improves with age.
Reputed to be England's strongest ale, it is produced
in numbered limited editions (mine was No. D11422)
and is said to last for 25 years when maintained at
55°F. Technically a barley wine–style ale (big, full, complex, alcoholic, and fruity), its taste is apparently not
the only thing that benefits from aging. The first bottles from the 1960s have been offered by collectors for
$1,000. I hope history is a good guide; I have stored
14 bottles in my refrigerator, dating from 1988 and
1989.

THOMAS KEMPER AUCTION BLOCK
AMBER (draft)   MB   1.5
(Seattle, Washington)
Rather tasteless, with a compensating hit of hops; flat and unin-
tegrated; not particularly fresh, even when imbibed less than 8
miles from the brewery; chewy caramel/malt mouthfeel appears,

preceding a burst of citrus sharpness (tang) at mid-glass; no head, no Brussels lace; a disappointment.

THOMAS KEMPER MAIBOCK
ROLLING BAY BOCK (seasonal) MB 2.4
(Seattle, Washington)
Deep and abiding roasted-coffee flavor with a hint of yeastiness; sharp and increasingly controlled fruitiness; solid, flat Brussels lace sticks to the sides of the glass—not wispy or broken up; comes into its own as it warms at the middle of the bottle; tawny brown, as in bock style, but not very strong, unlike the bock style; remains sharp, puckery, and astringent; a bit too watery at the end; some residual alcohol.

THOMAS KEMPER WINTERBRAU
Lager (seasonal) MB 1.2
(Seattle, Washington)
Mild spiciness, fruity, and a bit stale; tangy and mildly fizzy; begins to get full and mealy in character as you drink it; this is a beer that's meant to be cute and seasonal, but instead is too general to be distinctive; gets tantalizing and seductive at the end, but by then it's too late; as a drinking companion put it: *feh.* Compatible with pepper-hot chicken dishes.

3 MONTS FLANDERS GOLDEN ALE CB 3.3
(Saint-Sylvestre, France)
Overwhelmingly yeasty; full and sharp as it spreads all over your mouth; alcohol feel increases quickly and in quantity; heavy-duty encompassing, rounded sweetness helps temper spicy foods; a little cloying, with bitterness at the finish; some grittiness also at the end; pale color and underlying thinness are consistent. (Requires a corkscrew to open.) Match with spicy and/or highly seasoned chicken dishes.

THUMB BLONDE Ale CB 2.5
(Glasgow, Scotland)
Malty-sweet mouthfeel stays on the tongue and then slowly fades into the aftertaste; creeping bitterness becomes a player after 3 to 4 sips; perfumey, with a bit of citrus-grapefruit in both the aroma and taste; flavors play off one another toward the end as the hops become more discernible; name is more interesting than the beer, but still worth a go if you're in Scotland.

TIGER Lager CB 3.3
(Singapore)
Unusually foamy; light and texturally quite satisfying, almost sensual; turns sweetish in tandem with some foods; subtle and even-handed from the tip of the tongue to the throat; so smooth and easy going down that its 23 ounces are finished before you're aware they're gone; not filling or otherwise intrusive; Asian equiv-

alent of a tasty Miller or Bud; I found this hard to rate. Good with barbecued pork.

TIJUCA Pilsener CB 3.8
(Belem, Brazil)

Very grainy and full; well integrated; nice warmth; mild spritziness throughout; smooth and well behaved; consistent, and assertive in interest; flavorful; you look forward to each sip. Especially good with Mexican food.

TIMMERMANS PECHE Lambic CB 3.3
(Itterbeck, Belgium)

Slightly fruity; somewhat soft fizziness; peach aroma and hue; circumscribed sweetness, smell, and looks bear out the promise; sadly, it quickly loses fizz; mild acidity makes it palatable if not exciting with some meats; sticks a bit to the sides of the mouth, but not cloying or cottony; cloudy golden-peach color at the bottom; good choice for those desiring a little adventure. Match with veal scallops or chicken and dumplings.

TOBY Pilsener CT 2.2
(Toronto, Ontario, Canada)

Rich, musty, hoppy aroma and taste; mild, tangy background on the flat of the tongue; light rich amber color supports a long-lasting head with a foamy backbone and delicate Brussels lace; mild alcohol theme; thin and one-dimensional; leaves a furry thickness on the roof of the mouth; for those with very specialized tastes.

TOMMYKNOCKER PICK AXE
PALE ALE MB 3.7
(Idaho Springs, Colorado; Casper, Wyoming)

Taste and aroma are quite fruity, quickly followed on the second sip by a circumscribed bitterness; strikingly fresh hop aroma emerges and takes over; hops fortunately predominate throughout, balancing in sequence with the sweet malty flavor which in tandem gives the mouthfeel a wonderful, predictable balance at each swallow; especially noticeable at the finish, the four varieties of hops offer up a bitter flavor complexity that defines this fine pale ale. Good pairing with a thick hero sandwich filled with sliced Swiss cheese and Italian salami.

TOMMYKNOCKER RED EYE LAGER MB 3.9
(Idaho Springs, Colorado)

Good strong taste of hop-infused maltiness; smooth, hearty mouthfeel; hop sharpness is invigorating and cuts to the bone; seems to contain alcohol; clumps of bubble-impacted head float like ice floes on the surface of the light-amber body; aromatic character is fresh and malty; lovely, lonely, sweet malty flavor coalesces into a focused, satisfying mouthfeel at the end. A very accommodating brew that goes well with barbecued chicken breast.

TOOHEY'S PREMIUM EXPORT LAGER   CB   2.9
(Thebarton, South Australia, Australia)
Grainy and rough with an in-your-face attitude; faint hint of
cloves, unusual for a lager; not particularly carbonated or texturally prickly, also unusual for a lager; hoppy; harsh, rounded hop
taste is close to soothing at the back of the throat; light- to
medium-bodied; finishes lighter-tasting than it started, with a
previously missing hit of alcohol that ties it all together. A fish
and chips beer if there ever was one.

TOP OF THE HILL LAKE HOGAN
HEFEWEIZEN   BP   2.8
(Chapel Hill, North Carolina)
Lots of authentic phenolic flavors responsible for the good-tasting
clove-like character; strong suggestion of refreshing nutmeg presence as well, which ultimately dominates the taste; experience of
tartness is enhanced by the lemon-juice color of the body; finishes with a clove aroma and mouthfeel; overall, a rather pushy
wheat beer that fortunately has reason to be pushy. Enjoy this
with light snacks.

TORONTO LIGHT Pilsener   CT   1.8
(Guelph, Ontario, Canada)
Foamy crispness quickly fades to flatness on the tongue; a bit of
zestiness at the very back of the throat; not quite bland, but not
energetic, either; some hint of ingredients occasionally reaches
the taste buds; not a bad beer, just a "nothing" beer; some hoppiness at the end.

TOURMENTE WHEAT   MB   3.5
(Montreal, Quebec, Canada)
Dainty, spicy fragrance precedes a zesty clove taste brought along
with a tart yeastiness; piles of well-delineated rounded bubbles make
up a thick, slowly collapsing head; judicious arrangement of coriander and orange peel gives this wheat beer a flavorful flair; finishes with a reserved, mesmerizing spiciness and juicy orange aftertaste;
a nifty and entertaining brew. Drink with fresh grilled tuna.

TRAFFIC JAM BIKINI WHEAT   BP   3.0
(Detroit, Michigan)
Though skimpily named, Bikini Wheat is filled with fresh-tasting ingredients; a slight lemon presence jazzes up the mild honey
taste from start to finish; could have a sharper mouthfeel for the
style; yeast tartness is too subdued; smooth and tasty. Drink this
in hot weather with thin slices of smoked fish.

TRAFFIC JAM COAL PORTER   BP   4.0
(Detroit, Michigan)
Roasted and mildly bitter, like strongly brewed coffee; visually
appealing, too, with its intricate designs of Brussels lace and puffy

off-white head; this pun-happy/hoppy-porter is an exquisite accompaniment to made-on-the-premises blueberry-raspberry pie; the burnt taste of the beer is the perfect counterpoint to the tartness of the fruit; finishes well integrated and comforting.

B E E R   F A C T

*T*he Traffic Jam and Snug is Michigan's first licensed brewpub and the first place in the U.S. to serve dairy-brewed beer. The beer is made in the same vessels used to produce Cheddar cheese for the pub's Snug restaurant. "Snug," short for snuggery, is a British word meaning a comfortable place or room, especially a small private space in a public house, or pub.

TRAQUAIR HOUSE ALE   **MB**   **4.1**
(Innerleithen, Scotland)
Warm and mellow, in both aroma and taste; tangible alcohol; smooth molasses feel; warming ambiance with glowing deep-amber color; no head to speak of; as it warms, the aroma, taste, and texture come together to make a full-bodied, complex ale in which no one ingredient, including the alcohol, dominates; fruitiness is downplayed; typical hearty Scottish ale with prominent molasses presence; moderate chewiness adds to the fun; a good ale that deserves your attention. A fine match with smoked salmon or trout.

TRAQUAIR JACOBITE ALE   **CB**   **3.0**
(Innerleithen, Scotland)
A delightful swirl of tastes and flavors greets the first sips and sniffs: prune/plum; coriander, coffee; toffee presence is present soon thereafter, adding to the rich, full mouthfeel; concentrated caramel aroma is part of the enjoyment; flavors integrate further at room temperature; quickly filling, so sip this slowly and share a bottle with a friend.

TREMONT ALE   **MB**   **3.2**
(Boston, Massachusetts)
Rounded bitterness is cushioned by a mild, malty aspect with fruity undertones; subtle, almost-sweet hop character is noticeable at the back of the mouth; increasing bitterness imparts a gentle spicy mouthfeel; heightened hop bitterness at the end is crisp and distinctive; leaves a slight sour taste, mitigated somewhat by the hoppier, more vivacious finish. Seafood with this New England ale, of course.

TRESTLES LAGER   CT   1.0
(Dubuque, Iowa)
Ersatz taste quickly sinks into blandness; flowery/perfumey flavor emerges with shellfish; food spices up the beer, which is essentially flat; in the end, typical, unsatisfying, and safely generic;
a below-par example of a contract brewery product.

TRIPLE TOISON D'OR ALE   CB   2.5
(Mechelen, Belgium)
Very smooth, creamy texture; sturdy, fresh wine aroma; sharp
sourness; overall, more attractive texture than taste; some muddiness to flavor and color; faint citric fruitiness doesn't help. Goes
with shellfish.

TROEGS PALE ALE   MB   3.1
(Harrisburg, Pennsylvania)
Filling mouthfeel of subdued, prolonged hoppiness that unfortunately doesn't maintain its strong presence; hints of hoppy spiciness float throughout each sip; sly, underlying fruitiness adds
balance and taste perspective; less aggressive than a more traditional pale ale, but well within the acceptable hop zone nonetheless; mild floral aroma; snapless, but accommodating. Appropriate
with sharp cheeses and/or seasoned meats.

TROIKA ORIGINAL RUSSIAN BEER
Lager   CB   1.1
(Moscow, Russia)
Starchy, bitter, and old-tasting—not off to a flying start; unexciting and placidly hopped, in the Russian beer tradition; light-
straw color; no head to speak of, though it does display short-lived,
not particularly dainty, Brussels lace; integrity diminishes toward
the end, finishing wan, with a hint of dryness and hoppiness;
bottle came with sediment, which appeared to add a buttery taste
(diacetyl)—not a good sign.

TROPICAL PILSENER   CB   3.7
(Las Palmas, Canary Islands)
Sweetly pungent malt-grain taste; nice body; hint of sourness raises
it above the predictable; moderated sweetness; texturally well balanced and appropriately fizzy; an attractive beer with sweet-sour
complexity. Try with Chinese and Japanese shrimp dishes.

TROY CHERRY RASPBERRY ALE   BP   2.6
(Troy, New York)
This beer clearly has fruit in it, but it's subdued and carefully
balanced; light, airy, and fanciful; slight bitterness from the cherry
tartness; surprisingly soft on the palate; honest to the taste of the
whole cherries and raspberries, but without being oppressive; full-
bodied; close to a one-note brew, but the note is cheerful and
fresh-tasting. Best imbibed by itself on a warm, not hot, day.

TRUE NORTH CREAM ALE   MB   2.7
(Vaughan, Ontario, Canada)
Balanced hop-malt mouthfeel at the outset evolves into a mild
hoppiness that sits on back of the throat, where it becomes
smoother and maltier; hint of spice in the aftertaste includes a
touch of vanilla; sweet, faintly flowery aroma; classic golden body;
finishes with a declining, but complex bitterness; nice hop-grainy
character at the end. Goes nicely with lamb chops.

TRUE NORTH LAGER   MB   3.2
(Vaughan, Ontario, Canada)
Crisp and slightly bitter; hint of grain in the background adds
an attractive near-nutty flavor; incrementally increasing malty
taste nicely balances the minimal hop presence; light-gold body
sits patiently under the thick and frothy clean white head; grainy-
sweet mouthfeel lingers in the aftertaste; finishes maltier than it
began, as well as nuttier; very well done. Makes a good partner
with pork and rice dishes.

TSINGTAO Pilsener   CB   0.4
(Shanghai, China)
Flat and easily forgettable; ingredients are absent, or at least not
discernible; tastes like water.

BEER FACT

*B*eer was virtually unknown to the Chinese
until the middle of the 19th century. The city of
Tsingtao, which means "green island," was the
site of China's first commercial lager brewing operation, started by Germans in 1897.

TUBORG DELUXE DARK Lager   CB   1.1
(Portland, Oregon)
Surprisingly thin and tasteless, with and without food; a rounded
sharpness is this beer's main distinction; bland and flat—even the
color has a faded, unattractive darkness; a beer this dull is difficult to finish.

TUBORG LAGER   CB   2.4
(La Crosse, Wisconsin, et al.)
Sharp, bitter, and tingly; mild body, no head to speak of; in general, "thin" visual experience with opaque dull-gold color; sharpness and bitterness abate, but fizziness remains; an obviously
hoppy brew; label says "Export Quality," but brewed in the U.S.
by Heileman; acceptable for those with accepting palates. Compatible with pork.

TUCHER FESTBIER MARZEN (annual)   CB   2.0
(Nurnberg, Germany)

Initially appealing sweetish/burnt taste quickly dissolves into watery, bland palate; starts with promise and ends with a yawn when sampled with food; mellows somewhat at the end, returning to its initial appeal.

TUN TAVERN LEATHER NECK LAGER   BP   2.6
(Atlantic City, New Jersey)

Sweet; ongoing undercurrent of bitterness blends seamlessly into the smooth texture; interesting, complex maltiness is unusual for a lager; crisp and light-bodied; character evolves into a sharp-sour mouthfeel that balances things nicely; sweetens further at the end, finishing smooth and rounded; a good everyday beer to enjoy with friends around the bar. Add a handful of mixed nuts and the picture is complete.

TUSKER MALT LAGER   CB   2.3
(Nairobi, Kenya)

More aroma than flavor on initial sip; tasteless, like water, except for a back-of-the-mouth mustiness going down the throat; has freshness that turns boring, a touch of sweetness as it warms to room temperature; light but very hoppy. Does nothing for most foods. Okay with pizza.

TUSKER PREMIUM LAGER   CB   4.3
(Nairobi, Kenya)

Very pale color and thin, slightly lemony taste immediately cool you down in 100°F weather; the water feels especially fresh, clean, and inviting; very thirst-quenching; faint hop bitterness is pleasantly balanced by mild maltiness; the ingredients don't intrude, but allow the overall freshness to predominate; light-bodied, fluffy (cottony), and very, very accommodating; dainty hop finish—a perfect hot-weather beer without food or other distractions.

TUTZ Pilsener   CB   3.2
(Schiltigheim, France)

Fresh and crisp; understated hoppiness interacts in tandem with the understated maltiness; slight perfumey character on exhale; malt sweetness in the swallow; flavors are both nuanced and direct; lightbodied and dainty; too passively bitter—you have to search for its presence, it doesn't immediately come to you; warm, malty hit at the finish; calls itself "the freshest beer in the world." Goes great with potato leek soup.

TYSKIE PILS   CB   2.9
(Tychy, Poland)

Punchy and assertive fresh malt taste generously complements a fresh grainy mouthfeel; sharp and full of insistent carbonation; unlike other pilseners, a textural richness is present; zesty and tasty, even as the effervescence diminishes; subdued but obvious bitterness as the glass empties; finishes with an equal complement of hops and malt. A good companion with baked or pan-fried fish.

UB EXPORT LAGER   **CB**   **2.5**
(Bangalore, India)
Immediate aroma is fresh and pungent with underlying metallic smell, none of which is long-lasting; primacy of bitterness with reasonable malt balance; texture becomes watery too soon for comfort; while texturally flat in general, it does maintain an active fizziness that goes well with poultry and salads; both hops and malts are more noticeable at the end of the bottle.

UMPQUA PERRY'S OLD ALE (draft)   **BP**   **2.4**
(Roseburg, Oregon)
Fresh aroma; apple-cider taste, though somewhat hoppier; fairly rich and medium-bodied; malt overtakes the hops, ultimately making the beer more palatable; flinty malt aroma at the end helps integrate the maltiness on the tongue; vaguely fruity finish enhances the rating; needs to be more consistent to truly be a contender.

UNION PREMIUM Pilsener   **CB**   **2.3**
(Ljubljana, Slovenia; former Yugoslavia)
Sharp but underpowered; fair amount of fizziness; initial honey taste subsides into sour dryness with food; thin and shallow; refreshing, but limited by flat sour-honey taste; whiff of bruised Concord grapes—perhaps not surprising, as this comes from the wine-producing area of the country.

UPPER CANADA COLONIAL STOUT   **CB**   **2.3**
(Toronto, Ontario, Canada)
A cherry roastedness wafts up as the cap comes off the bottle, the taste, however, is slightly bitter, somewhat milky, and soft on the palate; aroma disappears fairly rapidly, as does the initial intriguing complexity; moderated bitterness takes over; not as thick as it should be; diminished deep-amber color; weak-textured and lacking backbone; finishes with coffee taste, burnt aroma, and overall blandness.

UPPER CANADA DARK ALE   **CB**   **3.2**
(Toronto, Ontario, Canada)
Fruity ranginess on first sip, with an undercurrent of mustiness; dry and pointed; clean, fresh taste parallels the mustiness and offers a soothing complement to food; taste wanes as beer warms and becomes more of a background to the food; quite serviceable. Match with hearty pork dishes.

UPPER CANADA LAGER   **CB**   **2.5**
(Toronto, Ontario, Canada)
Extra-sharp with fading flavor; refreshing and cooling deep in

the throat, eventual neutral taste is surprisingly invigorating against food; tall, thin pilsener glass seems to stretch and air out the beer, encouraging the coolness to blend and become evenly distributed; more a pretzels-and-nuts beer, or one to drink alone rather than with food.

UPPER CANADA LIGHT LAGER   CB   0.7
(Toronto, Ontario, Canada)

Typical, but subdued, lager taste; sharp but not prickly; flat and watery with food; plain and uninteresting—you quickly lose interest; too-full hoppy aftertaste spoils any interest you might have had.

UPPER CANADA PALE ALE   CB   2.0
(Toronto, Ontario, Canada)

Musty, malty aroma with soda-pop taste and texture—light-bodied and fizzy; remains flat-tasting and plain; sweetens unpleasantly on the roof of the mouth with food; light amber color with a hint of raspberry shading; some integration of malt and hops, but both are mild and uninvigorating; needs to be cranked up a notch or two to be worth a second try.

UPPER CANADA PUBLICAN'S
SPECIAL BITTER ALE   CB   2.2
(Toronto, Ontario, Canada)

Whiff of oxidation, followed by mild, increasingly strong bitterness; too much candy-coated taste; water too weak to support the strong input of the hops, although bitterness gradually decreases, paving the way for an appropriate balance as maltiness increases; light, thin copper color; understated boldness gives a hint of what this beer should be; malty aroma in the finish, but too placid. Pleasant accompaniment to a hero (submarine) sandwich.

UPPER CANADA REBELLION Lager   CB   3.8
(Toronto, Ontario, Canada)

Sweet roundness, with fullness and warmth in the throat; lovely honey taste surrounds and subdues high alcohol content and fits in seamlessly with food, as if the beer and food are one; not very complex, but predictable and evenhanded; with a little more zip, this could be a much better beer; as it is, it's a good choice for someone interested in something different, but not radically so; increased alcohol presence in the finish; light amber color; smooth and refined. Try with pork chops or breaded pork tenderloin.

UPPER CANADA TRUE BOCK   CB   3.7
(Toronto, Ontario, Canada)

Soft and warm-tasting, with a pleasant hop aroma that encourages you to sniff deeply; visually quite bubbly, but texturally not much effervescence; hearty, full, complex flavor with mild emerging maltiness; gently flowing alcohol ambiance; hint of wineyness in the alcohol detracts somewhat; moderate amount of Brussels lace provides an appealing backdrop to sparkling red-amber color; finishes with a pleasurable surprise—a light, malty, toasted aroma atypical of bock. Be careful when you get out of your seat—you know there's alcohol when you stand up; as the label notes, this bock "is not for the faint of heart."

UPTOWN CLAYMORE SCOTTISH ALE   **BP**   **3.2**
(Tempe, Arizona)
Sugar-crystal sweet, with caramel overtones; full-bodied; a bit of chocolate doesn't linger, but helps to move things along; well-presented malty presence arises like a nymph out of the sea at mid-glass; smooth, with minimal satisfying bite; complex, ongoing flavors keep your interest; gentle spiciness at the end is a pleasant surprise. Goes well with spaghetti and lightly seasoned meat sauce.

UPTOWN IPA   **BP**   **3.8**
(Tempe, Arizona)
Flowery and instantly hoppy; fruity, malty, zesty hop aroma and matching flavor tell you this is a stylish IPA; modulated fresh hoppy aftertaste; hefty windows of Brussels lace add to its quality character; hop-fruity aroma stays strong and accessible; finishes with a very well coordinated flowery/fruity/hop arrangement. Goes nicely with lettuce and tomato salad topped with croutons.

URSUS PREMIUM PILS   **CB**   **2.8**
(Cluj-Napoca, Romania)
Crisp character briefly carries along a definite vanilla component that changes to a lightly-hopped mouthfeel; rounded texture provides support for the well-placed malt aspects; mild, floral hop presence is established by mid-bottle; clean aroma is slightly sweet; fuller, more mouth-filling sweetness toward the end is smooth and pleasing; finishes light and feathery on the palate. Oddly, this is appropriate with hard candy.

UTENOS PORTER   **CB**   **2.4**
(Utena, Lithuania)
Chocolatey and mildly bitter; turns sugary-sweet with hot and/or spicy foods; winey mouthfeel is similar to lightweight brandy; relatively uncomplex and not much textural edginess; hints of rich flavor to come, but never delivers; some caramel overtones add interest at the end.

VAILIMA LAGER   **MB**   **3.5**
(Apia, Western Samoa)
Sharp and vaguely sour; off-taste background, but appealing in any event; complexity of the ingredients makes this South Pacific offering interesting, though a little unpredictable; German-strength hoppiness; well-integrated ingredients; becomes more

intriguing with food; nicely sweet, but not tacky or cloying, finish further encourages you to have another bottle of this brew (at the outset, I wouldn't have expected to say that); grows more pleasing as you drink it; label declares "brewed and bottled under German management."

VAILIMA LIGHT Pilsener   MB   **2.1**
(Apia, Western Samoa)
Prickly and fresh-tasting, with some sourness; quite light-bodied and thin; aroma and texture predominate over the flavor; some hoppiness; dry, undistinguished finish.

B E E R   F A C T

Vailima, meaning "water in the hand," is a small mountain village in Western Samoa. According to legend, the wife of a man dying of thirst carried water from a nearby stream to him in the palms of her hands. Scottish novelist Robert Louis Stevenson spent the last years of his life in Vailima, where his house still stands. Neighbors called him Tusitala—"Teller of Tales."

VALENTINS KLARES WEIZENBIER   CB   **2.3**
(Heidelberg, Germany)
Quick, bubbly, thick head that with its airiness is hard to tell apart from the body; hint of green taste and sourness is all that greets the palate; only after several sips does sweet wheat flavor surface; settles into routine fizz and strength with food; in the end, not all that interesting. Okay with a hamburger,

VELTINS PILSENER   CB   **2.4**
(Grevenstein, Germany)
Quite bitter, with essentially no malt balance or pilsener-like carbonation; smooth and full-bodied; strong and consistent hop presence; very slight hint of malt aroma; bitterness is less focused at the end; it's a struggle to drink this, but the effort is, more or less, worth it. Goes surprisingly well with meat sauces and thick sautés.

VERMONT WEE HEAVY SCOTCH ALE   MB   **1.5**
(Burlington, Vermont)
Like the gooey stuff that comes from local trees, this Vermont product is mellow and lightly syrupy; nicely touched with alcohol as well; however, there is a spoiled pungency to it that is clearly detracting; deeply malted within the Scottish ale style; but off-taste lurking throughout is a major flaw.

VICTORIA Pilsener   **CB**   **0.0**
(Mexico City, Mexico)
Thin, cranky, sour, and repellent—finally, a bad Mexican beer; green, without flavor—I didn't finish it; grossly overpriced; ties with Green Rooster (see page 144) as *numero uno* in the unpalatable class.

VICTORIA AVENUE AMBER ALE—
SCOTTISH ALE   **MB/BP**   **3.8**
(Riverside, California)
Pour this well-integrated amber ale and get ready for a heady, bountiful, aromatic mix of nutmeg, honey, lemon, and spices; smooth and gentle going down; lasting warm bitterness at the back of the throat; pleasant aftertaste gets a bit too sticky on the roof of the mouth; increasing, almost overwhelming, burnt maltiness becomes predominant, then evolves into a malty-nutty mouthfeel; sweetens a bit with spaghetti and clam sauce.

VICTORY HOPDEVIL ALE   **MB**   **2.8**
(Downingtown, Pennsylvania)
Clean, fresh smell of hops is immediately apparent, and quite welcome; ditto for the taste; flavor complexity continues, featuring a minimal maltiness that sweetens along the way; pale-copper color comes with a frosty-white head; don't let the name mislead you—this is a good, even-tempered, rather restrained ale; it may be a one-note beer (hops), but it plays a balanced song of flavor; however, it does fade too much at the end. Drink it with well-seasoned seafood.

VICTORY PRIMA PILS   **MB**   **2.8**
(Downington, Pennsylvania)
Sharply bitter and sensually mouth-puckering; full, hoppy aftertaste makes you feel as if you're rolling around in a bin of just-processed hops; light-bodied; head is consistent, firm, and long-lasting; a stream of mild sweetness at the end takes the edge off the bitterness. Try this with a sausage or wiener on a roll with sauerkraut.

VIENNA LAGER   **CT**   **2.5**
(Milwaukee, Wisconsin)
Orange taste; rather undistinguished and a little off the mark; does nothing for food; hops try to push themselves into awareness; nothing terrible about this beer, just nothing to write home about.

VIKING LAGER   **MB**   **2.2**
(Victoria, British Columbia, Canada)
Fruity, highly carbonated combination with a fresh, uninhibited taste; slightly filling without food; a bit of thickness disappears after the first few sips; in the end, rather routine, with little distinction.

VLAS KOP ALE   **CB**   **2.6**
(Ichtegem, Belgium)
Contrasting perfumey honey-sweetness and apple pie/clove taste
set the stage nicely; suggestion of cinnamon is equally welcome;
surprisingly faint yeast presence; pale-straw liquid is thin and
tastes a bit musty; appealing and picturesque big-bubbled, frothy
head; overall, this is an odd but not unattractive beer, with a
strange, almost tentative arrangement of ingredients; if you want
to concentrate on what you're drinking, try this.

B E E R   F A C T

*V*las Kop means "flax head" or "towhead" in Flemish. It is widely used in Belgium to refer to boys
with white-blond hair.

VONDEL DARK ALE   **CB**   **0.3**
(Dentergem, Belgium)
Fruity, malty, and soft, with an especially foamy head; sour citrus taste as the beer settles in; clearly a lot of alcohol in this
drink; much too sweet and alcoholic for food; too filling and
slightly upsetting to my stomach; I found this hard to finish,
indeed close to unpalatable; there is precious little to recommend it.

WARSTEINER Pilsener   **CB**   **3.9**
(Warstein, Germany)
Immediately distinctive; gentle, flowery hoppiness; solid, lingering taste that is nicely balanced between malts and hops; very responsive and complementary to food, remaining well mannered
and even-tasting all over the palate; improves in character as a
meal progresses. Appropriate with spicy Thai food, hot Italian
sausages, or salads with assertive dressings.

WARSTEINER PREMIUM VERUM
Pilsener   **CB**   **3.0**
(Warstein, Germany)
Foamy, creamy, small-bubbled head sets the stage for thin, golden
sharpness underneath—but this prelude doesn't last long; hops
are noticeable; light and fizzy in the middle; slight bitterness at
the back of the mouth; holds its essence throughout, including
heady, memorable, slightly flowery aroma; texture outweighs flavor; light by German standards; remains interesting, if not entirely attractive. Good with meat loaf, hot dogs, or wurst with
sauerkraut.

B E E R   F A C T

*I*n Germany, "premium" is the middle of five standard classifications based on price, not quality. There is no industry or government standard for the premium designation, and as a result, no uniform relationship between what you pay and quality. American premium pilseners tend to offer lower adjunct levels than their non-premium—read: lower-priced—counterparts. Because standards are lacking for what is essentially advertising hyperbole, microbreweries and brewpubs do not use "premium" in their labeling.

WARTECK LAGER   CB   3.2
(Basel, Switzerland)

Smartly hopped and crisp on first sip, along with noticeable grainy taste; some acid undertones; maintains freshness throughout a meal; can be too assertive by itself, but just right for some foods; dryness is pervasive; distinctive; appears to have a relatively high alcohol content. Match with pork dishes.

WASATCH HEFE-WEIZEN   MB/BP   2.8
(Park City and Salt Lake City, Utah)

Sharp and unabashed, this playful *hefe-weizen* hits the taste buds directly and accurately; downplayed yeastiness provides a firm support for the easygoing citrus taste; full of flavor and appropriately dry; thirst-quenching, too; vaguest hint of clove is in there somewhere; citrus-yeast presence lingers; an easy intro to the style. Enjoy this with a crisp freshly made salad, heavy on the greens.

WASATCH IRISH STOUT   MB/BP   2.5
(Park City, Utah)

Fizzy and sharp; thin and bitter; stimulates the appetite, even after a big meal; bitterness combines with pungent roastedness and a lingering burnt taste on the roof of the mouth; ingredients never really integrate—they remain separate without coming together in a cohesive whole; fullness starts at the front of the mouth and disappears at the back; no head, no Brussels lace, just a deep brown sitting in the glass, awaiting some excitement; at the end, the roasted barley aroma is all but gone. Try with Indian food or rice dishes.

WASATCH RASPBERRY WHEAT   MB/BP   2.8
(Salt Lake City, Utah)

It's got raspberry aroma and taste, all right—the instant the cap comes off the bottle; aroma is fuller and sweeter than the thin, somewhat harsh taste; refreshing, with a mild yeasty sharpness that quenches thirst; uniform sun-tea color is appropriately cloudy; raspberry aroma throughout is a pleasant treat each time you lift the glass to your lips; forceful hop backbone overpowers plain food; flavor intensity weakens about halfway through, allowing the yeast's citrus bitterness to emerge; there is a rigidity to the overall presentation; don't let this beer sit in the glass too long—drink it quickly, before its energy and pizzazz are sapped (label calls this a malt beverage with raspberry juice concentrate). An interesting accompaniment to crêpes Suzette.

WASATCH SLICKROCK LAGER   MB/BP   2.7
(Park City, Utah)

Lazily fruity, with a tantalizing roughness and a quick, oxidized mouthfeel that disappears without a trace; imbalanced toward the hops, the taste is sharp and vibrant, though not overly flavorful; remains thick and fruity with food; cloudy pale color supports pencil-thin but well-designed head; bitterness mutes interplay of the ingredients; on the positive side, its harsh hop grittiness is a strong match for salty snacks; well made. Tasty with an Italian hero sandwich.

WASATCH WHEAT   MB/BP   0.3
(Park City, Utah)

Lemon-honey aroma with a distorted honey flavor that quickly turns ugly; musty, inconsistent, and then watery; eventually settles into a tea-like taste that lacks redeeming tannins and textural warmth; a baked-bread aroma shows itself briefly, offering the only sign of attractiveness; fruitiness never comes into full bloom, aroma never connects with the taste; unredeeming mild malt aroma at the end; hard to finish; inconsistent and unpredictable; poorly done; like a homebrew that failed; stay away.

WATCH CITY SATURNALEA
STRONG ALE   BP   3.4
(Waltham, Massachusetts)

Big-bodied, strong and malty; delicious dollop of alcohol fills the mouth almost immediately, accompanied by an apple-tinged fruity taste; dynamic duo of yeasty tartness and bitter hops propels this assertive, reddish-brown ale; bottle-conditioned for two months increases complexity (also means there's yeast at the bottom of the bottle); balanced and blended with loving care; smoothly sweet and remarkably refreshing, Saturnalea draws rings around its competitors. Savor this without food or other barroom distractions.

WATNEY'S CREAM STOUT   CB   3.9
(London, England)

Mellow roasted palate with continued inviting ambiance; restrained maltiness reflects its origins; beautiful dark-brown, almost black, color adds to the pleasure; retains strength with food; close to chocolates in taste; rich roastedness and depth enhance spicy foods; versatile and sophisticated with several appealing faces, but with solid core; no bitterness, which it could have used; finish is a bit too watery. A good choice with hamburgers, roast beef, or Buffalo-style chicken wings.

WATNEY'S RED BARREL Lager   CB   3.9
(London, England)

Lovely mellow wine taste; touch of bitterness; surprisingly sweet aftertaste; extraordinarily smooth; a bit too light to be closer to perfection. Match with beef or pork stews, steak and kidney pie, and other hearty main dishes.

TAP TIP

Dark and Tan

*A*Dark and Tan is the same as a Black and Tan (see page 148), but with Watney's Red Barrel lager substituted for the Harp. A subtle, indirect, mildly burnt taste marks the first sips of the delectably deep-brown mixture; sheets of Brussels lace decorate the glass; dry, acceptably rough finish. Retains its burnt zest with a burger and fries.

WATNEY'S STINGO CREAM STOUT   CB   3.5
(London, England)

Mellow and soft with dry-wine aroma; faint, palatable burnt taste; warm, with a hint of sweetness; doesn't really do justice to light or mildly flavored foods; a classic stout. Good with moderately sweet desserts such as a fruit tart or pound cake.

WEEPING RADISH BLACK RADISH
DARK LAGER   MB/BP   2.2
(Manteo, North Carolina)

Mildly toasty with a pleasant aftertaste; vague, weak malt presence; pronounced, undifferentiated taste reminiscent of the brewer's amber and golden lagers; mild burnt taste comes and goes quickly at mid-bottle, then the beer resumes its plodding, unexciting course; not worth the effort. Serve with popcorn.

WEEPING RADISH COROLLA
GOLDEN LAGER   MB/BP   2.7
(Manteo, North Carolina)

Immediate yeast aroma and taste—smells as if you just entered a bakery; bitter on the front of the tongue; quickly turns dry, in the manner of champagne; light and airy; thick, creamy long-lasting head; Brussels lace covers sides of glass in curving sheets;

a respectable light, mildly bitter beer with staying power; a pleasant summer drink. Goes well with a mixed green salad or a French salade niçoise.

B E E R   F A C T

Weeping Radish gets its name from the Bavarian vegetable favored by the local clientele. Served sliced and salted, the resulting moisture makes it appear as if the radish is weeping.

WEEPING RADISH FEST BEER
AMBER LAGER   MB/BP   2.1
(Manteo, North Carolina)

Hop-bitter and softly malty with gentle, very faint hint of toastedness; minor fizziness helps lessen the bitterness; predictable and uncomplex from start to finish; Brussels lace is bunched together rather than in pleasing patterns; unexciting; flavor diminishes by the end of the rather large bottle; disappointing; not worth trying with food.

WEIHENSTEPHAN EDEL—PILS   CB   2.6
(Freising, Germany)

Balanced malt and hop sweetness precedes faded, faintly bitter aftertaste; bold and crisp; gentles and mellows with food; light-golden color accurately reflects the lightness of this beer; not one of the brewery's better efforts. Goes with raw oysters or sushi.

WEIHENSTEPHAN EXPORT DUNKEL   CB   4.1
(Freising, Germany)

Smooth, long, malty swallow, with a splash of orange tang at the end; full-bodied and nicely modulated in both taste and texture; yeast fruitiness is a major player; well balanced, temperate, but very flavorful; charming mild roastedness on its own, or with hearty food; accommodating mellowness lingers on; a fine, comforting drinking partner that grows better after each sip. An accompaniment to lamb roasts and chops.

WEIHENSTEPHAN WEIZENBIER   CB   3.8
(Freising, Germany)

Faint clove aroma turns into a strong, refreshing, sharp clove taste mixed in with a crisp, full head of foam; dry and pleasantly tickly on the upper palate; firm, with evenly distributed ingredients; full-bodied and lush with subtle yeastiness; hazy light-blond color is muted (label says: "crystal-clear"); a compelling tartness surfaces as the glass is drained; a very good representation of wheat beer from the self-described "Oldest Brewery in the World." An appropriate match with roast beef.

WEINHARD'S BLUE BOAR PALE ALE   CB   2.6
(Portland, Oregon)
Pleasantly bitter, texturally smooth, and not malty at the outset; bitterness stays evenhanded and consistent throughout; finishes flat and fizzless; thins and turns slightly watery; this is meant to be an Irish-style beer, but it's not smooth, red, or malty-sweet enough. Try it with a grilled steak and baked potatoes.

WELSH FELINFOEL DOUBLE DRAGON
ALE   CB   4.1
(Llanelli, Wales)
Sweet-wine taste; touch of bitterness fits nicely into the sweetness; appealing smooth rich-amber color; attenuated fresh effervescence; sweet-smelling; clean rather than fizzy after swallowing; versatile; hearty, strong, and determined to help out with hearty, strong, rich foods—succeeds nicely in that respect. Try with a meal of thick-sliced roast beef, gravy, and mashed potatoes, and a gooey concoction for dessert.

BEER FACT

*F*elinfoel has redesigned its label so that its products are now sold under the name "Welsh," with "Felinfoel" displayed less prominently. In 1935, the company was the first in Great Britain to can its beer.

WELSH FELINFOEL DRAGON ALE   CB   4.0
(Llanelli, Wales)
Sharp and biting on first sip; gently increasing honey-tainted sweetness and mellowness trickle upward as the ale warms; fullness reaches appetizing midpoint, then stops and stays there; moderately lasting head with small bubbles tops a dusty-brown body with orange undertones; remote fruitiness adds mystery to this tender ale; alcohol remains warming and unobtrusive; yeasty aroma at finish. Goes well with chowders and grilled chicken.

WELSH FELINFOEL HERCULES ALE   CB   4.0
(Llanelli, Wales)
Combination wine-beer taste is quite winning; thin and thick at the same time; sweet and bitter; alcohol strength copes well with tangy food; finishes on an upbeat, hoppy note, warming as you swallow the last drop; good cold-weather warmer. Surprisingly appropriate with barbecued dishes.

WELSH FELINFOEL ALE   CB   3.9
(Llanelli, Wales)
Nicely balanced, with controlled sweetness laced with mild, fruity citrus taste; full-bodied and soft with a tart edge that revives at

every sip; yeast cloudiness and fruitiness are full and consistent; sweeter at the bottom of the bottle as the alcohol becomes more noticeable; mature balance of sweet and sharp; nicely put together. A near-perfect accompaniment with grilled tuna or salmon steak.

WELSH FELINFOEL BITTER Ale   CB   2.4
(Llanelli, Wales)
Rich without bitter bite on first sip; flat and uniform rather than complex in texture and taste; no aroma; prickly mouthfeel; somewhat tentative; not intrusive—surprising for a bitter; if possible, sample a few sips before ordering a pint of your own. Accompanies fresh fruit, such as mangoes and apple slices.

WELSH FELINFOEL PORTER   CB   1.8
(Llanelli, Wales)
Flat, thin, and without zip; no aroma; remains uninteresting; some maltiness in the nose as you drink it; hoppy finish is not typical of porter, nor is it thick, or dark, or sweetish; watery and untasty.

WEST END EXPORT LAGER   CB   3.3
(Thebarton, South Australia, Australia)
Crisp, dry, and reasonably well hopped; immediate impression of a substantial quality lager, including a taste of bitterness alongside a sweetish character; attractive full grains; agreeably balanced until the end, when hops begins to weaken; an enjoyable brew with a backbone. An excellent choice with grilled salmon or tuna steaks.

WESTMALLE TRAPPIST Ale   AB   4.3
(Abbey of Westmalle, Belgium)
Yeasty and fresh, with mouth-filling, rounded alcohol taste; gentle golden color; dainty texture, with substance and follow-through; a hint of fresh fruit is a delightful counterpoint; graduated upsurge of alcoholic potency continues at the end, underpinned by the gently swirling yeast performing its bottle-conditioned duty; a good example of the style—flavorful and well-balanced. Try it at brunch with ham and eggs.

WESTON PALE LAGER   BP   2.4
(Weston, Missouri)
Crisp, fresh hop mouthfeel; faint layer of sweet malt underlies the sharper, pushier hop character; briefly tastes like the inside of a freezer; ingredients become more integrated as the yellow-amber body warms; ultimately loses its already minimal assertiveness; more balanced at the end; okay, but not great.

WHISTLER BLACK TUSK ALE   MB   2.1
(Whistler, British Columbia, Canada)
Bitter coffee taste quickly diminishes, leaving a flat, tasteless mouthfeel in its wake; unpasteurized—a real problem, as it loses

flavor and textural presence even more rapidly as a result; dark-amber color gives the impression of trying to help coax out more taste substance merely by the way it looks; if this had an IQ, it would be dull normal; not bad, just nothing to get excited about.

WHISTLER PREMIUM LAGER   MB   1.2
(Whistler, British Columbia, Canada)
Sugar-sweet and smooth, with the obvious presence of hops; feels flat and uninteresting; apple-cider color and, alas, apple-cider weak; no pizzazz, no fizz, no sharpness; no complexity, either; this is not a lager or, perhaps, even a beer; somewhat malty at the end; this bottled brew is pasteurized and appears to have weakened on the shelf.

WHITBREAD ALE (draft)   CB   3.9
(London and Sheffield, England)
Dark, sour, bitter taste remains yeasty; bracing aroma and full body; a little too sharp, but palatable; especially refreshing on tap, with thick, chewable head topping off the body like cream froth on hot chocolate; bitter, firm in the mouth, and full-bodied; one of the better draft beers I have had. Tasty with black bean or vegetable soup accompanied by crusty bread.

WHITEFISH BROWN ALE (draft)   BP   1.6
(Whitefish, Montana)
Genuine roasted taste is demanding on first sip, but fades fast; fresh malty initial aroma recalls the beach; in the meantime, taste continues to diminish, flattening and weakening; the flavor changes character, turning into a brew that tastes like toasty Kool-Aid; weak and watery, with carbonation predominating at the end; not offensive, but not pleasing, either. Food doesn't help this disappointing brew.

WICKULER PILSENER   CB   3.7
(Wuppertal, Germany)
Dry and flavorful; fresh-off-the-farm aroma precedes an equally attractive grainy taste and texture; gradually and comfortably increases in bitterness, but not overwhelmingly so; finishes with a more defined malt-hops balance and integration; hefty sheets of Brussels lace chase the classic golden liquid down the sides of the glass; a visual and gustatory delight. Drink this with egg salad on a sunny spring day.

WIDMER ALT (draft)   RB/BP   3.3
(Portland, Oregon)
Tart fruitiness with a gradual slide into compact fizziness; citrus fruitiness is quite appropriate for food; pleasant sharpness merges midway through the (large) glass; well made, with good potential in its responsivity to a variety of foods, ranging from cold cuts to shrimp salad.

TAP TIP

The Draft Difference

Naturally carbonated, usually unpasteurized (pasteurization prolongs shelf life but saps the beer of flavor and charm), and a lot fresher than the bottled variety, draft beer is a delight for the senses. Generally, tapped beer has more character than the same brand in a bottle. Compare the two and taste for yourself. Because it is not pasteurized, draft is much more perishable. The good part is that unpasteurized beer allows more of the essence and complexity to come through. That's why brewers prefer their customers to drink from the tap, rather than from a can or bottle. An increasing number of breweries are now marketing what they call draft beer in cans and bottles. It is just not the same. The fact is, once you try freshly brewed draft beer, it's hard to enjoy anything else, regardless of style, brand, or price.

WIDMER BIG BEN PORTER MB/BP **2.1**
(Portland, Oregon)
Subtle molasses and licorice flavors are fitted together seamlessly; faintly effervescent; increases in maltiness and sweetness; flavor weakens and diminishes too soon; flattens texturally; tastes a bit tarry; a disappointment at the end.

WILD BOAR SPECIAL AMBER Lager CT **2.2**
(Dubuque, Iowa)
Sweet molasses presence, but texturally flat and uninteresting; core is faithful to typical malty-sweet amber style; fades in the finish.

WILD GOOSE AMBER Ale MB **2.6**
(Cambridge, Maryland)
Mild, alluring caramel aroma and taste make for an attractive opening; texturally full and very satisfying; simultaneously warm and bitter; strong caramel-popcorn aroma wafts up as the beer warms; decided caramel color; small bubbly head emphasizes underlying thinness; eventually emerges mildly malty, as a good amber should; fades a bit in the end, with sour overtones; a step or two away from being a classy brew.

B E E R   F A C T

*T*he term "amber" is often used by brewpubs and microbreweries in the United States to indicate the beer's color: copper, tawny, reddish-brown.

WILDCATTERS REFINED STOUT   CT   2.6
(San Antonio, Texas)

Circumscribed, contained roastedness; moderate malty sweetness; soft, smooth-textured mouthfeel focuses on tongue and palate; bitterness joins up with the roastedness, making for a balanced, flavorful taste, especially at the end; has all the earmarks of stout, but is restrained in its presentation—a good choice for the novice who wants to begin to appreciate the real thing. Drink alone or with light foods, like shellfish.

WILLIAMSBURG AMERICAN
PALE ALE   MB   1.6
(Williamsburg, Virginia)

Mild, hoppy-fruity aroma is followed by a more pronounced hop taste whose caramel undertone quickly fades; so does the already minimal hop bite; hint of plastic doesn't help; existing fruit character is deadened and lifeless; bitter hop aftertaste, though not delightful, does hang around awhile; needs work.

WILLIAMSVILLE BORDER PORTER   MB   3.5
(Fernandina, Florida)

A full taste of coffee fills the mouth—soft and penetrating; smooth chocolate flavor supplants the coffee while a sedate hoppiness emerges and underpins it all; bold and subtle at the same time; meant to replicate traditional English porters, this version comes very close; finishes with a soothing mixture of chocolate and coffee tastes, with a quick spot of malt to round things off; a well-done beer. Drink this with game—venison, for example.

WIT White/Wheat   CT   3.1
(St. Paul, Minnesota)

Honey-lemony taste—sort of like cloudy, weak-colored, but tasty tea; the gentle flavor ultimately becomes clear—orange peel and coriander; sweet musty aroma; naturally cloudy, the hazy hue settles between that of ale and wheat beer, with far less visual texture than wheat beer; ebb and flow of sweetness and tartness moves playfully over the tongue and the roof of the mouth; yeasty aroma is apparent at the end, as are clumps of yeast floating on the bottom of the glass (indicative of bottle-conditioning); interesting and light; satisfying without food, but hard to match with food; finishes with a slight thickness at the roof of the mouth that leaves you a little thirsty.

WIT BLACK Ale   CT   3.4
(St. Paul, Minnesota)
Gentle caramel aroma is followed by a fuller, mouth-filling sweet
caramel-malt taste; undefined spiciness punctuates the smooth,
almost creamy texture; dark-brown body supports a patient half-
inch-thick tan head—a pretty picture; ingredients become more
integrated toward the end; spices and some of the hoppiness absorb the increasing roasted presence; beguiling and different. Try
this with glazed pork or ham.

WITKAP-PATER SINGEL ABBEY ALE   AB   4.0
(Ninove, Belgium)
Fruity clove taste along with lovely soft texture resulting from a
gentle fizziness; fluffy, thick, foamy head produces lasting, irreg-
ularly shaped, but attractive Brussels lace; bottle-conditioned and
highly yeasty, as befits the style; light and fulfilling; head sits patiently and evenly on top of the cloudy straw-colored body; smooth
bittersweetness glides down the throat, leaving a faint clove aftertaste; combination of ingredients weakens somewhat at the
end, allowing for a taste of the individual components rather than
the earlier blending; aroma keeps flavorful pace with the taste;
well made and lovely to look at; buy two, so you can taste and
look longer. Try this with freshwater fish with a delicate sauce,
and make sure to drink it slightly warm.

WOLAVER'S BROWN ALE   CT   2.9
(Fort Bragg, California)
One of the first of the new breed of organically produced beers,
Wolaver's Brown is malty and nutty with a fresh, sharp mouthfeel on the roof of the mouth; pleasantly fizzy and refreshing;
balancing bitterness arises underneath the maltiness, creating interest missing earlier; increasing hoppiness near the end; organically grown hops and malts help give this an intriguing mixture
of taste sensations; finishes with malt in the aftertaste, immediately preceded by a touch of hops. Try it with soft cheeses.

WOLF CANYON ANO NUEVO
IMPERIAL STOUT   BP   3.1
(Santa Fe, New Mexico)
Smooth and soft, with a definite alcohol presence; rich coffee
aroma; complex, but predominantly sweet; reveals layers of chocolate, subtle hops and a malt fullness; bitterness gradually emerges
at the end, along with a pinch of burnt taste; well made. A good
appetite-builder, so have a pint before the meal arrives.

WOLFBRAU Pilsener   CB   3.3
(Osnabruck, Germany)
Lemon-honey tea aroma is soothing but flat; no head; tastes like
fresh coffee grounds, but without the bitterness, making this very
distinctive, if not outstanding; malt appears to be toasted; hops

remain sweet, with subterranean bite; interesting and different; cloudy weak-tea appearance; I would drink this again, but perhaps with tea biscuits or crackers; finishes with a full honey sweetness; intriguing; worth the effort to locate.

WOLFSBRAU AMBER LAGER CB 2.5
(Calgary, Alberta, Canada)

Warm, rosy upsurge with tickle of tiny bubbles at the back of the throat; simultaneously mildly sweet and sour with comforting, surprising heftiness; unassuming and appealing in a bland sort of way; benign balance of malt and hops. Fine with most types of sandwiches.

WRIGLEY RED Scottish Ale CT 2.8
(brewed for Old Chicago in Boulder, Colorado)

Amber sweetness and toasted flavor; fresh-tasting and appropriately sweet; chewy and more integrated as you drink it; Gold Medal winner at the 1993 Great American Beer Festival. A perfect match for fish and chips.

WURZBURGER HOFBRAU FESTBIER CB 3.0
(Würzburg, Germany)

Sweet, thickish malty character is thinned nicely by an undertone of consistent mild spiciness; flavor suggests a light clove-citrus combination; tastes milder than it smells; little bit of orange rind adds some bitterness and perks things up after a while; fawn-colored body; ends with a balancing of malt and spice. Goes nicely with fresh-baked sponge cake.

WURZBURGER HOFBRAU
OCTOBERFEST Lager (annual) CB 2.5
(Würzburg, Germany)

Medium-sharp texture and medium-caramel taste on first sip settle into muted fruity/sweet balance; weak overall; somewhat thin-flavored for most foods; musty, demanding odor is too prominent; gets more ingratiating and full as it warms; a mixed bag but worth trying.

WYE RIVER BLACK CRAB BEER Lager MB 0.6
(Baltimore, Maryland)

Hardly fruity and hardly hoppy; weak, flat tea taste; cloudy gold body; essentially bland and tasteless; no texture, either; goes nowhere.

WYNKOOP BOCK MB/BP 4.0
(Denver, Colorado)

Deep, fruity aroma and deep coffee-chocolate taste, with the emphasis on the coffee; appropriately and distinctively malty, not to mention alcoholic; smooth, strong, and rich-tasting; finishes with an invigorating parallel arrangement of malt and alcohol, both of which vie for, and deserve, your attention; essentially a double bock in strength and flavor profile; well made and well worth the price. It's a luxury to drink this without interference from food, or from anything else for that matter.

WYNKOOP IRISH CREAM STOUT   MB/BP   3.0
(Denver, Colorado)
Romantic, delicate roasted flavor tantalizes on first sip, followed by smooth, fresh but uncomplicated taste; stays mellow with maltiness that unfortunately remains a bit too hidden and too flat texturally; could be thicker and more flavorful, but an intriguing example of an American-made cream stout.

WYNKOOP JED FEST Lager (annual)   MB/BP   3.7
(Denver, Colorado)
Fresh and thoroughly flavorful; retains a fruitiness that is beguiling and a bit sweet; too sharp and sour with meats or heavy meals; maintains a fresh, mildly fruity fragrance and taste; drink this before a meal or with light fare such as fish or chicken.

XINGU BLACK BEER Stout/Lager   CB   4.0
(Toledo, Brazil)
Watery caramel taste with complementary nonintrusive aroma; not as thick or chewy as expected, but enough texture to please my palate; gets enticingly mellower and properly sweeter as more is imbibed; good blend of bitterness and sweetness; solid and enjoyable. Good with Buffalo-style chicken wings and other hot, spicy snacks.

B E E R   F A C T

Xingu is bottom-fermented like a lager, but in all other respects (taste, texture, color), it resembles stout.

YBOR BROWN ALE   MB   3.0
(Tampa, Florida)
Subtly malty sweet, with a toffee character that's smooth and mellow; complementing hop character is sublime and polished; caramelized-sugar aroma; gets maltier and sweeter as it warms, but always stays controlled and restrained; mellow and comforting, with a malty punctuation at the end; a sweet, gentle ale. Does a good job with medium-done steaks.

YEBISU ALL MALT Pilsener   CB   2.7
(Tokyo, Japan)
Fresh, but flat; slightly acidic; clearly a malt beer, with dry ambiance; mellow and smooth; nice easygoing sipping companion with which to pass the time while you wait for your meal; essentially no fizz; leaves some scrawny Brussels lace.

YEBISU STOUT DRAFT (bottle/can)   **CB**   **2.4**
(Tokyo, Japan)
Thick and light with minimal fizziness; overall impression of lightness; poorly balanced; pale-golden color. Try it with chicken.

B E E R   F A C T

*T*he legendary 14th-century Japanese deity and prophet Yebisu is reputed to be the "bringer of good luck and prosperity."

YI KING Pilsener   **CB**   **2.1**
(Guangzhou, China)
Bland and flat, with yeasty sharpness around the edges; thin body; no head; warms into mellowness at mid-bottle; too wine-like in taste; final swallow is more palatable than the first.

YOUNG'S LONDON PORTER   **CB**   **3.2**
(London, England)
Deep, rich, and dark; a typical porter: palatable bitterness, balanced texture, and moderated sharp burnt taste; thins out a little bit at the end; traditional dry weak-coffee flavor. Good with meat-and-potato meals.

YOUNG'S OATMEAL STOUT   **CB**   **4.3**
(London, England)
Appealing chocolate malt aroma on first sip; roasted flavor spreads out across the tongue; round and full-bodied; gets thicker, more chocolatey, and sweeter as it warms; brown-black color adds to the ambiance; remains a medium-dry beer; easy to drink two to three bottles, with or without food; has substance and class. Good with steak and potatoes.

YOUNG'S OLD NICK Christmas Ale
(annual)   **CB**   **3.9**
(London, England)
Smooth, creamy, and voluptuous barley wine with deep sweet burnt taste—yummy; nice smoky-amber color; retains physically soft, warm texture throughout; unfortunately, a bit too mild for most foods. Savor as an *apéritif* or *digestif*.

YOUNG'S OLD NICK BARLEY WINE   **CB**   **2.2**
(London, England)
Made with soft water (as is true of most beers in England); ale yeasts interact with malt to produce fruity (banana) esters; increasing alcohol warmth, but not as strongly alcoholic as other barley wines; flat on the tongue; unusually weak for the style; unsatisfying.

YOUNG'S RAM ROD Ale   CB   3.6
(London, England)

Dark and musty; sharp; hearty; rich malty presence; tingly on your tongue; strong flavor, aggressive in its strength. A good match with prime rib or roast beef.

YOUNG'S SPECIAL ALE   CB   3.0
(London, England)

Soft and creamy, with mild pinprick of carbonation; fruity, flowery mouthfeel—more a physical than a taste sensation; some warmth, fullness, and caramel candy sweetness emerge with food; this beer doesn't identify its intentions, resulting in some uncertainty about what to expect.

YOUNG'S WINTER ALE (annual)   CB   4.0–4.3
(London, England)

Pungent chocolatey burnt-caramel taste with accompanying aroma; smooth; its complexity achieves a nice balance; gentle medium head; retains warmth at the end; improves as you drink it; a tad too watery. Match this with spicy foods.

YOUNGER'S TARTAN SPECIAL ALE   CB   4.1
(Edinburgh, Scotland)

Yeast-wine aroma is followed by a deep yeasty flavor that's close to divine; moderate carbonation plays nicely against a smooth, easygoing texture; malt, hops, and yeast are all used in balance and moderation; caramel in the malt emerges gently at the appropriate time at mid-bottle; alcohol is present and creeps up on you before you know it; a good, carefully calibrated ale that presents itself shyly and subtly. Drink with strong-flavored meat or cheese.

YUCHAN Pilsener   CB   4.0
(Beijing, China)

Nice rice influence; malt and hops are secondary; very tasty, alone as well as with poultry; invigorating and appealing; helps work up the appetite; enjoyment is primary; try this, if you can find it. Not surprisingly, a good match with Chinese food, but also tasty with Western-style chicken and vegetable main courses.

YUENGLING PORTER   CB   4.1
(Pottsville, Pennsylvania)

Airy; moderately bold, with slightly less body than it should have; pleasant subdued roasted flavor, especially in the finish; mellow, warm, and comforting; delightful and satisfying. Quite drinkable on its own, but also compatible with seafood.

YUENGLING TRADITIONAL LAGER   CB   3.3
(Pottsville, Pennsylvania)

Crisp and cold on the roof of the mouth, with a quick malt rush; pleasant, somewhat prickly fizziness; malt flavor is sweet and well balanced against the unobtrusive hops; smooth, yet with a certain roughness; slightly and nicely chewy; label proclaims "Original Amber Beer." Good with spicy Chinese or Indian rice dishes.

BEER FACT

*Y*uengling, still family-owned, is America's oldest brewery. Operations began in 1829.

ZAGORKA LAGER   CB   0.9
(Zagora, Bulgaria)

Sterile and flat on first sip; slightly rancid-tasting; so uncomplex as to be uniform in taste, texture, and lack of appeal; hint of fruitiness relieves, but doesn't excuse, tedium at the end.

ZAMBEZI PREMIUM EXPORT LAGER   CB   2.5
(Zimbabwe)

Somewhat crisp and tart; not much fizz or zestiness; becomes more full-bodied as you drink it; malt finally offers a charming sweetness, though the aftertaste is musty and lingers too long; no head; faded golden body; overall, reminiscent of a commercial American pilsener, but with more character; tries very hard to be a good companion. Brewed for cooling off in the shade.

ZHUJIANG Lager   CB   2.9
(Guangzhou, China)

Tart, slightly honey-flavored, and crisp; full and rounded, with a solid core; soothing and mellow; feels silky around the edges; nice network of grains helps increasingly flat texture return some interest; roughly, rather than delicately, balanced; a lot of yin and yang in this brew, but in the end a bit too thickishly sweet. Compatible with seafood pasta.

ZIEGENBOCK AMBER BEER   CB   2.6
(Houston, Texas)

Puckering at first; then settles down into a predictable, uncomplicated mouthfeel that doesn't vary from sip to sip; carefully distributed malt flavor flows generously in and around the mild hoppiness; the overall effect, however, is similar to strong water; steady as she goes; dryness in the mouth at the end; a beer that aims to suit every taste.

ZIPFER PREMIUM MALT LIQUOR   CB   3.2
(Vienna, Austria)

Lots of mouth sensations with this one: high carbonation level, sharp, and quite bitter; things calm down and sweeten somewhat after two or three sips; decreased effervescence, too; tasty sweet bitter balance is achieved at mid-bottle; clearly uses quality ingredients to best advantage; finishes less sharp, but still engages your interest; nicely done. Good accompaniment to a sausage or premium-quality hot dog.

ZYWIEC FULL LIGHT Pilsener   CB   1.5
(Zywiec, Poland)
Slightly cloying honey-like texture with matching aftertaste; bland; no fizziness—just flat throughout; slight sharpness comes along at mid-bottle; lacks depth and complexity; rather watery; finishes with some warmth; overall, unexciting and uninviting.

NONALCOHOLIC BREWS FOR THE DESIGNATED DRIVER

There were skeptics in 1989 when major breweries like Budweiser and Miller jumped into the nonalcoholic beer market. But sales immediately shot skyward: The year after nonalcoholic brews were introduced as major players, total sales leaped 90%, representing 1% of all beer industry sales. Those figures have changed little over the past several years, but there are now more players.

Truth be told, there is nothing new about nonalcoholic brews; they've been around commercially for at least 60 years (and, it is certain, for far longer than that—millennia, say—as even a brief historical review of homebrewing and cultural attitudes toward alcohol will reveal). Two leading European brands, Beck's Haake-Beck and Heineken's Buckler, have been available for more than half a century.

In the United States, Cincinnati's Hudepohl Brewing Company introduced Pace Pilsner in 1983, marking the debut of the first nonalcoholic brew. At present, there are upwards of forty on the market. Required by U.S. law to be labeled "brew," they contain no more than 0.5% alcohol by weight, which is the legal definition of nonalcoholic. Otherwise, the ingredients are the same as those found in beer.

In this section I have rated some of the legally designated "brews" on the market, as well as a type of nonalcoholic beverage not generally featured in this country: malt beverages. Popular in South America, malt beverages contain no alcohol at all and

> **NOTE:** These brews are ranked in comparison to one another; the ratings should not be compared with those given to beers that contain alcohol.

can properly be enjoyed by designated drivers—or anyone else interested in beer-like flavor and complexity without having to bother with the effects of fermentation. In fact, commercially produced nonalcoholic brews in this country must be identified as malt beverages on the label.

BAVARIA MALT BEVERAGE   **CB**   **3.3**
(Lieshout, Holland)
Sharp all over the mouth, and grainy as well; restrained textural mouthfeel maintains its edge from sip to swallow; moderate bitterness compensates for the lack of alcohol; well-placed hit of

malt in the background significantly adds to the pleasure; stays relatively complex for a nonalcoholic brew; remains tasty until the last drop; a good choice.

BITBURGER DRIVE ALKOHOLFREI   CB   3.8
(Bitburg, Germany)

Grainy, bitter, and dry—all nicely calibrated and balanced; bitterness diminishes gracefully on the roof of the mouth; there is a purity of flavor, with a clean, thin mouthfeel that is complemented by the ongoing right-off-the-vine Concord grape aroma; pale blond body has substance and character; almost chewy at the end; a very decent nonalcoholic brew.

BUCKLER   CB   2.2
(brewed by Heineken in Amsterdam, Holland)

Tingly mouthfeel with fullness on the tongue and on the roof of the mouth; sharper and less sweet than many of the others; becomes one-dimensional and flat with spicy foods; turns bland and somewhat old-tasting on the palate; like weak tea at the end.

CERVEJA CHEERS   CB   3.5
(Leca do Balio, Portugal)

Like a freshly mowed front yard, Cheers has a charming alive-in-the-morning grassy aroma and taste; with moderate effervescence, it presents a fuller, more finished mouthfeel than many other nonalcoholic brews; strong grainy flavor doesn't weaken or diminish; intermingling of malt and grain produces an unusually interesting approach to the style.

CERVEJA PRETA DOCE   CB   2.8
(Ponta Delgada, Azores)

This entry is deeply imbued with molasses aroma and flavor, but more overwhelmingly so than you've ever experienced; very, very sweet; more like a food item than a beer; overtones of corn, as in corn syrup; rich mahogany color reinforces the chewy, almost succulent taste; no hint of hops, but plenty of malt; tread carefully with this one, but if you want something unusual, this is it.

CLAUSTHALER   CB   3.8
(Frankfurt, Germany)

Sharp maltiness with suggestion of hop bitterness; flat and texturally uninvigorating; maintains flavor and integrates ingredients in a more unified package than many other brews; malty aroma is present even with strongly flavored or spicy foods; blond color with a hint of ruby; more filling and more beer-like than the others, though still far from the real thing; mildly hoppy finish adds to this brew's distinctiveness.

COORS NON-ALCOHOLIC   CB   2.2
(Golden, Colorado)

Appealing malt-grain mouthfeel, particularly on upper palate;

graininess effortlessly wends its way along, with nothing else available to intrude; noisily effervescent; light in taste and color; warms and sweetens at the end; not a total waste of your money.

EXTRACTO DE MALTA
MALT BEVERAGE   CB   3.9
(Hamburg, Germany)
Rich chocolatey flavor reminiscent of a malted or milk shake; pungent malty aroma with attenuated sweetness; accompanying bitterness is nicely tuned and balanced; flavor level is maintained with or without food; in the end, lacking fermentation, any oomph is overwhelmed by thick mouthfeel and soda-fountain character (syrupy viscosity); heavily hopped; comes within drinking distance of real beer.

FIRESTONE   CB   1.8
(Los Olivas, California)
Nicely balanced hop and malt character with onrushing crispness; while it maintains some backbone, it also exudes an off-putting harshness; malty aroma at the end, with a weak tea finish.

HAAKE BECK   CB   3.5
(Bremen, Germany)
Fresh and invigorating; honeyed maltiness with a touch of hops doesn't allow sweetness to go too far; retains firmness and consistency missing from some other brews; maintains pleasantly beer-like presence with food; small bubbles make the head interfere with the taste of the light-golden body; fades a bit at the end.

HAMM'S NA   CB   2.5
(Milwaukee, Wisconsin)
Hoppy; some texture, but quickly surfacing flat taste on the roof of the mouth; faint sourness threads its way throughout; eventually tastes similar to a ballpark pilsener; tastes more like real Hamm's than any of the other brews taste like their alcoholic counterparts; a nonalcoholic brew with some pizzazz.

HENNINGER GERSTEL BRAU   CB   3.4
(Frankfurt, Germany)
Faintly bitter, with a complementary dose of graininess; filled with flavor, at least in the context of a nonalcoholic brew; not very complex; moderate amount of staccato sharpness on the tongue makes up, somewhat, for the lack of alcohol; thick, foamy head nicely caps the pale-straw body; above average for the category.

KALIBER   CB   2.8
(brewed in London, England, for Guinness)
Tasty and highly malty; pleasantly attractive, clean, mid-range golden color; becomes very watery with most foods; mild honey sweetness; emerging honey and malt integration suggests this

brew should be imbibed alone or with relatively bland food; malt finish lingers on the roof of the mouth.

MALTA GOYA (non-alcoholic)   CB   1.1
(Wilkes-Barre, Pennsylvania)

Full-bore molasses-sweet taste arrives on a silky smooth, brown-black body; lots of corn taste, too; pushy flavor finds every crevice in the mouth and stays there; overwhelming character is much too much of a good thing; too strong and overpowering; if you like this sort of brew, a sip or two will do just fine.

MALTINA   CB   3.4
(Lima, Peru)

Burnt-caramel taste is not unpleasant; deep, deep brown, almost black color; silky smooth and pleasantly sweet; solid textural ebb and flow; malt is restrained and slightly bitter; complements and surrounds food in a gentle cocoon of softness; sweetness has the potential to become overpowering after two or three glasses; thickens on the tongue; without fermentation, its potential is not reached.

MOLSON EXEL   CB   3.3
(Vancouver, British Columbia, Canada)

Grainy, almost coffee-flavored; fuller taste than many other non-alcoholic brews; smells a little like soap; turns mildly sour, smooths out with smoked foods; matches up to some alcoholic beers with its projection of hop and malt taste and faint beer odor—as if there actually is a small portion of real beer in there somewhere, although I wouldn't seek it out in a bar or elsewhere; finishes with mild honey presence and appealing graininess; in general, Canada seems to produce better nonalcoholic beers than does the U.S.

MORENITA MALTA   CB   2.6
(Osorno, Chile)

Soft, mushy, and on first several sips, tasteless; dark, brooding color; some warmth and presence emerge with spicy foods; plain, with a certain charm that makes you come back for more; neutral-tasting throughout; thickish at the end, with no carbonation.

MORENITA MALTA ESPECIAL   CB   3.3
(Concepcion, Chile)

Softer and sweeter, with a more chocolatey auburn color, than Morenita Malta; malts are ascendant here along with a languid, almost syrupy texture; grows into some mild grittiness at the back of the mouth, while attractive, balmy sweetness remains in front; head is only a trifle creamier than the body; perhaps a tad too sweet for comfort with most foods; a filmy aftertaste remains in the mouth after drinking most of the unusually large bottle.

N.A. PEVO CB 2.6
(Popovice, Czech Republic)
Grainy and sharp at the back of the throat; pleasant mild bitterness
easily accommodates the continuous, refreshing grain flavor; light
mouthfeel and light in texture; very sparkly, not unlike well-carbonated
club soda, complete with bitters and a twist of lemon; finishes tastefully balanced; bouncy, doughy sweetness in the aftertaste; a beer
to drink when you are thirsty. Goes with a green salad.

B E E R   F A C T

*P*rohibition in the U.S. tested the resourcefulness
of many brewers. In order to stay in business,
beer makers marketed nonalcoholic drinks and
"near-beer." Catchy brand names attracted the attention of the public: Vivo (Miller), Famo (Schlitz), Lux-
O (Stroh's). Anheuser-Busch cleverly called its brew
Pivo, which is the word for "beer" in Russian and Polish,
and very similar to the Czech term.

O'DOUL'S CB 3.1
(brewed by Anheuser-Busch in St. Louis, Missouri)
Quick pilsener feel without the usual accompanying spritzy texture; soft, foamy head is full of air, letting you get quickly to the
pale-golden, light-tasting body; mild, faint hoppiness at the back
of the throat reminds you that this is a "brew," not a beer; some
flavor emerges with food, but it's essentially one-dimensional and
not complex; possesses a core-taste solidity that others lack; Silver Medal winner at the 1993 Great American Beer Festival.

O'DOUL'S AMBER CB 3.3
(brewed by Anheuser-Busch in St. Louis, Missouri)
A noticeable hoppiness invigorates a fresh, playful aftertaste; proper
touch of caramel-sweet balance reflects the underlying maltiness;
crisp, clean, close to bold-tasting; more full-bodied and complex
than many nonalcoholic brews; finishes smooth and gentle on the
tongue; a step or two above many of the others in this category.

OTTAKRINGER NULL KOMMA
JOSEF ALKOHOLFREI CB 0.6
(Vienna, Austria)
Strong grain aroma and taste, with a sharp, disconcerting bitterness that impels the taste forward; turns too grassy too soon, giving off a mouthfeel reminiscent of undeveloped sweet peas—raw
and not yet ready for growth, much less harvesting; clear pale-
blond color; sweetens and settles heavy in the stomach; thick-
tasting; quite unappealing.

PABST NON-ALCOHOLIC
MALT BEVERAGE   CB   2.4
(Tumwater, Washington)

Light and straightforward; fresh-tasting and crisp all over the mouth; similar in character to beer served at baseball games; becomes somewhat watery at mid-bottle; agreeable and tempting; finishes with a graininess that is gentle on the palate; 1997 Great American Beer Festival Gold Medal winner in the Non-alcoholic Malt Beverages category.

PAULANER THOMAS BRAU   CB   3.3
(Munich, Germany)

Mild-tasting and not very complex; drinker-friendly honey-grain aroma is noticeable from start to finish; no carbonation of any consequence; malt-based sweetness flows quietly and gently, taking your thoughts off the fact that no alcohol is present; a rather uneventful brew, but relatively satisfying nonetheless.

RED BARON MALT BEVERAGE   CB   0.9
(Wilkes-Barre, Pennsylvania)

Cherry-flavored; very wine-like in taste, texture, and mouthfeel; not fizzy at all; almost like liquid Jell-O, but not as sweet; clearly a before-dinner drink; not complex; simple and uninteresting.

SCHLOSS JOSEF ALSATIAN
MALT BEVERAGE   CB   3.1
(Schutzenberg, France)

Quite malty and light-tasting; relatively zestless, it obviously lacks alcohol; tiny, fizzy bubbles provide visual interest through the straw-colored body; grainy and noticeably intense with fast foods like a cheeseburger or chicken sticks; finishes smooth and warm; moderately flavorful, this is an above-average nonalcoholic brew; available only at Trader Joe's specialty food stores.

SCHLOSSGOLD ALKOHOLARMES
BIER   CB   3.4
(Linz, Austria)

From start to finish, the light grainy aroma and strong grainy taste define the main characteristics of this unchanging light-golden malt beverage; refreshing, easy to drink, and not filling; gradual increase of restrained but tasty maltiness; has a whipped-cream-like rocky head; finishes sweet, with a touch of sugar at the tip of the tongue; accommodates to a variety of foods—spicy, bland, or in-between.

SHARP'S   CB   0.8
(brewed by Miller in Milwaukee, Wisconsin)

Fruity, vaguely citrus taste with minimum texture; no significant malt or hop presence; flavor goes flat early on, as does the head; more like a cross between lemon juice and a fruit-flavored soda;

cereal grain provides some sweetness; finish is watery and thin, without its previous hint of graininess; tastes and feels empty.

ST. PAULI   CB   2.8
(Bremen, Germany)
Incredible, almost overpowering malt aroma quickly followed by pronounced honey taste; medium-bodied but very flat; honey flavor continues throughout, with no hops or, of course, alcoholic counterbalance; malt texture remains, especially at the back of the throat; lacks complexity; watery base with visible flecks of grain sprinkled throughout; in the end, the taste is superior to the texture (none), color (wispy blond), and aroma (quickly fading).

TEXAS LIGHT DARK   CT   2.4
(San Antonio, Texas)
Rather grainy, with a close-to-oat taste that is strong and direct and, of course, not interfered with by any alcohol; roughness on the tongue adds to its charm; somewhat lifeless without the alcohol; not much more than the grain taste and occasional glimpses of malt; deep brown body with shades of orange and red; finishes with a nutty aroma that leaves a fond farewell.

TEXAS SELECT   CB   0.3
(San Antonio, Texas)
Very light, very weak, very uninteresting—and that's just the beginning; sour and unpleasantly musty; corn presence predominates, resulting in an overwhelmingly pallid grainy taste and ambiance; degenerates into dirty-water mouthfeel with food; some feistiness, but the effort is not worth it.

UPPER CANADA POINT NINE   CB   2.9
(Toronto, Ontario, Canada)
Musty and very grainy-tasting, with honey overtones; subdued but pervasive hop presence; more full-bodied than other nonalcoholic beers, with a corresponding degree of complexity; substantial hop taste stays throughout, making up in strength and punch for the lowered alcohol content; aroma is sweeter and pleasanter than the flavor, which retains a rough, unpolished mouthfeel; distinctive and curiously appealing—finishes with a malted milk or milk shake taste.

WARSTEINER PREMIUM FRESH   CB   3.9
(Warstein, Germany)
Complex, sharp, and grainy, reminiscent of its big-sibling Warsteiner Premium Verum, the one *with* alcohol; slight bitterness; dry and lightly malted; faint citrus taste is unusual for a nonalcoholic brew; highly effervescent; delightful aroma of freshly mowed grass at the finish. A good thirst-quencher to have along with light summer fare.

APPENDIXES

BEERS BY STATE: AN ALPHABETICAL LISTING

NAME	LOCATION	RATING	STYLE
ALASKA			
Alaskan Amber	Juneau	3.8	Alt
Alaskan Frontier American Amber Ale	Juneau	0.7	Ale
Alaskan Pale Ale	Juneau	1.0	Ale
Midnight Sun Fireweed Honey Wheat Beer	Anchorage	1.9	Wht
ARIZONA			
Ballyard Brown Ale	Phoenix	2.5	Ale
Bandersnatch Big Horn Premium Ale	Tempe	3.4	Ale
Bandersnatch Milk Stout	Tempe	4.0	Sto
Bandersnatch Pale Ale	Tempe	1.8	Ale
Cougan's Marzen	Glendale	2.2	Mar
Cougan's Porter	Glendale	2.6	Por
Crazy Ed's Original Chili Beer	Cave Creek	0.6	Lag
Crazy Ed's Black Mountain Gold	Cave Creek	2.5	Lag
Dark Mountain Porter	Vail	1.4	Por
Four Peaks Scottish Amber Ale	Tempe	1.1	Ale
Gentle Ben's Copperhead Ale	Tucson	0.6	Ale
Gentle Ben's MacBlane's Oatmeal Stout	Tucson	2.2	Sto
Gentle Ben's Red Cat Amber	Tucson	2.3	Ale
Gentle Ben's TJ's Raspberry	Tucson	2.4	Ale
Hops Amber Ale	Scottsdale	2.4	Ale
Hops Bock	Scottsdale	3.1	Boc
Hops Pilsner	Scottsdale	3.2	Pil
Hops Wheat	Scottsdale	2.3	Wht
Mogollon Superstition Pale Ale	Flagstaff	2.0	Ale
Mogollon Wapiti Amber Ale	Flagstaff	2.9	Ale
Uptown Claymore Scottish Ale	Tempe	3.2	Ale
Uptown IPA	Tempe	3.8	Ipa
CALIFORNIA			
Acme Pale Ale	Fort Bragg	1.4	Ale
Alpine Village Hofbrau Lager	Torrance	2.3	Lag
Alpine Village Hofbrau Pilsner	Torrance	2.3	Pil
Anchor Liberty Ale	San Francisco	3.7	Ale
Anchor Old Foghorn Ale	San Francisco	3.4	Ale

NAME	LOCATION	RATING	STYLE
ANCHOR OUR SPECIAL ALE (ANNUAL)	SAN FRANCISCO	2.5–4.0	ALE
ANCHOR STEAM	SAN FRANCISCO	3.9	STM
ANCHOR WHEAT	SAN FRANCISCO	3.8	WHT
ANDERSON VALLEY BARNEY FLATS OATMEAL STOUT	BOONVILLE	4.0	STO
ANDERSON VALLEY DEEP ENDERS DARK PORTER	BOONVILLE	3.8	POR
ANDERSON VALLEY HIGH ROLLERS WHEAT	BOONVILLE	3.6	WHT
ANDERSON VALLEY POLEEKO GOLD LIGHT ALE	BOONVILLE	3.7	ALE
ARROGANT BASTARD ALE	SAN MARCOS	2.3	ALE
BEAR REPUBLIC HEFEWEIZEN	HEALDSBERG	3.3	WHT
BELMONT LONG BEACH CRUDE	LONG BEACH	2.1	POR
BELMONT MARATHON WHEAT ALE	LONG BEACH	1.8	WHT
BELMONT STRAWBERRY BLONDE	LONG BEACH	2.2	ALE
BELMONT TOP SAIL ALE	LONG BEACH	2.8	ALE
BISON CHOCOLATE STOUT	BERKELEY	2.1	STO
BUCKHORN BOCK	TORRANCE	1.6	BOC
CALIFORNIA LIGHT BLONDE ALE	TORRANCE	0.0	ALE
COAST RANGE MERRY MAKER ALE	GILROY	1.5	ALE
DRAKE'S ALE	SAN LEANDRO	2.1	ALE
FIRESTONE	LOS OLIVAS	1.8	NA
FIRESTONE DOUBLE BARREL ALE	LOS OLIVOS	2.6	ALE
HE'BREW GENESIS ALE	BOONVILLE	0.8	ALE
HOPPY HOLIDAZE FLAVORED ALE (ANNUAL)	LARKSPUR	2.8	ALE
HUBSCH LAGER	DAVIS	1.4	LAG
HUBSCH MARZEN	DAVIS	2.4	MLT
HUMBOLDT PALE ALE	ARCATA	2.1	ALE
HUMBOLDT RED NECTAR ALE	ARCATA	2.8	ALE
JAMAICA BRAND RED ALE	BLUE LAKE	3.3	ALE
JAMAICA BRAND SUNSET INDIA PALE ALE	BLUE LAKE	1.1	IPA
JOHN BARLEYCORN BARLEY WINE STYLE ALE	BLUE LAKE	3.0	BAR
JUMPING COW AMBER ALE	PASO ROBLES	2.3	ALE
KARL STRAUSS AMBER LAGER	SAN DIEGO	2.9	LAG
KARL STRAUSS BLACK'S BEACH EXTRA DARK PORTER	SAN DIEGO	4.0	POR
KARL STRAUSS DOWNTOWN AFTER DARK BROWN ALE	SAN DIEGO	3.3	ALE
KARL STRAUSS GAS LAMP GOLD ALE	SAN DIEGO	2.7	ALE

NAME	LOCATION	RATING	STYLE
KARL STRAUSS PORT LOMA LIGHTHOUSE LITE LAGER	SAN DIEGO	1.1	LAG
KARL STRAUSS RED TROLLEY ALE	SAN DIEGO	3.1	ALE
KB AUSTRALIAN LAGER	MENDOCINO	2.9	LAG
LAGUNITAS DOG TOWN PALE ALE	PETALUMA	3.4	ALE
LIND RASPBERRY WHEAT	SAN LEANDRO	0.9	WHT
LOS GATOS OKTOBERFEST (SEASONAL)	LOS GATOS	0.1	ALE
LOST COAST DOWNTOWN BROWN ALE	EUREKA	3.2	ALE
LOST COAST STOUT	EUREKA	3.3	STO
MAGNOLIA SPUD BOY IPA	SAN FRANCISCO	3.5	IPA
MAGNOLIA THUNDERPUSSY BARLEYWINE	SAN FRANCISCO	3.9	BAR
MANHATTAN BEACH BOHEMIAN PILSNER	MANHATTAN BEACH	2.5	PIL
MANHATTAN BEACH HOPHEAD IPA	MANHATTAN BEACH	2.6	IPA
MARIN OLD DIPSEA BARLEYWINE STYLE ALE	LARKSPUR	3.0	ALE
MENDOCINO BLACK HAWK STOUT	HOPLAND	3.4	STO
MENDOCINO RED TAIL ALE	HOPLAND	2.3	ALE
MENDOCINO YULETIDE PORTER (SEASONAL)	HOPLAND	2.5	POR
MOONLIGHT TWIST OF FATE BITTER ALE	WINDSOR	3.3	ALE
MOYLAN'S INDIA PALE ALE	NOVATO	2.9	IPA
NAPA VALLEY RED ALE	NAPA	3.5	ALE
NORTH COAST BLUE STAR GREAT AMERICAN WHEAT	FORT BRAGG	2.3	WHT
NORTH COAST OKTOBERFEST ALE	FORT BRAGG	0.8	ALE
NORTH COAST OLD NO. 38 STOUT	FORT BRAGG	3.1	STO
NORTH COAST RED SEAL ALE	FORT BRAGG	2.4	ALE
OLD RASPUTIN RUSSIAN IMPERIAL STOUT	FORT BRAGG	3.1	STO
OLDE RED EYE RED ALE	TORRANCE	0.4	ALE
PRIMO	VAN NUYS	2.2	LAG
RAZOR EDGE LAGER	UKIAH	2.5	LAG
RECCOW T'MAVE	SAN FRANCISCO	2.5	LAG
RHINO CHASERS AMBER ALE	CHATSWORTH	3.7	ALE
RHINO CHASERS AMERICAN ALE	CHATSWORTH	2.2	ALE
RHINO CHASERS LAGER	CHATSWORTH	3.7	LAG
RIVERSIDE 7TH STREET STOUT	RIVERSIDE	3.1	STO
RIVERSIDE GOLDEN SPIKE PILSNER	RIVERSIDE	0.9	PIL
RIVERSIDE PULLMAN PALE ALE	RIVERSIDE	2.4	ALE
RIVERSIDE RAINCROSS CREAM ALE	RIVERSIDE	0.5	ALE

NAME	LOCATION	RATING	STYLE
SACRAMENTO RED HORSE ALE	SACRAMENTO & CITRUS HTS	3.3	ALE
SAMUEL ADAMS TRIPLE BOCK	CERES	4.7	BOC
SAN ANDRES EARTHQUAKE PALE ALE	HOLLISTER	3.0	ALE
SAN ANDRES KIT FOX AMBER	HOLLISTER	1.1	ALE
SAN ANDRES SEISMIC ALE	HOLLISTER	1.8	ALE
SANTA BARBARA PACIFIC PALE ALE	SANTA BARBARA	2.9	ALE
SANTA BARBARA RINCON RED ALE	SANTA BARBARA	2.6	ALE
SANTA CRUZ LIGHTHOUSE AMBER	SANTA CRUZ	1.1	LAG
SANTA CRUZ LIGHTHOUSE LAGER	SANTA CRUZ	0.3	LAG
SEABRIGHT BANTY ROOSTER IPA	SANTA CRUZ	2.4	IPA
SIERRA NEVADA BIGFOOT BARLEY WINE STYLE ALE (ANNUAL)	CHICO	0.2–1.3	BAR
SIERRA NEVADA CELEBRATION ALE (ANNUAL)	CHICO	2.3–3.9	ALE
SIERRA NEVADA PALE ALE	CHICO	3.2	ALE
SIERRA NEVADA PALE BOCK	CHICO	2.5	BOC
SIERRA NEVADA PORTER	CHICO	2.6	POR
SIERRA NEVADA STOUT	CHICO	2.5	STO
SIERRA NEVADA SUMMERFEST (ANNUAL)	CHICO	3.5–3.8	ALE
SLO GARDEN ALLEY AMBER ALE	PASO ROBLES & SAN LUIS OBISPO	2.4	ALE
SOLANA BEACH PIZZA PORTS PORTER	SOLANA BEACH	2.8	POR
SPENCES PALE ALE	CHATSWORTH	2.2	ALE
ST. STAN'S AMBER ALT	MODESTO	3.8	ALT
ST. STAN'S DARK ALT	MODESTO	3.9	ALT
ST. STAN'S FEST BIER	MODESTO	3.5	ALT
ST. STAN'S GRAFFITI WHEAT	MODESTO	1.9	WHT
STEELHEAD EXTRA PALE ALE	BLUE LAKE	3.3	ALE
STONE PALE ALE	SAN MARCOS	2.6	ALE
VICTORIA AVENUE AMBER ALE— SCOTTISH ALE	RIVERSIDE	3.8	ALE
WOLAVER'S BROWN ALE	FORT BRAGG	2.9	ALE
COLORADO			
BOULDER PALE ALE	BOULDER	3.6	ALE
BOULDER PORTER	BOULDER	2.7	POR
BOULDER STOUT	BOULDER	2.2	STO
BRECKENRIDGE AVALANCHE AMBER	BRECKENRIDGE	0.4	ALE
BRECKENRIDGE CHRISTMAS ALE (ANNUAL)	DENVER	4.0	ALE
BRECKENRIDGE INDIA PALE ALE	DENVER	2.4	IPA
BUFFALO GOLD PREMIUM ALE	BOULDER	2.9	ALE

NAME	LOCATION	RATING	STYLE
Carver Iron Horse Stout	Durango	2.6	Sto
Carver Old Oak Amber Ale	Durango	2.5	Ale
Carver Raspberry Wheat	Durango	0.5	Wht
Coopersmith's Albert Damm Bitter	Fort Collins	3.0	Ale
Coopersmith's Christmas Ale	Fort Collins	3.2	Ale
Coopersmith's Horsetooth Stout	Fort Collins	4.0	Sto
Coopersmith's Imperial Stout	Fort Collins	3.0	Sto
Coopersmith's Mountain Avenue Wheat	Fort Collins	1.8	Wht
Coopersmith's Not Brown Ale	Fort Collins	2.7	Ale
Coopersmith's Poudre Ale	Fort Collins	2.4	Ale
Coopersmith's Punjabi India Pale Ale	Fort Collins	3.8	Ipa
Coopersmith's Sigda's Green Chile	Fort Collins	2.2	Ale
Coors	Golden	1.4	Pil
Coors Extra Gold	Golden	1.8	Pil
Coors Non-Alcoholic	Golden	2.2	Na
Coors Winterfest (annual)	Golden	3.1	Lag
Crested Butte Red Lady Ale	Crested Butte	2.3	Ale
Durango Dark	Durango	2.7	Lag
Flying Dog Doggie Style Ale	Denver	1.9	Ale
Golden City Centurion Barleywine Ale	Golden	0.2	Bar
Great Divide Saint Brigid's Porter	Denver	2.9	Por
H.C. Berger Red Raspberry Wheat Ale	Fort Collins	2.6	Wht
H.C. Berger Whistlepin Wheat Ale	Fort Collins	2.7	Wht
Hubcap Razzle Dazzle Berry	Vail	1.0	Ale
Il Vicino Wet Mountain India Pale Ale	Salida	3.3	Ipa
Ironworks Condor Lager	Lakewood	2.0	Lag
Keystone	Golden	0.9	Pil
Killian's Red Ale	Golden	2.0	Ale
New Belgium Abbey Belgian Style Ale	Fort Collins	4.1	Ale
New Belgium Blue Paddle Pilsener	Fort Collins	3.8	Pil
New Belgium Fat Tire Amber Ale	Fort Collins	3.9	Ale

NAME	LOCATION	RATING	STYLE
Oasis Capstone Esb	Boulder	3.3	Esb
Oasis Pale Ale	Boulder	2.5	Ale
Odell 90 Shilling Ale	Fort Collins	3.7	Ale
Odell Curmudgon's Nip Barley Wine	Fort Collins	2.2	Bar
Odell Easy Street Wheat	Fort Collins	3.7	Wht
Odell Levity Ale	Fort Collins	2.8	Ale
Pasquini's Red Ale	Denver	3.8	Ale
Rockies Buffalo Gold Premium Ale	Boulder	3.7	Ale
Tabernash Amber Colorado Lager	Longmont	2.5	Lag
Tabernash Weiss	Longmont	3.0	Wht
Tommyknocker Pick Axe Pale Ale	Idaho Springs	3.7	Ale
Tommyknocker Red Eye Lager	Idaho Springs	3.9	Lag
Wrigley Red	Boulder	2.8	Ale
Wynkoop Bock	Denver	4.0	Boc
Wynkoop Irish Cream Stout	Denver	3.0	Sto
Wynkoop Jed Fest	Denver	3.7	Lag
CONNECTICUT			
Hammer & Nail American Ale	Watertown	3.4	Ale
Hammer & Nail Extra Special Bitter Ale	Watertown	3.7	Ale
New England Atlantic Amber	Norwalk	3.1	Alt
New England Holiday Ale	Norwalk	4.0	Ale
Olde Wyndham Frog 'n Hound Cream Ale	Willimantic	2.3	Ale
DELAWARE			
Dogfish Head Chicory Stout	Rehoboth Beach	3.2	Sto
Dogfish Head Shelter Pale Ale	Rehoboth Beach	1.4	Ale
FLORIDA			
Firehouse Key Lime Wheat	Miami	2.8	Wht
Firehouse Pilsener	Miami	0.2	Pil
Indian River Amberjack Alt	Melbourne	2.2	Alt
Kelly's Havana Red Ale	Key West	2.4	Ale
Kelly's Southern Clipper Wheat	Key West	0.7	Wht
Key West Lager	Key West	0.4	Lag
Key West Sunset Ale	Key West	2.2	Ale
Sarasota Ipa	Sarasota	2.5	Ipa
Steel Reserve 211 High Gravity Lager	Tampa	2.5	Lag
Studley Ale	Fernandina Beach	0.0	Ale

NAME	LOCATION	RATING	STYLE
TAMPA BAY OATMEAL STOUT	TAMPA	0.8	STO
WILLIAMSVILLE BORDER PORTER	FERNANDINA	3.5	POR
YBOR BROWN ALE	TAMPA	3.0	ALE
GEORGIA			
DOGWOOD WHEAT	ATLANTA	3.0	WHT
RED BRICK ALE	ATLANTA	2.4	ALE
SWEETWATER EXODUS PORTER	ATLANTA	0.4	POR
HAWAII			
KONA PACIFIC GOLDEN ALE	KAILUA-KONA	2.6	ALE
IDAHO			
SUN VALLEY GOLD LAGER	HAILEY	0.5	LAG
SUN VALLEY HOLIDAY ALE	HAILEY	3.9	ALE
SUN VALLEY WHITE CLOUD ALE	HAILEY	3.8	ALE
ILLINOIS			
FLOSSMOOR STATION IMPERIAL ECLIPSE STOUT	FLOSSMOOR	3.4	STO
GOOSE ISLAND DUNKEL WEIZEN BOCK	CHICAGO	2.2	BOC
GOOSE ISLAND HONKERS ALE	CHICAGO	2.7	ALE
GOOSE ISLAND MILD ALE	CHICAGO	2.9	ALE
OLD CHICAGO LAGER	CHICAGO	1.2	LAG
INDIANA			
BAD FROG ORIGINAL LAGER	EVANSVILLE	1.4	LAG
BROAD RIPPLE EXTRA SPECIAL BITTER	INDIANAPOLIS	2.6	ALE
COOK'S GOLDBLUME	EVANSVILLE	0.5	LAG
DUESSELDORFER PALE ALE	INDIANAPOLIS	2.9	ALE
GERST AMBER	EVANSVILLE	3.2	LAG
GRINGO EXTRA LAGER	EVANSVILLE	0.8	LAG
MAGNUM MALT LIQUOR	FORT WAYNE	0.7	MLT
MISHAWAKA HOP HEAD ALE IV	MISHAWAKA	3.3	ALE
SCORPION MALT LIQUOR	EVANSVILLE	2.4	MLT
STERLING	EVANSVILLE	1.5	PIL
IOWA			
ALIMONY ALE	DUBUQUE	3.9	ALE
BUFFALO BILL'S PUMPKIN ALE	DUBUQUE	2.4	ALE
CHERRYLAND CHERRY RAIL LAGER	DUBUQUE	2.9	LAG
CHERRYLAND GOLDEN RAIL LAGER	DUBUQUE	2.8	LAG
CHERRYLAND SILVER RAIL LAGER	DUBUQUE	2.2	LAG
DARRYL'S PREMIUM LAGER	DUBUQUE	2.6	LAG
JOHN'S GENERATIONS WHITE ALE	SOLON	2.9	WHT
MILLSTREAM LAGER	AMANA	3.8	LAG
MILLSTREAM SCHILD BRAU AMBER	AMANA	2.7	LAG
MILLSTREAM WHEAT	AMANA	0.3	WHT

NAME	LOCATION	RATING	STYLE
SIMPATICO AMBER	DUBUQUE	2.4	LAG
SIMPATICO GOLDEN LAGER	DUBUQUE	1.2	LAG
STONE CITY MANSION STOUT	SOLON	2.9	STO
STONE CITY STONE BLUFF PILS	SOLON	0.9	PIL
TRESTLES LAGER	DUBUQUE	1.0	LAG
WILD BOAR SPECIAL AMBER	DUBUQUE	2.2	LAG
KANSAS			
FLYING MONKEY AMBER ALE	MERRIAM	2.0	ALE
FLYING MONKEY PALE ALE	MERRIAM	2.1	ALE
FLYING MONKEY WHEAT BEER	MERRIAM	1.3	WHT
FREE STATE OATMEAL STOUT	LAWRENCE	1.2	STO
PONY EXPRESS HONEY BLONDE ALE	OLATHE	0.7	ALE
PONY EXPRESS NUT BROWN ALE	OLATHE	2.6	ALE
PONY EXPRESS RATTLESNAKE PALE ALE	OLATHE	1.6	ALE
PURGATORY PORTER	WICHITA	2.4	POR
75TH STREET ROYAL RASPBERRY WHEAT	OLATHE	3.3	WHT
KENTUCKY			
BLUEGRASS HELL FOR CERTAIN BELGIAN SPECIAL ALE	LOUISVILLE	0.4	ALE
OLDENBERG PIOUS PALE ALE	FORT MITCHELL	2.5	ALE
OLDENBERG PREMIUM VERUM	FORT MITCHELL	2.6	LAG
THE SPIRIT OF ST. LOUIS ALE	FORT MITCHELL	1.6	ALE
LOUISIANA			
ABITA AMBER	ABITA SPRINGS	2.6	LAG
ABITA GOLDEN	ABITA SPRINGS	2.3	LAG
ABITA IRISH RED ALE	ABITA SPRINGS	1.4	ALE
ABITA TURBO DOG	ABITA SPRINGS	3.8	ALE
ACADIAN VIENNA AMBER	NEW ORLEANS	3.2	LAG
DIXIE	NEW ORLEANS	3.5	LAG
DIXIE BLACKENED VOODOO LAGER	NEW ORLEANS	2.4	LAG
DIXIE CRIMSON VOODOO RED ALE	NEW ORLEANS	2.3	ALE
MAINE			
ALLAGASH WHITE	PORTLAND	3.6	WHT
GEARY'S LONDON STYLE PORTER	PORTLAND	3.0	POR
GEARY'S PALE ALE	PORTLAND	2.4	ALE
GRITTY MCDUFF'S BEST BITTER	PORTLAND	2.3	ALE
HAMPSHIRE SPECIAL ALE (ANNUAL)	PORTLAND	2.4	ALE
MAGIC HAT NOT QUITE PALE ALE	PORTLAND	2.4	ALE
MAGIC HAT RED ALE	PORTLAND	2.4	ALE
OLD THUMPER EXTRA SPECIAL ALE	KENNEBUNK	2.5	ALE
SEA DOG BROWN ALE	BANGOR	2.5	ALE

NAME	LOCATION	RATING	STYLE
SEA DOG WINDJAMMER			
BLONDE ALE	BANGOR	3.8	ALE
SHIPYARD BROWN ALE	KENNEBUNK & PORTLAND	2.5	ALE
MARYLAND			
BLUE RIDGE HOPFEST			
BROWN ALE	FREDERICK	3.9	ALE
BLUE RIDGE SNOWBALL'S CHANCE	FREDERICK	2.4	ALE
BLUE RIDGE SUNRAGE			
SOUR MASH	FREDERICK	2.0	ALE
BREWER'S ALLEY MAIBOCK	FREDERICK	2.7	BOC
BRIMSTONE HONEY RED ALE	BALTIMORE	2.6	ALE
BRIMSTONE RASPBERRY PORTER	BALTIMORE	1.9	POR
CLIPPER CITY INDIA PALE ALE	BALTIMORE	0.7	IPA
DEEP CREEK GOLDEN ALE	FREDERICK	0.2	ALE
DEEP CREEK YOUGHIOGHENY			
RED AMBER ALE	FREDERICK	1.1	ALE
DEGROEN'S PILS	BALTIMORE	1.1	PIL
DEGROEN'S WEIZEN	BALTIMORE	2.4	WHT
HATUEY	BALTIMORE	2.3	LAG
MOJO HIGHWAY GOLDEN ALE	FREDERICK	3.3	ALE
OLIVER'S SCOTTISH ALE	BALTIMORE	2.2	ALE
OXFORD WHITE OX WHEAT ALE	BALTIMORE	3.2	WHT
SCHMIDT'S	BALTIMORE	2.4	LAG
WILD GOOSE AMBER	CAMBRIDGE	2.6	ALE
WYE RIVER BLACK CRAB BEER	BALTIMORE	0.6	LAG
MASSACHUSETTS			
BAILEY'S ALE	NANTUCKET	3.1	ALE
BERKSHIRE TRADITIONAL			
PALE ALE	SOUTH DEERFIELD	3.4	ALE
HARPOON ALE	BOSTON	2.7	ALE
HARPOON OCTOBERFEST	BOSTON	4.0	LAG
HARPOON PILSNER	BOSTON	2.2	PIL
NORTHAMPTON OLD BROWN			
DOG ALE	NORTHAMPTON	3.3	ALE
PAPER CITY CAPTAIN ELIZUR'S			
HERITAGE RED ALE	HOLYOKE	3.2	ALE
PICKWICK ALE	BOSTON	2.5	ALE
SAMUEL ADAMS OCTOBERFEST	BOSTON	3.7	LAG
TREMONT ALE	BOSTON	3.2	ALE
WATCH CITY SATURNALEA			
STRONG ALE	WALTHAM	3.4	ALE
MICHIGAN			
ALTES GOLDEN LAGER	FRANKENMUTH	1.3	LAG
BELL'S AMBER ALE	KALAMAZOO	0.0	ALE

NAME	LOCATION	RATING	STYLE
BULL ICE MALT LIQUOR	DETROIT	1.0	MLT
COLT 45 MALT LIQUOR	DETROIT	0.3	MLT
FRANKENMUTH DARK	FRANKENMUTH	3.1	LAG
FRANKENMUTH GERMAN-STYLE BOCK	FRANKENMUTH	2.4	BOC
FRANKENMUTH PILSNER	FRANKENMUTH	1.2	PIL
GOEBEL GOLDEN LAGER	DETROIT	2.1	LAG
HARD GAUGE BEER	DETROIT	0.8	LAG
KALAMAZOO TWO HEARTED ALE	KALAMAZOO	3.2	ALE
MCSORLEYS ALE	DETROIT	2.0	ALE
OLD DETROIT AMBER ALE	FRANKENMUTH	3.8	ALE
OLD MILWAUKEE	DETROIT	0.8	LAG
PERRY'S MAJESTIC LAGER	FRANKENMUTH	2.6	LAG
PIELS DRAFT	DETROIT	1.0	PIL
RED BULL MALT LIQUOR	DETROIT	1.4	MLT
SCHAEFER	DETROIT	2.3	PIL
SCHLITZ	DETROIT	1.8	LAG
STROH'S	DETROIT	2.4	LAG
TRAFFIC JAM BIKINI WHEAT ALE	DETROIT	3.0	ALE
TRAFFIC JAM COAL PORTER	DETROIT	4.0	POR
MINNESOTA			
AUGSBURGER BOCK	ST. PAUL	2.5	BOC
AUGSBURGER DARK	ST. PAUL	1.8	LAG
AUGSBURGER GOLDEN	ST. PAUL	1.1	PIL
AUGSBURGER ROT LAGER	ST. PAUL	2.3	LAG
AUGSBURGER WINTER FESTBIER	ST. PAUL	2.6	LAG
AUGUST SCHELL BOCK	NEW ULM	2.2	BOC
AUGUST SCHELL ORIGINAL DEER BRAND	NEW ULM	3.8	LAG
AUGUST SCHELL PILSNER	NEW ULM	2.8	PIL
BARLEY BOYS ED'S RED PALE ALE	ST. PAUL	2.4	ALE
BARLEY BOYS JACK'S BLACK PORTER	ST. PAUL	3.7	POR
BARLEY BOYS PHIL'S PILS	ST. PAUL	2.8	PIL
BLACK TOAD DARK ALE	ST. PAUL	1.8	ALE
GATOR LAGER	NEW ULM	2.3	LAG
GLUEK DARK BEER	COLD SPRING	2.7	PIL
GLUEK PILSNER	COLD SPRING	0.5	PIL
GRAIN BELT	ST. PAUL	2.8	LAG
JAMES PAGE IRON RANGE AMBER	MINNEAPOLIS	3.4	LAG
JAMES PAGE BOUNDARY WATERS WILD RICE BEER	MINNEAPOLIS	4.1	LAG
JUMPING COW AMBER ALE	NEW ULM	2.3	ALE
NAKED ASPEN BROWN ALE	COLD SPRING	3.3	ALE

NAME	LOCATION	RATING	STYLE
Naked Aspen Honey Wheat	Cold Spring	2.2	Wht
Pig's Eye Pilsner	St. Paul	2.5	Pil
Redding Premium Golden Ale	New Ulm	1.1	Ale
Rhino Chasers Winterful (seasonal)	St. Paul	2.5	Ale
Schmaltz's Alt Ale	New Ulm	3.3	Alt
Slo Garden Alley Amber Ale	New Ulm	2.4	Ale
Soulard Our Special Lager	Cold Spring	2.5	Lag
Spanish Peaks Black Dog Ale	New Ulm	2.5	Ale
St. Croix Maple Ale	New Ulm	2.8	Ale
Stoney Creek Lager	St. Paul	0.7	Lag
Summit Great Northern Porter	St. Paul	2.8	Por
Summit India Pale Ale	St. Paul	2.7	Ipa
Wit Black	St. Paul	3.4	Ale
Wit White/Wheat	St. Paul	3.1	Wht
MISSOURI			
Boulevard "Bully" Porter	Kansas City	3.8	Por
Boulevard Nutcracker Ale	Kansas City	2.8	Ale
Boulevard Wheat Beer	Kansas City	2.3	Wht
Budweiser	St. Louis	1.1	Pil
Busch	St. Louis	1.0	Lag
King Cobra Malt Liquor	St. Louis	2.2	Mlt
Michelob Classic Dark	St. Louis	1.8	Lag
Michelob Dry	St. Louis	2.1	Lag
Michelob Pale Ale	St. Louis	1.9	Ale
Morgan Street Doppelbock	St. Louis	1.9	Boc
O'Doul's	St. Louis (Anheuser-Busch)	3.1	Na
O'Doul's Amber	St. Louis (Anheuser-Busch)	3.3	Na
Schlafly Barleywine	St. Louis	3.0	Bar
Schlafly Hefeweizen	St. Louis	1.1	Wht
Schlafly Oatmeal Stout	St. Louis	4.0	Sto
Schlafly Pale Ale	St. Louis	2.5	Ale
Schlafly Robert Burns Scotch Ale	St. Louis	3.5	Ale
75th Street Brown Ale	Kansas City	2.5	Ale
Weston Pale Lager	Weston	2.4	Lag
MONTANA			
Kessler Ale	Helena	2.3	Ale
Kessler Lorelei Extra Pale Lager	Helena	3.2	Lag
Minott's Black Star Amber Export	Whitefish	1.9	Lag

NAME	LOCATION	RATING	STYLE
MINOTT'S BLACK STAR GOLDEN LAGER	WHITEFISH	2.4	LAG
NICHOLAS ALE (SEASONAL)	HELENA	3.1	ALE
SPANISH PEAKS BLACK DOG ALE	BOZEMAN	2.5	ALE
WHITEFISH BROWN ALE	WHITEFISH	1.6	ALE
NEVADA			
BOILER ROOM RED	LAUGHLIN	3.0	BOC
GREAT BASIN RYE PATCH ALE	SPARKS	3.3	ALE
NEW HAMPSHIRE			
NUTFIELD NOR'EASTER ALE	DERRY	3.5	ALE
NUTFIELD OLD MAN ALE	DERRY	2.9	ALE
PORTSMOUTH BLACK CAT STOUT	PORTSMOUTH	2.4	STO
SMUTTYNOSE OLD BROWN DOG ALE	PORTSMOUTH	2.5	ALE
NEW JERSEY			
RIVER HORSE CREAM ALE	LAMBERTVILLE	3.2	ALE
RIVER HORSE HOP HAZARD PALE ALE	LAMBERTVILLE	3.2	ALE
TUN TAVERN LEATHER NECK LAGER	ATLANTIC CITY	2.6	LAG
NEW MEXICO			
ASSETS DUKE CITY AMBER LAGER	ALBUQUERQUE	1.9	LAG
ASSETS HEFE WEIZEN	ALBUQUERQUE	2.2	WHT
ASSETS SANDIA STOUT	ALBUQUERQUE	2.5	STO
BLUE CORN PLAZA PORTER	SANTA FE	2.3	POR
DUKE CITY ALE	MANZANO	2.8	ALE
ESKE'S ALT BIER	TAOS	1.4	ALT
ESKE'S BOCK	TAOS	3.8	BOC
ESKE'S EL JEFE WEIZEN	TAOS	3.0	WHT
ESKE'S SPECIAL BITTER	TAOS	3.5	ALE
ESKE'S TAOS GREEN CHILI	TAOS	2.7	LAG
RIO GRANDE OUTLAW LAGER	ALBUQUERQUE	2.8	LAG
SANTA FE CHICKEN KILLER BARLEY WINE	SANTA FE	1.3	BAR
SANTA FE FIESTA ALE	SANTA FE	1.9	ALE
SANTA FE NUT BROWN ALE	SANTA FE	2.6	ALE
SANTA FE OLD POJOAQUE PORTER	SANTA FE	3.5	POR
SANTA FE PALE ALE	SANTA FE	2.3	ALE
SECOND STREET INDIA PALE ALE	SANTA FE	1.4	IPA
SIERRA BLANCA PILSENER	CARRIZOZO	2.4	PIL
WOLF CANYON AÑO NUEVO IMPERIAL STOUT	SANTA FE	3.1	STO
NEW YORK			
BIG HOUSE MA BARKER	ALBANY	0.2	ALE
BROOKLYN BLACK CHOCOLATE STOUT	BROOKLYN	4.1	STO
BROOKLYN BROWN DARK ALE	BROOKLYN	3.1	ALE

NAME	LOCATION	RATING	STYLE
Brooklyn East India Pale Ale	Brooklyn	4.1	IPA
Buffalo Blizzard Bock	Buffalo	0.9	Boc
Carnegie Hill Golden Ale	New York	2.3	Ale
Carnegie Hill Hefe-Weizen	New York	2.1	Wht
Checker Cab Blonde Ale	New York	1.3	Ale
Commonwealth Hefe-Weizen	New York	2.4	Wht
Commonwealth Hudson River Porter	New York	2.5	Por
Commonwealth Octoberfest	New York	2.4	Lag
Genesee 12 Horse Ale	Rochester	3.4	Ale
Genny Beer	Rochester	2.5	Lag
Genny Cream Ale	Rochester	2.7	Ale
Highfalls India Pale Ale	Rochester	2.9	IPA
J.W. Dundee's Honey Brown Lager	Rochester	2.4	Lag
Michael Shea's Irish Amber	Utica	3.0	Lag
New Amsterdam Amber	Utica	3.6	Lag
New Amsterdam India Pale Ale	Utica	2.4	IPA
New Amsterdam New York Ale	Utica	3.3	Ale
Ommegang Belgian-Style Abbey Ale	Cooperstown	4.0	Ale
Ommegang Hennepin Belgian-Style Ale	Cooperstown	4.2	Ale
Post Road Pale Ale	Utica	3.6	Ale
Post Road Real Ale	Utica	3.6	Ale
Post Road Snowshoe Ale	Utica	1.5	Ale
Samuel Adams Cream Stout	Utica	2.3	Sto
Saranac Adirondack Amber	Utica	2.2	Lag
Saranac Adirondack Season's Best (annual)	Utica	3.4	Ale
Saranac Black & Tan	Utica	3.8	Sto/Lag
Shan Sui Yen Sum	Utica	2.5	Pil
Southampton Saison	Southhampton	2.5	Ale
Troy Cherry Raspberry Ale	Troy	2.6	Ale
NORTH CAROLINA			
Cottonwood Lift Your Kilt Scottish Ale	Boone	3.5	Ale
Huske Hardware House Rough House India Pale Ale	Fayetteville	3.3	IPA
Pete's Gold Coast Lager	Winston-Salem	3.2	Lag
Pete's Summer Brew Pale Ale	Winston-Salem	2.7	Ale
Pete's Wicked Ale	Winston-Salem	3.8	Ale
Pete's Winter Brew	Winston-Salem	2.1	Ale
Midnight Dragon Gold Reserve Ale	Winston-Salem	1.5	Ale

NAME	LOCATION	RATING	STYLE
MIDNIGHT DRAGON MALT LIQUOR	WINSTON-SALEM	1.1	MLT
MIDNIGHT DRAGON ROYAL RESERVE LAGER	WINSTON-SALEM	0.5	LAG
PINEHURST VILLAGE DOUBLE EAGLE SCOTCH ALE	ABERDEEN	3.3	ALE
TOP OF THE HILL LAKE HOGAN HEFEWEIZEN	CHAPEL HILL	2.8	WHT
WEEPING RADISH BLACK RADISH DARK LAGER	MANTEO	2.2	LAG
WEEPING RADISH COROLLA GOLDEN LAGER	MANTEO	2.7	LAG
WEEPING RADISH FEST BEER AMBER LAGER	MANTEO	2.1	LAG
OHIO			
BANKS BEER	CINCINATTI	2.1	LAG
BLUE MOON HARVEST PUMPKIN	CINCINATTI	2.5	ALE
BREWMASTER'S BREWER'S PRIDE PORTER	CINCINATTI	1.6	POR
BRUIN PALE ALE	CINCINATTI	1.0	ALE
CHRISTIAN MOERLEIN BOCK	CINCINATTI	2.6	BOC
CHRISTIAN MOERLEIN-CINCINNATI SELECT BEER	CINCINNATI	2.5	PIL
CROOKED RIVER BLACK FOREST LAGER	CLEVELAND	3.2	LAG
CROOKED RIVER SETTLERS ALE	CLEVELAND	2.4	ALE
GREAT LAKES CONWAY'S IRISH ALE	CLEVELAND	2.9	ALE
HOSTER HEFE WEIZEN	COLUMBUS	2.5	WHT
LITTLE KING'S CREAM ALE	CINCINATTI	2.0	ALE
MAIN STREET ABIGAIL'S AMBER	CINCINATTI	2.8	ALE
MAIN STREET STEAMBOAT STOUT	CINCINATTI	3.5	STO
MAIN STREET WOODY'S AMERICAN WHEAT	CINCINATTI	2.3	WHT
MOERLEIN'S CINCINATTI BOCK BEER	CINCINATTI	2.9	BOC
OREGON			
BRIDGEPORT BLUE HERON PALE ALE	PORTLAND	2.4	ALE
BRIDGEPORT OLD KNUCKLEHEAD BARLEY WINE STYLE ALE	PORTLAND	4.0	BAR
DEAD ARMADILLO ROASTED RED	LAKE OSWEGO	2.5	LAG
DESCHUTES BACHELOR BITTER	BEND	3.1	ALE
DESCHUTES BLACK BUTTE PORTER	BEND	3.7	POR
DESCHUTES MIRROR POND PALE ALE	BEND	1.2	ALE

NAME	LOCATION	RATING	STYLE
DESCHUTES OBSIDIAN STOUT	BEND	2.5	STO
FULL SAIL BROWN ALE	HOOD RIVER	2.8	ALE
FULL SAIL GOLDEN ALE	HOOD RIVER	2.3	ALE
FULL SAIL WASSAIL WINTER ALE (ANNUAL)	HOOD RIVER	2.9	ALE
GOLDEN VALLEY RED THISTLE ALE	MCMINNVILLE	1.0	ALE
HAIR OF THE DOG ADAMBIER	PORTLAND	3.8	ALE
HAIR OF THE DOG GOLDEN ROSE-BELGIAN TRIPEL STYLE ALE	PORTLAND	4.0	ALE
HENRY WEINHARD'S DARK	PORTLAND	2.3	LAG
MACTARNAHANS SCOTTISH STYLE AMBER ALE	PORTLAND	3.8	ALE
MCMENAMINS BLACK RABBIT PORTER	PORTLAND	2.7	POR
MCMENAMINS HAMMERHEAD AMBER ALE	PORTLAND	2.0	ALE
MCMENAMINS NEBRASKA BITTER	PORTLAND	2.9	ALE
MCMENAMINS RUBY RASPBERRY ALE	PORTLAND	3.0	ALE
MCMENAMINS TERMINATOR STOUT	PORTLAND	2.1	STO
OREGON ORIGINAL HONEY	PORTLAND	1.5	ALE
PELICAN DORYMAN'S DARK ALE	PACIFIC CITY	1.3	ALE
PHILADELPHIA'S IPA	PORTLAND	2.9	IPA
PHILADELPHIA'S TUGBOAT STOUT	PORTLAND	1.0	STO
PORTLAND BAVARIAN STYLE WEIZEN	PORTLAND	1.8	WHT
PORTLAND SUMMER PALE ALE	PORTLAND	1.4	ALE
ROGUE GOLDEN ALE	NEWPORT	2.4	ALE
ROGUE MAIERBOCK ALE	NEWPORT	3.9	BOC
ROGUE MEXICALI ALE	NEWPORT	2.5	ALE
ROGUE MOGUL ALE	NEWPORT	3.6	ALE
ROGUE NEW PORTER	NEWPORT	3.7	POR
ROGUE OLD CRUSTACEAN BARLEY WINE	NEWPORT	3.6	BAR
ROGUE SHAKESPEARE STOUT	NEWPORT	4.8	STO
ROGUE SMOKE ALE	NEWPORT	2.0	ALE
ROGUE ST. ROGUE RED ALE	NEWPORT	4.4	ALE
SAMUEL ADAMS WINTER LAGER (ANNUAL)	PORTLAND	2.2–3.9	LAG
SAXER THREE FINGER JACK HEFEDUNKEL	LAKE OSWEGO	2.3	LAG
SILETZ NUT BROWN ALE	SILETZ	3.7	ALE
SPENCER'S MCKENZIE PALE ALE	SPRINGFIELD	3.7	ALE
ST. IDES MALT LIQUOR	PORTLAND	1.1	MLT
STEELHEAD BOMBAY BOMBER IPA	EUGENE	2.2	IPA

NAME	LOCATION	RATING	STYLE
STEELHEAD EXTRA PALE ALE	EUGENE	3.3	ALE
TANNEN BOMB (ANNUAL)	MCMINNVILLE	3.8	ALE
TUBORG DELUXE DARK	PORTLAND	1.1	LAG
UMPQUA PERRY'S OLD ALE	ROSEBURG	2.4	ALE
WEINHARD'S BLUE BOAR PALE ALE	PORTLAND	2.6	ALE
WIDMER ALT	PORTLAND	3.3	ALT
WIDMER BIG BEN PORTER	PORTLAND	2.1	POR
PENNSYLVANIA			
BLUE HEN TRADITIONAL	PHILADELPHIA	2.9	LAG
BUNKER HILL LAGER	WILKES-BARRE	1.8	LAG
DOCK STREET AMBER	PHILADELPHIA	3.1	ALE
DOCK STREET BOHEMIAN PILSNER	PHILADELPHIA	3.5	PIL
DOCK STREET ILLUMINATOR	PHILADELPHIA	3.1	LAG
ERIN'S ROCK STOUT & AMBER LAGER	WILKES-BARRE	2.4	LAG
ESQUIRE EXTRA DRY	SMITHTON	0.9	LAG
INDEPENDENCE FRANKLINFEST	PHILADELPHIA	2.3	LAG
LANCASTER MILK STOUT	LANCASTER	2.3	STO
LORD CHESTERFIELD ALE	POTTSVILLE	2.5	ALE
MALTA GOYA	WILKES-BARRE	1.1	NA
NEUWEILER BLACK & TAN	ALLENTOWN	2.5	POR/L
NITTANY ALE	PHILADELPHIA	3.0	ALE
OLDE HEURICH MAERZEN	PITTSBURGH	2.6	LAG
PENNSYLVANIA PENN PILSNER	PITTSBURGH	3.7	PIL
PRIOR DOUBLE DARK	NORRISTOWN	3.7	BOC
RED BARON MALT BEVERAGE	WILKES-BARRE	0.9	NA
RHEINGOLD PREMIUM	PHILADELPHIA	1.1	PIL
ROLLING ROCK	LATROBE	3.6	LAG
SAMUEL ADAMS CREAM STOUT	PITTSBURGH	2.3	STO
SAMUEL ADAMS DARK WHEAT	PITTSBURGH	2.7	WHT
SAMUEL ADAMS DOUBLE BOCK DARK	PITTSBURGH	3.7	BOC
SAMUEL ADAMS HONEY PORTER	LEHIGH VALLEY	3.3	POR
SAMUEL ADAMS OCTOBERFEST	PITTSBURGH	3.7	LAG
STEGMAIER 1857 PREMIUM LAGER	WILKES-BARRE	3.2	LAG
STEGMAIER PORTER	WILKES-BARRE	2.4	POR
STOUDT'S ABBEY TRIPLE	ADAMSTOWN	3.8	BOC
STOUDT'S HOLIDAY RESERVE BEER-SMOKED PORTER	ADAMSTOWN	3.4	POR
STOUDT'S HONEY DOUBLE BOCK	ADAMSTOWN	4.0	BOC
TROEGS PALE ALE	HARRISBURG	3.1	ALE
VICTORY HOPDEVIL ALE	DOWINGTOWN	2.8	ALE
VICTORY PRIMA PILS	DOWINGTOWN	2.8	PIL

NAME	LOCATION	RATING	STYLE
Yuengling Porter	Pottsville	4.1	Por
Yuengling Traditional Lager	Pottsville	3.3	Lag
RHODE ISLAND			
Private Stock Malt Liquor	Cranston	1.1	Mlt
TENNESSEE			
Blackstone Nut Brown Ale	Nashville	3.4	Ale
Bohannon Market Street Golden Ale	Nashville	2.1	Ale
Bohannon Market Street Oktoberfest	Nashville	0.3	Lag
TEXAS			
Ballantine Pale Ale	San Antonio	2.0	Ale
Bitter End Modulator Doppelbock	Austin	3.4	Boc
Blue Star Pale Ale	San Antonio	2.8	Ale
Blue Star Stout	San Antonio	3.5	Sto
Celis Dubble Ale	Austin	3.7	Ale
Celis Grand Cru	Austin	2.4	Ale
Celis Pale Bock	Austin	3.4	Boc
Celis White	Austin	4.0	Wht
Dallas Gold	Dallas	1.0	Pil
Falstaff	San Antonio	2.3	Lag
Jax	San Antonio	3.0	Pil
Kosmos Reserve Lager	Shiner	3.0	Lag
Lone Star	San Antonio	3.1	Lag
Madcap Zebra European Peach	Longview	2.7	Lag
Mexicali Beer	San Antonio	2.5	Pil
Olympia	San Antonio	2.1	Pil
Pabst Blue Ribbon Draft	San Antonio	2.1	Lag
Pearl Lager	San Antonio	2.3	Lag
Pecan Street	Shiner	2.5	Lag
Pilsener Club Premium	San Antonio & Galveston	1.0	Pil
Rattlesnake Premium	Shiner	2.4	Lag
Red Bone Red Lager	San Antonio	1.9	Lag
Saint Arnold Christmas Ale (seasonal)	Houston	3.1	Ale
Saint Arnold Kristall Weizen	Houston	3.2	Wht
Shiner Bock	Shiner	2.4	Boc
Shiner Premium	Shiner	2.5	Pil
St. Ides Malt Liquor	San Antonio	1.1	Mlt
Steel Reserve 211 High Gravity Lager	Longview	2.5	Lag
Texas Cowboy Vienna Lager	Dallas	0.5	Lag

NAME	LOCATION	RATING	STYLE
Texas Crude Bock	Longview	2.1	Boc
Texas Light Dark	San Antonio	2.4	Na
Texas Pride	San Antonio	0.1	Pil
Texas Select	San Antonio	0.3	Na
Wildcatters Refined Stout	San Antonio	2.6	Sto
Ziegenbock Amber Beer	Houston	2.6	Lag
UTAH			
Eddie McStiff's Canyon Cream Ale	Moab	0.0	Ale
Wasatch Hefe-Weizen	Park City & Salt Lake City	2.8	Wht
Wasatch Irish Stout	Park City	2.5	Sto
Wasatch Raspberry Wheat	Salt Lake City	2.8	Wht
Wasatch Slickrock Lager	Park City	2.7	Lag
Wasatch Wheat	Park City	0.3	Wht
VERMONT			
Catamount Amber Ale	Windsor	0.2	Ale
Catamount Pale Ale	Windsor	2.7	Ale
Catamount Porter	Windsor	3.8	Por
Long Trail Ale	Bridgewater Corners	3.3	Ale
Otter Creek Hickory Switch Smoked Amber Ale	Middlebury	2.9	Ale
Otter Creek Oktoberfest Autumn Ale	Middlebury	2.5	Ale
Vermont Wee Heavy Scotch Ale	Burlington	1.5	Ale
VIRGINIA			
Dominion Lager	Ashburn	1.0	Lag
Rock Creek Winter Passion Spiced Ale	Richmond	3.7	Ale
Sweetwater Kokopelli IPA	Centreville	2.7	Ipa
Williamsburg American Pale Ale	Williamsburg	1.6	Ale
WASHINGTON			
Bert Grant's Imperial Stout	Yakima	4.2	Sto
Bert Grant's India Pale Ale	Yakima	3.6	Ipa
Bert Grant's Scottish Ale	Yakima	2.0	Ale
Big Pig Ale	Seattle	2.5	Ale
Big Time Bhagwans Best India Pale Ale	Seattle	2.0	Ipa
Big Time Old Wooly Barley Wine	Seattle	2.8	Bar
Black Label	Seattle	2.1	Lag
Fish Eye IPA	Olympia	0.5	Ipa
Fish Tale Mudshark Porter	Olympia	2.7	Por
Fish Tale Wild Salmon Pale Ale	Olympia	1.2	Ale

NAME	LOCATION	RATING	STYLE
Fitspatrick Stout	Seattle	3.1	Sto
Hale's IPA	Seattle	4.4	Ipa
Hale's Amber Ale	Seattle	1.0	Ale
Hale's Pale Ale	Seattle	2.2	Ale
Hazel Dell Red Zone Pale Ale	Vancouver	0.2	Ale
Hood Canal Agate Pass Amber	Poulsbo	1.9	Lag
Jet City Ale	Seattle	2.4	Ale
Leavenworth Blind Pig Dunkel Weizen	Leavenworth	3.0	Wht
Leavenworth Hodgson's IPA	Leavenworth	2.5	Ipa
Lucky Lager	Tumwater	0.8	Lag
Maritime Flagship Red Ale	Seattle	3.0	Ale
Maritime Islander Pale Ale	Seattle	2.8	Ale
Maritime Nightwatch Ale	Seattle	3.0	Ale
Orchard Street Golden Ale	Bellingham	2.4	Ale
Osb Stock Ale	Bellingham	3.0	Ale
Pabst Non-Alcoholic Malt Beverage	Tumwater	2.4	Na
Pete's Gold Coast Lager	Seattle & N.Ca.	3.2	Lag
Pete's Summer Brew Pale Ale	Seattle	2.7	Ale
Pete's Wicked Ale	Seattle	3.8	Ale
Pete's Winter Brew Amber Ale	Seattle	3.1	Ale
Pike India Pale Ale	Seattle	3.8	Ale
Pike Pale Ale	Seattle	3.6	Ale
Pyramid Best Brown Ale	Seattle	2.9	Ale
Pyramid Pale Ale	Seattle	2.5	Ale
Pyramid Snow Cap Ale (seasonal)	Seattle	2.5	Ale
Pyramid Wheaten Ale	Seattle	3.3	Ale
Rainier Ale	Seattle	3.6	Ale
Rainier Beer	Seattle	2.7	Pil
Red Hook Ballard Bitter India Pale Ale	Seattle	3.0	Ipa
Red Hook Blackhook Porter	Seattle	4.0	Por
Red Hook Blonde Ale	Seattle	2.0	Ale
Red Hook Esb Ale	Seattle	3.1	Ale
Red Hook Wheat Hook Ale	Seattle	2.9	Ale
Red Hook Winterhook Christmas Ale (annual)	Seattle	3.6	Ale
Salmon Creek Sweet Stout	Vancouver	3.8	Sto
Smith And Reilly Honest Beer	Tumwater	2.7	Pil
Thomas Kemper Auction Block Amber	Poulsbo	1.5	Lag

NAME	LOCATION	RATING	STYLE
THOMAS KEMPER MAIBOCK ROLLING BAY BOCK	SEATTLE	2.4	BOC
THOMAS KEMPER WINTRBRAU (SEASONAL)	SEATTLE	1.2	LAG
WISCONSIN			
ADLER-BRAU PILSNER	APPLETON	0.9	PIL
AMBER—VIENNA STYLE	MONROE	3.1	LAG
AUGSBURGER PILSENER	MONROE	3.5	PIL
BERGHOFF FAMOUS BOCK	MONROE	2.4	BOC
BERGHOFF GENUINE DARK	MONROE	3.3	LAG
BERGHOFF OKTOBER FEST BEER (ANNUAL)	MONROE	2.3	LAG
BERGHOFF ORIGINAL LAGER—DORTMUNDER	MONROE	2.6	LAG
BIG APPLE PREMIUM	MILWAUKEE (PABST)	2.4	PIL
BRAUMEISTER PILSENER	MONROE	2.5	PIL
BUCKHORN	MILWAUKEE	0.1	PIL
CAPITAL DARK	MIDDLETON	3.2	LAG
CAPITAL BAVARIAN LAGER	MIDDLETON	3.3	LAG
CAPITAL OKTOBERFEST	MIDDLETON	2.5	LAG
CAPITAL WILD RICE	MIDDLETON	2.4	LAG
CRAZY HORSE MALT LIQUOR	LA CROSSE	1.9	MLT
DEMPSEYS ALE	MONROE	2.4	ALE
FOECKING PREMIUM	MONROE	0.3	LAG
GRAY'S HONEY ALE	JANESVILLE	2.5	ALE
HAMM'S	MILWAUKEE	2.5	PIL
HAMM'S NA	MILWAUKEE	2.5	NA
HARLEY-DAVIDSON HEAVY BEER	MONROE	2.4	PIL
ICEHOUSE ICE BEER MALT LIQUOR	MILWAUKEE	3.3	MLT
JAMES BOWIE KENTUCKY HILLS LTD. PILSNER	LA CROSSE	2.0	PIL
LAKEFRONT CHERRY LAGER	MILWAUKEE	2.7	LAG
LAKEFRONT CREAM CITY PALE ALE	MILWAUKEE	2.3	ALE
LAKEFRONT PUMPKIN LAGER	MILWAUKEE	3.8	LAG
LEINENKUGEL'S RED LAGER	CHIPPEWA FALLS	2.1	LAG
LEINENKUGEL'S BERRY WEISS	CHIPPEWA FALLS	2.1	WHT
LEINENKUGEL'S BIG BUTT DOPPELBOCK	CHIPPEWA FALLS	2.2	BOC
LEINENKUGEL'S ORIGINAL PREMIUM	CHIPPEWA FALLS	3.1	LAG
MAGNUM MALT LIQUOR	MILWAUKEE	0.7	MLT
MICKEY'S MALT LIQUOR	LA CROSSE	2.6	MLT
MILLER HIGH LIFE	MILWAUKEE	2.4	PIL
MILWAUKEE 1851	LA CROSSE	0.4	PIL
OLDE ENGLISH 800 MALT LIQUOR	LA CROSSE	2.9	MLT

NAME	LOCATION	RATING	STYLE
POINT MAPLE WHEAT	STEVENS POINT	2.2	WHT
POINT SPECIAL PREMIUM LAGER	STEVENS POINT	2.9	LAG
RED DOG	MILWAUKEE	1.1	LAG
RED, WHITE AND BLUE SPECIAL LAGER	LA CROSSE	3.2	LAG
RHINELANDER	MONROE	2.4	LAG
SCHLITZ MALT LIQUOR	MILWAUKEE	1.3	MLT
SCHMIDT	LA CROSSE	1.8	LAG
SHARP'S	MILWAUKEE (MILLER)	0.8	NA
SPECIAL EXPORT	LA CROSSE	3.4	LAG
SPRECHER AMBER	MILWAUKEE	3.5	LAG
SPRECHER PUB BROWN ALE	MILWAUKEE	2.9	ALE
STAG	LA CROSSE	2.1	LAG
STEEL RESERVE 211 HIGH GRAVITY LAGER	LA CROSSE	2.5	LAG
TUBORG LAGER	LA CROSSE, ET AL.	2.4	LAG
VIENNA LAGER	MILWAUKEE	2.5	LAG
WYOMING			
OTTO BROTHERS MOOSE JUICE STOUT	WILSON	3.0	STO
OTTO BROTHERS TETON ALE	WILSON	3.4	ALE
SNAKE RIVER ZONKER STOUT	JACKSON HOLE	2.2	STO
TOMMYKNOCKER PICK AXE PALE ALE	CASPER	3.7	ALE

BEERS BY COUNTRY: AN ALPHABETICAL LISTING

NAME	LOCATION	RATING	STYLE
ARGENTINA			
Bieckert Especial	Antartida	4.2	Pil
Cordoba-Dorada	Cordoba	3.7	Pil
Leon de Oro Cerveza Especial	Antartida	3.8	Lag
Palermo Estrasburgo	Quilmes	2.2	Lag
Quilmes Cristal	Buenos Aires	1.6	Pil
San Carlos Especial	San Carlos	2.3	Pil
Santa Fe Rubia Especial	Santa Fe	3.9	Lag
Schneider Cerveza Rubia Especial	Santa Fe	2.2	Lag
AUSTRALIA			
Australian Premium Lager	Brisbane	1.4	Lag
Big Barrel	Leabrook, South Australia	3.0	Lag
Boags Premium Lager	Hobart, Tasmania	2.2	Lag
Broken Hill Lager	Thebarton/Adelaide, South Australia	2.0	Lag
Broken Hill Old Stout	Adelaide, South Australia	1.2	Sto
Broken Hill Real Ale	Adelaide, South Australia	2.9	Ale
Castlemaine XXXX Lager	Brisbane, Queensland	3.3	Lag
Coopers Best Extra Stout	Leabrook, South Australia	3.4	Sto
Coopers Sparkling Ale	Leabrook, South Australia	2.5	Ale
Down Under	Perth, Western Australia	2.6	Lag
Foster's Lager	Melbourne, Victoria	3.4	Lag
Foster's Light Lager	Melbourne, Victoria	3.2	Lag
Gulf Beer	Indooroopilly, Queensland	1.4	Lag
Laguna Bay Australian Pale Ale	Indooroopilly, Queensland	2.8	Ale
Old Australia Stout	Thebarton, South Australia	3.8	Sto
Red Back Malted Wheat Beer	Fremantle, Western Australia	2.2	Wht
Reschs Pilsner	Sydney, New South Wales	2.9	Pil
Sheaf Stout	Sydney, New South Wales	2.5	Sto
Southwark Gold Lager	Thebarton, South Australia	2.1	Lag
Southwark Premium	Adelaide, South Australia	4.1	Pil
Swan Lager	Perth, Western Australia	3.3	Lag
Thomas Cooper Adelaide Lager	Leabrook, South Australia	2.4	Lag

NAME	LOCATION	RATING	STYLE
TOOHEY'S PREMIUM EXPORT LAGER	THEBARTON, SOUTH AUSTRALIA	2.9	LAG
WEST END EXPORT LAGER	THEBARTON, SOUTH AUSTRALIA	3.3	LAG
AUSTRIA			
EDELWEISS DUNKEL DARK	SALZBURG	3.0	WHT
EDELWEISS HEFETRUB	SALZBURG	2.4	WHT
EDELWEISS KRISTALLKLAR WEIZENBIER	SALZBURG	4.0	WHT
EGGENBERG URBOCK	SALZBURG & LINZ	2.0	BOC
GOSSER PALE	LEABEN GOSS	2.6	LAG
GOSSER STIFTSBRAU	GRAZ	3.5	LAG
MACQUEEN'S NESSIE ORIGINAL RED ALE	VORCHDORF	4.0	ALE
OTTAKRINGER GOLD FASSL PILS	VIENNA	2.9	PIL
OTTAKRINGER GOLD FASSL VIENNA LAGER	VIENNA	2.5	LAG
OTTAKRINGER NULL KOMMA JOSEF ALKOHOLFREI	VIENNA	0.6	NA
PUNTIGAMER DARK MALT DRAFT	GRAZ	2.5	MLT
PUNTIGAMER PANTHER DRAFT	GRAZ	3.1	LAG
SCHLOSSGOLD ALKOHOLARMES BIER	LINZ	3.4	NA
SKOL INTERNATIONAL	LINZ	1.2	PIL
STEFFL VIENNA LAGER	LINZ	2.1	LAG
STIEGL COLUMBUS PILS	SALZBURG	3.1	PIL
ZIPFER PREMIUM MALT LIQUOR	VIENNA	3.2	MLT
AZORES			
CERVEJA PRETA DOCE	PONTA DELGADA	2.8	NA
MELO ABREU ESPECIAL	PONTA DELGADA	3.0	PIL
BAHAMAS			
KALIK—BEER OF THE BAHAMAS	NASSAU	2.9	LAG
BARBADOS			
BAJAN BEER	BRIDGETOWN	2.7	LAG
BANKS LAGER	WILDEY	2.3	LAG
BELGIUM			
AFFLIGEM NÖEL CHRISTMAS ALE	OPWIJK	3.9	ALE
AFFLIGEM TRIPEL ABBEY	OPWIJK	3.6	ALE
ARA BIER ALE	ESSEN	3.8	ALE

NAME	LOCATION	RATING	STYLE
ARTEVELDE ALE	MELLE/GHENT	4.1	ALE
BARBAR BELGIAN HONEY ALE	QUENAST	3.7	ALE
BEL PILS	PUURS	3.8	PIL
BIOS COPPER ALE	ERTVELDE	1.4	ALE
BLANCHE DE BRUGES	BRUGES	3.9	WHT
BLANCHE DES NEIGES ALE	MELLE/GHENT	2.3	ALE
BOON GUEUZE	LEMBEEK	2.2	LAM
BOS KEUN SPECIAL PAASBIER	ESSEN	2.7	ALE
BRIGAND BELGIAN ALE	INGELMUNSTER	3.8	ALE
CHAPEAU FARO LAMBIC	WAMBEEK	2.6	LAM
CHAPEAU GUEUZE LAMBIC	WAMBEEK	1.1	LAM
CHIMAY PERES TRAPPISTES ALE-GRAND RESERVE	CHIMAY ABBEY	2.5	ALE
CHIMAY PERES TRAPPISTES ALE-PREMIERE	CHIMAY ABBEY	4.7	ALE
COCHONNETTE PETITE VAPEUR COCHONNE ALE	PIPAIX	3.1	ALE
CORSENDONK MONK'S BROWN ALE	SIGILUM MONASTERY, ERTVELDE	3.9	ALE
CORSENDONK MONK'S PALE ALE	SIGILUM MONASTERY, ERTVELDE	4.0	ALE
DE KONINCK ALE	ANTWERP	3.9	ALE
DELIRIUM NOCTURNUM	MELLE/GHENT	3.5	ALE
DELIRIUM TREMENS BELGIAN ALE	MELLE/GHENT	1.7	ALE
DENTERGEMS WHITE ALE	DENTERGEM	0.6	ALE
DOUGLAS SCOTCH BRAND ALE	ANTWERP	3.9	ALE
DUVEL	BREENDONK	2.9	ALE
ENAME DUBBEL ABBEY ALE	OUDENAARDE	4.0	ALE
FIRE FOX BELGIAN ALE	MELLE/GHENT	4.2	ALE
GOUDEN CAROLUS ALE	MECHELEN	3.9	ALE
GRIMBERGEN DOUBLE ALE	WATERLOO	4.0	ALE
GRIMBERGEN TRIPLE AMBER ABBEY ALE	WATERLOO	4.0	ALE
GULDEN DRAAK	ERTVELDE	3.8	ALE
HOEGAARDEN GRAND CRU ALE	HOEGAARDEN	0.9	ALE
HOEGAARDEN WHITE	HOEGAARDEN	2.6	WHT
ICHTEGEM'S OLD BROWN ALE	ICHTEGEM	3.9	ALE
KWAK	BUGGENHOUT	2.1	ALE
LA GUILLOTINE BELGIAN ALE	MELLE/GHENT	3.2	ALE
LEFFE BLOND ALE	LEFFE	3.1	ALE
LIEFMANS KRIEKBIER (SEASONAL)	OUDENAARDE	3.9	ALE

NAME	LOCATION	RATING	STYLE
LINDEMAN'S KRIEK-LAMBIC	VLEZENBEEK	2.0	LAM
LINDEMAN'S PECHE LAMBIC	VLEZENBEEK	1.3	LAM
LUCIFER	DENTERGEM	1.1	A/L
MAES PILS	WATERLOO	3.0	PIL
MAREDSOUS ABBEY ALE	DENEE	4.1	ALE
MARTIN'S PALE ALE	ANTWERP	3.5	ALE
MATEEN TRIPLE ALE	MELLE/GHENT	3.4	ALE
MORT SUBITE PECHE LAMBIC	ROBBEGEM	3.4	LAM
OERBIER ALE	ESSEN	3.2	ALE
ORVAL TRAPPIST ALE	FLORENVILLE	2.1	ALE
PALM ALE	BRUSSELS	3.2	ALE
PERTOTALE FARO LAMBIC	LEMBEEK	2.9	LAM
PETRUS OAK AGED DARK BEER	BAVIKHORE	2.8	PIL
PIRAAT ALE	ERTVELDE	4.0	ALE
RIVA BLANCHE ALE	DENTERGEM	2.2	ALE
RODENBACH ALEXANDER BELGIAN RED ALE	FLANDERS, ROESELARE	4.3	ALE
RODENBACH BELGIAN RED ALE	FLANDERS, ROESELARE	2.7	ALE
RUBENS GOLD	KONTICH	3.0	ALE
SCALDIS BELGIAN SPECIAL ALE	PIPAIX	3.7	ALE
SCALDIS NOEL ALE (ANNUAL)	PIPAIX	2.1	ALE
SEZOENS ALE	BOCHOLT	3.0	ALE
ST. SEBASTIAN CROCK ALE	MEER	2.6	ALE
ST. SIXTUS ABBEY ALE	WATOU	3.1	ALE
STEENDONK WHITE ALE	BREENDONK	3.9	ALE
STELLA ARTOIS	LEUVEN	2.5	PIL
STER ALE	MEER	3.1	ALE
TIMMERMANS PECHE	ITTERBECK	3.3	LAM
TRIPLE TOISON D'OR ALE	MECHELEN	2.5	ALE
VLAS KOP ALE	ICHTEGEM	2.6	ALE
VONDEL DARK ALE	DENTERGEM	0.3	ALE
WESTMALLE TRAPPIST	ABBEY OF WESTMALLE	4.3	ALE
WITKAP-PATER SINGEL ABBEY ALE	NINOVE	4.0	ALE
BELIZE			
CROWN LAGER	BELIZE CITY	2.3	LAG
BOLIVIA			
PACENA CENTENARIO	LA PAZ	2.6	PIL
TAQUINA EXPORT BEER	COCHABAMBA	2.5	PIL
BRAZIL			
ANTARCTICA	SAO PAULO	2.7	PIL
BRAHMA	RIO DE JANEIRO	3.8	PIL
BRAHMA CHOPP	RIO DE JANEIRO	3.7	PIL

NAME	LOCATION	RATING	STYLE
KAISER	QUEIMADOS	0.8	PIL
SCHINCARIOL PILSEN	SCHINCARIOL	0.2	PIL
SKOL CERVEJA PILSEN	RIO CLARO	1.0	PIL
TIJUCA	BELEM	3.8	PIL
XINGU BLACK BEER	TOLEDO	4.0	STO/LAG
BULGARIA			
ASTICA PREMIUM LAGER	HASKOWO	3.6	LAG
ZAGORKA LAGER	ZAGORA	0.9	LAG
CANADA			
ALGONQUIN COUNTRY LAGER	FORMOSA, ONTARIO	0.5	LAG
ALGONQUIN SPECIAL RESERVE ALE	FORMOSA, ONTARIO	2.9	ALE
ARCTIC AMBER LAGER	SAULT STE. MARIE, ONTARIO	0.8	LAG
ARCTIC BAY CLASSIC LAGER	VANCOUVER, BRITISH COLUMBIA	1.8	LAG
BEER	CALGARY, ALBERTA	0.7	LAG
BIG ROCK COCK O' THE ROCK PORTER	CALGARY, ALBERTA	2.4	POR
BIG ROCK COLD COCK WINTER PORTER	CALGARY, ALBERTA	3.1	POR
BIG ROCK GRASSHOPPER WHEAT ALE	CALGARY, ALBERTA	2.5	WHT
BIG ROCK MAGPIE RYE BREW	CALGARY, ALBERTA	0.4	LAG
BIG ROCK MCNALLYS EXTRA ALE	CALGARY, ALBERTA	1.3	ALE
BIG ROCK SPRINGBOK ALE	CALGARY, ALBERTA	2.1	ALE
BIG ROCK WARTHOG ALE	CALGARY, ALBERTA	2.5	ALE
BLANCHE DE CHAMBLY WHITE BEER ON LEES	CHAMBLY, QUEBEC	3.1	WHT
BRICK LAGER	WATERLOO, ONTARIO	3.1	LAG
BUCKERFIELD'S APPLETON BROWN ALE	VICTORIA, BRITISH COLUMBIA	3.3	ALE
BUCKERFIELD'S ARCTIC ALE	VICTORIA, BRITISH COLUMBIA	2.0	ALE
BUCKERFIELD'S PANDORA PALE ALE	VICTORIA, BRITISH COLUMBIA	2.9	ALE
BUCKERFIELD'S SWANS OATMEAL STOUT	VICTORIA, BRITISH COLUMBIA	3.8	STO
BUZZARD BREATH ALE	CALGARY, ALBERTA	1.7	ALE
CALGARY AMBER LAGER	TORONTO, ONTARIO	2.4	LAG
CANADA COUNTRY LAGER	VANCOUVER, BRITISH COLUMBIA	3.0	LAG
CANADIAN LAGER	VANCOUVER, BRITISH COLUMBIA	2.0	LAG
CLARK'S GREAT CANADIAN	VANCOUVER, BRITISH COLUMBIA	1.0	LAG
CLUB	TORONTO, ONTARIO	2.7	LAG
DRUMMOND DRAFT LAGER	CALGARY, ALBERTA	2.4	LAG

NAME	LOCATION	RATING	STYLE
DRUMMOND DRY	RED DEER, ALBERTA	0.8	LAG
EISBOCK ICE BEER	NIAGARA FALLS, ONTARIO	2.9	BOC
ELEPHANT RED LAGER	LONDON, ONTARIO	2.2	LAG
F AND A	TORONTO, ONTARIO	3.1	LAG
FOSTER'S LAGER	TORONTO, ONTARIO	3.4	LAG
GLACIER BAY LAGER	TORONTO, ONTARIO	1.1	LAG
GRANVILLE ISLAND ENGLISH BAY PALE ALE	VANCOUVER, BRITISH COLUMBIA	2.6	LAG
GRANVILLE ISLAND LAGER	VANCOUVER, BRITISH COLUMBIA	2.9	LAG
GRIZZLY	HAMILTON, ONTARIO	0.4	LAG
HENNINGER MEISTER PILS	HAMILTON, ONTARIO	3.2	PIL
JOHN LABATT CLASSIC	TORONTO, ONTARIO	3.8	LAG
KEY DARK	VICTORIA, BRITISH COLUMBIA	1.2	LAG
KIRIN DRAFT	VANCOUVER, BRITISH COLUMBIA	3.9	PIL
KODIAK PREMIUM LAGER	SASKATOON, SASKATCHEWAN	2.5	LAG
KOKANEE GLACIER PILSENER	CRESTON, BRITISH COLUMBIA	3.4	PIL
LA FIN DU MONDE	CHAMBLY, QUEBEC	3.3	ALE
LA GAILLARDE ALE ON LEES	CHAMBLY, QUEBEC	2.4	ALE
LABATT'S	VANCOUVER, BRITISH COLUMBIA	3.1	PIL
LABATT'S 50 ALE	VANCOUVER, BRITISH COLUMBIA	3.7	ALE
LABATT'S BLUE PILSENER	VANCOUVER, BRITISH COLUMBIA	3.1	PIL
LABATT'S VELVET CREAM STOUT	EDMONTON, ALBERTA	3.1	STO
L'EAU BENITE TRIPLE	CHAMBLY, QUEBEC	2.4	ALE
LOWENBRAU PREMIUM DARK	TORONTO, ONTARIO	2.8	LAG
LOWENBRAU PREMIUM LAGER	TORONTO, ONTARIO	2.7	LAG
MILLER HIGHLIFE	TORONTO, ONTARIO	2.2	PIL
MOLSON BRADOR MALT LIQUOR	TORONTO, ONTARIO, ET AL.	2.7	MLT
MOLSON EXEL	VANCOUVER, BRITISH COLUMBIA	3.3	NA
MOLSON EXPORT ALE	TORONTO, ONTARIO, ET AL.	3.2	ALE
MOLSON GOLDEN ALE	MONTREAL, TORONTO, ET AL.	2.4	ALE
MOLSON ICE LAGER	VANCOUVER, BRITISH COLUMBIA	3.5	LAG
MOLSON SPECIAL DRY	TORONTO, ONTARIO	2.5	LAG
MOOSEHEAD CANADIAN LAGER	ST. JOHN, NEW BRUNSWICK	1.1	LAG
MOUNTAIN CREST	TORONTO, ONTARIO	0.9	PIL
OKANAGAN SPRING PREMIUM LAGER	VERNON, BRITISH COLUMBIA	1.1	LAG
OKANAGAN SPRING ST. PATRICK STOUT	VERNON, BRITISH COLUMBIA	1.3	STO
O'KEEFE ALE	TORONTO, ONTARIO	3.1	ALE
O'KEEFE'S EXTRA OLD STOCK MALT LIQUOR	VANCOUVER, BRITISH COLUMBIA	2.9	MLT

NAME	LOCATION	RATING	STYLE
Old Style Pilsner	Vancouver, British Columbia	2.4	Pil
Old Vienna Lager	Toronto, Ontario	3.0	Lag
Pacific Draft	Vancouver, British Columbia	1.7	Pil
Pasadena Lager Natural Draft	Vancouver, British Columbia	1.0	Lag
Quelque Chose Something	Chambly, Quebec	3.9	Ale
Raftman	Chambly, Quebec	2.9	Ale
Red Baron	Waterloo, Ontario	1.9	Lag
Rickard's Red Draught	Calgary, Alberta	2.5	Ale
Schooner Lager	Montreal, Quebec	1.8	Lag
Sleeman Cream Ale	Guelph, Ontario	3.0	Ale
Sleeman Lager	Guelph, Ontario	2.7	Lag
Sleeman Original Dark Ale	Guelph, Ontario	2.3	Ale
Steeler Lager	Hamilton, Ontario	0.5	Lag
Toby	Toronto, Ontario	2.2	Pil
Toronto Light	Guelph, Ontario	1.8	Pil
Tourmente Wheat	Montreal, Quebec	3.5	Wht
True North Cream Ale	Vaughan, Ontario	2.7	Ale
True North Lager	Vaughan, Ontario	3.2	Lag
Upper Canada Colonial Stout	Toronto, Ontario	2.3	Sto
Upper Canada Dark Ale	Toronto, Ontario	3.2	Ale
Upper Canada Lager	Toronto, Ontario	2.5	Lag
Upper Canada Light Lager	Toronto, Ontario	0.7	Lag
Upper Canada Pale Ale	Toronto, Ontario	2.0	Ale
Upper Canada Point Nine	Toronto, Ontario	2.9	Na
Upper Canada Publican's Special Bitter Ale	Toronto, Ontario	2.2	Ale
Upper Canada Rebellion	Toronto, Ontario	3.8	Lag
Upper Canada True Bock	Toronto, Ontario	3.7	Boc
Viking Lager	Victoria, British Columbia	2.2	Lag
Whistler Black Tusk Ale	Whistler, British Columbia	2.1	Ale
Whistler Premium Lager	Whistler, British Columbia	1.2	Lag
Wolfsbrau Amber Lager	Calgary, Alberta	2.5	Lag
CANARY ISLANDS			
Tropical Pilsener	Las Palmas	3.7	Pil
CHAD			
Gala De Luxe Export Beer	Logone	1.5	Lag
CHILE			
Andes Pilsener	Santiago	1.2	Pil
Austral Polar Pilsener	Punta Arenas	2.8	Pil
Cristal Pilsener	Limache	1.3	Pil
Dorada Pilsener	Talca	3.3	Pil
Escudo Pilsener	Osorno	2.9	Pil

NAME	LOCATION	RATING	STYLE
ESCUDO SCHOP	SANTIAGO	2.4	PIL
IMPERIAL PILSENER	PUNTA ARENAS	2.7	PIL
KUNSTMANN LAGER	VALDIVIA	2.7	LAG
LIMACHE CERVEZA TIPO CRUDA	LIMACHE	3.2	PIL
MORENITA MALTA	OSORNO	2.6	NA
MORENITA MALTA ESPECIAL	CONCEPCION	3.3	NA
PAULANER PREMIUM LAGER	SANTIAGO	3.0	LAG
ROYAL GUARD CERVEZA-TIPO DORTMUND	SANTIAGO	2.5	LAG
ROYAL GUARD PILSENER	SANTIAGO	3.8	PIL
SCHOP OSCURO	OSORNO	3.4	PIL
CHINA			
CHANGLEE LAGER	SANSHUI	2.6	LAG
CHINA CLIPPER	GUANGZHOU	2.5	LAG
CHINA GOLD	GUANGZHOU	1.8	PIL
CHUNG HUA PILSENER	GUANGZHOU	3.4	PIL
DOUBLE HAPPINESS	GUANGZHOU	2.3	LAG
EMPERORS GOLD	GUANGZHOU	3.5	PIL
GENGHIS KHAN	GUANGZHOU	1.1	LAG
GOLDEN DRAGON	GUANGZHOU	3.1	PIL
GREAT WALL	HEBEI	2.9	LAG
HUA NAN	GUANGZHOU	3.8	LAG
JINDAO	QINGDAO	4.0	LAG
LONGXIANG	BEIJING	2.1	PIL
MON-LEI	BEIJING	2.6	LAG
NINE STAR	BEIJING	2.9	LAG
PANDA	SHANGHAI	3.5	PIL
SNOWFLAKE	SHENYANG	2.3	PIL
SUN LIK	HONG KONG	3.5	PIL
SWEET CHINA	GUANGZHOU	0.2	LAG
TSINGTAO	SHANGHAI	0.4	PIL
YI KING	GUANGZHOU	2.1	PIL
YUCHAN	BEIJING	4.0	PIL
ZHUJIANG	GUANGZHOU	2.9	LAG
COLOMBIA			
CERVEZA AGUILA	BARRANQUILLA	2.3	PIL
CLAUSEN EXPORT	BOGOTA	2.8	PIL
LEONA CERVEZA	BOGOTA	2.2	PIL
CONGO			
NGOK' MALT LIQUOR	POINTE NOIRE	1.8	MLT
COSTA RICA			
IMPERIAL	SAN JOSE	1.3	LAG

NAME	LOCATION	RATING	STYLE
CYPRUS			
Keo	Limassol	3.1	Lag
CZECH REPUBLIC			
Black Lion Premium Dark	Hradecky	3.1	Lag
Budweiser Budvar	Budejovice	3.5	Pil
Crystal Diplomat Dark Beer	Wurtenberg	3.8	Lag
Gambrinus Lager	Pilsen	2.9	Lag
Karel Iv Lager	Karlovy Vary	3.6	Lag
Kozel Premium Czech Malt Liquor	Velke Popovice	3.0	Lag
Lobko Bohemian Lager Vysoky	Chlumec	4.1	Lag
N.A. Pevo	Popovice	2.6	Na
Pilsner Urquell	Pilsen	3.5	Pil
Radegast Original Lager	Nosovice	3.1	Lag
Staropramen	Prague	3.9	Pil
DENMARK			
Buur Beer Deluxe	Randers	3.4	Lag
Carlsberg	Copenhagen	3.3	Lag
Carlsberg Elephant Malt Liquor	Copenhagen	3.1	Mlt
Ceres Royal Export	Arthus	3.3	Lag
Faxe Premium	Faxe	2.7	Lag
Giraf Malt Liquor	Odense	2.3	Mlt
Green Rooster	Copenhagen	0.0	Lag
DOMINICAN REPUBLIC			
Presidente Pilsener	Santo Domingo	3.5	Pil
ECUADOR			
Club Premium	Quito	2.1	Lag
Pilsener	Quito	4.0	Pil
EL SALVADOR			
Pilsener of El Salvador	San Salvador	2.5	Pil
Regia Extra	San Salvador	2.4	Lag
ENGLAND			
Adnams Suffolk Extra Ale	Southwold	3.1	Ale
Bass Pale Ale	Burton-on-Trent	3.8	Ale
Bateman's Dark Victory Ale	Wainfleet	3.8	Ale
Bateman's XXXB Ale	Wainfleet	3.7	Ale
Boddington's Gold	Manchester	2.3	Ale
Bulldog	Reading	3.3	Ale
Chester Golden Ale	Cheshire	2.9	Ale
Churchill Amber	Redruth	3.3	Lag

NAME	LOCATION	RATING	STYLE
Churchill Lager	Redruth	3.6	Lag
Double Diamond Ale	Burton-on-Trent	2.5	Ale
Fuller's ESB Export Ale	London	2.5	Ale
Fuller's London Pride	London	3.8	Ale
George Gale Prize Old Ale	Horndean	3.9	Ale
Greenall's Bitter	Warrington	2.4	Ale
Greenall's Cheshire English Pub Beer	Warrington	3.1	Ale
Guru Lager	London	2.2	Lag
Hardy Country Bitter	Dorchester	2.3	Ale
Hobgoblin Traditional English Ale	Witney	3.8	Ale
Irish Brigade	Warrington	3.0	Ale
John Bull	Burton-on-Trent	2.4	Ale
John Courage Amber Beer	Staines	3.5	Lag
John Courage Export	Bristol	2.8	Lag
John Peel Ale	Blackburn	2.8	Ale
Kaliber	London	2.8	Na
King & Barnes IPA	Horsham	2.7	IPA
Kingpin Lager	Mansfield	1.0	Lag
Lal Toofan Indian Pilsener	Trowbridge	2.1	Pil
Landlord Strong Pale Ale	Keighley	2.9	Ale
Lcl Pils	Newcastle-upon-Tyne	2.4	Pil
London Light	London	2.2	Pil
Lynx Pilsner	London	2.1	Pil
Mackeson Triple XXX Stout	London	4.1	Sto
Marksman Lager	Mansfield	3.3	Lag
Marston's Albion Porter	Burton-on-Trent	2.8	Por
Master Brew Premium Ale	Faversham	2.1	Ale
McMullen's Ak Original Bitter	Hertford	2.8	Ale
Melbourn Bros. Apricot Beer	Stamford	3.8	Lag
Merriman's Old Fart	Leeds	2.5	Ale
Monkey Wrench Ale	Harrogate	4.2	Ale
Moonraker Old Ale	Manchester, Middleton	3.3	Ale
Mordue Workie Ticket	Newcastle-upon-Tyne	3.4	Ale
Morland "Old Speckled Hen" English Fine Ale	Abingdon	4.1	Ale
Newcastle Brown Ale	Newcastle-upon-Tyre	3.3	Ale
Norvig Ale	Wisbech	2.4	Ale
Old Peculier Ale	Masham	3.8	Ale

NAME	LOCATION	RATING	STYLE
Pope's "1880"	Dorchester	3.6	Ale
Royal Oak Pale Ale	Dorchester	4.4	Ale
Ruddles Bitter	Rutland	1.4	Ale
Ruddles Country Ale	Rutland	2.3	Ale
Samuel Smith Oatmeal Stout	Tadcaster	4.0	Sto
Samuel Smith Tadcaster Taddy Porter	Tadcaster	3.7	Por
Samuel Smith's Imperial Stout	Tadcaster	4.0	Sto
Samuel Smith's Lager	Tadcaster	4.0	Lag
Samuel Smith's Nut Brown Ale	Tadcaster	3.4	Ale
Samuel Smith's Old Brewery Pale Ale	Tadcaster	3.0	Ale
Samuel Smith's Winter Welcome Ale (annual)	Tadcaster	2.3–3.8	Ale
Sarah Hughes Dark Ruby Ale	Sedgeley	2.2	Ale
Shepherd Neame India Pale Ale	Faversham	3.2	IPA
Swale Indian Summer Pale Ale	Sittingbourne	2.6	Ale
Thomas Hardy's Ale-1989	Dorchester	0.4	Ale
Watney's Cream Stout	London	3.9	Sto
Watney's Red Barrel	London	3.9	Lag
Watney's Stingo Cream Stout	London	3.5	Sto
Whitbread Ale	London & Sheffield	3.9	Ale
Young's London Porter	London	3.2	Por
Young's Oatmeal Stout	London	4.3	Sto
Young's Old Nick (annual)	London	3.9	Ale
Young's Old Nick Barley Wine	London	2.2	Bar
Young's Ram Rod	London	3.6	Ale
Young's Special Ale	London	3.0	Ale
Young's Winter Ale (annual)	London	4.0–4.3	Ale
ESTONIA			
Saku Estonian Pilsner	Eesti	3.0	Pil
Saku Estonian Porter	Eesti	2.7	Por
ETHIOPIA			
Asmara	Asmara	2.1	Lag

NAME	LOCATION	RATING	STYLE
FINLAND			
KOFF	HELSINKI	3.6	LAG
LAPIN KULTA	HELSINKI	2.2	LAG
LENINGRAD COWBOY LAGER	HELSINKI	2.3	LAG
FRANCE			
ADELSCOTT MALT LIQUOR	SCHILTIGHEIM	4.2	MLT
BIERE DU DESERT	DOUAI CEDEX	3.7	ALE
BRASSEURS BIERE DE PARIS	BONNEUIL	1.3	LAG
BRASSEURS GRAND CRU	BONNEUIL	3.5	LAG
BREUG LAGER	ROUBAIX	2.7	LAG
CH'TI BLOND BIERE DE GARDE	BENIFONTAINE	3.3	BDG
DESPERADOS	SCHILTIGHEIM	0.1	PIL
FISCHER D'ALSACE AMBER	SCHILTIGHEIM	3.2	MLT
GRAIN D'ORGE BIERE DE GARDE	RONCHIN	2.6	BDG
JENLAIN FRENCH COUNTRY ALE	JENLAIN	2.3	ALE
KRONENBOURG BIERE DE NOEL (ANNUAL)	STRASBOURG	2.8	LAG
KRONENBOURG PALE	STRASBOURG	3.1	LAG
LA BELLE STRASBOURGEOISE	SCHILTIGHEIM	2.9	LAG
SCHLOSS JOSEF ALSATIAN MALT BEVERAGE	SCHUTZENBERG	3.1	NA
SCHUTZ BIERE D'ALSACE PILS	SCHILTIGHEIM	2.4	PIL
SCHUTZENBERGER JUBILATOR	SCHILTIGHEIM	3.8	BOC
SEPTANTE 5 MALT LIQUOR	ROUBAIX	3.7	MLT
SEPTANTE ROUGE	ROUBAIX	2.2	ALE
SUPER 49 MALT LIQUOR	ROUBAIX	2.8	MLT
TERKEN BIERE DE LUXE MALT LIQUOR	ROUBAIX	2.9	MLT
TERKEN BRUNE MALT LIQUOR	ROUBAIX	2.5	MLT
3 MONT FLANDERS GOLDEN ALE	SAINT-SYLVESTRE	3.3	ALE
33 EXPORT	PARIS	3.1	LAG
36.15 PECHEUR	SCHILTIGHEIM	0.3	LAG
TUTZ	SCHILTIGHEIM	3.2	PIL
GERMANY			
AKTIEN JUBILAUMS PILS	KAUFBEUREN	2.8	PIL
AKTIEN ST. MARTIN DUNKLER DOPPELBOCK	KAUFBEUREN	2.8	BOC
AKTIEN WEIZEN	KAUFBEUREN	2.6	WHT

NAME	LOCATION	RATING	STYLE
ALTENMUNSTER EXPORT	MARKTOBERDORF	2.0	LAG
ALTENMUNSTER MALT LIQUOR	MARKTOBERDORF	1.9	MLT
ARNOLD PILSNER	BAVARIA	1.3	PIL
AVENTINUS WHEAT-DOPPELBOCK	MUNICH	3.3	BOC
AYINGER BAVARIAN WHEAT	AYING	2.9	WHT
AYINGER CELEBRATOR DOPPELBOCK	AYING	3.7	BOC
AYINGER DUNKLES UR-WEISSE	AYING	4.0	WHT
AYINGER JAHRHUNDERT BIER	AYING	2.9	LAG
AYINGER MAIBOCK	AYING	2.0	BOC
AYINGER OKTOBERFEST-MARZEN	AYING	3.9	LAG
BARRE BRAU	LUBBECKE	3.8	PIL
BECK'S	BREMEN	3.1	PIL
BECK'S DARK	BREMEN	2.6	PIL
BECK'S OKTOBERFEST (SEASONAL)	BREMEN	3.7	LAG
BERLINER PILS	BERLIN	2.5	PIL
BERLINER RATSKELLER LAGER	BERLIN	2.2	LAG
BITBURGER DRIVE ALKOHOLFREI	BITBURG	3.8	NA
BITBURGER PILSENER	BITBURG	3.3	PIL
BOLTEN ALT	KORSCHENBROICH	4.0	ALT
BROYHAN PREMIUM	HANNOVER	1.8	LAG
CASSEL SCHLOSS	NOERTEN-HARDENBERG	1.7	LAG
CLAUSTHALER	FRANKFURT	3.8	NA
DAB TRADITIONAL GERMAN DARK BEER	DORTMUND	1.7	LAG
DEININGER KRISTALL WEIZEN	HOF	2.2	WHT
DINKELACKER	STUTTGART	2.9	PIL
DINKELACKER DARK	STUTTGART	3.4	LAG
DORTMUNDER AKTIEN ALT	DORTMUND	1.2	ALT
DORTMUNDER UNION DARK	DORTMUND	0.1	LAG
DORTMUNDER UNION ORIGINAL	DORTMUND	3.6	PIL
DRESSLER	BREMEN	2.0	PIL
EDELWEISS LUXURY GRADE MALT LIQUOR	DRESDEN	1.4	MLT
EINBECKER UR-BOCK	EINBECK	2.7	BOC
EKU DARK HEFE WEISBIER	KULMBACH	3.8	WHT
EKU EDELBOCK	KULMBACH	3.7	BOC
EKU KULMBACHER PILS	KULMBACH	3.9	PIL

NAME	LOCATION	RATING	STYLE
EKU KULMBACHER RUBIN	KULMBACH	1.9	LAG
EKU KULMINATOR URTYP HELL MALT LIQUOR	KULMBACH	0.2	MLT
ERBACHER GERMAN LAGER	ERBACH	2.4	LAG
ERDINGER WEISSBIER HEFETRUB	ERDING	4.4	WHT
ERDINGER WEISSBIER-DUNKEL	ERDING	4.0	WHT
ERDINGER WEIZENBOCK	ERDING	3.8	BOC
ETTALER KLOSTER DUNKEL	ETTAL	4.5	LAG
EXTRACTO DE MALTA MALT BEVERAGE	HAMBURG	3.9	NA
FEST BIER	BAYREUTH	2.4	MLT
FIEDLERS BOCK IM STEIN	KOBLENZ	2.5	BOC
FIEDLERS PILS IM STEIN	KOBLENZ	2.3	PIL
FLENS	FLENSBURG	2.6	LAG
FURSTENBERG	DONAUESCHINGEN	3.3	PIL
GLOSSNER HOPFENGARTEN PILS	NEUMARKT	3.6	PIL
GLOSSNER TORSCHMIED'S DUNKEL	NEUMARKT	3.2	LAG
GOLFER'S CHOICE GERMAN ALE	SCHWABISCH GMUND	2.6	ALE
GRENZQUELL GERMAN PILSNER	HAMBURG	3.1	PIL
HAAKE BECK	BREMEN	3.5	NA
HACKER-PSCHORR WEISSE BOCK	MUNICH	3.3	BOC
HACKER-PSCHORR WEISSE DARK	MUNICH	2.5	LAG
HACKERBRAU EDELHELL MUNICH LAGER MALT LIQUOR	MUNICH	3.3	LAG
HENNINGER DARK	FRANKFURT	2.5	LAG
HENNINGER GERSTEL BRAU	FRANKFURT	3.4	NA
HENNINGER KAISER PILSNER	FRANKFURT	3.0	PIL
HENNINGER LIGHT	FRANKFURT	1.9	PIL
HERRENBRAU PILSENER MALT LIQUOR	BAYREUTH	2.4	MLT
HERRENHAUSER PILSENER MALT LIQUOR	HANNOVER	1.2	MLT
HOFBRAU BAVARIA DARK RESERVE	KULMBACH	2.5	LAG

NAME	LOCATION	RATING	STYLE
HOFBRAU BAVARIAN LIGHT RESERVE	KULMBACH	2.7	LAG
HOFBRAU MUNCHENER OKTOBERFEST	MUNICH	3.3	LAG
HOFBRAU ROYAL BAVARIAN LAGER	MUNICH	3.1	LAG
HOLSTEN	HAMBURG	3.0	PIL
HOLSTEN DRY	HAMBURG	2.9	PIL
ISENBECK	HAMM	3.4	LAG
JEVER PILSENER	JEVER	3.0	PIL
JULIUS ECHTER HEFE-WEISSBIER	WURZBURG	3.0	WHT
KAISER PILSNER	FRANKFURT	0.5	PIL
KAISERDOM EXTRA DRY	BAMBERG	3.9	LAG
KAISERDOM RAUCHBIER SMOKED BAVARIAN DARK	BAMBERG	3.9	LAG
KAPUZINER WEIZEN KRISTALLKLAR	KULMBACH	3.1	WHT
KLOSTER SCHWARTZBIER-MONKHOF	KULMBACH	2.9	LAG
KLOSTERBOCK MONKSHOF	KULMBACH	2.3	MLT
KRONEN CLASSIC ALL DARK	DORTMUND	2.1	LAG
KROPF DARK DRAFT	KASSEL	2.6	LAG
KROPF DRAFT	KASSEL	2.3	LAG
KROPF EDEL PILS	KASSEL	2.5	PIL
LANDSKRON PILS	RADEBERG	3.8	PIL
MAISEL'S HEFE WEISSE	BAYREUTH	4.0	WHT
MAISEL'S WEIZEN	BAYREUTH	2.0	WHT
MAISEL'S WEIZEN KRISTALL-KLAR	BAYREUTH	2.5	WHT
MAXIMATOR DARK DOPPELBOCK	MUNICH	3.5	BOC
OBERDORFER DARK HEFEWEIZEN	MARKTOBERDORF	3.1	WHT
PADERBORNER PILSENER	PADERBORN	0.2	PIL
PAULANER ALT MUNCHER DUNKEL	MUNICH	3.9	ALT
PAULANER BAVARIAN ALPINE EXTREME ALE	MUNICH	2.6	ALE
PAULANER HEFE-WEIZEN	MUNICH	2.9	WHT
PAULANER MUNCHEN NR. 1 LAGER	MUNICH	2.2	LAG
PAULANER OKTOBERFEST	MUNICH	3.8	LAG

NAME	LOCATION	RATING	STYLE
PAULANER SALVATOR DOPPELBOCK	MUNICH	4.0	BOC
PAULANER THOMAS BRAU	MUNICH	3.3	NA
PINKUS ORGANIC MUNSTER ALT	MUNSTER	1.5	ALT
PINKUS HOME BREW WEIZEN	MUNSTER	1.3	WHT
PINKUS ORGANIC UR PILS	MUNSTER	1.9	PIL
PSCHORR-BRAU WEISSE	MUNICH	3.5	WHT
RED STAR SELECT	BERLIN	2.2	LAG
REICHELBRAU BAVARIAN DARK	KULMBACH	3.1	LAG
RIEGELER SPEZIAL EXPORT	KAISERSTUHL	2.9	LAG
RITTERBRAU PALE	DORTMUND	4.0	LAG
SAILER PILS	MARKTOBERDORF	2.8	PIL
SCHLENKERLA SMOKED BEER-MARZEN	BAMBERG	3.7	ALE
SCHULTHEISS BERLINER WEISSE	BERLIN	3.0	WHT
SCHULTHEISS GERMAN PILSENER	BERLIN	0.3	PIL
SCHWEIZERHOF-BRAU LAGER	MARKTOBERDORF	2.9	LAG
SPATEN FRANZISKANER HEFE-WEISSBIER	MUNICH	2.6	WHT
SPATEN FRANZISKUS HELLER BOCK	MUNICH	3.1	BOC
SPATEN MUNCHEN CLUB-WEISSE	MUNICH	3.5	WHT
SPATEN MUNICH OPTIMATOR DOPPELSPATEN BOCK	MUNICH	3.4	BOC
SPATEN OKTOBERFEST UR-MARZEN	MUNICH	2.8	LAG
SPATEN PILS	MUNICH	2.5	PIL
SPATEN PREMIUM	MUNICH	3.3	LAG
ST. GEORGEN KELLER BIER-UNGESPUNDET-HEFETRUB	BUTTENGEIM	2.3	LAG
ST. PAULI	BREMEN	2.8	NA
ST. PAULI GIRL	BREMEN	3.4	PIL
ST. PAULI GIRL DARK	BREMEN	3.5	PIL
STEINGADENER WEISSE DUNKEL	KAUFBEUREN	2.9	WHT
STEINHAUSER BIER	FRANKFURT	3.5	PIL
TUCHER FESTBIER MARZEN	NURENBERG	2.0	LAG

NAME	LOCATION	RATING	STYLE
VALENTINS KLARES WEIZENBIER	HEIDELBERG	2.3	WHT
VELTINS PILSENER	GREVENSTEIN	2.4	PIL
WARSTEINER	WARSTEIN	3.9	PIL
WARSTEINER PREMIUM FRESH	WARSTEIN	3.9	NA
WARSTEINER PREMIUM VERUM	WARSTEIN	3.0	PIL
WEIHENSTEPHAN EDEL-PILS	FREISING	2.6	PIL
WEIHENSTEPHAN EXPORT DUNKEL	FREISING	4.1	LAG
WEIHENSTEPHAN WEIZENBIER	FREISING	3.8	WHT
WICKULER PILSENER	WUPPERTAL	3.7	PIL
WOLFBRAU	OSNABRUCK	3.3	PIL
WURZBURGER HOFBRAU FESTBIER	WURZBURG	3.0	LAG
WURZBURGER HOFBRAU OCTOBERFEST (ANNUAL)	WURZBURG	2.5	LAG
GREECE			
AEGEAN HELLAS	ATALANTI	4.2	LAG
ARIS GREEK LAGER	THESSALONIKI	2.5	LAG
ATHENIAN-THE GREEK BEER	ATHENS	0.8	LAG
MARATHON-THE GREEK BEER	ATHENS	3.8	LAG
MYTHOS HELLENIC LAGER BEER	SINDOS	3.0	LAG
SPARTAN LAGER	ATALANTI	4.0	LAG
GUATEMALA			
CABRO EXTRA	GUATEMALA CITY	1.7	PIL
DURANGO	DEL SUR	0.8	PIL
FAMOSA 1896 LAGER	GUATEMALA CITY	2.7	LAG
MEDALLA DE ORO LAGER	GUATEMALA CITY	2.3	LAG
MONTE CARLO LAGER	GUATEMALA CITY	2.8	LAG
MOZA BOCK	GUATEMALA CITY	2.9	BOC
HAITI			
PRESTIGE STOUT	PORT-AU-PRINCE	4.0	STO
HOLLAND			
ALFA	SCHINNEN	3.1	PIL
BAVARIA LAGER	LIESHOUT	3.0	LAG
BAVARIA MALT BEVERAGE	LIESHOUT	3.3	NA
BRAND	LIMBURG	2.5	PIL
BUCKLER	AMSTERDAM (HENIKEN)	2.2	NA
CHRISTOFFEL BIER LAGER	ROERMOND	2.5	LAG
CHRISTOFFEL ROBERTUS	ROERMOND	2.6	ALE
DUTCH GOLD LAGER	BREDA	2.7	LAG
EUROPEAN EXPORT LAGER	ASSEN	3.0	LAG
GROLSCH	GROENLO	3.1	PIL

NAME	LOCATION	RATING	STYLE
GROLSCH AUTUMN AMBER ALE	GROENLO	3.6	ALE
GROLSCH DARK LAGER	GROENLO	3.2	LAG
GROLSCH DRY DRAFT	GROENLO	3.0	PIL
HEINEKEN LAGER	AMSTERDAM	3.4	LAG
HEINEKEN SPECIAL DARK	AMSTERDAM	2.4	LAG
JOSEPH MEENS' HOLLAND PREMIUM	SCHINNEN	1.0	LAG
LA TRAPPE ALE	TILBURG	3.9	ALE
LEEUW PILSNER	LIMBURG	3.2	PIL
ORANJEBOOM PREMIUM LAGER	BREDA & ROTTERDAM	3.4	LAG
PETER'S BRAND PILSENER	AMERSFOORT	2.3	PIL
REMBRANDT MASTERPIECE LAGER BEER	NIJKERK	2.3	LAG
ROYAL BRAND	WIJLRE	3.4	LAG
ROYAL DUTCH POST HORN	BREDA	3.9	LAG
SKOL HOLLAND PILSENER	ROTTERDAM	2.2	PIL
SWINKELS	LIESHOUT	2.4	PIL
HONDURAS			
PORT ROYAL EXPORT	SAN PEDRO SULA	1.3	PIL
SALVA VIDA	SAN PEDRO SULA	2.6	LAG
HUNGARY			
BORSOD PREMIUM	BOCSARLAPUJTO	2.5	PIL
KOBANYAI VILAGOS SOR	BUDAPEST	2.3	PIL
ICELAND			
GULL	REYKJAVIK	2.5	PIL
INDIA			
COLTS BERG	BANGALORE	2.1	PIL
FLYING HORSE ROYAL LAGER	BANGALORE	2.7	LAG
GOA PILSNER DRY	GOA	2.9	PIL
GOLDEN EAGLE LAGER	MADRAS	3.5	LAG
HIMALAYAN BLUE PREMIUM LAGER	SIKKUM, MALLI	2.5	LAG
KALYANI BLACK LABEL PREMIUM LAGER	BANGALORE	3.5	LAG
KINGFISHER LAGER	BANGLORE (BREWED IN ENGLAND)	2.8	LAG
RAJ INDIAN BEER	BANGALORE	2.4	LAG
SAND PIPER EXTRA GOLD LAGER	HARVANA, DHARUHERA	2.5	LAG
TAJ MAHAL LAGER	CALCUTTA	3.1	LAG
UB EXPORT LAGER	BANGALORE	2.5	LAG
INDONESIA			
ANKER PILSNER	DJAKARTA	2.9	PIL
BINTANG PILSENER	SURABAYA	3.9	PIL

NAME	LOCATION	RATING	STYLE
IRELAND			
BEAMISH IRISH CREAM STOUT	CORK	3.7	STO
BECKETT'S ALE	DUBLIN	3.3	ALE
GUINNESS EXTRA STOUT	DUBLIN	3.8	STO
GUINNESS PUB DRAUGHT	DUBLIN	3.9	STO
HARP LAGER	DUBLIN	3.5	LAG
KILKENNY IRISH BEER-EXPORT	KILKENNY, ST. FRANCIS ABBY	3.0	LAG
MACARDLES TRADITIONAL ALE	DUBLIN	2.4	ALE
MURPHY'S IRISH STOUT	CORK	2.5	STO
MURPHY'S STOUT	CORK	3.5	STO
PORTERHOUSE RED ALE	DUBLIN	3.0	ALE
SATZENBRAU PREMIUM PILS	DUBLIN	3.0	PIL
ST. BERNARD GERMAN LAGER PILSNER	DUBLIN	3.2	PIL
ISRAEL			
MACCABEE	NETANYA	1.8	LAG
ITALY			
CASTELLO	SAN GIORGIO DI NOGARO	2.2	PIL
D'AQUINO ITALIAN BEER	INDUNO	2.3	PIL
DREHER PILSENER	MILAN	2.1	PIL
MCFARLAND GOLDEN FIRE	MILAN	3.9	ALE
MESSINA PILSENER	MILAN	4.1	PIL
MORETTI BIRRA FRIULANA	UDINE	1.3	PIL
MORETTI LA ROSSA ALL MALT	UDINE	3.1	LAG
MORETTI LA ROSSA DOPPIOMALTO	UDINE	2.7	LAG
PEDAVENA PILS CLASSICA	ITALY	2.1	PIL
PERONI	ROME	3.1	LAG
RAFFO	ROME	3.9	PIL
IVORY COAST			
MAMBA	ABIDJAN	3.1	MLT
JAMAICA			
DRAGON STOUT	KINGSTON	3.3	STO
RED STRIPE LAGER	KINGSTON	2.2	LAG
JAPAN			
ASAHI DRAFT	TOKYO	1.1	PIL
ASAHI SUPER DRY DRAFT	TOKYO	2.5	PIL
ASAHI Z DRAFT	TOKYO	3.7	PIL
KIRIN DRAFT	TOKYO (NOT FOR EXPORT)	2.0	LAG
KIRIN ICHIBAN MALT LIQUOR	TOKYO	4.0	MLT
KIRIN LAGER	TOKYO	3.9	LAG
SAPPORO BLACK MALT LIQUOR	TOKYO	4.0	MLT

NAME	LOCATION	RATING	STYLE
SAPPORO BLACK MALT LIQUOR	TOKYO (NOT FOR EXPORT)	4.1	MLT
SAPPORO DRAFT	TOKYO	2.4	PIL
SUNTORY DRAFT	OSAKA	2.2	PIL
SUNTORY GINJO DRAFT	OSAKA	2.6	PIL
SUNTORY GOLD DRAFT 100% MALT BEER	OSAKA	3.3	PIL
YEBISU ALL MALT	TOKYO	2.7	PIL
YEBISU STOUT DRAFT	TOKYO	2.4	STO
KENYA			
TUSKER MALT LAGER	NAIROBI	2.3	LAG
TUSKER PREMIUM LAGER	NAIROBI	4.3	LAG
KOREA			
CAFRI PREMIUM BEER	SEOUL	3.4	PIL
CASS FRESH	SEOUL	3.4	ALE
CROWN	SEOUL	2.2	LAG
OB LAGER	SEOUL	2.5	LAG
LEBANON			
ALMAZA PILSENER	BEIRUT	3.9	PIL
LIBERIA			
MONROVIA CLUB BEER	MONROVIA	3.0	LAG
LITHUANIA			
UTENOS PORTER	UTENA	2.4	POR
LUXEMBOURG			
DIEKIRCH	DIEKIRCH	2.9	PIL
MEXICO			
AZTECA	TECATE	0.3	PIL
BARRIL CLARA	MEXICO CITY	3.8	PIL
BARRIL OSCURA	MEXICO CITY	4.0	PIL
BOHEMIA PILSENER	MONTERREY	1.7	PIL
BRISA	GUADALAJARA	2.8	LAG
CARTA BLANCA	MONTERREY	3.6	LAG
CHIHUAHUA	MONTERREY	2.7	LAG
CLARA ESTRELLA DORADA	GUADALAJARA	0.6	LAG
CORONA EXTRA	MEXICO CITY	0.8	PIL
DOS EQUIS CLARA-LAGER ESPECIAL	GUADALAJARA	3.2	LAG
HOMBRE	CIUDAD JUAREZ	2.9	LAG
INDIO OSCURA	MONTERREY	1.6	LAG
MODELO ESPECIAL	MEXICO CITY	2.9	LAG
MONTEJO	YUCATAN, MERIDA	2.5	PIL
MONTEZUMA DE BARRIL	MEXICO CITY	3.3	LAG
NAVIDAD CERVEZA COMMEMORATIVA (ANNUAL)	MONTERREY	0.1–3.4	PIL

NAME	LOCATION	RATING	STYLE
NOCHE BUENA (ANNUAL)	ORIZABA	2.4–3.3	LAG
PACIFICO CLARA	MAZATLAN	3.1	PIL
SOL	GUADALAJARA	2.5	PIL
SUPERIOR	GUADALAJARA	3.1	PIL
TECATE	MONTERREY	3.0	PIL
VICTORIA	MEXICO CITY	0.0	PIL
NEW GUINEA			
SOUTH PACIFIC SPECIAL EXPORT LAGER	PAPUA	2.0	LAG
NEW ZEALAND			
DB DRAUGHT	AUCKLAND	2.3	LAG
KIWI LAGER	TIMARU	4.0	LAG
LEOPARD DELUXE	HASTINGS	3.0	PIL
LION RED	AUCKLAND	2.5	LAG
NEW ZEALAND LAGER	AUCKLAND	2.4	LAG
STEINLAGER	AUCKLAND	3.8	PIL
NIGERIA			
GULDER LAGER	LAGOS	2.5	LAG
STAR LAGER	LAGOS	1.0	LAG
NORWAY			
AASS BOCK	DRAMMEN	3.2	BOC
AASS CLASSIC	DRAMMEN	3.2	LAG
AASS JULE ØL	DRAMMEN	4.5	LAG
AASS PILSNER	DRAMMEN	2.9	PIL
FRYDENLUND	OSLO	2.5	PIL
HANSA DARK	BERGEN	4.1	PIL
HANSA LIGHT	BERGEN	2.6	PIL
MACK-ØL ARTIC BEER PILSENER	TROMSØ	2.9	PIL
NORWEGIAN ICE	TRONDHEIM	1.6	PIL
RINGNES EXPORT PALE	OSLO	4.0	PIL
RINGNES SPECIAL JUBILEE ALE	OSLO	2.7	ALE
PANAMA			
PANAMA CERVEZA ALLEMANA STYLE	PANAMA CITY	3.6	LAG
PERU			
CALLAO PILSEN	CALLAO	2.3	PIL
CRISTAL PREMIUM	CHICLAYO & LIMA	2.4	LAG
CUSQUENA PREMIUM PERUVIAN BEER	CUZCO	2.4	LAG
CUZCO	CUZCO	3.2	PIL
MALTINA	LIMA	3.4	NA

NAME	LOCATION	RATING	STYLE
PHILIPPINES			
Manila Gold Pale Pilsen	Cabuyao	3.1	Pil
Red Horse Malt Liquor	Manila	3.2	Mlt
San Miguel Dark	Manila	4.4	Pil
San Miguel Pale Pilsen	Manila	2.9	Pil
POLAND			
Dojlidy Porter	Bialystok	3.2	Por
Karmi Okocim Low Alcohol Content Beer	Brzesko	3.8	Lag
Krakus Light	Zywiec	2.1	Pil
Lech Pils	Lech	0.2	Pil
Okocim O.K. Full Light	Warsaw	2.2	Pil
Okocim O.K. Pils	Warsaw	0.3	Pil
Okocim Porter	Okocim	3.1	Por
Okocim Premium Beer	Okocim	3.1	Pil
Polander Beer	Koszalin	3.1	Lag
Tyskie Pils	Tychy	2.9	Pil
Zywiec Full Light	Zywiec	1.5	Pil
PORTUGAL			
Cerveja Cheers	Leca Do Balio	3.5	Na
Cristal	Leca Do Balio	2.2	Pil
Europa	Lisbon	3.1	Lag
Sagres Premium	Lisbon	2.1	Lag
PUERTO RICO			
India	Mayaguez	1.1	Lag
Medalla Light	San Juan	0.8	Pil
ROMANIA			
Ursus Premium Pils	Cluj-Napoca	2.8	Pil
RUSSIA			
Admeeral Tyeyskoye	Moscow	0.4	Lag
Moscova	Moscow	1.3	Lag
Ostankinskoye Beer	Moscow	2.7	Pil
Slavayansky	Moscow	0.3	Lag
Troika Original Russian Beer	Moscow	1.1	Lag
SCOTLAND			
Alba Scots Pine Ale	Alloa	2.8	Ale
Belhaven Scottish Ale	Dunbar	4.0	Ale
Fraoch Heather Ale	Alloa	2.9	Ale
Golden Promise Ale	Edinburgh	2.8	Ale
Grozet Gooseberry & Wheat Ale	Glasgow	3.1	Wht
Lorimer's Scottish Beer	Edinburgh	2.6	Ale
MacAndrew's Scotch Ale	Edinburgh	3.2	Ale

NAME	LOCATION	RATING	STYLE
MACLAY WALLACE PALE ALE	ALLOA	3.8	ALE
MCEWAN'S EXPORT INDIA PALE ALE	EDINBURGH	4.0	IPA
MCEWAN'S SCOTCH ALE	EDINBURGH	3.8	ALE
MERLIN'S ALE	BROUGHTON, PEEBLESHIRE	3.7	ALE
ORKNEY DARK ISLAND BEER	QUOYLOO	2.9	ALE
ORKNEY SKULLSPLITTER ALE	QUOYLOO	3.8	ALE
ST. ANDREWS ALE	DUNBAR	3.9	ALE
SWEETHEART STOUT	GLASGOW	3.5	STO
TENNENT'S LAGER	GLASGOW	1.8	LAG
THUMB BLONDE	GLASGOW	2.5	ALE
TRAQUAIR HOUSE ALE	INNERLEITHEN	4.1	ALE
TRAQUAIR JACOBITE ALE	INNERLEITHEN	3.0	ALE
YOUNGER'S TARTAN SPECIAL ALE	EDINBURGH	4.1	ALE
SINGAPORE			
ABC EXTRA STOUT	SINGAPORE	3.7	STO
ABC VERY SUPERIOR STOUT	SINGAPORE	3.6	STO
ANCHOR PILSENER	SINGAPORE	2.5	PIL
BARON'S STRONG BREW	SINGAPORE	2.9	LAG
TIGER	SINGAPORE	3.3	LAG
SLOVAKIA			
GOLDEN PHEASANT	HURBANOVO	3.9	LAG
SPAIN			
AGUILA IMPERIAL ALE	MADRID	3.8	ALE
AMBAR DOS ESPECIAL	ZARAGOZA	3.3	LAG
CRUZCAMPO LAGER	CAMPO	2.7	LAG
DAMM	BARCELONA & VALENCIA	3.8	PIL
ESTRELLA GALICIA ESPECIAL	LA CORUNA	2.5	PIL
KELER LAGER	SAN SEBASTIAN	3.4	LAG
SWEDEN			
CARNEGIE STARK-PORTER	SUNDSVALL	2.7	POR
PRIPPS LAGER	GOTHENBURG	2.9	LAG
SWITZERLAND			
BEER SWISS MOUNTAIN	APPENZELL	3.1	LAG
CAESARUS IMPERATOR HELLER BOCK	ZURICH	0.0	BOC
CARDINAL LAGER	FRIBOURG	4.0	LAG
GLARNER LAGER	ZURICH	3.1	LAG
HEXEN BRAU SWISS DUNKEL MALT LIQUOR	ZURICH	3.9	MLT
HOPFENPERLE	RHEINFELDEN	2.6	PIL
HOPFENPERLE SPECIAL	RHEINFELDEN	2.9	LAG

NAME	LOCATION	RATING	STYLE
HURLIMANN SWISS DARK LAGER	ZURICH	2.4	LAG
WARTECK LAGER	BASEL	3.2	LAG
TAHITI			
HINANO	PAPEETE	2.1	LAG
TAIWAN			
CHINA LUXURY LAGER	TAIPEI	2.9	LAG
TAIWAN BEER	TAIPEI	1.8	LAG
THAILAND			
AMARIT LAGER	BANGKOK	2.2	LAG
BANGKOK BEER	BANGKOK	1.6	PIL
SIAM ALE	BANGKOK	3.8	ALE
SINGHA	BANGKOK	2.5	LAG
SINGHA GOLD	BANGKOK	0.9	PIL
TOGO			
NGOMA MALT LIQUOR	LOME	2.1	MLT
NGOMA TOGO PILS	LOME	2.7	PIL
TURKEY			
EFES	IZMIR	0.9	PIL
EFES PILSENER PREMIUM BEER	ISTANBUL	3.3	PIL
UKRAINE			
RUSKI	KIEV	3.3	LAG
RUSSKOYE LAGER	KIEV	0.2	LAG
VENEZUELA			
ANDES	CARACAS	2.6	LAG
POLANDER BEER LAGER	CARACAS	3.1	LAG
POLAR	CARACAS	1.0	LAG
VIETNAM			
33 EXPORT	HO CHI MINH CITY	2.0	PIL
BGI	HO CHI MINH CITY	1.7	PIL
HUE BEER	HUE	0.6	LAG
SAIGON LAGER BEER	HO CHI MINH CITY	0.0	LAG
WALES			
BRAINS TRADITIONAL WELSH ALE	CARDIFF	3.9	ALE
THAMES FESTIVE ALE	LLANELLI	2.5	ALE
WELSH FELINFOEL ALE	LLANELLI	3.9	ALE
WELSH FELINFOEL BITTER	LLANELLI	2.4	ALE
WELSH FELINFOEL DOUBLE DRAGON ALE	LLANELLI	4.1	ALE

NAME	LOCATION	RATING	STYLE
WELSH FELINFOEL DRAGON ALE	LLANELLI	4.0	ALE
WELSH FELINFOEL HERCULES ALE	LLANELLI	4.0	ALE
WELSH FELINFOEL PORTER	LLANELLI	1.8	POR
WEST INDIES			
CARIBE	CHAMPS FLEURS, TRINIDAD	3.3	LAG
ROYAL EXTRA STOUT	CHAMPS FLEURS, TRINIDAD	3.4	STO
SHANDY CARIB	PORT OF SPAIN, TRINIDAD	0.2	LAG
WESTERN SAMOA			
VAILIMA LAGER	APIA	3.5	LAG
VAILIMA LIGHT	APIA	2.1	PIL
FORMER YUGOSLAVIA			
BELGRADE GOLD	BELGRADE, SERBIA	2.9	PIL
GOLDHORN CLUB	LASKO, SLOVENIA	3.4	PIL
KARLOVACKO	KARLOVAC, CROATIA	2.9	LAG
KARLSBEER	KARLOVAC, CROATIA	3.2	PIL
NIKSICKO PIVO	NIKSIC, MONTENEGRO	3.1	PIL
RED BREW-STER	LJUBLJANA, SLOVENIA	2.2	PIL
UNION PREMIUM	LJUBLJANA, SLOVENIA	2.5	PIL
ZIMBABWE			
ZAMBEZI PREMIUM EXPORT LAGER	ZIMBABWE	2.5	LAG

BEST BEERS BY STYLE

NAME	LOCATION	RATING
ALES		
CHIMAY PERES TRAPPISTES ALE-PREMIERE (RED LABEL)	BELGIUM, CHIMAY ABBEY	4.7
ROYAL OAK PALE ALE	ENGLAND, DORCHESTER	4.4
RODENBACH ALEXANDER BELGIAN RED ALE	BELGIUM, ROESELARE	4.3
WESTMALLE TRAPPIST	BELGIUM (ABBEY OF WESTMALLE)	4.3
YOUNG'S WINTER ALE (ANNUAL)	ENGLAND, LONDON	4.0–4.3
FIRE FOX BELGIAN ALE	BELGIUM, MELLE/GHENT	4.2
MONKEY WRENCH ALE	ENGLAND, HARROGATE	4.2
OMMEGANG HENNEPIN BELGIAN-STYLE ALE	USA, NEW YORK, COOPERSTOWN	4.2
ARTEVELDE ALE	BELGIUM, MELLE	4.1
MAREDSOUS ABBEY ALE	BELGIUM, DENEE	4.1
MORLAND "OLD SPECKLED HEN" ENGLISH FINE ALE	ENGLAND, ABINGDON	4.1
NEW BELGIUM ABBEY BELGIAN STYLE ALE	USA, COLORADO, FORT COLLINS	4.1
TRAQUAIR HOUSE ALE	SCOTLAND, INNERLEITHEN	4.1
WELSH FELINFOEL DOUBLE DRAGON ALE	WALES, LLANELLI	4.1
YOUNGER'S TARTAN SPECIAL ALE	SCOTLAND, EDINBURGH	4.1
BELHAVEN SCOTTISH ALE	SCOTLAND, DUNBAR	4.0
CORSENDONK MONK'S PALE ALE	BELGIUM, ERTVELDE, SIGILLUM MONASTERY	4.0
ENAME DUBBEL ABBEY ALE	BELGIUM, OUDENAARDE	4.0
GRIMBERGEN DOUBLE ALE	BELGIUM, WATERLOO	4.0
GRIMBERGEN TRIPLE AMBER ABBEY ALE	BELGIUM, WATERLOO	4.0
HAIR OF THE DOG GOLDEN ROSE BELGIAN TRIPEL STYLE ALE	USA, OREGON, PORTLAND	4.0
MACQUEEN'S NESSIE ORIGINAL RED ALE	AUSTRIA, VORCHDORF	4.0
NEW ENGLAND HOLIDAY ALE	USA, CONNECTICUT, NORWALK	4.0
OMMEGANG BELGIAN-STYLE ABBEY ALE	USA, NEW YORK, COOPERSTOWN	4.0
PIRAAT ALE	BELGIUM, ERTVELDE	4.0

NAME	LOCATION	RATING
WELSH FELINFOEL DRAGON ALE	WALES, LLANELLI	4.0
WELSH FELINFOEL HERCULES ALE	WALES, LLANELLI	4.0
WITKAP-PATER SINGEL ABBEY ALE	BELGIUM, NINOVE	4.0
AFFLIGEM NÖEL CHRISTMAS ALE	BELGIUM, OPWIJK	3.9
ALIMONY ALE	USA, IOWA, DUBUQUE	3.9
BLUE RIDGE HOPFEST BROWN ALE	USA, MARYLAND, FREDERICK	3.9
BRAINS TRADITIONAL WELSH ALE	WALES, CARDIFF	3.9
CORSENDONK MONK'S BROWN ALE	BELGIUM, ERTVELDE, SIGILLUM MONASTERY	3.9
DE KONINCK ALE	BELGIUM, ANTWERP	3.9
DOUGLAS SCOTCH BRAND ALE	BELGIUM, ANTWERP	3.9
GEORGE GALE PRIZE OLD ALE	ENGLAND, HORNDEAN	3.9
GOUDEN CAROLUS ALE	BELGIUM, MECHELEN	3.9
LA TRAPPE ALE	HOLLAND, TILBURG	3.9
LA TRAPPE TRAPPIST ALE QUADRUPEL	HOLLAND, TILBURG	3.9
LIEFMANS KRIEKBIER	BELGIUM, OUDENAARDE	3.9
MCFARLAND GOLDEN FIRE ALE	ITALY, MILAN	3.9
NEW BELGIUM FAT TIRE AMBER ALE	USA, COLORADO, FORT COLLINS	3.9
QUELQUE CHOSE SOMETHING	CANADA, QUEBEC, CHAMBLY	3.9
ST. ANDREWS ALE	SCOTLAND, DUNBAR	3.9
STEENDONK WHITE ALE	BELGIUM, BREENDONK	3.9
SUN VALLEY HOLIDAY ALE	USA, IDAHO, HAILEY	3.9
WELSH FELINFOEL ALE	WALES, LLANELLI	3.9
WHITBREAD ALE	ENGLAND, LONDON & SHEFFIELD	3.9
YOUNG'S OLD NICK	ENGLAND, LONDON	3.9
ABITA TURBO DOG	USA, LOUISIANA, ABITA SPRINGS	3.8
AGUILA IMPERIAL ALE	SPAIN, MADRID	3.8
ARA BIER ALE	BELGIUM, ESSEN	3.8
BASS PALE ALE	ENGLAND, BURTON-ON-TRENT	3.8
BATEMAN'S DARK VICTORY ALE	ENGLAND, WAINFLEET	3.8
BRIGAND BELGIAN ALE	BELGIUM, INGELMUNSTER	3.8
CRYSTAL DIPLOMAT DARK BEER	CZECH REPUBLIC, WURTENBERG	3.8
FULLER'S LONDON PRIDE	ENGLAND, LONDON	3.8
GULDEN DRAAK	BELGIUM, ERTVELDE	3.8

NAME	LOCATION	RATING
Hair Of The Dog Adambier	USA, Oregon, Portland	3.8
Hobgoblin Traditional English Ale	England, Witney	3.8
Maclay Wallace Pale Ale	Scotland, Alloa	3.8
MacTarnahans Scottish Style Amber Ale	USA, Oregon, Portland	3.8
McEwan's Scotch Ale	Scotland, Newcastle	3.8
Old Detroit Amber Ale	USA, Michigan, Frankenmuth	3.8
Old Peculier Ale	England, Masham	3.8
Orkney Skullsplitter Ale	Scotland, Quoyloo	3.8
Pasquini's Red Ale	USA, Colorado, Denver	3.8
Pete's Wicked Ale	USA, Washington, Seattle; North Carolina, Winston-Salem	3.8
Sea Dog Windjammer Blonde Ale	USA, Maine, Bangor	3.8
Siam Ale	Thailand, Bangkok	3.8
Sierra Nevada Pale Ale	USA, California, Chico	3.8
Sun Valley White Cloud Ale	USA, Idaho, Hailey	3.8
Tannen Bomb (annual)	USA, Oregon, McMinnville	3.8
Victoria Avenue Amber Ale (Scottish Ale)	USA, California, Riverside	3.8
Anchor Liberty Ale	USA, California, San Francisco	3.7
Anderson Valley Poleeko Gold Light Ale	USA, California, Boonville	3.7
Barbar Belgian Honey Ale	Belgium, Quenast	3.7
Batemans XXXB Ale	England, Wainfleet	3.7
Biere Du Desert	France, Douai Cedex	3.7
Celis Dubble Ale	USA, Texas, Austin	3.7
Hammer & Nail Extra Special Bitter Ale	USA, Connecticut, Watertown	3.7
Labatt's 50	Canada, B.C., Vancouver	3.7
Merlin's Ale	Scotland, Broughton, Peebleshire	3.7
Odell's 90 Shilling Ale	USA, Colorado, Fort Collins	3.7
Rhino Chasers Amber Ale	USA, California, Chatsworth	3.7
Rock Creek Winter Passion Spiced Ale	USA, Virginia, Richmond	3.7
Rockies Buffalo Gold Premium Ale	USA, Colorado, Boulder	3.7
Schlenkerla Smoked Beer-Marzen	Germany, Bamberg	3.7
Spencer's Mckenzie Pale Ale	USA, Oregon, Springfield	3.7
Tommyknocker Pick Axe Pale Ale	USA, Colorado, Idaho Springs	3.7

NAME	LOCATION	RATING
AFFLIGEM TRIPEL ABBEY	BELGIUM, OPWIJK	3.6
BOULDER PALE ALE	USA, COLORADO, BOULDER	3.6
GROLSCH AUTUMN AMBER ALE	HOLLAND, GROENLO	3.6
PIKE PALE ALE	USA, WASHINGTON, SEATTLE	3.6
POPE'S "1880"	ENGLAND, DORCHESTER	3.6
POST ROAD PALE ALE	USA, NEW YORK, UTICA	3.6
POST ROAD REAL ALE	USA, NEW YORK, UTICA	3.6
RAINIER ALE	USA, WASHINGTON, SEATTLE	3.6
ROGUE MOGUL ALE	USA, OREGON, NEWPORT	3.6
YOUNG'S RAM ROD	ENGLAND, LONDON	3.6
COTTONWOOD LIFT YOUR KILT SCOTTISH ALE	USA, NORTH CAROLINA, BOONE	3.5
DELIRIUM NOCTURNUM	BELGIUM, MELLE/GHENT	3.5
ESKE'S SPECIAL BITTER	USA, NEW MEXICO, TAOS	3.5
MARTIN'S PALE ALE	BELGIUM, ANTWERP	3.5
NAPA VALLEY RED ALE	USA, CALIFORNIA, NAPA	3.5
NUTFIELD NOR'EASTER ALE	USA, NEW HAMPSHIRE, DERRY	3.5
SCHLAFLY ROBERT BURNS SCOTCH ALE	USA, MISSOURI, ST. LOUIS	3.5
ALTS		
BOLTON ALT	GERMANY, KORSCHENBROICH	4.0
PAULANER ALT MUNCHER DUNKEL	GERMANY, MUNICH	3.9
ST. STAN'S DARK ALT	USA, CALIFORNIA, MODESTO	3.9
ALASKAN AMBER	USA, ALASKA, JUNEAU	3.8
ST. STAN'S ALT AMBER	USA, CALIFORNIA, MODESTO	3.8
ST. STAN'S FEST BIER	USA, CALIFORNIA, MODESTO	3.5
SCHMALTZ'S ALT ALE	USA, MINNESOTA, NEW ULM	3.3
WIDMER ALT	USA, OREGON, PORTLAND	3.3
NEW ENGLAND ATLANTIC AMBER	USA, CONNECTICUT, NORWALK	3.1
BARLEYWINES		
BRIDGEPORT OLD KNUCKLEHEAD BARLEY WINE STYLE ALE	USA, OREGON, PORTLAND	4.0
MAGNOLIA THUNDERPUSSY BARLEYWINE	USA, CALIFORNIA, SAN FRANCISCO	3.9
ROGUE OLD CRUSTACEAN BARLEY WINE	USA, OREGON, NEWPORT	3.6
JOHN BARLEYCORN BARLEYWINE STYLE ALE	USA, CALIFORNIA, BLUE LAKE	3.0
BIERE DE GARDE		
CH'TI BLOND BIERE DE GARDE	FRANCE, BENIFONTAINE	3.3

NAME	LOCATION	RATING
GRAIN D'ORGE BIERE DE GARDE	FRANCE, RONCHIN	2.6
BOCKS		
SAMUEL ADAMS TRIPLE BOCK	USA, CALIFORNIA, CERES	4.7
PAULANER SALVATOR DOPPELBOCK	GERMANY, MUNICH	4.0
STOUDT'S HONEY DOUBLE BOCK	USA, PENNSYLVANIA, ADAMSTOWN	4.0
WYNKOOP BOCK	USA, COLORADO, DENVER	4.0
ROGUE MAIERBOCK ALE	USA, OREGON, NEWPORT	3.9
ERDINGER WEIZENBOCK	GERMANY, ERDING	3.8
ESKE'S BOCK	USA, NEW MEXICO, TAOS	3.8
SCHUTZENBERGER JUBILATOR	FRANCE, SCHILTIGHEIM	3.8
STOUDT'S ABBEY TRIPLE	USA, PENNSYLVANIA, ADAMSTOWN	3.8
AYINGER CELEBRATOR DOPPELBOCK	GERMANY, AYING	3.7
EKU EDELBOCK	GERMANY, KULMBACH	3.7
PRIOR DOUBLE DARK	USA, PENNSYLVANIA, NORRISTOWN	3.7
SAMUEL ADAMS DOUBLE BOCK DARK LAGER	USA, PENNSYLVANIA, PITTSBURGH	3.7
UPPER CANADA TRUE BOCK	CANADA, ONTARIO, TORONTO	3.7
MAXIMATOR DARK DOPPELBOCK	GERMANY, MUNICH	3.5
BITTER END MODULATOR DOPPELBOCK	USA, TEXAS, AUSTIN	3.4
CELIS PALE BOCK	USA, TEXAS, AUSTIN	3.4
SPATEN MUNICH OPTIMATOR DOPPELSPATEN BOCK	GERMANY, MUNICH	3.4
AVENTINUS WHEAT-DOPPELBOCK	GERMANY, MUNICH	3.3
HACKER-PSCHORR WEISSE BOCK	GERMANY, MUNICH	3.3
AASS BOCK	NORWAY, DRAMMEN	3.2
HOPS BOCK	USA, ARIZONA, SCOTTSDALE	3.1
SPATEN FRANZISKUS HELLER BOCK	GERMANY, MUNICH	3.1
BOILER ROOM RED	USA, NEVADA, LAUGHLIN	3.0
CHRISTMAS/WINTER BEERS		
BRECKENRIDGE CHRISTMAS ALE	USA, COLORADO, BRECKENRIDGE/DENVER	4.0
YOUNG'S WINTER ALE	ENGLAND, LONDON	4.0–4.3

NAME	LOCATION	RATING
AFFLIGEM NÖEL CHRISTMAS ALE	BELGIUM, OPWIJK	3.9
UPTOWN IPA	USA, ARIZONA, TEMPE	3.8
ROCK CREEK WINTER PASSION SPICED ALE	USA, VIRGINIA, RICHMOND	3.7
RED HOOK WINTERHOOK CHRISTMAS ALE	USA, WASHINGTON, SEATTLE	3.6
SARANAC ADIRONDACK SEASON'S BEST	USA, NEW YORK, UTICA	3.4
COOPERSMITH'S CHRISTMAS ALE	USA, COLORADO, FORT COLLINS	3.2
BIG ROCK COLD COCK WINTER PORTER	CANADA, ALBERTA, CALGARY	3.1
COORS WINTERFEST ALE	USA, COLORADO, GOLDEN	3.1
NICHOLAS ALE	USA, MONTANA, HELENA	3.1
PETE'S WINTER BREW	USA, MINNESOTA, ST. PAUL	3.1
SAINT ARNOLD CHRISTMAS ALE	USA, TEXAS, HOUSTON	3.1
ANCHOR OUR SPECIAL ALE	USA, CALIFORNIA, SAN FRANCISCO	2.5–4.0
PYRAMID SNOW CAP ALE	USA, WASHINGTON, SEATTLE	2.5
NOCHE BUENA	MEXICO, ORIZABA	2.4–3.3
SAMUEL SMITH'S WINTER WELCOME ALE	ENGLAND, TADCASTER	2.3–3.8
SIERRA NEVADA CELEBRATION ALE	USA, CALIFORNIA, CHICO	2.3–3.9
SAMUEL ADAMS WINTER LAGER	USA, OREGON, PORTLAND	2.2–3.9
NAVIDAD CERVEZA COMMEMORATIVA	MEXICO, MONTERREY	0.1–3.4
INDIA PALE ALES (IPA)		
HALE'S IPA	USA, WASHINGTON, SEATTLE	4.4
BROOKLYN EAST INDIA PALE ALE	USA, NEW YORK, BROOKLYN	4.1
MCEWAN'S EXPORT INDIA PALE ALE	SCOTLAND, EDINBURGH	4.0
COOPERSMITH'S PUNJABI INDIA PALE ALE	USA, COLORADO, FORT COLLINS	3.8
PIKE INDIA PALE ALE	USA, WASHINGTON, SEATTLE	3.8
UPTOWN IPA	USA, ARIZONA, TEMPE	3.8
BERT GRANT'S INDIA PALE ALE	USA, WASHINGTON, YAKIMA	3.6
MAGNOLIA SPUD BOY IPA	USA, CALIFORNIA, SAN FRANCISCO	3.5
SHEPHERD NEAME INDIA PALE ALE	ENGLAND, FAVERSHAM	3.2

NAME	LOCATION	RATING
LAGERS		
AASS JULE ØL	NORWAY, DRAMMEN	4.5
ETTALER KLOSTER DUNKEL	GERMANY, ETTAL	4.5
TUSKER PREMIUM LAGER	KENYA, NAIROBI	4.3
AEGEAN HELLAS	GREECE, ATALANTI	4.2
JAMES PAGE BOUNDARY WATERS WILD RICE BEER	USA, MINNESOTA, MINNEAPOLIS	4.1
LOBKO BOHEMIAN LAGER VYSOKY	CZECH REPUBLIC, CHLUMEC	4.1
WEIHENSTEPHAN EXPORT DUNKEL	GERMANY, FREISING	4.1
CARDINAL LAGER	SWITZERLAND, FRIBOURG	4.0
HARPOON OCTOBERFEST	USA, MASSACHUSETTS, BOSTON	4.0
JINDAO	CHINA, QINGDAO	4.0
KIWI LAGER	NEW ZEALAND, TIMARU	4.0
RITTERBRAU PALE	GERMANY, DORTMUND	4.0
SAMUEL SMITH'S LAGER	ENGLAND, TADCASTER	4.0
SPARTAN LAGER	GREECE, ATALANTI	4.0
XINGU BLACK BEER	BRAZIL, TOLEDO	4.0
AYINGER OKTOBERFEST- MARZEN	GERMANY, AYING	3.9
GOLDEN PHEASANT	SLOVAKIA, HURBANOVO	3.9
KAISERDOM EXTRA DRY	GERMANY, BAMBERG	3.9
KAISERDOM RAUCHBIER SMOKED BAVARIAN DARK	GERMANY, BAMBERG	3.9
KIRIN LAGER	JAPAN, TOKYO	3.9
ROYAL DUTCH POST HORN	HOLLAND, BREDA	3.9
SANTA FE RUBIA ESPECIAL	ARGENTINA, SANTA FE	3.9
TOMMYKNOCKER RED EYE LAGER	USA, COLORADO, IDAHO SPRINGS	3.9
WATNEY'S RED BARREL	ENGLAND, LONDON	3.9
AUGUST SCHELL DEER BRAND	USA, MINNESOTA, NEW ULM	3.8
HUA NAN	CHINA, GUANGZHOU	3.8
JOHN LABATT CLASSIC	CANADA, ONTARIO, TORONTO	3.8
KARMI OKOCIM LOW ALCOHOL CONTENT BEER	POLAND, BRSESKO	3.8
LAKEFRONT PUMPKIN LAGER	USA, WISCONSIN, MILWAUKEE	3.8
LEON DE ORO CERVEZA ESPECIAL	ARGENTINA, ANTARTIDA	3.8
MARATHON-THE GREEK BEER	GREECE, ATHENS	3.8
MELBOURN BROS. APRICOT BEER	ENGLAND, STAMFORD	3.8
MILLSTREAM LAGER	USA, IOWA, AMANA	3.8

NAME	LOCATION	RATING
PAULANER OKTOBERFEST	GERMANY, MUNICH	3.8
UPPER CANADA REBELLION	CANADA, ONTARIO, TORONTO	3.8
BECK'S OKTOBERFEST	GERMANY, BREMEN	3.7
RHINO CHASERS LAGER	USA, CALIFORNIA, CHATSWORTH	3.7
SAMUEL ADAMS OCTOBERFEST	USA, PENNSYLVANIA, PITTSBURGH	3.7
WYNKOOP JED FEST	USA, COLORADO, DENVER	3.7
ASTICA PREMIUM LAGER	BULGARIA, HASKOWO	3.6
CARTA BLANCA	MEXICO, MONTERREY	3.6
CHURCHILL LAGER	ENGLAND, REDRUTH	3.6
KAREL IV LAGER	CZECH REPUBLIC, KARLOVY VARY	3.6
KOFF	FINLAND, HELSINKI	3.6
NEW AMSTERDAM AMBER	USA, NEW YORK, UTICA	3.6
PANAMA CERVEZA ALLAMANA STYLE	PANAMA, PANAMA CITY	3.6
ROLLING ROCK	USA, PENNSYLVANIA, LATROBE	3.6
BRASSEURS GRAND CRU	FRANCE, BONNEUIL	3.5
DIXIE	USA, LOUISIANA, NEW ORLEANS	3.5
GOLDEN EAGLE LAGER	INDIA, MADRAS	3.5
GOSSER STIFTSBRAU	AUSTRIA, GRAZ	3.5
HARP	IRELAND	3.5
JOHN COURAGE AMBER BEER	ENGLAND, STAINES	3.5
KALYANI BLACK LABEL PREMIUM LAGER	INDIA, BANGALORE	3.5
MOLSON ICE	CANADA, BRITISH COLUMBIA, VICTORIA	3.5
SPRECHER AMBER	USA, WISCONSIN, MILWAUKEE	3.5
VAILIMA LAGER	WESTERN SAMOA, APIA	3.5
SAMUEL ADAMS WINTER LAGER	USA, OREGON, PORTLAND	2.2–3.9
LAMBICS		
MORT SUBITE PECHE LAMBIC	BELGIUM, ASSE	3.4
TIMMERMANS PECHE	BELGIUM, ITTERBECK	3.3
MALT LIQUORS		
ADELSCOTT MALT LIQUOR	FRANCE, SCHILTIGHEIM	4.2
SAPPORO BLACK MALT LIQUOR	JAPAN, TOKYO (NOT FOR EXPORT)	4.1
KIRIN ICHIBAN MALT LIQUOR	JAPAN, TOKYO	4.0
KOZEL PREMIUM CZECH MALT LIQUOR	CZECH REPUBLIC, VELKE POPOVICE	4.0
SAPPORO BLACK MALT LIQUOR	JAPAN, TOKYO	4.0
HEXEN BRAU SWISS DUNKEL MALT LIQUOR	SWITZERLAND, ZURICH	3.9
SEPTANTE 5 MALT LIQUOR	FRANCE, ROUBAIX	3.7

NAME	LOCATION	RATING
ICEHOUSE ICE BEER MALT LIQUOR	USA, WISCONSIN, MILWAUKEE	3.3
FISCHER D'ALSACE AMBER	FRANCE, SCHILTIGHEIM	3.2
RED HORSE MALT LIQUOR	PHILIPPINES, MANILA	3.2
ZIPFER PREMIUM MALT LIQUOR	AUSTRIA, VIENNA	3.2
CARLSBERG ELEPHANT MALT LIQUOR	DENMARK, COPENHAGEN	3.1
MAMBA	IVORY COAST, ABIDJAN	3.1
NONALCOHOLIC		
EXTRACTO DE MALTA MALT BEVERAGE	GERMANY, HAMBURG	3.9
WARSTEINER PREMIUM FRESH	GERMANY, WARSTEIN	3.9
BITBURGER DRIVE ALKOHOLFREI	GERMANY, BITBURG	3.8
CLAUSTHALER	GERMANY, FRANKFURT	3.8
CERVEJA CHEERS	PORTUGAL, LECA DO BALIO	3.5
HAAKE BECK	GERMANY, BREMEN	3.5
HENNINGER GERSTEL BRAU	GERMANY, FRANKFURT	3.4
MALTINA	PERU, LIMA	3.4
SCHLOSSGOLD ALKOHOLARMES BIER	AUSTRIA, LINZ	3.4
BAVARIA MALT BEVERAGE	HOLLAND, LIESHOUT	3.3
MOLSON EXEL	CANADA, BRITISH COLUMBIA, VANCOUVER	3.3
MORENITA MALTA ESPECIAL	CHILE, CONCEPCION	3.3
PAULANER THOMAS BRAU	GERMANY, MUNICH	3.3
O'DOUL'S	USA, MISSOURI, ST. LOUIS (ANHEUSER-BUSCH)	3.1
O'DOUL'S AMBER	USA, MISSOURI, ST. LOUIS (ANHEUSER-BUSCH)	3.1
SCHLOSS JOSEF ALSATIAN MALT BEVERAGE	FRANCE, SCHUTZENBERG	3.1
OCTOBERFEST/MARZEN/FALL BEERS		
AYINGER OKTOBERFEST MARZEN	GERMANY, AYING	3.9
ROGUE MAIERBOCK	USA, OREGON, NEWPORT	3.9
PAULANER OKTOBERFEST	GERMANY, MUNICH	3.8
BECK'S OKTOBERFEST	GERMANY, BREMEN	3.7
SCHLENKERLA SMOKED BEER-MARZEN	GERMANY, BAMBERG	3.7
SIERRA NEVADA SUMMERFEST	USA, CALIFORNIA, CHICO	3.5–3.8
HACKER-PSCHORR WEISSE BOCK	GERMANY, MUNICH	3.3

NAME	LOCATION	RATING
HOFBRAU MUNCHENER OKTOBERFEST	GERMANY, MUNICH	3.3
PILSENERS		
SAN MIGUEL DARK	PHILIPPINES, MANILA	4.4
BIECKERT ESPECIAL	ARGENTINA, ANTARTIDA	4.2
MESSINA PILSENER	ITALY, MILAN	4.1
SOUTHWARK PREMIUM	AUSTRALIA, ADELAIDE	4.1
BARRIL OSCURA	MEXICO, MEXICO CITY	4.0
PILSENER	ECUADOR, QUITO	4.0
RINGNES EXPORT PALE	NORWAY, OSLO	4.0
YUCHAN	CHINA, BEIJING	4.0
ALMAZA PILSENER	LEBANON, BEIRUT	3.9
BINTANG PILSENER	INDONESIA, SURABAYA	3.9
EKU KULMBACHER PILS	GERMANY, KULMBACH	3.9
KIRIN DRAFT	CANADA, BRITISH COLUMBIA, VANCOUVER	3.9
RAFFO	ITALY, ROME	3.9
WARSTEINER	GERMANY, WARSTEIN	3.9
BARRE BRAU	GERMANY, LUBBECKE	3.8
BARRIL CLARA	MEXICO, MEXICO CITY	3.8
BEL PILS	BELGIUM, PUURS	3.8
BRAHMA	BRAZIL, RIO DE JANEIRO	3.8
DAMM	SPAIN, BARCELONA & VALENCIA	3.8
LANDSKRON PILS	GERMANY, RADEBERG	3.8
NEW BELGIUM BLUE PADDLE PILSENER	USA, COLORADO, FORT COLLINS	3.8
ROYAL GUARD PILSENER	CHILE, SANTIAGO	3.8
STEINLAGER	NEW ZEALAND, AUCKLAND	3.8
TIJUCA	BRAZIL, BELEM	3.8
ASAHI Z DRAFT	JAPAN, TOKYO	3.7
BRAHMA CHOPP	BRAZIL, RIO DE JANEIRO	3.7
CORDOBA-DORADA	ARGENTINA, CORDOBA	3.7
PENNSYLVANIA PENN PILSENER	USA, PENNSYLVANIA, PITTSBURGH	3.7
TROPICAL PILSENER	CANARY ISLANDS, LAS PALMAS	3.7
WICKULER PILSENER	GERMANY WUPPERTAL	3.7
GLOSSNER HOPFENGARTEN PILS	GERMANY, NEUMARKT	3.6
AUGSBURGER PILSENER	USA, WISCONSIN, MONROE	3.5
BUDWEISER BUDVAR	CZECH REPUBLIC, BUDEJOVICE	3.5
DOCK STREET BOHEMIAN PILSNER	USA, PENNSYLVANIA, PHILADELPHIA	3.5
EMPERORS GOLD	CHINA, GUANGZHOU	3.5
PANDA	CHINA, SHANGHAI	3.5
PILSNER URQUELL	CZECHOSLOVAKIA, PILSEN	3.5

NAME	LOCATION	RATING
PRESIDENTE PILSENER	DOMINICAN REPUBLIC, SANTO DOMINGO	3.5
ST. PAULI GIRL DARK	GERMANY, BREMEN	3.5
STEINHAUSER BIER	GERMANY, FRANKFURT	3.5
SUN LIK	CHINA, HONG KONG	3.5
PORTERS		
YUENGLING PORTER	USA, PENNSYLVANIA, POTTSVILLE	4.1
KARL STRAUSS BLACK'S BEACH EXTRA DARK PORTER	USA, CALIFORNIA, SAN DIEGO	4.0
RED HOOK BLACKHOOK PORTER	USA, WASHINGTON, SEATTLE	4.0
TRAFFIC JAM COAL PORTER	USA, MICHIGAN, DETROIT	4.0
ANDERSON VALLEY DEEP ENDERS DARK PORTER	USA, CALIFORNIA, BOONVILLE	3.8
BOULEVARD "BULLY" PORTER	USA, MISSOURI, KANSAS CITY	3.8
CATAMOUNT PORTER	USA, VERMONT, WINDSOR	3.8
DESCHUTES BLACK BUTTE PORTER	USA, OREGON, BEND	3.7
ROGUE NEW PORTER	USA, OREGON, NEWPORT	3.7
SAMUEL SMITH TADCASTER TADDY PORTER	ENGLAND, TADCASTER	3.7
SANTA FE OLD POJOAQUE PORTER	USA, NEW MEXICO, SANTA FE	3.5
WILLIAMSVILLE BORDER PORTER	USA, FLORIDA, FERNANDINA	3.5
STOUDT'S HOLIDAY RESERVE BEER-SMOKED PORTER	USA, PENNSYLVANIA, ADAMSTOWN	3.4
SAMUEL ADAMS HONEY PORTER	USA, PENNSYLVANIA, LEHIGH VALLEY	3.3
DOJLIDY PORTER	POLAND, BIALYSTOK	3.2
YOUNG'S LONDON PORTER	ENGLAND, LONDON	3.2
BIG ROCK COLD COCK WINTER PORTER	CANADA, ALBERTA, CALGARY	3.1
OKOCIM PORTER	POLAND, OKOCIM	3.1
STEAM BEERS		
ANCHOR STEAM	USA, CALIFORNIA, SAN FRANCISCO	3.9
STOUTS		
ROGUE SHAKESPEARE STOUT	USA, OREGON, NEWPORT	4.8
YOUNG'S OATMEAL STOUT	ENGLAND, LONDON	4.3
BERT GRANT'S IMPERIAL STOUT	USA, WASHINGTON, YAKIMA	4.2
BROOKLYN BLACK CHOCOLATE STOUT	USA, NEW YORK, BROOKLYN	4.1
MACKESON TRIPLE XXX STOUT	ENGLAND, LONDON	4.1

NAME	LOCATION	RATING
ANDERSON VALLEY BARNEY FLATS OATMEAL STOUT	USA, CALIFORNIA, BOONVILLE	4.0
BANDERSNATCH MILK STOUT	USA, ARIZONA, TEMPE	4.0
COOPERSMITH'S HORSETOOTH STOUT	USA, COLORADO, FORT COLLINS	4.0
PRESTIGE STOUT	HAITI, PORT-AU-PRINCE	4.0
SAMUEL SMITH OATMEAL STOUT	ENGLAND, TADCASTER	4.0
SAMUEL SMITH'S IMPERIAL STOUT	ENGLAND, TADCASTER	4.0
SCHLAFLY OATMEAL STOUT	USA, MISSOURI, ST. LOUIS	4.0
GUINNESS PUB DRAUGHT STOUT	IRELAND, DUBLIN	3.9
WATNEY'S CREAM STOUT	ENGLAND, LONDON	3.9
BUCKERFIELD'S SWANS OATMEAL STOUT	CANADA, BRITISH COLUMBIA, VICTORIA	3.8
GUINNESS EXTRA STOUT	IRELAND, DUBLIN	3.8
OLD AUSTRALIA STOUT	AUSTRALIA, SOUTH AUSTRALIA, THEBARTON	3.8
SALMON CREEK SWEET STOUT	USA, WASHINGTON, VANCOUVER	3.8
ABC EXTRA STOUT	SINGAPORE	3.7
BEAMISH IRISH CREAM STOUT	IRELAND, CORK	3.7
ABC VERY SUPERIOR STOUT	SINGAPORE	3.6
BLUE STAR STOUT	USA, TEXAS, SAN ANTONIO	3.5
MAIN STREET STEAMBOAT STOUT	USA, OHIO, CINCINNATI	3.5
MURPHY'S STOUT	IRELAND, CORK	3.5
SWEETHEART STOUT	SCOTLAND, GLASGOW	3.5
WATNEY'S STINGO CREAM STOUT	ENGLAND, LONDON	3.5
WHEAT/WEIZEN		
ERDINGER WEISSBIER HEFETRUB	GERMANY, ERDING	4.4
AYINGER DUNKLES UR-WEISSE	GERMANY, AYING	4.0
CELIS WHITE	USA, TEXAS, AUSTIN	4.0
EDELWEISS KRISTALLKLAR WEIZENBIER	AUSTRIA, SALZBURG	4.0
ERDINGER WEISSBIER-DUNKEL	GERMANY, ERDING	4.0
MAISEL'S HEFE WEISSE	GERMANY, BAYREUTH	4.0
BLANCHE DE BRUGES	BELGIUM, BRUGES	3.9
ANCHOR WHEAT DRAFT	USA, CALIFORNIA, SAN FRANCISCO	3.8
EKU DARK HEFE WEISBIER	GERMANY, KULMBACH	3.8
WEIHENSTEPHAN WEIZENBIER	GERMANY, FREISING	3.8

NAME	LOCATION	RATING
Odell's Easy Street Wheat	USA, Colorado, Fort Collins	3.7
Allagash White	USA, Maine, Portland	3.6
Anderson Valley High Rollers Wheat	USA, California, Boonville	3.6
Pschorr-Brau Weisse	Germany, Munich	3.5
Spaten Munchen Club-Weisse	Germany, Munich	3.5
Tourmente Wheat	Canada, Quebec, Montreal	3.5

BEST BEERS
FOR NOVICES

Some beers have characteristics that make them especially easy to enjoy. I have listed seventeen of the best—from ale to weiss—for those who are interested in easing their way gently into the world of beer—sort of a beer menu for the beginner. These brews are likely to encourage a return for more. Of course, more knowledgeable drinkers, or the just plain curious, are welcome to sample these highly accommodating beers, too. (See the listings for a full discussion of each beer's qualities.)

NAME	RATING	COMMENTS
Beck's Dark	2.6	Available most anywhere
Brahma Chopp	3.7	Brazilian draft in a can
Cardinal Lager	4.0	Light and fluffy
Churchill Lager	3.6	Available in larger cities
Corsendonk Monk's Brown Ale	3.9	Worth it for the color alone
Cuzco	3.2	Fizzy and fruity
Dogwood Wheat	3.0	Spice-clove taste, banana aroma
Fish Tale Mudshark Porter	2.7	Creamy smooth, not intense
Hammer & Nail American Ale	3.4	Lots of familiar flavors here
Hofbrau Bavaria Dark Reserve	2.5	Friendly and gentle
Kalyani Black Label Premium Lager	3.5	Tart and sharp
KB Australian Lager	2.9	Full of verve and gumption
Old Peculier Ale	3.8	Readily available
Ruski	3.3	Has mini cult following
Summit Great Northern Porter	2.8	Unaggressive and easy-drinking
Suntory Gold Draft—100% Malt Beer	3.3	Thick and creamy
Wildcatter's Refined Stout	2.6	Restrained roastedness

TRY SOMETHING DIFFERENT

While each beer tries to create its own identity, several incorporate brewing features that in my judgment truly make them stand out from the rest. The following are some of those you are likely to remember for a long time—regardless of how much, or how little, you enjoyed them.

NAME	RATING	COMMENTS
Adelscott Malt Liquor	4.2	Mellow, whiskey-like, peat-smoked
Anchor Our Special Ale	2.5–4.0	Tastes like a liquid Christmas tree
Bajan Beer	2.7	Aggressively malty, softly fizzy
Bandersnatch Milk Stout	4.0	A virtual meal in a glass
Bos Keun Special Paasbier	2.7	Sugary-sweet and yeasty (a naughty label, too)
Cherryland Cherry Rail Lager	2.9	Juice is in the tasting
Ch'ti Blond Biere de Garde	3.3	Sweetly champagne-like
Cochonnette Petite Vapeur Cochonne Ale	3.1	Tart, yeasty, apple-brandy flavor
Dogfish Head Chicory Stout	3.2	Blossoming milk-chocolate and coffee flavors
Duvel	2.9	Complexity of fruitiness/alcohol
Ettaler Kloster Dunkel	4.5	Rich, flavorful, and oh, so satisfying
Firehouse Key Lime Wheat	2.8	Smells like lime aftershave, tastes like key lime pie
Flossmoor Station Imperial Eclipse Stout	3.4	Like a fruit-filled dark chocolate candy
Grozet Gooseberry and Wheat Ale	3.1	Potent mix of malts, wild spices, and gooseberries
Ichtegem's Old Brown Ale	3.9	Slightly sour, fresh fruitiness

NAME	RATING	COMMENTS
KAISERDOM RAUCHBIER—SMOKED BAVARIAN DARK	3.9	SMOKY LIQUID SAUSAGE
MONKEY WRENCH ALE	4.2	PLUMMY RAISIN-MALT TASTE
QUELQUE CHOSE SOMETHING	3.9	WARM THIS BEER TO ROOM TEMPERATURE FOR BEST RESULTS
SWEETHEART STOUT	3.5	MILK-GRAPE COMBINATION
TUSKER PREMIUM LAGER	4.3	THIRST-QUENCHING HINT OF LEMON

ODD
BEER NAMES

Sometimes what's *on* the label is more intriguing than what's *in* the bottle or can. Here are my favorite names, regardless of any other distinction (or lack of distinction).

NAME	RATING	COMMENTS
ALIMONY ALE (DUBUQUE, IOWA)	3.9	THERE'S NO RECONCILING IT; SOME CONSIDER THIS "THE BITTEREST BREW IN AMERICA."
ARROGANT BASTARD ALE (SAN MARCOS, CALIFORNIA)	2.3	THIS ALE DARES YOU TO DRINK IT.
BAD FROG ORIGINAL LAGER (EVANSVILLE, INDIANA)	1.4	THEY TRIED TO BAN THIS GESTURING FROG IN SEVERAL STATES, AND IT WASN'T FOR THE TASTE OF THE BEER.
BRAINS TRADITIONAL WELSH ALE (CARDIFF, WALES)	3.9	YOU DON'T NEED LOTS OF SMARTS TO ENJOY THE LIGHTLY CARAMELIZED TASTE OF THIS VISUALLY APPEALING ALE.
DEAD ARMADILLO ROASTED RED (LAKE OSWEGO, OREGON)	2.5	ROASTED? DEFINITELY. DEAD? WELL, NOT QUITE, THOUGH IT DOES WEAKEN ALMOST FATALLY AT THE END.
DELIRIUM TREMENS BELGIAN ALE (MELLE/GHENT, BELGIUM)	1.7	BOTH THE ALE AND ITS NAME OFFER MIXED MESSAGES HERE. I'VE SEEN, AND TASTED, BETTER ADVERTISING GIMMICKS.
HAIR OF THE DOG ADAMBIER (PORTLAND, OREGON)	3.8	IF THEY CHANGED THE NAME, I THINK THEY WOULD SELL A LOT MORE OF THIS VERY, VERY GOOD RICH-FLAVORED BEER.
HAMMER & NAIL AMERICAN ALE (WATERTOWN, CONNECTICUT)	3.4	FEISTY, WELL-CONSTRUCTED HOPPINESS.
HARD GAUGE BEER (DETROIT, MICHIGAN)	0.8	NOT ENGAGING, NO MATTER HOW YOU MEASURE IT.
JUMPING COW AMBER ALE (PASO ROBLES, CALIFORNIA AND NEW ULM, MINNESOTA)	2.3	IN THE END, RUN-OF-THE-MILL.

NAME	RATING	COMMENTS
La Fin de Monde (Chambly, Quebec, Canada)	3.3	Assertive and strong, it's not the end of the world, but the beginning of a pretty good beer.
La Guillotine Belgian Ale (Melle/Ghent, Belgium)	3.2	Yeasty and tart, but no need to lose your head over it.
Leinenkugel's Big Butt Doppelbock (Chippewa Falls, Wisconsin)	2.2	Too bad the flavor profile doesn't live up to the size of the anatomical profile.
Leningrad Cowboy Lager (Helsinki, Finland)	2.3	Made in Finland, named for a (former) Soviet city, and celebrating an American icon—they should have spent more effort making a better beer.
Merriman's Old Fart (Leeds, England)	2.5	Let's drink to "all the cantankerous old buddies who make life a misery."
Monkey Wrench Ale (Harrogate, England)	4.2	No other tools required for this top-notch rich and plummy ale with a raisin-malt twist.
Mordue Workie Ticket (Newcastle-upon-Tyne, England)	3.4	Pungent caramel sweetness
Morland "Old Speckled Hen" English Fine Ale (Abingdon, England)	4.1	A strong commemorative ale deserves a special name, even if it's named for a car.
Mort Subite Peche Lambic (Kobbegem, Belgium)	3.4	There's nothing sudden about the very much alive peach character of this worthy import.
Old Rasputin Russian Imperial Stout (Fort Bragg, California)	3.1	The days of the Czar may be gone, but the strong alcoholic presence of his stout, thankfully, is not.
Orkney Skullsplitter Ale (Quoyloo, Scotland)	3.8	Easier to drink than to pronounce, it recalls magic, mystery, and some unsavory moments on the battlefield.
Smuttynose Old Brown Dog Ale (Portsmouth, New Hampshire)	2.5	No pornographic nostrils here. Smuttynose is one of a small group of islands off the New Hampshire coast.
Thumb Blonde (Glasgow, Scotland)	2.5	Thumb's up for the name, not the beer.

VISITING THE SOURCE: MICROBREWERIES AND BREWPUBS

I t's a good idea to call before planning to visit a brewpub. Some establishments have seasonal hours, others may have changed their status from brewpub to microbrewery (or vice versa), and still others may have moved or gone out of business. Brewpubs serve beer-friendly food and in some instances also offer fresh beer on tap from other local brewpubs.

Abita Brewing   (RB/BP)
100 Leveson Street
Abita Springs, Louisiana
   70420
Phone: (504) 893-3143

**Allagash Brewing
Company**   (MB)
100 Industrial Way
Portland, Maine 04103
Phone: (207) 878-5385 or
   (800) 330-5385

**Anderson Valley
Brewery**   (MB/PB)
14081 Highway 128
Boonville, California 95415
Phone: (707) 895-3369

Appleton Brewing   (MB/BP)
(Adler Brau)
1004 S. Olde Oneida Street
Appleton, Wisconsin 54915
Phone: (920) 731-3322

Assets Grill & Brewing   (BP)
6910 Montgomery N.E.
Albuquerque, New Mexico
   87109
Phone: (505) 889-6400

Bandersnatch Brewpub   (BP)
125 E. Fifth Street
Tempe, Arizona 85281
Phone: (602) 966-4438

**Bear Republic Brewing
Company**   (MB/BP)
345 Healdsburg Avenue
Healdsburg, California 95448
Phone: (707) 433-2337

Belmont Brewing   (BP)
25 39th Place
Long Beach, California
   90803
Phone: (562) 433-3891

**Berkshire Brewing
Company**   (MB)
12 Railroad Street
S. Deerfield, Massachusetts
   01378
Phone: (413) 665-6600

**Bert Grant's Brewery
Pub**   (RB/BP)
32 N. Front Street
Yakima, Washington 98901
Phone: (509) 575-2922

Big Time Brewing   (MB/BP)
4133 University Way N.E.
Seattle, Washington 98105
Phone: (206) 545-4509

Bison Brewery   (MB/BP)
2598 Telegraph Avenue
Berkeley, California 94704
Phone: (510) 841-7734

**Bitter End Bistro and
Brewery   (BP)**
311 Colorado Street
Austin, Texas 78701
Phone: (512) 478-2337

**Blackstone Restaurant and
Brewery   (BP)**
1918 W. End Avenue
Nashville, Tennessee 37203
Phone: (615) 327-9969

**Blue Corn Cafe and
Brewery   (BP)**
4056 Cerrillos Road
Santa Fe, New Mexico 87505
Phone: (505) 438-1800

**Blue Star Brewing
Company   BP)**
1414 S. Alamo Street
San Antonio, Texas 78210
Phone: (210) 212-5506

**Bluegrass Brewing
Company   (BP)**
3929 Shelbyville Road
Louisville, Kentucky 40207
Phone: (502) 899-7070

Bohannon Brewing   (MB/BP)
134 Second Avenue N.
Nashville, Tennessee 37201
Phone: (615) 242-8223

Boiler Room Brew Pub   (BP)
2100 S. Casino Drive
   (in the Colorado Belle
   Hotel riverboat)
Laughlin, Nevada 89028
Phone: (800) 789-2893

**Breckenridge Brewery
& Pub   (MB/BP)**
600 South Main
Breckenridge, Colorado
   80424
Phone: (970) 453-1550

**Breckenridge Brewery
& Pub   (MB/BP)**
2220 Blake Street
Denver, Colorado 80220
Phone: (303) 297-3644

Brewer's Alley   (BP)
124 N. Market Street
Frederick, Maryland 21701
Phone: (301) 631-0089

**Bridgeport Brewing &
Public House   (MB/BP)**
1313 N.W. Marshall
Portland, Oregon 97209
Phone: (503) 241-3612

**Broad Ripple Brewing
Company   (BP)**
842 E. 65th Street
Indianapolis, Indiana 46220
Phone: (317) 253-2739

**Carnegie Hill Brewing
Company   (BP)**
1600 Third Avenue
New York, New York 10128
Phone: (212) 369-0808

Carver's Brewing (BP)
1022 Main Street
Durango, Colorado 81301
Phone: (970) 259-2545

Cisco Brewers (Bailey's) (MB)
5 Bartlett Farm Road
Nantucket, Massachusetts
  02554
Phone: (508) 325-5929

**Coast Range Brewing
Company** (MB)
7050 Monterey Street
Gilroy, California 95020
Phone: (408) 842-1000

**Commonwealth Brewing
Company** (BP)
10 Rockefeller Plaza
New York, New York 10020
Phone: (212) 977-2269

**CooperSmith's Pub &
Brewing** (BP)
No. 5 Old Town Square
Fort Collins, Colorado 80624
Phone: (970) 498-0483

**Cottonwood Grill and
Brewery** (BP)
179 Howard Street
Boone, North Carolina
  28607
Phone: (828) 266-1004

Cougan's at Arrowhead (BP)
7640 W. Bell Road
Glendale, Arizona 85308
Phone: (623) 878-8822

Crested Butte Brewing (BP)
226 Elk Avenue
Crested Butte, Colorado
  81224
Phone: (970) 349-5026

**Crooked River Brewing
Company** (MB/BP)
1101 Center Street
Cleveland, Ohio 44102
Phone: (216) 771-2337

Dallas Brewing (MB)
703 McKinney Avenue
Dallas, Texas 75202
Phone (214) 871-7990

Dark Mountain Brewery (MB)
13605 E. Benson Highway
Vail, Arizona 85641
Phone: (520) 762-5777

D. L. Geary Brewing (MB)
38 Evergreen Drive
Portland, Maine 04103
Phone: (207) 878-2337

**DeGroen's-Baltimore
Brewing Company** (MB/BP)
104 Albemarle Street
Baltimore, Maryland 21202
Phone: (410) 837-5000

**Deschutes Brewery
& Public House** (MB/BP)
1044 N.W. Bond Street
Bend, Oregon 97701
Phone: (541) 382-9242

**Dogfish Head Brewing
and Eats** (MB/BP)
320 Rehoboth Boulevard
Rehoboth Beach, Delaware
  19971
Phone: (302) 226-2739

Durango Brewing (MB)
3000 Main Street
Durango, Colorado 81301
Phone: (970) 247-3396

**Eddie McStiff's Restaurant
and Brewpub** (MB/BP)
57 S. Main Street
Moab, Utah 84532
Phone: (801) 259-2337

Eske's, A Brewpub (BP)
106 Des Georges Lane
Taos, New Mexico 87571
Phone: (505) 758-1517

Firehouse Brewing (MB)
7902 N.W. 64th Street
Miami, Florida 33166
Phone: (305) 718-9620

Fish Brewing (MB/BP)
515 Jefferson Street
Olympia, Washington 98501
Phone: (360) 943-6480

**Flossmoor Station
Brewery** (BP)
1035 Sterling Avenue
Flossmoor, Illinois 60422
Phone: (708) 957-2739

**FMI Brewing
(Flying Monkey)** (MB)
5151 Merriam Drive
Shawnee Mission, Kansas
66203
Phone: (913) 522-2834

Four Peaks Brewing (MB/BP)
1340 E. 8th Street
Tempe, Arizona 85281
Phone: (480) 303-9967

Free State Brewing (BP)
636 Massachusetts Street
Lawrence, Kansas 66044
Phone: (785) 843-4555

Gentle Ben's Brewing (BP)
865 E. University Boulevard
Tucson, Arizona 85719
Phone: (520) 624-4177

**Golden Valley Brewery
and Pub** (MB/BP)
940 E. 4th Street
McMinnville, Oregon 97128
Phone: (503) 472-2739

**Great Basin Brewing
Company** (MB)
846 Victorian Avenue
Sparks, Nevada 89432
Phone: (775) 355-7711

**Great Northern Brewing
Company (Minott's)** (MB)
2 Central Avenue
Whitefish, Montana 59937
Phone: (406) 863-1000

Hale's Ales (MB/BP)
4301 Leary Way
Seattle, Washington 98107
Phone: (206) 706-1544

Hammer & Nail Brewers (MB)
900 Main Street
Watertown, Connecticut
06795
Phone: (860) 274-5911

Hazel Dell Brewpub (BP)
8513 N. E. Highway 99
Vancouver, Washington
98665
Phone: (360) 576-0996

**H.C. Berger Brewing
Company** (MB)
1900 E. Lincoln Avenue
Fort Collins, Colorado 80524
Phone: (970) 493-9044

Hops! Bistro & Brewery (BP)
8668 E. Shay Boulevard
Scottsdale, Arizona 85260
Phone: (480) 998-7777

Hoster Brewing   (BP)
550 S. High Street
Columbus, Ohio 43215
Phone: (614) 228-6066

Hubcap Brewery &
Kitchen   (BP)
143 East Meadow Drive
Vail, Colorado 81657
Phone: (970) 476-5757

Humboldt Brewery   (RB/BP)
856 10th Street
Arcata, California 95521
Phone: (707) 826-2739

Huske Hardware House
Brewing Company   (BP)
405 Hay Street
Fayetteville, North Carolina
   28301
Phone: (910) 437-9905

Il Vicino Wood Oven
Pizza and Brewery   (MB/BP)
3403 Central Avenue, N.E.
Albuquerque, New Mexico
   87106
Phone: (505) 266-7855

Karl Strass Brewery   (MB/BP)
1157 Columbia Street
San Diego California (92101)
   (and other locations)
Phone: (619) 234-2739

Kelly's Caribbean Bar,
Grill and Brewery   (BP)
301 Whitehead Street
Key West, Florida 33040
Phone: (305) 293-8484

Key West Brewing
Company   (MB)
1107 Key Plaza #229
Key West, Florida 33040
Phone: (305) 295-0327

Kona Brewing Company (MB)
75-5629 Kuakini Highway
Kailua-Kona, Hawaii
Phone (808) 334-1133

Lagunitas Brewing   (MB)
1280 N. McDowell Boulevard
Petaluma, California 94954
Phone: (707) 769-4495

Lancaster Malt Brewing
Company   (MB)
302 N. Plum Street
Lancaster, Pennsylvania
   17602
Phone: (717) 391-6258

The Leavenworth
Brewery   (MB)
636 Front Street
Leavenworth, Washington
   98826
Phone: (509) 548-4545

Long Trail Brewing
Company   (MB)
Route 4
Bridgewater Corners,
   Vermont 05035
Phone: (802) 672-5011

Los Gatos Brewing   (BP)
130G N. Santa Cruz Avenue
Los Gatos, California 95030
Phone: (408) 395-9929

Lost Coast Brewery   (MB/BP)
617 4th Street
Eureka, California 95501
Phone: (707) 445-4480

Magnolia Pub and
Brewery   (BP)
1398 Haight Street
San Francisco, California
   94117
Phone: (415) 864-7468

**Magnotta Breweries
(True North)** **(MB)**
110 Cidermill Avenue
Vaughan, Ontario, Canada
Phone: (800) 461-9463

**Main Street Brewery and
Restaurant** **(MB/BP)**
1203 Main Street
Cincinnati, Ohio 45210
Phone: (513) 665-4677

**Manhattan Beach Brewing
Company** **(BP)**
124 Manhattan Beach
 Boulevard
Manhattan Beach, California
 90266
Phone: (310) 798-2744

Marin Brewing **(BP)**
1809 Larkspur Landing
 Circle
Larkspur, California 94939
Phone: (415) 461-4677

McMenamin's **(BP)**
432 N.W. 21st Street
Portland, Oregon 97209
(and other locations in
 Oregon and Washington)
Phone: (503) 223-3184

Mendocino Brewing **(MB/BP)**
13351 South Highway 101
Hopland, California 95449
Phone: (800) 744-1361

**Midnight Sun Brewing
Company** **(BP)**
7329 Arctic Boulevard
Anchorage, Alaska 99518
Phone: (907) 344-1179

**Mishawaka Brewing
Company** **(BP)**
3703 N. Main Street
Mishawaka, Indiana 46545
Phone: (219) 256-9993

**New England
Brewing** **(MB/BP)**
13 Marshall Street
Norwalk, Connecticut 06854
Phone: (203) 853-9110

North Coast Brewing **(MB/BP)**
444 N. Main Street
Fort Bragg, California 95437
Phone: (707) 964-2729

Northampton Brewery **(BP)**
11 Brewster Court
Northampton, Massachusetts
 01060
Phone: (413) 584-9903

Oldenberg Brewery **(MB)**
400 Buttermilk Pike and I-75
Fort Mitchell, Kentucky
 41017
Phone: (606) 341-7223

**Otter Creek Brewing
Company** **(MB)**
74 Exchange Street
Middlebury, Vermont 05753
Phone: (802) 388-0727

**Paper City Brewing
Company** **(MB)**
108 Cabot Street
Holyoke, Massachusetts
 01040
Phone: (413) 535-1588

**Pelican Pub and
Brewery** **(BP)**
33180 Cape Kiwanda Drive
Pacific City, Oregon 97135
Phone: (503) 965-7007

**Pike Pub and
Restaurant** (MB/BP)
1415 1st Avenue
Seattle, Washington 98101
Phone: (206) 622-3373

**Pinehurst Village
Brewery** (BP)
1200 Route 211 E
Aberdeen, North Carolina
28315
Phone: (910) 944-3820

**Pony Express Brewing
Company** (MB)
311 N. Burch Street
Olathe, Kansas 66061
Phone: (800) 745-9649

Portland Brewing (MB/BP)
Brewhouse Tap Room & Grill
2730 N.W. 31st Avenue
Portland, Oregon 97210
Phone: (503) 228-5269

**Portsmouth Pub and
Brewery** (MB/BP)
56 Market Street
Portsmouth, New Hampshire
03801
Phone: (603) 431-1115

Pyramid Ales (MB/BP)
91 S. Royal Brougham Way
Seattle, Washington 98134
Phone: (206) 682-8322

**River Horse
Brewery** (MB/BP)
80 Lambert Lane
Lambertville, New Jersey
08530
Phone: (609) 397-7776

**Riverside Brewing
Company** (MB/BP)
3397 Mission Inn Avenue
Riverside, California 92501
Phone: (909) 784-2739

Rogue Brewery (MB/BP)
748 S.W. Bay Boulevard
Newport, Oregon 97365
Phone: (541) 265-3188

**Sacramento Brewing
Company** (BP)
7811 Madison Avenue
Sacramento, California
95821
Phone: (916) 966-6274

**Salmon Creek Brewery
and Pub** (BP)
108 W. Evergreen Boulevard
Vancouver, Washington
98660
Phone: (360) 993-1827

**San Andreas
Brewing** (MB/BP)
737 San Benito Street
Hollister, California 95023
Phone: (831) 637-7074

Santa Barbara Brewing (BP)
501 State Street
Santa Barbara, California
93101
Phone: (805) 730-1040

**Santa Cruz Brewing Co. &
Front Street Pub** (BP)
516 Front Street
Santa Cruz, California 95060
Phone: (831) 429-8838

**Santa Fe Brewing
Company** (MB)
18 Sr 14 E. Frontage Road
Sante Fe, New Mexico 87505
Phone: (505) 424-3333

Sarasota Brewing Company (BP)
6607 Gateway Avenue
Sarasota, Florida 34231
Phone: (941) 925-2337

Schlafly/St. Louis Brewery (BP)
2100 Locust Street
St. Louis, Missouri 63103
Phone: (314) 241-2337

Sea Dog Brewing Company (MB/BP)
26 Front Street
Bangor, Maine 04401
(also in Camden)
Phone: (207) 947-8004

Seabright Brewery (BP)
519 Seabright Avenue
Santa Cruz, California 95062
Phone: (831) 426-2739

Second Street Brewery (BP)
1814 2nd Street
Santa Fe, New Mexico 87505
Phone: (505) 982-3030

SLO Brewing (MB/BP)
1119 Garden Street
San Luis Obispo, California 93401
Phone: (805) 543-1843

Snake River Brewing Company (MB/BP)
P.O. Box 3317
Jackson Hole, Wyoming
Phone: (307) 739-2337

Solana Beach Brewery (BP)
135 N. Highway 101
Solana Beach, California 92075
Phone: (760) 481-7332

Southampton Publick House (BP)
North Sea Road at Bowden Square
Southampton, New York 11968
Phone: (516) 283-2800

Spanish Peaks Brewing (MB/BP)
120 N. 19th Avenue
Bozeman, Montana 59715
Phone: (406) 585-2296

St. Arnold Brewing Company (MB)
2522 Fairway Park Drive
Houston, Texas 77092
Phone: (713) 686-9494

St. Stan's Brewing (MB/BP)
821 L Street
Modesto, California 95354
Phone: (209) 524-4782

Steelhead Brewery & Cafe (MB/BP)
199 E. 5th Street
Eugene, Oregon 97401
Phone: (541) 686-2739

Stevens Point Brewing Company (MB)
2617 Water Street
Stevens Point, Wisconsin 54481
Phone: (715) 344-9310

Stone City Brewing Ltd. (MB)
220 S. Dubuque Street
Solon, Iowa 52333
Phone: (319) 644-1360

Summit Brewing Company (MB)
910 Montreal Circle
St. Paul, Minnesota 55102
Phone: (651) 265-7800

Sun Valley Brewing   (MB/BP)
202 N. Main
Halley, Idaho 83333
Phone: (208) 788-0805

**Swan's Brewpub/
Buckerfield Brewery (MB/BP)**
506 Pandora Avenue
Victoria, British Columbia,
    Canada V8W 1N6
Phone: (250) 361-3310

Sweetwater Tavern   (BP)
14250 Sweetwater Lane
Centreville, Virginia 20121
Phone: (703) 449-1100

**Tampa Bay Brewing
Company   (BP)**
1812 N. 15th Street
Tampa, Florida 33605
Phone: (813) 247-1422

Top of the Hill   (BP)
100 E. Franklin Street
Chapel Hill, North Carolina
    27514
Phone: (919) 929-8676

Traffic Jam and Snug   (BP)
511 W. Canfield at 2nd
Detroit, Michigan 48201
Phone: (313) 831-9470

**Troegs Brewing
Company   (MB)**
800 Paxton Street
Harrisburg, Pennsylvania
    17104
Phone: (717) 232-1297

Troy Brewing Company (BP)
417- 419 River Street
Troy, New York 12180
Phone: (518) 273-2337

Tun Tavern   (BP)
Two Ocean Way
Atlantic City, New Jersey
    08401
Phone: (609) 347-7800

Umpqua Brewing   (BP)
328 S.E. Jackson Street
Roseburg, Oregon 97470
Phone: (541) 672-0452

**Uptown Brewery &
Restaurant by Streets of
New York   (BP)**
1470 E. Southern Avenue
Tempe, Arizona 85282
Phone: (480) 777-9600

**Wasatch Brewpub/
Schirf Brewing   (MB/BP)**
250 Main Street
Park City, Utah 84060
Phone: (435) 645-9500

**Watch City Brewing
Company   (BP)**
256 Moody Street
Waltham, Massachusetts
    02453
Phone: (781) 647-4000

**Weeping Radish
Bavarian Restaurant
& Brewery   (MB/BP)**
Highway 64E
Manteo, North Carolina
    27954
Phone: (252) 473-1157
(call for directions)

**Weston Brewing
Company   (BP)**
504 Welt Street
Weston, Missouri 64098
Phone: (816) 640-5245

Whitefish Brewing **(MB)**
P.O. Box 1949
Whitefish, Montana 59937
Phone: (406) 862-2684
(call for directions)

Widmer Brewing **(MB/BP)**
929 N. Russell Street
Portland, Oregon 97227
Phone: (503) 281-2437

**Williamsburg Brewing
Company** **(MB)**
189-B Ewell Road
Williamsburg, Virginia 23188
Phone: (757) 253-1577

**Wolf Canyon Brewing
Company** **(BP)**
9885 Cerrillos Road
Santa Fe, New Mexico 87505
Phone: (505) 438-7000

Wynkoop Brewing **(MB/BP)**
1634 18th Street
Denver, Colorado 80202
Phone: (303) 297-2700

**Ybor City Brewing
Company** **(MB)**
2205 N. 20th Street
Tampa, Florida 33605
Phone: (813) 242-9222